GW01006350

CONTEMPORARY WORLD ARCHITECTURE

CONTEMPORARY WORLD ARCHITECTURE is a comprehensive survey of international architecture at the turning point of a new century. Focusing on modern building types and the forces that shape them, it offers a critical study of more than six hundred buildings by key architects worldwide. Analysing thirteen separate building categories, it traces the pluralist paths of architectural thinking from the seventies to the start of the new millennium. The evolving story of these new forms, with their underlying quest for aesthetic consensus, is told by **HUGH PEARMAN**

Φ

CONTENTS Introduction 6, Visual Arts *Museums & galleries 20*, Performance *Opera houses, theatres & concert halls 66*, Learning *Schools, universities & libraries 102*, Religion *Places of worship 136*, Consumerism *Malls, shops & bars 170*, Living *Houses & apartments 202*, Workplace *Offices & business parks 246*, Industry *Factories & research centres 282*, Leisure *Theme parks, hotels & visitor centres 320*, Transport *Airports, stations & shipping terminals 352*, Sport *Stadia, gymnasia & pools 392*, The Civic Realm *Public space & structures 426*, Towers *Vertical cities 464*, Bibliography 488, Index 496

This book is about building types, but it is also an oblique search for consensus. The last thirty years have been pluralist times in architecture, after all, but pluralism is not a style, a dogma, a movement, nor an underlying structure. Pluralism is merely what happens when there is no defining orthodoxy. Any direct attempt to chase the chimaera of a new global style, a replacement for what some have seen as the united front of the old International Style – and which others regard as a giant mid-twentieth-century con-trick – is as likely to succeed as a quest for the Yeti. The beast may be out there somewhere, but it does not choose openly to reveal itself. Likewise, the mood of architecture is today caught fleetingly in sidelong glances and snatches of sound.

This study attempts no more than to condense thinking across thirteen broad categories of buildings at what is, by any measure, a significant moment in architectural history. The architecture considered ranges from the radical to the conventional, but as always certain preoccupations with elevational treatment tend to span the categories in a way that the plan and section generally cannot. There are ways of accommodating particular functions and activities – a concert hall auditorium, say, or a factory production line – that an architect challenges at his peril, whereas the outward appearance offers far greater freedom. But in comparing the

hundreds of examples of any given building type with those of other categories, there are moments of concurrence. An assonance, a half-rhyme, sometimes becomes apparent.

There are those architects who espouse the notion of the lightweight, all-enveloping structure – the city as monolithic building. There are those who work in a diametrically opposite way, breaking the building down into its component parts, turning a house into a township. Such concerns of the micro and the macro, the inter-relationship of private and public domains, are by no means new. However, the return to such thinking at the start of the twenty-first century is especially relevant in the light of three particular developments: the extreme importance placed on 'masterplanning' in the commercial sector, and the more cerebral activity of urbanism in the public realm; the concept of 'bigness' in specific developments, which is an architectural device in itself; and, related to both of these, the resurgence of the super-tall building, particularly as part of the city-making frenzy of the Pacific Rim. But to these three, there is a codicil: experimentation continues at its most intense in the design of individual homes. The tradition of domestic radicalism is unbroken.

To see how far architecture has moved during our chosen period, consider what was coming to an end, and what was beginning, at the start of

the 1970s. In 1972, Louis Kahn completed his Kimbell Art Museum at Fort Worth, Texas, a year after Richard Rogers and Renzo Piano won the competition for the Pompidou Centre in Paris, the prototype mediathèque. In 1974, Bruce Graham and Fazlur Khan of SOM completed the Sears Tower in Chicago, destined to remain the world's tallest for many years. In 1975, in Ipswich, England, Norman Foster completed the amoebic black glass form of the Willis Faber Dumas headquarters. In 1978 the Mexican architect Luis Barragán built his last house, and that same year, in Sendai, Japan, the Italian architect Carlo Scarpa died. He was buried in his masterpiece, the Brion family cemetery at Treviso, Italy, in a tomb designed by his son Tobia.

In the 1970s, it seemed as if one architectural world – the world not only of international modernism, but also of craftsmanship, of conservatism – had died with Scarpa while another world – the world of high-precision, machine-made, radical, architecture – was taking over. No comparison can readily be made between Scarpa's last significant work, the Banca Popolare di Verona, with its geologically incised plinth and hand-rendered facade of mixed lime and brick chippings, and Foster's impending Hongkong and Shanghai Bank headquarters, its components shipped and flown in from all over the world. Similarly the completion of a landmark building by

a Piano & Rogers, Pompidou
   Centre, Paris, 1971–7
b Luis Barragán, Plaza y Fuente
   del Bebedero, Las Arboledas,
   Mexico City, 1958–61
c Louis Kahn, Kimbell Art
   Museum, Fort Worth,
   Texas, 1966–72

a | c

b

Harry Seidler and Marcel Breuer, the heavyweight concrete split drum of the Australian Embassy in Paris, was almost wholly eclipsed by the exactly contemporaneous building of the comparatively lightweight steel and glass Pompidou Centre. Seidler's architecture, influenced by Oscar Niemeyer as well as Breuer (he had earlier worked for both), seemed to represent the fag-end of a movement. Others influential in the post-war years, such as Josep Lluis Sert in Barcelona, were undertaking their final commissions: the last knockings, it seemed, of a pre-war manifesto architecture that had first come to prominence in the hermetic world of CIAM – the Congrès Internationaux d'Architecture Moderne – founded in 1928 and swiftly appropriated by Le Corbusier and his disciples. All, then, was set to change, and yet the previous generation of architects was not to be so easily eclipsed. Who would have thought, after all that architecture has been through since then, that Kahn, Scarpa and Barragán would return to favour so strongly?

At the time, all that was being challenged. Yet as the critic Peter Reyner Banham noted in an introduction to the first, slim, volume devoted to Foster Associates in 1978: 'The collapse of the Modern Movement, when it finally happened, proved not to be as much fun as had been anticipated.' Banham was clear: the Modern Movement had collapsed, though he saw Foster as an example of a

modernism that, he noted, 'survived as the dominant element in the new pluralism'. In an endearingly typical case of Banham having his cake and eating it, modernism was thus both very dead and very much alive. But Banham was right in this sense: the term 'modernism' proved to be as stretchable as elastic.

The big question of what, if anything, was going to replace orthodox, International Style modernism went back rather further. In 1961 the American critic Thomas Creighton, intrigued by the stylistic diversity of new buildings in the USA and impressed by then-new mathematical theories of universal confusion, coined the phrase 'chaoticism' to describe this pluralistic activity, and saw the principles of chaos as a positive architectural force. Chaoticism briefly became a bandwagon: the architect Philip Johnson, always quick to latch on to a trend, found it suited his work and outlook admirably, serving as an academic justification for his dilettante approach. Others (Mies van der Rohe, Richard Buckminster Fuller, Raphael Soriano) disagreed, sometimes violently. Either way, the brouhaha soon died down, to be revived in the 1990s when chaos theory – along with a general interest in science and scientists – again became fashionable. So fashionable, that the critic Charles Jencks could tackle 'complexity science' as a force shaping architecture. Creighton's earlier outbreak of lucidity on the same

subject went unremembered, except perhaps by Johnson, who immediately embraced the new Deconstruction movement that was chaos theory's latest manifestation.

Conventionally, all such fussing about an architecture after modernism is dated back to the first time the hegemony of CIAM was challenged by those on the inside: which happened in the mid-1950s with the hugely influential Team X and those sympathetic to its aims. Alison and Peter Smithson and James Stirling in Britain, Giancarlo de Carlo in Italy, and Aldo van Eyck in The Netherlands formed the core of a breakaway movement. In 1957 the British architect and academic Colin St John Wilson underwent a road-to-Damascus conversion when he attended the 1957 RIBA discourse in London by Alvar Aalto, which he described as 'a profound revelation and the inspiration for a critical stance maintained and developed ever since'. In 1960, Wilson wrote a paper, 'Open and Closed', in the Yale architectural journal which sought to identify an alternative tradition of modernism, the tradition of Gunnar Asplund, Hans Scharoun, Alvar Aalto, Hugo Häring, and Frank Lloyd Wright. Not an architecture after modernism, in other words, but a continuing tradition that served far better to connect past, present and future – for the very good reason that a clean break with the past was not part of its ideological make-up.

a   c   e

b   d

The mid-1960s was the period when Foster and Rogers met at Yale, establishing a mutuality of interest that was to lead, back in London, to the practice Team 4. They, and virtually all other British architects later to prove noteworthy, had made the pilgrimage out west to see the 'Case Study' houses of the Eames, Ellwood, Koenig, Soriano and others. They had encountered Buckminster Fuller's passion for lightweight enclosure, and had come home with an enthusiasm for industrial components and a disdain of 'wet', heavy building methods little changed since medieval times. Meanwhile, in Britain, when Cedric Price first flexed the muscles of his 'anticipatory architecture' and felt able to dismiss the cerebral products of Wilson's Cambridge set, led by Sir Leslie Martin, as 'just the Middle Ages with power points'. It was the time when the Archigram Group, with its studious emphasis on impermanent, flexible, service-dominated buildings, was being established by Peter Cook. In the United States, Frank Gehry was drawing in the office of Victor Gruen, the inventor of the most influential building type of the post-war period: the edge-of-town shopping mall. At the same time, Marcel Breuer was developing a brand of highly-articulated Brutalism in projects such as the Koerfer House on Lake Maggiore, Switzerland, and the Whitney Museum in New York, while in Philadelphia, Robert Venturi was combining the two strands of

modernism he had experienced working for Kahn and Saarinen to come up with the Guild House, establishing a strand of symbolic architecture that would take another twenty years to reach a state of decadence in the work of Michael Graves and others.

So when the architectural historian Sir Nikolaus Pevsner, in a radio broadcast in 1966, proved sufficiently worried by the work in Britain of Stirling, Denys Lasdun and others to detect a cult of personality and to coin the term 'post-modern' to describe its difference from his beloved International Modern style, he was describing only the ripples on the surface. The legacy of the renegade Team X – his prime concern – was already being overtaken on both sides. On one side was the 1960s movement that came to be known as 'high-tech', inspired variously by Case Study houses, Archigram's projects, and nineteenth-century engineering. On the other side, the work of Venturi and others pointed to a rather different breed of post-modernism, the kind that would, eventually, provide Banham with all the 'fun' he claimed to be seeking in 1978, at which time an economic recession in the West meant that nothing much was being built anyway. But in architecture, such movements take time to bubble up into the public domain by being expressed in enough real and large commissions to alter our perception of how the built environment is developing. The 'fun' mostly

arrived in the 1980s, and proved rather wearing.

So the decade of the 1970s was the fulcrum, the time when the ambitious background boys elbowed their way to the front as the old order finally (or so it seemed) crumbled. This, then, is the natural starting point for an exploration of the sea change that has taken place in architecture, worldwide, in the thirty years leading up to the Millennium.

Mies van der Rohe repeatedly remarked that one cannot invent a new kind of architecture every Monday morning: however, in the final third of the twentieth century, it seemed at times as if the world was trying to disprove that assertion with movement after movement, style after style. We have seen new vernacular, new regionalism, new classicism, high-tech, post-modernism, organic architecture, deconstruction, eco-architecture, cosmological architecture, ultra-minimalism, and the inevitable return to the period of heroic, 'white modern' architecture by a new generation. The thirty years in question were quite long enough for the avant-garde to become absorbed into the mainstream. Thus high-tech – that photographs very dramatically and is the preferred architectural style of magazine picture editors everywhere, which partly explains its continuing appeal – came to be seen as just another style, virtually a kit of parts, to be called on by any competent architect when the need arose. This it mostly achieved in

a Foster and Partners, Hongkong and Shanghai Bank, Hong Kong, 1979–86
b Harry Seidler (with Marcel Breuer), Australian Embassy, Paris, 1973–7
c Marcel Breuer and Herbert Beckhard Architects, Koerfer House, Ascona, Ticino, Switzerland, 1963–7
d Charles & Ray Eames, Eames House, Pacific Palisades, California, 1949
e Marcel Breuer, Whitney Museum, New York, 1966

hands other than its progenitors. Buildings by Rogers, Foster, Nicholas Grimshaw, Jean Nouvel and Renzo Piano continued to be highly crafted one-offs, though Foster achieved something like a production-line effect with his lesser steel-framed, glass-clad buildings, and Piano developed an oft-repeated private language of terracotta panelling, that evolved over many projects. Instead, high-tech fell into the hands of more anonymous 'commercial' practices who took up the products and methods developed by, or in the wake of, these pioneers. In this sense, the dullards of the architectural business came closest to the future so enchantingly previewed in the Eames House: an architecture made of readily available component parts. Scores of tasteful shiny buildings in business parks the world over testified to the strength of the original vision, their cost per square metre falling almost as rapidly as the cost per gigabyte of computing power contained within them. As ever, it is the details that count: but as Mies discovered, the effect of over-familiarity with a given idiom is increasing pressure on the big names of the business to continue innovating, rather than refining. For a while these big names were European, but simultaneously American corporate steel-framed building techniques, refined over the century since William Le Baron Jenney and Louis Sullivan, were quietly conquering Europe in their wake. The big American practices regrouped,

took a global (as opposed to merely Middle Eastern) perspective, and by the century's end had achieved a new domination in Pacific Rim nations – though not without considerable challenge from the architectural powerhouses of Japan and, increasingly, Australia.

And so the European 'tin gods' started to appear wanting. Where do you go, once you have built the Pompidou Centre, Lloyd's of London, Willis Faber, the Hongkong and Shanghai Bank, Kansai Airport, the Institut du Monde Arabe? How do you follow the big early successes, apart from repairing them? Few architects of any persuasion, it seems, have the desire or the capability to alter their aesthetic approach radically in mid-career as Corbusier or Stirling or Saarinen did. Others, such as Jean Nouvel, Will Alsop or Eric Owen Moss, appear to over-compensate and become restless gadflies, each project having to reinvent the image of the architect. The lucky ones are those who, like Nicholas Grimshaw, turn out to be late developers, evolving an approach down the years that reaches fruition, and international acknowledgment, relatively late in life. Even so, Grimshaw found it difficult to follow up the *tour de force* of his Waterloo International Terminal in London, an accomplished work of great maturity. The work of Renzo Piano – whose built output is considerably more prolific and diverse than Rogers' – is the supreme example of architectural adaptability, given

his willingness to refine an approach using traditional materials on one hand, and to innovate in other areas, for instance stadium and airport design. The British architect Michael Hopkins – who proved able to move well away from the lightweight enclosure technology of his old partner Norman Foster, to the extent of rediscovering the elastic virtues of lime mortar at his Glyndebourne Opera House – may also come to be seen as a link between movements and dogmas, fit to be placed in Wilson's evolving 'alternative tradition'. Some of these fully paid-up modernists found a new seam of work in the context of historic buildings: Foster in London, Berlin and the Ruhr; Piano in the conversion of the Lingotto factory, Turin; and architects such as Yves Lion with his 1987 Franco-American Museum at Blerancourt, France – an addition to an existing building that is in the high-definition tradition of Scarpa.

This book addresses the broad movements in architecture over this period not by 'ism' – such categories are notoriously slippery and mutable, though they serve their purpose and are not ignored here – but by building type. The most basic changes in architecture occur not because of academic theory or pure experiment, but because of changes in the way people live, work, are governed, entertain themselves, regard the outside world, and, most importantly, fund their buildings. It is now axiomatic that form follows

| | b | | d | |
| a | | c | e | |

a Renzo Piano Building
   Workshop, Kansai
   International Airport, Osaka,
   Japan, 1988–94
b Michael Hopkins and Partners,
   Glyndebourne Opera House,
   Glyndebourne, Sussex,
   1989–94
c Frank O Gehry & Associates,
   Guggenheim Museum, Bilbao,
   Spain, 1991–7

d Venturi Scott Brown &
   Associates, Vanna Venturi
   House, Chestnut Hill,
   Philadelphia, 1963–4
e Richard Meier & Partners,
   Getty Center, Brentwood,
   California, 1984–96
f (pages 12–13) Frank O Gehry
   & Associates, Guggenheim
   Museum, Bilbao, Spain,
   1991–7

finance just as much as it follows fashion or function.

Aalto said: 'It is not what a building looks like on the day it is opened, but what it is like thirty years later that matters.' It took only fifteen of those thirty years for the Willis Faber building – Foster assisted by Michael Hopkins – to make its unprecedentedly rapid journey from radicalism to officially acknowledged heritage icon. And it took less time still for Deconstruction to move from being a parlour game played between Peter Eisenman, Jacques Derrida, and Bernard Tschumi, to the completion in 1997 of the melting forms of Frank Gehry's Guggenheim Museum in Bilbao, as purely sculptural a building as Frank Lloyd Wright's original in New York, though perhaps kinder to the works of art it contains: in essence a jewelled shrine intended for Picasso's *Guernica*. For some (including this writer) the Bilbao Guggenheim is one of the great buildings of the era, for others it has a darker purpose. Basque separatists were caught planting mortar-launchers in Jeff Koons' giant floral 'puppy' placed outside the building, resulting in a fatal shoot-out shortly before the museum's official opening in late 1997. The building had come to be seen as a symbol of American colonization – a franchise like McDonald's – rather than, as the Basque government had intended, a proud icon of cultural independence. That small, ugly incident was the downside of what had become one

of the phenomena of the 1980s and 1990s: the cult of the globe-trotting, international 'signature' architect. 'Richard Meier everywhere' as Rem Koolhaas laconically put it: he himself being of the same set.

Alison and Peter Smithson put forward the notion that, in urbanistic terms, a net of routes of equal value is a better way to traverse a city than a hierarchy of major, median and minor roads. Perhaps the pluralism of architecture in the late twentieth and early twenty-first centuries may be likened to that Smithsonian net – they are all leading somewhere and, once the congested terrain is traversed, the destination will become clear. That, at the time of writing, seems just about possible, if admittedly unlikely. The Argentine writer Jorge Luis Borges, pluralism's finest fantasist, invented a more frightening notion: the Garden of Forking Paths. Endless junctions, endless choice, no easy turning back, a future only of infinitely expanding possibilities. No conclusion, ever. This too, though powerfully attractive in some ways, does not quite hit the mark. To introduce a third metaphor: for all that architects have been rattling the bars of their cages these past few decades, they are still in cages, and the cages are becoming smaller.

There are only so many ways of making buildings. The laws of physics apply, while the laws of economics dictate that, whatever architects may want to

do, the building must cost only so much. Indeed, over-generous budgets tend to have the effect of improving finishes rather than the daring of the conception, not least because the architect is always shackled by the materials and labour skills available. Richard Meier's Getty Center in Los Angeles is Meier in smooth metal panels and riven travertine, but it is not discernibly different Meier. Moreover, litigation always awaits the architect who pushes the boundary too far – as it awaits the contractor and components producer who find they have been seduced by the architect or, more likely, the contract value, into taking on more than they can handle. These and a host of other reasons, mostly to do with the layers of aesthetic control now present in developed societies, go some way towards explaining why the design of a building that wins a competition, say, can bear only a passing resemblance to the finished product some years later. But more often, architects are self-censoring: a lifetime of operating within the constraints of the real world, coupled with the fierce desire to build, can lead to an under-ambitious approach in which – like stock markets anticipating a set of bad economic data, and pricing shares accordingly – the downside is considered before a line is drawn. This may help when it comes to getting architecture on the ground, but when nobody can possibly be offended, then equally nobody can possibly be

enthralled. The best buildings will always stir fierce emotions – for and against – which is why architects such as Daniel Libeskind and Zaha Hadid have tended to find themselves at the eye of a storm.

So has anything emerged from the muddle? These thirty years have seen a restless quest, by architects of extremely different opinions and beliefs, to find an architecture appropriate to the age. Banham was right, back in 1978, to predict the rise of a new modernism in the hands of the technology-based practitioners, starting (with due deference to SOM's Hancock and Sears Towers) in Europe but spreading rapidly over the Atlantic and Pacific. Banham was also pushing at an open door: everyone who did not wear a blindfold saw high-tech that way and surprisingly few people looked at the baroque characteristics of a Rogers building and saw post-modernism instead. Similarly, among his supporters, James Stirling was usually taken to be a modernist rather than the 'freestyle classicist' that some tried to label him. It seemed that it was the attitude of the author that counted, and anyway the real classicists had no intention of claiming Stirling as their own, since they were too busy fighting among themselves. As it happened, virtually no architect lumped into the post-modern category agreed with it. The same was true of deconstruction a decade later. To return to high-tech (also a term usually rejected by its practitioners),

discussion in the 1990s tended to ignore the roots of the movement by looking no further back than Paxton and Fox's Crystal Palace, 1850-1, or, at a pinch, Turner and Burton's Palm House at Kew, 1845-7. However an appreciation of the movement's true lineage – which goes way back through the Tudor 'prodigy houses', through the great Gothic cathedrals, to the late Romanesque, and is all to do with refining structure to achieve lightness and drama – does nothing to dispel the power of this ostensibly modern approach. This mode of designing and building is, it can be argued, more than just one of the forking paths in the garden, more than just another strand in the net, but a highlighted route.

The inescapable fashion element is a phenomenon of the architectural world that few would care to admit to. Apart from a few self-aware ironists, those who find themselves forming movements in architecture take their task very seriously indeed. Among the modernists there has always been a disinclination to admit to a spiritual or expressionist side to their work: everything must be discussed in functional terms. If you believe this then you also have to believe that beauty, where it occurs, is a mysterious by-product of an industrial process. If even a transparently conscious attempt at imagery – for instance, in the design of an airport terminal, usually a safe bet for some kind of aeronautical metaphor – is not to be

discussed, then it is hardly likely that architects will prove willing to consider their work in fashion terms, since this implies ephemerality and architecture, despite growing evidence to the contrary, is still regarded as the creation of permanent objects.

Nonetheless, architecture has always liked to eat itself as one style succeeds another. The re-facading of buildings down the centuries is sufficient proof of this: such as medieval timber-framed houses later clad in brick or stone, perhaps several times over. Unpeeling the layers became one of the most difficult challenges of building restorers in the 1990s. Re-facading continues today, on a large scale. When President Valéry Giscard d'Estaing inherited the new Pompidou Centre project in Paris from his eponymous predecessor, he disliked the design so much that he seriously considered encasing it in a skin of his choosing. But by then the building was too advanced to be changed so radically and he had to live with the original design. The tables were turned a quarter of a century later, when Richard Rogers, by then Lord Rogers of Riverside, won the competition to redevelop London's South Bank arts quarter – a collection of post-war concert halls and an art gallery where the 1960s Brutalist elements were widely (though by no means exclusively) disliked. Other entrants in the competitions added various modifying and linking elements to the existing complex. Rogers' solution

b

a   c

a Zaha Hadid, Vitra Fire Station, Weil-am-Rhein, Germany, 1988–94
b Bernard Tschumi Architects, Le Fresnoy, Tourcoing, France, 1995–7
c Foster and Partners, Sainsbury Centre and Crescent Wing, University of East Anglia, England, 1978, 1988–91

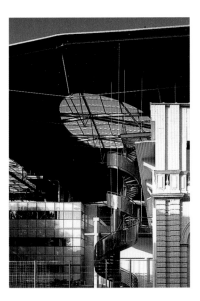

was to encase the least popular parts in a glass roof, so turning an area of separate buildings of a particular aesthetic into one very large building with a new dominant aesthetic (unbuilt at the time of writing). Similar thinking, if with a different aesthetic result, was shown by Bernard Tschumi when he came to remodel the fifty-year-old entertainment complex of Le Fresnoy in Tourcoing, northern France, 1995–7, as an art school. This he did by slipping a voluminous metal jacket over the entire cluster of refurbished buildings, oversailing them to create what he calls an 'in between' – precisely the result sought by Rogers in London. At Le Fresnoy, the outcome is unsettling: buildings that seemed to have a life of their own now appear in a great hangar as if put into storage, and suffer the indignity of being seen from angles and distances they were never intended to be. Nonetheless the surreal effect is curiously compelling.

Elsewhere, less extreme re-facading exercises were underway as developers removed twenty or thirty-year-old cladding systems from office blocks and cheaply produced the appearance of new buildings by re-cladding the structure in the latest style – or even sometimes, confusingly, in replicas of the original. Nothing more convincingly demonstrated how marginal the input of architects to commercial buildings had become: architecture was confined to the outside three inches of the building volume, a

suit of clothes to be removed and replaced as fashion and economic cycles dictated. Even seemingly untouchable buildings suffered this fate. In the case of the Sainsbury Centre at the University of East Anglia by Foster and Partners, it was the original architects who replaced the carapace and, in the process, altered the external appearance of their own building significantly. The ribbed silvery aluminium panels of the original, having begun to fail, were replaced with smooth white panels of a type not available at the time of construction, while the interior of the building remained largely unaltered. A subtle but noticeable chronological dissonance between inside and outside was thus set up. In the light of Tschumi's later work at Le Fresnoy, this was a double irony, since the rationale of Foster's original building was to throw a single roof over a number of disparate functions that would normally, in the university or gallery environment, be expressed as a series of separate buildings. The re-cladding of the Sainsbury Centre, an exercise that passed virtually without comment, can thus be regarded as a discourse on the very nature of contemporary architecture, and a prototype for the next generation of buildings – long predicted by techno-buffs – which will, we are assured, be capable of changing their appearance virtually at will as they respond to climate, light conditions, and the needs of their users.

Foster himself would probably prefer to see the exercise more pragmatically as little different from the lifetime maintenance schedules of aircraft, where the majority of components are replaced or upgraded by the end of the surprisingly long life of the average commercial flying machine.

During the last third of the twentieth century, there was rather more for architects to consider than the increasing impermanence of their built œuvre – which anyway was a change well signalled by the theorists of the 1960s from Cedric Price and the Archigram group onwards. New building types began to emerge, some more resistant to the attention of architects than others. The covered shopping mall, for all its eighteenth- and nineteenth-century roots, was reborn as an American invention of the 1950s, and achieved global dominance during the 1980s and 1990s. Mall-thinking came to inform the other great building type of the era, the airport terminal. If a Martian came to look at airports of the period, from Paul Andreu's rotunda of the Roissy 1 terminal at Charles de Gaulle airport in Paris, designed in the late 1960s, to Kisho Kurokawa's cruciform Kuala Lumpur airport designed in the late 1990s surrounded with its specially planted belt of rainforest, he might conclude that airports were mankind's way of working out a peculiar obsession with geometry. In a way, they are – a geometry concerned with

establishing the shortest walking distance within the terminal while allowing steadily growing numbers of planes to plug into it – but, working against this purity of design intent, they also became mankind's way of delaying the moment of departure long enough to force a bored captive market of passengers to shop, and for a very good reason: competition among international airports has driven down landing charges to a point where the operators can no longer generate a sufficient profit from passenger movements alone.

While the shopping mall proved a graveyard for many architectural ambitions, the airport – and transport buildings in general – became a way to make, or confirm, a reputation, second only to such cultural buildings as art galleries, concert halls and theatres. Both cultural and transport buildings, as it happens, learned much from the despised retail sector. This was not to do with expressed architecture, but the science of moving people around a building – a science developed into an art by the retail specialists, who were honour-bound to give each store the appropriate amount of passing trade and thus developed sophisticated methods to ensure the right distribution of shoppers, particularly in multi-level malls. The concept of the 'anchor store' was both to act as a destination in its own right and to work in concert with other 'anchors' and a mass of subsidiary shops

and restaurants in the bigger malls. These attractions in turn were balanced by the presence and accessibility of car parking. Thus the mall became a consumerist version of Ebenezer Howard's famous 'three magnets' diagram of the Garden City, and can be seen as the late twentieth century's greatest contribution to urbanism.

This may seem a curious conclusion, given the anti-urban qualities of many shopping malls, but it is noticeable, as the end of the century draws near, how many cultural centres have begun to be designed along remarkably similar lines. As America invented the modern shopping mall in the form of Victor Gruen's Northland Center in Detroit, 1949-54, and rapidly evolved it subsequently, so America invented the modern cultural mall in the form of New York's Lincoln Center, 1955-66, by Harrison, Johnson, Foster, Abramovitz, Saarinen and SOM, providing a choice of opera, ballet, symphonic music and drama like rival department stores in a mall. Just like a successful mall, the Lincoln Center has extended itself at intervals, providing other cultural attractions which add to the 'destination' status of the place. Like London's South Bank Centre, 1951 onwards, it has proved durable and adaptable. London's cultural mall slowly evolved over fifty years into a classic retail dumbbell shape: the South Bank Centre at one end, the Tate's Museum of Modern Art

at the other, and a gallimaufry of subsidiary attractions, including housing, cinemas, restaurants, shops – even a replica of Shakespeare's Globe Theatre, completed 1997 – closely associated. This cultural mall separates vehicles and pedestrians in the classic postwar manner of shopping centres, with the Thames-side walkway acting as the car-free zone and acres of car parks plugged into the vehicular spine route behind. The shift in London's centre of gravity that it represents – the most significant change this century in the way London functions – is a wholly unconscious tribute to the art of the retail designer, and an exact parallel with the Lincoln Center experiment, which itself colonized a rough end of town.

While the shopping mall was easing its tentacles into transport and cultural architecture, society at large was rather more concerned with another shift, particularly in the mature economies of the West: the decline of heavy industry and the rise of high-technology industries and office-based working. The very specific flow patterns of the traditional factory – raw materials in, finished products out – were modified to accommodate manufacturing at micro-scale which required conditions of absolute cleanliness and freedom from vibration, but which nonetheless had an astonishingly high rate of failure in the finished products, which had to be recycled. Factories thus came to resemble laboratories.

a   b

c

a   Eero Saarinen, Vivian Beaumont Theater, Lincoln Center, New York, 1958-65
b   Herzog and de Meuron, Tate Museum of Modern Art, Bankside, London, 1994-9: computer-generated graphic
c   Kevin Roche John Dinkeloo & Associates, Ford Foundation Headquarters, New York, 1963-8

Office buildings, in the meantime, found that gearing up for the electronic information revolution meant rediscovering their early twentieth-century roots, in the form of tall-ceilinged rooms arranged around an atrium. Despite the presence of this historical readymade, more research went into the design of offices than any other aspect of the built environment, from the ergonomic design of chairs and keyboards to the ability of the heating, lighting and air-conditioning to cope with the loads put upon them by rooms full of personal computers, fax machines and printers. The profession of 'space planner' was born to add a further layer of consultancy between architect and client. In many instances, the floorplates of the building would be determined by space planners (who themselves could be architects, but for arcane reasons usually not the architects of the whole building). Since all big office buildings came to share the same American-derived steel-frame construction system, and since others would nearly always come to fit out the finished building, once again only the external elevations were left for the named architects to have any fun with. Even there, their design role came close to being usurped by globalized cladding manufacturers and their engineers, while their traditional supervisory role was routinely removed by large construction management companies. 'Fast-tracking' became the buzzword as

huge office developments sprang from the ground on accelerated contracts while they were still in the process of being designed. Meanwhile the stock of the services engineer rose considerably as that of the architect fell. To this day, architects who are perfectly willing to sing the praises of certain structural engineers can hardly ever find it in their hearts to do the same for their services brethren – unwilling, perhaps, to accept that, at least for a time, the office building became less like a piece of architecture, and much more like a very large piece of office equipment.

The surroundings of many office blocks changed with the birth of the business park, spawned from the unlikely union of the grimy industrial estate and the research-based 'science park', usually university-linked. Business parks claimed to be about quality of the working environment but had more to do with easy access either to airports or motorway intersections, since they were aimed at international companies. Consequently many business parks, along with distribution depots and out-of-town shopping and entertainment centres, came to form elements of what are virtually new towns: either new towns springing up around airports, which themselves resemble cities, or the new towns umbilically connected to road junctions, which may be called 'intersection cities'. In many cases, both stimulants apply. At first, Charles de Gaulle Airport north of Paris was just

an airport in the fields. Today, the airport is only one element of the hugely expanded town of Roissy, a trading centre on a trade route and, as such, both historical and predictable in its growth pattern.

The exposed-services cliché of early high-tech buildings represented an attempt to architecturalize, and thus reclaim, the increasingly large services element of the building's budget. Research into the energy-efficient building – an immediate response to the oil crisis of the early 1970s – however ran ahead of available technology, which only began to seem capable of meeting the challenge of drastically reduced power consumption at the century's end. It was not until the advent of 'green' buildings, for offices, universities and the like, that a different language began to evolve: the architecture of wind towers and turbines, solar chimneys, cross-ventilation or tholos-like stack-effect atria, double-wall glazing, heat-sink heavy masonry or lightweight solar-powered skins. Architects became keen on 'green' buildings not only for environmental reasons, but because the green agenda allowed them to reclaim some lost design territory, take control of a larger proportion of spending on a building. A revival of interest in the use of timber – both structurally and, more frequently, as a cladding material – can also be seen as concealing a different agenda beneath its 'renewable' credentials. With timber cladding (indeed with the

use of most 'traditional' materials) the architect is once more in charge of design and out of the hands of the components manufacturers. Consequently a great deal of experimentation with traditional materials, used modernistically, began to take place from the mid-1990s. The other side of the coin was the first generation of 'green' high-tech buildings, where the use of a limited selection of suitable industrialized systems meant that a building by one architect could end up looking uncannily like a building by another, with such notable exceptions as the work of T R Hamzah and Yeang in Malaysia. This sameness may change as the industries develop more products. It is arguable – but perfectly possible – that the 'green' movement signals the biggest shift in the appearance of architecture since the advent of heroic modernism in the 1920s. Then again, stylistic inertia is a powerful force in its own right, with architects often readier to adapt old forms than to embrace new ones. This skeuomorphic tendency is inevitable and ancient: thus the Greeks faithfully copied all the details of timber temples into the new technology of stone.

Those modernists working with traditional materials could take heart from the 'regionalist' architects who gradually came to prominence: the adobe-influenced Antoine Predock in the southern United States and the Wright-influenced Bart Prince; Charles Correa and Raj Rewal in India; Geoffrey Bawa in Sri Lanka; Rasem Badran in Jordan; the school of Australian 'outback' architecture; the Hungarian organic tradition headed by Imre Makovecz. While in some cases such hand-made architecture has amounted to a manifesto statement against modernism, in others the painstaking use of seemingly retro materials was anything but. The growing appreciation of the work of Peter Zumthor in Switzerland, first with his archaeological shelters, then with his thermal baths complex at Vals, is evidence of the latter, as is much of the work of his fellow Swiss Jacques Herzog and Pierre de Meuron.

All styles, however, do not suit all building types. Even though Rafael Moneo could conceive an airport terminal as a broadly traditional building, few others do. Those experimenting with sappy forest thinnings and turf as building materials, along with those recycling discarded products such as whisky barrels, would not attempt to apply their approach to sports stadia or skyscrapers. A religious building, you might think, could be anywhere and be made of anything: but not so, it would seem that in most cases a certain opacity and solidity is required. Theatres and concert halls have acoustic and lighting demands that partly militate against lightweight architecture; the architecture of public spaces, in contrast, can be positively ethereal. Office buildings need natural light and often – as air-conditioning is seen to be an eco-logical evil – cross-ventilation; art galleries and museums, as much as shopping centres, must turn their backs on the world with windowless spaces, but can counterbalance those with their 'low' recreational elements – the cafés and shops. Schools must contain a certain variety of spaces and perform specific functions that tend to be expressed, by all architects everywhere, in a limited number of plan forms – relating the big communal space to cell-like teaching space, a form adopted increasingly by office space planners. Factories, however they are dressed up, must respond to the nature of the manufacturing process they shelter. Few homes look like offices, and even fewer offices look like homes. All this may seem truistic, but in the relentless categorizing of architectural styles – as if style was something that floated above the function of the buildings – it tends to be forgotten that buildings in their unformed state, as a set of needs, have their own demands, and that those demands may well suit one approach rather than another.

At the start of the twenty-first century, it is telling that the category broadly referred to as 'modernism' now contains such a plurality of approaches within its elastic sides. With its own tradition to draw on, the notion of the modern – which means a desire to express contemporary society in the buildings it occupies – has strongly reasserted itself after the

a b

c d

a Bart Prince with Bruce Goff,
   Shinenkan Pavilion for
   Japanese Art, Los Angeles
   County Museum of Art,
   1988–97
b T R Hamzah & Yeang, Menara
   Mesiniaga, Selangor, Kuala
   Lumpur, 1989–92
c Michael Hopkins and Partners,
   Inland Revenue Centre,
   Nottingham, England 1992–4
d Antoine Predock, Spencer
   Theater, Ruidoso, New Mexico,
   1994–6

period of doubt in the 1980s, as it did after a similar period in the 1950s. This is endlessly arguable: just what should be described as 'modernist', just what should form its own genus or species? But one should perhaps dig deeper. Beneath the busy surface of compatible or incompatible styles and approaches, of endless architectural diversification, of interest groupings, politics, beneath the horses-for-courses business of the right architect for the job, a very ancient game is still being played out. In its broadest sense, the battle is the same as it has been since the Renaissance: the classical versus the gothic. This is not a surface difference, but a fundamental, in-the-bones, thing. It is the symmetrical and completist architecture of one mode versus the chameleon, asymmetrical, accretive architecture of the other. This most basic of all architectural differences is quite capable of driving a wedge between practitioners seemingly in the same camp. Very few architects are aware of such essential forces driving them. If it is a game, then the rules are not so much learnt as instinctively understood. It is not a game with winners or losers: only ever players.

At the start of this introduction, I mentioned those relatively rare but always stimulating moments of concurrence when briefly – before things go haywire again – it appears that all the needles on all the dials are pointing in the same direction. One of these moments is experienced more often, and registers more strongly than others. Across all building types – even skyscrapers – one encounters the remarkable and increasing international popularity of the architectural approach that started in the Deconstructivist parlour but which, now greatly diversified, can be dubbed 'the displaced grid'. This is the skewing and overlaying of geometries in plan, section, or both, thus establishing tensions within what would conventionally be orthogonal structures, and which erupt sometimes violently but often beautifully into the expression of the building's exterior. Unlike other more shallow stylistic moments, this one has the potential to transcend fashion since it cannot easily be merely skin deep. Nor can it be in any respect functionalist. It necessitates an architectural repossession of the entire building form, and thus has hovering over it the ghost of a manifesto. It is moving, as high-tech did before it, from the hands of high-art practitioners into the mainstream. At the start of the new century, if there is a dominant element emerging from the past thirty years of pluralism, this looks a more likely candidate than most.

Building typologies continue to shift their ground, wax and wane in relative importance, and to overlap. We have seen how retail mall design has wormed its way into cultural, transport and leisure architecture. Sports buildings, meanwhile – encouraged by non-stop television coverage – have become highly fashionable, to the extent that they are now symbols of civic pride in much the same way as the theatre or city hall, and not only for those cities hosting the Olympics. Health buildings, no longer such an important category, are subsumed into the 'civic realm', where the cult of the 'signature bridge' shows how architects, having lost ground in some areas, can reclaim it in others.

In the next century the evolution of the office workplace will continue to fascinate: just how long can the big corporate headquarters survive as a building type? Similarly, how necessary will a physically cohesive university campus prove to be in an on-line age? One-off houses and places of worship will remain a testing-ground for ideas, and have not yet exhausted their capacity to surprise. Architects are still fascinated, as the Futurists were, by the dramatic possibilities of industry. The building type that can include all others, however, is only now moving to maturity after a century of development. The supertower – mixed-use, land-conserving, capable of meeting more and more of its own energy needs – will be the lodestone of the new century. Achieving the sustainable tower – which means the sustainable city – is the greatest challenge now facing architecture. If that can be got right, everything else will follow.

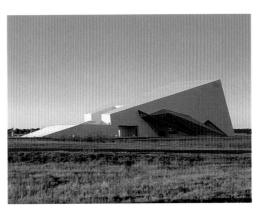

VISUAL ARTS *Museums & galleries* Exhibition spaces have long been exceptional buildings, their architecture drawing visitors as surely as their contents. But over the past thirty years, architecture has overtaken art. The museum has assumed a supreme role in moulding perceptions of a town or city, region or nation. With the onset of the science of arts economics, it has also become axiomatic that the arts are an industry, and a profitable one. As towns and cities once flaunted their cathedrals, factories and railway stations, so now they depend on the magnetic attraction of their galleries.

'Architects are both the victims and the beneficiaries of the political will.'
James Stirling, March 1991.

Nothing defines the cultural monuments of the late twentieth century more than the inability of most people, when asked, to vouchsafe correctly or even roughly what is inside them. The Sydney Opera House surely stages opera? Not primarily: the building is a performing arts centre which caters for concerts, ballet, theatre and cinema as well as opera. The Guggenheims in New York and Bilbao exhibit paintings and sculpture? Certainly, but that is not the reason why people visit these buildings. Does anyone who has been to see the Institut du Monde Arabe in Paris have much recollection of the contents disposed behind that masterly if occasionally troublesome Moorish diaphragm-mechanism solar wall? Very few. And so it goes on. What does James Stirling and Michael Wilford's Neue Staatsgalerie in Stuttgart, contain? A foolish question: one might as well ask what the dozens of museums built in Frankfurt during the 1980s, or the five hundred reputedly built in 1988 in Japan, were for, exactly.

Art museums are built for various reasons, few of them to do with art. They are built to provide a cultural destination for a provincial city with a dull reputation, or to refresh the waning arts credentials

of a capital needing to keep the overseas tourists pouring in, or to enhance the reputation of a seat of learning, or to satisfy the ego of a private collector or corporate billionaire. And they do all these things. Long ago Hans Scharoun and Mies van der Rohe placed the key pieces in Berlin's 'cultural forum' – respectively the Philharmonie concert hall, 1956-63, and the New National Gallery, 1965-8 – as different from each other as chalk from cheese, or music from silence. Mies' National Gallery in particular could have been a house or a Chicagoan corporate headquarters, being as it was the customary beautifully detailed box (with oversailing roof in deference to sunshading) set on a plinth. No matter: Scharoun created the unique landmark while Mies' presence was a political statement that one particular era had passed, and that the exiled architect – by then very aged – had returned. The name was what mattered. The 'cultural forum', built as it was close to the Berlin Wall, was itself a political act, assuming as it did (correctly, as it turned out) that a new centre would emerge round here when East and West were reunited.

Later, in one of those tricks that architecture loves to spring, Berlin returned to Chicago when Josef Paul Kleihues designed that city's Museum of Contemporary Art, 1991-6. Kleihues bought the Berlin notion of the grand, classically arranged city-block building, clad in limestone, and set it up on a

plinth, as Mies had done when he brought his Chicago preoccupations to Berlin. Despite the drawbacks of the Mies building – an inability to house permanent works in the glazed upper, pavilion level because of light damage, for instance – Mies is architecturally the clear winner on points. Curators, however, may well prefer Kleihues.

Art museums are pulled four ways: by the differing demands of their patrons, their public, their architects, and their curators. From a curatorial point of view, what matters most – apart from space, space, and more space – is carefully controlled daylighting, precise atmospheric controls, gallery design that allows easy display of a huge variety of different art forms, and all the relevant back-up facilities in terms of restoration workshops, storage, office space and so on. The patrons of such buildings are less concerned with the technicalities, and crave the cultural landmark, frequently as a means to urban regeneration. They may desire educational facilities such as lecture theatres, which curators are seldom interested in. Aesthetically the patrons tend to be more conservative than their architects. Meanwhile the public – apart from the few visitors who are going for the art rather than the 'experience' – wants soundbite-sized cultural entertainment and a good café. The upshot of all this is that, in all but a few cases, the modern art museum is effectively a multi-use building.

a	b
	d
	c

The jewel box versus the neutral container:
a   Jean Nouvel and Architecture Studio, Institut du Monde Arabe, Paris, 1981-7: library interior showing diaphragm wall
b   Josef Paul Kleihues, Museum of Contemporary Art, Chicago, 1991-6: gallery interior
c   MoCA, Chicago: gallery interior, looking out to garden
d   MoCA, Chicago: exterior view

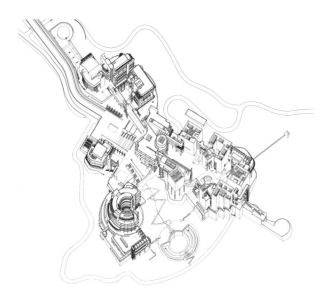

The whole process reached an apotheosis of sorts with the opening of The Getty Center in Los Angeles by Richard Meier in late 1997, allegedly America's first billion-dollar building (outside military complexes, presumably). This sprawling acropolis of an arts complex, thirteen years in the making, complete with its own techno-funicular railway from the city below, was accused by some critics of being simply too good – of making its host city seem scruffy, down-at-heel. Perched on its hilltop, gleaming white, overlooking both the city grid and the Pacific, the Getty is an ivory tower in the way that Frank Gehry's Guggenheim in Bilbao, completed only two months earlier, is not: Gehry engaged with his industrial surroundings in Bilbao with characteristic verve and relish. The two architects had become yin and yang, the cool rationalist versus the outright emotionalist, the aloof versus the committed, dividing the world up between them. Meier had built the Barcelona Art Museum, opened in 1996. Meier had built galleries everywhere. Gehry was called in by Bilbao: Gehry, too, had built everywhere.

But the white train at the Getty taking you to the acropolis gives the game away. Like a pilotless airport shuttle, it takes you to a no man's land where national boundaries, let alone the rough and tumble of a real city, are irrelevant. The Getty Center might as well be in space. Its fame is its wealth: its

unlimited ability to buy the greatest art in the world has distorted the art market considerably over many years – in the process increasing the value of its own collection. It may look white, but it is a black hole for art. The fact that it is wholly privately financed adds to its slightly sinister quality – as if some James Bond villain were seated in a control room at its centre, preparing to bring ruin on the world. Yet, in the end, it is just a complex of Richard Meier buildings and Meier – the master of brittle, perfect corporate architecture – was no doubt the ideal choice for a museum that operates as a global investor.

Politics and wealth are only part of the stately dance involved in the selection of architects. For instance Peter Eisenman's Wexner Center for the Visual Arts, at the Ohio State University, has attained a fame disproportionate to its setting or its function, simply because at the time, 1982–9, it was the largest project to be built by its famously egg-headed architect, and also because it was consequently one of the first built expressions of the style known as deconstruction. In other hands, this relatively modest insertion of new spaces between large existing buildings need not have excited much comment, but Eisenman was news. As well as creating a fractured structural grid for the project, and slicing a wall diagonally through the 3-D grid as you would expect from a founding father of deconstructivism, he

added the post-modern touches of cartoon-like brick towers and bastions, the main tower being split and displaced from top to bottom as if placed on a fault line. These towers were apparently a 'memory' of an armoury that occupied the site until 1958, but somehow this deliberately stage-set approach, abstracted though it is, is more shocking than all the games of displaced volumes that Eisenman plays inside, perhaps because it brings home to us that even an original thinker such as Eisenman was sufficiently conditioned by the architectural mores of his time to play the kind of post-modern joke that quickly palls.

The rest of the composition is to do with the now familiar business of overlaying various conflicting grids present in the area. Only architects derive such pleasure from fooling around with grids, which after all are an architect-made construct in the first place: the rest of humanity is merely bemused by such acts of self-examination. It became an Eisenman trademark, however, as well as being one of the signs by which one assesses any building for 'Decon' content, and it has this merit: it is a way of breaking down the bulk of a large building that can claim to be somehow rational rather than being driven purely by aesthetic considerations.

Thus Eisenman's later Columbus Convention Center in Ohio, 1989–93, wittily takes its cue from the tangle of railway tracks that used to exist on its

a   Richard Meier & Partners,
    Getty Center, Brentwood,
    California, 1984–97: courtyard
    with J Paul Getty Museum
    beyond
b   Getty Center: site axonometric

b

a

a   Richard Meier & Partners,
    Getty Center, Brentwood,
    California, 1984-97:
    gallery interior in the
    J Paul Getty Museum
b   Getty Center: plaza walkways

a | b

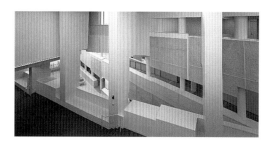

b   c   e

a   f

d

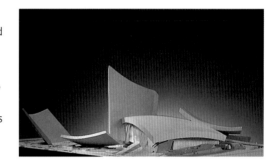

goods-yard site, a tangle encountered also in skeins of computer cabling. What would otherwise be a huge volume of a building is expressed as conjoined slices, snaking and undulating and presenting a very varied frontage to the main street. This is as valid as any other architectural scaling device.

As Eisenman built more, he loosened up a little: his Aronoff Center for Design and Art at the University of Cincinnati, Ohio, is less a dry academic exercise in the layering and rupturing of grids, more an intuitive response to the context of landforms and existing buildings – which means it is closer to the kind of thing a Gehry or a Behnisch might produce. Perhaps only Daniel Libeskind, of the crowd loosely described as 'Decon', is still inclined to plot out his buildings according to intellectual geometries of his own making, but even he has relaxed enough to produce gesturalist architecture such as his 'Spiral' design for an extension to London's Victoria and Albert Museum, and even more so with his 'shattered globe' design for the Imperial War Museum North in Manchester, north-west England. This is a fine example of the museum-as-urban-generator theory since Libeskind, the most cerebral of architects, was also paradoxically seen by his client as being highly commercial, to the extent that his architecture was deemed capable of drawing 400,000 visitors a year.

Stuttgart, never previously noted as a significant tourist honeypot, became one of the most visited cities in Germany following the completion in 1984 of the Staatsgalerie extension which James Stirling and Michael Wilford had won in competition in 1977, and which is notable far more for the quality and ingenuity of its external public spaces than it is for its frankly dull galleries inside. Frankfurt, with a reputation as a home of financiers and trade exhibitions, also consciously set out to reinvent its cultural image: not so much for tourist trade but to reinforce its position as a place for international companies to relocate to. Inward investment means moving quantities of people to a place they may not wish to go; people have certain demands when it comes to quality of life: museums, galleries, theatres and concert halls are therefore flung into the reckoning by those offering incentives of a more than purely fiscal nature.

The phenomenon is open-ended. Cities want signature architects to produce trophy buildings. Hence the success of such architects as Richard Meier, Frank Gehry, Arata Isozaki, I M Pei, Norman Foster. Theirs is a known and recognizable product. Buying such names – as Bilbao in northern Spain has bought Foster for its metro stations, Gehry for its Guggenheim, Wilford for its Abando transport interchange; and as San Francisco employed Mario Botta for its Museum of Modern Art – buys global renown.

The displaced grid and the displaced globe:

a Peter Eisenman, Wexner Center for the Visual Arts, Columbus, Ohio, 1982–9: view of entrance

b Peter Eisenman, Aronoff Center for Design and Art, University of Cincinnati, Ohio, 1988–96: interior view of circulation space

c Aronoff Center: entrance

d Wexner Center: aerial view

e Daniel Libeskind, Imperial War Museum North, Manchester, 1997: 'shattered globe' concept drawings

f Imperial War Museum North: model

Botta is a prime example of the phenomenon of collecting a signature style, since his chamfered-drum motif, present in so very many of his buildings, is as instantly recognizable (to those in the know) as a comedian's catchphrase. However, it must be remembered that the vast majority of the public are as much in the dark about private architectural languages as those who happen not to watch a particular cult TV programme, and so fail to pick up the conversational references of those who do. To the inhabitants of San Francisco, then, the arrival of a large and prominent public building by Botta must have seemed like an alien landing. Even to those familiar with Botta's mannerisms, the San Francisco Museum of Modern Art, 1989–95, is compellingly strange in its setting, the horizontal emphasis of its layered and banded brick carapace at odds with the soaring verticality of its high-rise neighbours, its solidity and introverted nature equally different from the delicacy of Fumihiko Maki's Yerba Buena Center over the road. The strikingly striped chamfered drum – which in other Botta works such as his cathedral at Evry, France (see 'Religion') constitutes the entire building envelope – is here consigned to the lesser function of a lightwell, bringing daylight down into the core of what is a very deep-plan building, where the horizontally striped theme continues in the interior of the great public lobby. As ever, Botta dramatizes

the drum by creating walkways around and across it. But from outside, the sharply angled form also manages to suggest a tower, almost as if the building proper is merely the footing for some great shaft which is either about to spring heavenwards from the suggested bud, or which has previously existed and been pruned. It leads the eye skywards.

The set-backs in the big brick box allowed Botta to naturally top-light as many of the galleries as possible via relatively conventional lantern rooflights and ceiling diffusers mounted in the flat roof sections. The building contains lecture halls, a large auditorium, cafés and a bookshop, as well as the galleries and sundry ancillary spaces. It is a considered piece of gallery-making and its sculptural form stems from that. For the city fathers, however, the Museum of Modern Art had another, now familiar, function – to act as the centrepiece of a 40-hectare urban regeneration project for a run-down district that had been officially recognized as a problem since the 1950s. The city threw cultural projects at the area, more or less piecemeal, and Botta's museum was merely the largest of them. It will take time to see if the Yerba Buena precinct benefits from the spin-off economic activity that arts buildings habitually generate: in the meantime Botta's great oculus at least provides a highly visible focus.

If a town or city is fortunate enough to be known already for one cultural strand, then a work by one of the world's architectural masters holds out the promise of a doubling of the audience. So Nîmes in southern France, on the Roman antiquity circuit, can now keep its visitors longer, and relieve them of more of their money, thanks to Norman Foster's mediathèque, the Carré d'Art, 1985–93. Everyone now purports to understand the beneficial economic impact, over a surprisingly wide area, of an arts magnet of this kind. So much so, that the very economic argument for arts provision – once scarcely given credence – is now presenting its own, more insidious threat: that capital spending on arts buildings is somehow an end in itself, irrespective of their contents or the need for continued revenue funding once they are built. But this attitude is difficult to drag into the daylight because it is overlaid by another, older attitude to such architecture: that it is good for the civic state. It has long been deemed virtuous partly at a local and regional level – the people are kept in touch with their own cultural history – and at a national and international level – the people are encouraged to look outwards to the world beyond, and the world beyond comes to them.

This is why, understandably enough, such buildings have been dubbed the cathedrals of our age, and have been so regarded since the burst of

a b   c
           e
       d   f

a James Stirling Michael Wilford & Associates, Neue Staatsgalerie, Stuttgart, 1977–84: exterior view. The loose public realm
b Neue Staatsgalerie: gallery interior
c Mario Botta, Museum of Modern Art, San Francisco, 1989–95: sections through central lightwell over lobby and through central axis
d MoMA, San Francisco: foyer space
e MoMA, San Francisco: gallery interior
f MoMA, San Francisco: aerial view

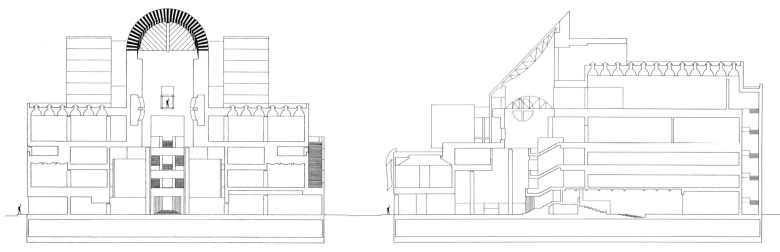

classically based museum building in the nineteenth century (Smirke in London and Schinkel in Berlin prime among them) offered a secular architecture of world culture at a time when no cathedrals were being built. The process of religious worship in most cultures requires its holy places, expressed in strongly architectural terms. For religion read art, in its broadest sense; for cathedral read gallery, museum, theatre or concert hall; for pilgrim read tourist; and there is your apt analogy, all tied up. It was true enough in the late eighteenth and nineteenth centuries for the moneyed classes, and, for all that it is now a cliché, it is even more true today. There is virtually an obligation placed upon members of the affluent society to travel. Their travelling has to be given a purpose. The cultural destination provides that purpose. And when historical remains and existing museological or art collections become overloaded, then the response is to create new destinations that are there because they are there. The architecture, not the collection, is the generator. There are certain rare exceptions: such as the pious hope that Picasso's *Guernica* might be moved from Madrid to the Bilbao Guggenheim in the Basque country; a move that, it was thought, would ensure mass movement of pilgrims to the new Gehry museum, and hence pay off its development costs more speedily. In theory the Bilbao Guggenheim was not predicated upon *Guernica*, and the calculations

of the museum's income potential were made, it is said, on the basis that the great work would not necessarily be there: but there is no doubt that, without it, the initial numbers of visitors to this previously little-visited industrial city were not stupendously high. Certainly, seeing a display of rather tired Damien Hirst works in the room originally designed to house *Guernica* – as one did in the Museum's opening exhibition – was to experience a piquant sense of bathos.

Although Meier's Getty Center in Los Angeles and Gehry's Guggenheim in Bilbao bestrode the world like some vast composite cultural colossus at the close of 1997, they are only part of a continuing tradition: the art gallery as urban regenerator and economic stimulant. Two other buildings serve as bookmarks in this open-ended history of the self-generating cultural building: the Pompidou Centre in Paris, 1971-7, and the Groninger Museum, Groningen, The Netherlands, 1990-4. The Pompidou Centre, won in competition in 1971 by Renzo Piano and Richard Rogers, signalled a sea-change in twentieth-century architecture, as a result of which the whole modern tradition can be said to have subtly altered. As with T S Eliot's theory of literary tradition, this backwards modification is highly important: the new work of art adjusts not only what comes after – rivers would run uphill if that were not the case – but

also our perception of what has gone before. What may have appeared to be the direction of a movement at one moment in time turns out to have taken a different route. We know this will happen again, that our cultural histories will have to be re-revised backwards down the centuries by some as yet unknown development. The deconstructivism movement of the late twentieth century, particularly as handled by Frank Gehry, caused vibrations right down to the root structure of modernism and forced us to look at the Pompidou with different eyes: its own place in the Pantheon was changed, and not just by changing fashion.

The Pompidou took to extremes Louis Kahn's famous notion of 'served and servant' spaces. It may therefore have more in common than it seems with Kahn's Kimbell Art Museum in Fort Worth, Texas, 1966-72, which was nearing completion at the time of the Pompidou competition. It also exemplifies an innate attribute of all grand public buildings, an attribute spun into space by Frank Lloyd Wright at New York's Guggenheim: new architecture as the prime cultural draw, rather than the contents. Famously, the Pompidou replaced the Eiffel Tower as the most popular destination in a city bright with cultural lodestars. But notoriously, what most visitors did was ride the snaking escalator tube slung on the outside, look out across Paris from the top, have a

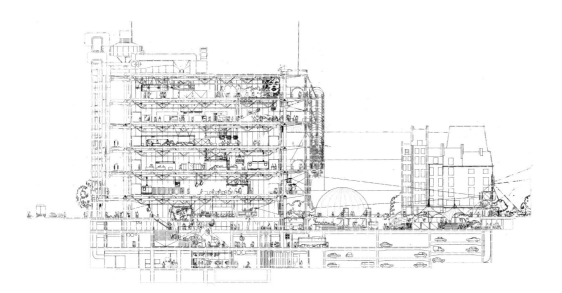

snack in the rooftop café, pose for photographs, and leave. Meanwhile, inside the long-span, sometimes rather low and gloomy, internal spaces, there was a national art collection, a library, temporary exhibitions, and IRCAM, a contemporary music centre, underground. These became something of a lost world. Despite the fact that this was the first of the modern mediathèques, a visually biased athenaeum, its serious functions (the reasons it was built) came to seem incidental compared with its generative quality as a giant urban climbing-frame. In an exact parallel, the spiral of Wright's Guggenheim was eventually emptied of its paintings and sculpture, which had never sat happily there. The collected art was put in real galleries built alongside by Gwathmey Siegel & Associates, 1982–92: the spiral was acknowledged as art enough in itself. Thus Wright's Guggenheim became another urban climbing frame, a pedestrian version of the unbuilt spiral of his 1925 'Automobile Objective', a mountain-top building which you were meant to drive up, see the view, drive down again. People had cars, their duty was to drive them somewhere, therefore Wright provided them with a destination. The Guggenheim crystallized this thinking and is now duly acknowledged as an end in itself.

However, for all that the Pompidou Centre became, it was never cynical in what it set out to achieve. The Pompidou architects believed with a passion in their cause. This was manifesto architecture, carried out by men at the idealistic beginning, not the glorious conclusion, of their careers. Piano and Rogers seemed genuinely taken aback and delighted when five times the projected numbers of annual visitors turned up, 25,000 a day, year after year, to a building that had been vilified through the design and construction processes, and routinely compared to an oil refinery upon completion. At one point it even threatened to revive the Franco-German hatreds of the Second World War when Krupps, renowned for its armaments manufacture, secured the contract to supply the heavy steelwork (Krupps' lorries had to arrive at night with the company name blanked out in order to maintain the peace). The huge popularity of the building – and this, in a sense, was what its architects found hard to credit – was largely due to the architecture and what that architecture did to the rest of the city, rather than to the activities within for which it had been expressly designed. Its rationale was, if not negated (the exhibition programme in particular proved highly successful) then at any rate set askew. Later to call in Gae Aulenti, architect of the city's highly successful Musée d'Orsay, 1980–6, to design the interiors of the Museum of Modern Art, was either a mistake or a clever touch, depending on your viewpoint. She treated the Piano and Rogers shell much as she

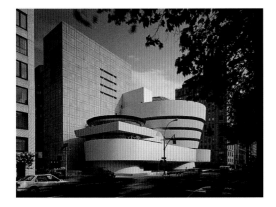

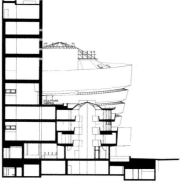

treated the impressive clear-span spaces of the old Gare d'Orsay and the Palau Naçional in Barcelona (the Museum of Catalan Art) – namely as big voids to be partitioned with dividing walls to hang things on. At the Pompidou, what appear to be solid floor-bearing walls are actually slightly flexible partitions themselves suspended from the trusses. The result was an appearance of permanence within an avowedly changeable structure; an effect that was dramatically removed from the original concept, actually implemented for a while, of having significant artworks stacked away on mechanized panels that could be summoned on request.

Whether regarded as art museum or viewing-platform, the Pompidou soon suffered from the numbers of feet tramping it. This, twenty years after its completion, led the authorities to consider a radical and undemocratic solution in the eyes of the architects: to limit numbers according to the ability and desire to pay. Even the open parvis which the building commands had begun to cause concern to the City of Paris – since that realm of happy buskers and laughing tourists had degenerated, it was said, into a honeypot for beggars and thieves, perhaps its tone should be improved by making it an exclusive area for paying guests. This soul-searching about just how public, and just how managed, a public 'gallery' should be, coincided with a major refurbishment for

the building, carried out by Piano in consultation with Rogers, in time for the Millennium. This work, oddly in some eyes, ossified much of the external appearance of the building in its original form rather than taking advantage of its design philosophy as an interchangeable kit of parts. The reorganization was largely confined to the interior, which raised the intriguing question as to just how many of the famous painted pipes on the Rue du Renard elevation still had a function beyond the sculptural. No matter: the exercise raised questions pertinent to any city considering a new arts centre and the way it mediates between the state and the people. The questioning of its original ideology drew attention to the thinking that informed its design.

The Pompidou Centre is the fulcrum on which all the architecture of the late twentieth century pivots and thus is the true starting point of this book. It realized the radical paper thinking of the 1950s and 1960s, and its continuity and change represents an enduring experiment. Therefore, any subsequent visual arts building has to consider what the Pompidou attempted, if only to reject it. Most did: the old notion that an arts building must, like a bank, architecturally represent stability rather than mutability soon reasserted itself. By the time London's National Gallery came to build its extension in 1986, its architect, Philadelphia-based Robert

Venturi, was forced into a contextual and deferential straitjacket which even his 'pop' sensibilities could not overcome, though the result was a more satisfactory building than his Seattle Art Museum, 1984–91, which is less of a building, more of a decorated hoarding. When Norman Foster came to build his own version of a mediathèque in Nîmes more than a decade after the Pompidou was completed, it was a formally arranged, effectively classical composition, highly resistant to change, only its transparency revealing its provenance. Even that clue vanished when Foster came to build his stone-panelled extension to the Joslyn Art Museum in Omaha, Nebraska, 1992–4, which in its undemonstrative, blank-box way is as deferential to its weak 1930s Beaux Arts parent as Venturi's London effort is to its weak 1830s Greek Revival parent. But at least these subdued later buildings function well as correctly top-lit galleries: the internal spaces of both engage the senses considerably more than their exteriors which – surely – is what an art gallery ought to be doing.

In similar vein, but structurally far more expressive, is Piano and Fitzgerald's Menil Gallery in Houston, Texas, 1981–6. Rogers, at the time of writing, had not designed another art gallery or museum since the Pompidou: his former partner Piano, in contrast, was able to reflect and develop his ideas. As at the Pompidou, the form of the building is dictated by

a   c
        e
    b d   f g

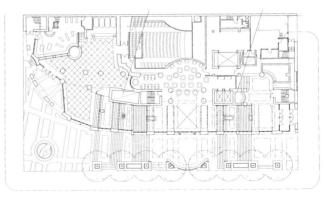

a Gae Aulenti, Musée d'Orsay,
   Paris, 1980–6: interior view
   showing galleries inserted
   into Orsay train shed
b Venturi Scott Brown &
   Associates, Seattle Art
   Museum, Seattle, 1984–91:
   exterior view
c Venturi Scott Brown &
   Associates, Sainsbury Wing,
   National Gallery, London,
   1986–91: plan
d Seattle Art Museum: site plan

e Sainsbury Wing: Exterior
   detail of connection between
   Sainsbury Wing and National
   Gallery
f Sainsbury Wing: oblique view
   of gallery at the north end of
   the central range of galleries
g Sainsbury Wing: interior of
   gallery at the north end of
   the central range of galleries
   Venturi's mannered interiors
   are unjustly neglected

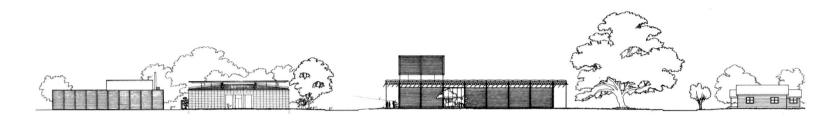

a

b

c

d

e

f

its most prominent element – in this case the ferro-cement light-deflecting blades that form the ceiling of the building, which are continued as a colonnade around its exterior where their ductile-iron trusses can be appreciated. Piano had learned about ferro-cement from boat building, and about the properties of ductile iron from his VSS Experimental Car project with Fiat, 1978–80, with the engineer Peter Rice. Technology transfer was thus alive and well at the Menil Collection, and applied to the one crucial element of all art galleries, the handling of light.

The most telling contrast to the act of late modern architectural soul-baring represented by the Pompidou, or Piano's equally rational if less exu-berant technology-led successor in Texas, is the Groninger Museum in Groningen, The Netherlands, 1990–4. The Groninger Museum set out from the first to seduce by appearance alone, unbothered by the standard of its contents, or even the technical niceties of displaying them to best effect. It may thus be counted a cheerfully cynical exercise. This agree-able northern Dutch university city with its ring of canals was well away from the tourist circuit and, worse, was best known as a centre for natural gas production which had become a relocation point for decentralized private companies and public utilities from the south. To be sent to the gas fields of Groningen had, to the horror of the city fathers,

come to mean a species of internal exile. An ambi-tious programme of arts events and new building was begun to correct this image, among them a pro-gramme of temporary 'video bus shelters' by invited stars such as Daniel Libeskind, Zaha Hadid, Rem Koolhaas and Coop Himmelblau. Intrigued by all this, the ambitious young director of the city's museum, Frans Haks, saw an opportunity for glory.

What happened next was completely unexpected to those who thought that the craze for turbocharged plastic laminates was a passing fad of the early 1980s associated with the Memphis group. The Groninger Museum, built on a new island in a basin of the city's main canal, sprang from the head of Alessandro Mendini, the Italian post-modernist designer much admired by Haks for, among other works, his architectural tea set for Alessi, where each piece was a miniature building. Haks had already decided that the various elements of the museum's collection and exhibition programme should be sepa-rately expressed: Mendini's response to this was to assemble an eclectic cast of characters to contribute an element apiece. These were himself, fellow design-ers Philippe Starck and Michele de Lucchi, and the American visual artist Frank Stella. No architects: 'We believe that in the coming decade artistic research based on the culture and technology of design will be more modern and decisive than

Top-light control mechanisms become the dominant symbol in Renzo Piano's Menil Collection and its adjacent Cy Twombly Gallery:

a   Piano and Fitzgerald, Menil Collection, Houston, Texas, 1981–6: site elevation
b   Menil Collection: exterior view
c   Menil Collection: gallery interior
d   Renzo Piano Building Workshop, Cy Twombly Gallery, Houston, Texas, 1992–5: elevation
e   Cy Twombly Gallery: interior of gallery
f   Renzo Piano Building Workshop, National Centre for Science and Technology, Amsterdam, 1992–7

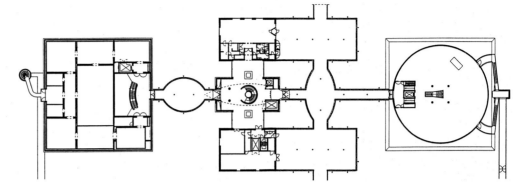

academic architecture, which is in decline,' Mendini announced in July 1988. He was obliged, however, to include his architect brother Francesco while a Dutch practice, the evocatively named Team 4, was retained to make it all buildable. As late as December 1992, Stella had to be dropped when his proposal for a massively complex and costly Teflon structure as a pavilion for 'old visual arts' threatened to drag the whole project down. Within days, architect Wolf Prix of the deconstructivist practice Coop Himmelblau was drafted in to save the day with fractured sheets of steel and shards of glass. This was a complete reversal of Stella's proposed soft organic shapes, not to mention an abandonment of two of Mendini's principles: to have an art gallery at least partly designed by a practising artist; and to have the main forms of the building determined by designers, not architects. But somehow, this U-turn scarcely seemed to matter. The museum forged ahead, despite construction problems with Prix's late contribution. When it opened, the Memphis-tinged architectural tea set appeared to have been smashed up at one end but there were acres of colourful laminate – even on the underside of the canal drawbridge, where it takes the form of abstracted Delftware – and it succeeded in its aims. Groningen was on the map, and more importantly back on the tourist itinerary. Haks achieved his apotheosis, and shortly afterwards he left.

The outcome of this extraordinary collaborative exercise is undeniably arresting. At the western end Starck's silver drum, housing ceramics, sits atop de Lucchi's square red-brick plinth containing the exhibition of the city's history – a rare example of separate authorship for consecutive layers of the same building. In the centre comes Mendini's blank gilded tower, used slightly bathetically for storage, flanked with lower blocks. To the east, the composition terminates with Coop Himmelblau's explosion. Here there are even fewer walls to hang pictures on than in Wright's Guggenheim, with the result that many are on flats suspended from the roof. Because the complex is built in a canal basin, and plunges below the waterline, it is deeper and more spacious than it first appears. Some of its internal finishes, particularly the multicoloured mosaic work to the main spiral staircase, are brilliantly handled. Yet the best pavilion – meaning the most thoughtful, providing a mysterious, white-veiled setting for the ceramic ware – is Starck's. In this context, relative understatement (not a characteristic normally associated with Starck) runs the risk of being overpowered, but the Starck drum holds its own and provides a necessary antidote to the Decon gymnastics.

Such detailed comments are, however, not what the Groninger Museum is all about. It functions on a larger scale. It works both nationally and

internationally. Its local collections and temporary shows contribute little or nothing to its popularity, something evidenced by the fact that when its collection and exhibition programme was housed elsewhere, little notice was taken of them. The idea of 'museum' as a place of study and reflection thus wholly shifted to mean merely 'museum building'. Again, the parallel is with religion. In just this manner the word 'church' had come over time to apply not to the congregation, but to the architecture that housed it. Groningen – an undeniable popular success – is the paradigm of the museum or gallery not as chaste muse, but as painted trollop. One hesitates to bracket them together, but one might make the same observation of Bruce Goff and Bart Prince's Shinenkan Pavilion at Los Angeles County Museum of Art, 1988–97, which is neither particularly good Goff (he died during its early design), nor particularly good Prince (he had yet to establish his own voice when he inherited the project), nor a particularly good exercise in Japanese iconography or Wrightian organic metaphor. Instead it comes over as a crude, seemingly self-parodying bit of museum advertising, which was by no means the original intention.

This is not a criticism that could be levelled at Daniel Libeskind's Jewish Museum in Berlin, 1993-7. A natural progression from his earlier

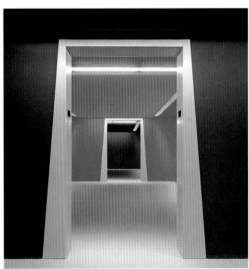

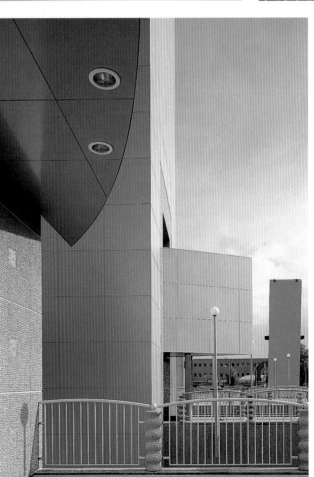

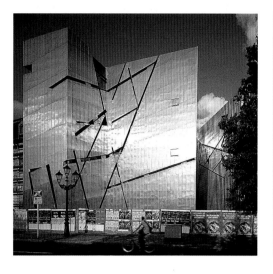

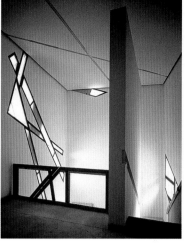

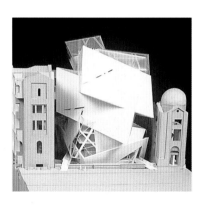

entry to Berlin's 'City Edge' competition, it appears at first to be a highly personal architecture, responding not only to the condition of the city but to the sense of absence, sorrow and anger that a Polish-born Jew such as Libeskind experiences when considering Berlin's recent past. Libeskind's personal mythology is notoriously complex. To say that his Jewish Museum resembles in plan a deconstructed elision of the geometric forms of the Swastika and the Star of David is at best a superficial comment, bearing in mind that its geometry was partly determined by drawing a matrix of lines between the addresses of prominent pre-war German Jews – and remembering also its mission to express the invisible, the Void. Libeskind's own summary is probably best:

'It is an attempt to give a voice to a common fate – the inevitable integration of Jewish/Berlin history despite the contradictions of the ordered and disordered, the chosen and not chosen, the vocal and silent, the living and dead.'

However, Libeskind's subsequent architecture uses related forms for entirely other, non-personal, reasons. His competition-winning 'Spiral' extension to London's Victoria and Albert Museum, while a freer composition as we have noted, applies the notion of fracture, of archaeological layering, to London as the Jewish Museum does to Berlin. Therefore the architect's response begins to take on the characteristics

of a style rather than a dogma – either a personal one or the broader deconstructivist view that aspires to the condition of anti-architecture and which, as more and more of it is built, becomes self-defeating by virtue of becoming another norm requiring a reaction. But what is an architect to do? You cannot, as Mies repeatedly remarked, invent a new architecture every Monday. And the Victoria and Albert Museum knew exactly why it had chosen Libeskind, and said so. It wanted a building of landmark status, that would pull in the visitors just as I M Pei's central glass pyramid at the Louvre in Paris acts as a mustsee tourist attraction.

Few architects have such a chance to design around a source of cultural reference as powerful as Libeskind's Jewish Museum. Henri Ciriani's 'Historiale de la Grande Guerre' in Peronne, France, 1987–92, which deals with the battlefields of the Somme and much else, in a building partly reminiscent of a gun emplacement, is a rare example; the entrance pavilion to the museum of cave-paintings at Niaux, France, by Massimiliano Fuksas, is another; along with a very few visitor centres – an entirely new building type, originating in the 1970s – such as Edward Cullinan's rough-hewn centre at Fountains Abbey in Yorkshire, England, or the Blasket Island Cultural Centre on the remote western coast of Ireland by Ciaran O'Connor and Gerard O'Sullivan of

b d
a
     e
c

Exploring the poetics
of memory:
a Daniel Libeskind, Boilerhouse
extension, Victoria & Albert
Museum, London, 1996–:
view of model
b Daniel Libeskind, Berlin
Museum with the Jewish
Museum, Berlin, 1993–7:
exterior view

c Massimiliano Fuksas, Entrance
Pavilion, Niaux Caves, Niaux-
Ariège, France, 1988–93
d Jewish Museum: view of
circulation space
e Jewish Museum: sections
and site plan

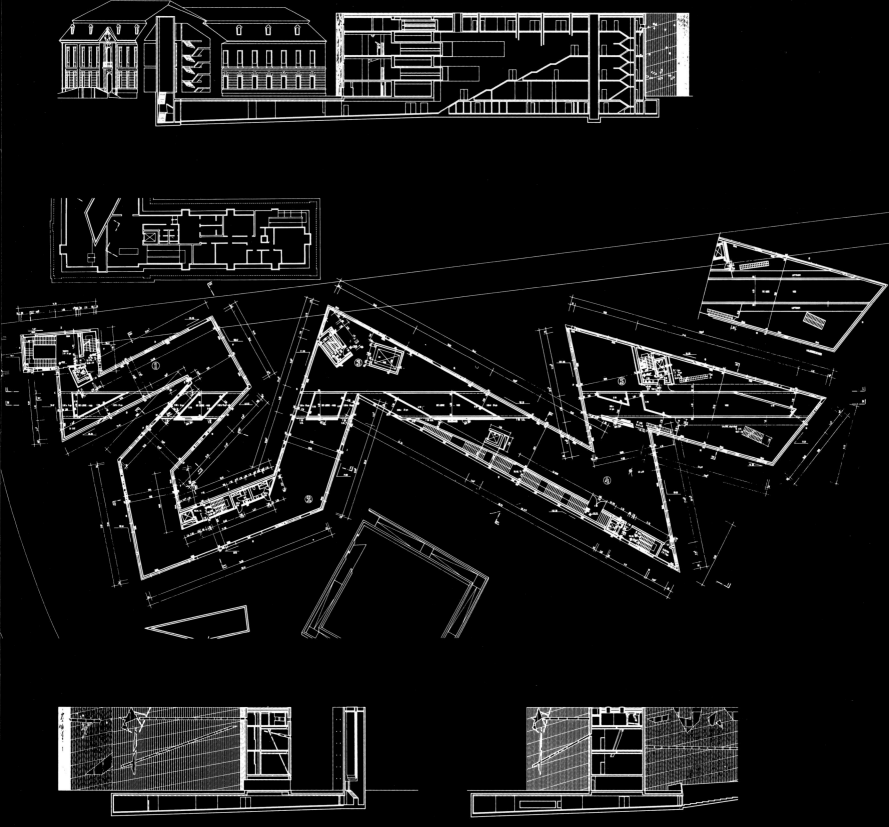

the republic's Office of Public Works (see 'Leisure'). These are buildings that respond both to their landscape and to a sense of history. They have a force born of necessity, something that could not be said, despite their mystic and sculptural qualities, of, say, Bernard Tschumi's 'folies' at La Villette, Paris, or Toyo Ito's 'Egg of Winds' and 'Tower of the Wind' in Tokyo. But even those open statements on the nature of uninhabited architecture have, arguably, greater power than a museum of very little but itself, which has come to be the dominant cultural building form at the close of the twentieth century.

As we have noted, Frank Gehry and Richard Meier became past masters at producing the kind of landmark museum and gallery buildings that the world's competing cities required. Meier, master of all

the 'Whites', designed museums that could equally be the headquarters of multinational corporations, applying his refrigerator aesthetic with equal *élan* everywhere: 'The Athenaeum' in New Harmony, Indiana, 1975–9, his Museum für Kunsthandwerk in Frankfurt, 1979–85, or its later Ethnological neighbour, his High Museum of Art, Atlanta, 1980–3. The Getty Center in Los Angeles, 1984–97, combines the genres – a container for art and business, or, art or business – brilliantly.

Gehry is different because his product is less immediately predictable, though just as instantly recognizable. Gehry also hit the world's museum circuit relatively late, but with immense impact. Once he had broken out of California – the Los Angeles Aerospace Museum, 1982–4, is the start-

ing point here – he took off. His break in Europe was due to client Rolf Fehlbaum, whose company, Vitra, made furniture in the out-of-the-way village of Weil-am-Rhein near Basel in Germany. Fehlbaum, who had discovered that commissioning famous names to design furniture pieces paid dividends, had previously worked with Gehry on his chairs contrived from cardboard-packing. In parallel with his furniture designs, Fehlbaum also began to commission a selection of the world's architects to design parts of his factory complex, beginning with Nicholas Grimshaw. Gehry was commissioned both to extend a factory building and to add a chair museum, to house the important Vitra historic collection. Later Fehlbaum added Tadao Ando and Zaha Hadid to his collection of architecture, respectively for a conference building

```
              g
a  c      d f
  b          e
```

and a fire station for the complex. But it was Gehry who made the biggest impact. The Vitra Design Museum, 1987–9, with its sinuous shapes struggling to emerge from the white rendered, zinc roofed aesthetic of his adjacent factory building, caught the imagination in a way that delighted Fehlbaum immoderately. Europe had discovered a form of Deconstructivism that could, unlike Tschumi's 'folies' at La Villette in Paris, be useful. Vitra at Weil-am-Rhein, previously a private industrial concern run by a hobbyist finding ways to stave off boredom, had become a place of pilgrimage with the opening of a public museum. Though connected with the factory, it was by no means merely a collection of its products – for Fehlbaum and his curator Alexander von Wegesack bought widely and wisely. Vitra

became a paradigm for the whole late twentieth-century museum or gallery culture. A place with no profile became famous overnight simply by commissioning a relatively small piece of distinctive public architecture, to house a collection that was amassed for the purpose. Perhaps Fehlbaum had noted the effect on Stuttgart of building Stirling and Wilford's Staatsgalerie, at any rate he made the crucial connection that it is not enough to build excellent and eye-opening buildings merely for private consumption: public access, and the veneer of culture, are the two essential preconditions. It must be noted that Fehlbaum had not founded Vitra: the son of the man who established the company he, like Alberto Alessi in Italy, inherited a viable business and was able to play a little, so gaining an

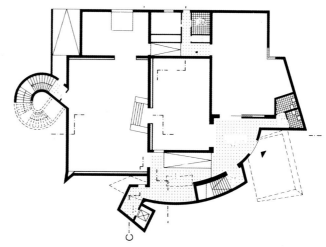

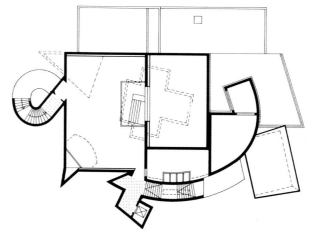

Meier and Gehry – yin and yang – were international brands by the 1990s:

a Richard Meier & Partners, High Museum of Art, Atlanta, 1980–83

b Richard Meier & Partners, Barcelona Art Museum, Barcelona, 1996

c Richard Meier & Partners, Museum für Kunsthandwerk, Frankfurt, Germany 1979–85

d Frank O Gehry & Associates, Vitra Design Museum, Weil-am-Rhein, Germany, 1987–9: exterior

e Vitra Design Museum: gallery interior

f Vitra Design Museum: plans

g Frank O Gehry & Associates, California Aerospace Museum, Los Angeles, 1982–4: main facade

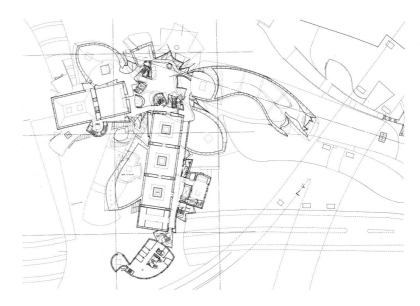

international profile never sought by his business-minded parents.

The fact that Gehry's Vitra Museum suffered in the damp climate of the upper Rhine valley – to the extent of needing remedial surface treatment six years after opening – did nothing to dampen his progress. In America, his University of Toledo Art Building, Ohio, 1990–2, and the Weisman Art Museum in Minneapolis, 1990–3, followed, emphasizing Gehry's increasing preoccupation with fluid forms and beaten-metal cladding. The process came to its head at the Guggenheim Museum, Bilbao, 1991–7, a very large cultural 'destination' that in its origins says as much about *fin-de-siècle* museum aspirations as Vitra's modest Basel venture. The Bilbao Guggenheim is the offspring of the international ambitions of two parents: the city, in its role as capital of the semi-autonomous Basque region of northern Spain, and the Solomon R Guggenheim Foundation, which following its initial all-American period had set its sights globally under its new director Thomas Krens. There was already a Guggenheim outstation in Venice, Italy: plans had been laid in 1991 for a Guggenheim in Salzburg, Austria, to be carved into the Monchsberg mountain by Hans Hollein. Hollein interested Krens but his scheme was beset with difficulties. Bilbao offered more, not least a huge building on a prominent site to be wholly paid for

and part revenue-funded by the Basque government. It was a dream deal for Krens, allowing transatlantic movement of exhibitions in a way previously denied him, and a true international presence for the first time. Bilbao was scarcely the centre of European civilization, but it was trying hard to reinvent itself and, anyway, there was no financial risk involved. It was equally a dream deal for Bilbao, who had not only a trophy architect in the shape of Gehry, but a trophy cultural brand name – Guggenheim – to add lustre. As ever, the aim of the city fathers was to change perceptions of what had previously been seen as a cultural backwater, a declining industrial centre (concerned with shipbuilding and heavy manufacturing) with a surrounding tourist industry considerably less lucrative than its counterparts in sunnier and drier southern Spain. Hence a multi-billion-dollar investment programme, conceived in the late 1980s for completion by the year 2000, which brought the world's architects flocking to a place some had never heard of, let alone previously visited. When the Basque Government's Minister of Culture, M Karmen Garmendia, remarked in 1996 upon the importance of the Guggenheim to his city, he put its economic impact first, and its 'visibility as a cultural centre' second. It would be, he said, 'a landmark and signature for our city, as well as one of the world's great art museums'.

Landmark and signature. The two words that encapsulate the museum and gallery building frenzy of the closing years of this century. The Bilbao Guggenheim is sited to act as a gateway to the city on the riverfront, embracing even the traffic-choked bridge of Puente de la Salve, exploiting its low-lying position with an explosive, architectonic flower-like roofscape. Gehry develops his persistent theme, expressing otherwise discrete building shapes within a connecting, sculptural and burnished envelope. The various elements focus upon a mighty central atrium. But there is even more than this. The political element that is inescapable in all big cultural building projects is here supercharged: for by building their Guggenheim, the Basque government thought it was declaring cultural independence from Madrid. A local architect, thinking small, could not have done this. But Gehry and the Guggenheim lent their signatures and built the landmark. In just this fashion, Frank Lloyd Wright originally solemnized what was an upstart on the New York art scene with his own signature and landmark. But in Bilbao, things did not work out quite as the politicians had planned.

The new Guggenheim instantly became the single most famous building in the world when it opened in autumn 1997. It was covered by all the world's media to saturation levels, its exposure helped rather than hindered by the fact that Basque

b

c

a

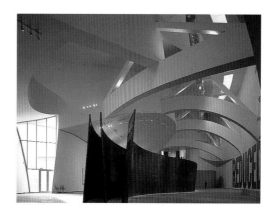

The single most evocative architectural image of the late twentieth century:

a Frank O Gehry & Associates, Guggenheim Museum, Bilbao, Spain, 1991–7: Richard Serra's *The Snake* sculpture in the long gallery

b Bilbao Guggenheim: site plan

c Bilbao Guggenheim: view of the museum from the opposite bank of the Nervion River

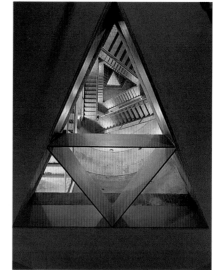

terrorists from the ETA group made a hamfisted attempt to conceal mortars in Jeff Koons' giant floral puppy installed in the museum's forecourt, intending to bomb the opening ceremony, carried out by King Juan Carlos. The discovery of this bomb plot, and the death of a policeman in the ensuing shoot-out, did more than focus the world's attention on Gehry's extraordinarily fine architecture, however – that was assured anyway. It highlighted an uncomfortable fact: that although the Basque government had commissioned the Museum, along with so much else in Bilbao, as an assertion of autonomous regional pride, it was regarded by some at least as an example of American cultural imperialism. The politicians had purchased a Guggenheim franchise much as one might buy a McDonald's franchise, and knowing that the direction of the museum – at least at first – was carried out entirely from New York only increased this feeling. Gehry's sinuous, swooping architecture in Bilbao, the culmination of a process of designing so many other arts buildings over the years, showed him at his best. Contrary to expectations the shape-making is not arbitrary – the spaces inside range from huge, warehouse-scale rooms for giant-scale conceptual art and installations, to intimate spaces for small drawings, even local artists. Nonetheless, as Gehry himself noted regarding his contribution to Disneyland Paris (see 'Leisure') his buildings are in

effect themed on himself. Gehry is an icon of America, his style too recognizable. The brouhaha surrounding the opening of the Bilbao Guggenheim served as a reminder of how the meaning of a cultural building has less to do with the architect than with the preconceptions of those who see it.

There are architects working within the cultural realm who do not depend upon an instantly recognizable style as Meier or Gehry (and to a lesser extent others such as Aldo Rossi, Mario Botta, Arata Isozaki and Norman Foster) do. Their response, though no less forceful, is more varied, more contextual. Hans Hollein, though obsessed by excavation – witness his European Volcanology Centre, 1997–2000, at St-Ours-les-Roches in the Auvergne, southern France, which takes up themes first aired in his plans for a Salzburg Guggenheim – is unpredictable in his overall responses: who could have foreseen the sinister, quasi-industrial forms of his Mönchengladbach Abteiberg Museum, 1972–82, or the blind wedge of his depressing Museum of Modern Art in Frankfurt, 1982–91, for instance? Rem Koolhaas of OMA is similarly inclined to go out on a limb, his designs united only by their uniform absence of anything that might conventionally be described as 'beauty'.

In America, the adobe-influenced Antoine Predock is now working on a scale that has obliged

c d   e

        f

a

b

      g

a   Hans Hollein, Abteiberg Municipal Museum, Mönchengladbach, Germany, 1972–82: entrance

b   Hans Hollein, European Centre of Volcanology, St-Ours-les-Roches, Auvergne, France, 1997–2000: model

c   Antoine Predock, Las Vegas Library and Discovery Museum, Las Vegas, 1986–90: exterior view

d   Las Vegas Library: interior view

e   Antoine Predock, American Heritage Center and Art Museum, Wyoming, Laramie, 1986–93: section through 'tepee'

f   American Heritage Center and Art Museum: exterior view at night

g   Antoine Predock, Nelson Fine Arts Center, Arizona State University, Tempe, 1986–9: exterior view

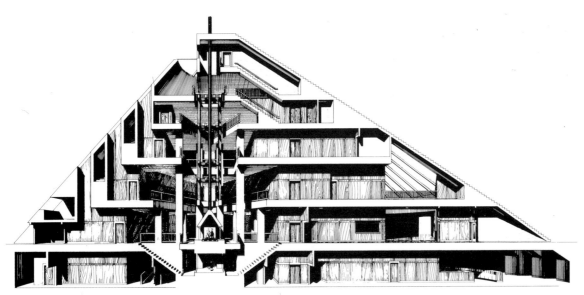

him to rethink his approach, but not to the extent that he abandons his response to context. Whether it works successfully writ large is another matter. His American Heritage Center and Art Museum, 1986-93, in Laramie, Wyoming, for instance, takes the form of a tepee and abstracts it into a form reminiscent of either a submarine's conning-tower or a moon rocket's nose-cone. A landmark, again, but here it has a function as the container of the visitor centre, part of an otherwise relatively conventional sequence of museum galleries, arranged as an offset tail to the conical head. Predock's handling of spaces here is very different to his Las Vegas Library and Discovery Museum, 1986-90, where the cone form again recurs, but is here subordinate to the whole, which, since it is for children, is broken down into child-scaled spaces. The Las Vegas building is as understated as the American Heritage Center is assertive, though both contain stairs to a viewing tower – at Laramie right on top of the big cone, in Vegas as the summit of a helical 'science tower'. At Predock's Arizona State University's Nelson Fine Arts Center, 1986-9, the forms break down still further into what is effectively a small village of linked forms. What he would do if released from his desert home ground to another part of the world with an utterly different cultural tradition is anyone's guess, and Disneyland Paris, where he designed a

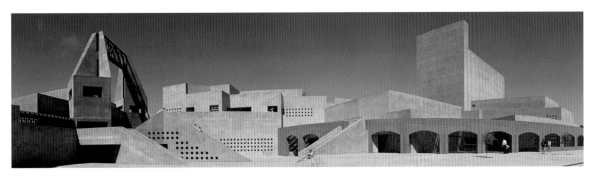

hotel with a Santa Fe theme, scarcely fulfils these criteria. One wonders also about how well the work of the Mexican architect Ricardo Legorreta travels. Legorreta's Marco Museo d'Arte Contemporaneo, Monterrey, 1991, takes the hot-climate response of a relatively featureless building around an open courtyard, using the coloured-render surface finish and abstracted 'vernacular' forms common to the region, first reinterpreted for the twentieth century by Luis Barragán. Legorreta shares certain concerns with museum architects the world over, not least his desire to blur the distinctions between exterior and interior and set up a public processional route: compare Ando and Kurokawa in Japan, Stirling in Stuttgart, or Evans and Shalev at the Tate Gallery's St Ives outstation, England. But certain architects are undeniably more 'regional' rather than international, and Legorreta's architecture is resistant to travel: though less so, perhaps, than the regionally-based work of architects such as Geoffrey Bawa in Sri Lanka, Balkrishna Doshi in India, or Turgut Cansever in Turkey. Against the New Internationalism in architecture must be set the New Regionalism, which may justifiably claim a higher moral standing. To try to separate cultural and climatic differences is needless. As Charles Correa once observed with admirable simplicity:

'In a warm climate, people develop a very different relationship to built form … ineffable indeed are the variations of light and ambient air, as we step from an enclosed room into a verandah, and thence perhaps into a courtyard, which itself may be shadowed by a pergola covered with plants, or by the spreading branches of a tree.'

In this vein one might also cite the more widely travelled Spanish architect Rafael Moneo as a responder to context rather than to inner forces – in particular his magical Museum of Roman Art at Mérida, 1980–5. The conventional response to the ruins Moneo faced would have been to design something light and transparent, a foil to the found object of the massive masonry. Instead, Moneo chose to work himself in thin Roman brick, and arched construction, but set on a different grid to the underlying remains, so that the disjunction between old and new is apparent. Moneo's museum, then, is not a reconstruction, but an evocation of the Roman architecture which you look down on as if from bridges.

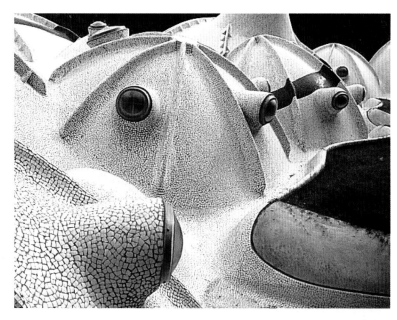

a	c	d
b		
		e
		f g

The smaller museums, away from the big cities, proved fertile ground:

a Balkrishna Doshi, Hussain-Gufa Gallery, Ahmedabad, India, 1993: roof detail

b Rafael Moneo, National Museum of Roman Art, Mérida, Spain, 1980–5: interior detail

c Evans + Shalev, Tate Gallery, St Ives, Cornwall, England, 1993

d Henri Ciriani, Museum of Archaeology, Arles, France, 1984–92: the blue defining wall evokes the intense colours of Roman buildings

e Museum of Archaeology: plans

f Museum of Archaeology: gallery interior

g Museum of Archaeology: Corbusian extrusions penetrate the blue-glass wall

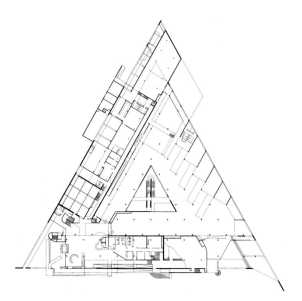

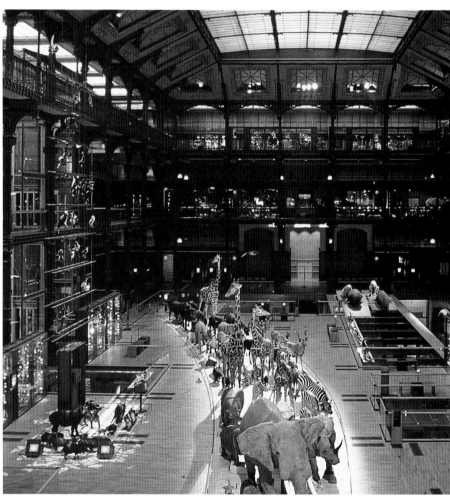

c   f
a
d
b
e

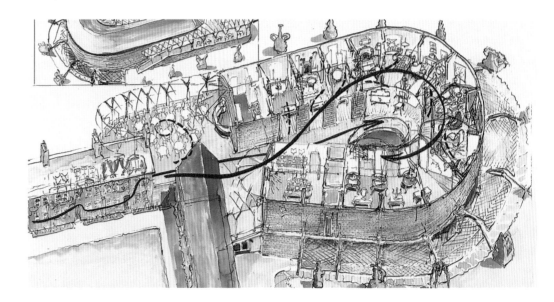

This semi-literal approach contrasts strongly with Henri Ciriani's Museum of Archaeology at Arles, southern France, 1984–92, where the great wedge of a building – its blue-glass defining wall punctured at intervals by early Corbusian extrusions – evokes instead the intense colours of Roman buildings and the organizing force of the Empire's troops and accountants.

Moneo's 'architecture as archaeology' is an approach one also finds in the museums of Rasem Badran and Abdul-Halim Ibrahim in Jordan and Saudi Arabia, or of Charles Correa in India – specifically, his National Crafts Museum in Delhi, 1975–90. At a pinch Correa might be accused of pastiche here – his museum sets out deliberately to be un-museum like by breaking down its galleries into forms based on village houses – but the effect, as with Moneo in Mérida, is assured when in lesser hands it would have veered into kitsch. In a similar vein, the Burrell Collection in Pollock Park, Glasgow, by a one-off team of architectural collaborators (Barry Gasson and John Meunier with Brit Andreson, realized by Barry Gasson Architects, 1972–83) is a gallery informed equally by its parkland setting, placed right up against a woodland edge, and by its contents, the eclectic art and sculpture collection of the shipowner Sir William Burrell, donated to the city in 1944. A low and meandering building, mixing its

materials (stone, glass, steel, timber) almost casually and incorporating some of Burrell's salvaged architectural pieces into its structure, this is the very opposite of the museum as conceived in Groningen. In contrast, it is modest to a fault, which meant that by the late 1990s it was out of step with current museological fashion and its visitor numbers had dropped off sharply. Studio Downie's beautifully understated Sculpture Pavilion, 1996, at Goodwood near England's Sussex coast – an ordering device of timber, glass and copper among the trees of a sculpture park – is in line of descent from the Burrell, which itself is part of a northern European tradition of modest, collection-based galleries that continues in the work of Scandinavian, and especially Norwegian, architects today. Two examples are the timber-clad Lillehammer Art Museum in Norway, 1992–3, by the internationally successful practice Snøhetta – a firm with both American and Norwegian partners, which has successfully climbed out of the regionalist pigeonhole – and Sverre Fehn's metaphorically composed Norwegian Glacier Museum in Fjaerland, 1989–91. Better still is Fehn's earlier, abstractedly simple, Scandinavian Pavilion at the Venice Biennale Gardens, which makes almost all the other pavilions on the site look as if they are trying much too hard.

Finally and somewhat unexpectedly in this quasi-regionalist context, comes a British selection,

starting with David Chipperfield's River and Rowing Museum at Henley-on-Thames (completed in stages, 1996–7) and Branson Coates' extension to the Geffrye Museum, East London, 1995–8. Branson Coates' offering, attached to an L-shaped building originally designed as almshouses, is a loop of what might be described as 'London vernacular', its form generated by the need to circulate people round the end of the museum and back, its visual references gleaned from the history of East London. At Henley, Chipperfield opted for a timber-clad building with steep pitched roofs. This in a sense was a tactic to get round the notoriously conservative planning authorities of Middle England (there is a reference to some of the Thames boathouses of the area) but Chipperfield also succeeded in making his building evocative of agricultural, barn-like buildings from widely different cultures, from Japan to New England via Borneo long houses. There is no such thing as 'international vernacular' – the phrase is an oxymoron – but this is nonetheless a building carrying multiple rural references in its simple forms. In contrast Tony Fretton produced a more English abstract vernacular when designing a rural gallery, ArtSway, in England's New Forest, 1996–7.

The archaeological approach has also been applied, with surprising success, to Paul Chemetov and Borja Huidobro's Galérie de l'Evolution,

a Studio Downie, Sculpture Pavilion, Goodwood, Surrey, England, 1996
b Charles Correa, National Crafts Museum, Delhi, India, 1975–90
c Barry Gasson Architects, Burrell Collection, Pollock Park, Glasgow, 1972–83
d Chemetov + Huidobro, Galérie de l'Evolution, Paris, 1982–90
e Snøhetta, Lillehammer Art Museum, Norway, 1992–3
f Branson Coates, Geffrye Museum extension, London, 1995–8: concept sketch

1982–90, in Paris. The whole idea here is to reveal a forgotten building, the 1877 Natural History Museum by Jules André, which had been closed since 1965, its collection of unfashionable stuffed animals gathering layers of dust in the dark for over twenty years. Yet behind the standard if imposing *belle-époque* facade was one of the most stunning iron and glass atrium interiors in all Paris. One of the great installation experiences of the early 1980s, when André's building began to be rediscovered, was the way the public was allowed in to one of the balconies overlooking the main floor, to gaze down at the dust-covered animals below, animated by a minimalist light and sound programme. The achievement of Chemetov and Huidobro is to retain some of that air of lost-world mystery in a completely renovated building, where the restored animals march diagonally across the atrium floor as if on their way to the Ark. This tableau forms the centrepiece of a new Natural History Museum, and, like all of President Mitterrand's '*Grands Projets*', the programme was funded generously.

The Galérie de l'Evolution, Aulenti's museums in Paris and Madrid, Adrien Fainsilber's Cité des Sciences et de l'Industrie at La Villete in Paris (created from giant unfinished abattoirs) 1980–6, and such projects as Herzog and de Meuron's Tate Museum of Modern Art at Bankside in London,

1994–9, are examples of an increasingly popular genre – the museum or gallery housed in a redundant or rediscovered structure. Such buildings have their own tradition, with Scarpa's 1964 Museo Castelvecchio in Verona the shining institutional example, while a large number of redundant warehouses and industrial buildings around the world have proved ideal for the large-scale aspirations of contemporary conceptual art and sculpture. Most notable in this area is the late sculptor Donald Judd's commandeering of the town of Marfa, Texas, as a continuing experiment in the siting of installation art. In particular Judd's precise and minimalist alterations of the buildings and spaces of a derelict US Army barracks with its artillery ranges outside Marfa – work continued by his Chinati Foundation – is a near-perfect fusion of art and architecture, all the more accomplished for being done by an artist rather than an architect, and somehow the better for being found space rather than purpose-built space.

When researching locations for its MoMA, London's Tate Gallery duly discovered that contemporary artists much prefer to work in the context of existing, preferably industrial, spaces, than to have to deal with purpose-designed buildings. This attitude mirrors that of theatre directors who see their art as best unfettered by the egos of architects (see 'Performance'). With sculpture and installation

b   d

a   e

c

work in particular developing rapidly, especially in size and scale, it transpired that, as with theatre design, it was becoming impossible to pin down the precise type of space that would be required. By the time all the agonizing had gone on and the venues built, artists' requirements would have moved on. Hence the Tate's choice of a Cyclopean brick-built former oil-fired power station (by Sir Giles Gilbert Scott, 1955–60, but early twentieth century in feel) for its most ambitious expansion to date: also the most ambitious art gallery thus far for Herzog and de Meuron, who at the time of their appointment were best known for the tiny glowing box of their Goetz Art Gallery in Munich, 1989–92. Similar thinking is apparent in the city of Gateshead's choice of a redundant riverside flour mill building for its new gallery of contemporary art (Ellis Williams architects, 1994–2001). Two previous ventures into this realm had proved highly successful: Renzo Piano's conversion of the titanic old Fiat works at Lingotto, Turin, into a cultural and trade centre (see 'Performance'); and the Powerhouse Museum, 1986–8, in Sydney by New South Wales public works architects, Denton Corker Marshall, and Neil Burley. The latter is a conversion of a waterside tramway generating centre into a museum of technology and decorative arts, the interiors of the generator halls being rather more interesting than the rather flimsy external treatment.

a Adrien Fainsilber, Cité des Sciences et de l'Industrie, Parc de la Villette, Paris, 1980–6: interior of exhibition space

b Herzog and de Meuron, Tate Museum of Modern Art, Bankside, London, 1994–9: computer-generated graphic of exterior view

c Frederick Fisher and Partners Architects, PS1 Contemporary Art Centre, New York, 1988–97

d Aldo Rossi, Bonnefanten Museum, Maastricht, The Netherlands, 1990–4

e Herzog and de Meuron, Goetz Art Gallery, Munich, Germany, 1989–92

a Gustav Peichl, Federal Art
  Gallery, Bonn, Germany,
  1986–92
b Office for Metropolitan
  Architecture, Kunsthal,
  Rotterdam, The Netherlands,
  1987–92: view into foyer
c Axel Schultes, Kunst Museum,
  Bonn, 1985–92: exterior detail
d Alvaro Siza, Galician Centre for
  Contemporary Art, Santiago de
  Compostela, Spain, 1988–95:
  gallery interior

a

b   d

c

Such thinking informs the creation of New York's PS1 Contemporary Art Center, 1988–97, run by arts entrepreneur Alanna Heiss, which after twenty-five years of using sundry abandoned warehouse spaces, moved into premises converted out of a rambling Romanesque former nineteenth-century school complex by the Los Angeles architect Fred Fisher, making it one of the largest galleries for contemporary art shows in the world. In contrast to the shoestring-budget previous life of this institution, the new centre was bankrolled to the tune of $8.5 million by New York City's Department of Cultural Affairs, so institutionalizing what had originally been spontaneous. Fisher's trademark is to reveal the existing building and to understate his own interventions, and so works at the opposite end of the visual spectrum to his erstwhile employer, Frank Gehry.

One might be forgiven for concluding that there is no such thing as a museum or gallery typology when one has to compare such European examples as Aldo Rossi's Bonnefanten Museum in Maastricht, 1990–4, with its strange empty shell-case of a dome; the Kunsthal in Rotterdam by Rem Koolhaas of OMA, 1987–92, with its deliberate crudeness in the handling of volumes; or the daunting museum plaza in Bonn where Gustav Peichl's Federal Art Gallery, 1986–92, with its defensive row

of freestanding columns and tepee rooflights faces the disrupted grid of Axel Schultes' Kunstmuseum, 1985–92, both now threatened by the move of political power to Berlin. After these and such other visually rich fare as the Groninger Museum, a gallery so relatively understated as Alvaro Siza's Galician Centre for Contemporary Art at Santiago de Compostela, Spain, 1988–95, is like a grapefruit sorbet after a *confit de canard*. At last: a gallery that is all to do with a sequence of interior spaces, its simple stone-clad external walls jumbling themselves comfortably into the medieval townscape without a trace of bombast.

In Japan, museum-making has been even more frenetic, with both imported and home-grown architects pitching in. Kenzo Tange, the elder statesman of Japanese architecture, contributed his Yokohama Museum of Art at Kanagawa, 1983–9, which is as formally classical in its way as his immensely important Peace Centre at Hiroshima, 1946–94, but with some of the tricksy post-modern touches of its era that serve to lessen its organizational force. The running has mostly been made by a younger generation, such as Kazuhiro Ishii, with his San Juan Bautista Museum in Ojika, 1996, a museum both wrapped around and overlooking a historic replica ship; Toyo Ito with the Yatsuhiro Municipal Museum at Kumamoto, 1988–91, which is

the modern expressionist's reply to Mies in Berlin, its wing-like lightweight roof forms visually sheltering the glass container beneath; Hiroshi Hara's Ida City Museum in Nagano, 1988, exploring his academic concern with vernacular forms that can be abstracted into large-floorplate modern buildings; Yoshio Taniguchi's Toyota Municipal Museum of Art in Toyota City, 1995, a minimalist landscape-centred building; and Arata Isozaki's Mito Cultural Complex in Tokyo, 1986–90. Isozaki's building is notable not so much for its rather lumpen collection of symbolist museum buildings as for the fractal spiral of its 100-metre-tall 'Art Tower', like a solidified twisted strip of photographic film.

Nothing – but nothing – unites the styles of these Japanese architects, all of whom are roughly of the same generation. So the supposedly exotic imports, such as English architects Branson Coates for their 'Art Silo' of the Penrose Institute of Contemporary Arts in Tokyo, 1993, or Mario Botta's 'Watari-Um' contemporary art gallery, 1985–90, in the same city with its trademark banded masonry, are relatively modest in comparison. As Botta wrote to his client, Mrs Watari: 'In the Babel of urban languages that changes daily, I wanted to test the durability of a strong, primary image, an architecture generated by the building's own inner logic, its geometry and the effects of light. These things came

a   d
          f
b   e g
c   h

a Hiroshi Hara, Ida City
   Museum, Nagano, Japan,
   1988

b Toyo Ito, Yatsuhiro Municipal
   Museum, Yatsuhiro,
   Kumamoto, Japan, 1988–91

c Kazuhiro Ishii, San Juan
   Bautista Museum, Ojika,
   Japan, 1996

d Yoshio Taniguchi, Toyota
   Municipal Museum of Art,
   Toyota City, Japan, 1995

e Branson Coates, Art Silo,
   Penrose ICA, Nishi Azabu,
   Tokyo, 1993

f Mario Botta, 'Watari-Um'
   Museum, Tokyo, 1985–90:
   plan

g Watari-Um Museum: exterior

h Watari-Um Museum:
   contextual view

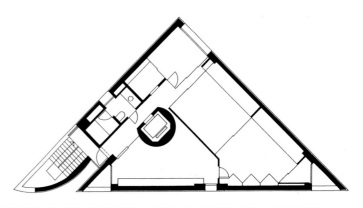

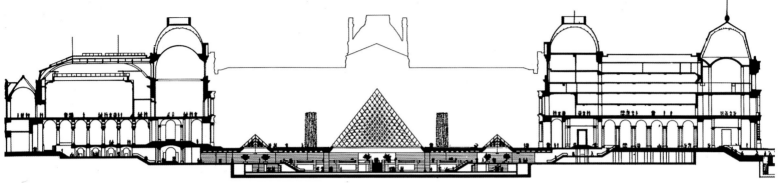

before a consideration of its urban impact.' Seen in an isolated photograph, where the building appears impactful indeed, the image makes you wonder at Botta's assertion. But pull back to see it in the context of Tokyo, and it all but vanishes in the scrum, just as a zebra's stripes act as camouflage.

All museum and gallery design, in theory, comes down to one eternal concern: the handling of space and light. These are the fundamentals of all architecture, but when it comes to the display of art, any mistakes here are unforgivingly prominent. This, apart from the extreme public prominence of such buildings, is why architects fight to have them in their portfolio. Technically they are relatively complex, particularly when it comes to diffusing natural light into top-lit galleries (the aim of nearly all curators) and maintaining the appropriate climate controls and security. But it is the successful manipulation of natural light that distinguishes the best architects from those who are merely show-offs. Arguably the most adept at this difficult art as the twentieth century drew to its close were the Sino-American architect Ieoh Ming Pei, and the Japanese architects Kisho Kurokawa and Tadao Ando.

Pei and Kurokawa make an interesting and fundamental contrast. Pei's weakness, if it can be described as such, was his famous addiction to deceptively simple geometric forms. From the triangle

or diamond stereometry of the East Wing of the National Gallery of Art in Washington, 1971–8, (a building thus overlaying the conception and construction of the Pompidou Centre) via the triangulated crystalline Bank of China in Hong Kong, 1985–90, to, as an inevitable conclusion, the pyramid of the Louvre redevelopment in Paris, 1983–9, Pei became the master of the eternal form, derived very clearly from his early Miesian predilections, but overlaid with a Chinese love of order and placement (this is not to be confused with Feng Shui, sometimes at odds with the harsh angularity of Pei's buildings). Kurokawa, in contrast, took a course of seeming architectural complexity, the very opposite of Pei's route. Where Pei espoused geometry, Kurokawa was wedded to what he called Metabolism, a term that meant whatever he chose to make it mean, but which, later in life, he defined as 'the principle of life' – a catch-all phrase that, according to his personal myth, included 'symbiosis with nature', 'abstract interrelationships' and 'asymmetry'. This last gives the clue: to take a Western analogy, the best way to think about the contrast between Pei and Kurokawa is to consider the differences between a Classicist and a Goth. The former imposes a rational, usually symmetrical order upon nature or townscape: the latter is accretive, evolutionary, and can claim to derive much of its force from an observation of the

a
b
c
   d

e
  f
  g

Pei's purism contrasts with Freed's willingness to work allusively:

a Pei Cobb Freed & Partners, Louvre Pyramid, 1983–9, and Richelieu Wing, Paris, 1988–93: section through Louvre

b Louvre Pyramid: exterior view

c Richelieu wing: interior of gallery

d Pei Cobb Freed & Partners, East Wing, National Gallery of Art, Washington, DC, 1971–8: interior view

e Pei Cobb Freed & Partners (James Ingo Freed), US Holocaust Memorial Museum, Washington, DC, 1989–93: section

f US Holocaust Memorial Museum: photographs of Holocaust victims line the walls

g US Holocaust Memorial Museum: Hall of Witness

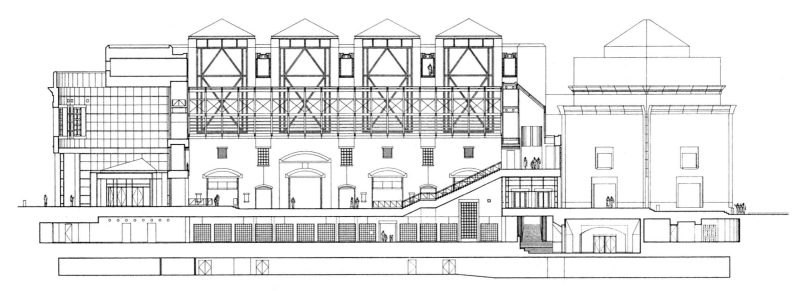

given forms of country or town. Thus a Pei museum is as different from a Kurokawa museum – as an object to contemplate and as a sequence of spaces to stroll through – as a Greek temple is from a medieval monastery. Although to compare the work of these two architects using a Western cultural analogy might seem otiose, the classical or gothic split is merely a way of describing what appears to be a universal cultural phenomenon. In the case of Kurokawa, some of his work has been compared with the principles of free arrangement to be found in Japanese garden-making. However, one should not submit too readily to the temptation to over-generalize. Pei's practice, after all, has given us the US Holocaust Memorial Museum in Washington, 1989–93 – which although possessing a handful of repeated geometrical elements such as a freestanding octagonal auditorium and a sequence of pyramidal-roofed towers, is inside, a fragmented series of compartmentalized spaces. Although there is a central 'Hall of Witness', this space is as different from the expansive open spaces of the National Gallery East Wing or those beneath the courtyard of the Louvre as can be imagined. And for a good reason: at the Holocaust Museum, Pei's partner James Ingo Freed was dealing with forms that were deliberately evocative of some of the places associated with the Holocaust. The external pyramidal towers echo the

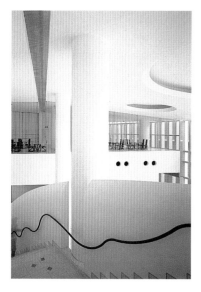

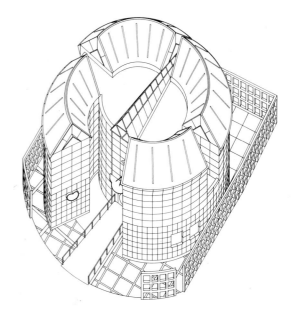

watchtowers of concentration camps: the gantry-bridges spanning the building at high level bring to mind the Warsaw Ghetto: within, sinister doors and enclosed, claustrophobic spaces are fully intended to echo some of the horrific experience of those imprisoned and killed. This, then, is programme architecture as much as Libeskind's in Berlin, though more overtly symbolic. The Pei practice could also respond to a context, though to suggest that its titanically-scaled brick-built extension to the Portland Museum of Art in Maine, 1981–3, is, as some have suggested, self-effacing, is fanciful in the extreme. The Portland building, playing Kahnian facade games of circle and semicircle, completely overwhelms its parent.

Those looking for a classically planned museum from Kurokawa, will, against all the odds, be rewarded if they search long enough. The Metabolist is mostly true to his organic, gothic, instincts. Like Pei, he shows a late fondness for Platonic forms – the cone, the sphere, the cube – but arranged as almost random elements within a composition: a way of museum-making he shares with Antoine Predock in his desert fastnesses. He is on record as saying that he likes his compositions to have no core, no apparent centre, and some, like the fanciful shape-making of his Ehime Prefectural Museum of General Science, 1991–4, or the earlier and more sober Nagoya City Art Museum, 1983–7,

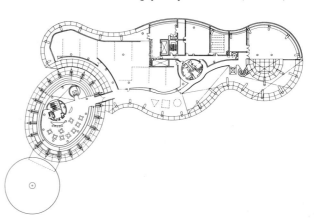

fulfil this aim. Yet his Honjin Memorial Museum of Art in Japan, 1989–90, is a strongly circular (in fact oval) form, with an axial approach. Similarly his Hiroshima City Museum of Contemporary Art, 1984–8, focuses its longhouse elements upon the obvious focus of a circular form approached, in classical fashion, up a grand flight of steps set on the axis. And in his later museum designs, at Wakayama in Japan, and at Louvain-la-Neuve in Belgium, a tendency to set up formal approach avenues begins to appear. Perhaps, like his old master Kenzo Tange, Kurokawa could not resist the lure of the formal and grandiose when given large projects to work upon later in life, although he was never tempted by the post-modern formalism of Arata Isozaki, as evidenced in his Museum of Contemporary Art in Los Angeles, 1981–6, or his Okanoyama Graphic Art Museum, 1982–4 – a decorative design that shows a decadent descent from his earlier, modular Art Museum in Takasaki, 1970–4, which in turn can be accused of an over-reliance on the repetition of a geometrical, 12-metre cube module. As for Kurokawa, though it might be heretical to suggest it, throughout his sixties an almost Beaux-Arts overlay began to descend upon the randomness of his planning.

So our representative Classicist and Goth have more in common than might at first appear.

Both also understand fully the importance of the handling of light, though here the true contest at the century's end was not between Pei and Kurokawa, but between Pei and Ando. Pei liked to saturate the public spaces of his museums with light, and was moreover of the view that, once inside the usually sealed environment of a gallery, the visitor was owed not only a reasonable level of light ('I'm old – I want to be able to see the pictures,' he is reported to have said on commencing his final phase of work in the Richelieu Wing of the Louvre) but also a sensation of the outside world. This proved to be a very important step forward because, in the 1980s, curatorial demands in art galleries had increasingly led to spaces that were all but hermetically sealed.

It is instructive to compare the interiors of three gallery buildings from this period: Pei Cobb Freed's Richelieu Wing, James Stirling and Michael Wilford's Clore Gallery at the Tate in London – the gallery as sealed space, with only one little window look-out for orientation; and the Sainsbury Wing of London's National Gallery, by Venturi Scott Brown and Associates – where the intention was to create galleries based upon the lantern-skylight model of Sir John Soane's Dulwich Picture Gallery, 1811–14, but where Venturi was not allowed to place an orientating window as he desired. 'There should be a

Japanese architects saw the art museum as a potent testing ground for ideas:
a Kisho Kurokawa, Wakayama Prefectural Museum, Wakayama, Japan, 1990–4: interior of circulation space
b Kisho Kurokawa, Ehime Prefectural Museum of General Science, Ehime, Japan, 1991–4: interior

c Kisho Kurokawa, Honjin Memorial Museum of Art, Ishikawa, Japan, 1989–90: interior
d Kisho Kurokawa, Fukui City Museum of Art, Sukui, Japan, 1993–6: exterior
e Wakayama Prefectural Museum: axonometric
f Fukui City Museum of Art: plan

g Arata Isozaki & Associates, Museum of Contemporary Art, Los Angeles, 1981–6: exterior view
h MoCA, Los Angeles: gallery interior
i Arata Isozaki & Associates, Okanoyama Graphic Art Museum, Hyogo, Japan, 1982–4: gallery and circulation spaces

a		e	g	h
				i
b				
c	d		f	

a   c | e

b

   d

great window at the end of the central gallery toward Pall Mall to disentomb the effect: the curators wanted the wall for a big picture which you can't read from a distance,' Venturi later commented. Despite this, and despite being necessarily handicapped by the extreme levels of daylight filtration demanded by the curators of the Renaissance collection, the gallery interiors of the Sainsbury Wing do allow some idea of what is happening, climatically, outside. Pei, however, wanted much more than this. Like Venturi, he wanted to 'disentomb the effect'. The existing windows in the Richelieu Wing allowed the necessary orientation, but he wanted more: he wanted visitors to be able to look up and see the sky as they perambulated, at the same time that direct sunlight was kept off the pictures. In addition, knowing the frailty of automated active shading devices and the tendency of museums and galleries not to indulge in routine maintenance, he insisted of his engineers that the natural top-lighting system should be fixed. All these apparently conflicting demands were resolved by the joint teams from Pei's office and the engineers Ove Arup, under Peter Rice: the cruciform fibrous plaster blades forming the ceilings of the Richelieu Wing galleries, tested on computer models, do the job almost miraculously and it is possible to see the sky with its clouds and planes. Light levels are almost

worryingly high for those used to the tomb effect of other galleries protective of their ancient canvases: there is even the odd splash of sunlight on the floor.

If Pei became the master of the technical handling of natural light with his last work at the Louvre, Tadao Ando emerged as the master of the poetics of light – falling both externally and internally, on solid and on water. In the Nariwa Museum, 1992–4, in the Naoshima Contemporary Art Museum and annexe, 1988–92, 1993–5, the Forest of Tombs Museum, 1989–92, and in the fascinating Chikatsu-Asuka Historical Museum in Osaka, 1990–4 – a building conceived as a grand flight of steps – Ando, using few materials, particularly concrete, glass and stone, has achieved a quality both luminous and numinous. In this respect he may be compared to that other master of light and manipulator of museum space, Carlo Scarpa (1906–78). Scarpa's Museo Castelvecchio in Verona, 1964, is one of the twentieth century's greatest examples of how creative power, and the juxtaposition of old and new, can enhance a museum's collection and atmosphere, rather than serve the ego of architect or than civic state. To be a master both of exhibition design and of architectonics: Scarpa still represents that particular Holy Grail and few, if any, present-day architects can attain it.

All Ando buildings, whatever their function, are temples:
a Tadao Ando, Chikatsu-Asuka Historical Museum, Minamikawachi-gun, Osaka, Japan, 1990–4
b Tadao Ando, Naoshima Contemporary Art Museum and annexe, Naoshima, Kagawa, Japan, 1988–92, 1993–5: view of courtyard

c Tadao Ando, Forest of Tombs Museum, Kumamoto, Kamoto-gun, Kumamoto, Japan, 1989–92: view of courtyard
d Tadao Ando, Nariwa Museum, Nariwa, Okayama, Japan, 1992–4: exterior view
e Naoshima Contemporary Art Museum: plan

PERFORMANCE *Opera houses, theatres & concert halls* The form of the auditorium based building places strong constraints upon architects. Paradoxically one of the most introverted of building types – for the performance of opera, theatre, dance and music, and the projection of film – it must also acknowledge its important public and celebratory role. While the auditorium often reflects both the social hierarchy of the society that builds it, and the complex science of acoustics, the most important design aspect is more instinctive: magically to enable the possibility of catharsis

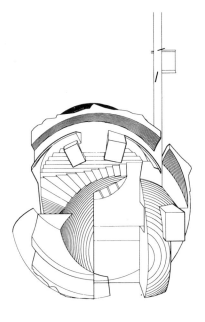

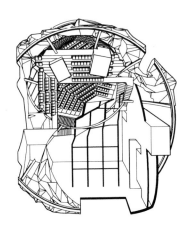

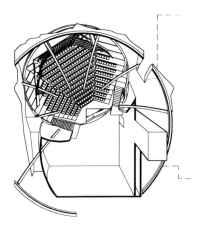

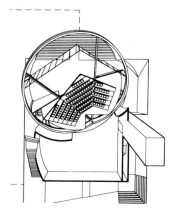

'We think, but we try not to think too much.'
Günter Behnisch, March 1997.

The auditorium-based building is as highly
charged an urban form as the art gallery, and as
such it places strong constraints upon architects.
Paradoxically, one of the most introverted of building
types – encompassing theatre, concert hall, opera
house and cinema, plus often the financially expedient addition of conference trade – must also
acknowledge its important public and celebratory
role. Within, the auditorium does two things. It acts
as the 'room' in which audience and performers (or
images) interact. It also defines the social hierarchies
of the society that builds it – seating and performance space arranged according to wealth, status,
or notions of democracy. Such buildings are among
the most demanding to design, both technically
and aesthetically.

They are especially difficult because technical competence can only go so far in determining the
feel of the space. A concert hall or opera house can
be acoustically brilliant, a theatre wonderfully comfortable, with uninterrupted sightlines, but the
atmosphere can still end up all wrong. Indeed, the
conclusion of many radical theatre, opera and dance
directors at the end of the twentieth century is that
comfort, sightlines and acoustics are in a sense

secondary to the main point: that performances –
particularly theatre – can be staged successfully anywhere, in even seemingly hostile conditions, so long
as the audience is piled into the same space as the
performers. Hence the frequent use of former warehouses and factories as galleried auditorium spaces:
hence the way that purpose-built 'experimental' theatres endeavour to replicate that black-box flexibility.
Such an approach is partly historical, acknowledging
the way theatre originally evolved in Europe as an
art form in existing, often galleried, public spaces
such as inn courtyards.

In this context, the Californian architect Eric
Owen Moss' project to insert a modest theatre
among his various developments in once seedy
Culver City, Los Angeles, is worth noting – particularly in view of the continuing discussion in this chapter
about the relationship of actor and audience. The
Ince Theater project, which began in 1993, shows an
architect manipulating the intersecting circles of the
audience's and the actors' domains with assurance –
not least because he works not just on plan, but in
three dimensions. The circles thus become intersecting spheres, a device that brings actor and audience
into the same 'room' while still defining the territories
of each. Externally, the modelling produces a curvilinear building that achieves the second objective of a
theatre – to advertise itself in the civic realm. The

There is a continuing quest by
architects to contain
performers and audience in
the same room:
a   Eric Owen Moss, Ince Theater,
    Culver City, California, 1993–:
    sectional perspectives
b   Ince Theater: model
c   Ince Theater: model

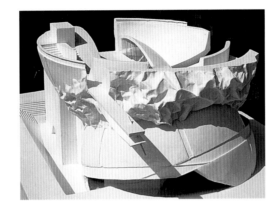

buildings surrounding it – including those already transformed by Moss – are rectilinear and the contrast of building typologies is clear. Finally, Moss intends his theatre to be an objective in itself, with broad steps running up its exterior and a high-level link built across to nearby office buildings. In this he is treading the same ground as Mario Botta and Tadao Ando do in certain of their projects – seeing the building as a public route, an urban stepping-stone. In the case of a theatre, this public function plugs it into the movement patterns of the city, breaking down some of the barriers between art and life.

The Ince Theater was conceived as a home for both live performances and cinema – a balancing act that, as we shall see, is often problematic, though less so in a small (450-seat) auditorium of the kind proposed by Moss. A further distinction needs to be made between speech-theatre and opera-theatre. Although plenty of experimental opera companies exist, the bulk of the operatic repertoire was composed in a limited period (broadly speaking, from the mid-eighteenth to the mid-twentieth centuries) which has an immediate effect upon the design freedom of architects working in this medium. Grand opera and grand opera houses, with proscenium arches, go together. They are the most predictable, and most costly, of all auditorium types. Concert halls are also usually predictable in form – a

symphony orchestra plus choir and organ is an absolute given, and everything else can be calculated from there; the needs of chamber music venues are also pretty much a given. Cinemas are the easiest of them all, since no interaction between audience and performers is required, though even here perceived intimacy is an advantage. But the acting of plays has undergone such transformations in the twentieth century – and particularly during the post-war years – that theatre architects have been obliged to follow the directors into the unknown, sometimes with disastrous consequences.

There is no time when architects did not miss the point entirely; some eighteenth- and nineteenth-century theatres were fiercely criticized by actors, directors and audiences alike for being monuments to ego rather than instruments of performance, and it has long been customary for architects to concentrate most on the public areas for effect – note Hans Poelzig's extraordinary Expressionist Grosses Schauspielhaus in Berlin, 1918-19, a dripping cave of stalactites. But in this century, it is most usually the attempts to house 'national' companies which have gone most wrong. The Royal Shakespeare Company's Memorial Theatre at Stratford-upon-Avon, designed by Elizabeth Scott in 1930-2, proved that a theatre can be completely 'dead' no matter how many people you consult. Years of modifications were

necessary to bridge the chasm it created between actor and audience, and the lessons had still not been learned when the RSC came to build a new London home in the Barbican (Chamberlin, Powell and Bon, completed 1981). Similarly Eero Saarinen's Vivian Beaumont Theater, 1958-65, in New York's titanic Lincoln Center, 1955-66, comprising an opera house, ballet-operetta theatre, concert hall and the theatre (built on fourteen acres) fell into the trap of trying to be dual-purpose: complex machinery was designed to allow it to transform from a proscenium theatre to a thrust-stage theatre. The compromise was apparent, and within a decade the machinery had permanently seized up anyway. Finally, Britain's National Theatre by Sir Denys Lasdun, 1967-77, was criticised for being too epic in scale in its open Olivier Theatre, and too deadening in its proscenium-based Lyttelton Theatre. Nobody complained about the 'black-box' experimental space of its third auditorium, the Cottesloe Theatre, inserted at a late stage of design.

Not all countries or regimes worried about what went on inside, however: national theatres elsewhere were conceived as huge buildings like city halls or airport termini. While Lasdun was agonizing over the nature of theatre in London, Leandro Locsin was building the sub-Brazilian elevated concrete box of the 1969 Theatre for the Performing Arts in

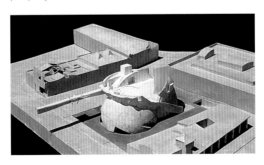

a

b

c

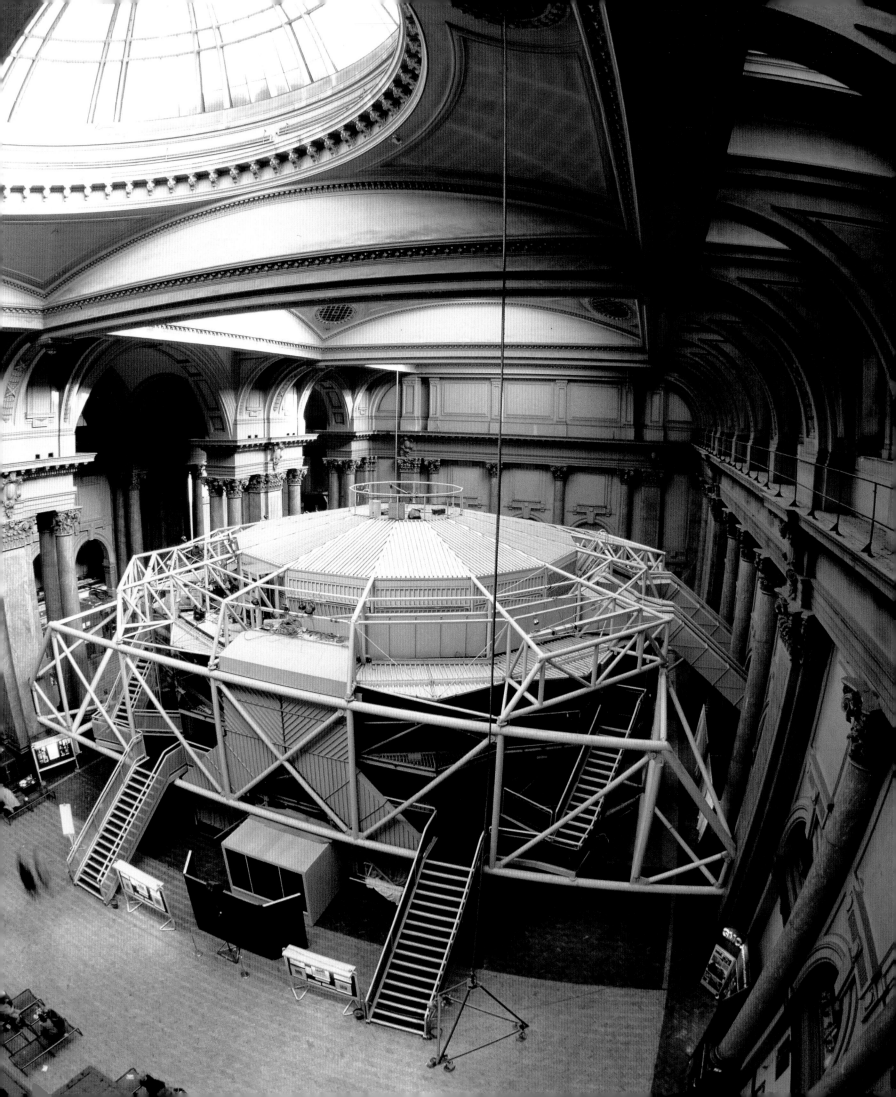

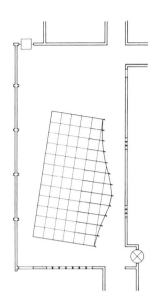

Manila, part of his masterplan for the Cultural Centre of the Philippines. From the approach side, it looks as if Boeing 747s should dock with it, but the other side holds a genuine surprise: the huge canti-levered volume of the foyer space hangs suspended over a lake. It is awesome, but it is primarily a politi-cal building – theatrical in a sense not appreciated by most directors and actors.

Given these precedents, it is not surprising that a reaction should take place, and then a counter-reaction. The radical post-war directors had rediscovered the immediacy of Shakespearian theatre – effectively the thrust stage, but also the in-the-round format, most notably at Manchester's Royal Exchange Theatre by Levitt Bernstein architects, with designer Richard Negri and director Michael Elliott, 1972–6. This last was a reaction against the institu-tionalization of the theatre – 'Shouldn't we STOP building for posterity?', Elliott asked at the time, in the light of the emerging National.

His theatre, a freestanding self-contained 'spaceship' placed in the echoing void of the nineteenth-century Royal Exchange building, had a successor some years later in the form of the 'Glass Music Hall' in Amsterdam, 1988–90, by Pieter Zaanen with engineer Mick Eekhout. This is a 200-seater glass-box chamber music hall, with one wall bowed to improve the acoustics, dropped casually onto the floor of H P Berlage's Stock Exchange, 1903, as if it were a giant display case. Its layout, however, is very conventional in comparison with Elliott's fer-vent espousal of in-the-round performance, and this reflects the trend in theatres generally: the successors to Elliott's generation have rediscovered the merits of older theatre forms, not only the conventional end-on stage as designed so transparently by Zaanen and Eekhout, but also the hierarchical late nineteenth-century proscenium-arch theatre form. Central to this apparent ideological somersault is a reappraisal of the notion of the 'democratic' auditorium. It is a pow-erful and ancient concept, true: the semicircular amphitheatres of Ancient Greece, most notably at Epidauros in the Peloponnese, are the pure origina-tors of the genre. They are auditoria where every seat carries a roughly equal value, in terms of status, of acoustics, and of sightlines. They are also the enemies of compactness, being in effect one half of a stadium. But most importantly – from the point of view of those staging 'intimate' rather than 'spectacle' theatre – they have to be full, virtually to capacity, in order for a rapport between actor and audience to develop. Any gaps in the wall of faces are immediately apparent.

This need not matter absolutely in those the-atres where a successful thrust-stage or in-the-round auditorium has been developed, so that the audience wraps around the performers. Those democratic theatres that fail are those that place too many of the audience at too great a distance from the front of the stage – as in the inter-war 'cinema theatres' of the United States or the Soviet Union, where it was fatally decided that the tunnel or fan auditorium created by projection needs could successfully double as a live theatre. It has also been noted that, where all seats are supposedly equal and so of broadly equal price, those prices tend to be on the high side – thus disenfranchizing the poor from coming to the theatre, and negating the whole concept of 'democ-racy'. Hence the reappraisal of the once-despised form of the bourgeois nineteenth-century theatre.

Such places were frequently built on very tight urban sites – mostly for reasons of land availability and cost. The audience tended to be stacked up in tiers, the higher being the cheaper. The columns introduced to support these tiers creat-ed zones of poor sight: seats thus affected were even cheaper. These theatres, while they served as three-dimensional diagrams of society's stratifications, nonetheless catered for the poor up in the 'Gods' (their lowliness expressed by their height, often gained by a separate staircase) and the rich in the front stalls. But for today's directors, these old theatres offer more than a broad pricing policy: their vertical arrangement has the double merit of

Theatre as cuckoo in the nest: Manchester's is radical, Amsterdam's a conventional box:
a Levitt Bernstein, Royal Exchange Theatre, Manchester, England, 1972–6
b Pieter Zaanen and Mick Eekhout, Glass Music Hall, Amsterdam, 1990: the glass box inside H P Berlage's Stock Exchange of 1903
c Glass Music Hall: plan

a
b c

bringing the rearmost seats closer to the stage, while a thin audience can line the visible edges of the tiers and provide a workable atmosphere for the performers – something impossible in a sparsely populated open auditorium. Finally, the notion that radical theatre needs radical architecture in order to work freely also came to be questioned in the late twentieth century: would it not succeed still better, some argued, if it could be seen to work in a theatre type associated with middlebrow entertainment?

London's Royal Court Theatre, a small late nineteenth-century proscenium auditorium famed for its ambience as much as the continuing success of its 'experimental' performances, is one such model. Peter Brook is adept at finding them – as witness his rediscovery of the 1904 Majestic Theater in Brooklyn

for a 1988 season, or his equivalent smaller base in Paris. Wherever these theatres were built – which means all over Europe and much of the United States – they are returning to favour. In the case of the Majestic, it later received its official makeover in a design by Hardy Holzman Pfeiffer that is an interesting and rare case of 'arrested decay'. Money was spent on new seating (Brook-style benches rather than individual seats) and basic upgrading of lighting and acoustics, rather than on tarting up the interior. Its appearance is therefore semi-distressed – in places with sprayed fire-resistant coatings left fully visible on old iron girders – with flaking layers of old paintwork sanded down and left revealed like a palimpsest of the theatre's past. The same architects created a striking new theatre complex at the Hult

Center for the Performing Arts in Eugene, Oregon, 1982, where the practice's interpretation of a 'traditional' interior for the Silva Concert Hall was to line it with a form of plaster basket-weave. In its disorientating, hallucinogenic way it is in the tradition of Poelzig. However, for the smaller Soreng Theater in the same complex, a flexible auditorium, a more standard response of a 'black box' with exposed services, was provided. Externally, with its mix of glass curtain walling, zig-zag roofs and stone-clad elements, it shouts less loudly, in keeping with its late 1970s, early 1980s period.

Such relative modesty could not be claimed for Barton Myers' Center for the Performing Arts in Cerritos, California, 1993, which looks like a fantasy Mongolian encampment with its cluster of towers

a	d f
b c	e g

a Hardy Holzman Pfeiffer, Brooklyn Academy of Music (BAM) Majestic Theater, Brooklyn, New York, 1987: interior of auditorium: theatre as found object

b Hardy Holzman Pfeiffer, Hult Center for Performing Arts, Eugene, Oregon, 1982: exterior view

c Hult Center: detail of the basket-weave of the auditorium ceiling Performance spaces serve as urban landmarks:

d Barton Myers Associates (with BOORA and ELS Design Group), Center for the Performing Arts, Portland, Oregon, 1982-7

e James Stirling Michael Wilford & Associates, Music School and Theatre Academy, Stuttgart, Germany, 1986-96

f Cesar Pelli, Blumenthal Performing Arts Center, Charlotte, North Carolina, 1987-92: exterior view

g Blumenthal Center: section

and flagpoles, its bright colours and abstract patterning. But then, this was a flagship urban regeneration scheme, and like many such ventures it tried too hard not only in its outside appearance, but also in its interior – an all-purpose auditorium, capable of being configured for flat-floor events, traditional concerts, opera and drama. Myers pulled out rather fewer post-modern stops to rather better effect in his two auditoria Center for the Performing Arts in Portland, Oregon, 1982–7, where there was something of a historic context to work in, not least a statutorily protected picture palace next door. The appliqué facades with their cut-out ziggurat motifs place the building as firmly in the 'PoMo' 1980s as the old movie house (now a concert hall) next door is 1920s.

Better than Myers for civic bombast is Cesar

Pelli's Blumenthal Performing Arts Center in Charlotte, North Carolina, 1987–92, another twin-auditorium affair dressed up to look rather like a shopping mall, particularly in the way the big lumps of the theatres are wallpapered into the overall complex just as department stores (another inward-looking building typology) try to lose some of their bulk in large retail complexes. Rather more considered landmark-making is apparent in Stirling and Wilford's Stuttgart Music Academy, 1989–96, where the concert hall is placed at the base of a battered cylindrical tower engaged with the rectilinear block of the academy behind (this is further discussed under 'Learning' since the building is principally a college).

The proscenium form is still common enough in many of these new theatres and concert halls, but

surely none is so bizarre as Aldo Rossi's reconstruction of the Carlo Felice Theatre in Genoa, 1983–90. This externally re-classicises an eighteenth-century building largely destroyed in the Second World War and expresses the tall new flytower as a fenestrated block topped with a cornice. Inside, however, things are very different. Rossi's concept here is to treat the flanks of the auditorium as if they were the sides of a street, complete with stone facings, windows with shutters, and balconies. The auditorium roof becomes the sky, complete with pinpoint halogen lights serving as stars. The stage area thus becomes a continuation of the 'street', its false perspective funnelling through the proscenium arch. The idea is at odds with the whole notion of the theatrical 'room' though it has historical precedent in the streetwise roots of

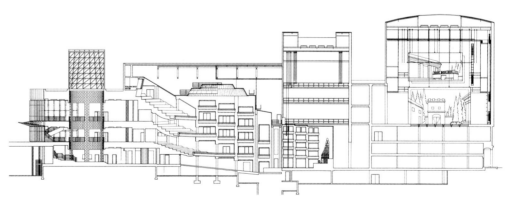

a James Stirling Michael Wilford
& Associates, Music School
and Theatre Academy,
Stuttgart, Germany, 1986–96:
view towards the stage
b Stuttgart Academy:
auditorium

a   b

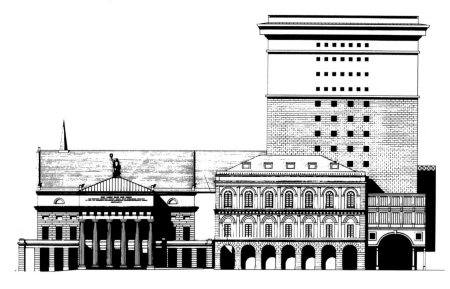

theatre, something that Rossi most fruitfully explored in his earlier, iconic, temporary floating theatre, the Teatro del Mondo (Venice and Dubrovnik, 1979–80). The Teatro del Mondo worked as an image of theatre rather than as theatre itself; built cheaply out of scaffolding and timber, it acknowledged the buildings built to serve the earliest emerging European theatre tradition. His later Lighthouse Theatre (Toronto, 1988) was a related scenographic exercise but made a serious attempt to make a link between the theatres of Ancient Greece and modern times through the amphitheatre form.

In this allusive tradition, the Beckett Theatre at Trinity College Dublin, by De Blacam and Meagher, 1990–4, followed on from their earlier insertions in timber at the college, which happened to include a galleried atrium reminiscent of an Elizabethan inn courtyard next to the eighteenth-century dining hall. This became a semi-official theatre space, while the 'black box' Beckett Theatre nearby with its timber-clad, jettied external appearance, tucked into a crevice of the existing complex, formed the official counterpoint. At the same time in Japan, Tadao Ando had also turned to history in the search for a 'universal theatre', even though it was designed for just one troupe. The Kara-Za Theatre, 1985–8, is appealing because it exists only as a set of drawings for a polygonal building, as wide as it is

tall, to be built out of common scaffolding poles and boarding wherever it is needed. Its relative complexity means that it cannot be struck and moved around on tour like a circus Big Top – but it is transient rather than permanent, and this as much as its form reminds one of the earliest Elizabethan theatres. Like so many practitioners of theatre, Ando had noted that in his own country's oldest theatres, actors and audience were crowded into the one intense space. 'I wished to create a theatre that would ring to the sound of a human voice,' he said. He sees theatre in sacred terms – as a place removed, in Buddhist terms, from this world.

Kara-Za is not your comfortable airconditioned, mall-friendly American idea of theatre, but comfort, some believe, is the enemy of good drama. Iain Mackintosh, of the consultancy Theatre Projects, tells the story of when the Royal Shakespeare Company director Adrian Noble staged a Japanese version of Twelfth Night at the Ginza Saison Theatre in Tokyo. Noble was at a loss to explain why the audience totally failed to respond. It was a new, well-equipped, theatre. Later, Noble realized the root of the problem: the seats were so deep and high-backed that the audience had lost contact with one another. Each individual was as isolated as if they were at home watching television. His suspicions were confirmed when he discovered that Peter

a c   e f
          g
          h
b d   i

Brook, who had earlier staged his Carmen at the same theatre, had built right over this airline-type seating with his own rudimentary benches. For Brook, inter-audience contact – thigh-to-thigh, on hard benches – was as important as actor-audience contact: and both were more important than mere comfort. As Stephen Daldry, director of London's Royal Court, later remarked: 'If people want comfortable seats, my opinion is that they should not go to the theatre.' A place where an alert audience shares the same space and breathes the same air as the performers: this is what is described, by Daldry and others as with Ando, as 'sacred space'.

All those who design theatres tend to come to similar conclusions, some expressing them more overtly than others. James Stirling and Michael Wilford, at their Cornell University Performing Arts Center, Ithaca, New York, 1982–8, saw the complex as an Italian hill town, with the auditorium expressed as a 'church'. Antoine Predock played a subtler game at his Mandell Weiss Forum in San Diego, 1988–91. Observing that: 'Going to the theater should be a ritual, a ceremony', he accordingly designed a long and stately approach along a freestanding mirror-glass wall, 270 feet long and 13 feet high, in which theatregoers would see themselves reflected as their feet crunched on the gravel and dry eucalyptus leaves. The point of arrival takes them quite literally

through the looking-glass. 'Depending on the level of light, one sees through the mirror or is reflected in it. Sometimes at night a glowing light from behind the looking glass reveals furtive impressions of movement visible to approaching patrons. The mirrored wall becomes a threshold between the reality of the everyday and the dreamlike, mythic power of the theater.'

Dealing in such magic has to be largely intuitive – yet those who have studied the science of the theatre, from Shakespeare's time onwards, claim to detect a geometrical rationale, based upon the circle and the triangle, that underlies all the best theatre design, consciously or otherwise. There are some interesting assonances, for instance, between the auditorium of Predock's Mandel Weiss forum with its thrust stage and semicircle of seating, and Lasdun's Olivier Theatre at London's National, designed more than 20 years previously. Predock's is smaller and simpler, but the intention and layout in both cases is near-identical.

It was when designing the National, and in search of sacred space, that Lasdun found himself simultaneously researching Epidauros and questioning practitioners such as Brook – who was provoked at one point to exclaim that you could put on a very good performance on a bombsite. The theatre, designed in 1967 and completed in 1977 on London's South Bank, was destined to be instantly

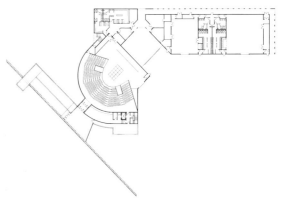

Architects plunder the tub of historical references:

a   Aldo Rossi, Carlo Felice New Theatre, Genoa, Italy, 1983–9: elevation
b   Aldo Rossi, Teatro del Mondo, Venice, 1979–80
c   Carlo Felice Theatre: interior of auditorium
d   Tadao Ando, Kara-Za, Sendai, Miyagi, and Asakusa, Tokyo, 1985–8
e   De Blacam + Meagher, Beckett Theatre, Trinity College, Dublin, 1990–4: exterior view of entrance
f   Beckett Theatre: elevation
g   Denys Lasdun, National Theatre, London, 1967–77: interior of Lyttleton Theatre – Epidauros reinvented
h   Antoine Predock, Mandell Weiss Forum, San Diego, 1988–91: exterior view
i   Mandell Weiss Forum: plan

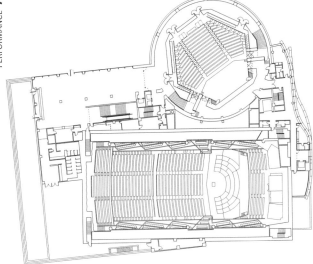

unfashionable – its author was from an older generation of modern individualists, working in heavyweight concrete. It was the theatre's misfortune to arrive on the scene just as concrete, as a facing material, was at the depths of public unpopularity.

Or so the legend of the National went. Actually, much evidence contradicts this version. The theatre's public spaces were taken to instantly by the public, and architects at the time were friendlier towards it than the growing myth of the building later suggested. Moreover, the initial hostility of directors and actors to the two main theatre spaces – with the usual complaint regarding lack of interrelation between actor and audience – mellowed somewhat over the years as productions were devised to suit the spaces. But on the level of its external appearance, it is undeniable that, by the mid-1980s, the National had become a symbol of hated 'modern' architecture in the mind of many public commentators. It is equally undeniable that by the mid-1990s it had moved back into favour and was deemed to be a piece of living history. It was statutorily listed as a structure of architectural and historic importance in 1995, on the very day that its director, Richard Eyre, announced a programme of improvements and alterations by the architects Stanton Williams, which Lasdun resisted: a compromise was eventually reached.

As a stratified building with recessive facades but with a Hawksmoor-like mastery of solid and void, the National emerged almost archaeologically from the earth of the city – again, one can find parallels with Predock's Mandel Weiss theatre in San Diego, and with his later projects such as the unbuilt Maryland Center for the Performing Arts, 1994, which emerges from the ground like an uptilted rock stratum, and his similar Spencer Theater at Ruidoso, New Mexico, 1994–6. Lasdun's National is readable from outside as two main theatres, differently aligned, under one roof. It is self-evidently there for just one purpose – again like Predock in San Diego, where the curved back wall of the auditorium is fully expressed. In this both are very unlike, say, the Sydney Opera House, finally completed only in 1973, where Utzon's forms could cloak almost any activity and where the symbolic, readily logographical, form of the building is everything. Compare this with the characteristically bravura shell of Frank Gehry's Disney Concert Hall in Los Angeles, 1989–2001, home to the LA Philharmonic, which is designed to leave passers-by in no doubt that here is a building of cultural importance, even if it is not wholly clear from the outside what goes where. However, Predock had an answer to this inside-outside problem, too, in the crystalline form of his unbuilt Baltimore Performing Arts Center, 1994 (in association with

Ayers Saint Gross). He conceived a carapace for a twin-theatre complex that was transparent (he called it an 'urban chandelier') within which the limestone and metal monoliths of each theatre and their support spaces would be apparent, like objects caught in amber. At the same time the overall shape of the envelope – a quartz-like mountain, its shape generated by the intersecting grid-lines of the city – would form the necessary civic symbol.

The design problem of the multiple auditorium complex can be tackled in numerous other ways. In Nagaoka, Japan, Toyo Ito's 'L-Hall' (L for Lyric), 1993–6, contains a 700-seat concert hall and 450-seat theatre and many studio spaces, the whole being partly earth-sheltered in the flat landscape. Ito expresses the two lumps of auditorium architecture in opposite ways: a glowing, translucent white oval signals the shape of the concert hall auditorium, a black box the flytower of the theatre. These contrasting elements are then tied together by a gently undulating roof that ripples beneath both forms, and shelters all the other spaces, from public foyers to private offices. The roof is pierced at intervals to bring daylight into the plan, and the complex, signalled by its twin crowns, is approached by pedestrians along an arched walkway that rises obliquely up the mounded parvis of the building. It is a relatively simple diagram which, on a larger scale,

a b c   e

         f

   d

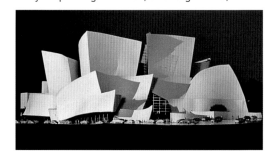

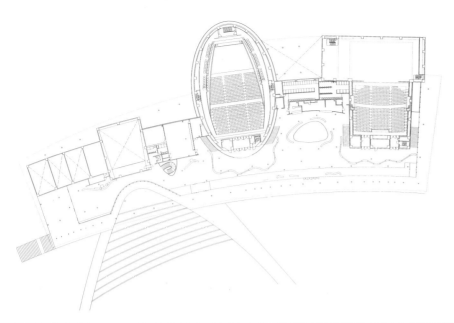

a   Arata Isozaki & Associates,
    Kyoto Concert Hall, Kyoto,
    Japan, 1991–5: plan
b   Kyoto Concert Hall: interior of
    auditorium
c   Kyoto Concert Hall: the
    embracing wall
d   Frank O Gehry & Associates,
    Walt Disney Concert Hall, Los
    Angeles, 1989–2001: the
    mystic Gehry envelope
e   Toyo Ito, L-Hall, Nagaoka,
    Niigata, Japan, 1993–6: plan
f   L-Hall: the sweep of the
    exterior, with the revealed
    auditoria above

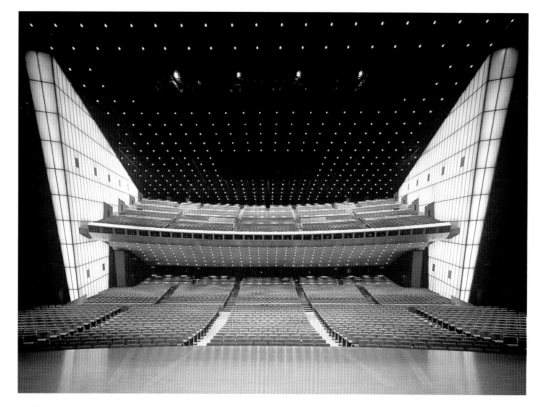

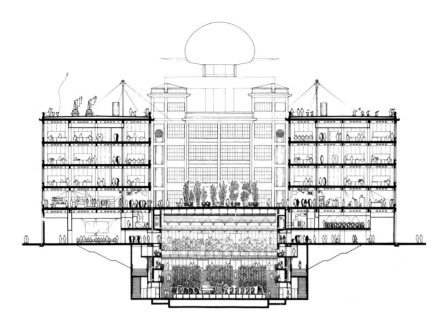

applies also to Arata Isozaki's Kyoto Concert Hall, 1991–5, where a 'classic' rectangular hall and a freer circular chamber music hall are handled with confidence as two great solids: the cube and the cylinder, tied relatively loosely together with an undulating and bifurcating glass curtain wall. Elsewhere – most notably in his 1990 arts complex at Mito – Isozaki chose to design a random element, the twisted, fractal 'Art Tower' to act as the symbol for a place that also happens to include twin concert halls.

The device of expressing the forms of the auditoria applies on the grandest scale to Rafael Viñoly's Tokyo International Forum of 1990–6 (also discussed in 'Civic Realm'). Viñoly's diagram of the great public foyer leading into each of the four auditoria is not so dissimilar to Ito's, even if the external architecture is very different: but for Viñoly, the foyer spaces dominate and the boxes of the auditoria are subsidiary; for Ito it is vice-versa. Viñoly's theatres are nonetheless soberingly large. Taken as a whole, using the public spaces as well as the auditoria, the International Forum can accommodate 36,000 people at one event. Taken separately, the halls step down from Hall A, which holds 5,000 and is used for large-scale events and concerts; Hall B, a flexible space for 3,000, used for banqueting; Hall C, an adaptable 1,500-seater for music (lined entirely with resonant Karim wood, the very colour of fine

Cremonese string instruments); and Hall D, a 600-seat experimental 'black box' theatre. It is part of the brilliance of Viñoly's concept that the descending size of these theatre boxes exactly mirrors the angle of the site boundary determining the main facade of the building, so allowing the perfect ellipse of his public forum space.

At this gargantuan end of the performance space market, one other option still remains – to express each building separately as a discrete entity. This is what Renzo Piano did with his Rome Auditoria, 1994. Piano designed a grouping of three beetle-like halls of different sizes (2,700, 1,200 and 500 seats), clustered with their heads together round a circular plaza. Built to the north of the city near the 1960 Olympics site, the complex encompasses more than the performance spaces. These are perched high over a plinth that contains, at the end housing the smallest hall, shops, restaurants and five cinemas, a library, museum and research centre, even a flower market as part of an overall landscape strategy that includes the exposed remains of a Roman villa on the site.

The complex is notable, among much else, for the fact that Piano succeeded in making the largest concert hall a homage to Scharoun's Berlin Philharmonie in the way the seating is disposed around the orchestra. The smallest hall is an

adaptable space recalling his and Richard Rogers' sunken 1970s IRCAM auditorium in Paris next to the Pompidou Centre: while the medium-sized hall for chamber and contemporary concerts is given a flexible seating arrangement and adjustable acoustics achieved with moveable ceiling segments. This was a solution Piano had used on his earlier 2,000-seat concert and congress hall in the Lingotto building in Turin, 1983–95, one of two main sunken auditoria beneath one of the courtyards of the colossal old Fiat factory. Like the horrific four-poster bed of Edgar Allen Poe, the ceiling of the Lingotto concert hall can be lowered until the balcony tier of seating vanishes altogether, in the process reducing the reverberation time from an orchestral 1.9 seconds to the 1.5 seconds preferred for chamber music recitals. Unlike the big, fractally arranged orchestra room in Rome, the Lingotto version is a classic acoustic shoe-box – a form that was also the cheapest to excavate and integrate with the grid of the existing building above. The separate 480-seat auditorium is effectively a miniaturized version, without the clever ceiling.

Going underground removes one problem with concert halls, which is that they are introverted forms that must attempt to achieve *civitas* by addressing and augmenting their surroundings. This duty takes on high political importance in the case of the opera house. Of all arts buildings, this type

a   Rafael Viñoly, Tokyo
     International Forum, Tokyo,
     1990–6: interior of Hall A
b   Tokyo Forum: interior of the
     3,000-seat Hall B
c   Renzo Piano Building
     Workshop, Lingotto Factory
     conversion, Turin, Italy,
     1983–95: section through
     Lingotto auditorium
d   Lingotto: the virtuous
     black box

c   d

a

b

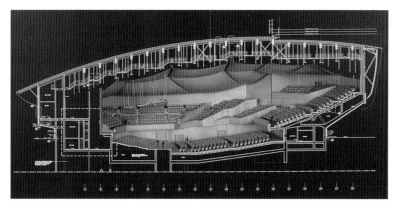

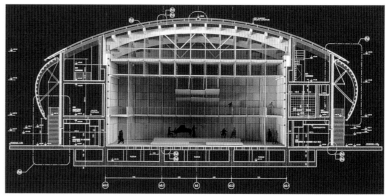

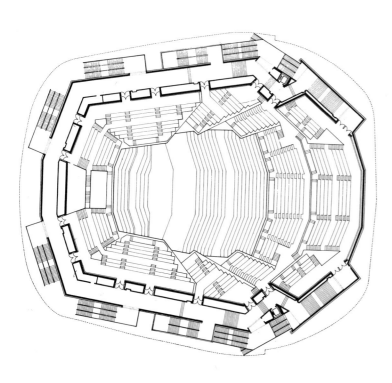

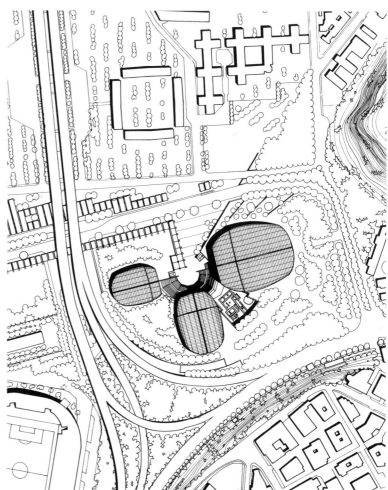

a c

b d   f

e

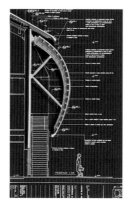

represents the ultimate test of a city's, and a nation's, virility – and of an architect's stamina. Only prosperous societies can afford opera houses, because only in prosperous societies can people afford to go to the opera. Even so, opera as an art form invariably requires heavy state subsidy. For all these reasons, the prospect of a new opera house tends to polarize opinion. The accusation of élitism sticks only too easily, and architecture tends to suffer as a result.

In some countries, therefore, new opera houses have to be introduced by stealth – in the United Kingdom, for instance, it is politically expedient to call them something else, such as 'lyric theatres'. The proposed Cardiff Bay Opera House by Zaha Hadid was abandoned at least partly due to

hostility to its function, although it was scheduled to stage a greater proportion of musicals and rock concerts than straight opera. The new Salford Opera House in the north of England, designed by Michael Wilford, was cannier, dropping the 'opera' tag before going public. It has been named 'the Lowry Centre' after the local artist because it will also include a gallery of his work.

Elsewhere, such camouflage is not
always necessary. In Seville, Spain, the building of a new city opera house was seen as a natural and inevitable consequence of staging Expo 92 – along with the new airport, railway station, and road system. This concept of the opera house as an essential piece of cultural infrastructure also tends to reduce the weight of expectation placed upon it: the

cylindrical Seville building, built by a non-heroic firm of local architects, modestly addresses the riverside. It is seen not as a landmark structure but as an everyday container for performance, and was built very quickly. Similarly, relatively little fuss attended the building of Bilbao's much larger opera house and concert hall, 1993–9, by Madrid-based Federico Soriano and Dolores Palacios – perhaps because it was overwhelmed by its neighbour, Frank Gehry's Guggenheim. Yet the concert hall is a fine conception, a rusting hulk of a building intended to recall the heavy industry of the old Euskalduna shipyards that were once here. The architects refer to it as a 'ghost ship' and declare:
'Its plates and rivets appear rusty: we shall merely clean up the old inside and set up, as if in the hold of

a Renzo Piano Building
   Workshop, Rome Auditoria,
   Rome, 1994: sectional model
b Rome Auditoria: plan of
   the 2,700-seat hall
c Rome Auditoria: cross-
   sectional model
d Rome Auditoria: site plan
   of 'beetle-like' halls
e Rome Auditoria: cross-
   sectional detail
f Michael Wilford & Partners,
   Lowry Centre, Salford, England,
   1992–2000

a ship, the rooms and large areas required for its use. We shall transform this rusting hulk which we have shored up as if in dry dock, into a music centre.'

It is also large, containing three halls, intended to be used for conferences as well as concerts, but Soriano and Palacios separate the uses, and their entrances and exits, so that each function has its own 'front door' and dedicated section of the cavernous building. It does not set out to be pretty, rather evocative. In an urban context that includes Gehry and Calatrava on song, a beauty contest was perhaps best avoided.

The relatively rapid gestation of the Bilbao opera and concert centre and Carlos Ott's Opéra Bastille in Paris is rare: the norm is for such projects to be very protracted. The Finnish National Opera House in Helsinki, by architects Hyvämäki-Karhunen-Parkkinen, took twenty years from inception to completion in 1993. The Essen Opera House in Germany took thirty. It was designed by Alvar Aalto in 1959, revised by him in 1964 and 1974, but built wholly posthumously, being completed only in 1990. In Sydney, Amsterdam or London, the story is much the same. The Amsterdam story is particularly apposite: originally the Austrian architect Wilhelm Holzbauer won the competition for a new Amsterdam City Hall in 1968 at the same time as a new opera house by the elderly and distinguished Dutch modernist

Bernard Bijvoet was being mooted elsewhere. Neither made much progress, and in 1979 (the year of Bijvoet's death at ninety) the city fathers decided to combine both projects in one building by Holzbauer at Waterlooplein on the banks of the Amstel. This proved immensely controversial – the most contentious new public building in The Netherlands for centuries. Building the opera and town hall meant flattening a famous flea-market district but worse, the result was rightly seen by public and architects alike as a bland compromise. Riots ensued. The anti-opera movement became known as 'Stopera'. The bureaucracy did not back down, the complex was built by 1987, but the name stuck: Amsterdam Opera to this day is known as the 'Stopera', and the dullness of the eventual huge architecture justifies the initial outrage. Bureaucracy grips the auditorium in the form of an L-shaped office block wrapping round it. A facade of repeating spindly post-and-beam elements scarcely rises to the occasion, while a covered mall gives a shopping-centre feel to the whole. Bijvoet, an underrated original contributor to the Modern Movement and a fine theatre designer, did not deserve to be associated even tangentially with the project, while the younger Holzbauer's reputation suffered a considerable setback. The end result has an air of weariness, typical of the buildings that emerge from these political,

financial and artistic struggles. The scars of battle have scarcely faded.

In London, they gave up: plans for a National Opera House in the 1960s, designed by Lasdun to sit as half of a pair with his National Theatre, were shelved. Instead, the cramped existing Royal Opera House is finally being expanded to designs by architects Jeremy Dixon and Edward Jones, which leave the E M Barry auditorium of 1857–8 largely intact. It was a 'sacred space' that worked. In the end, nobody had the nerve to gamble on a new one. Opera houses are very intensively used buildings – particularly when a ballet company is also present – and much of their function is surprisingly akin to that of a factory-distribution complex. Sets of successful productions can last for decades, and must be dismantled and stored. Sets of particular scenes must be lined up and trundled on in double-quick time. The mechanisms, revolves, and palletized storage systems that allow this to happen with speed and efficiency represent a colossal investment that the public hardly ever gets to see in action. As with all investments in new technology, it carries the risk of immediate obsolescence: a problem that the earlier labour-intensive manual methods of erecting and striking scenery did not face. The old ways, however, represent a high running cost, and opera houses always want to reduce

Grand opera makes for
political football and
(usually) long delay:
a Hyvämäki-Karhunen-Parkkinen,
Finnish National Opera House,
Helsinki, 1993
b Carlos Ott, Opéra Bastille,
Paris, 1983–90

c Jeremy Dixon Edward Jones,
Royal Opera House, Covent
Garden, London, 1996–9:
model
d Wilhelm Holzbauer with
Architectenbureau Dam,
Bijvoet en Holt, Opera House,
Waterlooplein, Amsterdam,
1982–8

	b	d
a		
	c	

their running costs, even if it involves high levels of capital spending to achieve this aim.

Sometimes, as in Helsinki, in Amsterdam and at London's Royal Opera, enhanced public spaces result from the long drawn-out process of getting an opera house built. Helsinki has its new, somewhat sterile, public square, Amsterdam its mall, London's Royal Opera House development reinstates a corner of the Covent Garden piazza, originally by Inigo Jones. But whatever the urbanistic benefits, politics usually ensure that this is one building type that will never have an easy ride. As cultural statements, opera houses are torn between their role in the public realm and the truth of their existence as publicly subsidised venues for an art form associated with the rich. Architects accepting a commission

to design an opera house must prepare to be vilified and, usually, expect to be very old – or dead – before the project is completed.

There are exceptions. Jean Nouvel was allowed to be pretty brisk when it came to extending the Lyons Opéra, 1989-93, and pretty radical too: his reward, on opening night, was to walk out on stage to be greeted with boos and catcalls from an audience bemused by the all-black interior and funereal light levels. But opera audiences are notably conservative, and the place continues to function smoothly enough. What tends to be forgotten, in discussions of Nouvel's engagement with the sensibilities of the opera-going public, is the extraordinary way he turned a horizontally-arranged cultural building vertically. The existing Italianate building was built by

Chenavard and Pollet in 1831, faced the Hôtel de Ville across the Place de la Comédie, and consisted of two arcaded storeys and an attic pavilion. Nouvel sandwiched the existing structure between two layers of his own design. The attic storey was removed, and replaced with a six-level barrel-vaulted pavilion to house costume and scenery workshops, ballet rehearsal spaces right on top, offices and restaurants (he cited the rounded form of a lute as inspiration). He dug just as far below ground, scooping out a 200-seat arena, rehearsal rooms for the opera players, and storage. By the time he had finished, a low-lying building had taken on – internally especially – the characteristics of a tower block, its internal volume tripled from the original. With operatic stars descending from the heights, and the chorus

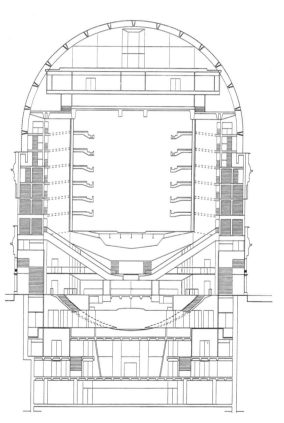

a d e
b c f g

Expansion of the existing Lyons Opéra was only possible vertically:
a Jean Nouvel, Lyons Opéra House, Lyons, France, 1989–93: the expanded opera house
b Lyons Opéra House: interior of auditorium
c Lyons Opéra House: roof-top ballet rehearsal space
d Lyons Opéra House: cross section

Glyndebourne is a revival of the companionable horseshoe auditorium:
e Michael Hopkins & Partners, Glyndebourne Opera House, Glyndebourne, Sussex, England, 1989–94: longitudinal section through auditorium and flytower
f Glyndebourne Opera House: exterior view
g Glyndebourne Opera House: auditorium

ascending from the depths – in order to meet at the same point backstage to effect an entrance – the reliance on reliable liftgear is absolute. Performers on the opera circuit are routinely astonished at how they are expected to circulate at Lyons.

In the context, however, Nouvel was responding to a straitjacket. The building, historic and protected, is guarded by its peristyle on three sides and is jammed up against unmoveable buildings to the rear. Expanding at ground level was impossible. Within the vertical envelope he created, Nouvel then slung his black cube of an auditorium (at 1,300 seats, still quite a small capacity by opera standards) high in the remade structure, accessing it from the foyers via escalators, double flights of stairs, and suspended walkways. A startling zone of bright red

plush must be traversed between the black zones of circulation areas and auditorium. Perhaps some of the audiences feel they are being dragged into unwelcome realms of irony. In its way, however, Nouvel's auditorium is as conventional as it could be: high (30 metres, with galleries cut right back so as not to impinge on the volume) and flanked with tiers of boxes on six levels. With circulation beneath its belly, it also functions as a discrete object within the whole structure. And finally, the big barrel vault on top, with its almost vertiginously airy ballet rooms, serves as a neat way to conceal the flytower. One remains entirely unaware of it. The louvres of the barrel roof glow red at night in a lighting scheme devised by Yann Kersale – a more intense red, when the building is full to capacity. Nouvel is to be

applauded for resisting the temptation to apply radial fanlight detailing or faux suspension rods to his tympani: the facade reads horizontally, reflecting the floor levels within.

Other opera houses that break the rules by being built swiftly may be found first in Paris and at Glyndebourne, England, where Michael Hopkins' opera house, 1989–94, rose rapidly and (relatively) cheaply because it was wholly privately financed. Glyndebourne, in the hills of Sussex, has no urban context: the Opéra Bastille in Paris has little else. And although Glyndebourne (built in handmade brick jointed with ductile lime mortar so as to avoid ugly expansion gaps) deals with the introverted auditorium problem by flanking it with windowed offices and placing curving open galleries at the rear, it

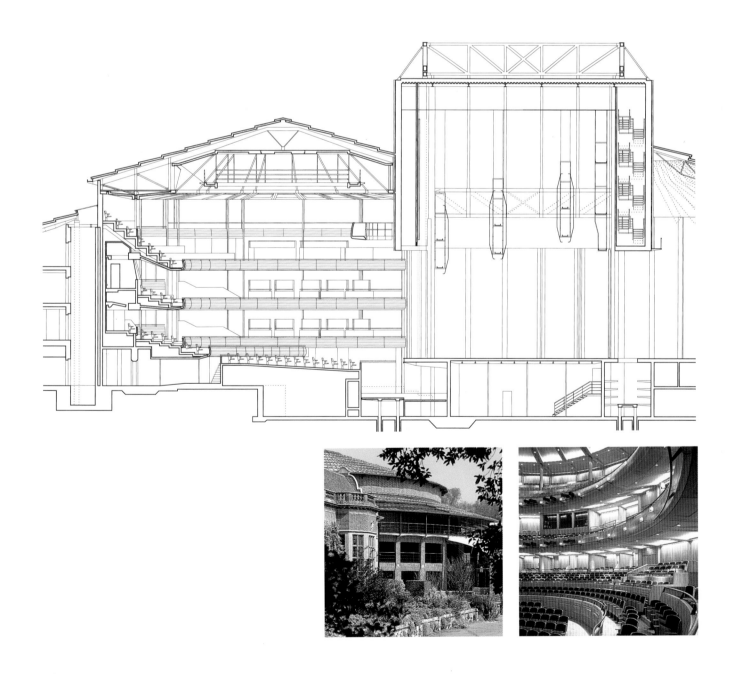

makes no attempt to conceal the inevitable flytower. Early designs which handled this lump as a third concentric circle to add to those of auditorium and backstage areas were dropped in favour of an austere lead-clad box topped with exposed Vierendeel beams. No artifice: the modernist principle that materials and forms should express their function is key to Hopkins' thinking, however traditional some of his buildings may seem. Inside, the timber-lined auditorium has been likened by Dr Germaine Greer to sitting inside a musical instrument. An interesting proposition, particularly in view of the fact that the plan form of the auditorium and stage area – from which the form of the opera house followed – was initially proposed by Ian Mackintosh of Theatre Projects as a modern interpretation of the eighteenth-century principle of intersecting circles. One circle is the horseshoe-shaped auditorium, the other the performance zone, and the area of intersection – where the circles overlap, and where the musicians sit – enables the audience to, in Mackintosh's words, 'assist at the celebration' of opera. Although Hopkins abandoned certain elements of Mackintosh's 1990 plan, he retained the principle of the zone of intersection, and it suited him to follow the concentric-circles form not only to achieve an intimate auditorium, but also to reduce the external bulk of the building, which thus ended up as an oval.

Little of this finesse is apparent at Paris' latest opera. It is now legendary that Parisians and visitors alike prefer the exuberant charms of the existing 1861 Opéra Garnier. Much of this is to do with the way the two houses deal with public space. The Opéra Garnier has lots of it, inside and out, reflecting the fact (quite literally, in its mirrored salons) that to go to the opera in Napoleon III's Paris was to go on parade. The Opéra Bastille, 1983-90, by contrast, fails badly, despite its spacious semicircular foyers. Squeezed onto a cramped urban site like a fat man in a tight suit, it addresses the immense square of Bastille, but this is not publicly usable space: it is a traffic maelstrom. In contrast, the area around Garnier was built deferentially after his opera house, giving it an appropriate setting. Inside, Ott cannot compete with the succession of processional public spaces provided by Garnier more than a century previously. The older building acknowledges that the experience of opera is mostly to do with public interaction; the newer sees it merely as another auditorium-based performance. Outside, it is too big and too crude, with a confusing multi-level entrance. In public image terms it cannot compete either with its predecessor or with its contemporary, the Cité de la Musique, 1985-95, by Christian de Portzamparc.

This, an element in the vast La Villette urban park with its science museum, exhibition hall, rock arena and 'follies', was intended to be a 'Beaubourg for music' – as important as the Pompidou Centre had been for the visual arts. Portzamparc was on the up, following the success of his Paris Opera Dance School in Nanterre, 1983-7, which demonstrated his talent for the bold, simple plan – in that case a comet-shaped configuration with a 'head' of the teaching and performing areas and a 'tail' of accommodation, the whole arranged to maximize the opportunities of its parkland setting. At La Villette, Portzamparc built his musical township in two phases: the western section, opened in 1990, houses the National Conservatory of Music and Dance, while the giant wedge of the eastern section includes a 1,200-seater concert hall and a museum of music. The first part is virtuoso shape-making with a sinusoidal roof rippling over one wing and a small concert hall housed in a freestanding chamfered cone that recalls both an ancient Greek tholos and the late-Corbusian feature of similar shape. The newer half of the Cité is perhaps the more interesting, however, because this is more in the public domain, conceived by the architect as an internalized streetscape, spiralling round the elliptical form of its auditorium. It is not quite as marked as in Garnier's opera house, but the plan of the Cité de la Musique shows a similar concern with the public promenade space around, and focusing upon, the auditorium, but capable of

a
b
d
c
e

Christian de Portzamparc's Cité de la Musique is the cultural stormtrooper of Paris' regeneration:
a Christian de Portzamparc, Cité de la Musique, La Villette, Paris, 1985-95: site plan
b Cité de la Musique West: a loggia separates the teaching blocks from the student residences
c Cité de la Musique East: interior of 1,200-seat concert hall
d Cité de la Musique West: four elegant blocks under an over-hanging roof form the *Conservatoire*
e Cité de la Musique West: foyer to the concert hall which forms an inner street through the building

a
b

c d
e

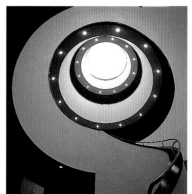

independent life without it. This is culturally induced town-making. It can be reliably dated by the bold incision Portzamparc laid across his spiral plan in the form of a giant tilted Vierendeel truss acting as a raised walkway and visible spine – his version of the late 1980s and early 1990s architectural obsession with fault lines and displacement.

He then proceeded to win the 1997 competition for Luxembourg's Philharmonic Hall with a form that is one great oval edged with slender *pilotis*. This suggests an oval auditorium within, but no: it is rectilinear. Portzamparc's design acknowledges that the oval form has become a legible sign, meaning 'music venue', and instead of making it only one part of a larger complex, he reverses the usual procedure. The usual small second hall is a curving form attached to the main building by the nose, like a pilot fish to a whale. The usual architectural morphic resonance is applied here and on the other side of the world, Arata Isozaki was making a related form in his Nara Convention Hall, 1992–8. This is another great oval, smoothly rounded rather than with a curtain of *pilotis*, with a streamlined attachment (of foyer space). Here, the great ellipse contains a pair of concert halls in the customary major and minor keys. Whereas the smaller, 450-seat one is a box, the internal shape of the larger 1,700-seater does conform faithfully to the boat shape of the building.

The dissonance between performance and social interaction – so well understood by J L C Garnier in nineteenth-century Paris – is tackled and treated in contemporary form at Tel Aviv's opera house. This is just one element in a huge urban composition – the Tel Aviv Performing Arts Centre, 1989–94, also including a theatre, concert hall, offices and housing, designed in well-mannered mainstream modern style by Yacov Rechter (appropriately enough, one might think, given that the architectural history of Tel Aviv in the twentieth century is a history of international modernism). Rechter deliberately left large unresolved spaces in his design for the public areas, on the declared principle that other architects would be invited to undertake this part of the project. The idea worked. Audaciously, the young and relatively untried architect Ron Arad with his then partner Alison Brooks were drafted in early on to apply their sculptural forms – more usually seen in furniture – to the opera house. They saw their task as not to dress up the existing architecture (in a sense, there was none) but to insert their own building within the maw of the Rechter project. Given that an austere commercial square provides the approach to the foyers, Arad's instinct was to challenge the tyranny of the modernist right angle with swooping and curving forms, and with a variety of textures and colours. The Arad insertions scarcely touch Rechter's

a   Yacov Rechter, Tel Aviv
    Performing Arts Centre, Tel
    Aviv, 1989–94: foyer by Ron
    Arad and Alison Brooks
b   Tel Aviv Performing Arts
    Centre: interior view looking
    up to skylight
c   Tel Aviv Performing Arts
    Centre: interior of auditorium
d   Tel Aviv Performing Arts
    Centre: plan
e   Tel Aviv Performing Arts
    Centre: aerial view

work, but inhabit its spaces. Different forms wrap round the back of the auditorium, melt and twist to form a bookshop, enclose box office and restaurant, clad bars and fly off elsewhere. In its way - particularly in its decorative exuberance, its brave choice of materials ranging from woven stainless steel to fused brass rods, sprayed concrete to glass - the Arad commission at Tel Aviv compares with the insertions of earlier times such as William Morris at London's Victoria and Albert Museum: a building meant to act as a permanent exhibition of the work of artists and craftsmen. Strangely, Arad and Brooks' work in Tel Aviv was anticipated by Rem Koolhaas and his Office for Metropolitan Architecture in their first significant built work, the National Dance Theatre in The Hague, 1984-7. But in that case, Koolhaas was simultaneously inserting rebellious elements into a Miesian grid-building that he himself had designed. Where Arad reacted to Rechter, Koolhaas reacted to himself, in a mannered attempt to exploit the collisions of seemingly irreconcilable architectural approaches.

The argument in favour of opera houses is, curiously enough, often presented as an economic one. When the brief was being drawn up for the Cardiff Bay Opera House in South Wales, a case had to be made for its economic significance. The spending power of visitors was important, as was

a

b

c

d

A new desire for urban drama made performance spaces increasingly controversial:

a   Office for Metropolitan Architecture, National Dance Theatre, The Hague, 1984-7: exterior view

b   National Dance Theatre: view from stairs looking down to entrance foyer and up to theatre bar

c   Zaha Hadid, Cardiff Bay Opera House, Cardiff, Wales, 1994-6: perspective view

d   Behnisch, Behnisch & Partner, Bristol Centre for Performing Arts, Bristol Docks, England, 1997-2000: model

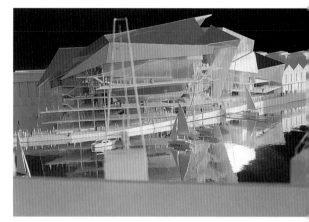

the creation of a couple of hundred jobs in a high unemployment area, but neither factor could justify the high cost of building such a large and advanced lyric theatre. What the arts economist Adrian Ellis pointed to instead was the matter of inward investment. Wales was one of the highest-scoring areas of the United Kingdom when it came to getting overseas firms – particularly in the form of high-volume assembly plant – onto its patch rather than elsewhere in Europe. Ellis argued that the opera house could be justified if it could be shown to be instrumental in attracting just a few more similar companies to the area on the 'quality of life' principle. This was a powerful line to take. Cardiff, in its former docks and industrial bay area, was aware that earlier such regeneration exercises – most notably London's Docklands – had allowed for scarcely any cultural input, at the same time neglecting the transport infrastructure that would allow the new docklands settlers speedy access to the old cultural centre of London's West End and South Bank. But as Ellis himself later remarked, such economic arguments, true so far as they went, were also a form of sophistry. If the Welsh decided they wanted an opera house, then they should just go ahead and build it, he suggested. Everything else would follow.

The furore that followed Zaha Hadid's winning of the competition to design the Cardiff Bay Opera House – and successfully re-submitting it to a subsequent appraisal panel – suggested that the Welsh were not at all sure if they wanted an opera house, or, if they did, whether they wanted this one. Mishandled and refused its funding from Britain's National Lottery-funded Millennium Commission, Cardiff became the first and most celebrated failure of a government policy to create a series of landmark cultural buildings throughout the United Kingdom. As is commonplace with architectural competitions, it later spawned an inferior replacement project, the undesired product of a strange kind of collective guilt.

Why some cultural buildings are built with apparent ease, and some, apparently equally viable and equally well funded, fall by the wayside is an enduring mystery of architecture. Partly Hadid's failure (apart from being female and foreign-born) was to be first on the block with what appeared to the general public to be a new style: broadly speaking, Deconstructivism. Later, Daniel Libeskind's considerably more extreme exercise in that area, to add an extension to London's Victoria and Albert Museum, met with less resistance from the powers that be. And finally, Günter and Stefan Behnisch's competition-winning design for a concert hall in Bristol's docks area – another skewed-plate architectural composition, emerging from a different yet related tradition – met relatively little adverse comment. So in two years, over three projects, in one country, a broad-based architectural movement had shifted from being outrageous to perfectly acceptable.

The Behnisch Bristol Centre for Performing Arts, 1997–2000, is an example of a building form that presents fewer difficulties than opera houses, both technically and politically. The history of concert-going is relatively more populist, there are more precedents of orchestras being formed in, and arising from, poor areas. Orchestral music has long been thought capable of exerting a classless appeal. Such reasoning is mostly nonsense – the artificiality of grand opera holds no fears for a generation raised on rock videos, for instance, while the visual appeal of an orchestra playing is limited. No matter: concert

halls are also relatively cheap. No need for such large and costly flytowers and underground scenery storage. No complex mechanisms, no wings or side-stages required unless dance is also to be performed there. Rehearsal space separate from the main auditorium is about the only luxury a concert hall can aspire to, beyond generous public foyers. Yet these buildings can command landmark status equal to their costlier cousins. If Sydney has its opera house, then Berlin has its Philharmonie, London its Royal Festival Hall, and Thousand Oaks, California, its Civic Arts Plaza.

The Civic Arts Plaza, by Antoine Predock (executive architects Dworsky Associates) was completed in 1994. It is municipal hall as landscape signifier. It mediates between the Ventura Freeway –

an eight-lane elevated concrete ribbon – and the groves and mountains of Southern California. You could whip past on the freeway and hardly know you had passed a town at all. Thus the Civic Arts Plaza was conceived as a way to anchor this scattered ribbon-development of buildings north of Los Angeles. Predock's response was to put the bulk of the complex – the 1,800-seat auditorium – right up close to the freeway, its monolithic end wall relieved by nothing more than a large rectangular relief of copper panels. Predock being adobe-influenced, the stark forms of the Plaza are neither surprising nor uncontextual: it is the scale that impresses, a scale and a deliberate coarseness of detail that can be read, through a blurry windshield, at speed. Away from the road, speed of motion reduced, the

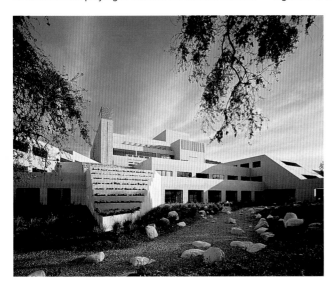

a c   e f
b
d

patterning becomes more complex for the eyes of arriving concert-goers. A 'pictograph wall' of embedded light sculptures refers to the art of the original native settlers of this area: a further attempt to apply a sense of place and history to a non-place. This is a beguilingly old-fashioned conception, not least because the auditorium element is only the most visible part of what is in fact a large local government complex.

The stand-alone concert hall can pose a more difficult challenge than such civic complexes. Like all auditorium-based building types, it must look inwards. Its public function – in particular the large number of people it must handle, is considerably larger than most theatres – provides the opportunity for an outer layer of space addressing the city. Not

all take this opportunity. While London's Royal Festival Hall, 1951, remodelled 1967, by Robert Matthew, Leslie Martin, Peter Moro and others may be rather tentative, Scandinavian-influenced modernism, it makes a virtue of transparency on all four sides and, furthermore, suspends the auditorium so as to create clear public space beneath, as Nouvel later did in Lyons. Many of its successors worldwide have achieved more architecturally, but relatively few of its successors have tackled the public realm quite so assiduously. In 1956 Hans Scharoun won the competition for the Berlin Philharmonie (completed 1963). Its organic, highly distinctive form, bears comparison with Jørn Utzon's design for the Sydney Opera House – also won in competition in 1956, but not finally completed until 1973. By that time (Utzon

had resigned in 1956, handing over the continuing design of the building to the Australian architects Peter Hall, David Littlemore and Lionel Todd) it had ceased to be an opera house, becoming instead a pair of concert halls – one large, one smaller. One of the results of this was to negate Utzon's most ingenious solution to the perennial opera house problem: what do you do with the great lump of the flytower? Utzon had concealed his two flytowers within two of his shell roof forms (each a segment of an imaginary sphere). With the need for large flytowers removed, the shells became what they have remained ever since: purely sculptural forms. They did at least give Eero Saarinen, the judge who championed Utzon as the winner, some useful ideas which he promptly used to design the curvaceous TWA

A strong tradition of lyric metaphor persists in the design of performance spaces:

a Antoine Predock, Civic Arts Plaza, Thousand Oaks, California, 1990–4: exterior view

b Antoine Predock, Baltimore Perfoming Arts Center, Baltimore, Maryland, 1994: sectional perspective

c Civic Arts Plaza, Thousand Oaks: interior of foyer

d Antoine Predock, Maryland Center for the Perfoming Arts, University of Maryland, College Park, Maryland, 1994: model

e Hans Scharoun & Edgar Wisniewski, Chamber Music Hall, Philharmonie, Berlin, 1968–87: view towards the stage of the Chamber Music Hall

f Philharmonie: exterior view

Terminal at Kennedy Airport in that same *annus mirabilis*, 1956. And time has shown that the functionality or otherwise of Utzon's shells does not matter a jot.

The influence of Scharoun resurfaced in 1997 when Günter and Stefan Behnisch won the competition for the Bristol Centre for Performing Arts, later named the Harbourside Centre, 1997–2000. It is a concert hall, and an important international commission for the Stuttgart-based practice. The centre starts from the same premise as Utzon's Sydney Opera House: its waterside setting is highly visible from higher parts of the city, therefore the roof becomes an important face of the building, and must be treated with as much care as a conventional elevation. Günter Behnisch cites Scharoun, however, not just for reasons of national solidarity, or because of the precedent of the similarly asymmetrical Berlin Philharmonie, but because Scharoun, for an architect of the elder Behnisch's generation, is a more comfortable model than the so-called deconstructivists – Hadid, Libeskind, Tschumi, Eisenman, Gehry, Coop Himmelblau – with whom his later work has a tendency to be bracketed. The younger Behnisch takes the same view. Perhaps the key is that both the Bristol and Berlin designs are concert halls informed by the notion of movement. Other parallels can be made: like Utzon at Sydney, Behnisch uses his roof

forms – here composed of tilted plates – to hide the lump of the flytower, which is necessary to handle theatrical musicals. Indeed the whole design slips and slides vertiginously over the water's edge, its roofscape seemingly chaotic, its form built up in skewed layers.

There is no reason why architecture composed in this highly tectonic manner should perform its function any less well than architecture of a more conventional shape. In the case of a multi-functional arts building such as this, it allows several differently sized and shaped spaces – always needed in such complex structures – to be housed comfortably within the overall envelope. Herman Hertzberger attempts the same trick with a multi-level undulating roof at his Chassé Theatre at Breda in The Netherlands, 1992–5 – a solid version of the 'glass wave' designed by Richard Rogers for London's South Bank complex. However, this rationalist explanation – for what Behnisch at least would deny was a deconstruction – is negated by his assertion that, had he been building in a tight urban area of London, for instance, rather than in the free-for-all post-industrial context of Bristol's docks area, he would be just as likely to come up with a sober rectilinear building to serve the same purpose. As if to prove his point, Herzog and de Meuron shortly after won a competition to design a large dance theatre in London's

Deptford that entirely conceals the theatre element within a taut-skinned glass shoebox, a trick also played by Fumihiko Maki in his unbuilt proposal for the Musicon concert hall in Bremen, Germany.

Not only is such orthogonality the antithesis of Behnisch, but also of those architects such as Holt Hinshaw Pfau Jones in California who – in their 1995 design for the San Jose Repertory Theater – made a virtue out of functionally expressing all the various lumpen elements of a theatre, grouping them round the skewed cube of the auditorium, even putting a rehearsal room up on the roof to keep the flytower company. But even that was conservative indeed compared with Itsuko Hasegawa's explosively playful Shonandai Culture Centre in the Tokyo suburbs, 1990, which is dominated by two spheres: one, a globe of the earth with its continents, contains the civic theatre while the smaller of the two houses a planetarium – which is less rare for that building type, as witnessed in Adrien Fainsilber's 'Géode' at La Villette in Paris. Metallic silver 'trees' and a mystical river wind their way through Hasegawa's complex, which is like a grown-up children's playground.

Smaller scale concert halls tend to be more homogenous, not least because their programme is less complex. But parallels between the various sub-genres can be made. The Kirishima International Concert Hall, 1994, in Japan by Fumihiko Maki is a

To express, or to conceal, the tell-tale forms?

a Herman Hertzberger, Chassé Theatre, Breda, The Netherlands, 1992–5: foyer

b Fumihiko Maki, Kirishima International Concert Hall, Kirishima, Japan, 1994

c Itsuko Hasegawa, Shonandai Culture Centre, Yokohama, Japan, 1990

a   b

c

medium-sized venue, clad in Maki's favoured stainless steel, with a faceted roof generated by acoustic reverberation times. Kirishima is the concert-hall equivalent to Hopkins' Glyndebourne Opera, and was built at the same time. Here there is no urban context, but a sylvan hilly landscape to command. Instead of the South Downs of Sussex, the gentle slope of the Kirishima Plateau of Southern Kyushu. Like Hopkins, Maki wraps public spaces around the rear of the auditorium, not in the form of galleries, but as foyers behind a tall glass wall, revealed relatively crudely by the breaking-down of the masonry flank walls of the building. Instead of the horseshoe shape of Glyndebourne's auditorium, Maki's is a leaf shape, contained within a built envelope with a pointed prow, as of a ship or spaceship. As at Glyndebourne, the relative isolation of the building, and the need to provide self-contained facilities for performers and audience and administration, results in a complex with a village-like quality, not least in Maki's case by the provision of rehearsal rooms around a courtyard (something present at the old Glyndebourne, but not at the new). A separate open-air concert bowl stands a short distance away with an aerofoil-section reflector roof over the stage. The startling superficial differences between Glyndebourne and Kirishima turn out to be just that – surface matters. Aside from the fact that the

English example stages opera (hence that tricky flytower problem) and Kirishima does not, the main differences are in the materials chosen as external finishes. Inside, both auditoria are timber-lined and both have been likened to the interiors of string instruments. You could never mistake Maki's faceted roof for Hopkins' shallow dome, but what is astonishing is not how different these two buildings for different cultures at opposite sides of the world are – but how similar: Kirishima is, after all, built for the performance of music from the Western tradition.

Kirishima also compares with
Tanglewood, Massachusetts, in the United States, especially in its campus character, its educational mission, and its dedication to smaller scale orchestras and chamber groups. At Tanglewood, the task was to preserve something of the *ad hoc* character of a rural festival that has achieved permanence, and it is no coincidence that the solution has parallels with that achieved by the Glyndebourne summer opera festival in England. The Seiji Osawa Hall at Tanglewood, 1989–94, by Boston architects William Rawn Associates, is a rather severe galleried concert hall in brick, timber and lead, with a barrel-vaulted roof. Probably intended to recall New England barns but actually possessing a rather 1920s stripped-classical air, its rectangular shape and broken

a b
   c

   d

The rural music box:
a   William Rawn Associates, Seiji Osawa Hall, Tanglewood, Lenox, Massachusetts, 1989–94
b   Seiji Osawa Hall: longitudinal section
c   Seiji Osawa Hall: the audience can sit on the grass and watch the performance
d   Seiji Osawa Hall: looking into the auditorium from outside

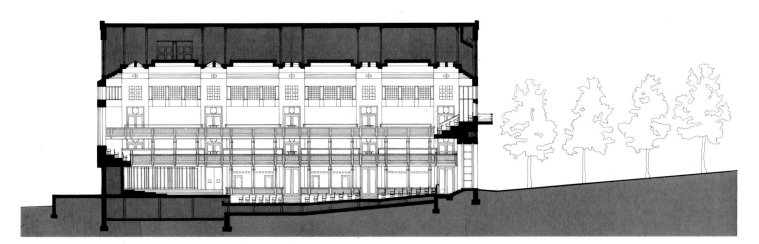

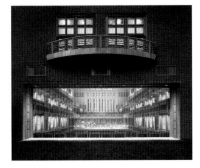

internal surfaces place it firmly in a conventional acoustical context. The surprise is that, at the far end from the stage, the building opens up via a massive slot in the end wall to allow audiences to spill out into the fields outside, getting progressively more casual in their seating arrangements. Thus a covered concert hall doubles as an open-air concert bowl, broadcasting sound and vision from its capacious interior, and supplemented with external loud-speakers. The traditional form and materials of the building in its sylvan landscape recall Hopkins' Glyndebourne, its function and positioning establishes links with Maki's Kirishima Hall, but the way Rawn's Tanglewood building allows the same performance to be enjoyed inside and outside simultaneously is more ambitious than either.

Opinions differ on the ideal shape for a concert hall auditorium. What may be perfect acoustically – for example, the rectangular shoebox shape, preferred and tirelessly promoted by the American acoustician Russell Johnson and also adopted by others, not least by Rawn at Tanglewood – does not always appeal to architects, or even to audiences who are not necessarily seeking aural per-fection. Usually a compromise has to be reached between the acoustic and aesthetic ideals. Johnson-led halls, such as I M Pei's Meyerson Symphony Center in Dallas, 1985-9, or Symphony Hall in Birmingham by the Percy Thomas Partnership, tend to be over-rigorous in feel. However, Pei's geometric exuberance and handling of light at the Meyerson Symphony Center make that hall as different as

could be in feel from the British example in Birmingham, where the hall is hidden within a regrettable conference complex. Pei cites Garnier – an architect whose work he came to admire when working in Paris on the Louvre – as an influence on the way he handles public space in Dallas, and the claim is not unjustified. Also like Garnier, the Meyerson concert hall defines its own space rather than having to accommodate itself to a space left grudgingly by others, which was Ott's misfortune in Paris. Michael Wilford's Lowry Centre in Salford enjoys a similar position in space, and a waterside setting for that Sydney reference, but shares the geometric simplicity of neither Utzon nor Pei: Wilford's complex and theatrical approach has, perhaps, more in common with Behnisch.

When architects reject the shoebox model, push the seating out at the sides and bring the back seats closer to the orchestra, the model usually cited is Scharoun's Philharmonie. Computer and laser modelling of such spaces supposedly reduces the risks: yet Birmingham's concert hall was acoustically acclaimed from day one while Manchester's later Bridgewater Hall, by RHWL, had a lengthy period of acoustic problems. Some halls are more forgiving than others, and better orchestras can cope with the differences. Music reviewers were swift to note that while Birmingham had the renowned CBSO under Simon Rattle, Manchester had to make do with the allegedly inferior Hallé Orchestra under Kent Nagano. Visiting orchestras had an embarrassing habit of not encountering the same acoustic problems as the home team.

Where the Japanese models differ from their Western counterparts is where, understandably enough, the buildings cater for indigenous rather than imported culture. Thus the National Noh Theatre of 1983 by Hiroshe Ohe is an exercise that in some ways can be compared with Western theatre's search for its Shakespearian soul. In this case, the different tradition produces an in-the-round format: more specifically a square stage at the centre of the auditorium, linked to the backstage area via a narrow bridge for entrances and exits. Hiroshe Ohe clads his largely traditional forms with curving and intersecting roofs of aluminium louvres.

In such unchanging theatrical traditions, the layout of a theatre can be prescribed. For opera and orchestral performance, as we have seen, there are certain givens, while play-acting is the most volatile medium of all: the history of recent theatre design is a history of architects lumberingly trying to pin down a quicksilver medium. By the time it is done, the genius director calling all the shots has departed, or changed his mind. As Günter Behnisch remarked, sometimes it is better not to think too much, just draw. Perhaps the most rigorous examination of what is meant by theatre is to be found in Provence. There, the late engineer Peter Rice, of Ove Arup, was called in to advise on the 'Theatre of the Moon'. Set in an ancient amphitheatre and open to the skies, there was only one thing to address: by the use of tracking reflectors, could the light of the moon be focused to allow night-time performances? The result was as magical a place as any deviser of theatrical entertainment has yet attempted.

Acoustic perfection can be of secondary importance to traditional intimacy:
a Pei Cobb Freed & Partners, Meyerson Symphony Center, Dallas, 1985–9: entrance
b Meyerson Symphony Center: interior
c Percy Thomas Partnership, Symphony Hall, Birmingham, England, 1986–91: auditorium
d Symphony Hall: exterior view
e Hiroshi Ohe, National Noh Theatre, Tokyo, 1983

| a | | c | d |
| b | | | e |

LEARNING *Schools, universities & libraries* From the kindergarten, the village school and the university to the national library, all buildings concerned with acquiring knowledge must reconcile two contradictory functions: the need to combine open, communal areas for collective learning, discussion and recreation, with small spaces for concentrated study. The antecedent of the monk's cell in a medieval monastery is still highly relevant, particularly in the case of training or residential colleges, while libraries have retained and, in some cases, enhanced their relative importance in the current on-line age.

'I think of the school as a secret society.'
Zvi Hecker, 1995.

An elementary school needs to be built.

An architectural competition is organized. So far, so commonplace – at any rate for those nations that habitually put such everyday buildings out to competition, rather than regarding them as processing plant, design-free zones. But then the stakes are raised: eighty-three architects from around the world take part. The 420 pupils planned for the school are to benefit from the kind of architectural attention normally focused only on great public buildings usually dedicated to the arts. Why?

The answer is politics. The Heinz-Galinski School is not only the first Jewish school to be built in Germany for sixty years, and completed fifty years after the end of the Second World War, but is in Berlin, of all places. The school cannot, for a while, be anything other than a symbol. Politicians and press make hay out of the whole enterprise, vying for points. And after opening day, when all the fuss has gradually subsided, it has to function as a school. The symbolism must, if cultural integration means anything, fade away until this is just another building performing a vital but humdrum task in a city suburb.

Zvi Hecker, the Israeli architect who won the competition in 1990 and completed it in 1995, made

a point that some might see as a defence of ghetto-ization, but which in fact sums up the whole nature of educational buildings, from schools to universities, training centres to libraries. 'I think of the school as a secret society,' he said. 'It doesn't have to be like a bank or public building, where routes are mapped out at the entrance. It's a family community.'

A related social and architectural agenda is apparent in the utterly different atmosphere of San Diego, California, where Tod Williams and Billie Tsien designed the Neurosciences Institute, 1993–5, to be a 'scientific monastery' in the words of its founder, Nobel Prize winner Gerald Edelman. Edelman had himself taught nearby at Louis Kahn's dauntingly monumental Salk Institute, 1959–65, and rejected that approach, with the approval of his architects. The Salk may be eternal architecture, a temple on its great empty plinth overlooking the sea, but as Billie Tsien remarked: 'People seem like litter in it'. So instead of being the grand 'signature' research complex of earlier times, the Neurosciences Institute is a deliberate clutter. There are three disparate buildings for different functions, each of which is itself broken down into forms that merge with the contours of the landscape, and which are arranged around a courtyard. It is wholly unlike the 'tabula rasa' approach of Kahn at the Salk. Family community? Monastery? Clearly the fact that similar thinking is apparent in

such vastly differing educational establishments as a Jewish school in the Berlin suburbs and a research institute up in the Californian hills, tells us that consideration of the act of learning itself – and the memory of it, since we have all been taught – now guides architects' tectonic thinking more powerfully than they might imagine. As much to the point, the rejection of monumentality shows a greater concern for what goes on in a place of learning, and a lesser concern with the face shown to the outside world.

In the case of Hecker's Berlin building, political and religious demands meant that this school cost around 15 per cent more than the state average, per square metre. Much of this money went on the integration of an advanced security system into the architecture, such that it is all but invisible. But Hecker did not mean 'secret society' in any fearful, sinister or historical sense: schools are like that, in fact, they have to be. They are inward-looking places of assembly and concentration, of interaction and also recreation. They can seem like prisons: they can also seem like magical walled gardens. The link between broad education and religious education – important in all strongly religious societies, but apparent even in humanistic form in non-denominational establishments – gives the clue as to the origins of these establishments and the persistence of certain layouts.

a b | c
d
e f

Villages of learning:
a Williams, Tsien & Associates, Neurosciences Institute, San Diego, California, 1993–5: exterior view
b Neurosciences Institute: view of courtyard
c Zvi Hecker, Heinz-Galinski School, Berlin, 1990–5: plan, the architect calls it 'a friendly meeting of whales'
d Heinz-Galinski School: courtyard
e Heinz-Galinski School: entrance
f Heinz-Galinski School: a junction of forms

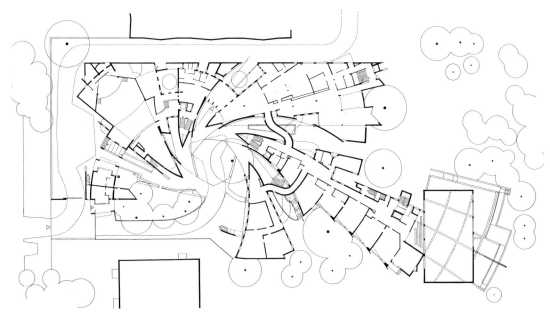

In its organization, the Heinz-Galinski School is undeniably unconventional. Hecker's concept has been described as a 'sunflower' – a sequence of discrete, roughly triangular, built elements radiating from an open circular focus. One might choose equally valid if sometimes contradictory similes: like the rays of the sun in a child's drawing, or the radiating pages of a book stood on end with its covers open: but again, Hecker came up with a telling analogy. Seeing it from the air, he remarked, it looked to him like a friendly meeting of whales. To him perhaps: the forms are indeed swimming head-to-head in comfortable proximity, discoursing perhaps, also sheltering – but their heads are the sharp noses of sharks rather than the unthreatening snouts of whales. The radial arrangement of six buildings implies a common central courtyard criss-crossed with people and activity – but again, this proves to be too simple an assumption. The blocks are joined by snaking walkways well away from their apexes, the focus is an entrance court, the open play area is at the back. While Hecker's obsession with the spiral form (also seen in his earlier 'Spiral' apartment building at Ramat Gan in Tel Aviv) is a fine way to generate a building complex, it appears rather differently up close, at head level rather than seen from an aeroplane. As with all buildings conceived as a geometrical game – something that architects of educational

buildings have a weakness for – the generative plan is not apparent, indeed can serve to confuse. The complex is not random, but it appears to be. At the focus those whale or shark heads take on the characteristics of razor-sharp, menacing knives, and the stark materials of the building (render and raw concrete and metal, mainly) are not overtly friendly. Yet there are compensations, not least in the variety of spaces to be discovered, internally and externally. As the critic and teacher Peter Cook has pointed out, the school is in fact a town – and for all its northerly latitude, a Mediterranean town at that. Fair enough: Zvi Hecker's school can pass as a casbah with its interlocking forms, interpenetrating spaces, and – for the stranger – utterly confusing layout. In Spain, the 1986–93 boarding school for the inland mountain town of Morella by Enric Miralles and Carme Pinós (Pinós was project architect) is arranged in similarly, apparently random fashion, and not just because this approach suits the higgeldy-piggeldy nature of upland townscapes: it forms a town within a town, a children's world.

What makes Hecker's and Pinós and Miralles' schools school-like, despite their somewhat brittle, high-architectural provenance and use of harsh, semi-industrial materials, is precisely that seeming randomness, that secret-society character. This perhaps saves the pupils and teachers from being

merely guinea pigs in an arcane game of architectural theory of the kind played out by Hecker, Frank Gehry or John Hejduk.

A family house is a secret society and a semi-closed community: teachers are 'in loco parentis' and thus the school is a substitute for the family house, and is equally introspective. The same applies to the child-care centres – effectively nursery schools – that large corporations increasingly tend to incorporate into their complexes. Thus Steven Ehrlich designed his Sony Child Care Center, 1992–4, in Culver City, California, as a protective oasis. It would have to be, here, in this curious edge-city close to the sundry urban interventions of Eric Owen Moss (see 'Performance' and 'Workplace') but in truth such schools – presenting a wall to the outside world and an open face to the private world of the children – tend to adopt this form almost everywhere.

Schools and colleges, in their disposition of spaces and in their relationship between teachers and pupils, descend directly from medieval seats of religious learning and their oriental equivalents: the inner sanctum of all places of learning is the library, as information resource and symbolic Ark of the Covenant. Similarly, all places designed within educational buildings for intense, solitary study have the characteristics of the monk's cell: hence the over-use by architects and others of the portrait of St Jerome

a

b

a Enric Miralles and Carme
   Pinós, Morella Boarding
   School, Morella, Spain,
   1986–93: view from the
   playground
b Morella Boarding School:
   interior of refectory

in his cluttered study by Antonello da Messina, *c*1475-6, and the subsequent woodcut by Albrecht Dürer, *c*1492.

This fifteenth-century idea of the working conditions of a fourth-century scholar in the deserts of Palestine is the enduring image of concentrated learning: undisturbed, reference material to hand, aloof from the unheeding bustle of everyday life. When Alvar Aalto came to design the Viipuri Library in Finland in 1927 he consciously drew inspiration from the idea of the reader sitting in a fantasy mountain landscape – plateaux, cliffs, numerous suns all over the sky – very like the notion of the saint-scholar in the miraculous desert. Aalto then internalized and top-lit this multi-level landscape to arrive at his building, with the commanding semicircular desk of the chief librarian symbolizing the mountain peak of solitary contemplation. And this was a public library, the most open of all its kind. One might compare it with the myth-making of Sir Denys Lasdun when designing the University of East Anglia in the early 1960s, where the ziggurat forms of his residential buildings were conceived as rocky outcrops in the lush landscape. These carry certain echoes of ruined rural Cistercian monasteries, but in their relentless geometric composition they anticipate more the spatial games of Zvi Hecker. As Alison and Peter Smithson commented in 1973: 'Could it be that why we like

Lasdun's East Anglia student clusters is because they are connective, they have a front and a back and counterpart space?' Bear in mind that, at this time, the heroes of college design across the Atlantic were still Gropius and Mies: in particular Mies with the modernist classical pavilion of his Crown Hall at the Illinois Institute of Technology, 1952–6, the ideal of the trophy educational building in a landscape.

The Smithsons had themselves defined the terms of the educational architecture debate in the late 1940s with their Hunstanton School in Norfolk, 1949–54, an early model of industrial-aesthetic school architecture disposed on a classical, Miesian model which they tirelessly propagated internationally through their membership of the breakaway Team X of CIAM – the Congrès Internationaux d'Architecture Moderne that had been the personal fiefdom of Le Corbusier and his disciples. Others pursued this grail into the field of prefabrication, and by the mid-1950s school building systems were widely available. In the United States, Ezra Ehrenkrantz's steel-framed SCBSD school-building system, developed in 1965, followed on from experiments in Britain's Hertfordshire schools, which in turn had led to the British CLASP system. As with standardized hospital building, however, any such systems are prey to changes in teaching or medical practice while any defect in design or materials is magnified by exactly

the numbers built. And like prefabricated housing systems, the real generator was neither architectural nor social, but the rather more basic need for economies of scale. Ehrenkrantz's system however – successfully deployed in California – confined itself to just four elements: structural roofdeck, air-conditioning, lighting and partitions. It left other architects free to decide the appearance of the external envelope. This anticipated the design of office blocks from the 1980s onwards, where architecture again was virtually confined to the skin.

Hunstanton perhaps cast a longer shadow than it deserved to, but it represents one enduring model: the rational, symmetrically arranged school building – rectangular, enclosing two courtyards with the main hall linking the perimeter classrooms at the centre. In plan, this disposition of space can take any number of different surface forms. One would not normally compare the 'New Brutalist' Smithsons in England with the rational formalist Aldo Rossi in Italy: but in their school designs their thinking is closely related. Rossi's secondary school at Broni, completed in 1981, is closely identifiable with the plan of Hunstanton: a quad traversed by a wing containing the central hall, the classrooms distributed around the perimeter. Elsewhere by the 1980s, this type had evolved into an atrium-based model with classrooms either side of a top-lit central space.

a | b
| e
| c d

Old plans, new clothes: the handling of educational spaces is near-universal:
a Aldo Rossi, Secondary School, Broni, Italy, 1979–81
b Foster and Partners, Lycée Albert Camus, Fréjus, France, 1991–3: section

c Hodder Associates, St Catherine's College, Oxford, England, 1992–4: exterior view
d St Catherine's College: external detail
e Lycée Albert Camus: view of brise-soleil canopy

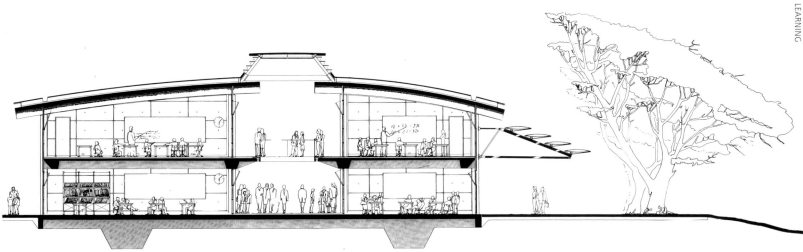

In this the type differs from the equally valid free-plan model exemplified by Walter Gropius and Maxwell Fry's Impington Village College, 1938-40, outside Cambridge, England (a type made all the easier by the flexibility of flat-roofed modules) and which has the merit of mimicking the organic way school complexes tend to expand themselves over time.

So there is a paradox. The basic forms of buildings devoted to learning are ancient and enduring, while at the same time the academic, aesthetic and political theories surrounding education have long made them architectural test-beds. But from the kindergarten to the national library, all buildings concerned with acquiring knowledge must reconcile two contradictory functions: the need for intense, undisturbed areas for collective or individual study, allied with more public spaces for open discussion and recreation. Particularly in the case of residential colleges, the antecedent of the medieval monastery is therefore still highly relevant. Just as the monastery is a self-contained community – a town by any other name – the concerns of educational buildings are urbanistic, and work on both small and large scales. There is no conceptual difference between the 'branch-and-leaves' spinal design of Lasdun's Hallfield School in London, 1947-51, and the equivalent, more complex, spinal design of his University of East Anglia. Had Lasdun been a dedicated self-publicist like the Smithsons, Hallfield might have become the famous European 1950s educational model rather than its contemporary, Hunstanton. But the two strands continue down to the present: Norman Foster's Lycée Albert Camus in Fréjus, France, 1991-3, being in line of descent from Hunstanton, while Mecanoo's Isala College at Silvode, The Netherlands, is in the Hallfield tradition: or rather, both belong to the same tradition of informally linked forms that owe not a little to Aalto. For the classically symmetrical answer to Lasdun's University of East Anglia, look no further than Arne Jacobsen's St Catherine's College, Oxford University, 1960-4, a building as rigorously inflexible as Hunstanton, complete and unalterable on its podium, sitting tightly as a Palladian country house in its manicured landscape, but with the tradition of the Oxford quad to justify its introverted nature. When Stephen Hodder came to extend St Catherine's with new student rooms, 1992-4, he found it necessary to leave Jacobsen entirely alone – as one would have to leave Kahn's Salk Institute alone – and build outside the sacred rectangle with a staggered block that nods to Jacobsen without apeing him. As at Hunstanton, Jacobsen's fenestration is the same all round, taking no account of aspect: though in his defence it is said that Jacobsen proposed sun-shading to the relevant elevations at St Catherine's, but that this was rejected

a
b   d
c

e

f

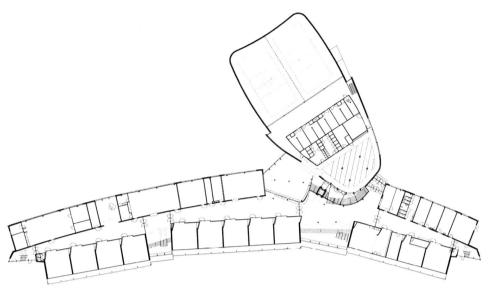

on the grounds of cost. Despite this evidence, Hodder had to fight to overturn an exactly similar cost-cutting proposal for his later extension. It seems that a blindness to the sun is normal in academic circles, since a similar story attaches to James Stirling's History Faculty at Cambridge University, 1964-7, where the great fan of patent glazing over the reading room faces into the sun, acting as an unwanted solar collector. There, the legend has it that the architect was forced by his client to rotate the building from his original desired (and sheltered) aspect. Unexpectedly, both stories are confirmed by the two universities concerned.

Mecanoo's Isala College in The
Netherlands, 1990-5, and the Science Center School in downtown Los Angeles by Morphosis, 1992, 1997-2000, are both case studies in the Janus-like nature of educational buildings. The LA example – designed to go right next to Frank Gehry's Aerospace Museum – offers one face to the clamour of its urban setting, and another to its landscaped 'underbelly', in this case an extension to the ready-made landscape of Exposition Park, known as the Rose Garden. As with the work of so many architects of this genera-tion, the school is an architectonic subversion of what is, in plan, a fairly simple rectilinear block. Much the same occurs in the quite different setting of the Isala College, though not in the way you

might imagine at first glance. On one side, it presents an almost formal face: a long, curving block cranked at intervals to provide facade variety and with one full-height section of differently expressed glazing signifying 'entrance'. This elevation faces the river and faces south: hence some solar shading to the classrooms. The other side comprises the private realm of schooling, the area usually hidden from public gaze. Here the forms become more intimate. The long curving block – here clad in rough-mortared clinker brick – sprouts a wing in two sections: the first clad in zinc, leading onto a curving section in vertically-striated copper cladding. The building defines and overlooks public spaces, but in actuality, it defies its visual clues. The formal elevation along the river does not announce the entrance: that is on the intimate side. The real entrance is thus tucked between the zinc-clad hall and the clinker-brick class-room wing to the north. The full-height glazing on the south turns out to be expressing a broad stair-well: it is intended for light and vision, not movement from inside to outside. But this apparent contrariness can also be fitted into theories of the secret-society nature of schools and colleges. Grand entrances are for public buildings that feel a need to indicate the point of entrance through their architectural vocabu-lary: 'secret' buildings need make no great play with their entrances for precisely the opposite reason. As

it happens, the understated entrance of Isala College is oriented towards the village from which the pupils come, so familiarity soon establishes itself. For all its variety of materials, the composition as a whole is far less hectic than Hecker's, and disposed to be open rather than defensive, not least because of its happy freedom from a need for tight security – and is in a rural-suburban setting rather than Heinz-Galinski's city-suburban context. The result is that Mecanoo's building, like Gropius and Fry's Impington Village College, serves very well as a simple diagram of what a school is. There, in the long, gently curving block, are the cell-classrooms, split between 'theoretical' on the southern side, and 'practical' on the northern. This block tapers towards its ends, which allows the broad central corridor to feel more spacious than it really is – but in essence it is a modified spine-corri-dor block. Plugged into this at an angle is a wing containing the large-volume spaces that schools need: hall (here with wavy timber Aalto-ish ceiling, gymnasium and cloakrooms). Set protectively in the crook of the building's arm is that symbolically loaded space, the library, and the point of intersec-tion between the big-space wing and the corridor block is celebrated by the full-height, top- and side-lit stairwell. It is a place of bustle and noise between classes, for all its sound-absorbent timber slat ceilings. The layout looks simple and, relatively

The grid is skewed, but the usual elements adhere:

a Mecanoo, Isala College, Silvode, The Netherlands, 1990-5: facade facing river
b Isala College: the entrance is situated to the right of the zinc-clad hall
c Isala College: vertically striated copper cladding surrounds the sports halls
d Isala College: circulation space
e Isala College: plan
f Morphosis, California Science Center School, LA Unified School District, Los Angeles, California, 1992, 1997-2000: computer generated model

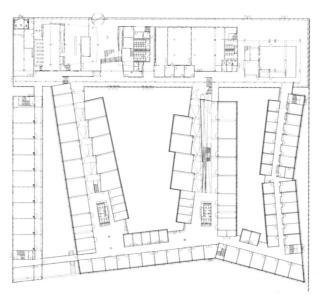

speaking, it is. It is resolving the relationship between the conflicting elements – private and public, cell and hall – which calls for ingenuity, and in this case it is received. With a few deft tweaks, the diagram has become architecture.

If Lasdun's University of East Anglia is the Hallfield School writ large, can the same be said for Mecanoo's contemporary Faculty of Economics at Utrecht Polytechnic, 1991–5? Yes and no: the plan, though quirky, is courtyard-based on the Hunstanton model. However the common facilities block – containing lecture halls, library, canteens and so forth – takes up one full side of this essentially square building, and is expressed in a different architectural language from the cellular classroom wings. Visually, the effect is very different from the school. Tight site planning led Mecanoo to consider this part of the university complex as a casbah (that analogy again, so appropriate for a private world) and consequently the open space at its centre, crossed by two wings, is carved up into three 'courtyards' – spaces in part so narrow that they take on the characteristics of light wells, or alleyways in a souk. These open spaces are each given their own quality. A bamboo jungle traversed by elevated walkways occupies the largest, central, space, ringed by glass curtain walling. A Zen garden occupies another space, the facades in that case clad in cedar-slat panels. The third and narrow-

est space is turned into a rocky pool, again with glazed but partially louvred elevations overlooking it. Like the Isala College and Morphosis' Los Angeles equivalent, the essentially simple diagram of the college is then wrenched slightly out of kilter, the geometry skewed, to prevent the monotony of rectilinearity and parallelism. The same technique is used in the internal streets within the blocks. Unusually the entrance is in the facade that appears to signal the public face. It is a much more muscular composition than the school, and it certainly escapes the criticism commonly levelled at campus universities of having no urban sense, of being too widely spaced: but it also can be read as a desperate attempt to make the best of a brief that demanded too much accommodation on too small a site. There was little elbow-room, but the elbow has been most vigorously applied.

This desire by 1990s architects to subvert the tyranny of the right angle – even when the right angle seems to be the logical solution to a problem – was based on the almost instinctive feeling that educational buildings are not factories, they have a humanizing function, and the spaces within and around them must be varied at all costs in order to provide stimulation. Partly this was in response to an earlier generation of school and college builders who had proclaimed the virtues of system-building and

modularity. At a time of huge expansion of educational buildings in post-war years, the system-built solution was an attractive one, and in retrospect was a noble endeavour. At tertiary educational level, the idea reached its apotheosis in the late 1960s University of Paris buildings at Jussieu – officially the Pierre and Marie Curie University. The architect Albert conceived a grid of linked pavilions on a podium, marching towards the river: with just one, taller block set at 45 degrees to the grid in clear space to act as a marker. Student unrest in 1968 led to a design modification: the six-storey pavilions were set up on very slender steel *pilotis*, leaving clear space beneath except at staircase access points. This was to protect university staff against intimidation from rioting students at ground level. The resulting, incomplete but very large complex was, spatially, eerily effective. The extreme slenderness of the columns, compared to the bulk of the steel-framed monolithic complex above, made it appear to float. The podium became a gloomy, Piranesian, strangely exciting, underworld. Curious, perhaps, that such a mechanistic complex was being built just when its relative, Baltard's nineteenth-century iron pavilion-based market hall of Les Halles, was being demolished. But planning policy in central Paris changed, as did the fashions in university buildings. Albert's incomplete grid was later cut off from the Seine by

a b

c

a   Mecanoo, Faculty of
     Economics and Management,
     Utrecht Polytechnic,
     The Netherlands, 1991–5:
     the Zen garden
b   Faculty of Economics
     and Management: plan
c   Faculty of Economics
     and Management:
     circulation space

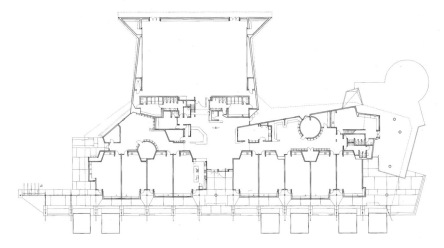

Jean Nouvel's Institut du Monde Arabe. The Jussieu complex languished unloved and unmaintained (the eternal Parisian problem) until one architect decided to respond positively to its spirit: Rem Koolhaas of OMA, who won the 1992 competition to add twin arts and science libraries to it. Koolhaas' library took the form of a part-buried cube, the arts stacked on top of the sciences, at the open south-east corner. Its concrete floorplates were designed as fractured, interconnecting ramps, like a square spiral cut out of paper. Koolhaas understood that the Jussieu grid contained an energy that could generate a new form of absolute rectilinearity: something that was at the same time static and eruptive, repetitive and filled with incident. But that was a response to a given context. Albert's fine version of that 1960s architectural obsession, the megastructure, was not about to suddenly influence a new generation of educational buildings. However its existence acted as a mute reproach to those architects who were starting to get very tricksy indeed in their attempts to 'humanize' the act of learning.

Perhaps at the back of everyone's mind was Rudolf Steiner (1861–1925) and his doctrine of anthroposophy: the world explained spiritually rather than rationally. Steiner schools – more than 170 of them, worldwide – are the most visible residue of his teaching. Steiner's Goetheanum at Dornach in

Germany, 1924–8, gives us the picture: a resolute rejection of the right angle, forms not so much organic as mineral. Later, engineering developments derived at least partly from natural forms provided a new impetus for the Steiner movement. In the mid-1990s, the Steiner School built in Stavanger, Norway, by Arbeidgruppen HUS, was a timber-clad, shingle-tiled, 'breathing' natural construction based upon the form of their hyperbolic paraboloid roof structures. As the hyperbolic paraboloid is a double-curved shell whose geometry is generated by straight lines, this can be said to be the ultimate Steineresque paradox. But by the end of the century, you did not have to be a nutty professor to subscribe to this kind of thinking: the desire for 'organic' forms in architecture had come to transcend most stylistic and technological boundaries, thus putting Frank Lloyd Wright right back on the agenda. For education – and particularly for the schooling of young children – it was seized upon worldwide. Some very folksy designs emerged: for a time it seemed as if the neolithic ring-hut was to be the architectural lodestone of the epoch. As with all such reactive movements, it settled down after a few years. In Britain, just as the 'Hertfordshire style' of light, prefabricated schools under the Gropius-inspired county architect Charles Aslin had dominated educational architecture post-Hunstanton in the 1950s, so did the 'Hampshire

style' – ranging from high-tech to folksy, but always concerned with human scale, communality and light. It came to dominate thinking about school building in the 1980s and 1990s under the county architect Sir Colin Stansfield-Smith. Both men enjoyed an influence reaching far beyond their respective parishes.

Elsewhere, other avenues were being explored, most interestingly one that led from Steiner towards the phenomenon of Deconstructivism. Two buildings give the flavour: Patkau Architects' Seabird Island School, 1988–91, at Agassiz, British Columbia, Canada; and Günter Behnisch & Partner's Hysolar Research Institute, 1987, at the University of Stuttgart, Germany. As its name implies, Seabird Island School is poetic architecture, its form inspired by its setting. Its form also derives from consultation with the Salish Indian communities which it serves. In its way it is as political a building as Zvi Hecker's in Berlin, for this was the first of a series of new schools for the native communities of northern British Columbia and therefore it was both an act of appeasement and an attempt at democracy. John Patkau remarked that, in any case, he was against the generalizing tendency of Western culture – that a response to place and local needs was for him more valid than an internationally recognizable architectural style. Here he was being true to the concerns of his old master, Arthur Erickson, who stated when

a c	d e
	f
b	g

designing his Museum of Anthropology, 1971–6, at the University of British Columbia:
'*Architects foremost should be listeners, since architecture is the art of relating a building to its environment and this requires listening to what the environmentalists say – listening to total context ... a building is not so much designed as it is decreed by the context.*'
Just as Erickson's 'listening' led to one of the more extraordinary examples of museum architecture, allegedly inspired by native villages (and this at a time when that hymn to modern technology, the Pompidou Centre, was going up in Paris) so his pupil Patkau derived an intensely individualistic building from his later discussions with the peoples of the Northwest Coast. Unsurprisingly, perhaps, some have seen echoes of Wright – particularly Taliesin West – in the tilting loggia and plenty of other 'organic' precedents can be cited, but this is unnecessary: mountain ridges, birds, crustacea are all echoed by its forms and all derive from its location. It is a very site-sensitive building. Beneath all the gymnastics, on plan it is surprisingly orthodox, the almost universal schools diagram asserting itself yet again. There is the straight edged primary facade, behind the loggia, with its entrance as is only right and proper. Behind it, the cellular classrooms. Then the circulation space, distorted by numerous interventions to avoid a sterile corridor-feel. Finally, plugged into the teaching block

in such a way as to form a stubby second wing, is the large hall. Dress it up as you will, this is what you always come back to. The fact that Seabird Island School has a political and ecological correctness to it – its timbers are of the manufactured laminated variety, for instance, rather than being the Douglas Fir you might expect (to protect the habitat of the grey spotted owl) – sends a signal to one audience, but does not impinge on the clear-sighted planning which serves the main audience: schoolchildren.

Similar thinking is apparent at another eco-aware educational building: Edward Cullinan Architects' Westminster Lodge for the Parnham Trust at Hooke Park College in Dorset, England, 1994–6. Cullinan, who has masterplanned complete university campuses at the University of North Carolina at Charlotte, and in East London's Docklands, here produced, with engineers Buro Happold, a small residential building, turf-roofed and made out of forest thinnings. Eight student rooms are arranged around a central seminar and conference room. The Trust teaches those training to work in the timber industries, and this experimental building was designed as a prototype for low-impact buildings to be sited in sensitive areas such as National Parks. What other architectural response would have been appropriate? By means of its innovative structure, it avoids the whimsical. For different reasons, so does the work of

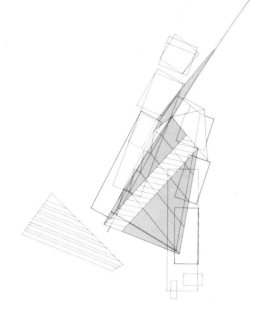

the 'vernacular' architect David Lea in designing student housing at the Royal Agricultural College, Cirencester: this is in the timeless tradition of Arts and Crafts architecture, such as the work of Baillie Scott (1865–1945).

At one end of the Seabird Island school, beneath an upraised section of roof, is a section of patent glazing set on a tilt – a standard product used in a non-standard way. Halfway round the world, in Stuttgart, Günter Behnisch had just produced a building that played exactly the same trick with the same kind of glazing system, a feature that seems somehow to have climbed out of the same box as Patkau's. The Hysolar Research Institute, 1987, emerged from two aspects of Behnisch's work: an unrivalled experience in the design of schools from the 1950s onwards, when he developed the principle of the free plan, at first in conjunction with prefabricated components; and the very slow, bureaucratic process of designing and constructing the West German government building in Bonn. When the Stuttgart commission arose, Behnisch took it as an opportunity to relax and work quickly, building upon the basis of his earlier educational work. As at Seabird Island, the restless roof forms, tilted planes and overlapping plates cover a perfectly logical sequence of spaces beneath, perhaps an extreme variation on the theme of two wings either side of an

atrium. As a bonus – since the purpose of the institute is to research the uses of hydrogen produced with solar power – the building was provided with a separate freestanding architectural element in the form of a tilted plane of solar panels. Behnisch claims that the building resulted from a process of improvisation. This must surely be true of all buildings, but presumably he meant the rather more *ad hoc* composition such as a jazz improvisation might produce: starting off in one direction, it might end up in quite another. It is notable that such an 'improvised' building, resulting from and looking like an architectonic experiment and devoted to the cause of technology, should share certain attributes with an organically considered building such as Patkau's. Far from being improvised, Seabird Island School resulted from four months of close consultation with those who would ultimately use it, and, aesthetically responds more to its setting than to the process (in this case, teaching) taking place within. Both Hysolar and Seabird Island are educational buildings, true, but beyond that there is little to link the programme of the two. One can only posit a stylistic *zeitgeist*.

In any event, Behnisch – who once he had abandoned grid-based prefab systems was wont to experiment restlessly with form – applied some of the lessons of Hysolar to a new school in Frankfurt, 1989–94. The overlapping planes and bits of

sculptural redundant structure are deployed again, in less extreme fashion, as the practice moved towards what was to become an oft-repeated gesture: at the point where the tectonic plates of the building intersect – the place of maximum spatial force – there is the entrance and the main, usually full-height, public space. It is a trick he has subsequently used on a variety of office buildings. But not all his later schools exhibit the same tendencies. In an earlier phase of his career, Behnisch had employed a radial plan, most notably in the 1973 Progymnasium at Lorch. He took up the idea afresh in designing a technical college at Ohringen in the mid-1990s, which takes the form of a two-storey open torus raised on *pilotis*. This gives the building a landmark quality (it is close to a busy motorway) and also serves to embrace and define its territory to protect it from the motorway. It may be compared with Shin Takamatsu's Misumi Elementary School, in Japan, begun in 1994, where classrooms are also arranged in a circle. In both cases, the thinking is the same as ever: larger volumes, such as a science block and a sports hall, are treated as separate objects connected to the main run of rooms. The respective plans may fruitfully be laid over those of James Stirling and Michael Wilford's contemporary Temasek Polytechnic in Singapore, 1991–5, a colossal complex that works in very much the same way. Where the Ohringen School

a b

d

c   e

The cloister becomes a circle:

a Behnisch & Partner, Hysolar
  Research Building, University
  of Stuttgart, Germany, 1987:
  conceptual plan
b Hysolar Research Building:
  exterior view
c Behnisch & Partner,
  Progymnasium, Lorch,
  Germany, 1973

d Shin Takamatsu, Misumi
  Elementary School, Misumi,
  Shimane, Japan, 1994–7:
  central courtyard
e Misumi Elementary School:
  interior of classroom

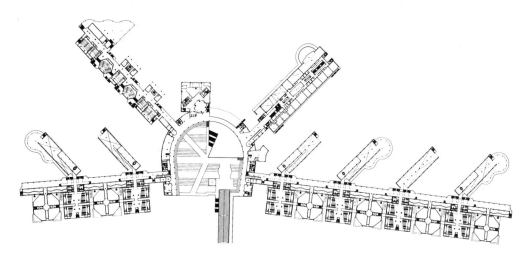

is a small building working on a large scale, Temasek is large-scale, large-size, with mighty volumes plugged into its equally mighty main horseshoe block. It is, however, a town rather than a megastructure.

The retreat from the idea of the megastructure was – with certain key exceptions – one of the characteristics of the 1970s and 1980s. Given a brief that required architects to provide facilities for a number of disparate activities, with very different spatial needs, within one complex, architects increasingly opted to express the forms as a cluster of elements, linked or merely proximate, forming academic villages. Against this trend – and thus showing that it was nearer the end of a line of architectural development rather than at the start of a new one – was Norman Foster's Sainsbury Centre, added to Lasdun's University of East Anglia campus, 1974–8. This is an art gallery, but it also houses a number of university functions including tuition rooms and dining facilities. Its purpose is educational as much as cultural. By placing all the elements under one big clear-span shell, clad with interchangeable aluminium sandwich panels that (as with all flexibly conceived buildings) were not interchanged except when they all needed replacing some years later, Foster was applying the 1960s concept of the 'serviced shed'. It could, he remarked at the time, have been several buildings instead of one. As it was, an invisible fault-line divided

Lasdun's bony university from Foster's shiny shed. The later masterplanning skills of the American architect Rick Mather were needed to re-urbanize the campus and – as much as possible – reconcile the two approaches.

Foster stuck to the big-enclosure idea. His Law Faculty in Cambridge, 1990–5, next to Stirling's History Faculty, stacked a library above basement lecture theatres, bringing daylight down to the lower levels via a side atrium overlooked by the open library decks. This was fine in principle, and is spatially dramatic, particularly as the light pours down through a curving latticework facade engineered by Tony Hunt: but the acoustic consequence, when the lecture halls turned out and students piled noisily up the stairs to the exit, was scarcely conducive to quiet study in the library above. This was not a problem encountered in the Foster practice's earlier less ambitious, monofunctional library at Cranfield University, 1989–92, in the English Midlands, which does its best to provide a centrepiece for a very sorry ragbag of existing buildings. Other architects had long since abandoned the idea of the big, all-encompassing enclosure in the educational context, for instance Stirling and Wilford at their Cornell University Performing Arts Centre, 1982–8, where the elements gather and discourse. At Temasek, where the volume of the library could have

been subsumed into the main horseshoe building, it is instead pulled out as a discrete entity, a square rising to a cross. Other wings with other functions – technology, business, design and applied science – run back from the horseshoe, bringing to mind the spokes of Jeremy Bentham's Panopticon as translated into nineteenth-century prisons and hospitals. Separate cylindrical residential blocks complete the picture. With a total population of some 13,000 people, Temasek Polytechnic effectively entailed the creation of a new town. Its similarity in plan to the relatively tiny Heinz-Galinski School reinforces the original and persistent idea: a school is a community. On this scale, however, it is expressed not so much as a secret society as a specialized urban district: an educational quarter to set alongside the financial centre, the retail and leisure area, the industrial estate, the housing.

Something of a similar task faced the Lyons-based architects Jourda and Perraudin when they came to design the Cité Scolaire, 1989–92, in their home town, and then the University of Marne-la-Vallée outside Paris. At Lyons – an education village including both elementary and secondary schools – we find again the sheltering, curving form. One reason was to design in sympathy with the undulating bank of the River Rhône on which it is sited, but the big curve of the classroom block (the classroom

a   Foster and Partners,
    Cambridge Law Faculty,
    Cambridge, England, 1990–5:
    a classic Fosterian supershed
b   James Stirling Michael Wilford
    & Associates, Temasek
    Polytechnic, Singapore,
    1991–5: plan
c   Temasek Polytechnic: a
    classic Stirling Wilford
    township

b   c

a

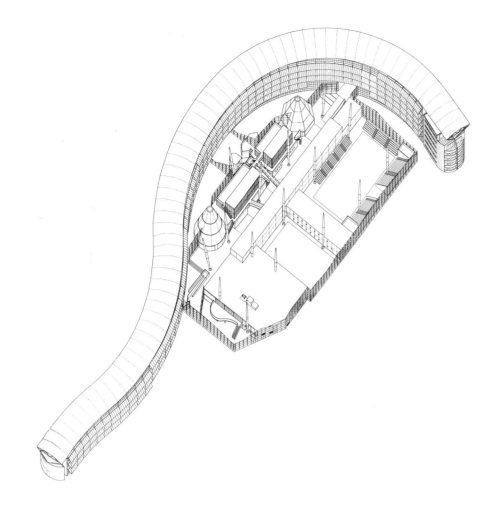

units sitting inside independently of facades and roof, allowing ready upgrading) also serves to enclose and define an intermediate area of mast-suspended grassed roofs beneath which lie the usual big halls but also stairs, galleries, mezzanines and service blocks. So this is an ingenious variation on a common theme, not to mention a very rare example of a suspended roof that is also planted – except in its glazed atrium roof section where grass gives way to glass, and the influence of the German engineer Frei Otto's 1960s cable-net structures becomes transparently visible.

Marne-la-Vallée, 1992–6, followed quickly. In the architectural zoo of this new satellite town outside Paris, Jourda and Perraudin contributed two new forms: a big radiused block of lecture theatres

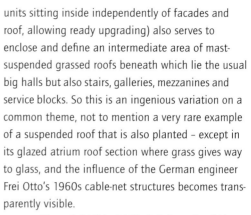

a   g

b d f h

c e

and restaurants, pinned vertically with one of the Kurokawa or Predock type of conical towers which equally became a Jourda and Perraudin trademark. They also dared to offer what on plan is a straightforward, rectilinear teaching building, curtain-walled in glass, with an absolutely central, linear atrium. In perspective there is more variation, since this block is built on a sloping site, allowing its cubic volumes a vertical displacement. If one were to combine these two buildings – the curving big-space block with the rectilinear cellular teaching block – one would arrive at a form such as the Centenary Building at the University of Salford, England, by Hodder Associates, 1994-5. This building contrives to be layered both horizontally and vertically, where the two sides of the building have utterly different characters, and where the central

atrium with its (few) linking gantries takes on the character of one of those recurrent casbah streets.

Others try different stunts. For his Law Faculty, 1990-6, at the University of Limoges, Massimiliano Fuksas creates an orthogonal building – respectful of its eighteenth-century neighbours – which is subverted by the bulges of lecture auditoria, clad in titanium and zinc, bursting literally out of the grid. On the whole this is less successful as a device than the wholly orthogonal sculptural massing of his Michel de Montaigne University Art School in Bordeaux, 1992-5, clad in patinated copper and wood, which clearly owes a debt to artists Richard Serra and Donald Judd.

The pull of landscape and tradition, as we have seen on Seabird Island, can be as powerful a

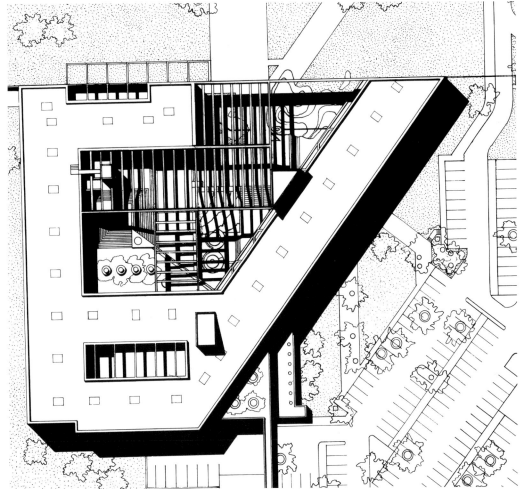

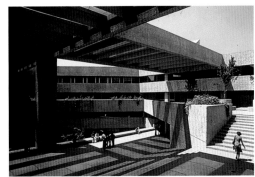

Layering and expressing the distinct forms of the teaching building:

a   Jourda & Perraudin, Cité Scolaire, Lyons, France, 1989-92: axonometric
b   Cité Scolaire: circulation space
c   Cité Scolaire: external detail of oversailing roofs
d   Hodder Associates, Centenary Building, University of Salford, England, 1994-5
e   Massimiliano Fuksas, Michel de Montaigne University Art School, Bordeaux, France, 1992-5
f   Teodoro González de León, Colegio de Mexico, Mexico City, 1974-6: site plan
g   Massimiliano Fuksas, Limoges University Law Faculty, Limoges, Haute-Vienne, France, 1990-6
h   Colegio de Mexico: external circulation

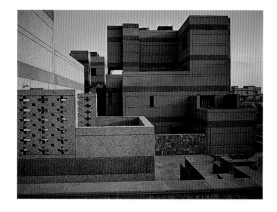

force in educational architecture as a building's programme. While the preceding examples derive their form from the expression of the spaces they enclose, an equally valid response is the contextual one. The stratified terraces of Teodoro González de Leôn's Colegio de Mexico, 1974–6, breathe the same air as Lasdun's East Anglia, or Giancarlo de Carlo's student residences at Urbino, 1962–6. They even share some regionalist characteristics with Geoffrey Bawa's University of Ruhunu, 1980–6, at Matara in Sri Lanka with its post-colonial feel, or Raj Rewal's masterly National Institute of Immunology in New Delhi, 1984–90, abstracted from local forms. But they are in turn as different as could be from the university 'trophy building', created to add focus and drama, such as Venturi Scott Brown's Gordon Wu Hall at Butler College, Princeton, 1980–3, Michael Hopkins' Queen's Building at Emmanuel College, Cambridge, 1993–5, or John Outram's Computational Engineering Faculty, 1993–7, at Rice University, Houston, Texas, with its Romanesque 'Robot Order' columns and 300-foot-long, 50-foot-high central gallery. This is not to say that these buildings lack function – Outram's plan at Rice is admirably rational, rather like a shopping mall with big anchor stores (lecture halls and auditorium) around a square at one end and smaller units leading off either side of a street – but their architects are also chosen for effect.

A better example can scarcely be imagined than Building 8 at the Royal Melbourne Institute of Technology, Australia. By Edmond and Corrigan, and completed in 1995, this is postmodern facade-making with a vengeance, its stridency quickly wearisome. Edmond and Corrigan are also stage designers, and this is a very theatrical building: a backdrop to a drama of modern student life. As it houses the faculties of architecture and design, one can only imagine what its future users will think of it. But it also imposes a kind of order on what was previously a collection of left-over spaces. Nearby, and even stranger, is Ashton Raggatt McDougall's Storey Hall, 1993–5 – a makeover of a nineteenth-century lecture hall given a fuzzy-logic treatment of fractal geometric forms in shocking colours and even, at one point, an upholstered ceiling. The theories of the Oxford mathematician Dr Roger Penrose are cited as an influence. Australia has no exclusive rights to bizarre academic architecture: Britain can offer the offbeat turbo-charged Gothic of De Montfort University's School of Engineering in Leicester by Short Ford & Associates, completed in 1993 (its shape though not its skin dictated by its experimental nature as a wholly naturally ventilated large college building) while Tokyo gives us the Aoyama Technical College, 1990, by Makoto Sei Watanabe. This can be compared to a large alien insect, or perhaps some mutated form of plant life,

From the urbane to the extrovert: academic assertiveness:

a   Raj Rewal, National Institute of Immunology, New Delhi, 1984-90
b   John Outram Associates, Computational Engineering Faculty, Rice University, Houston, Texas, 1993-7
c   Short Ford & Associates, De Montfort University Engineering Building, Leicester, England, 1993
d   Edmond + Corrigan, RMIT Building 8, Melbourne, Australia, 1990-5
e   Makoto Sei Watanabe, Aoyama Technical College, Tokyo, 1990
f   Ashton Raggatt McDougall, RMIT, Storey Hall, Melbourne, Australia, 1993-5

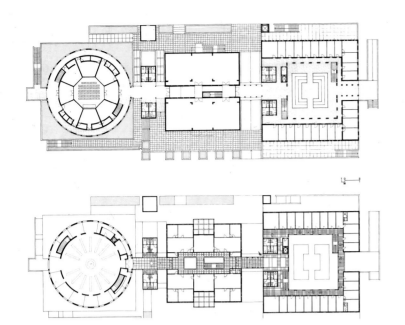

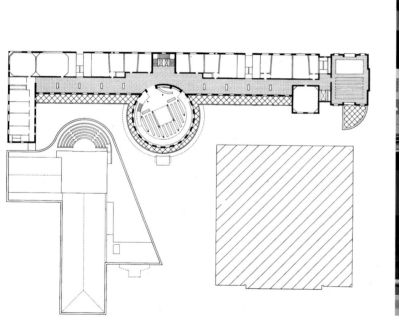

a   c   f

b   d

e

also fulfilling the functions of a school. Its rationale is to be made of elements that have grown beyond their necessary function, and have begun to jostle each other frictionally, thus adjusting their relationships accordingly to arrive at the building we see, the process arrested. It is the architect's personal metaphor for the chaotic urban nature of Tokyo and quite possibly – though it is briefly reminiscent of the work of Vienna's deconstruction kings, Coop Himmelblau – it could only happen here.

While the academic village is one thing, the all-embracing academic megastructure another, and the deconstructed object a third, there is also a fourth way in educational buildings, which is to do with monumentalism. Stirling and Wilford's Music School in Stuttgart, 1986–96, for 1,000 students, sets its great rotund tower against the rectilinear teaching block behind in memory of both Gunnar Asplund's Stockholm Public Library of 1928, and of Claude Nicholas Ledoux's 1789 Rotonde de la Villette in Paris. Unlike both of those, however, where the cylinder rises from the centre of the composition, Stirling and Wilford pull their drum forward and to one side, engaging it with the building rather than making it the geometrical centre. Its urbanistic function is to act as the positive counterpoint to the void of the circular courtyard in their earlier Staatsgalerie next door, which is of exactly the same diameter: its

academic function is to house a concert hall, library and seminar rooms. Stirling and Wilford's Science Library, 1988–94, at the University of California's Irvine campus also sets the ancient form of the drum with pierced openings against a rectangular block, though in this case the drum is relatively larger and its interior is itself an open courtyard, so combining in one form the two separate elements present in the Stuttgart work.

While the Music Academy sidesteps true Beaux-Arts planning, another monumental academy is happy to embrace it. This is the Research Centre of Crete, 1985–90, outside Heraklion by Panos Koulermos, who has taught at several eminent American, British and Italian schools of architecture. The research centre is a device to focus the otherwise scattered and visually unconnected surrounding buildings of the University of Crete. It has three elements, arranged along the grandest of implied axes – one which leads from the Minoan city of Knossos via the Venetian port of Heraklion to Athens over the sea. A square open courtyard study building leads into the atrium of a square enclosed laboratory building, which in turn leads into the cylinder containing library, seminar rooms and lecture auditorium – exactly the same mix as Stirling and Wilford's at Stuttgart, though this complex is only two storeys high.

Koulermos' architecture is stripped classical, with Minoan references in the fenestration. Elsewhere, notably in the British universities of Oxford and Cambridge, more mainstream historicism is apparent. At Magdelen College Oxford, Demetri Porphyrios has contributed the Longwall Quadrangle, 1991–5, new student residences in the medieval gothic-meets-classical manner of its parent college, while at Downing College Cambridge the classicist Quinlan Terry has gone to the books of Palladio for his Maitland Robinson Library, 1989. Such a scholarly exercise – nonetheless chastised by traditionalist critics for being 'incorrect' – bears only the most superficial resemblance to a turbo-charged classical seat of learning such as Hammond Beeby Babka's 1991 Harold Washington Library in Chicago, which boasts some references to early Louis Sullivan as well as colossally scaled classical motifs atop the rare treat of a fully glazed tympanum. It manages to make Michael Graves' Clark County Library in Las Vegas – a composition reminiscent of Ernst Sagebiel's immense stripped-classical civic buildings in late 1930s Berlin, though made of fragile stucco rather than durable limestone – look positively reticent: the last thing you'd expect from the arch post-modernist of the 1980s. Perhaps Graves could not compete with the Strip: contributing a building with a 'serious' function to the razzmataz of casinos, hotels and

Monumentality suggests both permanence and importance:
a Panos Koulermos, Research Centre of Crete and University of Crete, Heraklion, Crete, Greece, 1985–90: plans
b James Stirling Michael Wilford & Associates, Music School and Theatre Academy, Stuttgart, Germany, 1986–96: plan
c Research Centre of Crete: exterior view
d Stuttgart Music Academy: rehearsal in progress
e James Stirling Michael Wilford & Associates, University of California Science Library, Irvine, California, 1988–94
f Hammond Beeby Babka, Harold Washington Library, Chicago, 1991

a   b   c d   e f   g i   h j

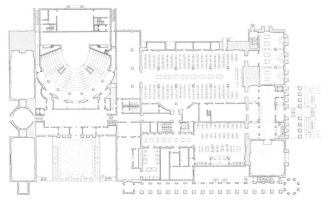

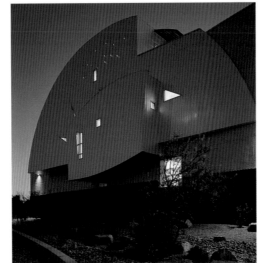

themed malls, he turned the classical volume control right down, as did other 'serious' architects building libraries and cultural buildings in the city. They include Antoine Predock for the Las Vegas Library (discussed with its Discovery Children's Museum in 'Visual Arts') and Meyer Scherer and Rockcastle with Tate and Snyder for the Sahara West Library and Fine Arts Museum – a rather less successful 'regionalist' attempt than Predock's.

The opposite of the trophy-building approach is the kind of architecture that manages to stitch the urban realm together as well as adding new elements. The buildings of Rick Mather and John Miller at the University of East Anglia (UEA), 1991–3, are urbanistic in this sense, serving to define outdoor spaces and form a series of events between previously isolated or unregarded sections of Lasdun's uncompleted campus. Mather's student residences – cranked straight blocks and an S-curved range – do this while simultaneously recalling the somewhat contradictory forms of both Gropius and Aalto, notably, their late 1940s halls of residence in Boston at the Harvard Graduate Centre and Massachusetts Institute of Technology respectively – the former rational and pragmatic and the latter sinuous and site-responsive. Such urban interventions – filling in the gaps, making sense of under-used space – is a skill that works irrespective of style. Mather repeated

a   Michael Graves, Clark County
    Library and Theater, Las Vegas,
    1990–4: exterior view
b   Clark County Library:
    circulation space
c   Michael Graves, Denver
    Central Library, Denver,
    Colorado, 1991–6: plan
d   Denver Central Library:
    contextual view

e   Eduardo Souto de Moura,
    Faculty of Geological
    Science, Aveiro University,
    Aveiro, Portugal, 1991–4:
    exterior view
f   Faculty of Geological Science:
    lecture room
g   Meyer, Scherer & Rockcastle
    with Tate & Snyder, Sahara
    West Library and Art Museum,
    Las Vegas, Nevada, 1990–4,
    1996–7: exterior view

h   Sahara West Library:
    foyer space
i   Rick Mather, University of
    East Anglia Buildings,
    Norwich, England, 1991–3:
    exterior view
j   UEA Buildings:
    circulation space

the trick in an older context with his student residences at Keble College Oxford, 1992–5, delineating a new quadrangle. Similar work can be seen in progress at the chaotic University of Aveiro in Portugal, where Alvaro Siza's library, 1995, and Eduardo Souto de Moura's Faculty of Geological Science, 1994, bring order and style – the former Aalto-ish, the latter in the Gropius camp – to the dispersed campus. Siza's library helps to create a centre for the university, a need felt by a large number of the world's educational institutions, many of which have either evolved piecemeal, or departed from their original masterplans. Thus the Melbourne campus of Deakin University was an inchoate collection of suburban-scale brick buildings from the 1970s and 1980s until a radiating complex of four new buildings was designed at its centre by Wood Marsh (project architects Pels Innes Neilson and Kosloff). The pinwheel arrangement of buildings – each differently shaped, one with curving precast concrete walls in homage to Harry Seidler – radiates from a central stair tower and serves to draw in the various movement paths running through the campus, while reading from outside as a defining central cluster. As the Australian critic Hamish Lyons wrote of the project – and it is true of all such projects – 'It is not so much a gesture towards some evolving masterplan or a furture urbanism as

about stamping an immediate authority upon an undistinguishable background.'

In Oregon, the interventions of the very eclectic firm Moore Ruble Yudell (in this case mostly Buzz Yudell rather than the better known Charles Moore) at the University of Oregon, Eugene, stitched together a 1914 campus in a knowing and successful reinterpretation of the architecture of that period, by means of a science complex, 1985–9. The faculty had asked Yudell to provide 'a community of scientists' on a site until then conspicuously lacking a sense of community. As Yudell put it:
'We asked how this functions and what is most important to that group of scientists in their daily life. How our physical form can support and even enlighten that process, or the lives of that group of scientists, and in turn how this building can be a citizen within its greater context. To me those issues have nothing to do with style.'

Behind his words lay the fact that, in the 1970s, the University of Oregon had been the subject of a study by the planning guru Christopher Alexander, holding a torch for public participation and his theories of 'pattern language' in the relationship of people and buildings. Moore Ruble Yudell acknowledged this prior work, but the task was clear enough: the original Beaux-Arts plan of the campus had been disrupted by later additions that bore little

relationship either to it or to each other. The resulting Science Complex provides suites for the disciplines of geology, biology, physics and computer science on the programmatic level, but, in Yudell's phrase, became a 'citizen' by re-urbanizing the campus. A four-storey entrance atrium provides the focus, supplemented by landscaped external courtyards – the whole working on the principle of 'open circulation' rather than dead-end spur routes to various departments. The library, as at Stirling and Wilford's Temasek Polytechnic, is pulled just clear of the main mass of the building although it is linked to it. While many might object to the consciously archaic surface treatment of the architecture, its planning logic and understanding of the hierarchy of spaces within such an institution is generally applicable. To each his own guru: where Yudell had Alexander preparing the ground for him in Oregon, and the historifying Charles Moore as master, Mather the modernist cites the theoretical townscape work of Camillo Sitte (1843–1903) as inspiration for his UEA work.

In thinking this way, it is sometimes necessary to create an urban context from scratch, with little on the ground to give a cue. One example would be Ralph Erskine's Stockholm University Buildings, 1973–83, comprising library, student centre and sports hall, which in virtuoso fashion create an area where no place of any note previously

Campuses functioning as urban signifiers:
a Moore Ruble Yudell, Oregon University Science Complex, Eugene, Oregon, 1985–9: exterior view
b Ralph Erskine, Stockholm University Buildings, Stockholm, 1973–83
c Oregon University Science Complex: interior view
d Wood Marsh (with Pels Innes Neilson and Kosloff), Deakin University, Melbourne, Australia, 1996

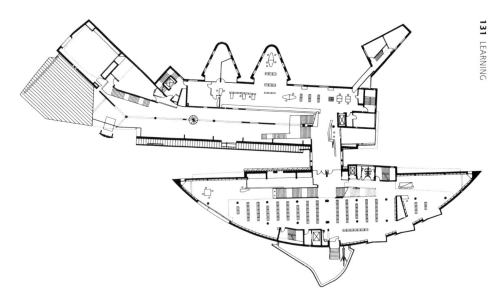

existed. In connecting his library to an existing acade-mic building, for instance, Erskine created a link based on the notion of a railway terminus. The huge library is based upon a rationalist grid, but elsewhere tectonic experiments recalling Erskine's 1940s and 1950s work (looking very fresh again in the late 1990s) serve to informalize the space. Erskine's work provided an inspiration to a small cabal of British architects, such that the most complete example of a whole educational complex inspired by his work emerged from a group within a large commercial practice, the Building Design Partnership. This is the St Peter's College Campus of the University of Sunderland, 1992-9, built upon a cleared industrial site of former shipyards sloping down to the River Wear, where there was no context to speak of. On this site, BDP architects headed by Tony McGuirk (who had previously worked for, and later collaborated with, Erskine) have produced a convincing example of an imagined Erskinian Scandinavian university: all loose-fit, big-roofed, rough-sawn timber and smooth patent cladding, angles askew, light flooding in, high-level walkways, with both intimate and large-scale open spaces. Some saw Aalto in it, and the similarity is undeniable, but in truth this loose assemblage of large forms, gathered as if in conversation around an irregular university square, has the tectonic and mixed-media qualities more readily associated with

Erskine – a Scandinavian-based Quaker architect who was himself British by birth.

The symbolic nature of research libraries and certain civic libraries, and their monofunctional nature, often sets them apart from the programmatic complexities of an educational complex, especially when architects choose to express them as freestand-ing objects. Where libraries stand alone, we expect them to act as markers, and such places as Will Bruder's Phoenix Central Library in Arizona, 1988-95 – an expressionist Sainsbury Centre for the written word, its ribbed copper cladding standing up to the adjacent freeway like a giant hangar or warehouse – do just that. Bruder's library brought him inter-national attention, not least because of its joyous espousal of what was to become a very 1990s archi-tectural concern – bigness. The Phoenix library is big in every way. One can imagine it a great deal smaller, like Herzog and de Meuron's signal box in Basle, Switzerland: it is as if Bruder had designed at one scale and then pressed the zoom button on his photo-copier. Its biggest space, the fifth floor non-fiction reading room, covers 4,000 square metres - a prairie of bookstacks and readers' desks, accessed by a grand double staircase and a set of glass lifts. Its bigness and simplicity is also a function of its cost: as with the huge Euralille development by Rem Koolhaas and others, the single-minded vast enclosure proved to be

Cities without visible libraries are cities lacking soul:
a   Will Bruder, Phoenix Central Library, Arizona, 1988-95: view from the freeway
b   Phoenix Library: fifth floor reading room
c   Dominique Perrault, Bibliothèque Nationale de France, Paris, 1989-96
d   Bolles-Wilson & Partner, Münster City Library, Münster, Germany, 1987-93: plan
e   Münster City Library: view of circulation zone from first floor

a		c	d
			e
b			

a surprisingly cheap way of getting the floorspace, copper cladding or no. Phoenix is now known for its library, just as the previously unregarded city of Münster in Germany found itself on the map with its City Library, 1987–93, and civic offices, 1991–96, (discussed in 'Civic Realm') by Bolles-Wilson and Partner.

Where libraries are national, they become a matter of international status. Thus we have Dominique Perrault's rigidly geometric solution to housing the French National Library, 1989–96, by the Seine in Paris, comprising four L-shaped towers of books rising from the corners of a massive podium of reading rooms, the whole edifice clad in a forest's worth of tropical hardwood. Hence the appeal of Snøhetta's Great Library in Alexandria, Egypt, 1989–99, with its tilted circular disc of a roof and its curved rear stone wall incised with random lettering from a thousand cultures. Perhaps this also explains the disappointment felt by some at Colin St John Wilson's British Library in London, 1976–98, which is primarily concerned with programme and function, and very little to do with gargantuan external gestures: it reserves its surprises for the inside, especially the great Aalto-esque foyer. But Wilson's relatively low-key, Scandinavian-influenced architecture goes back to first principles: what is a library for? If it is to be a focus of learning, like a

medieval monastery, then the monastic form of successive linked spaces generated by their function and grouped around a common public court, is as valid as ever. Wilson's symbolic gesture is internal: at the back of the entrance foyer a glass tower of books rises, as if extruded from the book stacks beneath. The tower is a building within a building, housing the Library of King George III that was the effective origin of the British national collection. Rare books are a form of secret knowledge, accessible only to initiates, and which speak of history and continuity of culture.

The architect and theorist Richard MacCormac tackled the same issue with his Ruskin Library at the University of Lancaster, 1993–8, an almost Botta-like oval clamshell of a building, conceived as a metaphorical container for the John Ruskin archive. It is expressed as a completely separate entity from the university library he built there at the same time – just as architects Joanna van Heyningen and Birkin Haward had created a tiny banded brick casket, the 1988 Katharine Stephen Room, for the rare books collection of Newnham College, Cambridge.

Given Ruskin's importance in the field of nineteenth-century architectural criticism, and his call for architecture to recognize the past while avoiding sham revivalism, MacCormac developed a

sophisticated mythology for his building based on the notion of the building as island and refuge, its construction honestly expressed but amenable to colouration and abstract surface decoration. Central to its plan is the archive itself, expressed as a freestanding vertical cabinet, emerging through the glass and stone floor on axis, just as Wilson's historic archive at the heart of the British Library does. 'It is the great treasure chest ... it is an ark or reliquary, a tabernacle, a bookcase or, by inference, a great book,' MacCormac wrote of the Ruskin archive, his 'keep within a keep'.

Wilson's equivalent internalized gesture of the King's Library at the British Library is based on the assumption that only those who need to know – library users – will be offered the chance to understand the coded signal. It is a very British response. Contrariwise, Perrault's expression of the library as symbol (each tower can be read as an open book) glorifies the State and its literary patrimony as publicly as possible: a very French response. All libraries must, however, make a simple decision as to how they are arranged: should they seat the scholars among the books, allowing them to make their own free choice, or should they treat the library as a species of processing plant, with the raw material – books – fetched from storage for the purpose? The British and French National Libraries take the

a b
d e
f
c

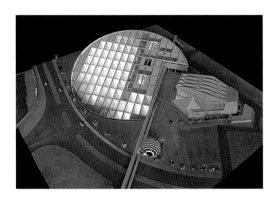

a De Blacam + Meagher, Cork
Institute of Technology
Library, Cork, Ireland, 1993-5:
circulation through bookstacks
and individual reading areas

b Cork Institute of Technology
Library: main reading area

c Snøhetta, Bibliotheca
Alexandrina, Alexandria,
Egypt, 1989-99: model

d Colin St John Wilson, British
Library, St Pancras, London,
1976-98: Reading Room

e British Library: exterior, looking
towards St Pancras Station

f British Library: circulation
space with the glass tower of
the King's Library stacks (right)

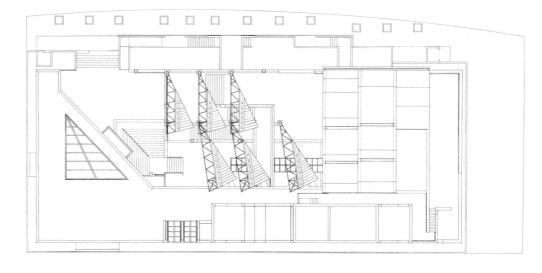

second course – although for scientific users, who rely far more than humanities readers on topical journals and reports, direct access is permitted in the British example (Perrault's library is for humanities only). University libraries, with their lesser resources, more usually adopt the latter.

An example of the library as wholly inward-looking place of learning, with an almost medieval layout, is De Blacam and Meagher's library at Cork Institute of Technology in the south of Ireland. This practice had previously turned to forms evocative of earlier times in their timber Beckett Theatre at Trinity College, Dublin (see 'Performance'). At Cork, the library is announced externally by a very simple curving rectangular brick facade, with absolutely minimal fenestration. Inside, it would be immediately understandable to a Renaissance, even a medieval, scholar. Rows of two-person booths, separated by tall timber screens, span most of the triple-height reading room, and there is also a variety of other study spaces, from the very private to the fairly public. Three levels of book stacks rise from this space, and at the other side is a periodicals gallery. The reader spaces are wired for computers. The materials are self-finished and austere (brick, block, concrete, timber and ply), daylight filters in from high-level clerestories, supplemented by both uplighting and task lighting. It is a diagram of

learning, a place for five hundred St Jeromes – in fact, a thousand or so with the equivalent second phase.

The definition of 'education', of course, grows steadily wider. By the late 1980s, what had previously been the unconsidered area of company training centres had become very much like traditional colleges. Some did not admit to the fact: Hiroshi Hara's 1990 Sotetsu Cultural Centre in Yokohama, for instance, does not let on that three-quarters of its baroque bulk (Hara's architecture customarily erupts into unexpected forms) is a research and training institute, complete with dormitories, for a railway company. Others are happy to express the collegiate ethos: Richard MacCormac's Cable and Wireless College in Coventry, England, 1989–93, with its Zen-influenced layout and echelon of green-tiled curving roofs inspired by a ceremonial ancient Chinese suit of jade pieces, was quickly compared to a monastery. Such places are closed to outsiders, accessible only to those who are to be initiated into the mysteries of the trade, profession, or craft. While there, they are immersed, living on site, all needs catered for. There are few areas in which such a place does not seem very like a religious order, and if not then certainly a residential school or university. But as we have seen, the line of descent of such institutions makes the comparison not merely plausible but inescapable.

c
a
b   d

Training centres assume a monastic aspect:
a   Hiroshi Hara, Sotetsu Cultural Centre, Yokohama, Japan, 1990: entrance
b   Sotetsu Cultural Centre: interior space
c   Sotetsu Cultural Centre: plan
d   MacCormac Jamieson Prichard, Cable and Wireless College, Coventry, England, 1989–93

RELIGION *Places of worship* Contemplative and inspirational space is required by each of the world's major religions. People respond to a spiritual setting, joining in congregations that can be either participatory or performance-led, depending upon liturgical requirements. Sometimes highly public spaces of ritual, sometimes spaces for meditation, retreat or prayer, these buildings designed for worship retain a high level of significance, helping to mould architectural thought. Successfully redirecting religious tradition is one of the most challenging tasks any architect can face.

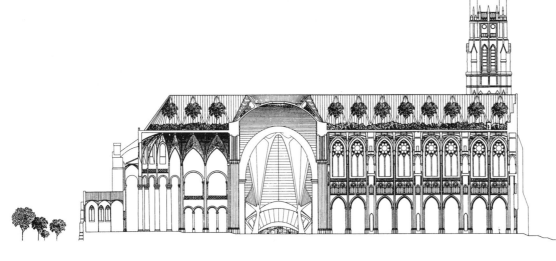

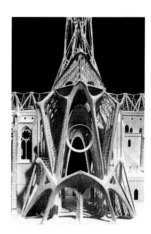

'I don't care about your church, I didn't ask you to do it. And, if I do it, I'll do it my way. It interests me because it's a plastic work. It's difficult.'

Le Corbusier accepting the commission to design the chapel at Ronchamp, 1950.

In Sicily there is a surviving ancient Greek

Doric temple that functions today as a Christian cathedral. In Seville, Spain, the great former mosque with its Giralda tower fulfils the same function. In London's Spitalfields district a single building has served successively as a Huguenot chapel, a synagogue and, today, a mosque. In Japan, a Shinto-influenced architect, Tadao Ando, has built Buddhist temples and Christian chapels. Frank Lloyd Wright designed both Christian and Jewish religious buildings. So did Louis Kahn, who also added a mosque to his portfolio. Sir Frederick Gibberd produced a Roman Catholic cathedral and a national mosque in the United Kingdom. Santiago Calatrava, from Spain, has worked for years on the Episcopalian Cathedral of St John the Divine in New York. It would appear that there is a certain amount of cross-talk between the architectures of different religions, and between the subdivisions within religions, and that this process of transfer is not confined to the monotheistic cultures.

One could argue that it is perfectly possible to design an all-purpose religious space that would be acceptable to all faiths, if perhaps not all at the same time. There would be difficulties, of course – the consultative process alone would be a nightmare – but the thing could be done. How to imagine the resulting architecture? As it happens, there is no need to imagine it, for it has already been done. Between January 1994 and October 1995, Tadao Ando designed and built a 'meditation space' next to the Paris headquarters of UNESCO (the United Nations Educational, Scientific, and Cultural Organization). His brief from the client was to design a building that would be 'a place of prayer for eternal, global peace for all peoples of the world, transcending their religious, ethnic, cultural and historical differences and conflicts'.

Ando's resulting small drum of a building is set in a sparse granite-paved courtyard washed with rippling water, and approached indirectly by ribbon walkways. Inside the drum (made of beautifully moulded stacked curving sections of concrete) is a granite floor of radiating sections, a chair – and light. Light falling through the two entrance apertures, light washing down the walls from the flat ceiling above, cast as a concrete disc slightly smaller than the container on which it is placed, and fixed by four equidistant tabs, so allowing a very narrow annulus of glazing. That is all. The granite flooring has in its previous existence borne the brunt of the atomic blast at Hiroshima, but one does not have to know this to appreciate the place, any more than one need necessarily know that some of the stones at Corbusier's Pilgrimage Chapel at Ronchamp, 1953–5, were salvaged from the burnt-out wreck of the previous chapel on the site.

There are certain aspects to religious buildings that trigger responses, consciously or subconsciously, in those who are of the faith. In Ando's Meditation Space, Buddhists and Muslems will acknowledge the presence of moving water and the surrounding courtyard, while Christians may think of a cloister. The circular form will be familiar to many, among them Jews, where participants in ritual gather round a central focus – while for others the circular form is symbolic of sanctuary, or of Christ's sepulchre. Christians may look up and find an echo of the Cross in the barely discernible cruciform supports of the circular ceiling or they may, along with other faiths, imagine the pendentives of a dome. Those who place importance upon the containers of wisdom, or of relics, can see the little building as just such a container. Those that set store by the notion of journey, or of overcoming difficulties to arrive at enlightenment, will find it in the oblique approach. The chair against the wall assumes some of the characteristics of altar, pulpit, Islamic mihrab or Jewish Aron Kodesh – not overtly, but it provides a visual point of reference.

a b   d e

c

Adding levels of meaning to existing complexes:

a Santiago Calatrava, Cathedral of St John The Divine, New York, 1991: longitudinal section

b Cathedral of St John The Divine: detail of model

c Tadao Ando, Meditation Space, UNESCO, Paris, 1994–5: Ando's circular pavilion sits in the courtyard of Marcel Breuer's 1958 UNESCO Headquarters

d Meditation Space, UNESCO: interior of chapel

e Meditation Space, UNESCO: view of ceiling

Whether or not Ando consciously endeavoured to fuse all these references is irrelevant – it is, after all, an Ando building, sharing characteristics with many other Ando buildings, and all of them possess a certain quality, both luminous and numinous. They are serious, austere, they deal in light, volume and tactility. He cannot help building temples, whatever their ostensible function may be.

His Meditation Space is universal in a way that a Japanese equivalent – Togo Murano's posthumous 1988 Meisokan Meditation Hall – is not. Meisokan, though as austere internally and quite as successful in its deployment of natural light as Ando's, is a clearly regional form based upon the pattern of a lotus blossom, and is set in a pond to emphasize the point. Despite its architect's pronouncement from as early as 1919: 'Be above style!', this architecture does not travel. Outside its homeland, it would seem contrived. Better is Benson and Forsyth's 1985 cylindrical Boarbank Oratory at Grange-over-Sands, Cumbria, England, a tiny room for private prayer that – although designed for an order of nuns – aspires to the condition of a universal meditation space *à la* Ando.

With the exception of Judaism, the world's religions have mostly sought, historically, to identify themselves through recognizable forms of architecture. Thus the layout of mosques may be traced back to the courtyard form of the House of the Prophet at Medina, the plan of many Christian churches to the Cross or the circular Sepulchre, non-conformist Christian churches to the Greek Temple (to distinguish them from the Gothic arches, towers and spires of state conformism). A Hindu mandir is a built mixed metaphor. Its pinnacles represent both the mountains of the religion's origins and, like Christian spires, upwards aspiration. Its foundations are feet, its pillars are knees, the inner sanctum is the stomach, the place of the idol is the navel, windows are ears, flags the hair, and so on. Its interior is not so far removed from the carved caves of the earliest mandirs. But its purpose is remarkably similar to Ando's UNESCO place of meditation. In a mandir, time is suspended and the mind becomes still. It focuses beneficial divine vibrations – not only for the faithful who visit it, but also as a harmonic generator for its surroundings (this is taken very seriously: no steel is allowed in the stone construction of a mandir, lest it interfere with the vibrations). Like some Buddhist pagodas, a mandir is meant to emanate enlightenment. But then again, that aspiration holds good for all the great religious buildings of the world. The downside scarcely needs mentioning: buildings symbolic of one religion can become targets for the hatred of another.

What style is most appropriate today for a given religion? When Will Bruder came to design his Kol Ami Worship and Learning Center for the Jewish community of Scottsdale, Arizona, 1997, he eschewed any obvious religious signifiers, opting instead to reflect the desert vernacular of the region in defiance of the building's suburban setting. This alone was enough, for it sets the building apart and suggests resonances with the religion's Middle Eastern roots. The first phase was completed in 1996. Bruder's main building material – large sand aggregate blocks – are laid deliberately offset rather than flush, giving the walls a rough-hewn quality. For the main synagogue volume, the walls are also battered, emphasizing the fortress-like feel of the complex. Two parallel wings of classrooms are attached, forming between them an elongated cloister with zigzag lightweight polycarbonate awnings. It might be argued that Bruder's architecture implies that the Jewish community is on the defensive and ghettoized, turning its back on its surroundings. But an inward focus is apparent in the buildings of all religions, with the place of worship in particular needing to be free from outside distractions. Many religious buildings – think of Durham Cathedral in England, or Albi in France – are also fortresses.

It is a brave architect, then, who attempts an open-aspect church. Fumihiko Maki pulled it off with

a

b c

d

Searching for the
appropriate form:

a Murano Mori Architects,
   Meisokan Meditation Hall,
   Niigata, Japan, 1988: the
   lotus-shaped building is set
   in a pond

b Benson + Forsyth, Boarbank
   Oratory, Cumbria, England,
   1985: entrance to the
   prayer room

c Boarbank Oratory:
   interior of chapel

d Will Bruder, Kol Ami Worship
   and Learning Center for the
   Jewish community, Scottsdale,
   Arizona, 1997

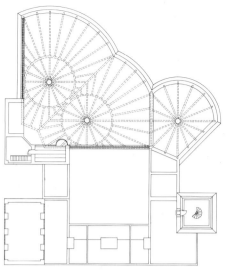

his Tokyo Church of Christ in the Tomigaya district, opened in 1995. A triangular concrete section, the end wall of the entrance lobby, is surmounted by a cross and gives the impression that it is a half-raised curtain, revealing the door of the building. The main structure is a big shed with a curved roof and a glazed end – but the end is an opaque double curtain wall, sandblasted and ceramic-fritted on the outside and with a sandwich layer of glass fibre membrane within, so the changing intensity of external light is all you experience. Given that the church faces onto a busy freeway, this acoustic and visual separation is welcome. Light also pours down from light slots along the edge of the roof along the outward-leaning sidewalls. The use of light, of birch finishes, and of a particular northern European kind of pendant light fitting, gives this Japanese church a very Finnish feel. However, the overall shape of the building is distinctly oriental. In this it contrasts with Arata Isozaki's Tokyo Christian College Chapel in the Inba district, built in 1989 for an evangelical Protestant denomination, where the architect has consciously adopted a Byzantine form of three domes and a freestanding bell tower. The structure of the domes is of laminated wood. Its difference from its (mostly) Roman Catholic and Orthodox counterparts is that there is not one main dome over the nave: the smallest one is the entrance foyer while the other

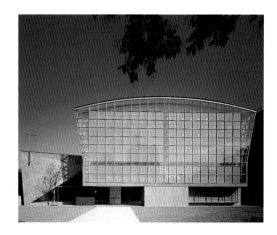

two are interlinked, so giving the roof a double focus. Still, its purpose is immediately apparent, unlike the subtler statement of Maki's.

The basilica form persistently recurs in this way as a memory both of the early Christian church and of its Ottoman connections, though it can be quite drastically modified. The Swiss architect Justus Dahinden, for instance, visited the form in two churches in quite different locales: first Mityana Cathedral, 1972, in Uganda, East Africa, the three equal portions of which represent segments of a dome. Like three nuns in conversation, these head-pieces also address a larger community comprising a convent, school and so on. Dahinden thus dismantled the traditional dome, and in so doing arrived at forms not unlike the straw huts of the area. Then in Italy in 1996 he took the knife to the dome again, this time at the church of St Maximilian Kolbe in Varese, 1996. Here the dome is half hollowed out, but the external form is allowed to continue round to form two arms, embracing the semicircular court-yard at the centre. Externally it is all rather crudely done: internally, the timber structure of the half-dome is a delight.

Building in the 'appropriate' style can often result in confusing signals. In Britain in the late nineteenth century, when the fast-expanding Jewish middle class was swelled by poor refugees from

Central Europe, architects began to search for a style for their new synagogues. Nathan Solomon Joseph, commissioned to design the new Central Synagogue in London in 1867, rejected Gothic as being Christian, and neo-classical as pagan. The correct style, he concluded, was Moorish – the architecture, as he saw it, not so much of Islam as of all Semitic peoples. But there was a need to relate to the con-text of the British religious infrastructure. So for a time synagogues were built that combined elements of Gothic and Moorish – ogee and pointed arches, rose windows, topped with minarets. At other periods an Egyptian style was attempted for synagogues, but no clear consensus was ever reached. A dispersed reli-gion – particularly one that periodically suffered per-secution – was finally unable or unwilling to set itself apart with a readily distinctive style. Elsewhere in the world, this could lead to some brave experiments – Frank Lloyd Wright's Beth Sholom Synagogue in Elkins Park, Pennsylvania, 1954–9, being an example of architecture expressive of a religion's symbolism. However, in its rationale and much of its organiza-tion, the irregular hexagon of the Beth Sholom syna-gogue was not so very different from Wright's foursquare Unity Temple, 1904–6, in Oak Park, Illinois – particularly in its combination of worship and educational areas within the same complex, a feature common to his circular Annunciation Greek

Orthodox Church, 1956–63, at Wauwatosa, Wisconsin. This conjoining of worship and broader community functions was to become a near-universal element of new churches by the end of the century.

Style cross-referencing has been common-place: six years after Joseph declared Moorish to be the best possible style for synagogues, the competi-tion for the expiatory church of the Sacre Coeur in Montmartre, Paris, 1873–1919, was won by Paul Abadie with a design he called 'Romano-Byzantine'. Similarly the architect John Francis Bentley built Westminster Roman Catholic Cathedral in London, 1895–1903, in Byzantine style to distinguish it from the Gothic of nearby Westminster Abbey. The idea in both cases was to return to the 'pure' architecture of the early church around the Mediterranean, in which the Arab influence could not be denied. As we have seen, this approach is an enduring one. National characteristics generally overlay the received form, whether it be the carrot spires and onion domes of German churches, or the extraordinary Hungarian organic tradition as best exemplified by the churches of Imre Makovecz, which deploy their overwhelming fairytale imagery regardless of denomination: as in his Siofok Lutheran Church, 1986–7, and his Roman Catholic church in Paks, 1987. In the United States, what might be termed a related 'forest tradition' of chapel building is apparent in the work of Fay Jones,

a Arata Isozaki, Tokyo Christian College Chapel, Tokyo, 1989: overt historicism can be seen in the Byzantine form of the three domes and bell tower
b Tokyo Christian College Chapel: interior of chapel
c Tokyo Christian College Chapel: plan

d Fumihiko Maki, Tokyo Church of Christ, Tokyo, 1995: Maki's Church of Christ, in contrast with Isozaki's Christian College Chapel, exhibits low-key symbolism

a	c	d
b		

a one-time apprentice to Frank Lloyd Wright and colleague of Bruce Goff. Jones' 1980 Thorncrown Chapel at Eureka Springs, Arkansas, with its Wrightian latticework detailing, is perhaps more successful than the attempt at woodland gothic represented by his Mildred B Cooper Memorial chapel in Bella Vista, 1982, which has a Goff-like whimsy to it. Both, however, stand like extensions of the trees around them, appearing to be open to the air (in fact they are both glazed-in). Jones' later Leonard Community Chapel in Fort Worth, Texas, 1990, returns to the themes of the Thorncrown Chapel in more solid form: it is no preparation for the shock of discovering that Jones has turned to brick cylinders and basilica-like domes for his latest exercise, the Lindsey Wilson College Chapel in Columbia, Kentucky, 1997.

By the late twentieth century, as in medieval times, much religious architecture has come to be associated with structural virtuosity. The difference between Coventry Cathedral, 1951–62, as originally drawn by Sir Basil Spence under the influence of Albi, with fat stone columns – and as ultimately developed and built, with slender tapering cruciform concrete columns rising to a fractal version of fan-vaulting, is down to the engineering of Ove Arup. Like Auguste Perret's Notre Dame at Le Raincy, near Paris with its prefabricated concrete-mesh walls, 1922–3, it is

Gothic in its sensibilities, if modern in its construction methods. At the same period as Spence's and Arup's cathedral, the Spanish born, Mexican-based architect-engineer Felix Candela was going much further in placing engineering at the service of church architecture. As early as 1951, Candela's astonishing thin-shell concrete constructions, with roof skins as thin as 16 millimetres were, he maintained, a matter as much of intuition as of calculation, 'in the manner of the old master-builders of cathedrals'. His Church of Santa Maria Miraculosa in Mexico City, 1954–5, (with Enrique de la Mora) has been compared with Gaudí, but can seem almost vorticist from some angles. In Italy, Candela's only peer in concrete engineering, Pier Luigi Nervi, concluded his career with the vast Papal Audience Hall in Rome, 1970–1, while in Scotland architects Gillespie Kidd and Coia were forcing the envelope of the church into provocative structural forms, culminating in their St Benedict's Drumchapel, 1964–70, its concave copper roof seeming from inside the church to be a suspended timber hull.

During the same fertile post-war period, Walter Netsch of Skidmore, Owings and Merrill contributed his notable Air Force Academy Chapel, 1959–63, in Colorado Springs. This, to an extent like Ando's UNESCO Meditation Space, had the task of being inter-denominational – but in the United

States at that time this meant merely Protestant, Roman Catholic, and Jewish, with the majority Protestants on top under the glorious roof, and Catholics and Jews given smaller, purpose-designed spaces tucked into the dark lower level. Even this crudely hierarchical division of space astonished some commentators at the time for its perceived radicalism – fears were expressed that rival strands of Protestantism and Judaism would have difficulty rubbing shoulders in their own allotted areas, let alone in proximity to separate faiths. As it turned out, the three chapel spaces beneath the extraordinary seventeen pointed blades of the tetrahedral roof structure, intersected with strips of abstract stained glass, were successfully commissioned with scarcely a murmur of protest. Perhaps it was in the end simply the fact that, viewed from outside or in, the chosen roof construction – aluminium-clad steel space frames – was thoroughly appropriate for an air force establishment, echoing as it did the wings and fuselages of the hardware the cadets were familiar with. This was the period immortalized in Tom Wolfe's *The Right Stuff*: the blades or spires seem ready to blast off into the clouds at the speed of sound, even of light.

Another who wrought religous symbolism from structural virtuosity was Kenzo Tange. His 1960–4 St Mary's Cathedral in Tokyo – built in the same period as his Olympic buildings in that city –

a   b
         d

     c

The organic origins of gothic infiltrate all styles:

a Imre Makovecz, Lutheran Church, Siofok, Hungary, 1986–7

b Skidmore, Owings and Merrill (SOM), Air Force Academy Chapel, Colorado Springs, 1959–63

c Fay Jones + Maurice Jennings, Thorncrown Chapel, Eureka Springs, Arkansas, 1980

d (and page 147) Fay Jones + Maurice Jennings, Skyrose Chapel, Rosehills Memorial Park, Whittle, California, 1997

e (page 146) Fay Jones + Maurice Jennings, Mildred B Cooper Memorial Chapel, Bella Vista, Arkansas, 1982

drapes metal-clad hyperbolic paraboloid shells from a cruciform arrangement of glazed roof ridges. It is not Tange's best building by any means, but the kite-shaped floor plan that results is an ingenious reworking of the standard nave-and-transept arrangement of churches through the ages, and the external form is undeniably arresting. Lesser hands, provoked by such virtuosity, tried some of the same tricks more or less successfully. So the matter of architecture and engineering combining in religious architecture for awesome effect had become very familiar, almost a cliché, by the start of the last third of the twentieth century. This was symptomatic of those religions, predominantly Christian, that deemed it necessary to appear up-to-date rather than those, like Islam and Hinduism, that relied upon traditional forms. This striving for effect degenerated into the pursuit of form-making almost for its own sake. Germany's Gottfried Böhm practised in the tradition of Expressionist ecclesiastical reform architecture established by his father Dominikus Böhm (1880–1955) predicated on an abandonment of historical forms and the melding of congregation and altar. However, Gottfried Böhm's form-making became ever more assertive. His Pilgrimage Church at Neviges, West Germany, 1963–8, is a concrete mountain range of a building which, though powerful, exerts a less subtle force than Le Corbusier's Pilgrimage Chapel at

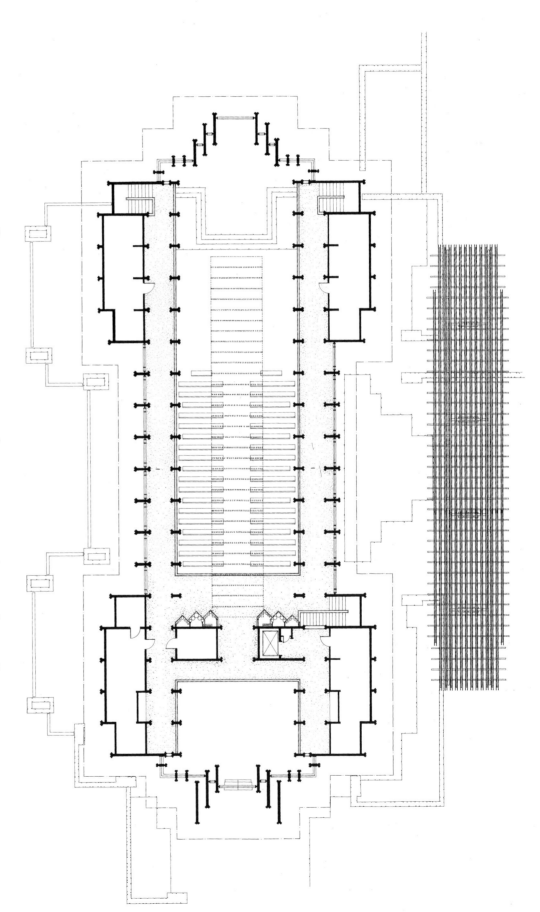

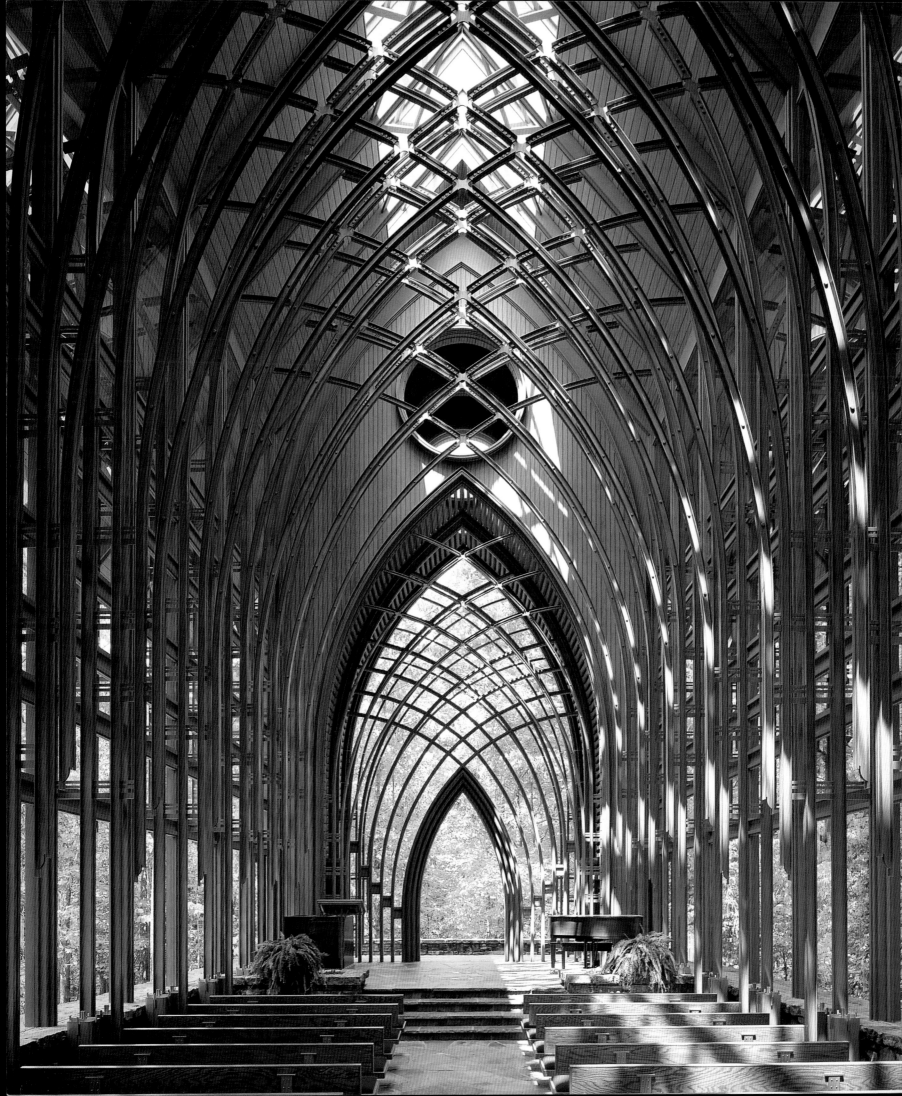

Ronchamp, 1953-5, or his later Monastery of Ste Marie-de-la-Tourette near Lyons, 1957-60. Even Alvar Aalto was not immune from this bug: witness one of his last works, the Riola church in Bologna, Italy, 1966-78, in which he seems to parody and make crude his own lifetime's concerns with the undulating form and the play of light.

Modern technology did not necessarily make things better, although Philip Johnson made a brave attempt with his 'Crystal Cathedral' in Garden Grove, California, 1977-80. Johnson had been the author of a number of religious buildings during his long career, in his usual restless ragbag of styles – notable among them his spiralling 90-foot tall Chapel of Thanksgiving in Dallas, 1976, where light pours in through stained glass panels placed in the diminishing spiral of the roof, giving the building a somewhat Islamic air (this was a device used to equal effect by HOK in their considerably larger 1993 Mormon church in Independence, Missouri, where the spiral is finally twisted into a spire). The Crystal Cathedral is at the opposite extreme to the Dallas chapel. It is a cathedral for the age of the TV evangelist – in this case one particular TV evangelist, the Reverend Robert H Schuller, who enjoyed an audience of millions. Services are therefore televised, which means the 'cathedral' is a filmic backdrop set. This at least partly explains its camp characteristics, such as a choir whose seating forms part of a giant organ console, the organ pipes rising above them in twin timber-clad towers. Fortunately Johnson's later ideas for an otherwise conventional Gothic tower built of glass (see 'Workplace') did not materialize here. Instead there is a more abstract and, from a distance, rather fine 286-foot campanile which evokes the feel of Perpendicular Gothic in its 'bundle of rods' arrangement, like stainless-steel prisms or icicles. Externally the Crystal Cathedral is a rather lumpen mirror-glass arrangement: internally the mirror glass makes for the usual drab view of the outside world but, by reflecting 92 per cent of the sun's rays, allows for the huge volume to be naturally ventilated. Visual interest is instead sustained by the complex tracery of the tubular steel space frame.

Even a church on this colossal scale was not enough for the doughty Johnson. Aged 90, he designed the Cathedral of Hope for Dallas, Texas, unveiled in 1996 and scheduled for completion in

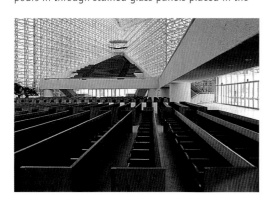

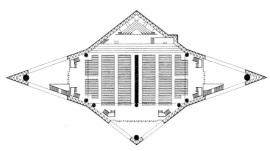

a   c   d e
b

2004. This, for a 2,000-strong congregation mostly of lesbian and gay worshippers, is best thought of as a twin-auditorium concert hall, for it displays the classic pairing of large and small auditoria, in this case arranged either side of a large central lobby – the smaller hall being the existing church, the lobby and large new building being by Johnson. Between the old building and new is a tall freestanding screen wall doubling as an open bell tower. The style of the 'cathedral' (the term has a looser meaning in the United States than in the rest of the world, being applied to any large church) is the last of many to be espoused by Johnson during his lengthy career: it is a version of deconstructivism, the fractal variety, the coloured concrete buildings appearing like icebergs or detached chunks of craggy cliff-face. This apparent design looseness is in fact scarcely more unorthodox than Spence's saw-tooth walls at Coventry, since the interior is arranged conventionally and symmetrically. Johnson acknowledged that this would be his swan-song, to the extent of calling it 'the crowning jewel in my lifetime of work'.

Despite such examples, by the last third of the century attitudes had begun to change. In Christian cultures, a return to less strident forms became apparent, along with a desire to recapture something of the timeless qualities of space and light associated with traditional church building. What this came down to in practice was either a return to vernacular, or a reappraisal of the work of the 'alternative' modernists – the grouping including Wright, Asplund, Lewerentz, Aalto, Scharoun, and

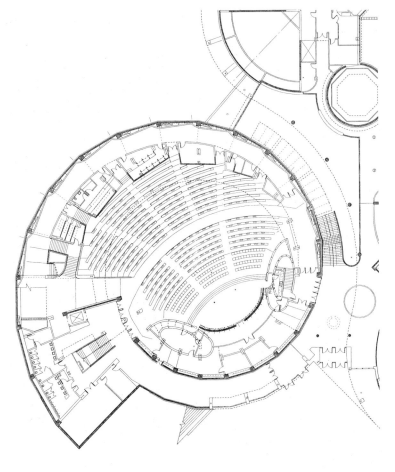

The understated metaphor versus showbiz glitz:

a Philip Johnson and Alan Ritchie Architects, 'Crystal Cathedral', Garden Grove Community Church, Calfornia, 1977–80: the vast interior of the church

b Crystal Cathedral: plan

c Alvar Aalto, Riola Church, Bologna, Italy, 1966–78

d Hellmuth Obata + Kassabaum, Reorganized Church of Jesus Christ of Latter Day Saints, Independence, Missouri, 1988–93: exterior view

e Reorganized Church of Jesus Christ of Latter Day Saints: plan

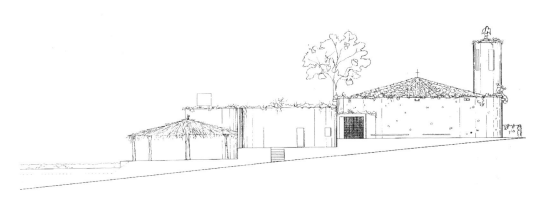

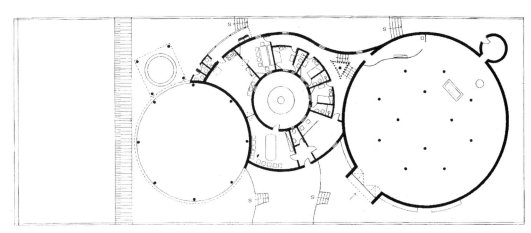

a b   f g

c   h

d

  e

others who constitute a different line to that offered by Corbusier, Mies, and the CIAM axis. In this context, Jørn Utzon's church at Bagsvaerd, near Copenhagen, 1974–6, is instructive. Here is a church that eschews structural gymnastics, instead choosing to recognize the affinity between churches and industrial buildings in the rural landscape. At a casual glance you might assume that it had an agricultural function but this, after all, is in the suburbs, not the prairies. It is quite a small church but its scale speaks of bigger things – such as the uncompleted Beauvais Cathedral in northern France or the equally abruptly terminated Lancing College chapel in southern England. It has a nave and clerestory windows, and it makes its effect through a conjunction of the industrial aesthetic (corrugated aluminium roofing) and a high level of finish on its concrete surfaces – subtly patterned precast cladding to the exterior walls, and a boardmarked *in-situ* thin-shell concrete roof to the nave interior. In its mode of presentation, Bagsvaerd was not a church such as one had seen previously, but it was recognizably a church for all that.

Considerably rougher, and deliberately so, is the slightly later church in Minas Gerais, Brazil, by the Roman born, Brazilian adoptive, architect, scenographer and theorist Lina Bo Bardi. Bo Bardi saw in Brazilian ideals a greater hope than was possible in the reconstruction of everything she had seen

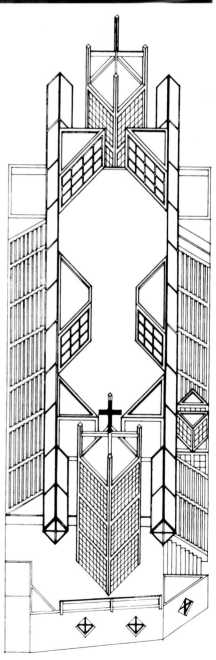

destroyed in her native country during the Second World War. She was to be cruelly disappointed. By the time she came to sketch out the Church of Espírito Santo do Cerrado, 1976–82, she had moved away from the sculptural modernism she had previously shared with Oscar Niemeyer and others – most notably in the São Paulo Art Museum, 1957–68. This church is Bo Bardi's reaction against what she saw as the failed experiment of industrialization and socialism in Brazil, where all the evils of the First World's industrial revolution had been compressed into a few years, and the state had become decadent. Bo Bardi's response to this was to reject 'Western' culture with its gadgets, consumerism and finesse – and also, one might say such triumphalist, highly engineered church architecture as Niemeyer's Brasilia Cathedral, completed in 1970, or the flash neon-lit resort-architecture of the Sacred Heart Church in Carlos Paz, Argentina, 1976–84, by Miguel Angel Roca. She did not assume the William Morris view that a return to craftsmanship was the answer: craftsmanship, she asserted, had never existed in Brazil, only what she described as 'a sparse domestic pre-craftsmanship'. She had already experimented with primitivism in housing projects: she now applied her theories to a church. It appealed to her because it was in a very poor district, was commissioned by Franciscan monks, and had no budget – all its materials and labour

were to be given. 'It was all given freely,' she said, 'not in the sense of a catholic pietism, but astutely, as how to arrive at things by very simple means.'

The church as built, though rough and ready, was fully drawn up by the architect and is, in the event, deceptively sophisticated in its simplicity. Three intersecting circles of diminishing size form the complex: respectively the worship area with its stubby cylindrical bell tower; nuns' cells and meeting rooms around a little circular cloister; and a covered open yard, fenced around like a cattle pen and with a beaten earth floor, for public gatherings. The final element, naturally enough for Brazil, is a contiguous · football field. Supports for the main church space are of local rough timber, the main wall material is local brick, the roofs are of colonial pantiles. But Bo Bardi had not worked in vain. At the outbreak of war, she worked with Gio Ponti on *Domus* magazine, and rubbed shoulders with the exquisites of the Italian and South American arts set: the neo-primitive church interior with its carefully considered openings for light – a narrow circlet where roof touches wall, a triangular section taken out of the roof over the altar, high pierced openings all round – is thoroughly designerly. A sketch by the architect of a 'simple' wooden seat (in fact highly architectonic) gives the game away even more. Although she foreswore being part of what she called a 'folkloric élite', Bo Bardi

No good architect can ever achieve true artlessness; but Bo Bardi came close:

a Lina Bo Bardi, Espírito Santo Do Cerrado Church, Uberlândia, Minas Gerais, Brazil, 1976–82
b Espírito Santo Do Cerrado Church: exterior view
c Espírito Santo Do Cerrado Church: site elevation
d Espírito Santo Do Cerrado Church: plan

e Espírito Santo Do Cerrado Church: interior of chapel
f Jørn Utzon, Bagsvaerd Church, Copenhagen, 1974–6
g Miguel Angel Roca, Sacred Heart Church, Carlos Paz, Argentina, 1976–84: exterior view
h Sacred Heart Church: axonometric

a   d e

b   c

could not help her upbringing, her training, or her own previous professional career. She had produced a piece of fine architecture that did its damnedest to appear nothing of the kind.

Relevant in this context are the philosopher-designers of the Utopian architectural teaching community known as the Open City at Ritoque in the extreme south of Chile, whose building methods aspire to the artisanal, who build directly without drawings (usually), and whose rationale is an architecture freed from economic power. But one might also mention the way Edward Prior conceived St Andrew's Church in Roker, England, in 1905, as a 'rational', Saxon-influenced building – artisanally expressive, but in the event partly overlaid with Arts and Crafts decoration. In the case of Bo Bardi's church, the plan – enclosed worship space, semi-open community space, wholly open parvis, here given over to sport – is however a timeless diagram of the ideal relationship between church and town.

The Mexican architect Ricardo
Legorreta attempted a different, though related, primitivism when he came to design the new cathedral in Managua, Nicaragua, 1993–5. This is not a rejection of the prevailing ethos of the host nation, as Bo Bardi's was. Instead, it is a response to a natural catastrophe, the earthquake that destroyed much of the Nicaraguan capital, including the previous

cathedral, in 1972. Rebuilding it was as symbolically important an event as the rebuilding of Coventry Cathedral in England after the wartime Blitz. This is appropriately monumental architecture, wrought out of a reasonably simple material for an impoverished nation, poured concrete. Interestingly, Legorreta's response to the demands of the Second Vatican Council in the early 1960s, calling for greater active involvement of participants, and a reaching out to the community, has resulted in a great internal space reminiscent in some ways of a mosque. Outside, the cross of the boardmarked concrete tower is strangely subverted by the sequence of domed rooflights, Arabian in feel, that are echoed both in the larger companion domes of the semicircular sacristy and the Veneration Chapel. The cruciform motif is everywhere – in ceilings, columns, light fittings – but the arrangement of domes suggests something beyond the 'Spanish influence in Nicaragua' offered by the architects. The resulting space, however, has fulfilled its purpose admirably: it has become a community building in which – like Seville's mosque-turned cathedral or many Hindu events – the act of religious worship feels almost incidental to the wider activities going on.

This searching for the roots of indigenous religious buildings became apparent everywhere. In La Jolla, California, Charles Moore designed his

rural Church of the Nativity, 1985–9, as a take on Spanish missionary architecture. In Chester, England, George Pace – as eclectic in his own way as America's Moore, but confined in his work almost exclusively to church architecture – gave the city's cathedral a detached Bell Tower, 1968–75, based on Saxon and Romanesque precedents, its stress patterns calculated by primitive computers. And in the Georgian settlement of Clinton, New Jersey, Allan Greenberg produced the Church of the Immaculate Conception, 1994–6, as an eighteenth-century classical basilica, complete with campanile – but its masonry, rather than being loadbearing, clads a steel frame.

More extreme examples of roots-ism were being designed elsewhere, however. In the grounds of a hotel in Karuizawa, Japan, the Californian community architect Kendrick Bangs Kellogg produced in 1988 an 'organic' wedding chapel comprising a sequence of leaning concrete arches of varying sizes joined with fishscales of overlapping glass and acrylic panels, the whole curving and undulating, suggestive of a cavern or igloo, rising from a plinth of loose stone walls. It is ironic that a building so strongly reminiscent of the forms of the extremely early church, rough and basilica-like, complete with the suggestion of round-topped Romanesque arches, should be created for the greater glory of nothing more than the Hoshino Hot Springs Resort Hotel.

Supercharged regionalism
compared to a cautious use
of the vernacular:
a   Ricardo Legorreta, Managua
    Metropolitan Cathedral,
    Nicaragua, 1993–5:
    exterior view
b   Managua Cathedral: shrine

c   Managua Cathedral:
    view towards altar
d   Moore Ruble Yudell,
    Church of the Nativity,
    Rancho Santa Fé, California,
    1985–9: exterior view
e   Church of the Nativity:
    view towards altar

Islamic cultures, though placing much more store by tradition in their mosques, threw up some interesting variations on a theme in the post-war period. In a sense modernism never made much headway, since Hassan Fathy rediscovered traditional vernacular architecture and applied it to a mosque as early as 1948, at New Gourna, near Luxor in Egypt. Its form, and its rammed-earth construction, were to prove highly influential to succeeding generations of architects in North Africa and the Middle East. Not surprisingly, perhaps, one of the very few 'modernist' mosques came from the hand of a Westerner: Louis Kahn's Sher-e-Bangla mosque in Dhaka, Bangladesh, 1962–83. Kahn's characteristic late forms – monumental brick pierced with vast semicircles, with a nod to pointed arches in parts – seem strangely appropriate, though a little redundant when applied to a cubic form at the top of the minaret, which consequently looks like a microphone. In a sense, the commission came about by accident: Kahn was planning and rebuilding the government centre of Dhaka, and the religious building came as part of the package. Since the Dhaka work found Kahn at his most historicist (especially Roman-influenced) the range of cultural references deployed by this Estonian-born architect in his mosque is complex to say the least.

Islam's answer to Gottfried Böhm comes in the form of Zlatko Uglien's Sherefuddin Mosque in Visoko, Bosnia, completed in 1980. Expressionism is to the fore, both in the 'organic' shapes of the main building and in its minaret with its melting cowl. Bosnia, in geographical if not political terms, is close to Hungary, a nation with its own tradition of organic architecture – particularly as applied to the sequence of churches in the 1970s and 1980s by Imre Makovecz and compatriots such as Gyorgi Csete and Istvan Kistelegdi. The geometrical and modular basis of much mosque design in theory lends itself to modern reinterpretation, but comparatively seldom receives it except in the most 'westernized' nations such as Saudi Arabia, where the examples are unconvincing. A better example elsewhere is the Jondishapur University Mosque in Iran by Kamran Diba: a sequence of rounded brick forms owing little to tradition. It was completed in 1974, when Iran was a Western-oriented state. Also by Diba (in collaboration with Parvin Pezeshki) is the tiny and abstracted Place of Prayer in the grounds of Tehran's Carpet Museum: two open-roofed concrete cubes, one inside the other and slightly rotated to face Mecca. It was built in 1978, the year before the fall of the Shah and the reversal of his programme of Westernization. At this very moment of transition, Jahangir Mazlum's Al Ghadir Mosque, 1977–87, also in Tehran, shows how broadly modernist geometrical forms were starting to revert, in his case through rich applied

a
b

c   e

d   f

g

Evolving the ancient symbol:
a Jahangir Mazlum,
   Al Ghadir Mosque, Tehran,
   1977–87: interior
b Al Ghadir Mosque:
   exterior view
c Zlatko Uglien, Sherefuddin
   Mosque, Visoko, Bosnia, 1980

d Rasem Badran, Qasr Al Hokm
   Palace of Justice and Al Jame
   State Mosque, Riyadh, 1992:
   exterior
e Abdel Wahed El-Wakil,
   Corniche Mosque,
   Jeddah, Saudi Arabia, 1986
f Al Jame Mosque:
   courtyard interior
g Al Jame Mosque: plan

brickwork and decoration. Although Saudi Arabia can produce a building such as the Palace of Justice Mosque in Riyadh, 1992, by the Jordanian architect Rasem Badran – a highly successful fusion of traditional Nadji architecture with modern techniques – more normal are historicist mosques such as those designed by the London-based architect Abdel Wahed El-Wakil: most notably, his Al Qiblatain Mosque of 1987 in Medina. The divergent approaches of Badran and El-Wakil have equal validity (the latter's has more in common with Hindu temple builders), though Badran is the more interesting to those who believe that architecture is simultaneously capable of being progressive and traditional. Badran's mosque, though rich in ornament to minimalistically inclined eyes, in fact starts gently to abstract the elements of its tradition, which is entirely in keeping with a desert architecture. One might cite the precedent of Arthur Shoosmith's Garrison Church in New Delhi, 1928–30, which abstracts the image of the square-towered Anglican church in brick rather as Edwin Lutyens produced the eternal form of the Cenotaph, the empty tomb. Again, one can point to the return of traditional forms. The British may not exactly have ushered in an age of radical architecture during their stewardship of India, but the promise of Shoosmith's Garrison Church seemed to have faded by the time AGK Menon came to design St Mary's Cathedral in Varanasi, 1990–3 –

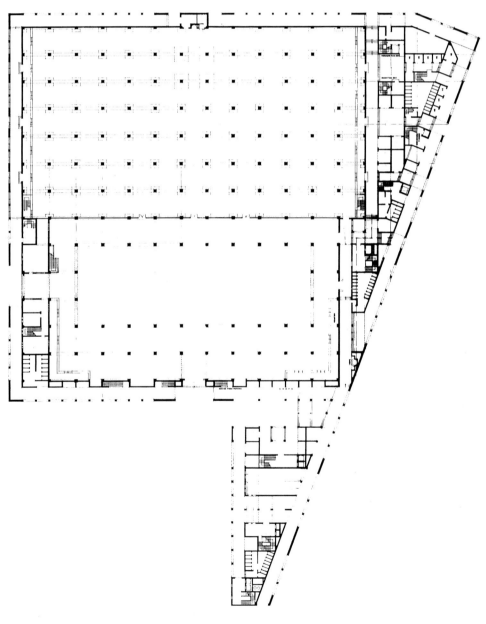

based on rather mosque-like interlocking cubic forms, nonetheless recalling early Christian basilicas, but with Hindu-influenced detailing.

This line of church architecture of predominantly solid form may be seen deployed with success in Sir William Whitfield's mighty 1982 brick Chapter House for St Alban's Cathedral, England. The Chapter House demonstrates that it is possible to graft a substantial new building onto an ancient one without resorting to the get-out of a glass box, by instead evoking the forms of earlier times. No-one has ever tried to bracket Sir William with California's Steven Holl before, but Holl's Chapel of St Ignatius in Seattle, 1997, is another play with elemental forms, in this case in an entirely new building. The roofscape of this Jesuit chapel is like the eroded forms of a Byzantine church, sliced and skewed, with a separate campanile: like Corbusier at Ronchamp, Holl clearly delights in the plasticity of his forms. Inside, however, it is an utterly conventional rectangular plan, the varying roof heights and shapes coupled with the play of light serving to highlight the most important areas – the tallest section, of course, being focused on the altar. That Holl then chose to construct the walls of his church out of great shaped precast concrete sections, fitting them together like pieces of a child's jigsaw and then colouring them ochre, finally rendering the lifting holes precious with

gilded caps, is more than artifice. Like Bruder in Arizona, Holl wanted solidity, the idea of the strong masonry walls of the ancient place of worship. This longing is equally apparent in the bastion-like church by Alvaro Siza at Forno, Portugal, where the white forms are elemental indeed, austere to an extreme both inside and out – but somehow legible as a church despite the lack of any of the usual signals.

Mosque architecture in turn received
a stimulus in the 1990s, with the completion of the Islamic Centre Mosque in Rome, 1975–95. In a city where the main industry for a millennium has been the Papacy and its administration of the Roman Catholic church, this was no mean undertaking. But the Muslim population in Italy was on the increase, and neither the Italian government nor the Rome Municipality wished to deny it. The site, however – donated by the city – was never intended to cramp the style of the Vatican: it is two miles from the city centre. A competition to design an Islamic Centre was won jointly in 1975 by Sami Mousawi (Iraqi-born, partly English-based, Bauhaus-modern by inclination) and the older Paulo Portoghesi (Italian architect and academic, an eclectic often pigeon-holed under 'post-modern') with the structural engineer Vittorio Gigliotti. So architects of differing persuasions found themselves yoked, a not infrequent occurrence in political competitions where

juries are split (consider the saga of Amsterdam's Opera House). Twenty years later, however, this particular scratch design team was still together and had completed the centre with its meeting halls, the largest Islamic library in the West, and its mosque. Mousawi had managed to find in Islamic architecture a connection to Western modernism – especially its theoretical and often actual rejection of excess, but also in its love of geometrical forms. Portoghesi found it suited his historicist approach; he had previously worked with Gigliotti on the complex intersecting circular geometries of the Church of the Sacra Famiglia in Salerno, 1968–74, where poured concrete was used to dramatic effect in the roof vaults.

Both men luxuriated in the symbolic aspects, as expressed by the dome, the minaret, the colonnade and the courtyard – forms not so far removed from the architecture of Renaissance Italy. As built, the *tour de force* at the Rome Mosque, however, is the expression of concrete columns and trusses as 'trees', treated in an organic, almost Art Nouveau or Secessionist, manner. This – as opposed to the more common and rigid use of steel 'trees' to support the roofs of large public areas – exploits the plastic qualities of concrete to combine structure and ornament in a way that would please Louis Sullivan, if not Adolf Loos. First encountered in the colonnade or *riwaq*, the columns each consist of four bunched

a Stephen Holl, Chapel of
   St Ignatius, Seattle, 1997:
   chapel interior
b Chapel of St Ignatius:
   chapel exterior
c Paulo Portoghesi, Sami
   Mousawi and Vittorio Gigliotti,
   Islamic Centre Mosque,
   Rome, 1975–95

a   b   c

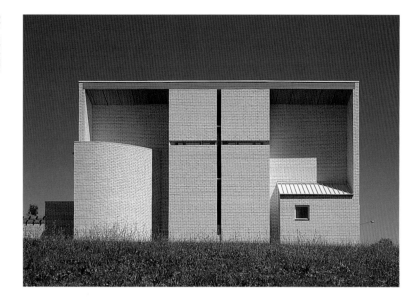

elements, square in cross-section, that branch out and curve to support the roof. When encountered in the main prayer hall, this system is elaborated. Clasped by a ring at the first level of furcation – the swelling of the column and the ring signalling a capital – the trusses then loop off, ribbon-like, to form intersecting open vaults. Notable beneath the hall's sixteen smaller domes, this system becomes very effective indeed where it delineates the main dome comprising seven stepped concentric rings. The result is to dematerialize the usually prominent pendentives of a large dome. Although, at a casual glance, the looping trusses can look like spaghetti, closer inspection reveals the very ingenious structural rationale of the system, which is closely related to the effect provided by a canopy of trees with its spreading branches. At the earlier Salerno church, Portoghesi and Gigliotti had concerned themselves with the expression of mass: here they pare down the concrete mass as far as possible to create a tracery of light. Comparisons have been made with the Baroque Ecclesiastical architecture of Borromini (on whom Portoghesi is an expert) and Guarini. The architect John Melvin has identified three churches to which the Rome Mosque owes a large debt: Borromini's St Carlo alle Quattro Fontane and St Ivo della Sapienza; and the mathematician-architect Guarini's St Lorenzo in Turin. Melvin concludes that

Portoghesi and Mousawi have introduced Counter-Reformation Baroque to the Islamic tradition, blended with references to those modern masters such as Kahn who interpreted classicism afresh. Yet the overall effect is convincingly Muslim, not merely the self-evident details such as minaret, water-tinkling courtyard and the abstracted decorative use of calligraphy and intertwining arabesques. The relatively lengthy gestation period of the Islamic Centre appears to have helped, rather than hindered, its design.

Not to be completely outshone by the new mosque down the road, the Vatican held its own competition for a church to mark the Millennium – its contribution to the year 2000 celebrations around the world. It is a pilgrimage church, since every year representatives of the Roman church travel to hear the Pope, and this, in the poor Tor Tre Teste district on the edge of town, is both a marker on this continuously unrolling calendar, and a way to engage with the deprived communities of Rome. The invited competition was between Tadao Ando, Günter Behnisch, Santiago Calatrava, Peter Eisenman, Frank Gehry and Richard Meier. No Muslim architect was invited, and no Italian, but there was no bar on other faiths or other nations.

Richard Meier won. His church is relatively small but succeeds in expressing its embedded importance by fairly simple means. For once it is not quite

another Meier refrigerator building, and in this it is unlike his previous religious building, the Hartford Seminary of 1978–81, which claims a Corbusian influence but which might as well be the business park headquarters of a computer company. In Rome he breaks out of the fridge. Although there are orthogonal elements in the associated community centre with its auditorium, it depends for its effect on three curving, overlapping shells – the idea of the Trinity – sheltering and containing the side chapel, baptistry and main worship area. The three shells are made of poured concrete, their interstices glazed. Meier is trying nothing that has not been tried by many other architects in the post-war years.

He certainly attempts nothing so radical as Calatrava's suggested 'opening wings' design, which would have transformed a conical structure into the suggestion of a great angel. Nor does he engage with the neighbourhood as Behnisch did, who saw the real need as being outside the church boundaries. Nor does he aspire to the monk-like calm of Ando with his triangular building, cruciform rooflight, and sunken meditative colonnade. Similarly the idea of expressing the Trinity architecturally is common enough – you see it, for instance, in the church of St Thomas Aquinas at Charnwood, Australia, 1987–9. There, architects Mitchell Giurgola and Thorp opt to divide the white walls of the sanctuary into three,

The Trinity used as an
architectural ordering device:
a Mitchell Giurgola & Thorp
   Architects, St Thomas Aquinas
   Church, Charnwood,
   Australia, 1987–9
b Richard Meier & Partners,
   Rome 2000 Millennium
   Church, Rome, 1996–2000:
   model view shows the interstices between the three shells

c Rome 2000 Millennium
   Church: site plan
d Rome 2000 Millennium
   Church: the three shells
   represent the Trinity

a   b   d

c

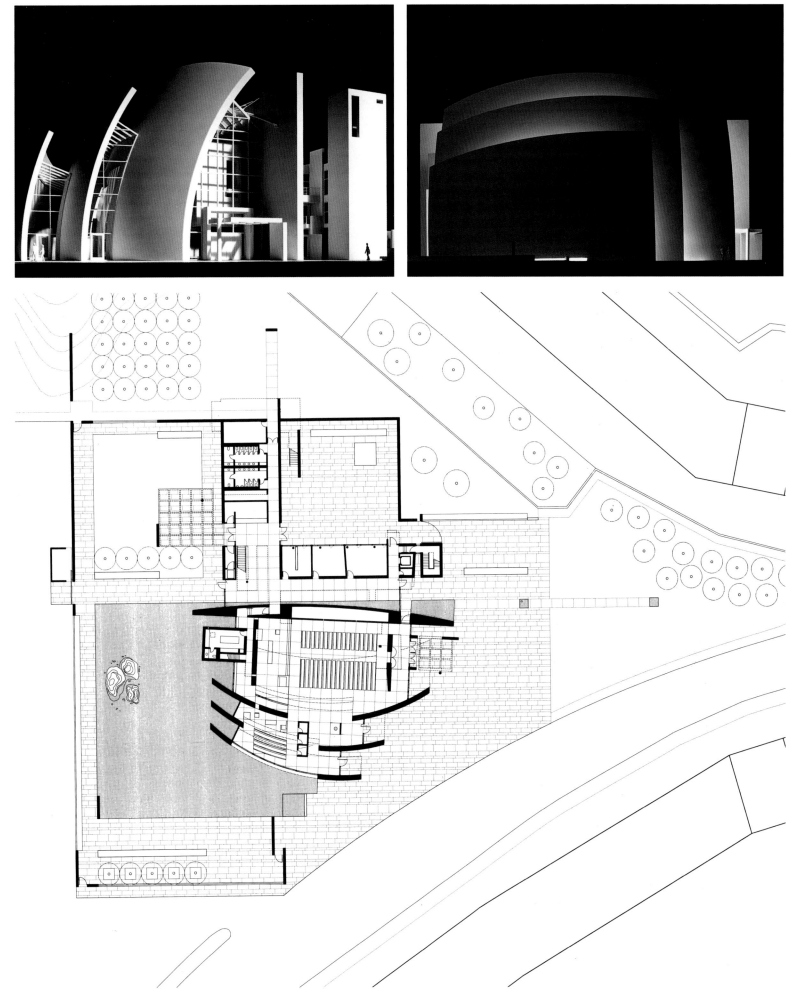

creating a central niche for the altar. Those less attuned to such subtleties are left in no doubt as to the building's function: the rear wall of the sanctuary is incised with a full-height, full-width glazed cross. Meier's Rome 2000 church can be seen as a summation of a line of thought in contemporary church design, taking ideas of arch and dome and tower and layered walls and the play of light, and recasting those thoughts on a fairly modest scale.

New cathedrals – with a requirement for monumentality built into the brief, whether or not this is openly expressed – have sometimes tended in the post-war years to adopt a circular form not so much in memory of the primitive Church, but because of the liturgical changes requiring participation between clergy and worshippers. This is a requirement for

which the old form of long-nave cathedral, designed for a largely passive congregation, is singularly unsuited. Parallel experiments at this time with 'theatre in the round' made this an architectural and theatrical, as much as a liturgical, movement. Hence Niemeyer's great 'opening flower' of the Brasilia Cathedral, 1970, and hence Frederick Gibberd's related exercise in Liverpool, England, 1960-7. The circular church (and sometimes synagogue) building form continues to be applied – often in the teeth of the appalling acoustic problems inherent in circular places of assembly. But like the self-conscious engineering of the early post-war period, it has come to seem a cliché. In theory, fashions should have much less hold over religious buildings than other types, but in truth the Christian churches in particular have

been slaves to architectural fashion as they struggle to update their image. So when Mario Botta came to design Evry Cathedral in France, 1988–95, a bit of back-tracking was required.

Botta is one of those late twentieth-century architects who has made most fruitful use of the circular form. Just before the commission at Evry, he had designed the new church at Mogno in his home patch, the Ticino. The original church and part of this Maggia Valley village had been destroyed by a spring avalanche in 1986. There Botta designed the elliptical ark-like form of his church with its banded masonry and sharply sloping glass roof, the angle of the slice through the drum being such that the oval of the building's plan becomes a disc for the roof. This disc, split in two, faces down the valley

a   c   e   f
                       g
    b d

while the tall prow of the church (the bows of the ark, if you like) faces away from the village towards the higher ground that was the source of the avalanche. Inside, two arches of Cyclopean scale form the spine of the building while the walls, massively thick at ground level, gradually taper towards the top, giving the interior a funnel shape. At their thickest point behind the altar, a Romanesque apse is virtually quarried out, its banded stonework recalling the rural chapels of the Normans. 'The attempt,' remarked Botta, 'more symbolic than actual, [was] to handle huge forces.' Sheltered within this dam-like stone shell, one looks up past the arches and sees the sky. The interior plan is rendered more subtle by the fact that the rectangular nave plan of the lost church is carved out of the thickness of the oval plan of the new one. Angled, deeply incised, doors lead defensively from a walled courtyard into the church either side of the arch-spine. The building, like the windowless fortress-churches of frontier districts, appears more secure than it is, for it is still a puny relative to the forces that could be ranged against it. But its task is to represent sanctuary and security.

Having designed the Mogno church in response to a natural calamity, Botta then with seeming casualness took what amounted to a mould of the tapering interior of Mogno, inverted it, and expressed it externally as the cone-shaped roof of the Church of Beato Odorico, Pordenone, 1987–92; placed a cylinder within a cube for a church at Sartirana, 1987–95, and finally re-applied the Mogno form, on a large scale, at Evry Cathedral, 1988–95. No-one could accuse Botta, as they might Jean Nouvel, of being profligate with his shape-making and materials. Evry is so similar to Mogno, that it appears to deny it its allegedly site-specific reason for being. It is circular in plan, with a more complex variant of Mogno's glazed roof on the angle. The great thickness of the walls here used for ancillary rooms and stairs, with a related apsidal arrangement behind the altar, has a funnelling effect on the interior, and is plugged into an enclosing courtyard. But for Botta, the surroundings at Evry are no less potentially hostile than those at Mogno. The difference is that, while Mogno shelters the community symbolically against the forces of nature, Evry does exactly the same against the forces of modern architecture. For Botta, Evry's New Town represents the

Botta's architecture is ready-made for churches. The ark, the sanctuary, the tomb:

a Mario Botta, Church, Mogno, Switzerland, 1986–96: the elliptical drum is sliced by the disk forming the roof

b Mario Botta, Church, Sartirana, Switzerland, 1987–95: altar

c Mogno Church: the striations of light from the skylight crossing the masonry bands evoke strong comparisons with Evry Cathedral

d Sartirana Church: the cylinder within the cube

e Mario Botta, Church of Beato Odorico, Pordenone, Italy, 1987–92: looking up towards the top of the cone

f Church of Beato Odorico: view from beyond the altar

g Church of Beato Odorico: the 'beehive' cone of the church

very worst kind of modernist planning – rigidly functional, with no room, as he says, for anything but working and sleeping. 'The objective,' he declared, 'was to offer the city a call to believers that could, *even more importantly*, [my italics] have strong meaning for non-believers ... For them, the cathedral can be seen as a moment of silence and meditation, not necessarily religious or as a response to the need for certain functions, but as a place where any citizen may pause for a while.' In short, Botta wanted to recapture the perceived community role of the medieval cathedral, with the modernist housing estates around standing in for the hovels of the peasants of the Dark Ages. Nevertheless, there are some highly original touches, although most had previously occurred on his secular buildings: Botta designed

Evry with a circlet of trees running round the perimeter on top, with a covered walkway beneath the tree-line. While the glazed roof aspires to heaven, the building thus has a more prosaic function as a vantage point. In a way, Botta has evolved his own myth of church-making that, while clearly personal, he applies with exactly as much flexibility or rigidity as those designing mosques. For them, it is the symbolism of the Prophet's House: for him, it is the sheltering cave and the hillside above. And if proof were needed of the old dictum that museums are the cathedrals of today – why, Botta took the form of Mogno and Evry and made it the centrepiece of his Museum of Modern Art in San Francisco, 1989–95, (see 'Visual Arts') and for identical reasons: to assert its presence in the city, to constitute a point of

reference, to bring light washing down from above, to set up a dialogue with the community, and to act as an ark of tradition against the glassy vacuousness of the business district round about. There is even an apsidal detail at the root of the great circular atrium beneath that slanting eye-on-the-sky (which at one point Botta wanted to crown with trees). Wasting not a single idea, Botta then took the idea of the walkway round the roof, as used at Evry, and applied it right back down the scale for his little chapel at Monte Tamaro in the Ticino. This time he used the Mogno giant arch element externally, as a bridge leading to the apex of the roof. Like any medieval church builder, Botta has his specialized vocabulary: it is simply that it is personal to him, rather than to any generalized tradition or system of belief.

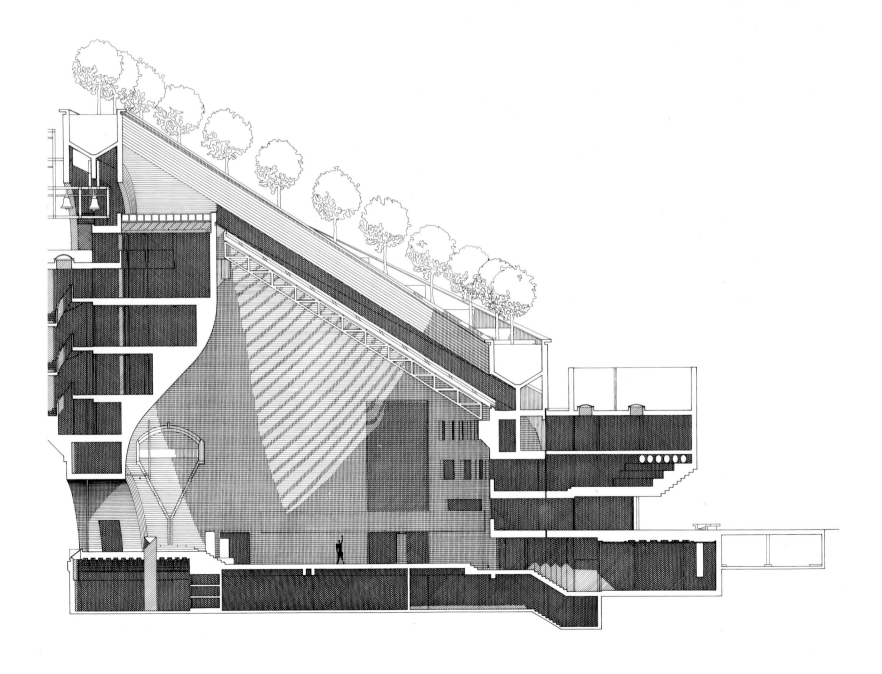

a   Mario Botta, Evry Cathedral,
    Evry, France, 1988–95:
    cross section
b   Evry Cathedral: a cross sits at
    the apex of the sliced drum
c   Evry Cathedral: the altar
d   Evry Cathedral: a circlet
    of trees runs around the
    roof perimeter
e   Evry Cathedral: the interior
    of the cathedral

a	b d
	c e

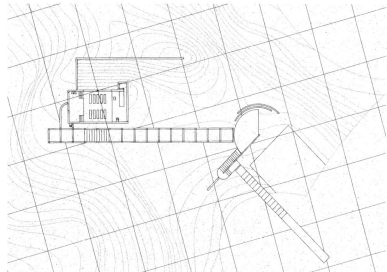

Perhaps the same could be said of Tadao Ando, except that his churches are conceived within a tradition of simplicity and austere forms. There is a kind of shared thinking, for instance, between Ando's 'Church on the Water', Hokkaido, 1985-8, and Roland Rainer's Parish Community Centre, 1973-6, at Puchenau, near Linz in Austria. One can make similar comparisons between Ando's Chapel on Mount Rokko, 1985-86, and Corbusier's monastery of La Tourette, 1957-60 - most notably the simple, raw concrete, rectangular chapel - or between his Water Temple, 1989-91, and Carlo Scarpa's Brion Cemetery, 1969-78; or even between his 'Church of the Light' at Ibaraki, 1987-9, and aspects of Ricardo Legorreta's Managua Cathedral in Nicaragua. This tradition of unostentation, of delight in basic materials used well, in the juxtaposition of light and dark, is possibly the most enduring aspect of religious buildings down the centuries - whether achieved by the hands of believers or non-believers. For an architect of faith working in the austere monastic tradition, an example would be the Belgian monk-architect Dom Bellot. But it is clearly nonsense to suggest that the best religious architecture comes from personal faith. The best religious architecture comes from the best architects, regardless of faith.

Ando, though his approach is characteristic whatever the building, does not produce the same response for Christian and Buddhist buildings. The Water Temple on Awaji Island, 1989-91, is for the Shingon Buddhist sect. As Ando used the form of the crucifix architecturally in his churches, here he employs such Buddhist symbols as the lotus flower and vermilion-hued interiors. But perhaps only he would place the temple hall beneath an oval pond filled with lotus plants, and then devise a means of entry which involves descending a staircase leading down through the water. It is a meditation space of an original quality. As remarked earlier in this chapter, Ando cannot help building temples. His seminar building at Vitra in Weil-am-Rhein could be a chapel; his Japanese Pavilion at Expo 92 in Seville was a great timber temple - unlike any of his other work. The qualities are consistent, but the architectural expression of those qualities varies greatly according both to client and context.

In the Christian Protestant area, those churches that most successfully carry forward a tradition are to be found in Scandinavia, where the work of Gunnar Asplund, Sigurd Lewerentz, Alvar Aalto and others is a constant source of reference for today's architects, who appear gratifyingly not to be overawed by their illustrious predecessors. Lutheran churches are paid for out of taxes, which ensures a continued building programme, which is mostly decided by competition. The Danish practice Fogh

Ando's contemplative approach succeeds across sects and denominations:
a Tadao Ando, Church of the Light, Ibaraki, Osaka, Japan, 1987-9
b Tadao Ando, Church on the Water, Yufutsu-gun, Hokkaido, Japan, 1985-8
c Tadao Ando, Chapel on Mt Rokko, Nada, Kobe, Hyogo, Japan, 1985-6: plan
d Tadao Ando, Water Temple, Tsuna-gun, Hyogo, Japan, 1989-91: interior of temple
e Water Temple: aerial view

a   b c
            d
            e

and Følner and the Finnish architects Gullichsen, Kairamo & Vormala and Juha Leiviskä are notable: Fogh and Følner for Egedal Church, Kokkedal, Denmark, 1990; Gullichsen, Kairamo & Vormala for their Church at Kauniainen, 1983; and Leiviskä for his Church and Parish Centre at Kuopio, Finland, 1986–92, which has become justly celebrated. Its planar architecture allows a distinctly northern use of natural light – a church of this form would simply not work in southerly climes. The vertical layering of brick and glass, culminating in the bell tower, gives emphasis to the sequence of broken forms – the church at its head, diminishing to a tail of ancillary buildings, the worship area angled 15 degrees from the axial spine of the complex, so generating drama. It is a suburban church, but it somehow summarises both the long tradition of Scandinavian rural churches and the twentieth-century Scandinavian tradition of humane modernism. It is also recognizably a church rather than an exercise in ostentation; the mature work of an architect well versed in the genre. It is the handling of light that makes the difference: Leiviskä's Kuopio church is as much an instrument of light as the best concert halls are instruments of sound.

And finally death, which brings Roman Catholicism to the foreground. Other religions may do more to celebrate, grieve over, or venerate the dead at the moment of the funeral rite: some may produce fine funerary monuments, and in the nineteenth century the High Anglican tendency in England became architecturally obsessed with the trappings of death; but only the Roman Catholic Church can make of death an entire architectural discipline. Tombs, monuments, ossuaries, landscape: 'necropolis' is merely Greek for 'city of the dead', and therefore requires urbanistic and architectural skills comparable to a living city. When death, and the remembrance of the dead, is not a taboo subject, then the architecture of death is not morbid, but both pragmatic and poetic. Hence the existence of such places as Aldo Rossi's San Cataldo Cemetery in Modena, Italy, 1971–81. Rossi had an admirable black humour about the commission – a competition win. The cemetery appears to include an apartment block – a brick cube with punched windows. But the windows are unglazed, and the wind whistles through as if through a skeletal ribcage; the galleried centre is open to the sky. This is the bone-house, the above-ground equivalent of the catacombs of ancient times. It is, Rossi observed, a place for zombies. There is a conical chapel, and regimented rows of ancillary accommodation. Of the whole composition, he said: 'I refer to it as the great cemetery, but in actual fact all cemeteries are great because they are the place of death.' Those interested in architectural 'isms' may note that Rossi was a neo-rationalist, which means anti-modernist or more specifically anti-technologist. The Modena Cemetery is regarded as the finest built example of what was in essence a 1960s academic movement. But the occurrence of architecture in the landscapes of the dead is natural enough, particularly when it is expressed as family vaults and chapels. Examples recur the world over, though one will suffice here: Richard England's chapel at the Addolorata Cemetery in Malta, 1987. With its deceptively simple, angled geometric shapes, this is a building of small size but large scale, visible and clearly definable from quite a distance. 'In order to know a place, one must know its memories,' he said. In Malta's case, the memories are of more cultures and religions than almost any other nation on earth.

Only a Mediterranean Roman Catholic nation would put up tourist signs to a recent tomb. But those driving near Treviso in Italy will find just such signs guiding them to Carlo Scarpa's masterwork, the Brion Cemetery at San Vito d'Altivole, 1969–78. The Brion cemetery (a large family plot wrapped round an existing village cemetery, including Scarpa's own tomb) is so famous as to need little description. Indeed it is so famous that it is, in a strange way, regarded not as a place of death but of life, a much-visited piece of landscape architecture. Part of its genius, perhaps, lies in the fact that this is architecture designed to be at one with

a b

c

d e

a   Aldo Rossi, San Cataldo
    Cemetery, Modena, Italy,
    1971–81: 'the great house of
    the dead'
b   Gullichsen, Kairamo &
    Vormala, Church at
    Kauniainen, Finland, 1983
c   Richard England, Chapel,
    Addolorata Cemetery,
    Malta, 1987

d   Fogh + Følner, Egedal Church,
    Kokkedal, Denmark, 1990
e   Juha Leiviskä, Männistö
    Church and Parish Centre,
    Kuopio, Finland, 1986–92

the landscape to an extent that its eventual ruin is designed in: the erosion and fragmentation of the sculptural concrete built forms and its partial inundation with water, inherent from the first, will be – if it is allowed to take its course – entirely appropriate. The forms are also non-religious in their imagery, which is abstract, though the way the matching tombs of the Brions, man and wife, lean together under their sheltering arch is clear enough. The whole arrangement with its sequence of spaces is a representation of the passage to the next life. In the twentieth century, perhaps only Edwin Lutyens achieved such an emotive, non-denominational, architecture of death – in Lutyens' case the Cenotaph ('empty tomb') in London's Whitehall, 1919–20, and the Memorial to the Missing of the Somme at Thiepval in France, 1932. Nothing could possibly be the same after the madness of the Great War, least of all the certainties embodied by the established Church. It was a reaction against organized religion that led to the downplaying of Christian imagery in many of the war memorials of the time. Lutyens' Memorial to the Missing of the Somme is pure architecture – arch piled on arch – on a grand scale, the open halls of the building lined with the names of those whose bodies were never recovered. Like Rossi's ossuary, it is a building left open for the elements and ghosts to move around. The bones may not be there – they

could not be – but the names, with all their cumulative resonance, are. Just as powerful, in the modern context, is Takefumi Aida's 1988 Tokyo War Memorial Park, which suggests ruin and desolation but also the hope of redemption and reconstruction.

Of similar power to the coupled tomb of the Brions is the primitivist pairing of tombs at the Open City in Ritoque, Chile. The graves are of one child who died by fire, and another who drowned. The first is a broken brick dome spiralling into the ground, the second a broken brick dome spiralling into the sky. The nearby Cenotaph at the Open City (they use Lutyens' term) is a room cut into the earth, and roofed by the sky, in spirit if not in form like a Mycenaean tholos. Related thinking, though expressed in more finished architectural terms, is to be found at the Igualada Cemetery, Barcelona, 1985–97, by Enric Miralles and Carme Pinós. This project – similar to Rossi's at Modena – reclaimed a dried-up, once industrial valley as a landscape of the dead, conveying the idea of a procession into the earth. The buildings that house Rossi's 'zombies' are here ship-like and stately, both of and separate from the earth. There is a notion of descent and ascent, death and rebirth, in materials as well as form: living trees are contrasted with a ground treatment of random timber railway sleepers, trampled underfoot like bodies after the massacres of the Somme.

a	d
b	f
c	e

Cemeteries expressed as points of departure:

a Carlo Scarpa, Brion Cemetery, Treviso, Italy, 1969–78: two tombs lean towards each other

b Brion Cemetery: detail of tombs showing water channel in landscaped garden

c Brion Cemetery: screen of intersecting circles

d Enric Miralles and Carme Pinós, Igualada Cemetery and Chapel, Igualada, Barcelona, 1985–97: plan

e Igualada Cemetery: view of cemetery buildings and landscaped walkways

f Igualada Cemetery: concrete wall with niches

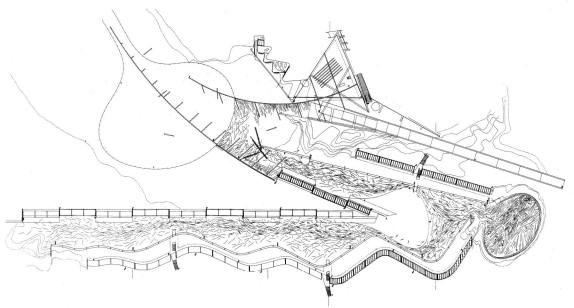

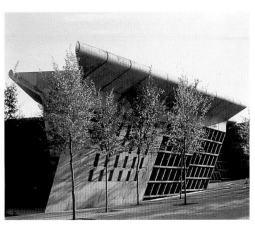

CONSUMERISM *Malls, shops & bars* Retail design embraces building types as diverse as the one-off bar or restaurant, the 'statement' fashion store, covered inner-city arcades and the giant themed edge-of-town shopping mall – both the smallest and largest elements of the urban environment. Crucial to the advance of consumerist architecture are the relationships of interiors to frontages, and of the shopfront to the streetscape in the crowded heart of existing cities. A new retail mall must contribute to the diverse and convivial life of the urban centre, rather than draining it dry.

'The merchant has always been and will always be most successful where his activity is integrated with the widest possible palette of human experiences and urban expressions.'
Victor Gruen, 1973.

There are shops, and there is retail. A 'shop' –
a term which includes bars and restaurants – can be the most designed object on earth, subject to the attentions of the best and most fashionable architects, and has a glorious, brief, life. One thinks of Los Angeles watering holes such as the 1986 Kate Mantilini Restaurant in Beverly Hills by Morphosis, or RoTo's Nicola Restaurant of 1992-5, or of Branson Coates' series of Tokyo bars in the 1980s, or of any hotel restaurant by the designer Philippe Starck. Retail, in contrast, is a huge and multi-headed organism. Retail means zoning. Retail means high-streets, malls, edge-of-town superstores, great big metal sheds, enormous car parks. Retail has a relatively long, and usually inglorious, life. One thinks of the West Edmonton Mall in Canada, or the Mall of America in Minnesota, both involving Maurice Sunderland architects – themed private kingdoms. The world of big retail is a world where architects with famous names seldom venture. Small wonder: it is a highly specialized discipline which, like hospital design, a relatively few practitioners guard jealously,

working closely with an equally tightly drawn circle of financiers and developers. Retail developments scarcely ever show up in architectural awards schemes, nor, usually, do their originators want them to.

A perusal of the standard art-historical accounts of twentieth-century architecture reveal that retail gets short shrift if it is mentioned at all. It is as if it does not exist, yet by any standards the shopping mall, to take one manifestation of the genre, has since the Second World War had a greater impact than almost any other building form, both on the way people conduct their lives and on the appearance and usage patterns of towns and cities. For example: if a modern mall is carved out of a town with an inherited medieval street pattern, then the maximum force for physical change is dictated not so much by swarms of people and their cars, nor even by the very large areas needed for the big stores, important though these are – but by the turning circle of the maximum permitted length of delivery truck, which is enormous. Towns have to be broken up to accommodate this dimensional need.

Why the curious silence about retail developments, save for those rare nineteenth-century examples that fall within the art-historical ambit because of their use of advanced materials – the Galleria in Milan, say, or the great Parisian department stores of

the *belle époque*? Robert Venturi has noted the 'mental-aesthetic blackout and photographic cropping' used by architectural historians to focus in on the things they want to see, to the exclusion of the rest of the built environment. Venturi notes the way Japanese temples and shrines are described as discrete objects when they are sited – especially in the case of Kyoto – in teeming and highly commercial urban surroundings. This, of course, exemplifies Venturi's 'complexity and contradiction' theory. In general American architects and some critics are more comfortable with commercialism than their European counterparts – and Venturi's and Denise Scott Brown's 1972 homage to the Las Vegas commercial strip, *Learning from Las Vegas*, is rightly celebrated. But when Venturi and Scott Brown returned to the Strip in 1994, they found that it had changed. The original Strip, rising from the desert, had been urban sprawl 'at its most pure'. By the mid-1990s, the Strip had been built up and renamed Las Vegas Boulevard. '[It] has become in some ways the equivalent of the shopping mall that accommodates the pedestrian in safe and explicitly artificial environments,' Venturi noted. He was making no overt value judgements – his commentary suggests that he saw this as merely part of the evolution of cities over time in all kinds of ways. Vegas had changed from pop culture to gentrification, from pop taste to 'good'

a   c
          d

b

Impermanence offers the
radical an outlet:
a Branson Coates, Caffè Bongo,
   Tokyo, 1986
b Branson Coates, Bohemia
   Jazz Club, Tokyo, 1986
c RoTo Architects,
   Nicola Restaurant,
   Los Angeles, 1992-5
d Nicola Restaurant:
   interior view

a c   f g

b d   h

e

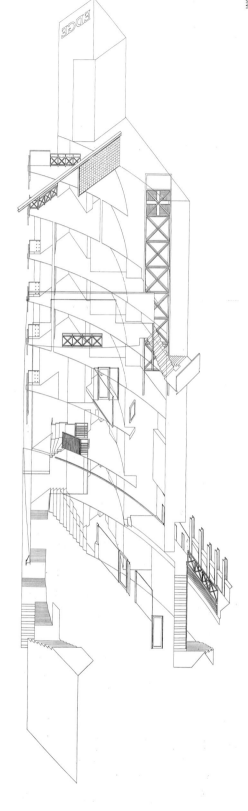

taste, from electric to electronic and, most tellingly, from 'folk art, vivid, vulgar, and vital, to unconvincing irony'. Strips become malls, malls become edge-cities. All of which suggests that shopping mall designers are the first architectural–planning troops sent in by the authorities in an attempt to impose order on retail chaos – hence the love of crude theming as exemplified by Jerde Partnership International's 1985 Horton Plaza in San Diego, which attempted to revitalize a wrecked area in Hispanic post-modern style. It can be compared with such related developments as William Lim's Central Square in Kuala Lumpur, 1990, where the seemingly random placing of primary-coloured PoMo motifs serves to cloak a breaking-down of the bulk of the development into smaller forms that are derived from the shop-houses of the neighbourhood. Lim also designed Singapore's Golden Mile shopping centre of 1974: the trouble is that the 'regionalism' of such architects tends to be overlaid by the perception of theming that is now endemic to most such complexes, which in turn leads to the impression that they could be anywhere in the world. To my knowledge Lim has not yet designed shopping malls in the United States; however Jerde has come to the Far East in a big way with its Canal City Hakata in Fukuoka, 1996. Thankfully, the theme there is not an American's take on Orientalism: instead it is all to do with geology and the elements

– an excuse for layered, striated and highly coloured building forms. It may be more crudely made but intellectually this is possibly no more false than, say, Branson Coates' tongue-in-cheek historicism of 'The Wall' of 1990 (the matter of theming versus narrative architecture is considered in 'Leisure'). In contrast, consider the very tough and rigorous retail development (bars, shops and offices) known as the 'Azabu Edge' in Tokyo by Ryoji Suzuki, 1987. This explores the notion of a city's edge condition rather more fruitfully, and incorporates thoughts on archaeology and stratification just as much as Coates or Jerde, if utterly differently. At the time of construction, this roughhewn, brutalist building overlooked a wasteland. Now it is part of a wall of buildings along a new road, but embodies the memory of that frontier moment. And this is the essence of shopping buildings on the city fringes. Roughly brought to heel by horny-handed, dusty-booted retail architects and developers (whose work is seldom published), the tamed Strip is then ripe for the attentions of aesthetically minded urbanists and signature architects (whose work is always published). It is unusual to find an architect such as Suzuki who combines the two roles of retail pioneer and darling of the magazines.

Tadao Ando's 'Collezione' building of 1986–9 in Tokyo is a different animal entirely, being a fashion building for fashion retailers on a very fashionable

Malls and theme parks enjoy a symbiotic relationship:

a William Lim Associates, Central Square, Kuala Lumpur, Malaysia, 1990, in collaboration with Chen Voon Fee: randomly placed coloured PoMo blocks
b Jerde Partnership International, Horton Plaza, San Diego, 1985
c Central Square: outdoor café on terrace
d Jerde Partnership International, Canal City Hakata, Fukuoka, Japan, 1996
e Design Partnership (William Lim, Koh Seow Chuan and Tay Kheng Soon), Golden Mile Complex, Singapore, 1974
f Branson Coates, 'The Wall', Tokyo, 1990
g Ryoji Suzuki, 'Azabu Edge', Tokyo, 1987: exterior view
h Azabu Edge: exploded axonometric

street. Car parking, a pool and gymnasium occupy the basement levels, followed by shops on ground and first floors, showrooms and gallery on the second, and the owner's flat on top. The whole is an especially good Andoan exercise in intersecting geometries – here the circle and the square – and the play of light against concrete, rising from the cool depths to the brightness of the sky. In contrast to Ando's very exclusive and concentrated building, Fumihiko Maki's nearby 'Spiral' of 1985 attempts a broader mixed-use agenda in a more outgoing way. Maki combines retail elements (design shop, bar, café and restaurant) with an art gallery and a multi-use auditorium for theatre and music. From the street it is a series of stepped, fragmented forms, a reflection of the urban chaos of the surrounding city; inside, the elements are pulled together by the visually floating spiral ramp that gives the building its name: a modest exercise in Japanese vertical city-making.

The American model – the model of a nation with lots of cheap land for continuing sprawl and transformation – strikes few chords in crowded, expensive Japan, and scarcely more in crowded, tightly regulated Europe, but seems just the business for the emerging economies of the Far East where, as we are constantly being reminded, large cities mushroom virtually overnight to create vast megalopolises by the weekend – halted only by the occasional economic

crisis. What took Europe two centuries, and Las Vegas thirty years, is telescoped into – maybe – a decade in some parts of the Pacific Rim. Or so we are told, but such an attitude is questionable. Manchester, England, for instance, achieved a rate of growth during parts of the nineteenth century that would impress even the Koreans, growth that was fuelled by the same precipitate flight from poor countryside to wealthy city. Then as now, the rapid growth of the city was arrested at intervals by recession as it over-reached itself, as Korea and its neighbours did at the end of the twentieth century; but it always dusted itself down and carried on. The old industrial centres have just had longer than the Pacific Rim nations to get over first industrialization, and then post-industrialization. But always, the retail mall is an intrinsic part of the process of transformation. The nineteenth-century cities spawned their iron and glass arcades. A century or so later, the cleared heavy industrial sites – so handy for low-cost, low-rise development and hectares of car parking – were first colonized by retail malls. 'Architecture' in the normally accepted sense, was largely absent. But then, it was not the famous architects of the nineteenth century who built the arcades.

The modern shopping centre has a hero, Victor Gruen, and a pivotal date: 1948. While in Holland and Britain – more specifically, in Rotterdam

and Coventry – planners and architects were devising ways to separate vehicles and pedestrians in the new precincts arising from the ashes of war, Gruen – a Viennese refugee architect born Viktor Grünbaum in 1903, who had studied under Peter Behrens in the 1920s before fleeing the Nazi Anschluss in 1938 – found himself grounded in Detroit by bad weather in 1948. He went to see one of the sights of the city, the great J L Hudson department store. 'Hudson's is for Detroit what the Eiffel Tower is for Paris,' Gruen later noted. He found that the store's directors, in particular one Oscar Webber, were undecided over the future of Detroit's suburban Strip. On the one hand, there were customers out there. On the other, to open a store in that tacky hinterland would degrade the proud name of Hudson. Over subsequent meetings, Gruen and Webber sketched out the modern shopping centre as a solution. Gruen's first stab, 1948-50, was, he later admitted, comical: he envisaged the large 'magnet store' – Hudson's – as one of a necklace of smaller stores on a roughly oval plan, with car parking both in the middle of the resultant egg shape and outside it. Luckily, the Korean War with its materials shortages intervened to provide valuable thinking time. Gruen's next attempt became Detroit's Northland Center, 1949-54. Northland put the magnet store at its centre, grouped tenant buildings around it in a logical,

Shops become a chic
urban rendezvous:
a Tadao Ando, Collezione,
   Minato, Tokyo, 1986-9
b Fumihiko Maki, Spiral
   Building, Tokyo, 1985

linked fashion, with landscaped, pedestrianized garden courts and an impressive programme of public art. Parking was on the outside, and an underground service road kept the stores supplied invisibly. No insurance company would fund the Center, on the grounds that it was too big, so Webber built it out of the firm's capital. Analysts predicted a $50 million turnover after five years: it did $100 million of business in its first year.

Northland was still – for all its external colonnades and linking covered ways – open to the skies outside each store, as was Gruen's equally celebrated Fort Worth Center in Texas, 1955. With his next project, however, Gruen established the canonic form of the enclosed, multi-level shopping centre. The Southdale Center in Minneapolis, 1953-6, responded to a continental climate where temperatures swing from minus 30 degrees Celsius in winter to plus 42 degrees Celsius in summer. Gruen was inspired by nineteenth-century arcades as he drew, roofing over an internal mall, pierced with glazing for natural light, providing a stable microclimate. It was a supreme marketing coup. Southdale also brought the shops together around an atrium in a single building – another first, as was the addition of entertainments such as a children's zoo. Two magnet department stores – the local rivals, Daytons and Allied – were placed either end of the mall, with smaller shops in

between, so originating the classic dumbbell plan of most such centres since. To save money on the roof, the footprint of the Center was reduced by building upwards – two levels above ground, plus a half-basement. Harry Bertoia created the big abstract sculptures. A new building type had arrived.

Gruen himself quickly realized that his edge-of-town invention was a Frankenstein's monster (though he never used that term). Like Venturi years later, he understood that shopping malls were merely the first step towards town-making. Thinking first of 'shopping towns' in contrast to lesser centres he scornfully dubbed 'machines for selling', he then conceived the idea of the 'multifunctional centre' where the car would be largely unnecessary as everything – living, working, recreation – would be in close proximity. He became a government advisor and a theorist on the subject. Gruen was neither an intuitive academic nor an art-architect (at best his architecture was competent International Style) but a brilliant planner. His 1973 book *Urban Environment - Survival of the Cities* may have had none of the architectural impact of Venturi's Las Vegas bombshell of the year before, but it anticipated the idea of the sustainable, compact modern city as endlessly discussed in the 1990s.

The twin cities of Minneapolis–St Paul, however, did not become that sustainable city. They saw instead only more and more shopping centres and

cars. By 1992, when the extraordinarily ambitious Ghermezian family of developers (the Triple Five Corporation) opened their 'Mall of America' – the biggest in the United States – in the city, there were already nine other competing centres including Gruen's pioneer. The Mall of America added 4.2 million square feet of space, four magnet stores, 350 other shops arranged along four themed malls, a central seven-acre leisure park ('Camp Snoopy') with a half-mile roller-coaster and flume ride, scores of restaurants, forty-four escalators and 12,750 parking spaces, arranged in huge buildings either end of the rectangular complex. Were it not for a financial recession, it would have been larger at opening. The main architect for the West Edmonton Mall, Maurice Sunderland Architects of Calgary, also planned the Mall of America, but the work was later handed over to the Jerde Partnership of Venice, California.

Such mall design is conventionally regarded as building rather than architecture, and to a certain extent this is true. The Mall of America has a very coherent plan – a perimeter rectangle, with the magnet stores pushed out diagonally at each corner, and the covered leisure park filling in the middle. Weirdly enough, this hollow *parti* is reminiscent of Gruen's first, abandoned, 'egg' design for a Detroit shopping centre in the 1940s – but the centre has been given a recreational purpose, which itself is

a

a Victor Gruen, Eastland
   Shopping Center, Harper
   Woods, Missouri, 1958: after
   the success of his Southdale
   Center, Gruen, the grandfather
   of enclosed edge-of-town malls
   went on to design many more
   retail centres

b (pages 177–8) Maurice
   Sunderland Architects with
   Jerde Partnership
   International, Mall of America,
   Bloomington, Minnesota,
   1986–7: retail gigantism
   at its most extreme

Gruen's idea of a leisure zone writ large. Such a deep-plan, low complex offers the architect little in terms of facade treatment, but even that little is not exploited. It is the tragedy of shopping centres that individual stores always want their own architects. Thus each of the four prominent corners of the complex has a different skin treatment: Sears is PoMo, Macy's classical, Bloomingdales corporate white marble, Nordstrom a bricky Tudorbethan. The flanks of the rest of the centre are mostly stripy brickwork. The best architecture there is engineering, as expressed in the glazed roof of the leisure centre and the railway-station roof design of the nineteenth-century themed West Avenue. But for High Architecture or even 'good' architecture, look elsewhere. This is true of all such centres, which is why some of the largest, and most intensively used buildings on earth have a mysterious critical invisibility. Can we learn from such places? Venturi asked himself that question on revisiting Vegas, but elected not to answer it. The journey from Rome to the Las Vegas Strip, he implied but did not state, was rather more fruitful than the journey from Strip to Boulevard.

If, then, we regard the shopping mall as a piece of Ur-city – one step up from the fascinating protozoan slime of the Strip, a primitive life form which might one day evolve into something sophisticated – what of its variants? It is routinely accepted, for instance, that the huge out-of-town shopping malls can suck the life-blood out of traditional city centres. By the early 1980s, Europe's planning gurus were warning about the dangers of what was then virtually an exclusively North American phenomenon known as the 'doughnut effect'. If everything – shopping, office parks, middle-class homes – moves to the suburbs, then, so the wisdom went, the centre cannot hold together. It collapses, into dereliction, vandalism and crime.

From Edmonton in central Canada

(sucked dry by the mighty West Edmonton Mall) to Gateshead in northern England (sucked just as dry by the virtually unheralded arrival of Europe's biggest shopping mall, The Metro Centre, in the mid-1980s) the doughnut effect seems real enough in terms of ghostly town centres, even if the predicted crime wave does not necessarily occur. There are strategic consequences to such places. While the old centre of Gateshead became eerily empty, with 1960s multi-story car parks demolished through lack of use, it was a different picture on the town's bypass – which happens to be the A1 London–Edinburgh trunk road. This became snarled up with queues of traffic heading for the Metro Centre. Permanent road signs were erected to warn of possible delays.

The edge-of-town problem is, however, only one, albeit daunting, aspect of retail design today.

There are broadly seven main types of shopping centre, each with many variations. First is the open mall, which is a purpose-built version of a traditional shopping street, but usually with vehicles and pedestrians segregated. Second is the 'black box' enclosed mall, where the idea is not only to provide cover from the weather but to concentrate attention on the brightness of individual shop fronts and so encourage buying rather than strolling. Third is the daylit covered mall, which abandons that theory in favour of the attraction of the well-tempered environment, drawing on such historical precedents as nineteenth-century arcades, and in particular the lofty Galleria in Milan, and which can consist of several vertically stacked layers around atria. The fourth category contains the mega-malls such as Gateshead, Edmonton, and Minneapolis, which take the principles of the in-town daylit covered mall and reproduces them, usually at only one or two levels, on a vast scale, often on cleared fringe industrial sites and often with a large entertainment element as well as shops and restaurants. Fifthly, the 'speciality centre', which – usually in popular tourist areas – eschews big stores and multiples in favour of small, preferably one-off, units selling high-value goods, combining these with lots of cafés and restaurants. Sixth is the village-like, cheaply built 'factory shopping centre' or 'Designer Outlet village' where cut-price fashion brands are hawked. And

finally, there is what might be called 'intersection city', a phenomenon that springs up on key road junctions and consists usually of discrete large-scale sheds separated by acres of car parks, and which typically includes furniture and toy stores, discount food stores, fast-food outlets, a multiplex cinema, a hotel, some distribution warehouses, perhaps even some light industry. Intersection City can take wide variations. One such is the American–Australian invention of the 'megaplex' – multi-screen cinema and leisure complex, which invaded Europe as a mutation of the out-of-town shopping idea. What previously was shopping with cinema and leisure attached became cinema and leisure with shopping attached.

To these seven, you could add the big department stores, such as La Samaritaine or Printemps in Paris, Selfridges or Harrods in London, or Macy's, Bloomingdales, and Hudson's in the United States. Although department stores form the large-floorplate 'anchors' (also called 'magnets') of conventional shopping malls, some are large enough to be regarded virtually as shopping centres in their own right. It can be argued that a shopping centre is just a department store writ large; contrariwise there was a trend in the 1980s for ailing department stores to be converted into multi-tenanted shopping centres. However, the traditional big store survived: new ones were built such as Hans Hollein's Haas Haus in Vienna of 1985–90, and old ones extended successfully, as with the Stockmann department store extension in Helsinki by Gullichsen, Kairamo and Vormala, 1989.

The first six of the main shopping centre categories outlined above can be seen as logical developments of conventional *ad hoc* streets with individualized shop fronts, of the kind that first emerged in the eighteenth century. Malls are, after all, just arrangements of streets with shops on them. However, the seventh category, Intersection City, comes from a different lineage. It accommodates almost all the different manifestations of commerce combining elements of the industrial estate, the business park, the retail park and the transport-related distribution centre, familiar to us from the canal and railway eras. All Intersection City lacks is housing, or it would be more akin to a tarmacked garden suburb. But in its simplest form it is not a city at all, merely a superstore like Carrefour (meaning 'crossroads') or

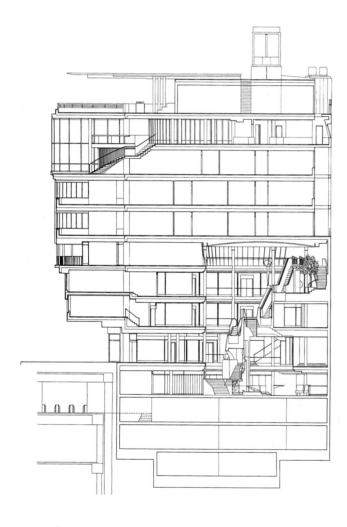

a b
c

e
d f
g

Mammouth in France. The first name tells you where to expect to find them – an idea borrowed by one of Britain's biggest Intersection Cities, Cross Point outside Coventry. The second name tells you how big they are. In Europe, the French undoubtedly pioneered Intersection City – they have been active in the retail sheds sector since the 1960s and a key example of the genre is the 200-shop Cité Europe, 1995, at Coquelles near the French terminal of the Channel Tunnel. This was designed by Paul Andreu of the Aéroports de Paris practice (the link with transport buildings is significant) together with Pierre Michel Delpeuch and François Tamisier.

The seven categories break down in other ways. When, for instance, does a 'speciality centre' such as Ghirardelli Square of 1964 in San Francisco (Wurser, Bernadi & Emmons, with Lawrence Halprin & Associates) become a 'festival marketplace' such as Boston's 1976 Faneuil Hall (Benjamin Thompson + James Rouse), for instance? The answer is that 'festival marketplace' is more of a brand name, coined by the American developer James Rouse to describe the developments – usually involving the conversion of old buildings – at which he and Thompson became adept. Then, at what point does a straightforward megamall transform into a 'theme centre', like West Edmonton Mall, which features more submarines than the Canadian Navy? There are elements of theming in all of them, particularly in the food courts. Whatever the jargon of the day, all types of shopping centre have a habit of learning from, and merging with, other types.

The new urban store versus the transport-node strip:
a Hans Hollein, Haas Haus, Vienna, 1985–90: cross section
b Haas Haus: the atrium has an Art-Deco quality
c Haas Haus: the building wraps around the street corner
d Architecten Bureau van den Broek en Bakema (M D Booy & O M van Strijp), Renovation of the Lijnbaan Centre, Rotterdam, 1996–7
e Benjamin Thompson + James Rouse, Faneuil Hall, Boston, 1976
f Wurser, Bernadi & Emmons, Ghirardelli Square, San Francisco, 1964 (with Lawrence Halprin & Associates): the original 'speciality centre'
g Aéroports de Paris (Paul Andreu, Pierre Michel Delpeuch, François Tamisier), Cité Europe, Calais, France, 1995

Rotterdam's Lijnbaan Centre, first conceived by the city planner Cornelis van Traa and designed by Johannes van den Broek and Jacob Bakema in the mid-1940s (and recently renovated in the 1990s by the same architects), might claim to be the first modern open shopping centre, as it removes vehicles from sight, giving the mall over wholly to pedestrians. However, similar thinking was occurring in the bombed cities and new towns of Britain at the time, most notably Coventry and Harlow. In Europe, the segregated centre was seen as an in-town thing. Gruen, as we have seen, designed his for the edge of town, catering for a car-owning population: Conversely, then, Gruen is, therefore, the begetter of the 'doughnut effect'. But all of these were in turn undoubtedly influenced by the segregatory principles of 'Radburn planning', dating from the 1920s and which, involving Lewis Mumford and first being put into effect in Radburn, New Jersey, in 1929, could be said to be an all-American trend.

For a while, 'dark' malls – selling
machines – became the norm, but the rules soon changed. In 1970 the Houston Galleria by Hellmuth, Obata + Kassabaum (HOK) had revived the old notion of the glazed arcade, and put an ice rink in the mall – a feature that was later to become a shopping centre cliché – and a running track around the roof. Gallerias became, and remained, the thing,

with Toronto's Eaton Centre by Bregman and Hamann with Craig Zeidler Strong, 1977–80, eventually becoming a place of pilgrimage for a generation of notebook-filling European retail architects. Even the rigorous 'real' architects of the new UK city of Milton Keynes, obsessed with their 1970s concept of a linear mall marching on for ever (at 650 metres it is still the world's longest) were prepared to let in daylight through clerestory glazing. Just about every mall everywhere then had to be daylit, even underground oddities such as Pei, Cobb Freed & Partners' Carrousel du Louvre in Paris, lit by an upside-down pyramid on axis with the more famous one in the Louvre courtyard, its glazed upturned base incorporated into a traffic roundabout. Older 'dark' centres are now routinely opened up in order to compete with their newer rivals while the first-generation open malls from the 1950s and 1960s are equally routinely retrofitted with glazed canopies.

Although invented in the 1960s, the 1970s saw the speciality centre take off as a way to bring life and tourists back into abandoned buildings: first in San Francisco, then Boston, then London, and then select locations worldwide. The big idea of the speciality centre was to abolish the sacrosanct anchor store by making a combination of food outlets the effective crowd-pulling anchor. A speciality centre may also decide not to provide car parking,

though this can be risky unless it is right at the tourist heart of things.

The West Edmonton Mall is on a 121-acre site and includes more than 800 outlets, of which eleven are big department stores. Not enough different store chains exist in European countries to fill an equivalent of all the space that Edmonton provides. In comparison, a speciality centre is minute: for instance Sydney's Harbourside Festival Markets by Architecture Oceania and RTKL Associates is just 15,000 square metres, and that in turn is three times the size either of San Francisco's Ghirardelli Square or of Covent Garden Market in London. Arguably the sunken Forum des Halles in Paris, by Vasconi & Pencreac'h, 1979, is a speciality centre: that manages a relatively large 40,000 square metres. But its size was dictated largely by its site – the huge hole in the ground left by the excavations of the Les Halles quarter, which became a touchstone for architectural debate in France in the 1970s (see 'The Civic Realm').

From a North American standpoint, European cities have survived remarkably intact precisely because of what are perceived as rigid zoning and green belt laws restricting the spread of out-of-town malls, despite the threat of the Metro Centre. The downside of this is that retail competition is reduced: prices in European shops can be twice as high as their equivalents in the United States.

a b c |
     d   e
          f

a Architecture Oceania and RTKL Associates, Harbourside Festival Markets, Sydney, 1988
b Vasconi & Pencreac'h, Forum des Halles, Paris, 1979: going underground in the city
c Lambert Scott and Innes, Castle Mall, Norwich, England, 1993
d Hellmuth, Obata + Kassabaum (HOK), Houston Galleria, Houston, Texas, 1965–70, 1986: the Houston Galleria and Eaton Centre spawned a host of imitators
e Bregman & Hamann with Craig Zeidler Strong, Eaton Centre, Toronto, 1977–80: the exterior is a nondescript office tower
f Eaton Centre: the galleria is a place of pilgrimage for retail architects

	c e
a b	d f

a GHM Rock Townsend, 'Hello' store, Co-op Shopping, Cardiff, 1995: restaurant interior

b 'Hello' store: entrance canopy

c SITE, Best Stores, Inside Outside Showroom, Milwaukee, Illinois, 1984: the wall breaks away to reveal a 'ghost' shop

d SITE, Best Stores, 'Notch' Showroom, Sacramento, California, 1977: the store seems to have inhabited the remnants of a larger crumbling building

e SITE, Best Stores, Indeterminate Facade, Houston, Texas, 1975: the corner is undermined alarmingly

f SITE, Best Stores, Tilt Showroom, Towson, Maryland, 1978: the whole facade is lifted and tilted, as if by a giant hand

'Planners and preservationists conspire against a population that would prefer greater convenience and lower prices' as the *Wall Street Journal* succinctly put it in 1995, apropos the English city of Norwich. Norwich was hailed by many as a beacon of hope, its Castle Mall shopping centre ingeniously inserted right into the centre of the urban doughnut. This top-lit but largely underground multi-level centre is the dirigiste planner's answer to the West Edmonton Mall and its brethren. Castle Mall's architects, the previously local practice of Lambert Scott and Innes, soon found themselves advising the City of Moscow on the tricky problem of threading big commercial malls into historic areas. But such successes bring their own problems: the centre may be alive, but thousands of cars then come right into the centre instead of staying out on the edges. Despite the best attempts at creating public transport alternatives, it is almost impossibly difficult to separate shoppers from their cars. If you do so forcibly, then trade suffers, and that will never do.

The family of shopping centre types constantly expands. Stand-alone food superstores become virtual department stores, mini-malls flanking the open food floors of many a new supermarket, but this is only the start. The 'Hello' store on the rural fringe of Cardiff, Wales, designed by GHM Rock Townsend, is simply a food store and a non-food store, treated very differently architecturally, pushed together. At the point of collision, the forces generate a street of smaller shops running through the middle, with a restaurant on an upper level. The floor area of the food hall equates to a traditional market square, while the specialist units around the walls – wine shop, butcher, baker, delicatessen – correspond to the specialist shops you tend to find around the edges of squares in old market towns. What makes 'Hello' different from a French perimeter-road tin shed of equivalent floorspace is the addition of architecture of a relatively complex and, at certain points, expensive nature. This indicates perhaps that this particular architectural language is maturing, or maybe that profit margins in some countries are high enough to afford a level of architectural indulgence. Thus the famous 1970s examples of Best stores in the United States by SITE architects and Venturi, or Sainsbury's stores in Britain by an assortment of architects including Nicholas Grimshaw and Partners (Camden Town, London, 1985-8) and Dixon Jones (Plymouth, 1992-4).

The 'Factory Shopping' village evolved towards the end of the twentieth century. They developed from the cut-price shops where clothes factories supplying chain stores traditionally sold their rejects and over-stocks. Originally placed beside the factory compounds, they came to be grouped together – sometimes on cleared industrial sites, sometimes in semi-rural positions – in largely *ad hoc* fashion. Economic recession in the early 1990s hastened their development as their perceived cheapness became desirable. Rapidly they became alternative outlets for (mainly) well-known fashion labels – selling at wholesale prices. Leisure elements – rides, zoos, restaurants – were introduced to reinforce the family image. The buildings remained stylistically impoverished, if honest, until mainstream developers began to take an interest, and the size of such places began to interest planning controllers. By the late 1990s, signature architects had become involved, with even Richard Rogers designing a 210,000-square-foot factory outlet centre on an old industrial site in Ashford, southern England, next to a new international railway station. Ambitiously aimed at shoppers from France and Belgium as well as England, the Ashford centre – in another eerie reinterpretation of Gruen's original abandoned oval shopping-centre plan – was designed as a linked series of tensile-roofed pavilions arranged elliptically around an enclosed central space. Factory shopping outlets, like speciality centres, rely on many small units and a large element of catering to compensate for the lack of a department store 'magnet'. For this reason and to keep costs down, they develop as simple single-storey discrete units, clustered like an

African village. While supermarkets transformed themselves into department stores that also sell petrol as a loss-leader, traditional filling stations, in search of the profits they could no longer make from petrol alone, expanded to become niche supermarkets, thus plugging the gap at the bottom and contributing still further to the relentless rise of car-borne shopping. The presence of car parks at such filling stations, plus occasionally more adventurous architecture, indicated that people drove there specifically to shop, rather than, as previously, merely making small impulse purchases while waiting at the pumps.

There are two options for the traditional town centre in the face of such competition. One, already well-developed, is to become, in effect, an open added-value speciality centre (or 'festival destination'), leaving the high-volume, low value shopping to the edge-of-town boys. This, combined with up-market housing, is virtually the only option left for smaller towns. The other is the Norwich way, or on a larger scale the Indianapolis way, which is to thread mall routes through, by or under existing city streets and blocks, linking up at node points corresponding to the crossings of greenfield malls, and picking up on traditional pedestrian routes across town. The big malls have always been introverted, a linked sequence of mostly blank boxes that only come alive

inside. Using stealth techniques to ease them into the grain of existing cities can make a virtue out of what was previously a defect. Or so it is piously hoped. Surprisingly, the model of Milan's Galleria Vittorio Emanuele, 1861-7, by Giuseppe Mengoni, though routinely cited, is very seldom properly followed through. The Galleria, though comprising two streets in cruciform pattern, is here rendered public on a large scale, in the tradition of the city block with an inner courtyard. The block thus has street facades on both outside and inside, with the inside being treated architecturally as if it was an open street, in free Renaissance style, despite its wondrous glazed and domed roof. Thus inserted into a commercial block, with comparatively little impact on the world outside, and with retail as the ground level of a mixed-use sandwich, Mengoni's Galleria is a better model for modern malls even than its supporters – seduced by the marvellous roof and the grandeur of the public space – imagine. In the 1990s the only architect to rise successfully to the challenge set by Mengoni was Santiago Calatrava, who successfully introduced a galleria of original form into the massive commercial and retail block in Toronto, known as BCE Place, 1987-92. Calatrava's organic forms – conceived as a forest canopy – make a sense of place out of a street with some otherwise very bland facades indeed. The trick was not just to span the gap at the

top of the buildings – Calatrava does that with a fairly standard curve – but to create a narrower, almost gothic, vault within it, springing from bifurcating trunks or columns running the length of the mall and so serving to impose an architectural rhythm on the facades. It is five storeys – 27 metres – high. Calatrava's work is sometimes compared to that of Antoni Gaudí, and this comparison is nowhere more apparent than in the central square of this scheme with its nine intersecting barrel vaults rising from an arched brick substructure and the impressive device of two enormous angled wings of glass that can be tilted open. In a sense this is architecture as social Band-Aid – Calatrava's overlaid architecture partly conceals and serves to heal the dull overscaled corporatism of the buildings it strides between – but it is also a building in its own right, defining space and allowing retail activity such as restaurants and cafés to spill out into the 'open'. It is the Barcelona Ramblas for an extreme climate. Remarkably, it came about not as a conventional architectural competition for a part of this commercial development, but as an invited contest for public art that could serve to humanize the leftover spaces between the blocks.

Such virtuosity is, however, rare in retail schemes, and Calatrava's can be seen as much as an office atrium as an enclosed shopping street. Given that the plan of a shopping mall, while derived from

a	b	c
		d

Dealing with a perennial problem: the black hole of the mall roof. A light-reflecting superstructure helps:

a Building Design Partnership, Bentalls Centre, Kingston-on-Thames, England, 1985-92: detail of the coffered panels of the glazed vaulted roof

b Bentalls Centre: overlooking circulation and glass lifts in the mall

c Santiago Calatrava, Toronto Galleria, Toronto, 1987-92: detail of the roof structure

d Toronto Galleria: Calatrava's Gaudíesque vaults serve to mediate and conceal the corporatism of the buildings it links

a street, is also closely related to the plan of an atrium-based department store, why do malls so seldom achieve what is conventionally regarded as a high quality of architecture – something that plenty of stand-alone department stores have managed? The problem is seemingly intractable: studying the world's shopping centres is one of the most depressing things it is possible to do for anyone with an enthusiasm for architecture. Part of the problem is the introverted nature of the beast. It generally turns its back on all around it, concentrating its energies on the mall within. Its largest volumes – the biggest stores – usually require large windowless facades, in order to maximize display space inside and control the lighting. To compensate for the fortress-like appearance that results, the public entrances to the malls are generally glitzed up as far as possible so as to entice shoppers – though this is not deemed so necessary in edge-of-town examples where everyone is expected to arrive by motor vehicle and therefore presumed to want to go there anyway. Finally, almost any cohesive architectural theme is immediately overwhelmed by the stridency of the competing corporate identities and frontage variations of the shops within the mall. The architect can seldom win: in those malls (usually the small, specialist centres) where a shop-front design code is introduced and enforced, the result is usually anaemic and unduly repetitive. Yet the opposite of

design control – the genuinely anarchic free-for-all of the Venturian Strip – is emasculated by being compressed and contained within a space. The only escape left to mall architects is the grand gesture – usually an arresting feature in the mall such as trees or rides or fountains, and especially the gallery roof – as in BDP's Bentalls Centre in Kingston-on-Thames, just outside London, 1985–92. This is one of the better UK examples inside, rather than out. The perennial problem of the glazed vaulted roof becoming a black hole after dark is solved with a coffering device of perforated white metal dotted with fibre-optic lighting at the intersections, so providing solar shading during the day and a reflective surface for uplighting, highlighted by the optic points, at night. Such gestures are not easily achieved, since shopping malls are giant pieces of equipment incorporating smoke-venting in the event of fire. The roof is the conventional place for such equipment: to leave the roof clear, you either have to extrude the vault upwards to allow extraction ducts to plug in the sides above the main mass of the building (the prime example here is Richard Rogers' Lloyd's of London building) or, if resources do not allow that, you must arrange your smoke extraction through the backs of stores – the Bentall's model. In such circumstances, architecture becomes dependent upon the goodwill of those enforcing local fire regulations.

Architectural detailing in retail malls
is necessarily crude. The malls work at primary levels of detailing – all subtlety is lost in the competitive maelstrom – that usually do not bear close scrutiny. The task to find either a local identity or a widely applicable architectural language (the generic galleria barrel-vaulted roof) that can somehow both read urbanistically and pinion the squirming retail monster beneath is made more difficult by the fact that neither retailers nor financiers – the clients – care either way: all they want is profitable space for shops and cars.

So by the start of the twenty-first century, forty-five years after Gruen enclosed the Southdale Mall in Minneapolis, the archetypal urban example is the Sun Dong An Plaza in Beijing, China, by RTKL Associates of Los Angeles, 1992–6. This is international mall-land, with little regional touches. Just as Cesar Pelli placed vaguely pagoda-like tips on his Petronas Towers in Kuala Lumpur, just as hordes of Western architects make their window openings pointed when designing otherwise identikit hotels and office blocks in the Middle East, so the Sun Dong An Plaza sports slightly hipped 'oriental' roofs. Those aside, it could be anywhere in the world. It is a canonic example of the mall being used to impose order on previously existing chaos, for its site is the famous Dong An open-air food and clothing market,

established in 1903. This behemoth of a development, costed at US$300 million, was a touchstone of China's runaway economy in the late 1990s, signalling its desire for profitable Western-led developments at the expense of tradition. So importantly was it regarded that the contract to build it was signed in the Great Hall of the People in June 1992; approvals were granted in three months; work on site began in October 1993; and it was open for business by late 1996. It was an astonishingly rapid programme even by North American fast-track standards, and it created the single largest retail centre in Beijing. For all its hamfisted attempts at a regionalist style, it contrives to be on a dense city scale. It incorporates office blocks and – at its southern end – new facilities for the Ji Xing Theatre and Beijing Opera. It acknowledges the outside streets to the extent of having small outward-facing shops running round its flanks. It provides open space in the form of roof gardens. Not much more can be said – malls are malls, the world over – but it seems a model of constraint compared with other examples of the genre in the Pacific Rim, such as The Mines Shopping Fair in Selangor, Malaysia, by the Buchan Group of Brisbane, Australia, 1997. This themed mall – close to Kuala Lumpur and the new airport, and within striking distance of six rapidly expanding new townships – has boats on a canal moving through one

Mall theming taken to extremes:
a   Buchan Group, The Mines Shopping Fair, Selangor, Malaysia, 1997: campanile tower
b   The Mines Shopping Fair: traditional references are mixed with contemporary glitz to produce unadulterated kitsch
c   The Mines Shopping Fair: boats take shoppers along canals
d   RTKL Associates, Sun Dong An Plaza, Beijing, 1997

a	d
b	
c	

mall, and a hallucinogenic cyclorama playing on the dome of another, and everywhere debased motifs of the area, sanitized for tourists and locals alike. It is quite open about its kitschness. Arguably this is what shopping malls do best.

So what happens when an architect of noted aesthetic sensibilities is given a 100 per cent retail mall to create? First, you get an attempt mildly to subvert the conventional layouts of such places – Rogers prefers the curving layout, as seen not only in his 1990s factory outlet village, but also in his design for a huge semicircular mall in London's Royal Docks (part of his Royal Docks Strategic Plan, 1984–6) where the main spine mall is intersected by subsidiary radiating spines, chopping up the mass into variously sized units. Rogers made the Venturian

move from mall to city with ease: his 1991 master-plan for Berlin's Potsdamerplatz is remarkably similar to the *parti* of the Royal Docks centre, and on an even larger canvas he turned the semicircle into a circle to produce his Lu Jai Masterplan in Shanghai in 1992 (see 'Workplace'). This generative principle also recurs in the practice's business park projects. The fan-shaped, radiating grid of streets: for Rogers, it works at all scales and for all building typologies. It is a further confirmation of the ancestry of the retail mall as, simply, a covered street.

Aldo Rossi, when given a commission for a big edge-of-town supermarket set in the middle of the usual acres of car parking, had to deal with the equally usual problem of how to urbanize a blank box. Where other architects pour their energies into

the principle facade, making essentially one-dimensional buildings, Rossi chose instead to soar heavenwards, giving the eponymous Centro Torri, 1985–8, a cluster of tall square-plan brick towers, together advertising the name of the store. Far more numerous, and far bigger, than the heating and ventilation needs of the store demanded, the towers with their ceramic lettering were for Rossi – like those he saw on factories round about – an appropriate typology, given the equally introverted nature of a factory building. They also solved one of the perennial problems of such places, which is how to give a ground-hugging building type sufficient presence to command the empty spaces it is beached in. In Coventry, England, architects Lifschutz Davidson gave their brick-box Sainsbury's store, 1995, a

All malls need not look the same; some are more expressive than others:
a Aldo Rossi, Centro Torri, Parma, Italy, 1985–8: exterior
b Centro Torri: interior
c Jean Nouvel, Euralille (Triangle des Gares), France, 1991–6: exterior
d Euralille (Triangle des Gares): circulation space
e Jean Nouvel, Mediapark project, Cologne, Germany, 1991

strongly uptilted tensile fabric canopy, illuminated at night, to act as their signalling device.

Jean Nouvel tried the same thing in two ways with his retail mall at Euralille in France, 1991–6, originally called 'Triangle des Gares', and his 'Quartier 207' office and retail development for Galéries Lafayette and others in Berlin, 1991–6. These coincident projects gave Nouvel the chance to reflect on the nature of city-making. As he observed in a conference at the Pompidou Centre in 1992: *'In the face of economic pressure, political factors connected to unemployment and consumption, what's the good of talking about aesthetics, proportions, harmony and ways of life? Responses conditioned by finances or traffic flow undoubtedly have serious political underpinnings. They make the architecture*

of cities a game played by everyone, without anybody knowing the rules or the value of the cards.'

For all his talk of displacement and discontinuity forming one of the bases of his work, however, Nouvel as a good Parisian felt appropriate respect for that part of a city's character formed by advertising and consumption. His 1991 competition-winning Mediapark project in Cologne envisaged the use of electronically-projected signage and logos to animate the all-glass facades of the principle buildings: they would provide the ornament to otherwise ornament-free sleek-tech architecture. As with most such schemes (one thinks of the original competition-winning entry for the Pompidou Centre competition by Piano and Rogers), this building-as-sign-matrix idea is a recurring one that tends to get diluted in the

execution of 'real' architecture – but which happens entirely naturally in *ad hoc* fashion in the commercial and entertainment districts of most world cities, where existing buildings are smothered in a visual frenzy of neon signs. Even in brash Euralille – a vast commercial development masterplanned by Rem Koolhaas by and over the new TGV station at Lille in northern France – Nouvel had difficulty getting his commercial images to stick. His plan to enliven the tops of the marching line of office towers with wrap-round commercial signs was rejected in favour of art works. 'It would seem that nowadays in the city we orientate ourselves by works of art rather than publicity signs,' he remarked – an interesting inversion of the traditional view of urban degeneration, particularly given that Nouvel regarded such signs as a form

a   c   e

b   d

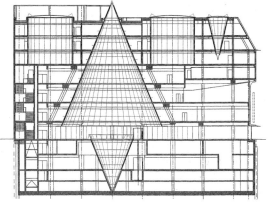

of art anyway. Nor was he eventually allowed to deck the carapace of the commercial centre beneath with advertising signs – his model was a Formula 1 racing car, festooned randomly with sponsors' logos. With the interior design of this very large mall given to others, it seemed that there was little for Nouvel and his collaborator Marc Pandavoine to do beyond provide the shell space with its runway-like malls. His transparent curtain-walling system to the flanks of the centre, however, work as intended, allowing advertising slogans and logos to hang down from the floor slabs behind near the entrance – giving way to light refracting foils and holograms along the Avenue Willy Brandt where Nouvel's stubby towers are sunk through the canopy like knives stuck in cheese. There, art rather than commerce has won out, as Nouvel had accurately predicted. The acres of oversailing roof above the centre, which allows filtered daylight to penetrate, is unrelated to the malls below and so will allow whatever internal changes are needed in the future. This is one of those developments that has a greater importance than at first appears, for one of the 'givens' of conventional mall design is that the galleria roof with its crossing-point domes forms a visible and fixed element of the roofscape: not so here. In general, the Euralille centre is fully in accordance with Koolhaas' notions of Bigness and congestion culture ('Above a

certain scale, it is no longer a matter of architecture, but that the building itself becomes a kind of urbanism,' as Koolhaas said of his adjacent Grand Palais conference centre and concert hall; see 'The Civic Realm'). Curiously enough, it is exactly this principle that has always guided the design of retail malls, consciously or unconsciously.

In Berlin, the task was rather different. Nouvel had a large urban block to work on where the principal tenant – Galéries Lafayette – provided a ready-made and historically significant model for the department store. The interior of Lafayette's 1900 store by Chanut is arguably the finest of the sequence of great stores built in Paris that began in 1876 (Bon Marché, by Boileu and Eiffel), continued through Magasins du Printemps, 1881-9, by Paul Sédille and, after the Galéries Lafayette, concluded with La Samaritaine, 1905, by Franz Jourdain. An evolution of the Parisian arcades or 'passages' of the early nineteenth century, the principal point of these buildings was their spacious atriums rising to dramatic glazed roofs. Of these and their brethren, Lewis Mumford had commented: 'If the vitality of an institution can be measured by its architecture, one can say that the department store was one of the most vital institutions of the epoch from 1880 to 1914.' Given such precedents, Nouvel had a lot riding on his Berlin design, particularly as it was in a prime loca-

tion on two major routes, Friedrichstrasse and Französische Strasse. He realized that the design 'had to create an event'. The way he did this was to make a smooth curtain-wall facade wrapping round the corner; to throw open the ground floor to the street; and, once inside, to create an atrium that plunged down as well as up. Up in a glazed cone to the roof – so making the store appear to rise to the sky, when in fact the cone pierces through the offices above; and down in a smaller cone to the levels of car parking. By playing with light projections on these angled and curved glazed surfaces, the effect becomes weirdly displacing. In the office levels, smaller inverted cones act as lightwells or atria. As completed, it is (as usual) not quite the giant electronic matrix that Nouvel at first envisaged, inside and out, with his idea of giant ever-changing pixelated signboards on the external facades dwindling to old-fashioned large banners. Of the unbuilt design, he said:
'This building stands mid-way between abstraction and figuration, between the atmospherics of natural light and the spectacle of artificial projection. It plays a scenographic game of seduction and desire, juxtaposing the visible and the hidden, the intelligible and the perceptible.'

But retail has a habit of asserting itself over the desires of architects. The people behind such schemes have a habit of slapping down their

a c
    e
b d

The creative admission of daylight:
a Jean Nouvel, Galéries Lafayette, Berlin, 1991-6: section
b Renzo Piano Building Workshop, Bercy 2 Shopping Centre, Charenton le Pont, Paris, 1987-90: interior view

c Galéries Lafayette: the rational exterior curtain wall
d Bercy 2 Shopping Centre: aerial view
e Galéries Lafayette: the interior of the conical atrium

architects' wilder and costlier ideas, while in Berlin a tight planning policy forbade breaking out of the standard city-block envelope of a certain area and height. So Galéries Lafayette in Berlin turned out to be Quartier 207: a block of shops and offices, not quite the revolution in urban perceptions it first promised to be.

Renzo Piano also became involved with retail design on the city-block scale. His Bercy 2 shopping centre in Paris, 1987–90, can in retrospect be seen as a dry run for the later, larger, Kansai International airport terminal, and involved the same Piano associate, Noriaki Okabe. The necessarily large windowless bulk of the centre – a corner block, hemmed in by autoroutes – is rendered palatable by expressing it as a curved, semi-toroidal form clad in stainless steel. The rectangular panels are thus made to clad a double-curved shape, which meant that thirty-four variations in panel size were necessary. In effect, Piano and Okabe found a visually simple (if technically complex) geometric resolution of the need to clad large-span spaces – Bercy II has 100,000 square metres of shops and services. Inside, in a not untypical Piano theatrical coup, what appears from the outside to be a giant high-tech car fender becomes the interior of a great ship's hull, complete with plywood purlins. However, he was in a sense only retreading ground previously explored by Cesar Pelli

with Gruen Associates in the 'Blue Whale' of the Pacific Design Center, a huge furniture mart in Los Angeles, 1971–5, and its later, less well-known second phase, a green ziggurat, 1984–8, with showrooms and conference centre. In both phases, the glass skin is stretched as tightly as possible over the unadorned structural shapes beneath, with no flourishes, sliced off at the ends and corners as if with a knife. The taut skin of the first phase was built at the same time as the guts-on-the-outside arts palace of the Pompidou Centre in Paris by Piano and Rogers. Pelli liked to observe that, per square foot, his cost a quarter as much. This is the problem all architects face with retail buildings, which is why they all prefer to design art galleries. However, Piano bit the bullet at Bercy and came up with an all-sheltering form that looks a great deal less brittle than Pelli's earthquake-resistant glass skins (and probably still costs more). Yet there are places when even retail developers allow for higher than usual costs, and will spend on architecture, as when Mario Botta was tempted out of his Ticino base to provide Florence with a shopping centre. Only in extreme cases, with watchful planning authorities, do such wonders occur: usually the bottom line of the accounts sheet is the key determinant of design quality. This is not only in order to attract tenants with competitive rents, while also maximizing the developer's profit, but also

a Cesar Pelli with Gruen
  Associates, Pacific Design
  Center Phase 2, Los Angeles,
  1984–8
b Mario Botta, Esselunga Centro
  Commerciale, Florence,
  1988–92: trainshed allusion

The sophisticated
minimalism of Pawson
and Jiricna pre-selects
the customers:
c John Pawson, Jigsaw,
  London, 1996: shop interior
d Eva Jiricna, Joseph,
  London, 1989
e Jigsaw: minimal circulation

because new shopping centres mean lucrative land purchases and spin-off trade for towns and cities that may be struggling to balance their own books. It is difficult for any city to turn down the money promised by a big new mall.

Searching like Nouvel in Berlin for low-cost visual impact, the German architect Rüdiger Kramm achieved more than his French colleague with his slightly earlier 'Zeil-Galerie Les Facettes' in Frankfurt, 1990–3. As in Nouvel's Berlin Galéries Lafayette, a French word was used to define shopping chic, but the 'facettes' in question were the zig-zag perforated metal panels Kramm placed as a large screen on the street, activated by weather sensors to act as the matrix for a changing computer-driven colour light display. It is rather endearingly low-tech, but it works. Because Kramm's specialist small-unit arcade was internalized, with no need for window space on the outside to display goods, the big screen slung on the outside was a way of providing an elevation to the otherwise narrow slot of the arcade's entrance. Inside, it is one of the tallest shopping centres in the world. Four levels are usually considered daring by retail developers – here there are twelve, four of them below ground. Pompidou-style escalators move between the levels in the narrow slot of an atrium.

Kramm and his associated artists and technicians were able to make an impact on shopping by

treating architecture as a mode of ephemeral display. More normally, if an architect wishes to create effect, it is as an interior designer of specific individual retail units that wish to convey a unique brand image. Thus we have high-style architects such as Eva Jiricna and John Pawson doing such stores as the Joseph shops in London's Brompton Cross, 1989, or the flagship Calvin Klein store in New York, 1995. Like restaurants and bars, these are in a sense themed interiors – but themed on architecture itself rather than any outside influence. When Rick Mather produced his 1980s and early 1990s series of Chinese restaurants for the Zen chain in London, Montreal and Hong Kong, a theme of running water emerged. There was an excuse: it is a Chinese symbol of good fortune – but as handled by Mather it was refined from a relatively simple cascade into a series of gravity-defying trickling glass bowls spiralling in the air above the diners. Zaha Hadid's Moonsoon restaurant in Sapporo, Japan, 1989–90, was selling the Zaha experience. In Jiricna's shops in London, Paris and New York, the theme is the sequence of extraordinarily delicate steel-and-glass spiral staircases. In Pawson's case, extreme minimalism is the luxury fit-out deployed: luxury because of the quality of materials and the discipline it imposes on the shop staff. Frank Gehry does a restaurant in Japan: it takes the form of a giant fish. Alfredo Arribas'

Barcelona bars are as eclectic as the Australian designer Mark Newson's restaurants or Philippe Starck's hotels, and it is that very eclecticism, their film-set inspiration, that brands them and their brethren. Arribas' 1994 Estandard bar, restaurant and nightclub complex in Barcelona, with its different moods for different spaces and levels within the same building envelope, is comparable with Newson's 1997 'Mash & Air' restaurant and bar complex in Manchester, England for the entrepreneur Oliver Peyton, followed in 1998 by a London equivalent. Peyton, like Nigel Coates' Tokyo clients in the 1980s, was partial to collecting designer names: after Newson, he signed up Zaha Hadid for another restaurant in Knightsbridge. Such retail outlets, like fashion stores, are relatively ephemeral pieces of interior design, more than shopfitting but less than architecture: they generally last only as long as the particular economic cycle that created them, and sometimes not even that.

Minimalist shop interiors, such as John Pawson's Calvin Klein store in New York, or Claudio Silvestrin's outlet for the same company in Paris, 1997, were commissioned because minimalism was at that time fashionable: at other times more baroque, stagey designers and architects are favoured, as with Coates' flagship store for Jigsaw in London's Knightsbridge of 1990. Somewhere in

between came the curiously disorientating effect of Shiro Kuramata's 1988 Issey Miyake Men department within Tokyo's Seibu store: an exercise in the creative use of expanded metal sheet, used both structurally (to support shelves and hangers) and as a finishing material both for walls and the vaulted ceiling. This was radical indeed compared with his 1984 Miyake Boutique in New York's Bergdorf Goodman store, which merely explored the possibilities of terrazzo. Later he returned to the defining curved ceiling for one of his last works, the Kiyotomo Sushi Restaurant in Tokyo, which in its sparse furnishings, simple materials and careful handling of light, evinces a thoroughly Japanese sensibility in a wholly contemporary setting. But for all that, such interiors are clearly stage sets, changeable at the whim either of the fashion designer or of the store or restaurant owner. It is a Faustian pact: the designer is given a freedom not possible in more 'permanent' and larger architectural works, but he or she knows the work will die sooner rather than later.

It is rare for an architect to be allowed to design an entire building, with elevations, as a shop, which at any rate ensures an average longevity for the product. This is something the classicist Allan Greenberg achieved with his Tommy Hilfiger fashion store in Los Angeles, designed in 1996 in full nineteenth-century historicist mode with a sweeping

In the 1980s, restaurants became urban theatre. In the 1990s, restaurant culture exploded worldwide, replacing shops as the fashionable architect's standby:

a Conran Roche, Bibendum, Michelin Building, London, 1986
b Alfredo Arribas, Velvet Nightclub, Barcelona, 1994
c Kuramata Design, Kiyotomo Sushi Restaurant, Minatoku, Tokyo, 1988

d Mark Newson, 'Mash & Air' restaurant and bar, Manchester, England, 1997
e Zaha Hadid, Moonsoon Restaurant, Sapporo, Japan, 1989–90
f Frank Gehry, Fishdance Restaurant, Kobe, Japan, 1986–7
g Rick Mather, Zen Restaurant, Pacific Place, Hong Kong, 1989

a	d	f	g
b			
c	e		

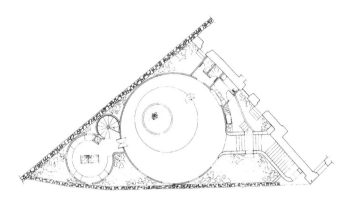

staircase under a central dome. Even ephemeral interiors can, however, prove to have staying power. Philippe Starck's 1984 Café Costes in Paris, with its declared intention of being 'Sad and Beautiful as the Buffet of Prague's Railway Station' proved very influential, not least on the series of basement restaurants created by Terence Conran and CD Design in London in the 1990s such as Quaglino's and Mezzo. Conran, a designer and retailer as well as a restaurateur throughout his career, successfully mingled the serving of food with the selling of goods in a number of his developments, most notably the 1986 Bibendum Restaurant and Conran Shop complex carved out of the old Michelin Tyre building in London's South Kensington – a building that, as with his 1997 Bluebird Café in Chelsea, came ready-themed with an automotive motif. Starck tended to make up his own themes as he went along: his revamp of the Royalton Hotel in New York with its restaurant, 1988, is Starck's hallucinogenic take on the idea of clubbishness. The boutique hotel (see 'Leisure') is part of the same culture as the high-design clubs, bars and restaurants discussed here. Thus Melbourne, which produced the 1993 Adelphi Hotel on Flinders Lane by Denton Corker Marshall, is celebrated for its glass-bottomed rooftop pool that cantilevers out over the facade: but its basement bistro, in fashionable 1990s displaced-grid style, is

more frequented. The same city gave us Tom Kovac's 1994 Capitol Nightclub and, more interestingly, his 1995 Sapore restaurant, which is another 'organic' cavern-like rejection of the designer chic afflicting that city's restaurant quarter, as it afflicted the restaurant quarter of every affluent city in the world. Kovac's swooping plasterwork world may be compared with some of the work of London-based Ron Arad, though perhaps a more genuine exercise in retail non-design would be Lina Bo Bardi's 'Bar of the 3 Arches' and Coaty Restaurant in Salvador, Brazil, completed in 1987 as virtually her last design.

Equally consciously, if more artfully, created are the interiors the Muji chain of 'no-brand-goods' stores, which began in Japan in the 1980s as a corrective to rampant consumerism, and which has proved successful worldwide as a recognizable brand in its own right. A good mid-period Muji interior was the Aoyama branch of 1993 by Tagashi Sugimoto (creator of the identity for the whole chain) and the Super Potato design group. It made a virtue of the use of two salvaged materials: steel panels from scrap merchants and reclaimed timber. With many local variations, this rough-hewn look became the trademark of Muji everywhere, but to use recycled materials in Japan at this time was a strong political statement, since the nation was under fire from environmentalists for its devil-may-care use of rare

tropical hardwoods, much of it used by the construction industry merely for moulding concrete.

Sometimes a retail group can adopt a given image that can be interpreted by many designers and architects – as the Benetton chain of clothes stores tends to – or it can go to the opposite extreme and employ no fixed house style, as first Fiorucci and then Diesel stores attempted. But in general, the rule is that customers must have a sense of what store they are in. The design of the interiors is crucial to that act of recognition. In food stores, the time-and-motion experts have developed strict ideas on internal organization that anyway leave architects with little to do but draw the standard layout and reserve their best effort for the exterior. In Europe in the late 1980s this came to be a Holy Grail, to the extent that emphasis on interior and graphic design diverted attention from the lifeblood of all shops – the quality and type of goods being sold. When recession bit, svelte interiors did not show up on the balance sheet.

But in contrast to the demands of the chain stores, there are the occasional shops that are pure architecture. James Stirling's and Tom Muirhead's Electa Bookshop in Venice's Biennale Gardens, sailing like a vaporetto between the rows of trees, is large-scale, small-size architecture, doing all the things you would expect a large, complex building to do in terms of structure, roof treatment, natural and

a   b | c d

          e f

a   Lina Bo Bardi, Marcelo Carvalho Ferraz and Marcelo Suzuki, Misericórdia Slope, ('Bar of the 3 Arches', Coaty Restaurant), Salvador, Bahia, Brazil, 1987: plan
b   Coaty Restaurant: an existing tree forms the centrepiece
c   Tom Kovac, Capitol Nightclub, Melbourne, Australia, 1994
d   Denton Corker Marshall, Adelphi Hotel, Melbourne, 1993

Eventually the symbols of retail became detached from their settings entirely: 'virtual shopping' was born, along with a heavy dose of consumerist irony:
e   Mark Fisher, set design for U2 'Pop Mart' Tour, various locations, 1997–8
f   'Pop Mart': view at night during the performance

artificial lighting, glazed curtain wall, ground condition and acknowledgment of context – but for something that is little more than an enlarged kiosk. The boat–shop concept was taken a stage further by Michael Hopkins & Partners in his tiny demountable summer ticket office, 1994, for Buckingham Palace in London, which is as close to a wooden sailing boat as it is possible for a rectilinear building to be, and which can be packed away in winter.

Consumerism has its own style, its different elements being separately recognizable to anyone who ever exchanges money for goods. Consumerist design thus increasingly escapes from the malls and the stores into virtual reality, where you can buy goods electronically by navigating round a 'virtual mall' with its own architecture. This can then be applied back to a form of reality, as one of the world's most successful rock bands, U2, did on their 'PopMart' tour of 1997–8 (sets by the architect Mark Fisher). Even when 'permanently' housed, there is something about buying and selling that gives a temporary feel to any architecture set up to contain it. Retail is an animal that can morph itself into new shapes and guises: architects have to deal with a volatile element that is capable of slipping invisibly right out of the mall and re-forming somewhere else entirely. Whereupon, the city wakes up and attempts to impose a new order.

LIVING *Houses & apartments* Privately commissioned individual houses or apartments, followed by social housing projects, continue to be among the best ways for an architect to establish a reputation. The house has always been a radical testing ground for original design ideas which can subsequently be developed on projects of increasing scale and complexity: a house is a city in microcosm. The bespoke house, or apartment, is not merely a fashionable interior – whether it be deconstructivist, minimalist or functional – but is a potent urban generator.

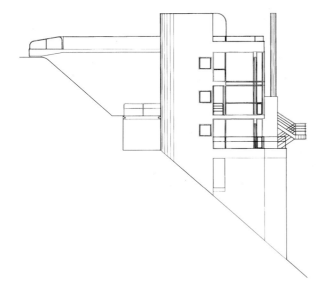

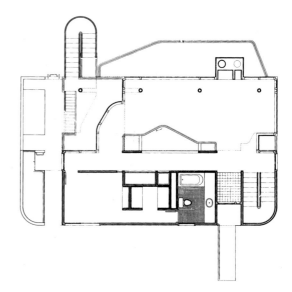

'The idea of all these houses I build is not to create a containment (but) to allow nearly everything to come together in a fluid sense as a complete whole. That's all in the handling of space.'
Frank Lloyd Wright, 1955.

One of the more intriguing images of, and
opaque commentaries on, the modern house is the last painting by the opium-addicted artist Christopher Wood before his suspected suicide in 1930, *Zebra and Parachute*. The zebra stands, un-expectedly but meekly enough, on the roof terrace of a house clearly recognizable as Le Corbusier's Villa Savoye at Poissy, 1929–31, still being completed at the time of painting but well known to the Paris-based Wood. Critical commentary on the painting has tended to focus on the animal – why is it there? What does it mean? – and generally concludes that it represents the spiritual or poetic aspect of the sup-posedly rational Modern Movement – the antithesis of machine-living. As Alan Powers has pointed out, most pioneering modern houses of the time pos-sessed a Zebra – a displaced, anachronistic element such as an ornate fireplace or window surround or chandelier or animal skin (Berthold Lubetkin always took care to include such an item in his housing – a pair of antlers, rough-hewn countryish chairs, peasant bedspreads, even a classical caryatid). But too much

attention is paid to the zebra, while the other myste-rious element is overshadowed – the descending parachute in the top right of the picture with a limp – presumably dead or dying – figure suspended from it.

One can imagine the zebra clattering down Corbusier's great ramp to the meadows around the house. One can sense the lifeless airman crumpling amid the dandelions and cow-parsley. But you do not have to imagine any event outside the captured moment which – as some historians of art rather than architecture have surmised – is perhaps to do with reaching the point of no return in the transition from the representative to the abstract. Wood had taken his representative art as far as it could go. The dangling airman, as Sebastian Faulks has suggested in his biography of Wood, therefore acknowledges, quite literally, the death of figuration.

At this remove, we can only marvel at the aptness of Wood's choice of subject matter, for what he instinctively guessed, we know now with the cer-tainty of hindsight: that the Villa Savoye defines the moment at which the modern house matured as a complete work of art and craft. It achieved this, rela-tively few years after the modernizing, mechanizing and cleansing impetus given by the Great War. It was an intense period of prototyping in the hands of, amongst others, Adolf Loos, J J P Oud, Gerrit Rietveld, Mart Stam, Josef Frank, Giuseppe Terragni,

Alvar Aalto, Walter Gropius, Marcel Breuer, Mies van der Rohe: Rudolph Schindler and Richard Neutra in the United States; and Corbusier himself. In a way, the Villa Savoye's function as an out-of-town party villa for a wealthy Parisian socialite helps its cause, for the house – untrammelled by the exigencies of day-to-day living – can stand as a universal exemplar, as much a place of pilgrimage as Corbusier's later chapel at Ronchamp.

However, while Le Corbusier was at pains to establish connections between his work and that of classical architecture, the European moment of tran-sition as seen with such deadly clarity by Wood had very little to do with the work of the heirs to the nineteenth-century Arts and Crafts tradition, as prac-tised pre-eminently in America by Frank Lloyd Wright. Wright's Barnsdall, Millard, Storer and Ennis houses from the early 1920s would have taken their place in the modernist pantheon much earlier were it not for their intrinsic use of ornament: which is why his rela-tively unadorned Fallingwater House, 1935, still enjoys greater acclaim. It is telling that Schindler worked in Wright's office from 1917 to 1921, and supervised the building of the Barnsdall House – without which, one suspects, Schindler's Lovell Beach House, 1925–6, at Newport Beach, California, would have been the poorer. Neutra, like his Vienna-born colleague Schindler, also passed through Wright's

a b

c

e

d

An early return to white
1930s modernism:
a Richard Meier & Partners,
   Douglas House, Harbor
   Springs, Michigan, 1971–3:
   elevation
b Douglas House: plan
c Douglas House: external
   stair and deck
d Douglas House: internal
   voids and layers
e Douglas House: in context

office and this informed the other Lovell House in Los Angeles, 1927–9, which with its cable-suspended slabs was structurally more audacious than the European brethren it stylistically resembled. Although it is commonplace to assert that the 'Wright style' had no successors, the sheer numbers of architects who had contact with the man, and assisted in his work, of necessity felt his influence, some directly. John Lautner, who worked at Taliesin in the late 1930s and set up his own office in Hollywood in 1939, was always happy to acknowledge the debt his buildings clearly owe to Wright (and, later, Saarinen). As if driven by memories of Fallingwater, he was constantly building houses upon rocks, doing so right up to the early 1990s. He never forgot the Wrightian metaphor of the cave, either, normally making his

houses a process of transition from the dark interior out to some stunning outlook.

Living so long – but somehow remaining friendly with his clients in a way that Wright did not always manage – Lautner was able to update some of his houses in the light of evolving technology. A prime example is his Sheats House in Los Angeles, first built in 1963, where the living area was at first conceived to be entirely open to the view across the city – an invisible air curtain, Lautner thought, would provide the necessary climatic protection. This Wright-like optimism proved misplaced, so he installed floor-to-ceiling glazing with the thinnest mullions then possible. By the late 1980s, frameless silicon-sealed glazing had arrived: so Lautner returned to the Sheats house (by then in different

a

b　c

The spirit of Wright:
a　John Lautner, Sheats–Goldstein House, Los Angeles, 1963, 1989–96: view of the pool and house
b　Sheats–Goldstein House: frameless silicon-sealed glazing allowed the mullions of the 1963 Sheats House to be removed
c　Office for Metropolitan Architecture, Villa dall'Ava, St Cloud, Paris, 1985–91: Le Corbusier deconstructed

ownership) to make the inside to outside distinction almost as insubstantial as he had originally envisaged. This was not so much remodelling as 'perfecting', he said.

However, like Wright, Lautner was able to wear down his clients. Celebrated Lautner compositions such as the Arango House overlooking Acapulco Bay, Mexico, 1973–7, with its extraordinary cantilevered terrace complete with edge-moat, tends to conceal comparative failures of the same period such the Hope House in Palm Springs, originally designed in 1973 for Bob Hope. This was designed with an exposed concrete shell roof engineered by Felix Candela, very reminiscent of the outspread wings of Saarinen's TWA Terminal at Kennedy Airport. The shell roof was later modified to a steel-

frame structure with timber sheathing – a mistake, since it caught fire from welders' sparks, burnt away completely, and had to be rebuilt. By which time, the fight had gone out of the Hopes, who trimmed back Lautner's design considerably. The atrium, 60 feet in diameter with an openable roof – conceived as the ultimate party space – became an open courtyard. The house took six years to complete, even in its truncated form, and stands as a member of that curious architectural club – buildings designed for one material and method and completed in another, for which the form is unsuitable.

Client economics may force the architect's hand this way sometimes, but in other cases the architects themselves indulge in games with appropriate forms and materials. Rem Koolhaas and his

Office for Metropolitan Architecture enjoy this kind of fun more than most. This may be why, when OMA's Villa dall' Ava at St Cloud, Paris, was designed, 1985–91, Koolhaas thought of the Villa Savoye and then subverted the image. The house, with its strips of windows raised on its *pilotis*, is clad not in white render but corrugated metal, horizontally applied. Where Le Corbusier offset the rectilinear nature of the main block with curving roof forms, Koolhaas does the same in bright orange plastic perforated fencing of the kind seen around roadworks. And where Christopher Wood depicted Corbusier's Villa with a zebra, certain photographs of the Villa dall' Ava mysteriously show a real baby giraffe strolling around. In fact, the plan of the house is entirely different from the Villa Savoye, and it is replete with other architectural references from Mies to Pierre Koenig, but the visible mutation shows the enduring power of that particular Corbusian moment.

The Villa dall' Ava is one of a multitude of the Villa Savoye's mutated offspring; a not dissimilar example, this time faced in plywood rather than crinkly metal, is Dirk Alten's little suburban house extension in Braunschweig, Germany, grandiosely named The Eagle, 1989–92, which also has a touch of Rietveld about its window shutters. The name is most probably a reference to the first manned moon-landing craft: the famous radio message 'the Eagle has landed' describes exactly its resolute anti-contextualism. Alten previously worked for Koolhaas' Office of Metropolitan Architecture, so the line of descent is clear.

After the Villa Savoye, the next logical step for the 'modern' house was to establish a more than nodding acquaintance with industrialization. The United States led the way, first with Lawrence Kocher and Albert Frey's 'Aluminaire' House of 1931 at Syosset on Long Island – also known as the Harrison House. With its slender aluminium frame members and thin corrugated cladding in the same metal, rendered in a distinctly Corbusian aesthetic, this showed the possibilities of mechanized production, and eerily also anticipated certain aspects of Koolhaas' Villa dall' Ava. More radical still was George and William Keck's 'Crystal House' at the Century of Progress Exhibition in Chicago of 1934. This was an astonishingly prescient structure with an external space-frame that was as factory-made as Bruno Taut's celebrated 'glass house' of the 1914 Cologne Werkbund was hand-crafted. Moreover it was a considerably less bespoke item than Pierre Chareau's iconic Maison de Verre in Paris of 1931.

Next came the Californian 'Case Study' houses from the 1940s to the 1960s, and in particular Charles and Ray Eames' 1949 house at Pacific Palisades, made from off-the-peg industrial components. The majority

c	d f
a	g
b	
	e

The descendants of Case Study confirmed the enduring appeal of the Californian dream:

a Dirk Alten, The Eagle, Braunschweig, Germany, 1989–92: entrance stair

b The Eagle: shutters enclose the ribbon window

c Richard and Su Rogers, House in Wimbledon, London, 1968–9

d John Winter, Winter House, Highgate, London, 1969

e Simon Unger and Tom Kinslow, 'T House', Wilton, New York, 1988–94

f Jonathan Ellis-Miller, Prickwillow, Cambridgeshire Fens, England, 1989–93

g Jonathan Ellis-Miller, Mary Reyner Banham House, Cambridgeshire Fens, England, 1997: plan

of modernist houses in the closing years of the century make due acknowledgement to these two predecessors: the Villa Savoye 'white house' model in masonry and glass with its plastic qualities, and the component-based Keck–Eames model – steel and glass, and anything but plastic in form or potential. Architects' borrowings from the early industrial aesthetic are generally modified by the 'floating slab' influence of Mies van der Rohe's Farnsworth House, 1946–50, at Fox River, Illinois – the planar qualities of which are very different from the box-like form of the Eames house with its overt acknowledgement of De Stijl, more specifically Rietveld and Mondrian. The torch is carried down through the generations. Thus Richard Rogers devised the unbuilt Zip-Up House, 1968–71, as a manifesto prefabricated house, a reaction to the laborious, Victorian building techniques he and Team Four had encountered in the earlier Creek Vean House, 1966–8. He achieved a relatively high degree of prefabrication in the house he built for his parents in Wimbledon, 1968–9, using yellow composite aluminium panels for the walls (these inspired by the sides of insulated trucks). Thus too, the English architect John Winter, who in the 1950s made the journey to Pacific Palisades and worked briefly for the Eameses before returning to Britain to become the priest of the English high-tech movement, enthused his assistants with the spirit of Case Study – to the

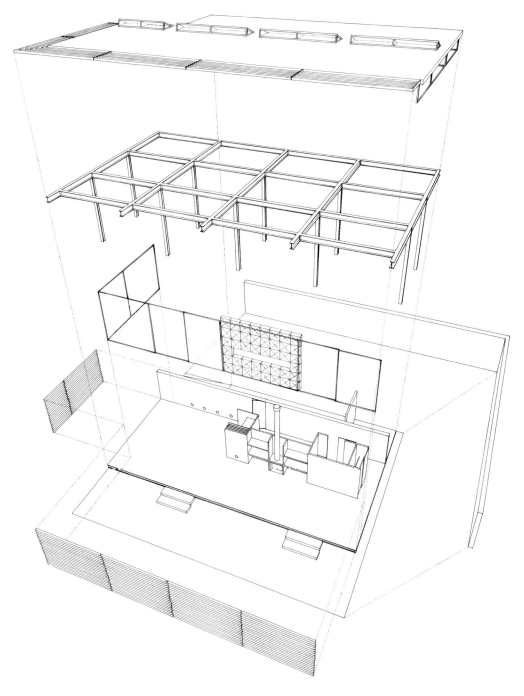

extent that in the early 1990s one of them, Jonathan Ellis-Miller, built himself a steel-framed home in the agricultural village of Prickwillow. The building in the flatlands of the Cambridgeshire Fens is a miniaturized homage to Case Study seen through a Miesian filter. Then, in 1997, he produced a larger and more sophisticated house and studio next door for Mary Banham, widow of the critic and adoptive Californian Peter Reyner Banham. These houses are curiously at home in the utterly different geography of the English Fens – a fact ascribed by Ellis-Miller to the kinship such places have with the *ad hoc* homes made by self-builders in such remote farming areas.

Winter himself, in the meantime, having occupied his own house, 1969, clad in Cor-Ten oxidizing steel in London's Highgate for over a quarter of a century, saw the rust revival come around in the form of Simon Ungers and Tom Kinslow's 'T House' in Wilton, New York, 1988–94, which owes nothing at all to Case Study or Mies and which was incorrectly thought by some at the time to be the first house ever built out of weathering steel. The powerful form of the 'T House' derives from the fact that a 13-metre-long library for ten thousand books is expressed as a rectangular volume cantilevered at high level and at right angles to the living accommodation beneath. Many sculptors, but relatively few architects, make use of the patination possible with untreated steel;

its colours changing from vivid orange to dark brown over time. When used with flush glazing, as at Winter's house, however, it creates a whitish bloom on the glass.

Three more models emerged in the post-war years: the mass-produced house, as predicated by Richard Buckminster Fuller with his Dymaxion and Wichita prototypes, and the 'junk house' – exploiting cheap, readily available materials such as fencing materials to dress up basic structures, plus a use where possible of found materials – a strand that is also American in origin, which leads from Bruce Goff through Frank Gehry in his 'chicken wire' phase – his own house, Santa Monica, 1978 – to Eric Owen Moss, and which has indissoluble links with 'organic' architecture. To compare Goff's last built work – the Al Struckus House of 1979 in Woodland Hills, California – with the work of emerging Hungarian organic architects of the same period such as Gyorgi Csete and Imre Makovecz, is to realize that internationalism in architecture is as much a matter of morphic resonance as of manifestos, exhibitions and publications.

An offshoot from the junk or organic house design movement is the eco-home. This can be a technologically biased construction, either actively power-generating or – as with T R Hamzah and Yeang's 'Roof-Roof' house in Selangor, Malaysia of 1983-4 – passive, making a virtue out of the need

for solar shading. More commonly though, the eco-home places the notion of recyclability, maximum insulation and power generation above aesthetic considerations, but the two are not mutually exclusive: just as there is an assonance between all the homes made of old oil drums and car tyres and bottles, scattered across the American deserts, so there is to the homes of alternative communes in forested areas, those who incorporate old railway cars, shipping containers and trailers into homes in isolated coastal regions, and those – such as the 300-population Findhorn community in northern Scotland – who, in 1962, started their community with trailer homes ('caravans' in English) but who have since turned to other large containers provided by industry, in their case huge whisky tuns. The 'Barrel House' by Andrew Yeats, 1995, is one of the more sophisticated examples, rising two-and-a-half levels and using the Douglas Fir staves of the recycled tuns structurally rather than as mere cladding. Such eco-communities (compare also the Open City at Ritoque in Chile, an architect-led equivalent) depend not so much on a style or choice of materials and forms – though image plays a bigger role than their designers would perhaps care to admit – as the notion of communality and freedom from capital constraints.

That architecture of a high order can result from such recycling exercises is shown most

a   b

c

Eco-junk meets collage culture:
a Frank O Gehry & Associates, Gehry House, Santa Monica, 1978 (renovated 1992–3)
b T R Hamzah & Yeang, 'Roof-Roof' House, Selangor, Malaysia, 1983–4
c Andrew Yeats, Eco Arc, The (Whisky) 'Barrel House', Findhorn, Scotland, 1995

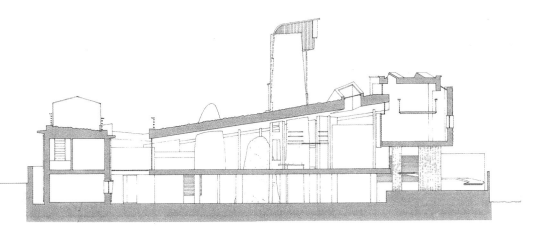

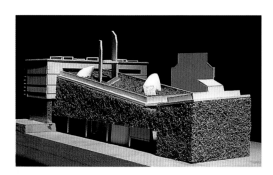

wonderfully by Goff's mast-suspended Bavinger House, Oklahoma, 1950, and the nearby Joe Price house and studio, Bartlesville, built in phases, in 1956, 1966 and 1974. But for all their site-specificity and use of found materials, these are once again single homes for relatively wealthy clients. Price, for example, was of the family that had commissioned the Price Tower at Bartlesville from Wright, and he was later to 'collect' other architects including Bart Prince and Kisho Kurokawa. This is hardly on the same level of eco-commitment as, say, the 'earth-ships' built from the mid-1970s onwards by Michael Reynolds in Taos, New Mexico, which are made from old tyres and aluminium drinks cans, bolstered with rammed and bermed earth, usually U-shaped with one glazed south-facing elevation supplemented with photovoltaic panels for energy self-sufficiency. The results are strangely beautiful, if less openly architectural than Goff's.

Such 'garbage houses', built by affluent and healthy Westerners, act as a gloss on the large percentage of the world's poor population that has absolutely no choice in the method of housing construction other than to use recycled materials and practise low-energy consumption. To adopt the construction techniques and materials of the shanty town is in a sense insulting to the inhabitants of such places, however correct the principle may be

energy-wise. Even so, this kind of eco-awareness takes its place as one element in the architectural development of the living place: successfully enough to begin to feed back into the mainstream, where the house or apartment continues to be a sure-fire way for a young architect to establish a reputation. In London, architects Sarah Wigglesworth and Jeremy Till set 'high' architecture against 'low' materials in their design for a low-energy house and studio, 1998–9, where the external walls are of straw bales visible behind polycarbonate, the structural cross walls are of rubble-filled gabions, and the elevation facing a busy railway track is of stacked sandbags. This is in a sense a house partly in the 'garbage' tradition, and partly in the tradition of Eames and Walter Segal in its use of cheap readymade components. This experimental home on the urban fringes is far removed from the sleek, Corb-influenced modernism of another London triumph from the period – Richard Paxton and Heidi Locher's studio apartment block on Clerkenwell Green, 1997, where a street elevation in the tradition of 1930s modernism conceals the architect's own home behind, arranged somewhat in the manner of a Roman atrium house. It is, however, modified for the British climate by having a motorized opening glass roof over the courtyard and living area, a dramatic device successfully concealing the fact that, being locked in by

b   c

            e

a   d   f

Low-grade materials and sustainability do not exclude 'high' architecture:

a   Sarah Wigglesworth Architects and Jeremy Till, The Bale House, Islington, London, 1998–9: model

b   The Bale House: section

c   Paxton Locher, Clerkenwell House, London, 1997: plan of Paxton Locher apartment and office space and entrance to other apartments

d   Clerkenwell House: entrance facade

e   Clerkenwell House: living space under sliding glazed roof – the Roman atrium rediscovered

f   Clerkenwell House: courtyard with glazed roof open

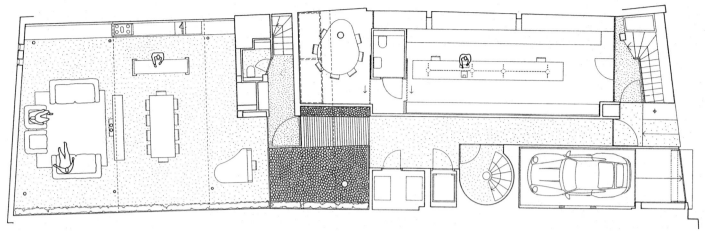

surrounding buildings, it has no conventional outward-facing windows. Paxton and Locher pulled this off where others would easily have failed; as Paxton remarked at the time: 'The theatrical edge of Modernism can be a dangerous place.'

The home, then, continues to be a test-bed for design ideas that can subsequently be developed on projects of increasing scale and complexity: a house is a city in microcosm. Those design ideas are usually recycled, since absolute originality is as rare in housing as in other building types. But the importance of the house as a honing tool for architectural ideas means that, for this reason if no other, the architectural home has nothing whatever to do with the cult of the interior designer and decorator. As with the distinction between 'shops' and 'retail', however, there is a sharp distinction to be made between 'houses' and 'housing'. Housing can be a social project of the kind familiar to us from the mid-nineteenth century onwards, with examples of extreme size and scale such as Emile Aillaud's attempts to personalize system-built estates in France in the 1950s and 1960s. These were experiments that, though often informal in layout, paved the way for the neo-classical experiments in prefabrication by Ricardo Bofill's Taller de Arquitectura such as the Arcades du Lac at St Quentin-en-Yvelines, France, 1978–83, the Espaces d'Abraxas at Marne-la-Vallée near Paris,

1978–82, and similar exercises in Montpellier and Montparnasse, Paris, through to the mid-1980s. None of these could have been predicted from Bofill's earlier, less megalomaniac and more spritely housing schemes of a regional character in Spain such as his Walden 7 complex outside Barcelona, 1973–5.

Such thinking must be compared with the large-scale housing experiments of the Smithsons in England (Robin Hood Gardens, East London, completed 1972) or the related but larger scale experiment of Gallaratese 2 in Milan, 1967–73, by Carlo Aymonino and Aldo Rossi or – as perhaps the most successful attempt to humanize the megablock – Ralph Erskine's Byker Wall development in Newcastle-upon-Tyne, 1969–80. All these were attempts to lend dignity to mass housing, to create less regimented plans and sections than, say, the influential early built experiments in Germany by Gropius (Dammerstock, Karlsruhe, 1927–8; Siemensstadt, Berlin, 1929–30, both of which placed identical blocks in parallel lines, in the latter case with generous open space). The influence of Le Corbusier's later series of Unité d'Habitation blocks, no less than his monastery of La Tourette, necessarily informed many of these projects, not least because they were early attempts to produce the very kind of self-propelled communities now seen as vital to the well-being of cities.

But 'housing' can also mean a suburban estate, laid out by private developers to maximize returns and beloved of film-makers in search of dark doings beneath the squeaky-clean surface (*The Stepford Wives*, *Halloween*, *Edward Scissorhands* and so forth). Suburbanism is the ubiquitous housing movement of the twentieth century, made possible first by improvements in public transport – so allowing rapid commuting into the old city centres – and then by the growth in car ownership, which relieved the isolation of these communities for those who looked after the home. Suburban housing – like shopping malls – has traditionally received little attention from art historians, who prefer their examples to be of one-off architecture rather than oft-repeated buildings. Its defining characteristic – heavy land consumption, the land for each home fenced off like a pioneer farmstead – was always unfashionable, and came also to be seen as ecologically and environmentally unsound in densely populated nations by the century's end. Instead, high-density city living was heavily promoted in an attempt to save the remaining countryside for amenity and food production. However, the taste for suburban living cannot be killed: the mix of town and country, allied to the freedom of the private car, is just too beguiling for too many.

a b   e

         f

c d

Housing can equally be the kind of astonishing high-rise social housing clusters that sprang up from the 1970s onwards in Hong Kong (a graphic response to land shortage) and from the 1980s onwards in the rest of the oriental countries of the Pacific Rim as workers flocked from country to city. Housing can mesh in with the urban grain of the city, or it can disrupt it, turn its back on it – a characteristic shared both by many large problematic social housing estates of mid-century, and by the guarded apartment complexes, with their secure parking and health clubs, that have become such a feature of the world's wealthier cities as city-centre living became fashionable again in the 1990s.

Occasionally, however, the two categories – one-off house or house type and housing project – coincide. The German–Austrian model housing exhibitions set the example – the *Weissenhofsiedlung* (housing estate) in Stuttgart in 1927, directed by Mies on behalf of the Deutscher Werkbund, and its successors in Breslau, 1929, and Vienna, 1932, employed most of the leading European modernist architects of the day. Rather more eclectic in its approach was the International Building Exhibition (IBA) in Berlin in 1984, directed by Paul Kleihues, by which time post-modernism, or at any rate anti-modernism, was at its peak, and the new historical urbanism (as exemplified by the work of Rob Krier)

Social and private housing schemes assume a civic importance beyond their function:

a Ralph Erskine, Byker Wall, Newcastle-upon-Tyne, England, 1969–80: the successful attempt to humanize the housing 'megablock'

b Byker Wall: exterior detail

c Ricardo Bofill, Les Espaces d'Abraxas, Marne-la-Vallée, France, 1978–82

d Ricardo Bofill, Walden 7 Complex, Barcelona, 1973–5

e Rob Krier, Apartment Building, Ritterstrasse, Berlin, 1977–80

f Mark Horton, House on a Hilltop, San Francisco, 1995

was being propagated. In several cases, the architects had the task merely of dressing up otherwise identically massed blocks, something that was never wished upon the architects of the *Werkbundsiedlungen*.

Housing projects do, however, sometimes evolve virtually unplanned. In San Francisco, after the Oaklands Hill district was razed by fire in 1991, such an extraordinary collection of new individual homes sprouted afterwards that it could be considered as, *ipso facto*, an exhibition. It was an exhibition in some cases of ostentation – insurance payouts were gener- ous, the clients were wealthy, square footage was often sought at the expense of appropriate massing, scale, and detailing – but in other cases it was gen- uine experimentation of the kind tried out in the critic and publisher John Entenza's earlier Case Study programme in which Eames, Saarinen, Koenig, Neutra *et al* participated. In the case of Oaklands Hill, the architects were anything but birds of a feather: Frank Israel, Charles Moore (Moore Ruble Yudell), David Baker, James Gillam, Savidge Warren Fillinger ... work- ing amid styles ranging from hacienda and assertive post-modern to hard-edged industrial. Stanley Saitowitz's McLane-Looke House uses corrugated metal *à la* Koolhaas, as does Jim Jennings in his Becker House (to distinguish a block containing work- space and children's rooms from the main living block); Philip Banta's XYZ House is a not entirely suc

cessful reworking of Neutra; while Mark Horton's House on a Hilltop, another linked pair of forms, car- ries references from Utzon through Botta to Alvaro Siza (and unlike the others dares to have furniture by hands other than the universally desired pieces by Eames, Bertoia, Corbusier and Mies). None of these uses the canyon topography as successfully, say, as Schindler's Janson House of 1949 in Hollywood Hills or a later example such as Richard Meier's Douglas House at Harbor Springs, Michigan, 1971–3. Yet to pick out such examples is in a way invidious, since the West Coast of the United States, like the west coasts of Ireland and Australia, is dotted with such enclaves of rich people's retreats, some of which are by good architects but most of which are not. Unlike the Villa Savoye – which was diminished when the Parisian suburbs encroached – such places work as an ensemble; good jostling alongside bad.

Perhaps one response to the jostling suburb is not to design your house in conscious reaction against it, but to extract the suburban qualities you desire and re-direct them. This kind of response can vary from the updating of a vernacular, as seen in the Middle East and India, to the randomizing of forms and the introduction of alien elements: at which latter art, the Miami-based practice of Arquitectonica has proved itself adept. Their Casa Los Andes in Lima, Peru, 1983 5, took the one element that bound

Topography is an architect's
best friend:
a Jim Jennings, Becker House,
   Oakland, California, 1996:
   views out across the San
   Francisco area
b Becker House: the house is
   approached at its upper level

b

a

	e	
a	c	d
b		
	f	
		g

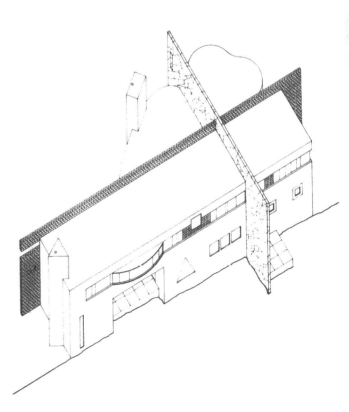

a   c d e

b

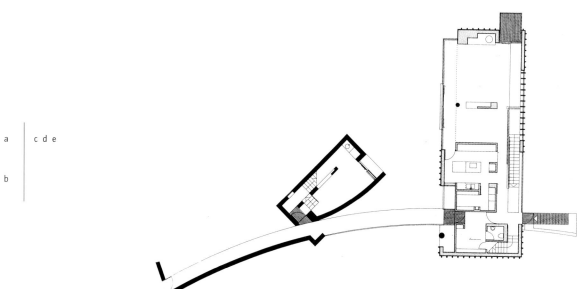

together all the varying house styles in the suburb – the high, strong boundary wall. The result is a cruciform spine to a building that is sternly rectilinear on one side, and which bursts out into a looser assemblage of forms on the other. While the white render and faded pink tiles of the area are taken as the basic palette, other elements are introduced, such as intense red and yellow. The whole composition is then set askew in the oblong box of a site within a green garden. The Bauhaus-modern feel of the straight elevation is belied by a sinusoidal pink form efflorescing in one corner of the intersecting walls, and acting as the entrance lobby and stairwell. If a house could be described as being Calvinist and Catholic at the same time, then this house is it. As artists of all disciplines discover, one has to know the rules in order to break them: this is as successfully achieved by Arquitectonica as by Koolhaas and OMA. A rural equivalent to the Casa Los Andes is Studio Granda's Haus im Vordertaunus in Wiesbaden, Germany, 1989–92, where an internationalist Iceland-based practice produced a convincing fantasia on the vernacular of the Rhineland, quite possibly unconsciously.

In house design perhaps more than any other discipline, regional variations in architecture become more apparent, according to climate, local materials, and the traditional ways of dealing with

them. Yet it is equally true that a handful of international styles of house design, handed down from Le Corbusier, Mies, Wright and Eames, seem capable of settling in all their variations anywhere in the world. In contrast to these, Mario Botta's many houses in the Ticino district, such as the Casa Rotonda of 1981–2 at Stabio, have become almost a local vernacular of their own. Arquitectonica successfully build upon the Miami Beach aesthetic of the 1930s (Atlantis apartments, 1980–2). Glen Murcutt in Australia is the leader of a number of architects who respond in part to their national legacy of farm buildings and sheep stations with their steel frames and corrugated-metal roofs: Murcutt's Ball-Eastaway House at Glenorie, 1981–3 – an extruded shed raised on stilts among the trees – is one example; Clare Design's Thrupp and Summers House at Nambour, 1986–7, with its more expansive interior is another; while the Gartner House at Mount Tamborine, 1989–90, by Gabriel Poole brings a touch of chinoiserie to the type; but the supreme example is the Newman house at Balgownie, 1988–91, by James Grose of Grose Bradley. Here is a house which looks at a glance like an animal shed – perhaps a winter shelter for cattle, an impression heightened by the row of agricultural rotary ventilators along the roof ridge. Grose himself sees it as a mix of the generic shearing shed and the jumble of long metal-clad

buildings of the BHP Steelworks – the products of which constitute the principal materials of the house. The Newman House is separated laterally into three zones, the central zone being higher – like the traditional basilica plan. The ends of the 'nave' with their animalistic, paired eye-like windows and bent steel legs, give the building a multivalent imagery. The quality of internal space and light is exceptional.

Outside of this shed-influenced architecture, other houses completed in Australia during the period point to an emerging regional, rather than Euro-American, aesthetic sensibility (although note that Australian shed-architecture itself became so influential as to inspire copies on other continents, for instance Schaudt Architekten's 1996 Jungerhalde row-housing in Konstanz, Germany, which takes the Eames principle of readymade industrial components and marries it to an outback aesthetic – all in a suburban context). Although it has been noted that most Australian architects emerging in practice from the 1970s onwards had received some of their training at either pluralistic British schools of architecture or post-modern inclined American schools, buildings such as these show a distinctly Australian aesthetic emerging from the welter of international references. Prime among these, perhaps, is the Athan House at Monbulk, 1986–8, by Maggie Edmond and Peter Corrigan. These two architects subsequently

An example of the emerging 'modern vernacular':
a Studio Granda, Haus im Vordertaunus, Wiesbaden, Germany, 1989–92: view of pavilions
b Haus im Vordertaunus: plan
c Clare Design, Thrupp and Summers House, Nambour, Queensland, Australia, 1986–7: exterior
d Thrupp and Summers House: interior
e Grose Bradley, Newman House, Balgownie, Australia, 1988–91

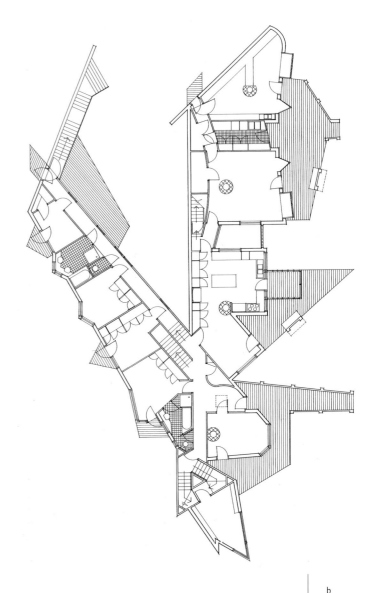

Regionalism thrives: certain
areas became famed for their
one-off houses:

a Glen Murcutt, Ball-Eastaway
   House, Glenorie, Australia,
   1981–3
b Edmond + Corrigan, Athan
   House, Monbulk, Australia,
   1986–8: jagged forms
c Athan House: the building
   addresses the site topography
d Athan House: entrance
e Athan House: plan

a | b
  | c
  | d e

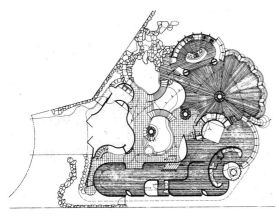

developed an aggressive post-modern style for their 1995 Building 8 at the Royal Melbourne Institute of Technology (see 'Learning'). The Athan House promises something else. Resolutely anti-International Style, to an extent it partakes of Robert Venturi's complexity theory, and Nigel Coates-ish 'narrative architecture', as well as the disassembly-of-elements that preoccupies Frank Gehry and thus, if it must be pigeonholed, would be filed in the Deconstruction slot. But Peter Corrigan appears not to be one for movements in architecture. Declaring himself an Australian patriot, a lover of suburbia and of theatricality, Corrigan aspires to and here achieves a unique architecture – unique in its choice of materials, colours and patterning, as well as in form. It is essentially V-shaped in plan, a footprint taken merely as a starting point for explorations of the meeting point of inside and outside, building and ground condition. With its sharp prow, it has been likened to a ship sailing through the woodland.

The Athan House is best left in its own category – something that can be said of few buildings and even fewer houses but which is equally true of John Outram's Rausing House, 1981-6, in Sussex, England, and Bart Prince's houses in California. Outram, like Edmond and Corrigan, constructs and pursues his own very personal iconography; in his case it is a 'myth-making' architecture, derived very

broadly from classicism and the Romanesque, but now standing alone and inimitable. The Rausing House, built for a very wealthy UK-based Swedish industrialist, is an example of what can emerge when a client gives a (relatively unproven) architect his head. Its linked pavilions of nougat-like masonry (including a material invented by Outram, called 'Blitzcrete', of broken brick set in concrete and then sliced) are evidence of a highly original mind at work – as are the rich interiors of the Rausing House with such sumptuous materials as panelling made of burr elm edged with polished aluminium. Bart Prince, while working in the Wright-Goff tradition, has a wider sphere of vision. His own house at Albuquerque, New Mexico, 1983-4, is a science-fantasy dwelling – a spaceship perched on a polychromatic masonry plinth – while his other houses such as the Mead-Penhall House, also in Albuquerque (industrial-insect imagery) and the Joe and Etsuko Price House, Corona del Mar, California, 1983-90 (timber–copper organic) confirm that this is a man who designs without a book of the modern masters at his elbow.

Such one-offs do little to unsettle the two main thrusts of architect-designed houses: internationalist and regionalist. The regionalist tendency in particular continues to be a powerful force. In Arizona, Antoine Predock's architecture sprang from

the pueblo adobe dwellings of the area, though by the time he came to design the Zuber House in Paradise Valley, Phoenix, 1987-9, he had graduated to heavyweight concrete and blockwork. Increasingly his homes took on distinctive forms of their own, but always reflected the topography and landscape tones of their setting. At first this would seem to be the opposite approach of Joshua Schweitzer, a former employee of Frank Gehry, whose house, The Monument at Joshua Tree, California, 1987-90, is a linked group of stuccoed pavilions painted in intense colours. But in reality, the harsh light of the rocky desert landscape with its huge skies subdues this relatively tiny grouping to the extent that, from any distance, it seems an entirely natural outcrop. Like many others, Schweitzer pays due deference to the pioneering work of Luis Barragán in and around Mexico city, notably such works as the Egerstrom House and stables in Mexico City of 1968 or his late masterpieces, the Gilardi House, 1976, and the Meyer House, 1978. The first two are noted for their use of intense colours, the last shows Barragán in plainer and more austere mood. All three are brilliant exercises in landscape as much as architecture. Ricardo Legorreta, one of the inheritors of the Barragán mantle, draws heavily upon tradition without slavishly copying it. While his Akle House at Valle de Bravo, Mexico, 1994, on a vertiginous site is deliberately traditional

a b   d
              e

     c

with its steep tiled roof, exposed log beam-ends and ochre stucco, it is also entirely supported upon a massive exposed concrete frame, peeping beneath the traditional dressings like a hooped petticoat underpinning a Victorian gown. Legorreta's son Víctor has built a house for himself and his wife Jacinta on the outskirts of Mexico City that, with its unostentatious exterior and magical inner space, is a reworking of the courtyard-based walled house. Away from home in Los Angeles, however, Ricardo Legorreta upped the scale and the image for his Greenberg House, 1991, and employed more abstract forms without losing sight of the tradition.

In Argentina, Miguel Angel Roca, whose work sometimes recalls Barragán in its use of native-derived forms and strong colours, nonetheless has a different and more internationalist sensibility. His Vespasiani House in Córdoba, Argentina, 1984–90, is like Lutyens or Prior in its butterfly plan, with a touch of Venturi in the great entrance portico, entering the house on the diagonal. But Roca has another sly reference to make: beneath the portico ripples a gridded glass wall, curving seemingly at random. It is, in fact, a slice through Mies van der Rohe's famous unbuilt glass tower in Berlin, transposed most oddly to suburban Argentina. The house is also placed up on a Miesian plinth, but a solid one: Roca has no desire to make the house appear to float.

Regionalism came more openly to the fore in the work of Hassan Fathy and his followers in Egypt and elsewhere, Raj Rewal in India (Asian Games Housing, New Delhi, 1982) Balkrishna Doshi (Hyderabad housing, 1976) and in the work of Black Forest architects Mahler, Günster, Fuchs in Germany, with their series of timber-clad barn-like sheltered housing blocks for the elderly on the riverfront in Neuenberg, 1993–6. Regionalistic tendencies are also present, arguably but persuasively, in the work of such classicists as Allan Greenberg in New England and the aptly named Robert Adam in Old England – both responding to a particular tradition. Adam's own house, Crooked Pightle, in Crawley outside Winchester, is a successful exercise in understated domestic classicism, working through implication rather than bravura. A similar claim might be made of the classical-vernacularist Demetri Porphyrios, whose architectural responses range from a farmhouse and stables in Windsor, England, to a resort village at Pitiousa on the Greek island of Spetses. In such places, God is not so much in the details as in the planning, and Porphyrios conceived of the place as a sequence of spaces rather than as a collection of individual buildings. It is in one sense a manifesto-town, like the settlement of Seaside in Florida, 1980 onwards, masterplanned by Andres Duany and Elizabeth Plater Zyberk, with individual buildings by

a Bart Prince, Joe and Etsuko
  Price House, Corona del Mar,
  California, 1983–90: plan
b Price House: exterior detail
c Joshua Schweitzer, The
  Monument, Joshua Tree,
  California, 1987–90
d Raj Rewal, Asian Games
  Housing, New Delhi, 1982
e Demetri Porphyrios, Belvedere
  Farm Village, Windsor, England
  1989–91

Legorreta and Predock
are both inheritors of the
Barragán tradition:

a Víctor Legorreta, Víctor and
   Jacinta House, Mexico City,
   Mexico, 1996
b Ricardo Legorreta,
   Greenberg House, Brentwood,
   California, 1991
c Ricardo Legorreta, Akle House,
   Valle de Bravo, Mexico, 1994
d Antoine Predock, Zuber House,
   Phoenix, Arizona, 1987–9:
   exterior view
e Zuber House: courtyard
f Zuber House: looking towards
   the city from the deck

a	c		e	
b			d	f

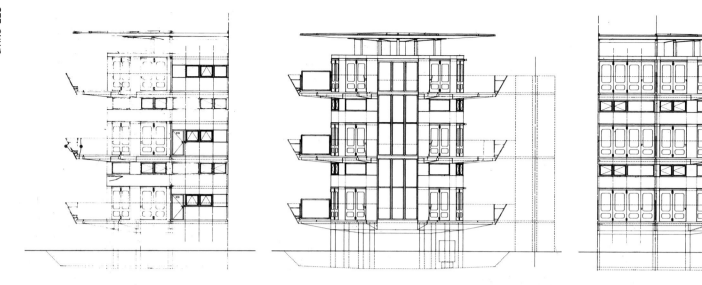

other architects including Leon Krier (Belvedere, 1988) and Tony Atkin (Beach pavilion, 1987) where the aim is to rediscover the virtues of traditional townships and reinforce them with covenants and design codes. Or like Lucien Kroll's masterplan for 'Ecolonia' at Alphen aan den Rijn in The Netherlands, 1995 onwards, a European Union-funded demonstration project for low-energy housing designed by nine firms of Dutch and Belgian architects working with nine developers. Or even like the town of Celebration in Florida, a Disney venture masterplanned by Robert Stern and Jaquelin Robertson – with buildings contributed by Aldo Rossi, Robert Venturi, Philip Johnson and others (see 'Leisure'). These places are little different in principle from the model villages built either by enlightened industrialists or patrician landlords from the eighteenth to the twentieth centuries – except that today they tend to become vehicles for anti-modernist fervour. But in another sense, Porphyrios at Spetses was doing nothing more radical, say, than Francis Spoerry did when laying out the Mediterranean resort of Port Grimaud from the 1960s onwards: expressing holiday centres through the medium of regional architecture and individual homes rather than via alien resort hotels.

Even Jean Nouvel takes his place in this local-vernacular aspect of housing: his Pierre et Vacances apartment villas at Cap d'Ail, France,

1987–91, his Hotel Les Thermes at Dax, France, 1990–2, and his Hotel St James in Bordeaux, France, 1987–9, all draw on regional architectural characteristics, respectively houses clinging to cliffs like mineral outcrops, big resort houses shuttered against the sun, and rusting agricultural sheds. But in housing, Nouvel is perhaps better known for his social housing experiment of 'Nemausus' in Nîmes, 1985–7, which followed on from his earlier housing scheme at Saint-Ouen and is not remotely contextual. Nemausus is, in plan, a very familiar model: two parallel blocks of deck-access flats raised on *pilotis* with cars beneath. The difference comes both in the internal layout of the apartments, and in the architectural expression of low-cost industrialized components. Far from being standardized, the flats come in seventeen types (for the total of 114 units). They can be one, two, or three levels inside, and are all double-aspect – the access deck on the northern side and balconies to the south. The use of industrial metal cladding, doors and stairs on the outside of the six-storey blocks is an attempt at 'utility building' but is also a knowing nod at precedents such as the Eames House. Similarly the decks and balconies are treated highly architecturally, the mesh balustrades tilted outwards and terminated on each side short of the prow of each building, which is fully glazed from top to bottom. The horizontal mesh sun-louvres at roof level, however, continue

all the way round. The end effect is another knowing reference – linked to the white-modern 'steamship' aesthetic of the 1920s and 1930s, but reinterpreted for the post-*Star Wars* generation. The composition of each block depends upon the success of outside community living. Nemausus turned the plan of Le Corbusier's Unité d'Habitation inside out, as so many architects in the 1950s and 1960s had done, to create 'streets in the sky' on the outside rather than inside of the building. On the balcony sides, the industrial doors extend to the full width of each apartment, so allowing it to be opened up fully to the Mediterranean climate. This is fine if neighbour relations are amicable, since the screening between each apartment's slice of deck is rudimentary, but not so good if they are not. 'Challenging orthodox attitudes', as Nouvel claimed to have done with Nemausus, is always a dangerous thing to attempt with social housing, since the architect must somehow carry with him hundreds of other individuals whom he has never met and never will. How many of the tenants at Nemausus, one wonders, appreciated the industrial imagery (red warning lights, factory panic-buttons for bellpushes, raw interior finishes, punched-metal stairs) as a wry commentary on Corbusier's celebrated and misunderstood dictum, 'a house is a machine for living in'? One of the more revealing weaknesses of architects in the late

Less radical than it looks:
a Jean Nouvel, Nemausus Housing, Nîmes, France, 1985–7: section across site
b Nemausus Housing: two parallel blocks of deck-access flats
c Nemausus Housing: courtyard
d Nemausus Housing: detail of stairwell
e Clare Design, Cotton Tree Housing, Sunshine Coast, Australia, 1992–5: Cotton Tree is a social housing scheme which is both flexible and sustainable, for families and single occupiers
f Cotton Tree Housing: interior of apartment

a		e f
b		
c d		

twentieth century was to take a contemporary-art aesthetic (in which the notion of 'installation' is key, and cross-cultural references abound) and apply it not only to the wealthy private patrons who collect such art and architecture, but also to social housing. The user response is inevitably different, and cannot be programmed.

Yet social housing of all types creates its own folk memory. When the notorious 'crescents' of the concrete 1960s system-built Hulme Estate in Manchester, England, degenerated into modern slums inhabited by squatters, the estate became known not only as a black spot for drugs dealing and crime, but also for an extraordinary flowering of creative culture as the illegal tenants set up studios and crafts-based businesses within the generous spaces of the neglected blocks. The solution of the authorities in the 1990s was exactly the same as the response of Victorian authority to the 'rookeries' of a century or more earlier: the perceived slums were demolished. The difference was that in the 1990s, many of the displaced tenants were then offered the chance not only to go legitimate, but to have a say in the design of the replacement buildings. Irony of ironies, 'Homes for Change' (by Mills Beaumont Leavey Channon, 1993-6), the building that evolved from this process, was a densely urban, part system-built, deck-access block, in direct line of descent from

the demolished housing. The clothes of the buildings, in particular timber cladding and mesh balconies, no more disguised the origin of the building type than did Nouvel's industrial appurtenances in Nîmes: but in the case of the Manchester housing, it was as a direct result of tenant consultation (and included a workshop element, another nineteenth-century idea). This did not prevent the inevitable process of entropy from beginning afresh: within a few months of the first buildings being completed, reports began to circulate of graffiti and security grilles beginning to appear.

What all such experiments come down to is funding, or the lack of it. Lack of money – always the case with publicly funded housing – means lack of space, particularly in places where land costs are high. Social housing is therefore nearly always an exercise in achieving density of population, both within a given area and within a given building. Whether that density is dressed up in the industrial aesthetic of Nouvel or the Cyclopean classicism of Bofill makes, in the end, little difference. Ultimately the poor are packaged in a way that the rich are not. The trade-off, for the architect, is always the same: if a certain number of homes has to be provided within a development for a set price per square metre, then how much of the available money should be spent on good quality materials

and fittings, and how much should be devoted to providing more generous spaces? The answer is nearly always that space is the most desirable attribute of housing, therefore attempts must be made – through simplification, through repetition, through use of industrialized components, by building tall – to maximize the interior volume of each individual home and to maximize the usable outdoor space for gardens, play areas and so forth. Oddly, this laudable emphasis on space can go too far: it is not unusual to find social housing with relatively generous room sizes – and cheaply built to achieve that – virtually alongside private-sector speculative housing where rooms are smaller but materials generally better. That dissonance reflects the fact of who is making the investment in each case, and what the perceived value of the home to the occupier is: as a place to live, as an investment, as a status symbol.

Rules are never absolute: there are strongly architectural developments that defy conventional categorization, such as Piet Blom's extraordinary 'Tree' Houses, 1973-8, in Helmsond, The Netherlands, where each house takes the form of a cube balanced on one point, arranged in series around the t'Speelhuis community centre like an architectural forest. But this raises a further point: the difference between nationalities when it comes to attitudes between the public and private sectors. In a society

a c e g

f

b d

a Piet Blom, 'Tree' Houses, Helmsond, The Netherlands, 1973-8: detail
b Kisho Kurokawa, Nagakin Capsule Tower, Tokyo, 1970-2: contextual view
c 'Tree' Houses: exterior view
d Nagakin Capsule Tower: interior of capsule
e Mills Beaumont Leavey Channon Architects, 'Homes for Change', Hulme Estate, Manchester, England, 1993-6: deck access block
f 'Homes for Change': model
g 'Homes for Change': exterior

where housing is habitually though not exclusively rented in both sectors and across all classes (France and The Netherlands are examples), there is not such a sharp distinction in attitude as there is, for instance, in the United States or United Kingdom, where property-owning is a way of life that defines class and status. There, the difference between private housing and social housing is instantly apparent. In the case of Piet Blom's 'Tree' houses (and many another Dutch residential quarter) you would not know, or need to know.

However, the old desire for economies of scale constantly reassert themselves: hence Richard Rogers' experimental project for an industrialized housing system in Korea, 1992 – a modular system of prefabricated housing units, deliverable by truck and stackable in virtually any configuration and to great heights if necessary. There was a more than passing similarity to the earlier work of the Japanese Metabolists (Arata Isosaki's unbuilt 'Clusters in the Air', 1962, and especially Kisho Kurokawa's Nagakin Capsule Tower, Tokyo, 1970-2) where, as with Rogers' scheme, the house modules were driven to the site and craned into position, in that case on twin concrete cores. Similarly the idea can be cross-referenced to Paul Rudolph's unbuilt 1967 Graphic Arts Center project in New York, which played with its room-elements in related fashion. But as Charles

Jencks pointed out in 1977, the notion of creating buildings by stacking boxes has recurred every five years or so since Walter Gropius suggested it in 1922: Kurokawa is one of the very few to have achieved it. In Rogers' case, the research showed that a production run of 100,000 units could be produced in factory conditions at 20 per cent of conventional construction costs. As is perhaps typical in such circumstances (Wright's Usonian Houses spring to mind) the ideas tend to be recirculated into homes for wealthier people: so Rogers returned to the stacked-units idea, though the construction principles were more Kahnian, for his large-scale Montevetro apartment building of 1994-9 in Battersea, London: Thames-side homes for the well-heeled, rather than humane housing for the Korean industrial workforce.

A more pragmatic solution to achieving urban density and economy of scale in social housing was provided by Renzo Piano's large Rue de Meaux housing complex in Paris, 1987-91, which explores facade-making with large terracotta tiles within a delicate rectilinear grid of glass-reinforced concrete panels. It fills an urban block – taking in some existing buildings – around a large courtyard and represents an intelligent modernist reworking of an ancient and highly effective European urban typology.

For one-off houses, clients – although rarely with an unlimited budget – are commissioning for

a d
b
c e
   f g

The rationalist grid meets the new organicism:
a Renzo Piano Building Workshop, Rue de Meaux Housing, Paris, 1987–91: elevation
b Rue de Meaux Housing: facade detail
c Rue de Meaux Housing: courtyard

d Ushida Findlay, Soft and Hairy House, Tsukuba, Japan, 1994
e Ushida Findlay, Truss Wall House, Tokyo, 1991–3: view from the street
f Truss Wall House: living space
g Soft and Hairy House: bathroom

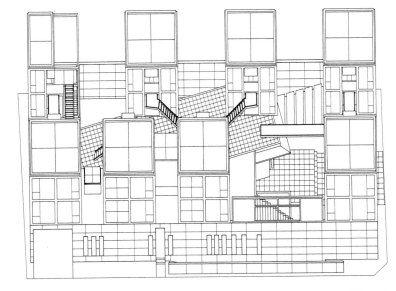

a   f

b d

c e

themselves and can make their own decisions as to how the balance is struck between space, quality of materials, and valuable objects such as furniture and electric gadgetry. A significant number of architect-designed private houses are on tight plots that place most emphasis on the architectonic quality of internal spaces, rather than on the extent or quality of outdoor space. This is especially true in Japan, where land is scarce and very valuable. Ushida Findlay's series of private houses in Tokyo from the late 1980s onwards (the Echo Chamber, the Truss Wall House, the Soft and Hairy House and so on) are exercises in a particular art of containment which is the exact opposite, for example, of the disassembled forms of a typical American house by 'Jumbly' architects such as Frank Gehry or Stephen Holl or Eric Owen Moss. The Truss Wall House, 1991–3, in Tsurukawa, a suburb of Machida-City in Japan, is – despite its startling Expressionist-Organic form – a typically Japanese response to an amazingly hostile urban environment. These are not the suburbs of the gently hissing summer lawns one associates with other world cities. These are places where people build homes on tiny plots jammed together like tombs in a cemetery – but without the associated calm. A clutter of electric wires festoons these streets at high level, traffic whips past, railways rattle close by, open gardens are rare and tiny. Unsurprisingly, such suburban houses

tend to turn in on themselves: there is nowhere else remotely comfortable to turn. Thus the Truss Wall House (a name that misleadingly implies something rectilinear) is focused on a small internal courtyard – itself something of a miracle, considering the tiny footprint of the building – and also manages a ramp to a little patch of roof garden.

Bedrooms are sunk partly below street level, the first-floor living room is double-height, and the house's fluid exterior is matched by an equally fluid interior, both in plan and section. Concrete sprayed onto mesh hung from vertical trusses achieves the plastic appearance. Inside, the parallels are as much with boat fit-outs as with conventional furnishing: as with boats, space is so limited that built-in furniture is the most efficient option. Recalling Art Nouveau and the work of such disparate architects as Gaudí and even Mackintosh, the house is conceived as a metaphor for a human organ: its spaces are like the auricles and ventricles of the heart, its people-circulation flows similarly, while its double walls contain air circulation as well as insulation.

It is worth recording that not all Japanese architects respond to such a crowded context in this introverted way. Shinichi Ogawa's Cubist House in Yamaguchi, 1990, for instance, is a glass cube containing a ground floor of four linked smaller solid cubes enclosing bedroom, kitchen, bathroom,

and so on. But the first floor – on top of these, attained by a perforated stainless steel ramp with glass landings – is the client's studio, agora-phobically open to view on all sides. It thus aggressively and belligerently does exactly what instinct suggests it should not. The house is, incidentally, not Cubist, merely cubic.

The architect Kazuhiro Ishii reacted against the increasingly exhibitionist architecture of new individual houses by returning to a consideration of the traditional Sukiya style. Just as humble homes had always acted as a corrective to the grandiose castles and temples of the élite, so Ishii wished to point up the decadence of much modern architecture. 'I suspect urban conditions in the Japan of today have reached a limit,' he wrote. 'Although our cities brim with vitality, from the standpoint of an environment for daily life, they are no more than artificialities heaped on top of other artificialities.' But Ishii, in designing a 1995 rural retreat for an old widow in hilly woodland near the Seto Inland Sea, was no Luddite: he used a Fuller dome, covered with Teflon film, at the centre of his plan, where it shelters the Buddhist shrine, next to the tea pavilion.

This, however, was a rich client's privilege. For most, the dense urban condition had to be faced, and the new generation of Japanese architects proved capable of a modernist restraint there too, as

a   Toshio Akimoto, Yakult
    company housing, Tokyo,
    1990: plan
b   Yakult Company Housing:
    dormitory block
c   Kazuo Sejima, Seiyaku
    Women's Dormitory,
    Kumamoto, Japan, 1991:
    communal living space
d   Yakult Company Housing:
    circulation between blocks
e   Seiyaku Women's Dormitory:
    street facade
f   Shinichi Ogawa, Cubist House,
    Yamaguchi, Japan, 1990

a

b   c

Tradition – plus a Bucky dome
recalling Bruno Taut:
a Kazuhiro Ishii, Sukiya-Yu,
   Seto Inland Sea, Japan, 1995:
   tea pavilion interior
b Sukiya-Yu: aerial view
c Sukiya-Yu: site plan
   and elevations

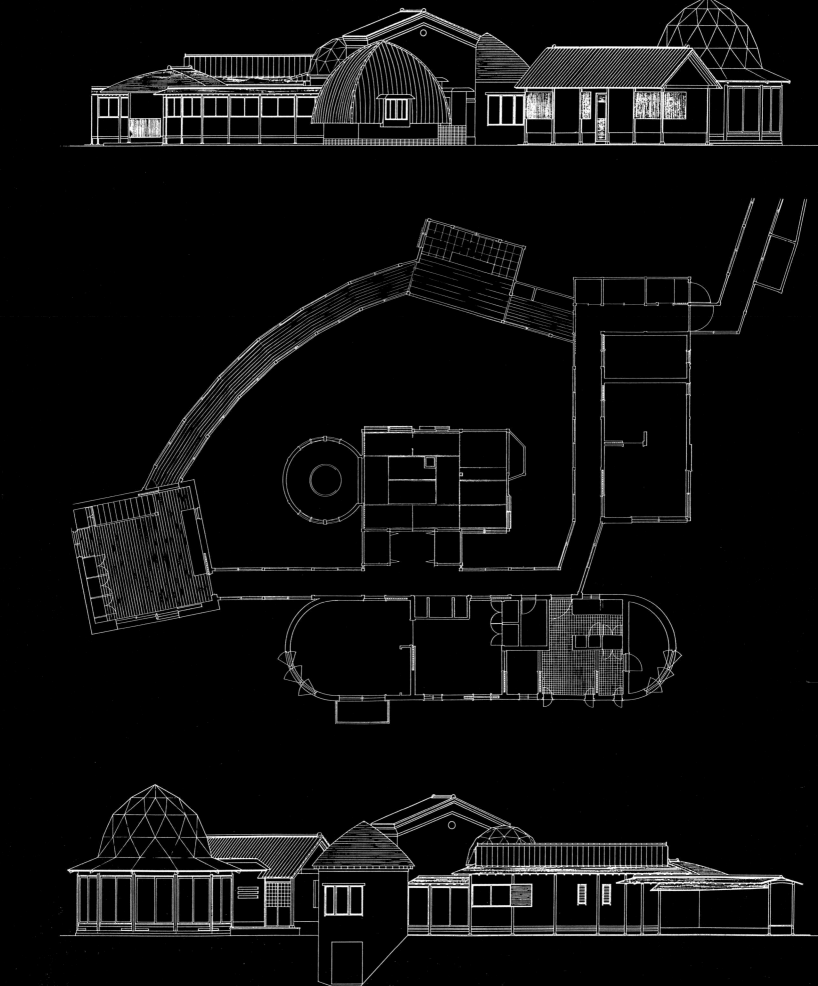

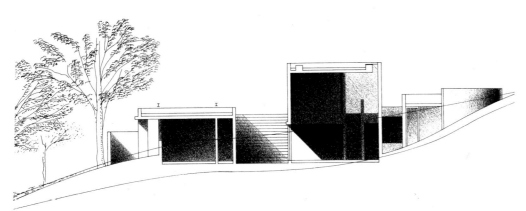

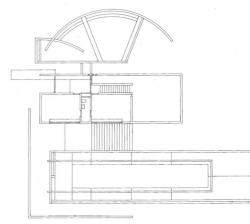

with Kazuo Sejima's Seiyaku Women's Dormitory in Kumamoto, 1991, or the tougher, industrial forms of the mid-1990s Yakult company housing in Tokyo by Toshio Akimoto, with its blind walls at ground level and raised plinth around which two-storey dormitory blocks gather like staircases round an Oxbridge quad. Tadao Ando internalized his 1983–5 Nakayama House in Nara for some of the same reasons that Ushida Findlay did at the Truss Wall House – though Ando's site was not quite so hemmed-in by the city. At Nara he simply created a rectangular concrete box divided in half longitudinally – half being the house, and half a prison-like yard, echoed in a smaller but equally enclosed roof terrace to the house. The sense of containment is absolute, and Ando used the split box on a number of other projects. Elsewhere, as at his Kidosaki House, 1982–6, things are less extreme, the great curve of the entrance wall acting as a sheltering hand rather than an abrupt barrier.

Just as space is routinely referred to as the ultimate luxury so, by the end of the century, an apparent absence of possessions had come to signify wealth rather than monastic austerity. The minimalist house is the ultimate statement of separation from normal humanity, for several reasons. Poor people like to display what little they own, for the very reason that it is all they have. Averagely wealthy people still accumulate clutter, and the art objects

that some of them collect and mostly hang on the walls, are different only qualitatively from the mass-produced bibelots of the lower orders (and that itself is arguable, in Jeff Koons' terms). But the very rich and very self-aware can live a life that is in itself a form of performance art, merely by dressing a certain way and inhabiting a certain kind of space. A small but élite band of minimalist architects designs the houses for these people, and also the shops that sell the kind of well-cut, unostentatious clothes they like to wear, and the restaurants where they like to dine. Their cars, one imagines, are German, and usually either black or silver.

If one was looking for a precedent – outside the monastic cell – for this kind of living, one would look inevitably at Mies van der Rohe's Farnsworth House in Illinois, 1946–50, and its Philip Johnson derivative at New Canaan, Connecticut, 1949–50. One would consider the 'traditional' Japanese house and its raked Zen garden. In both cases, the act of living is of symbolic or religious significance. There are rituals to be undertaken. The living is not easy – it is a disciplined act. Slobbing around is not an option. Yet for all that it is easy to poke fun at the minimalists – they are too easily characterized, as in Evelyn Waugh's Bauhaus-derived architect, Professor Otto Silenus (*Decline and Fall*, 1928), as humourless, emotionally suspect beings preying on

Some of Ando's houses are astonishingly austere:
a Tadao Ando, Koshino House and addition, Ashiya, Hyogo, Japan, 1979–81, 1983–4: section and plan
b Koshino House: view into living space
c Tadao Ando, Nakayama House, Nara, Japan, 1983–5: interior of living space
d Nakayama House: courtyard
e Nakayama House: aerial view

the affectations of the rich – the best of their work genuinely attempts to capture some of the attributes of home-making before consumerism became pervasive. It is therefore both paradoxical and fully understandable that only the wealthy (people for whom, like monks, money is not a problem) tend to indulge in this way of living. One could go further and wonder if it is a kind of subconscious act of contrition, but it is probably easier to conclude that, when you can have what most people would regard as everything, perhaps the neat response is to appear to have nothing. Nothing but land, and air, and water, and limitless space. This way of thinking is related to the ultimate symbol of power in the corporate office hierarchy – not to need an office, or a desk, when you have the wide world and all that is

in it. Emptiness implies fullness, the way that white contains all the colours of the spectrum.

In one sense the work of John Pawson and Claudio Silvestrin – partners at one point, later practising separately – or of less severe architects such as Richard Meier in the United States, David Chipperfield or Rick Mather in Britain (particularly with Mather's masterly Hampstead house of 1997, The Priory) – is historicist rather than contemporary. Their houses have the authentic casbah look but they can do with ease what their modernist ancestors only dreamed of – particularly in the way they use the new technology of structural and electronic glass. Even Future Systems' Hauer-King house in London's Canonbury, 1995, deemed very radical at the time, was content to echo Chareau and Lubetkin in its

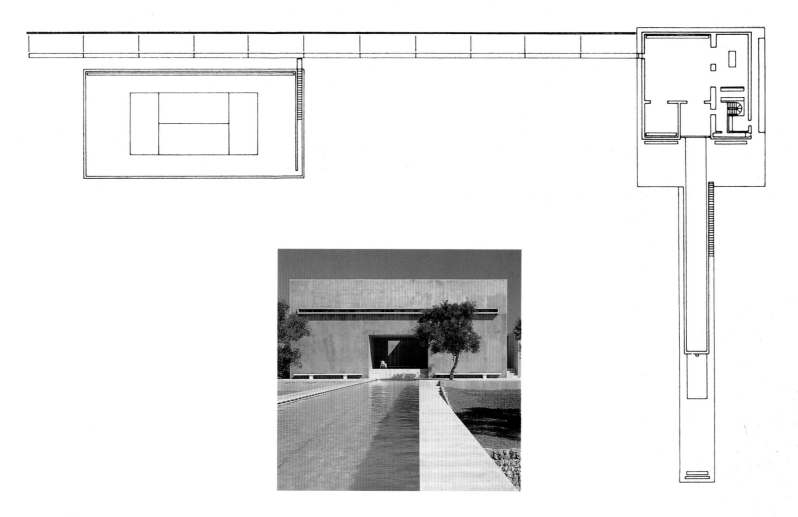

a   c e
          d
b

The architect's bag of references is both geographic and historical:

a John Pawson and Claudio Silvestrin, Neuendorf House, Mallorca, Spain, 1987–9: plan

b Neuendorf House: exterior view

c Anthony Hudson, Baggy House, Devon, England, 1993–4: contextual view

d Future Systems, Hauer-King House, Canonbury, London, 1995

e Hudson Featherstone Architects, Baggy House Pool, Devon, 1997

glass-block front elevation. While Meier, Chipperfield and Mather fruitfully explored and developed the heroic white-modern architecture of the 1920s and 1930s, Pawson and Silvestrin's Neuendorf House in Mallorca, Spain, is as much an exploration of the ancient architecture of that island as any adobe-inspired exercise by Antoine Predock in Arizona. It is only a holiday home yet, like so many fortresses in the area, it is approached with reverence up a long, stepped path, cars being kept at a distance. Another approach is invisibility: while plenty of architects choose to express, overtly or covertly, references from architects of the past in their work – a heroic example such as Anthony Hudson's 1994 'Baggy House' on the cliffs in Devon, England, is bursting with references to Mies, Voysey, Mackintosh *et al* – an increasing trend is

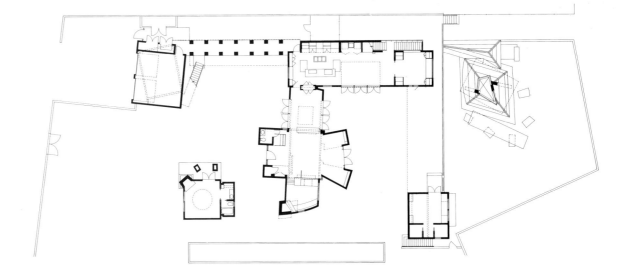

for earth-sheltered housing, scarcely visible from its surroundings, which draws its luxury not from its internal spaces or its external architecture but solely from the views it commands. An early example of this type is the Hill House at La Honda, California, 1977–9, perched high on a ridge, by Steven Badanes and John Ringel in the 'alternative' practice known as Jersey Devil. A later example is by Future Systems on the Pembroke coast in Wales, 1997–8, which acts as an 'eye' out over the sea. Exclusiveness here comes from a combination of secrecy and perfect siting.

The antidote to such refined exercises in architectural editing and excision is, as implied earlier, the houses constructed by the 'Jumblies'. Disassembled, deconstructed, call it what you will, Jumbly architecture, from Gehry in California (Schnabel House, Brentwood, 1986–9) to Daryl Jackson in New South Wales (Beach House, Bermagui, 1989–90) can be seen as an expression of engagement with the disorder of modern life, rather than retreat from it. Thus RoTo's Qwfk House in New Jersey, 1989–95, while nominally obscure, is physically joyous. RoTo (Michael Rotondi and Clark Stevens, both formerly key members of Morphosis) has a more complex approach than merely the architecture-as-complexity-theory. The Qwfk House, also known as the Teiger House, is L-shaped in plan, but bursts out all over in all kinds of materials – a

a
b   d

c

Once more, houses aspire to townships:
a Frank O Gehry & Associates, Schnabel House, Brentwood, California, 1986–9: plan
b Daryl Jackson, Beach House, Bermagui, New South Wales, Australia, 1989–90: exterior
c Bermagui Beach House: interior
d Schnabel House: exterior

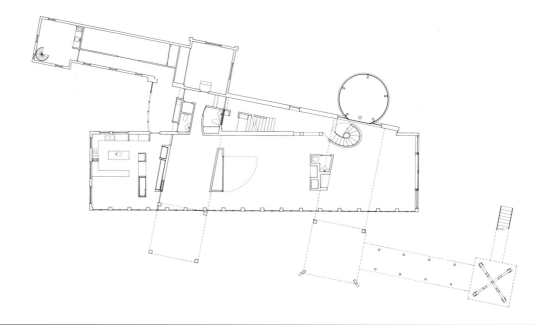

a
b
c
d e

rare example of extreme Californian architecture making it across to the conservative East Coast, to be compared in some respects with the Sag Pond House, 1990–94, on Long Island by Argentinian-born Diane Agrest and Mario Gandelsonas, which dissassembles the various components of the house in a manner not unrelated to Gehry. But then RoTo have built not only elsewhere in the States, but also in Japan, and are capable of moving from primitive hut architecture to the sophisticated plate-tectonics of their Warehouse C centre in Nagasaki. Rather more ordered though, in its celebration of industrial bits and pieces just as Jumbly, is John Young's Deckhouse in Hammersmith, London, 1986–9. Young, the partner of Richard Rogers most concerned with the sourcing and development of components, designed a house

that – though with its own strong sense of domestic ritual – is another modern alternative to extreme minimalism. Indeed, like all the products of the Rogers stable, it is positively decorative – consider the use of circular industrial heating units as roundels, a theatrical lighting rig, and brightly coloured exposed structural members. Its celebration of the bathroom – the space around which the house revolves – may be very 1990s, but in feel the place is historicist, with its references not only to Eames but also to Neutra, Chareau and Prouvé. Just as the speculative builders of Victorian times frequently made themselves a house in a row that was a little bigger and finer than its for-sale neighbours, so Young's Deckhouse is the bookend to a row of apartments built by the Rogers

Partnership as a way of funding their own office development alongside.

The house continues its Janus-like progress. It becomes increasingly apparent that however frantic the headline form-making becomes there are constraints that tie all but a few architects to derivatives of layouts and styles that have evolved over centuries – those constraints being as much to do with experience and appropriateness as bureaucratic interference. It is not just the prevalence of architect-designed furniture from the middle years of the century that gives so many house interiors an over-familiar feel: it is the fact that, ultimately, the house as a building type cannot be endlessly re-invented. Its variants can, however, be re-combined and reinterpreted.

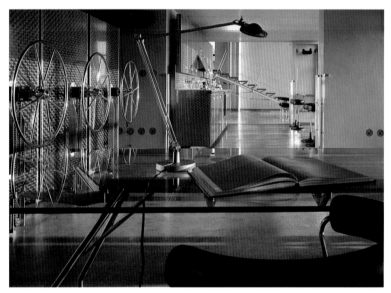

The abstracted domesticity at Sag Pond versus the anti-domesticity of the Deckhouse:

a   Agrest & Gandelsonas Architects, House on Sag Pond, Long Island, New York, 1990–3: plan

b   House on Sag Pond: exterior view

c   House on Sag Pond: interior of living space

d   John Young, Deckhouse, Hammersmith, London, 1986–9: view of dining space with views beyond to the Thames

e   Deckhouse: use of industrial baroque details

WORKPLACE *Offices & business parks* The office building survives, despite the threat of low-cost electronic links, the steady rise of self-employment, and the ecological need to reduce car journeys and power consumption. The corporate headquarters building is in rude health, both in and out of town, and the growth of science and business parks has become a worldwide phenomenon, employing millions. But more interesting than either, perhaps, is the 'boutique office' – the small-scale building that allows for alternative ways of working closer to home.

'The role of the architect is to transform society and take it forward, to give people a desire to discover new ways of living and working.'
Gaetano Pesce, 1994.

Two contradictory sets of sociological data
make any consideration of future office architecture intriguing, if not downright dangerous. One set of forecasts shows an ever greater proportion of the world's working population becoming office-based, as blue-collar manual occupations decline and white-collar service activities become steadily more dominant. Another predicts the death of the office building, brought about by a combination of new information technology, greater self-employment, the need to reduce wasteful travel between home and work, and – in the public sector – the fashion for decentralization of public services into small, locally based buildings that appear more approachable and democratic. Yet for all this, the corporate headquarters building – now augmented by the explosive growth in direct-sales and telephone-helpline buildings – appears to be burgeoning. This has proved to be one of the most enduring of all building types, and one capable of embracing both the overblown corporatism of Philip Johnson's AT&T building in New York (the 'Chippendale Skyscraper') 1978–83, and the small-scale bricolage of Eric Owen Moss's

Gary Group Headquarters in Culver City, Los Angeles of 1988–90. From Kenzo Tange's Kafkaesque Tokyo Metropolitan Government HQ, 1991, to the hermit's caves of Balkrishna Doshi's Sangath studio development of 1981 in Ahmedabad, India.

The vast scale differences and surface treatments possible in office buildings are however mostly a factor of repetition: the individual workplace varies comparatively little across the various types of building on offer. As a typology, then, the office building is adaptable only up to a point. A seldom challenged assumption has it that no single aspect of the built environment has changed so radically in the last two decades of the twentieth century as this particular building type. In respect of the genre of edge-of-town workplaces, this is perhaps true. But in the urban centres, the process of change has mostly come down to three things: the need to accommodate computer-based working methods with their predictable, if in the short term dramatic, heat and cabling implications; the idea of the 'democratic' rather than hierarchical workplace, particularly when desk-sharing is in evidence; and the return, after a relatively short period in abeyance, of the atrium.

In terms of physical appearance, the notion of radical change means little more, perhaps, than that the designers of city centre standard speculative office blocks have finally adopted some of the

	b	c
a		d
		e f

The chameleon office transforms itself at will:
a Philip Johnson, AT&T building, New York, 1978–83
b Kenzo Tange, Tokyo Metropolitan Government HQ, Tokyo, 1991
c Eric Owen Moss, Paramount–Linblade–Gary Group Complex, Culver City, California, 1988–90: plan and section
d Paramount–Linblade–Gary Group: street facade
e James Stirling Michael Wilford & Associates, No 1 Poultry, London, 1986–97: exterior view
f No 1 Poultry: plan

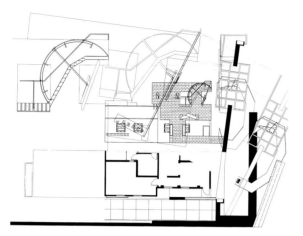

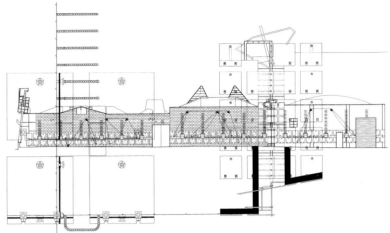

elements of the great American and European corporate headquarters. Frank Lloyd Wright's atrium-based Larkin Building of 1903 was the harbinger of this particular building type that was to mature in the 1960s and 1970s. The chasm that existed between the relative quality of commissioned headquarters and mere containers of net lettable space has therefore narrowed somewhat, and occasionally a great deal. James Stirling and Michael Wilford's muscular arrangement of drum and triangle at Number One Poultry in the City of London, 1986–97, looks very like a tailor-made office building, but is in fact speculative lettable office and retail space. Its strength derives from its unusual and strong-minded developer, the landowner Lord (Peter) Palumbo, and the legendarily lengthy planning battle he fought in order to build on that site. In general, though, the lessons learned by the speculative builders are mainly concerned with the quality of internal space, transparency, and external landscape. Their avatars include the vastly differing examples of Kevin Roche John Dinkeloo & Associates' Ford Foundation building in New York, 1963–8, and Herman Hertzberger's Centraal Beheer insurance company at Apeldoorn in The Netherlands, 1968–72.

Roche's building anticipates the grand corporate edifices of the late 1980s as much as it recalls Wright at Larkin – again there is the grand central

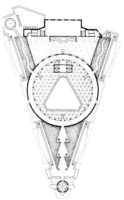

space, but here it is vastly enlarged, planted and side-lit, drawing in the outside world. In contrast, Larkin was a self-contained fortress. At Apeldoorn Hertzberger used his structuralist theories to produce a beehive of cells, an arrangement that offered both a more domestic scale and – within the grid framework provided – the opportunity for the users to customize their own spaces, still open-plan in format. From here to the 'democratic' offices of the 1980s was not a big step. Niels Torp's SAS headquarters in Frösundavik, Sweden, 1985–7, keeps its big space for the public areas and is otherwise cellular. Ralph Erskine's 'Lila Bommen' block in Gothenburg 1986–90, questioned the orthogonality of the atrium, an exploration that culminated in its immediate successor, the 'Ark' building in London's Hammersmith, 1988–91, now the UK headquarters of Seagram. Like Centraal Beheer, 'The Ark' mixed large open-plan spaces with smaller areas for *ad hoc* colonization. More originally, it subverts the idea of the forest-floor atrium, inherent to the genre since the Ford Foundation, by urbanizing it with a settlement of little buildings and alleys. The great space contained at the heart of the building's hull thus becomes apparent by degrees, rather than yielding all its dramatic potential at once.

Such discussions inevitably return to one cardinal rule of office design, with three sub-clauses.

The cardinal rule is that, with relatively rare exceptions, office design is to do with interiors: it is space-planning. The sub-clauses relate to those interiors – should they be cellular, open-plan, or Bürolandschaft (more of which later)? As with the classical orders of architecture, we can add another: composite, meaning a mix of these types. All office interiors of the twentieth century necessarily fall into one camp or other. So despite its regimented open-plan layout, the Larkin building anticipated many elements of later office blocks. In particular, its forbidding exterior, yielding internally to a tall narrow atrium overlooked by open galleries, is compellingly reworked in the Lloyd's of London building, designed by the Richard Rogers Partnership in 1976 and opened in 1986.

The Larkin building's floorplates were startlingly modern in proportion. It was mechanically ventilated, top-lit, with strongly expressed external stair towers and even such popular touches, nearly a century on, as a roof garden. Little had changed, aside from the sophistication of the structural columns and beams, by the time Wright came to build his Johnson Wax building in 1936. There, the atrium had expanded to become the main event, at a time when almost all other architects had temporarily abandoned the idea of the galleried space. In both buildings, workers were regarded as adjuncts to the fixtures and fittings. At Larkin, the desk workers were

constrained by the limited movement of the swing-out chairs attached to the desks. At Johnson, legendarily, it was necessary to sit with the correct posture on the (separate) three-legged chairs, or tip over backwards. Freedom of movement, let alone expression, was not on the agenda.

Then in the 1950s, spurred by the post-war economic reconstruction of Germany, came the notion of Bürolandschaft, purveyed by the Schnelle brothers. They took Wright's regimented open plan, and fruitfully rearranged it, soon with the help of the freestanding partitioning systems then beginning to appear. It meant office as landscape, rather than office as a clerical equivalent of the factory floor. It was meant to imply improved productivity and happiness. Designing Bürolandschaft was a highly technical and partly intuitive process. In the wrong hands, it became just a mess of scattered furniture. Inevitably, the cellular office made a swift return, sometimes in whole but more usually as part of a composite interior design – which usually means, in true hierarchical office fashion, that the lower orders stay out in the open (landscaped or not) while the management retreats back into its defensible cells.

The persistence of the Roman atrium plan in office design has been remarkable. There have been influential variations on this, such as the long narrow courtyard of Vasari and Buontalenti's Uffizi

a

b d
c e

The democratic workspace is wholly internalized:
a   Ralph Erskine, 'Lila Bommen', Gothenburg, Sweden, 1986–90
b   Ralph Erskine, The Ark, Hammersmith, London, 1988–91: the great space at the heart of the building becomes apparent by degrees
c   The Ark: built speculatively, the occupation of the entire building by Seagram ensured that the atrium did not become enclosed for fire separation
d   The Ark: the ship-like exterior
e   The Ark: plan

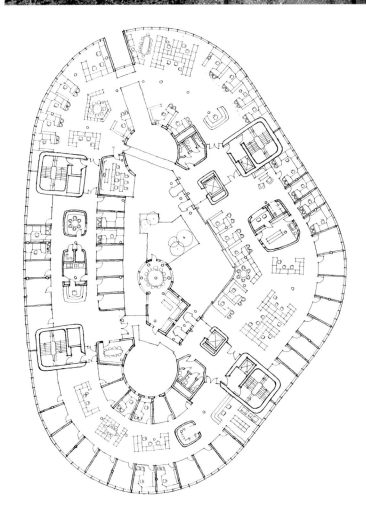

in Florence, begun in 1560, a programme with resonances for the many architects who see atria as internal streets. Sometimes the form expands to become virtually a city square – consider Sir William Chambers' late eighteenth-century Somerset House in London. Whatever the detail differences, the form of the office annulus with the private or public space at its centre – yielding light, air, and a tempered version of 'outside' that owes something to the monk's cloister – is immensely successful as a taxonomy. So much so, that the great mystery must be why it fell from fashion during mid-century, only to be rediscovered in the mid-1960s by such architects as Roche, John Portman with his hotels, and in Britain by the Cambridge-London axis of Colin St John Wilson and James Stirling. Once revived, however, it became one of the enduring images of the last third of the twentieth century. Although the atrium form might seem at odds with the other great development of the past hundred years – the skyscraper – it has now been successfully addressed in the form of the 'sky lobby': successive atria interleaving the office floors or – as in the case of Foster and Partners' Commerzbank building in Frankfurt, 1991–7 – by spiralling the atrium voids around the building as it rises, so giving all floors visual access to the spaces. This exemplifies the other aspect of the atrium's mutability during the period; popular though the ring-doughnut plan remains, the side atrium – the bite taken out of the circumference – came to be regarded as equally important. Once again, this was partly to do with hierarchy. In buildings with fine

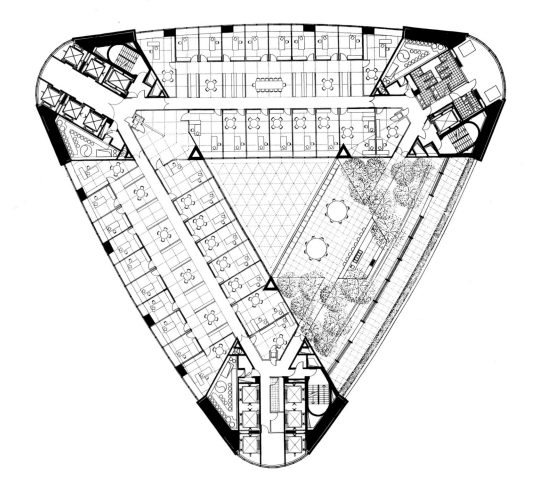

To every worker a window and a garden:

a Foster and Partners, Commerzbank, Frankfurt, Germany, 1991–7: atrium garden

b Commerzbank: contextual view

c Commerzbank: plan

d Commerzbank: view of atrium

internal atria, the spaces overlooking the atrium have a higher value, while those placed on the outside-facing walls – perhaps with perceived noise and pollution problems – can be seen as inferior. The side atrium addresses this problem while at the same time relating the building's interior to the city at large, thus partially overcoming the feeling that such places are turning their backs on the urban realm. In this sense the atrium becomes much more like a large conservatory, acting as an intermediate space between interior and exterior whilst preserving the visual links between the two. The distinction between the side atrium and the doughnut-plan atrium is the same as that between plaza and courtyard.

While such subtle morphological shifts were taking place in the city centre office building, a rather larger revolution was taking place on the outskirts of town. Many companies in the post-war years had built new headquarters out-of-town, so creating mini-townships of their own. This was particularly true of land-hungry industrial concerns: hence such notable buildings as Kevin Roche and John Dinkeloo's West Office for the Deere and Company headquarters in Moline, Illinois, 1975–8. The line here goes straight back to Eero Saarinen, who had designed the original HQ, 1957–64, before his death, upon which it passed to Roche and Dinkeloo as his successors. The West Office doubled the size of the

administration area, its facades of weathering steel derived from the original curtain wall, but were adapted to be more energy efficient. Though linked umbilically back to the main building, the West Office functions as an independent entity, its two low staggered wings enclosing a garden under a glazed roof expressed as a series of vaults. The block is sliced through by a route that echoes and exaggerates the slight displacement of the wings, kinking as it passes through the garden, the presence of the route acknowledged by triangular sections taken out of each wing to act as portals. In a way this internal focus is strange in the parkland setting of the Deere complex, but in fact the occupants of the building can face either way, the effect being like a temperate glasshouse in a botanical garden. Elsewhere, out-of-town company headquarters took on the role and scale of country houses, but the Deere building had more influence on current developments in a new building type: the office or business park.

The business park is another tempered 'outside' environment. Memorably captured by one developer in the phrase 'PhDs rolling in the grass', office parks emerged from their science-park roots because high-tech businesses used airports intensively, and the world's airports, being sited generally outside the cities they serve, offered hectares of flat land to build on. If not airports, then motorway intersections

would do. Seen in this light, office parks became the equivalent of nineteenth-century railway towns.

The business and science park as we understand it today was born in California in the early 1960s, when graduates of the University of California versed in the new skills of computer science wanted to establish their businesses in close proximity to the research facilities that the University could offer. The Californian headquarters of Hewlett-Packard evolved in exactly this way, cheek by jowl with the university. Here were the makings of what was to become Silicon Valley. Because university-based research is a globally mobile activity, reports of the Californian model soon flashed across the world. In particular it came to the attention of the scientists at Cambridge University in England. At the end of the 1960s, Trinity College, which owned a large area of unproductive land on the city's north-eastern edge, decided to create an equivalent of the American experience, as related by returning researchers. The idea appealed to city planners, who had long resisted heavy industry in the city (unlike Oxford, their great rivals) but who saw the clean, non-intrusive, futuristic idea of a science park as a legitimate way to generate economic growth.

Cambridge established a pattern: such parks generally began with relatively small businesses generated by the university itself, then acquired a name

a b

c

The workplace becomes a semi-rural retreat:
a   Kevin Roche John Dinkeloo & Associates, John Deere & Company West Office Building, Illinois, 1975–8: the out-of-town headquarters building, begun by Eero Saarinen in 1957

b   John Deere & Company West Office Building: two wings enclose a garden under glazed vaulted roofs
c   Arthur Erickson Architects, Napp Laboratories, Trinity College Science Park, Cambridge, 1979

that attracted small multinationals, so 'legitimizing' the area and attracting bigger multinationals. At this point developers, rather than universities and research groups, began to take an interest. Instead of building office blocks in traditional locations, they realized that they could build a different type of office building in a parkland setting out on the edges of towns, so attracting a different breed of occupier. Airports and motorway intersections were duly targeted. Retail soon followed where the offices had led, and leisure elements began to be included as well. Rapid decentralization from the city centre to the perimeter was soon under way.

Genres and sub-genres began to emerge. There are industrial parks, where the units are predominantly to do with manufacturing, storage and distribution. There are the research-based science and technology parks, such as the highly successful Sophia Antipolis on the French Riviera, or Tsukuba Science City in Japan. There are office parks, such as Stockley Park or Aztec West (Bristol) in Britain, its equivalent at Charles de Gaulle airport in Paris (indeed, at virtually every major airport in the world), or Yokohama in Japan. And, increasingly, there are 'Almost Everything Parks', invariably also at motorway or trunk road intersections near big cities, where all these elements converge – retail sheds, distribution warehouses, multiplex cinemas, office buildings,

research company headquarters, hotels. In the United Kingdom, the biggest of these Intersection Cities to date (see also 'Consumerism') may be found at Cribb's Causeway outside Bristol and at Cross Point outside Coventry. These are non-residential towns, utterly dependent upon the use of automobiles.

Two factors work against this trend, however. The first is the rediscovery of the traditional city, where land values have in recent years been falling. Tighter-packed office parks on reclaimed industrial land closer to the old centres are periodically mooted. The second is the research – carried out mostly as a joint project between Japan and Australia – into what is called 'The Multi-Function Polis' or MFP. First conceived in 1987 as a 'city of the future' for the Pacific Rim, this project went through a phase where people asked: why, given global electronic communications, does the MFP have to be gathered in one place like business parks or traditional cities? Could it not be a net of small nodes, linked electronically all around the Rim and indeed the globe? After endless conferences and papers, it was concluded that people still need to meet face to face in order to strike sparks off each other, and the MFP idea once again focused on the idea of a single, new urban centre, envisaged outside Adelaide in southern Australia. The trouble with such long-term research is

that cities have a habit of moving faster than the researchers. Workplaces, or work districts, emerge constantly, usually without the aid of heavyweight academic study or enlightened architectural input. Thus in 1992 Richard Rogers masterplanned a new quarter of Shanghai – Lu Jai – on ecological principles related to Radburn planning to create what the practice called a 'comprehensive design for a sustainable, compact twenty-four-hour city'. Scarcely had the ink dried on the plans when Shanghai, in the grip of economic boom, went ahead without Rogers and developed the land piecemeal and non-ecologically.

The MFP is really the Almost Everything Park with the added ingredients of housing and culture. To some extent, this means that the planning wheel has come full circle: for what is it but a New Town? This then raises another question: if all this, from the Californian experiments of the 1960s onwards, is really just about making segments of cities that are well connected both electronically and in terms of physical transport, then cannot existing cities absorb such functions perfectly happily? In response to this concepts emerge such as 'Millennium Point' in Birmingham, England, designed by Nicholas Grimshaw. This is a Japanese–French-style technopolis – which means a science and business park – shoehorned right into the old city centre where land

has been released by the collapse of old-fashioned industries. The old 'polis' thus returns to reclaim the new. The dense city is the winner, the spacious landscaped environment is the loser.

The effects of those early parks in California and Cambridge continue to ripple around the world, however. Every former Eastern bloc city, from Berlin to Brno, acquired its necklace of office parks. Increasingly, internationally renowned architects – such as Mario Bellini at Yokohama or Murphy Jahn at Munich – were asked to design them. It has become evident that, like shopping centres, in the long term they are a necessary phase in the evolution of the modern city, rather than a replacement for the traditional centre. Consequently, the architecture of individual buildings within them varies disconcertingly: cod-vernacular or faux-warehouse styles are frequently associated with, respectively, 'rural' and formerly industrial, particularly riverside, sites: science parks are fond of the image of high-tech; while more ambitious developers opt for an Expo-inspired approach of discrete pavilions in an intensive landscape. Like international Expos, these pavilions are by signature architects, on a masterplan that, likely as not, is drawn up by another big name.

An early example of the genre, Stockley Park near London's Heathrow, is a slice of history. Begun

Ways to dress up a standard floorplate:
a Arup Associates, Stockley Park, Heathrow, London, 1985–6
b Ian Ritchie, B8 Building, Stockley Park, Heathrow, London, 1988–90
c Foster and Partners, Stockley Park, Heathrow, London, 1987–9

a c

b

as a relatively low-key exercise with a family of unassuming pavilions developed by Arup Associates, it quickly grew in ambition, soon boasting contributions from Ian Ritchie, Norman Foster, Eric Parry, SOM, and rather more expansive and progressive buildings by the new generation who took over Arups. Such evolution partly reflected a desire to move away from the trading-estate origins of the business park towards something more akin to the landscape-with-buildings parks of the eighteenth century. But mostly it is to do with added value: perceived higher quality leading to actual higher rents and a better class of tenant.

In a final twist, some companies have gone right back to the Deere Company principle established by Saarinen and Roche, and formed their own out-of-town campuses which have become single-company townships. The most staggering growth was recorded by the Microsoft Corporation, which between 1984 and 1994 built 3.2 million square feet of office and research space on a 260-acre campus at Redmond, Washington. Seattle-based Callison Architecture began with an almost Hertzbergian cluster of small linked cruciform buildings dubbed 'starships' but soon found that the company's growth demanded more conventional and larger corporate-style office buildings. In spite of this the Microsoft campus has continued to evolve as just

that – a campus – to the extent that the company, for all its world domination, does not have an obvious architectural image, a key HQ building.

These continued to be as popular as ever. Philip Johnson provided a kind of grandfather clock with broken pediment for AT&T and (at roughly the same time) the camp perpendicular gothic of his Pittsburgh Plate Glass HQ in Pittsburgh, Pennsylvania. Michael Graves produced the awe-inspiring entrance portico of his Humana building in Louisville, Kentucky, 1982–6; Pei the unmistakable profile of his angular, looming Bank of China in Hong Kong, 1985–90, or the related First Interstate Bank in Dallas, 1984–6. In Japan, Hiroshi Hara produced an extraordinary collection of buildings including the hallucinogenic, vaguely Mediterranean, acropolis of the Yamato International Building in Tokyo, 1987, and the linked Grand Arch of his Umeda Sky Building in Osaka, 1993, which with its gantries and great central aperture looks as if it should launch rockets to Mars. Like Kenzo Tange's architecturally related Fuji Television Building in Tokyo, 1995 – another experiment in carving random holes out of a rectilinear grid – it is ugly in a way no truly functional structure taking this form would be, but that is not the point: it is right there, and you cannot help recognizing it.

After such examples, one warms to Microsoft. Just as the company produces software rather than

Corporate symbolism can
override all else:

a Philip Johnson, Pittsburgh
   Plate Glass Headquarters,
   Pittsburgh, Pennsylvania,
   1979-84
b Hiroshi Hara, Yamato
   International Building,
   Tokyo, 1987
c Michael Graves, Humana
   Building, Louisville, Kentucky,
   1982-6: exterior view

d Humana Building: the awe-
   inspiring entrance portico
e Hiroshi Hara, Umeda Sky
   Building, Umeda City,
   Osaka, Japan, 1993
f Kenzo Tange, Fuji Television
   Building, Tokyo, 1995

c d

a

b

e f

hardware, so its company image – insofar as it exists at all – is of landscape and water and general business park sprawl rather than of signature architecture. In a curious way it mirrors the older industry of the American Northwest represented by Boeing, which has evolved a 'university of the air' around its massive assembly plant in nearby Seattle. And for the same reason: companies undergoing explosive expansion, as Boeing did after it invented the wide-bodied passenger jet in 1969, need site planning and practical, rapidly built accommodation rather than glossy facades. Boeing's image, recognized worldwide, was the 747 'Jumbo' jet, a building in itself.

Similarly in England, the rapid growth of the Dyson domestic appliances company meant that plans for a company building of note – designed by architect Chris Wilkinson and engineer Tony Hunt – were overtaken by expansion as the firm became the fastest growing company in the UK and created its own campus on an industrial estate in rural Wiltshire. Again, the architecture proved less important than the clear image of James Dyson's designerly and increasingly ubiquitous cleaning machines. The difference was that Dyson – unlike the Boeing bosses or Bill Gates of Microsoft – had always hankered after a building that would express his company's ethos, and finally began to build it. In the meantime, he placed his staff at purpose-made giant tables of ten people each, and bought an Antonio Citterio Vitara chair (1997 cost: £400) for each employee, to ensure comfort and equality – office hierarchy being most usually expressed by a subtle gradation of chair types, from trainee to managing director. Dyson's philosophy of office design sounded very like that espoused by Microsoft or Disney Animation (see 'Leisure'): 'There are no department boundaries or borders or walls, ditches, moats, ha-has or minefields: freedom of movement and of expression is total,' Dyson wrote in 1997. 'I hope, in this way, to make everyone design-conscious, and to feel encouraged to make creative contributions.'

The middle way – a building that quietly expresses an unmistakable image of the organization it contains without shouting it from the rooftops – is exemplified by Carlo Scarpa's last building, the Banca Popolare di Verona, 1973–5. This is, as you would expect of Scarpa, as tailor-made and hand-crafted as a building can get. It has something of the

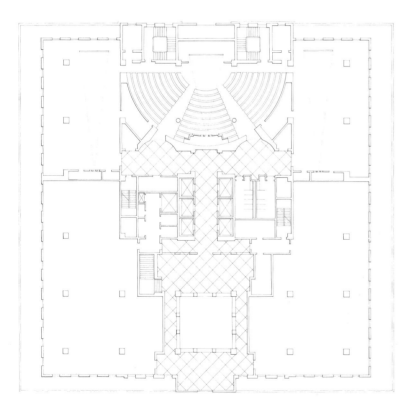

a b   d
       c e

Architecture skin-deep:
a   Michael Graves, Public Service Building, Portland, Oregon, 1980–3: plan
b   Public Service Building, Portland: exterior view Rejection of the orthogonal:
c   Ton Alberts and Max van Huut, NMB Headquarters, Amsterdam, 1979–87: the biggest gingerbread house ever created
d   NMB Headquarters: the rejection of the right angle in the interior, true to Steineresque Expressionism
e   Ton Alberts and Max van Huut, Gasunie Headquarters, Groningen, The Netherlands, 1989–94

feel of a painstakingly made boardroom interior brought out into the street, blinking in the sun. All Scarpa's tricks are here: of layering and incising, of sinking some apertures and projecting others, of relating the interior to the exterior, of using tactile materials and rich paint effects. Many a corporate building is all broad statement and no detail: Scarpa's Banca Popolare di Verona appears to work from the details up to the broad form. Such exercises in subtlety do not often commend themselves to the corporate mind.

While office park 'rurbania' continued to evolve on the fringes as an alternative form of workplace, the role of city-centre offices came under scrutiny. If the nature of the office is to be an internalized planning exercise, then what forms do office buildings contribute to the city at large? The uncomfortable fact is that the office block, like the shopping centre, usually does not want to be part of urban life. It generally gives little to the street in the form of shops, restaurants and public alleyways (an exception is the ground levels of North American superblocks, where an urban realm exists almost independently of what goes on up above). Nonetheless, this anti-urbanistic quality of the office building is contrasted with the desire of corporate clients to present a public image – something that is exceptionally difficult to design into a speculatively built block, where the final user is unknown. In the closing years of the century, certain architects began to ponder this. In the United States, after the shock administered to corporate America by the fame and

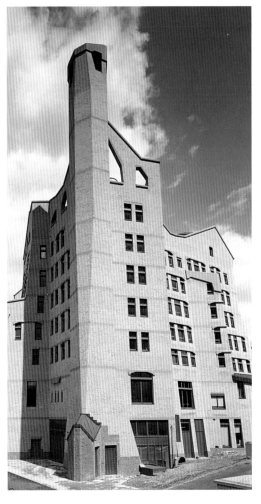

notoriety of Philip Johnson's AT&T building with its sumptuous entrance lobby, Michael Graves applied richly decorative facades to otherwise conventional blocks to house, among others, the Humana headquarters in Louisville, Kentucky Corporation, 1982-6 – arguably the lushest of them all – and the earlier Public Services Building in Portland, Oregon, 1980-3, which was not as lush as he'd originally wanted. In Europe, Ton Alberts and Max van Huut produced the anthroposophical NMB headquarters in Amsterdam, 1979-87 – a reaction against the tyranny of the right angle, true both to Expressionism and the thoughts of Rudolf Steiner – to house 2,000 banking staff. The general effect is to create what appears to be the biggest gingerbread house ever constructed. Where Graves relished large scale, Alberts and Van Huut try to break it down, both in the Amsterdam building and in their later, no less individual Gasunie Headquarters in Groningen, 1989-94.

Such buildings work on the macro-scale: driving the autoroute round Groningen, the Gasunie building stands in the flat landscape like a mesa in the Arizona desert. It is no less a declaration of the might of its occupants (northern Holland is built on natural gas, and the gas company funded the building of the city's bizarrely eclectic Groninger Museum, see 'Visual Arts') than Norman Foster's exaggeratedly detailed Hongkong and Shanghai Bank headquarters,

1979-86, or its looming neighbour, the aggressively angular Bank of China, 1985-90, by I M Pei. This is universal. Consider, for instance, Arquitectonica's Banco de Credito headquarters in Lima, Peru, 1982-8 – a large courtyard block of conventional plan, subverted both by its rocky landscape and by the free-form elements arranged around its inner facades. There is nothing so new in these examples apart from their differently extreme forms: they all represent an architecture of power and wealth.

This is most apparent in the world's financial centres, where show counts for a great deal but broad massing – the termite-hill aspect of such places – counts for more. Rogers' masterplan for Lu Jai in Shanghai, 1992, though overtaken by events, nonetheless represents a rare example of an attempt to impose order on the looming possibility (and, as it turned out, rapid arrival) of apparent chaos. The scheme remains as a valid diagram of how an office district can, so far as is possible, be 'sustainable' in the extraordinary growth conditions of the Pacific Rim. At this time, the population of Shanghai grew over a five year period from thirteen million to seventeen million as an industrial revolution overtook the country. Rogers' favourite motif of the radiating plan is here employed to create a Haussmann-like array of boulevards. As well as the radial routes there are three concentric rings of roads around a circular

park. The innermost is for pedestrians and bicycles; the middle ring is for trams and buses; and the outermost for cars. Conceived as a mixed-use community, with housing and shops as well as a preponderance of office blocks and towers, this diagram permits facilities within walking distance for inhabitants, while obliging those commuting by car to leave their vehicles at the perimeter (underground railways providing alternative transport). The buildings are massed in such a way as to create view corridors to the Huangpo River and Old Shanghai. The estimate was that Lu Jai would have an energy 'take' 70 per cent lower than a conventional commercial scheme of similar magnitude. Well, perhaps: it certainly proved that there is life in the century-old idea of segregatory planning, not to mention the equally venerable idea of the self-contained polis. By offering a solution to the urbanistic problem of the big office district – that the hundreds of thousands of desk spaces available result in a huge tidal drag of the population in and out every day, with associated pollution and congestion problems – the Rogers masterplan in a sense acknowledges the fate of mature business districts: that gradually, after the event of long-term building, car movements are discouraged and public transport increased. The inclusion of housing, however, is something that tends not to occur in

a   Arquitectonica, Banco de
    Credito, Lima, Peru, 1982-8:
    the architecture of power
    and wealth
b   Banco de Credito: exterior view
c   Arquitectonica, Banque de
    Luxembourg Headquarters,
    Luxembourg, 1989-94
d   Richard Rogers Partnership,
    Lu Jai masterplan,
    Shanghai, China, 1992
e   Pei Cobb Freed & Partners,
    Bank of China, Hong Kong,
    1985-90

```
          b c e
     a
          d
```

existing financial quarters, mainly because land is too scarce and expensive.

In this context, the architecture of individual office buildings becomes secondary, the ensemble effect being more important. In Hong Kong, Frankfurt, Atlanta, Dallas, the City of London, Manhattan, La Défense in Paris, and equivalent areas around the world, the appearance of commercial centres reflects their origins as teeming markets, where jostling, high-density existence is reflected in the clustering of the key buildings. To glance at the skyline of Hong Kong is to realize how deeply selective architectural photography must be in such places, where not only the relatively fine detail of Foster's Hongkong and Shanghai Bank building, but the coarser, larger scale of I M Pei's Bank of China, all but disappear in the throng. In the commercial arena buildings such as these are relatively rare: even when commissioned by the organization that is to use them, the need for speed generally means a standard approach of steel frame with clip-on skin, where the visible architecture goes no deeper than 6 inches into the depth of the building – always with the exception of a gorgeously tricked-out reception and lift lobby area. Such interventions that the architect can make, beyond the choice of surface materials, are therefore generally confined to modelling the mass of the structure.

It is paradoxical, then, that one of the canonic office buildings of the post-war era – Foster's Willis Faber Dumas (now Willis Corroon) building in Ipswich, England, 1970 – makes a play at not being architecture at all. By simply tracing the amoebic shape of the site in walls of black glass which, by day, reflect back the other buildings of the city around it, Willis Faber (to which Michael Hopkins, then with Foster Associates, contributed a great deal) seems to be an anti-building. With its deep plan and self-sufficiency of facilities – originally including a swimming pool for staff, and a lawn on the roof – it appears to exclude the town it reflects. By night, however, the lighting inside turns the walls transparent and all the workings are laid bare. Thus it becomes apparent that, all the time, the city was being observed by the workers within. And although the glass walls are a celebration of a particular moment in technological advancement – the building happened to be commissioned at the very moment when the Pilkington Glass Company had devised an early silicon-jointed frameless glazing system, which Foster then pushed to its limits – the night-time view reveals that the building is about more than its walls, that there is a tectonic quality to its open-plan interior that is almost wholly lacking in the skin-deep architecture of most commercial buildings.

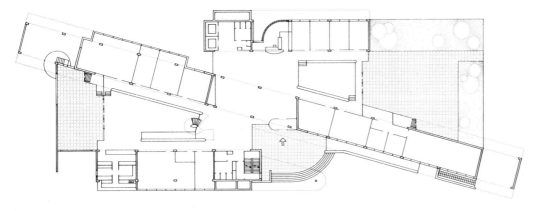

If Willis Faber represents one point of departure at the start of our chosen period, then so too, for very different reasons, does Herman Hertzberger's Centraal Beheer – another decentralizing insurance company headquarters, designed and built only three years earlier, 1968–72, which owes nothing to advances in technology, but a great deal to Hertzberger's theories about individual workspace. The Centraal Beheer is a deliberately rough-hewn building, designed in casbah-like fashion as a sequence of small modules building up to an indeterminate whole: a far more whole-hearted exercise in seeming non-architecture than the Foster building. For this reason, while Willis Faber looms large in any architectural appreciation of the modern office building – and little is ever said about how it functions internally – Centraal Beheer, with no particularly striking external aesthetic (so no stunning photos for the glossy magazines and books), tends to command the attention of space-planners and sociologists as the key building of the era.

In any Foster office building, self-discipline on the part of the worker is essential and personal space-making with its concomitant clutter is anathema. The appearance of his own office is testament to this. For Hertzberger, personal space-making and clutter were precisely the point of the exercise. The building is non-hierarchical to a fault – it does not even

have a single main entrance, which reinforces the village-like quality of its interior. And although open-plan in concept, it is divided up on a grid pattern with low walls, paths and furniture to allow each worker to colonize a part of it. Indeed, the workers appear to have seen this as a challenge and done their best to customize their own areas, even, in the early days, with makeshift partitions made of rope and bird-cages as well as the usual posters, plants and so on. All this freedom is given a focus in the galleried full-height social centre of the building, overlooked by restaurants and cafés. In contrast, the equivalent centre of Willis Faber is occupied by a succession of escalators rising through the building – though at the top, in the white space-frame pavilion overlooking the rooftop lawn, the clusters of Eames tables and chairs announce 'relaxation' in the usual controlled Fosterian manner. In the end, the difference was in the perceived nature of the companies themselves. At Willis Faber, it was stated from the outset that 'the pride taken in the immaculate running of the building ... would reflect on the company's working philosophy as a whole.' In contrast, Centraal Beheer also saw its building as a reflection on the co-operative company philosophy – and to this end was happy to allow the slightly anarchic consequences of Hertzberger's design. Hertzberger himself turned later to more assertive external architecture while not

abandoning his egalitarian views: his X-plan Benelux Merkenburo (trademark office) building in The Hague, 1990–3, has a distinctive and accomplished external form that is not merely the expression of interior function.

If Willis Faber remained committed to full open-plan, and Centraal Beheer to modified open-plan, neither as it happened was in tune with the emerging mood of the later 1970s and 1980s, which was a swing back to cellular office working. Office furniture and partitioning systems – not least Herman Miller's famous 'Action Office', designed in the 1960s – at first grappled with the problems of defining personal space and providing personal storage and working surfaces within the open-plan context. Later generations of furniture were more partition-based, creating relocatable walls that could be braced firmly between floor and ceiling. Because the upper tiers of management were the first to retreat back into small rooms, the cellular office came to be seen as a desirable objective for the ambitious office worker. Far from being democratic, the open floor therefore became associated with the lower orders. Promotion up the ranks – at first a matter of securing a bigger chair, more floor space, and increased amounts of storage compared with one's unpromoted colleagues – was finally symbolized by the acceptance into the élite of those entitled to their own cell,

Few architects can maintain
a non-architectural position
for long:

a Foster and Partners, Willis
   Faber Dumas Headquarters,
   Ipswich, England, 1970–5:
   the curtain wall
b Herman Hertzberger, Centraal
   Beheer I, Apeldoorn, The
   Netherlands, 1968–72: aerial
   view clearly showing 'honey-
   comb' of modules

c Willis Faber Dumas: interior
d Centraal Beheer: exterior detail
e Centraal Beheer: employees
   are able to personalize their
   own spaces
f Herman Hertzberger, Benelux
   Merkenburo, The Hague, The
   Netherlands, 1990–3: plan
g Benelux Merkenburo:
   exterior view

a c   f g

b d e

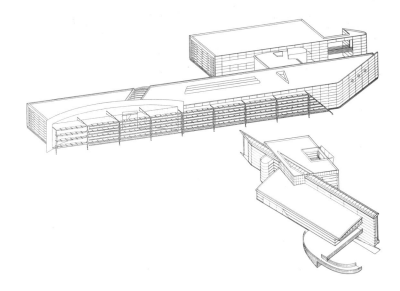

better still an inner cell guarded by an antechamber occupied by one's secretary. Upon attaining this Nirvana – vanishing from view of the general work-force as if received into Heaven – the aim then became to acquire a steadily larger cell in order to rise up the pecking order within the new cellular community. Because of the social distinctions it introduces, therefore, the worst kind of office layout for those committed to democracy is the 'mixed' system which is no different from the old front office and factory floor distinction of the industrial era. Far better perhaps, to espouse wholly one option or the other.

However, a new factor crept in during the late 1980s, spearheaded by IBM with its 'hot desk-ing' policy, which made the art of space planning into a science. This, driven by the recession-hit com-pany's need to reduce its worldwide overheads, was at first little more than a formalizing of the fact that many people in a large organization are relatively mobile, and at their desks relatively seldom, therefore that deskspace can be shared with others. The simple idea that people need not have one permanently designated personal space within an organization – because much time is spent in groups, in other branches, or working from home – was a big step for the personal ethos of a company and the way of lives of its staff, but did not radically alter the way office

buildings were created. It merely reduced the square metres necessary to process a given number of people, and put more emphasis on communal rather than individual work environments. That age-old cultural form – the open library floor flanked with carrels for intense study, the whole available for whoever comes along to use it – suddenly seemed highly relevant again.

The commercial need to reduce square footage coincided with the revolution in communica-tions equipment to create a new breed of aspira-tional manager – the freebooting new Action Man and Woman, toting mobile phone and lap-top com-puter, needing no office beyond the corner of a café table (an intriguing return to one of the sources of the modern office, the eighteenth-century coffee house). The New Action Employee still possesses the desired upper-management status of near-invisibility to the general workforce, but has the added bonus of emancipation from the desk, which therefore comes to be a symbol of slavery rather than power. Such mobile workers used to command relatively low status – sales people out on the road, generally – but have come to be seen as more glamorous, along the lines of foreign correspondents in the media. It is no coincidence that New Action Man and Woman arrived at a time when outside consultancies also came to enjoy very high status, being called in as

experts to advise on company policy in a way that no in-house team could hope to emulate. To be desk-bound, in this particular pecking order, is to seem unambitious. However, the desk – as we shall see later – has a powerful magnetic pull despite such developments.

Overriding all such social and hierarchical movements taking place in the white-collar labour market is a factor so enduring as to be regarded as permanent: the headquarters building as an expres-sion of corporate image. It has been said that a company that takes the time to commission a purpose-built headquarters is probably past its peak, since its attention is being diverted from the neces-sary business of growth. There may be some truth in this, but there is also research evidence that suggests the advertising power of signature architecture. Thus we find such buildings as Decq and Cornette's head-quarters for the Banque Populaire de l'Ouest outside Rennes in Brittany, France, 1988–90 – an exercise in what the architects insist is 'soft-tech', that answered the bank's expressed need for a new business culture in what had become a highly competitive financial services market. The main externally braced sheer glass facade, derived in part from the slightly earlier work of English high-tech exponents such as Nicholas Grimshaw and engineered by Peter Rice's RFR consul-tancy, was a new kind of architecture for France –

Office buildings must be
functional up to a point but
many are expressionist, too:

a   Decq + Cornette, Banque
    Populaire de l'Ouest,
    Rennes, France, 1988–90:
    exterior view

b   Jean Nouvel, CLM-BBDO
    Advertising HQ, St Germain,
    Paris, 1988–92: the oxidized
    steel hull is curiously
    contextualized on the riverside

c   Banque Populaire de l'Ouest:
    circulation behind the
    glass facade

d   CLM-BBDO HQ: studio interior

e   Banque Populaire de l'Ouest:
    axonometric

f   Frank O Gehry & Associates
    and Claes Oldenburg,
    Chiat–Day Headquarters,
    Venice, California, 1975–91

g   Richard Rogers Partnership,
    Channel 4 Headquarters,
    London, 1990–4

a c e

g

b d f

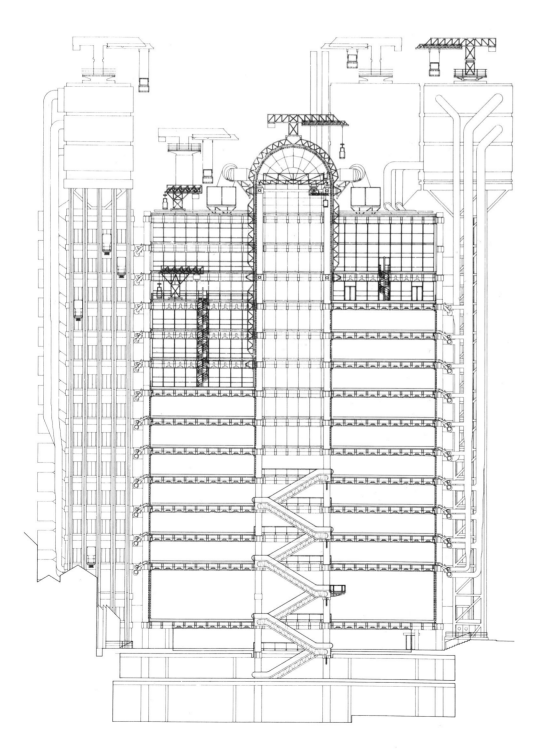

particularly rural France. It had bags of shock value, and did much to establish a new image for the bank. Grimshaw then proceeded to do exactly the same – in rather different form – in England's Celtic fringe with his *Western Morning News* building outside Plymouth, completed 1992 (see 'Industry'). A regional newspaper with a stuffy image was given a drastic image makeover. Although the ship or spaceship metaphor is clear in both, neither is as overt, for example, as Sumit Jumsai's 'Robot' building for the Bank of Asia in Bangkok, 1986. This is high-tech expressed in post-modern fashion, a visual joke fully in keeping with the spirit of the era. Purists may sniff, but from the corporate point of view its effect is the same as 'purer' architecture: it is a landmark. In which context, Arata Isozaki's Team Disney building in Orlando, Florida, 1987–91, (see 'Leisure') with its jumble of brightly coloured cubic forms jostling round a 120-foot-high central funnel, is relatively sophisticated stuff, though clearly from the same mid-eighties mindset as the Robot bank.

As a subtler example of advertising through architecture, consider Jean Nouvel's barge-like office building in St Germain, Paris for the advertising group CLM-BBDO, 1988–92. This is not at first overtly self-proclaiming: not in the installation-art sense of Frank Gehry and Claes Oldenburg's HQ for another advertising agency, Chiat–Day, in Venice, California,

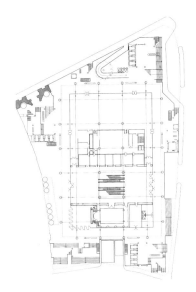
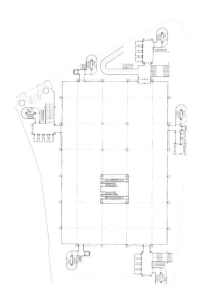

1975–91, with its giant pair of binoculars as centre-piece. Nor even like Richard Rogers' rather ostentatious Channel 4 television headquarters, 1990–4, in London, where (as with Isozaki in Orlando) the flamboyant entrance front is everything, but where the wings of offices behind are, in contrast, pedestrian. In comparison, the oxidized steel hull of the CLM-BBDO building is fairly reticent – until its roof opens up. This simple device (the skylights over the central atrium are contained in four large moveable panels flush with the pitch of the roof, hinging open at either side of a central pintle) means that the building appears to be stretching its wings for flight. This is a curiously contextual building for Nouvel – real snub-nosed barges are moored nearby, their hatches opening in similar fashion – but on a larger scale, the architecture becomes kinetic sculpture and the agency has its visual slogan.

No mention of Rogers can be made without due reference to the Lloyd's of London building, 1978–86, which together with Norman Foster's nearly contemporary Hongkong and Shanghai Bank, 1979–86, constitutes one of the most hand-crafted and, per square metre, expensive corporate buildings of the twentieth century. Although falling into the architectural pigeonhole labelled 'high-tech', and indeed being assembled to reasonably tight tolerances from components sourced globally, the highly

individual nature of these two buildings marks them out as almost Edwardian exercises in empire-building. Both reject the existing relatively simple and well-tried North American methods of producing such buildings – oddly perhaps, given their respective architects' knowledge and love of American architecture. Both do however try to reinvent an American idiom. In Rogers' case it is the rectangular, atrium-centred office building, in clear line of descent from Wright's Larkin Building in Buffalo. Foster's self-appointed task was to come up with a new kind of skyscraper, ninety years or so since the invention of the iron or steel skeleton frame in Chicago.

The Hongkong and Shanghai Bank is the more radical of the pair, in that the floors are hung in bunches from bridge-like trusses rather than evenly distributing their weight to a frame. It introduces a lofty atrium at its base, deriving its natural light not from the sky above but via a periscope arrangement of reflectors; and it deploys what was to become the familiar tactic of 'sky lobbies' higher up the building. The open ground level sweeps right under the curving glass belly of the building, effectively creating a covered public plaza. Lloyd's of London, in contrast, has an underlying conservatism belied by its startlingly modelled exterior. The Rogers practice, still committed to the idea of clear-span internal space derived from the external placement

The new baroque, verging on the rococo:

a Richard Rogers Partnership, Lloyd's Building, London, 1978–86: section
b Lloyd's Building: atrium
c Lloyd's Building: plans
d Lloyd's Building: amid Rogers' high-tech structure sits the original Lutine Bell

b	c
a	d

of services (a refinement of Louis Kahn's 'served' and 'servant' methodology) took an absolutely rectangular plan and produced a tall galleried interior, crisscrossed at the lower levels by escalators. Unusual, perhaps, to use a concrete frame for such a place, even though it rises to only a relatively modest twelve storeys at its highest, but that was forced upon the designers by nervous fire officers, fearful of an atrium blaze. The very fine finish to the *in-situ* concrete columns is one of the marvels of the interior. Externally, all the gymnastics are to do with the servant spaces being pushed to the perimeter. Lavatory pods, escape stairs, lifts, ductwork rising to openly expressed air-conditioning plant rooms, all combine to result in a huge amount of architectural movement over the glazed face of the building, which as a consequence recedes as a plane and which – since much of the glazing is opaque – imparts no clue as to what happens within except the sight of pinstriped gents and power-suited women whizzing up and down in glass lifts. While the fortress characteristic goes back to Larkin, here the severity of an inward-looking rectangular building is softened by the fact that its mass is cut back sharply and asymmetrically on three sides, allowing the glazed barrel vault of the atrium roof to be extruded through the centre as a separate element.

This highly sculptural modelling is one factor that saves Lloyd's of London from being a mausoleum – sitting amid the medieval streets of the City of London, glimpsed at intervals through narrow gaps, it never appears to be orthogonal in plan at all. The other factor is the constitution of the London insurance market, whereby brokers are constantly arriving to meet underwriters in the building, arrange some business, and then depart. Its appearance at busy times is of a giant beehive. Its black-ceilinged interiors with their turbine-like circular light fittings – combined with the sense experienced by some of being sealed in visually as well as atmospherically – led to some criticism, mostly in the early days (unfairly, given that this was a response to the declared preferences of the underwriters themselves). The interiors seemed gloomier than the light meter said they were. Yet (and this was undoubtedly a coincidence) Lloyd's actually is an institution that began life in a coffee-house: knowing this, the atmosphere deep into the working floors of Lloyd's seems strangely appropriate. Again, the contrast with Foster is instructive: from Willis Faber onwards, through the Hongkong and Shanghai Bank to the Commerzbank in Frankfurt and many another building, transparency has always been the Foster goal. The Rogers–Wright connections go further than plan form: witness the internalized nature of so many

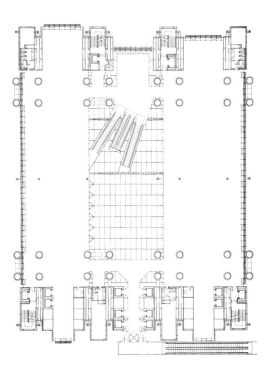

The Hongkong and Shanghai Bank was Foster's most highly articulated building:

a Foster and Partners, Hongkong and Shanghai Bank, Hong Kong, 1979–86: view into office floors

b Hongkong and Shanghai Bank: atrium interior

c Hongkong and Shanghai Bank: plan

b

c

a

Wright buildings and the sanctuary-like quality of his Kaufmann office of 1935-7 with its low level of filtered daylight.

In this context one might consider the work of the Californian architect Eric Owen Moss, whose architecture is a beguiling mix of *fin-de-siècle* 'displaced grid' mingled in the early days with a kind of bricolage and love of found materials. Moss' home patch, Culver City, is becoming pock-marked with his developments, from the Paramount–Lindblade–Gary Group headquarters, 1988-90, onwards. He is concerned with light as it affects mass, rather than lightness as an end in itself, and this is shown in his many collaborations with the developer Frederick Smith. These are gradually taking over various plots of waste ground and merging to form an alternative commercial district, surreally close to the themed environment of the Sony (formerly MGM) Picture Studios complex by Gensler Associates, 1990-94. Like Jean Nouvel, Moss likes to give his schemes resonant names: hence Samitaur of 1990-6 and Stealth of 1992-6, each successive scheme becoming more brooding. Note that in his related restaurant scheme The Box of 1990-4 - a raised, tilted volume very characteristic of fashionable architecture in the late 1990s - he uses the cubic corner window as a device. This is very reminiscent of the similar device in Scarpa's Canova Museum extension in Treviso of

1955-7 (though Scarpa, working at mid-century rather than at the end of the century, felt no need to place his box on a tilt). Taken as a whole, the Moss–Smith work in Culver City is gradually achieving piecemeal the kind of mixed-use commercial environment that occurs elsewhere either much more slowly (urban evolution over many years) or relatively rapidly (in a masterplanned urban development). It is corporate, in a way - there are real companies there - but they are blue-jeans corporate rather than blue-suit corporate. The official planned version of what might be called 'Mossville' could well turn out to look like Ricardo Legorreta's Plaza Reforma office complex of 1993 in Mexico City - an exotic and highly coloured composition dropped into an edge-of-town development area - or the yet more startling fragments of Legorreta's office complex in Monterrey, Mexico, 1991: one orange building is the domain of a wealthy businessman with his offices and inevitable art gallery, the other is speculative space.

Such places, lacking the size of their landmark cousins, are the workplace equivalent of 'boutique hotels' and became just as fashionable at just the same time. There were precursors such as Minoru Takeyama's Ni-Ban-Kan offices in Tokyo of 1970 - a colourful assemblage seen by some as a dry run for post-modernism but in fact betraying more of the 'pop' sensibilities of the early 1960s, which places

All these architects are in the business of urban repair. The result is the 'boutique workplace':

a Eric Owen Moss, Samitaur, Culver City, California, 1990-6
b Eric Owen Moss, Stealth, Culver City, California, 1992-6
c Eric Owen Moss, The Box, Culver City, California, 1990-4

d Mario Botta, Ransila Building, Lugano, Switzerland, 1981-5
e Ricardo Legorreta, Plaza Reforma, Mexico City, 1993
f Ricardo Legorreta, Office complex, Monterrey, Mexico, 1991
g Minoru Takeyama, Ni-Ban-Kan Building, Tokyo, 1970

```
        c │ d  g
a           e
b
          │ f
```

it in the same box as the Pompidou Centre in Paris. Mario Botta's 'Ransila' building in Lugano, 1981–85, its deep brickwork cut away in great zig-zags to reveal a glass skin beneath (this device became a post-modern cliché in lesser hands), is a trophy building of this kind: but it is positively self-effacing compared with Frank Gehry's 'Fred and Ginger' building for the ING Nederlanden Bank, 1992–6, in Prague which, with interiors by Eva Jiricna, is the boutique office building *par excellence*. An interiors project, Stephen Holl's offices for the financial trading company DE Shaw and Co in New York, 1991–2, fits the bill as a Zen-like environment for a sometimes frenzied activity; and even the helmet-like forms of Shin Takamatsu's developments in Kyoto (Takamatsu could be seen as a Japanese Eric Owen Moss in his adherence to one urban area) are of the genre. Takamatsu's 'Origin' series of commercial buildings, 1980–6, and 'Syntax' store, 1988–90, are one-offs of the most extreme variety. Takamatsu's designs are essentially buildings as defence mechanisms. More obviously boutique-like are the green cowls of Philippe Starck's 'Nani-Nani' building of 1989 in Tokyo and 'Le Baron Vert' in Osaka of 1990 (again, note the obligatory funny names), the latter subsequently joined by a red twin. Starck saw his buildings both as monsters and as forts – that is, defensive but capable of attack. They appear at a glance to be

merely scaled-up domestic products of the kind Starck throws out by the hundred, but in fact they yield some appealing and well-daylit small office floors.

Elsewhere, the goal of the 'democratic workplace' has been assiduously pursued, mainly in Scandinavia. Under architects such as Ralph Erskine and Niels Torp, the notion of the democratic office as defined by Hertzberger has been developed fruitfully. The idea that the crucial factor is the office environment, rather than its location, is one thing that has separated Scandinavian thinking from British and American real estate theory – which always maintains that location is of prime importance. Central to the development of the genre was Niels Torp's SAS building in Frösundavik, Sweden,

followed by his far larger headquarters for British Airways at Harmondsworth near London's Heathrow Airport. For BA, Torp saw the building as a village, comprising 'houses'. The houses are wings radiating from a central spine, but not uniform wings: the need for identifiable areas within the complex, the principle established by Hertzberger, is fully in evidence here, but the plan form of each wing was principally dictated by what Torp calls 'protected views' – both from the spine route, and from individual working areas. To protect those views, a percentage of cellular office space no greater than 12.5 per cent was envisaged; the cells in each wing are grouped to achieve these viewing corridors. Although some expansion of the cell percentage is possible, if a future management decides to renounce the predominance of

a b   d e
            f
  c

open-plan space, then a great deal of Torp's design energy will have been wasted.

He gives BA the equivalent of a village green at the focal point of his spine mall, with terraces forming a shallow auditorium, next to a 'contemplation area' within a small olive grove. A wall of changing art works ushers the visitor into the large circular restaurant area, expressed as another branch off the main spine. All public activities are focused on the mall, while Torp identified a whole series of 'internal focal points' along the wings. Although the external architecture of Torp's building is scarcely rabble-rousing (Hertzberger's extreme understatement at Centraal Beheer is surely preferable to this well-mannered corporate-business-park aesthetic) and the sprawling nature of the four-floor composition is

extremely wasteful of land resources, the point was to create a tranquil, semi-rural campus within a mile or so of the screaming hell of Heathrow, the hub of BA's worldwide operations. As with all such exercises, the commissioning of the HQ was an almost paternalistic attempt by the company in question to give itself a unified working environment of a uniformly high standard. No doubt endless market research had been carried out to show the productivity gains to be achieved by improved working conditions, but beyond that, the need was to place an architectural fix upon a very volatile business.

Such buildings and their equivalents worldwide are therefore evidence against the theory that the office building as a built form is in its death throes. In an on-line age, the argument goes, where is

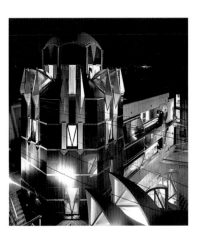

The architect's signature overcomes commercial inertia:

a Frank O Gehry & Associates, 'Fred and Ginger' Building, Prague, 1992–6
b Stephen Holl, D E Shaw and Company Office, New York, 1991–2
c Philippe Starck, Unhex Nani-Nani Building, Tokyo, 1989
d Shin Takamatsu, Origin I, Kyoto, Japan, 1980–1: street facade
e Shin Takamatsu, Origin III, Kyoto, Japan, 1985–6: aerial view
f Origin I & III: aerial view, Origin I to the foreground and Origin III to the rear

the point in travelling to work, usually to an office equipped with the very communications equipment that is meant to make such journeys unnecessary? The mobile New Action Man and Woman surely eschew such throwback working methods. Yet, at the start of the twenty-first century, with all possibilities open - including an unforeseeable reversal of town and country so far as working and living is concerned, with reverse commuting becoming more common-place - the office building nonetheless appears to be secure just so long as people need to meet to discuss their activities. Perversely, developments such as high-grade teleconferencing between companies and countries served for a while in the 1990s to anchor people and teams more firmly to their offices, since the relevant communications hardware was too costly and complex to install at home. More relevantly, such communications, by rendering physical travel less necessary, also tie people to the desk and the meeting room: they have less need to be out and about when they can see and talk to their client on-screen.

The big corporate blocks will continue to be produced, not least because of the perceived, if unquantifiable, benefits of joint human endeavour - call it morale, or company spirit. A sense of community is fostered by self-sufficient village-type HQ, such as Michael Wilford's for the Sto building products group in Germany - the key building there

being the expressively leaning, marching block of Sto Communications, 1993-7, or the considerably more formal arrangement of square hilltop pavilions and linking glazed internal streets for the Yapi Kredi Bank outside Istanbul, 1994-7, by John McAslan & Partners, which recalls Hertzberger. In a sense these all derive from such models as Sir Denys Lasdun's European Investment Bank on its Luxembourg hill-side, and once again the monastery, as much as the acropolis, suggests itself as the precedent. Self-containment is the aim.

Set against such communities, city centres offer the temptation of the landmark towers, such as the Australian examples by Harry Seidler and Denton Corker Marshall. Powerful corporate symbols, they assume national importance above a certain height. But - also above a certain height - buildings cease to be readable, detailed architecture, and instead become engineering, no more engaging than the smooth trunks of huge trees disappearing into the rainforest canopy. The most intriguing examples of office design are down on the forest floor: Balkrishna Doshi's Sangath Studio of 1981 in Ahmedabad, India, for instance - the architect's own partially earth-sheltered offices with white barrel-vaulted roofs, conceived as a small cluster of forms - or Eric Owen Moss' Paramount-Lindblade-Gary Group's headquarters, 1988-90, in Culver City, where

a c d e

b

f g

If the workforce is a family, what should the family home be like?

a Niels Torp, British Airways Headquarters Building, Heathrow, London, 1996-8

b John McAslan & Partners, Yapi Kredi Operations Centre, Istanbul, Turkey, 1994-7

c Niels Torp, SAS Headquarters, Frösundavik, Solna, Sweden, 1985-7: exterior view

d SAS Headquarters: internal street

e Michael Wilford & Partners, Sto AG Building K, Weizen, Germany, 1993-7: plan

f Sto AG Building: exterior view

g Sto AG Building: circulation space

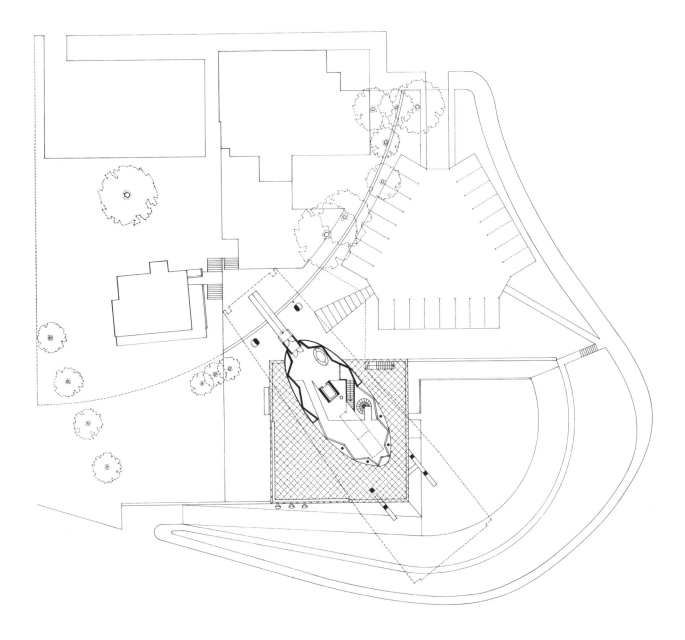

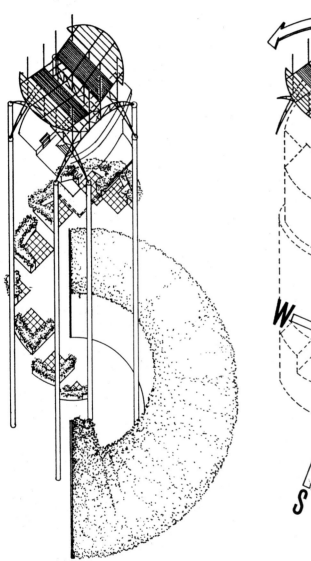

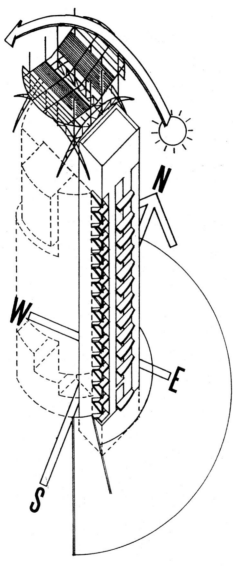

b   e f

a   c

d

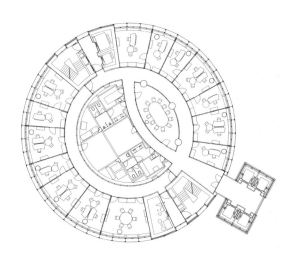

the imagery is post-holocaust, junk-festooned, semi-derelict, and therefore an antidote to the preening gloss of the conventional group HQ. And, as Oldenburg's binoculars on Gehry's Chiat–Day building proved, sheer size is not nearly as much of a guarantee of landmark status as the memorable image, on whatever scale.

All this assumes a historical tendency: to zone workplaces as somewhere different from other urban or suburban activities – living, shopping, entertainment. Most fruitful now, from the architectural point of view, is the challenge of the mixed-use development. Emerging from 1970s experiments with managed workspace, and energized by a growing move towards high-density urban living and the tendency to employ staff on flexible self-employed contracts, the mixed-use block will be the focus of intense design scrutiny in the early years of the twenty-first century. Whether it will be the European, Berlin or Paris model of layered, relatively low-rise courtyard development that will come to the fore, or the North American apartment-office-and-shops vertical alternative, or the late Corbusian Unité ideal, remains to be seen. This time, though, the forces stimulating mixed development are a little different: not mere convenience, but the urgent need to reduce movement of people, due to the sheer amounts of energy consumption and

pollution that such movement causes.

Two factors combine in the latter years of the century: the attempt to design an ecological office tower, along with earnest attempts to mix the uses within those towers in order to – in theory at least – reduce the pollution-generating potential of such behemoths. Arguably the skyscraper, though heavy indeed in 'embodied energy costs' and, usually, everyday energy consumption, is a form that reduces the pollution inherent in car travel to outlying office parks. City centres, generally speaking, are well served by public transport. The American model of mixing apartments with offices in the same tower looks good in principle but, generally, those living there are not also those working there – there is a two-way pattern of daily travel. In general, the quest to 'green' the skyscraper has been concerned with naturally ventilating it, and moderating the microclimatic effects that such very large buildings create. In this sense the work of the Malaysian architects Robert Hamzah and Ken Yeang has been exemplary. Yeang's own Selangor house of 1983–4 (the 'Roof Roof' House) tried out the principle of the 'environmental filter' that he and Hamzah later applied to office buildings. 'Roof Roof' is aligned to minimize exposure to the sun, and to maximize the cooling effect of the prevailing winds, while a louvred parasol, supported on columns, oversails the whole

complex. Its pool acts as a heat sink to regulate temperature extremes. The theory tested here was then applied to the cylindrical office tower Menara Mesiniaga, 1989–92, also in Selangor. Although other architects had long tinkered with the idea of the 'sky lobby' – Future Systems' 'Coexistence' tower project 1985, with its aerial parks was a relatively early design concept in this area, and was moreover designed to function as a self-contained community – Hamzah and Yeang can be credited with being first actually to build an ecologically designed office tower, complete with external, high-level open courts. These, hung with cascading plants, attempted with some success to take traditional ground-level sheltering devices and extrude them upwards. Planting and open terraces had been established for years on ground-hugging office buildings, and of course solar-shading devices were an ancient technology, but to take all these devices and express them vertically was a step in a new direction.

The cylindrical, or at any rate curved-sided, office tower came to be a symbol of a certain kind of eco-architecture. Where Hamzah and Yeang's Menara Mesiniaga was a mere fourteen storeys high, the RWE Tower in Essen, Germany completed in early 1997, by Ingenhoven Overdiek Kahlen & Partner (IOK) rises to over thirty – and is uncannily similar in plan and appearance to Foster's unbuilt 1982

Air conditioning sidestepped:
a T R Hamzah & Yeang,
   Menara Mesiniaga, Selangor,
   Kuala Lumpur, 1989–92:
   sketches of atrium gardens
   and solar movements
b Menara Mesiniaga:
   lobby interior

c Menara Mesiniaga:
   exterior view
d Menara Mesiniaga: entrance
e Ingenhoven, Overdiek, Kahlen
   & Partner, RWE Tower, Essen,
   Germany, 1997: exterior view
f RWE Tower: plan

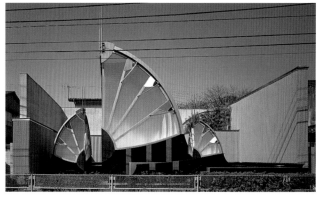

competition entry for the Humana tower in Louisville, Kentucky (won by Michael Graves). In Essen, there are no sky lobbies of the kind that mark out Foster's Commerzbank in Frankfurt, completed a few months later with a similar double-facade. And it was estimated at the time of opening that natural ventilation would only be effective for between 50 and 70 per cent of the time – which was conceded by IOK's partner Achim Nagel to be no better than a conventional seven-storey building could achieve, without even trying. But these were still relatively early examples, still lacking the skin of photovoltaic cells that, when these two towers were built, was a technology that promised drastically to reduce the energy consumption of such buildings. The climatic conditions of the Far East may prove the best testing-ground of such buildings, though the graceful office building known as the Telecom Tower in a suburb of Kuala Lumpur, 1997, by Hijjas Kasturi, was still at the intermediate stage: intelligently climate-controlled but not actively power-generating. Such large-scale buildings contrast with lower-tech examples such as Sauerbruch and Hutton's office tower for Berlin's social housing department, 1996–8, which depends upon a narrow plan for cross-ventilation and timber solar shading. A more pragmatic example of the 'breathing wall', however, is apparent in Daimler-Benz Haus by Renzo Piano, 1993–8, the tallest building in

Berlin's titanic Potsdamer Platz redevelopment (see 'Civic Realm'). Piano employs a double-skin glass wall on the south and west sides like IOK or Foster, but simply makes the outer skin of continuous opening louvres – their movement orchestrated by climate sensors – and the inner skin of manually openable windows, so that anyone can get cool air either from the cavity or, when conditions are right, from the world outside. This tower, though the flagship HQ building of the Daimler-Benz company which owns a huge chunk of the Potsdamer Platz area, is modest in other ways, being surprisingly reticent for so large a building. The mood after the fall of the Berlin Wall was against corporate triumphalism, and the overall masterplan for the area was conservative. Piano even employed exactly the same glass and terracotta cladding details for a smaller, triangular-plan office tower at the apex of the scheme – alongside a more solid, punched-window affair by Hans Kollhoff and Helga Timmermann – as if to emphasize the family nature of the development. Of the other contributions to the area, Richard Rogers' pair of deeply incised office, housing and retail blocks, 1992–9, succeed rather better in their handling of the Berlin urban block model than do the lumpen stripy speculative offices of Arata Isozaki to their south, 1993–7.

The Holy Grail of workplace design, hinted at by some of these buildings, is to achieve a largely self-sustaining building that can cool or heat itself without tearing holes in the sky: that is accessible by fuel-efficient public transport; that is part of a mixed-use development rather than being zoned in a white-collar workers' ghetto, with affordable housing available locally; that is laid out on broadly democratic principles, allowing free movement of personnel, the acknowledgement of family life, and the ability to work remotely when needed; that can be flexible enough to accommodate future changes in working methods; that can still communicate through its architecture a strong sense of identity. Some of these factors imply an urban – and a dense urban – solution. The future envisaged by Shin Takamatsu's Earthtecture Sub-1 in Shibuya, Tokyo, 1987–91, is one possibility: four floors of wholly subterranean space, dimly top-lit via sculptural metallic quarter-sphere 'towers', implying a retreat from a hostile environment. The other possibility, with more going for it, is the endless tower shooting skywards, a very Pacific Rim obsession (that is discussed further in 'Towers').

At the time of writing, some office buildings have achieved aspects of the criteria for social and environmental acceptability laid out above. Apart from small ecological home-offices, none – due to social, bureaucratic, and technological problems – had achieved them all. This is one of the most significant design tasks of the twenty-first century.

New cities: to go up, or down?
a Shin Takamatsu, Earthtecture Sub-1, Shibuya, Tokyo, 1987–91: view looking down into the subterranean environs
b Earthtecture Sub-1: quarter-sphere towers light the below-ground building
c Earthtecture Sub-1: stair detail
d Renzo Piano Building Workshop, Daimler-Benz building, Potsdamer Platz, Berlin, 1993–8

INDUSTRY *Factories & research centres* The nature of industry, and the buildings that contain its processes, has changed radically. Throughout the world, heavy industry has given way to light as a main employer, while both have been fundamentally affected by automation and new methods of distribution. Factories and assembly plant – even ancillary structures such as pumping stations and electricity sub-stations – increasingly have a public face. The rise of the pharmaceutical and electronics sectors has placed a heavy emphasis on research, and new forms of building have arisen to meet this need.

'It is only here, my friend, that the machinery and buildings can be found commensurate with the miracles of modern times – they are called factories.'
Letter from Peter Beuth in Manchester to Karl Friedrich Schinkel in Berlin, 1823.

'What the effects of automation will be remains to be seen'
Nikolaus Pevsner, 1976.

For the Californian architect Wes Jones – charged with the task of designing the vast central power–heat–chiller plant for the University of California at Los Angeles (UCLA) – the architectural handling of big pieces of mechanical equipment must at first have seemed paradoxical in a society where electronics had forged a new industrial revolution. As built, 1987–94, Jones' mechanistic building is in keeping with the tradition of modernist worship of heavy industry, and is therefore a throwback to the Italian Futurists and all that followed. Yet, he argues, mechanical forms are necessary in an electronic age. They provide a solid underpinning to the all-pervasive electronic miasma. Jones accordingly designed his chunk of industry – sited right at the heart of electronically biased academia – not as some well-mannered sleek container, but as an eruption of chimneys, ductwork and grilles, bursting out of a

brick facade with such energy that some of its panels are tilted forwards, as if yielding to the force within. It is a reminder that industry is notoriously untameable. It is also nostalgic.

The three years that elapsed between the Prussian civil servant Peter Beuth's visit to Manchester and his return in 1826 – this time accompanied by the architect Karl Friedrich Schinkel – demonstrates the speed at which industrialization can affect both the appearance of a townscape, and the living and working conditions within it. At the time of their joint visit, Manchester had reached the end of its first massive phase of industrial expansion – comparable to that experienced by Pacific Rim countries in the 1990s. Schinkel was intrigued by Manchester's infrastructure – its canal network with its transhipment points, its broad pavements, its elevated walkways – but was less complimentary about what he regarded as the non-architecture of the cotton mills ('monstrous shapeless buildings put up only by foremen without architecture – only the least that was necessary and out of red brick.') His perception was affected by the social unrest in Manchester. Unemployment was rife, Irish labourers were being shipped back home, property values were plummeting, and life was scarcely more agreeable for those left in work: '12,000 workers are now coming together to rise up. Many workers work sixteen hours a day, and then get

a weekly wage of only two shillings. Establishments that cost 500,000 pounds sterling are now worth only 5,000. A dreadful state of affairs ... there is a great English military presence in Manchester to ensure security.'

Small wonder – the memory was still fresh of the 'Peterloo' massacre of 1819 in the city, when a peaceful protest of 60,000 in favour of political reform was met by a cavalry charge that left eleven dead and up to 500 injured, inspiring Shelley's 'Masque of Anarchy' the following year. Industry is always inextricably tied to economics and politics, and for a time Manchester was both one of the most profitable and volatile places on earth – driving the wealth of the British Empire, but at the same time threatening to tip it into revolution. Beuth and Schinkel's visit was a type of above-board industrial espionage on behalf of a nation that consciously wished to modernize (Beuth headed the Department of Trade and Industry in Prussia's Finance Ministry; Schinkel was Privy Counsellor for Public Works). What intrigued both men during their tour was new technology, both in terms of manufacturing equipment and in architecture and engineering. Schinkel in particular noted the increasing use of cast iron and fireproof construction techniques in buildings, from mills to museums, and the advanced bridge, road and canal engineering of Thomas Telford. His diaries

of the journey usually do not mention working conditions: that social unrest in Manchester should have stirred his interest shows the extent of the troubles.

At intervals, this scenario repeats itself. Although Pevsner says nothing more in his 1976 A History of Building Types than that the impact of automation was yet to be felt on industrial architecture, he must have known well enough, even at the age of seventy-four, that change was in the air. The shift to automated manufacture was to have consequences as great as the arrival of Arkwright's Spinning Jenny in the Lancashire mills in the late eighteenth century, and was accompanied by comparable industrial unrest, if not outright massacre. And since automation is impossible without the making of computer components, one of the two building types that define industrial architecture at the end of the twentieth century – notwithstanding such examples to the contrary, as Wes Jones' energy plant at UCLA – is the microprocessor manufacturing plant, the other being the research laboratory. Neither of these has much in common with the buildings erected in earlier times to accommodate heavy industry, and the extensive storage such buildings demand for bulky raw materials and finished products.

For the purposes of this book, an industrial building is a building devoted to production, storage, distribution and research. Administration buildings

Revelling in the
industrial aesthetic:
a Holt Hinshaw Pfau Jones and
   Jones, Partners: Architecture,
   Chiller plant, University of
   California at Los Angeles,
   1987–94: industry at the
   heart of academia
b Chiller plant: street-level view
c Chiller plant: chimneys,
   ductwork and grilles burst
   forth from the brickwork

a   c

b

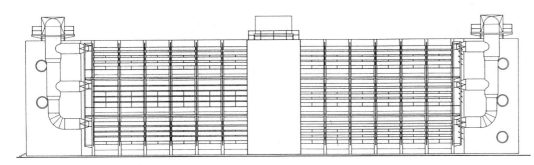

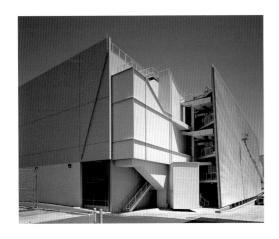

will normally be found in the 'Workplace' section unless they are architecturally part and parcel of the industrial facilities. Other ancillary buildings are, however, included here. Farm buildings also count – since agriculture is a form of production – as do those buildings connected with infrastructure – power and pumping stations, transmission-communications buildings and the like.

Yet the factory remains the building most associated with industry. Factories by nature have a flow pattern to them – materials arrive, are processed, and depart in new forms. Waste is generated and has to be dealt with on a separate loop, but the basic diagram is very simple – be it a steelworks or a video recorder assembly plant. The best architects and engineers have always striven to make that diagram clear – from Ledoux with his semicircular Royal Salt Works in Arc-et-Senans, 1775–6, to Wes Jones (first with Holt Hinshaw Pfau Jones, then in his own practice of Jones, Partners). Jones designed other industrial buildings, including an administration building for a concrete batching company in Oakland, California, and a film and tape archives building for Paramount Pictures in Los Angeles, both of which, like the UCLA energy plant, take care to reveal and celebrate the activities they serve. In the case of the concrete plant, the admin block derived its form from that existing of the batching plant with

its open steelwork, conveyor belts and hoppers. For Paramount, Jones mingled editing activities in the same building as the industrial business of film storage, and relieved the blank exterior of the building with an authentic Hollywood artificial sky backdrop, its support structure left exposed along with the building's chiller plant. Wes Jones quotes Heidegger: that what we must fear is not the dangers of technology, but our own desire to keep them hidden. He has been described as a child of the Cold War, his work the result of the fear of the mechanisms of the nuclear age, but this is fanciful: his outlook is not so different, say, from Britain's Nicholas Grimshaw, whose newspaper printworks for the *Financial Times* in London, 1987–8, was one of a series of buildings that exposed the industrial process to view, in this case through a very large glazed flank wall. 'We were astounded by the scale and beauty of the presses which were like great ship's engines, and felt they should be seen by the outside world,' remarked Grimshaw when recalling the project later.

This, coupled with Grimshaw's typical attention to the details of the glazing support structure – a system of external outriggers to brace the glass skin – led the fashion designer Jean Muir in 1989 to describe the building as 'an inlaid jewel box'. The building can also be read as a classically columnated facade, 16 metres high and 96 metres long, complete

a Nicholas Grimshaw and
Partners, Rank Xerox, Welwyn
Garden City, Hertfordshire,
England, 1988: elevation
b Holt Hinshaw Pfau Jones,
Paramount Studios Film and
Tape Archive, Los Angeles,
1989
c Rank Xerox: corner detail

d Holt Hinshaw Pfau Jones,
'Right Away Redy Mix',
Oakland, California, 1986–7
e Nicholas Grimshaw and
Partners, Igus Factory and
Headquarters, Cologne,
Germany, 1990–2: roof detail
f Igus Factory: roof detail

a c   d

b

          e f

with abstracted entablature. On this reading, the assemblage of the vertical structural arms, horizontal outriggers, and slender vertical tension rods have a depth, and together define a space. It is reminiscent of a fat Doric column built up from drums of stone, while the entablature is refined down to a double row of punched circular holes in the crowning horizontal bracing I-beams – the simple pattern of apertures carrying all the implied imagery of guttae, triglyphs and so forth. A distinctly Schinkelian shed, as opposed to its transatlantic cousin, the *New York Times* printing plant by Polshek and Partners, 1995–7, which is also located on a semi-industrial city edge, is similarly rectilinear, and similarly exposes the press through big windows (as did its predecessor, Albert Kahn's printing plant of 1929 in Brooklyn). Polshek's version appears as a deliberately brash decorated shed, right down to the corrugated metal cladding emblazoned with the paper's giant masthead at a jaunty angle. Using saturated colours to highlight other, smaller elements of the complex, such as the air handling machinery (yellow) and a paper store (bright blue), it eschews the jewel-like architectural detail in favour of effects that can be read at speed from passing cars.

Occasionally, well-known architects of galleries and offices are asked to produce factory buildings at the behest of image-conscious clients. More usually, factories are purely functional enclosures and their architects, if any, are virtually unknown outside the industrial sector. However, Grimshaw is an interesting case because he has managed, since 1972, to make factories an important part of his practice's work, and through them to win the commissions for transport buildings, offices, homes and galleries that are more usually the preserve of the 'signature' architect. He was the first architect of note to be commissioned by Rolf Fehlbaum at the Vitra furniture factory in Weil-am-Rhein, Germany, 1981, the first arrival at what was to become an international architectural zoo also featuring buildings by Frank Gehry, Tadao Ando, Zaha Hadid and Alvaro Siza. A later Grimshaw building, the research centre for Rank Xerox in Welwyn Garden City, Hertfordshire, England, 1988, with its active facade of automatic rotatable aluminium louvres and externally expressed ductwork for high-volume air handling, was notable for one other thing: it was designed in the certainty that the working practices within it would undergo rapid change, and that such changes were unpredictable. The client's best guess was that – since its future course was unknowable in the light of technological advances – up to a quarter of the total floor space might have to be redesigned and re-equipped every year. The solution – clear, unencumbered internal space, a simple doughnut plan, and an active light-

modifying facade coupled with flexible internal servicing – was perhaps the answer to Pevsner's 1976 warning of the looming effects of automation.

Grimshaw returned to Germany for the Igus plastics-moulding factory in Cologne, 1990–2. The line of development, right back to his early work, is clear: but the familiar prefabricated panels here take their place in a mast-supported structure with domed north-facing glass-reinforced plastic 'eyeball' roof lights. Inserted into a diamond pattern of steel roof beams, the roof lights give a grandeur to the factory floor that is a nod towards the loftier thin-shell domes of the hugely ambitious, historically important, and perpetually economically unviable, Brynmawr Rubber Factory in South Wales, 1946–51 (by the Architects' Co Partnership and Ove Arup). Brynmawr is routinely referred to, with some justification, as an industrial cathedral. It is notable that Grimshaw's client at Igus, Günter Blase, also refers to his factory as 'my cathedral'.

Religion is hardly the most obvious source of inspiration for the image of an industrial building, and so the question arises, what exactly is the most appropriate image for a factory? Some indication of what goes on within – either through revealing the actual process, or suggesting it through the built form – is a clear enough response. Philippe Starck takes this to extremes with his 1988 Laguiole knife

a

b c

d

e f

The art of architectural advertising:

a Nicholas Grimshaw and Partners, *Financial Times* Printworks, London, 1987-8: night view

b *FT* Printworks: interior

c *FT* Printworks: facade detail

d Polshek and Partners Architects LLP, *New York Times* Printing Plant, College Point, New York, 1995-7: night view

e *NY Times* Printing Plant: exterior

f *NY Times* Printing Plant: interior

factory in France – a simple silver-sided, glass-ended box of a building but for the fact that a giant knife blade sticks out of the roof at an angle. Starck said, apropos of the project: 'Architecture has no need of charity to survive and prosper if it can help industry and commerce in a dignified manner ... architecture can actually help an industry's reputation.' No doubt about the purpose of that building, a decorated shed if ever there was one. But elsewhere, appearances can deceive. Kisho Kurakawa's Wacoal headquarters in east central Tokyo, 1984, carries conflicting imagery: an entrance portico like a flying saucer leads to a building reminiscent of a streamlined steam locomotive of the kind worshipped by the Futurists, clad in white and silver. Two circular window apertures at its nose are combined into a

camshaft or piston motif. What mighty industrial enterprise goes on within? In fact Wacoal makes women's underwear and this building – facing the Imperial Palace – houses mainly office space and storage. In the case of the Igus Factory in Cologne, the glass-reinforced roof mouldings clearly express the nature of the plastics business within. What Günter Blase sought was clear enough: a factory with all the usual clear-span flexibility (hence the tapering latticework masts) but which would raise the profile of Igus, a company that was very successful but had zero public image. Blase wanted from Grimshaw exactly what Rolf Fehlbaum of Vitra had wanted at the start of his architectural odyssey a decade previously: status, for his company rather than necessarily for himself. The notion of the industrial building as a

corporate image-enhancer rather than lowest-cost option was undergoing one of its periodic revivals.

In the twentieth century, this tradition includes Peter Behrens' AEG Turbine Factory of 1908–9 in Berlin; Walter Gropius and Adolf Meyer's Fagus shoe-last factory in Alfeld, northern Germany, 1910–11; Hans Poelzig's Luban Chemical Factory of 1911–12 in what is now Poland; Erich Mendelsohn's hat factory in Luckenwalde, south of Berlin, 1921–3; the Van Nelle coffee, tea and tobacco factory, Rotterdam, 1926–9, by Johannes Brinkman, Leendert Cornelis van der Flugt and Mart Stam; and the Boots pharmaceuticals factory in Nottingham, England, 1930–32, by the engineer Sir Owen Williams, as well as the post-war example of Brynmawr, intended to act as a regeneration beacon for an impoverished

a
b c
f
d
e

The research building is the new factory:
a Frank O Gehry & Associates, Herman Miller Western Distribution Plant, Rocklin, California, 1987–9: the buildings are grouped around a 'town square'
b Herman Miller Western Distribution: exterior detail
c Herman Miller Western Distribution: view of atrium

d Antoine Predock, Center for Integrated Systems, Stanford University, Palo Alto, California, 1993–7: loggia
e Center for Integrated Systems: plan
f Center for Integrated Systems: little of the strong daylight of this area penetrates the solid facade

region. In the post-war years the Herman Miller company became a patron of good architecture, commissioning Grimshaw in England and, later, Frank Gehry for its Western Distribution plant in Rocklin, California, completed in 1989. The factory – relatively subdued by Gehry's standards – centres on a 'town square' as a hub, in response to the fact that by that time the company was a worker-partnership with a strong social agenda. Gehry admires and evokes industrial structures in much of his work: when designing the Advanced Technology Laboratories at the University of Iowa, completed 1993, he hit upon the university's craggy 1936 brick-built power house as 'the most animated and gutsy building on campus'. His laboratory block is just as uncompromising as any power plant: a rectangular,

limestone-clad box, windowless at the rear, against which are placed a low curved copper-clad wing on one side, and a more characteristically Gehryish jumble of offices on the other, finished in polished stainless steel. Contrast this with a similar university-based research facility: Antoine Predock's Center for Integrated Systems at Stanford University, Palo Alto, California, 1993–7. There, Predock chooses to make no reference to any industrial or electronic form, preferring instead to abstract and subvert the neo-Romanesque architecture of the original 1885 campus. Only the relative lack of fenestration in this stone and copper-clad building gives the game away: inside are labs and offices in which the strong daylight of the region is a positive disadvantage.

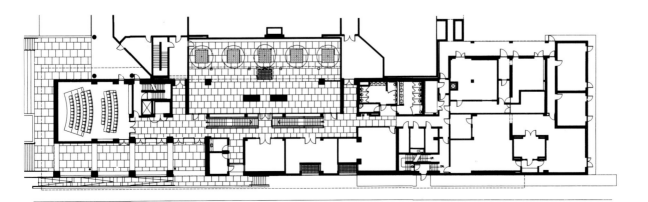

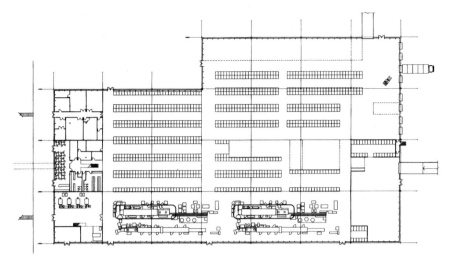

In the 1980s, a key building to note in the model-factory tradition was Norman Foster's Renault Distribution Centre, 1980-2, in Swindon, England. Renault was achieving good sales in Britain at the time and, wanting to expand, saw Foster as the architect to give physical form to its ambitions. As always, a strong client proved the key. Although Renault UK's bosses were unconcerned about the type of building they were to purvey, Renault France's Sebastien de la Selle had other ideas. De la Selle rejoiced in the resounding title of 'Co-ordinateur d'Expression Visuelle', and saw the distribution centre as a means to upgrade Renault's image. Accordingly the French side instructed the English side to consider the possibilities of architecture rather than merely building.

The resulting building – containing storage, offices, staff restaurant and a showroom – uses a structural 'umbrella' module of the kind that was to be refined into the 'trees' of Foster's later Stansted Airport in Essex. Here, however, the structure of each module broke through the roof as a mast. Each square bay was therefore self-supporting and in theory capable of being grouped in any configuration, though the confines of the site dictated a largely rectilinear building, cut away at one end. As part of his research, Foster had travelled to Quimper in Brittany to see Richard Rogers' recent Fleetguard

factory, 1980 – the first Rogers building since he and Renzo Piano had gone their separate ways after the Pompidou Centre in Paris. Fleetguard – part of the Cummins engine empire – had been given to Rogers on the recommendation of Kevin Roche, who had designed many of the company's factories in the United States. With its busy, bright red mast-and-strut exposed structure, it was known locally either as 'the spider' or 'the circus'. Foster, however, noticed what was for him a visual infelicity: the depth of the flat roof was such that much of the roof structure disappeared from view as one approached the building. It was, he pointed out, 'really a flat roof structure with appliqué'. This was perhaps a little hard – Fleetguard was composed of a series of repeatable modules not unlike Foster's instinctive first ideas for Renault at Swindon. The plan adopted a similar rectilinear layout with a cutaway at one end, and the brief from Cummins was for a factory, pure and simple, with little in the way of public interface; but Foster had seen something he could improve on, and accordingly rejected his own flat-roofed design, and introduced the undulating roofscape that so distinguishes the Renault depot. The masts emerge from the low point of each dished bay and are clearly visible from within the building through rooflights. By extending the structure out into the open to create a porte-cochere, Foster also visually explained the structural system –

again, a trick he was to refine and repeat at Stansted. There is no doubt about it – the yellow masts of Foster's Renault centre at Swindon are much more satisfyingly handled than the red masts of Rogers's Fleetguard plant at Quimper. The fact that the latter informed the former only extended a relationship that, just a few years previously, had seen Foster and Rogers working together as Team Four on the Reliance Controls building, 1965-6, also in Swindon. They had been recommended for the project by James Stirling, and were influenced in turn by the work of such disparate talents as Craig Ellwood and the Californian Case Study house programme, and by Ezra Ehrenkrantz's steel-framed system for schools – both in the United States – and the Smithsons' Hunstanton School in Britain, the water tower of which was directly quoted. Foster also established a working relationship with the structural engineer Anthony Hunt on the Reliance Controls building, while for both Rogers and Foster it marked a turning point – the move away from massive construction to lightweight, industrialized systems. This was what Rogers called 'shaking off Yale', where both architects had met as students. The 'follow-my-leader' relationship has continued throughout the two mens' careers as both find themselves designing similar types of buildings at similar times, even occasionally in close proximity.

a   b   c
                e
            d

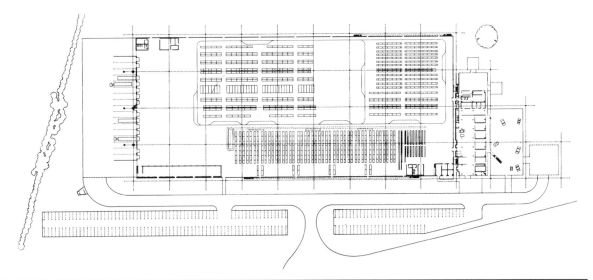

Very much of a period: the
1980s obsession with masts:

a   Richard Rogers Partnership,
Fleetguard Manufacturing and
Distribution Centre, Quimper,
France, 1980: entrance

b   Fleetguard: plan

c   Foster and Partners, Renault
Distribution Centre, Swindon,
England, 1980–2: plan

d   Renault: Foster was chosen
to design a signature building
to improve Renault's image
in the UK

e   Renault: the showroom

Renault's expansionist phase at this time extended to Mexico, where, in the desert landscape of Gómez Palacio near Durango, the company commissioned Ricardo Legorreta to build a factory, completed in 1985. Unlike Foster's Swindon building, which is principally a distribution centre, Legorreta's houses production lines actually making the cars. And where Foster's building was a celebration of the roof, Legorreta's is a celebration of the wall, and the roof does not feature as an architectural event at all. Inspired by the desert and its apparent infinity, his choice was to make a building that was of its surroundings rather than acting as a foil to them. 'The desert is magic, it is not possible to describe it; it only absorbs you,' said the architect later. 'I found myself with desert and walls, walls that never end. I did not want to soften this emotion.' The language is as different from Foster's rational descriptions as is the architecture. What makes Legorreta's factory interesting is the fact that such a building type can be emotional in a non-mechanistic sense.

It is, like most factories, a low-lying box, albeit a large one occupying 500,000 square feet. The main north–south axis has the entrance at one end. On the east of the spine is the main assembly building, engine-testing area, research offices, and storage – including a blue water-splashing courtyard as a cooling element. On the western side is a restaurant, also arranged around a courtyard, and landscaped open spaces. Everything comes down to the handling of the vertical surfaces. As Legorreta said:

'A wall is much more than a linear enclosing element. When thickened, it provides security and thermal mass; when stretched, extruded or duplicated, it offers shelter from the sun; when punctuated with opening, it provides light, access, and visual connection; when covered in vibrant colours, it radiates. This factory is a multidimensional celebration of the wall.'

Although this much is true of a great deal of hot-zone architecture, and especially Legorreta's œuvre, it is also particularly suitable as a strategy for the largely windowless nature of a factory building. Small windows are not punched but extruded as box forms, or shaded with angled freestanding walls in front of them. Outside, the colour is a recessive ochre while inside – again, typical of Legorreta – they become bright and saturated. Overall, the assembly of boxy forms is wholly in keeping with the architecture of the region. There are correspondences between all of Legorreta's buildings, but perhaps the most surprising cross-cultural reference is between the Renault factory and his Marco Contemporary Art Museum in Monterrey, completed in 1991. Museums, like factories, are predominantly top-lit 'black box' buildings, with the need for relatively

a

b

c

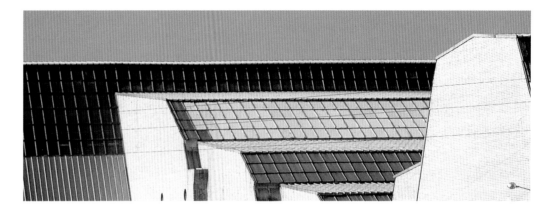

little fenestration, and that mostly for orientation. Like factories, they need a variety of different spaces for different activities and effects. Although taller than the earlier Renault plant, the ochre forms of the Marco with their small punched and extruded windows and perforated masonry screens share much of the same language. In similar fashion the refined brick skin of Rafael Moneo's Diestre transformer factory in Saragossa, Spain, 1963–7, anticipated the arts buildings he was later to become best known for.

The question, then, arises as to what, exactly, a factory is. For Ledoux at Arc-et-Senans – and for others during the Industrial Revolution such as Robert Owen with his New Lanark in Scotland and New Harmony in Indiana, United States – a factory was a focus for a complete community, the heart of a hamlet or town. This reaction against the horrors of unregulated industrialization was a continuing concern of the time, leading to a number of paternalistic if not wholly Utopian industrial communities. Ledoux quickly lapsed into fantasy at his saltworks. What began as a geometric arrangement of the production areas, the administrative offices, and workers' housing arranged in blocks around a semicircle – this much was built in his capacity as the King's Architect – became in his subsequent theoretical developments a new town with a huge church and market square, all the usual public buildings and some unusual ones

including a House of Morals, a Temple of Love (or brothel), and sundry other elements given over to conciliation, happiness and so on. Hierarchical and *ancien régime* as Ledoux's plan was, it also anticipated certain aspects of a new, freer society.

The more pragmatic industrial communities of Robert Owen succeeded better for a while: indeed, New Lanark, arranged in relatively *ad hoc* fashion in a rural valley not far from Glasgow, became a place of pilgrimage for everyone from the Tsar of Russia downwards. In turn it inspired such developments as Bruno Renard's Le Grand Hornu complex near Valenciennes in Belgium, 1822 – which took the paternalism of Owen and married it to the large-scale geometries of Ledoux, being a huge oval range within a rectangle. Such exercises were early attempts not only at caring for workers, but also in worker control – if they lived on the premises, with facilities for their families laid on, then they could easily be accounted for. Such cradle-to-grave worker complexes were to be enthusiastically adopted by the Japanese in the post-war years, but in general during the twentieth century the residential and manufacturing elements became separate entities.

One result of this separation was the idea of the separate but adjacent model village – as at Port Sunlight near Liverpool for the Lever soap empire, begun in 1888; Bourneville, Birmingham, for the

chocolate manufacturer Cadbury, begun 1879; and New Earswick, York, for the confectioners Rowntree, begun 1902. These were harbingers of the Garden City movement and indeed houses at New Earswick were made available to people outside the business that spawned them. New towns, and increased mobility, generally phased out the idea that industrialists should provide homes of any kind for their workforce: between them the state and the private sector would deal with the housing issue. There remain exceptions, such as Giancarlo de Carlo's densely plotted exercise in low-rise worker housing at Matteotti Village, 1970–5, for the employees of the Terni Company in the town of that name: the product of a *dirigiste* local administration rather than the usual market forces.

What usually remains a given in the evolution of the industrial building is its form. Factories clearly have to model themselves on the industrial processes taking place within them and this tends to lead to buildings that are disposed either in relatively long and narrow elements – suitable for goods that undergo successive processes, and of course production lines – or deep-plan virtually square buildings, which allow for freer circulation and back-loops within the process. Courtyards may be introduced into the plan to combine these two types – a template that has the virtue of being

a   Ricardo Legorreta, Renault
    Factory, Gómez Palacio
    Durango, Mexico, 1985:
    Legorreta's factory suits
    the nature of its desert
    surroundings
b   Renault, Mexico: courtyard
c   Rafael Moneo, Diestre Factory,
    Saragossa, Spain, 1963–7

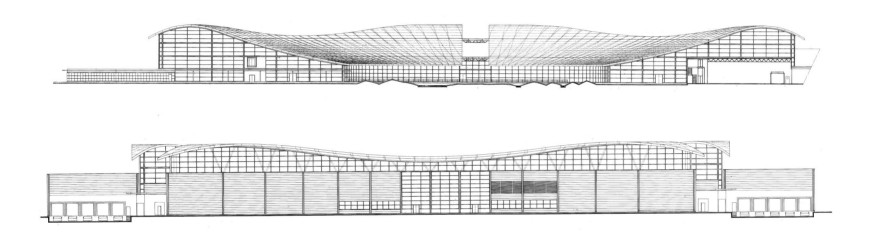

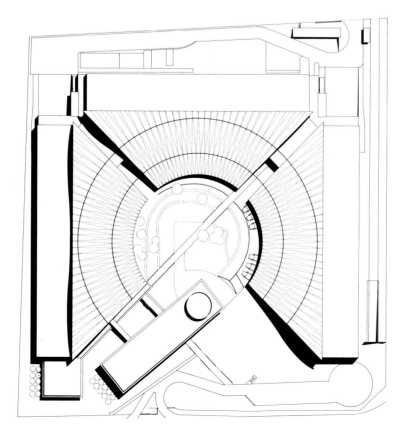

a   d | e   f
   b |
   c |

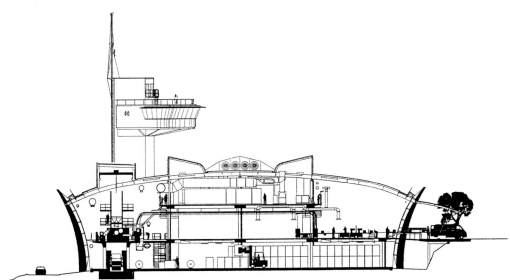

relatively frugal on land requirements. From the earliest industrial centres – medieval farm and barn complexes (merely another way of expressing in built form production, storage and distribution), through the later works of printers, dyers and weavers, to today's automated plant, these same forms tend to dominate. Indeed, the disposition of elements within and around a Cistercian monastery anticipate by hundreds of years the ideal self-sustaining worker communities of Ledoux, Owen and others, in plan being sophisticated and efficient diagrams of the process of living, working, and producing.

There is of course a difference between rural industrial centres and those in cities. The unexpected successor to the economic powerhouse of the medieval monastery, for instance, would be a place such as the necessarily introverted and highly staffed reprocessing plant of British Nuclear Fuels (BNFL) at Sellafield in Cumbria, 1950s to 1990s, much of it designed in serviced-shed form by BDP from 1980 to 1990 – an apparently sprawling, but in fact ingeniously organized, industrial complex demanding an almost feudal allegiance from the workforce of the surrounding towns and villages – which are economically dependent upon it, there being little other local employment. Having, like a monastery, an air of mystery and power to it, BNFL even spawned the kind of building more usually associated with ruined abbeys

than factories – a visitor centre to handle tourists.

In contrast to such a land-hungry rural development (estuarial refineries the world over may be compared) compare the car maker Fiat's titanic Lingotto factory in Turin, designed by Giacomo Matté Trucco, 1915–21. There, the production process spirals upwards from the raw materials intake at ground level, with railway marshalling yards alongside to provide the necessary mobility, to a final rooftop test-track for the finished vehicles. This almost Futurist vision lacked only the final element of cars being whisked away by cargo airships. Le Corbusier was fascinated by the Fiat factory, and both the ramps within the Villa Savoye and the rooftop exercise track on the Marseilles Unité may be traced back to it. The form of the Turin building – in essence a very long rectangle with subsidiary transverse blocks forming inner courtyards – is however true to the lineage of industrial developments, and in its vertical stacking is not so very different from nineteenth-century multi-level textile mills. Its conversion into a multi-purpose, culture-based centre from the late 1980s onwards in the hands of Renzo Piano proved to be a lengthy and at times controversial business. When a building's form is dictated so completely by its original function, finding a suitable new use is no easy task.

By the late twentieth century, architects – who as a general rule are employed on industrial

projects as mere facilitators of built square footage – were sometimes inclined to challenge the time-honoured form of the factory building. Where Grimshaw's *FT* Printworks was sternly rectangular, his *Western Morning News* building in Plymouth, completed 1992, is in the alternative tradition of factory as a landmark statement. True, it housed the offices of a newspaper group as well as its production plant and so had more of a public face. Even so, adapting the externally braced glass wall of the earlier building to the flaring bows of its ship-like building – complete with aircraft-carrier-style bridge – was an extreme example of expressionism triumphing over functionalism, to the extent that its curving internal office floors do not occupy the prow, which is left as a void. 'The thing about modernism is that it was to do with the shortest distance between two points,' the classicist Quinlan Terry was heard to observe, in apparent perplexity, after visiting the *Western Morning News*. Not so here, although it is noticeable that only the desk-workers occupy the curving part of the building. The machine hall at the rear, taking up more than half the building, is a virtually square production area.

Related exercises in structural and aesthetic virtuosity include Valode and Pistre's L'Oréal Factory at Aulnay-sous-Bois, France, 1988–91. One of the practice's declared aims – to personalize

Breaking away from the box:
a Valode and Pistre, L'Oréal Factory, Aulnay-sous-Bois, France, 1988–91: view from central garden
b L'Oréal: elevations
c L'Oréal: plan
d L'Oréal: exterior view
e Nicholas Grimshaw and Partners, *Western Morning News*, Plymouth, 1992: its ship-like imagery makes it a strong landmark statement
f *Western Morning News*: section

industrialized building methods – is achieved here, and with some flair. Its appearance to an extent belies its underlying plan – this starts off as a hollow square, the familiar courtyard typology – but successfully subverts that with a few well-handled interventions. Standard long rectangular blocks form the perimeter of the site on three sides, while the fourth is shortened and angled inwards as a discrete object, thus making a wedge-shaped incision into the plan. However, these are not immediately obvious. What you notice are the very complex curves of the aluminium roof wrapped over the main production floors which line the courtyard and sweep down to a circular garden at the centre. Virtuoso engineering is clearly apparent: this is the work of the late Peter Rice. The 'petals' of the roof are almost sublimely complex in construction terms, but yield shapes of great purity and beauty – appropriate, perhaps, for a factory that makes cosmetics. Nor is the roof a merely architectonic gesture, for it allows a very high level of natural daylight into the deep floors from high level clerestories.

Such architecture is possible for the production plant of companies making high-image, high-value goods, but it is a great deal less easy to convince the manufacturers of high-volume low-margin goods, where overheads are constantly being driven down and money spent on high aesthetics is

a Jean Nouvel, Poulain Factory,
   Blois, France, 1989–91:
   land art
b Poulain Factory: facade detail
c Jean Nouvel, Cartier Factory,
   Saint-Imier, Switzerland,
   1989–92: a jewel casket
   in the landscape
d Cartier Factory: elevation
e Cartier Factory: interior

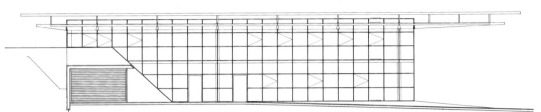

regarded as money wasted. At the luxury end of the market, fellow travellers of Valode and Pistre's L'Oréal plant are Jean Nouvel's factories for Poulain at Blois, 1989–91, and for the watchmakers Cartier at Saint-Imier in Switzerland, 1989–92. For Poulain, Nouvel thought along similar lines to Legorreta in Mexico, to the extent that the main issue is the wall. In black picked out with red (a favourite Nouvel colour scheme), the walls arrange themselves across the landscape in a consciously 'land art' fashion that is also a wry commentary on the standard profiled-metal factory box. At Saint-Imier, home of Swiss horological skills, the Cartier factory is, like Grimshaw's print-works, a jewel casket – in this case a block of black glass surmounted by an oversailing lid. The lid denotes luxury as much as the costly glass, since it projects far more than is necessary for solar shading in this cool climate. Its almost decadent structural redundancy is parallelled by Nouvel's Fondation Cartier in Paris, 1991–4, an administration building with a contemporary art gallery funded by the same client, where elements of the glass facade not only continue their sideways march beyond the envelope of the building, but are also expressed as freestanding screens – again, an unexpected link with Legorreta and his shielding screens at Renault.

The 'luxury factory' – remember also in this context the Vitra furniture complex at Weil-am-Rhein

a   c d

b   e

outside Basel – may be defined as one that steps architecturally outside the rigours of the technical brief. This is a grey area – only in unadorned sheds is architecture absent, and even there the expression of manufacturing processes – not to mention the engineering prowess apparent in, for instance, long-span construction – can have a powerful 'unconscious' impact. Why else would legions of architects, critics and photographers from the earliest years of the century onwards have been seduced by the might of the machine and the allure of the industrial structure? In contrast, however, consider two factories: Herzog and de Meuron's warehouse for Ricola at Laufen, Switzerland, 1986–7, and Coop Himmelblau's Funder Factory in St Veit, Austria, 1988–9. Both are relatively modest attempts to subvert the standard industrial box, in both cases on a tight budget. The Ricola warehouse, placed somewhat surreally in a former chalk quarry with soft craggy cliffs all round, is in plan simply the usual rectangular box with a loading bay for lorries at the front. Inside the structure is the usual arrangement of girders, spanning to a central line of columns. The usual automated storage equipment is used. Cheap materials have been used to divert attention to the building's skin. A busy cornice of slender sticks crowns walls of tilted horizontal bands of proprietary boarding, the bands diminishing in width from top to bottom. Shiny square panels of

a   d   e
            f
b   g
  c

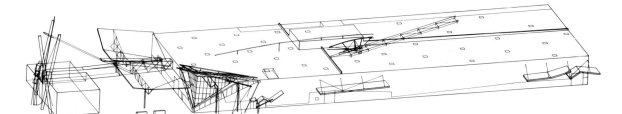

flush-fitted galvanized steel clad the loading bay. That is all, but – as with the same practice's Basel railway signal box – the use of a familiar material in an unfamiliar context gives the building a sense of the uncanny.

In Austria, Coop Himmelblau's Funder

Factory – a paper-coating works – achieves much the same thing by other means. Again, there is the standard rectangular box with a frontal canopy. The practice's Wolf Prix and Helmut Swiczinsky then play their familiar game of bursting wildly out of the frame, but at selected points only, notably one of the front corners. Although some of the interventions – for instance the asymmetrical angular red canopies tacked on at intervals – are functionally almost completely useless, the separate power plant with its chimney stacks is treated more seriously as a sculptural object. The architects successfully challenge the assumption that a pair of chimneys should be either parallel or vertical, which is as good a way as any of creating a corporate identity for a company engaged in a dull but necessary process.

The architecturally considered factory is primarily a continental European phenomenon. It is not encountered very much in the United Kingdom – sadly, given the twentieth-century precedents of Boots in Nottingham and Brynmawr in South Wales – and this is sometimes ascribed to the 'short-termism'

that afflicts much of British industry, coupled with the perceived need to maximize dividends to shareholders rather than invest in buildings or even equipment. There are certain exceptions. Not being British, the Cummins engine company felt free to appoint architects of merit for the Scottish heavy engineering plant it commissioned in the mid-1970s at Shotts in Lanarkshire. Cummins' home town of Columbus, Ohio, is notable for its buildings – not just industrial buildings – by the likes of SOM and Roche and Dinkeloo. Previously in Britain it had commissioned Kevin Roche, John Dinkeloo and Associates for its engineering factory in Darlington. This was a classic Miesian box, in Cor-Ten weathering steel, completed in 1967. The Miesian factory proved to be an import with staying power: by 1974 the tobacco products company Wills had completed its own Cor-Ten complex outside Bristol by Skidmore, Owings and Merrill with Yorke Rosenberg Mardall, an Anglo-American pairing that had just produced the head office for the Boots company in Nottingham, completed 1968. But come 1975, Mies seemed old hat to some of the British, so Ahrends Burton and Koralek – principally Peter Ahrends – ignored precedent with a highly articulated composition that 'wrapped' an existing factory on the site, added new production areas, defined the perimeter by means of a splayed, tensioned aluminium wall giving an undulating effect,

True architect-designed manufacturing plants are rare; the opportunities offered are even more seldom taken:

a Coop Himmelblau, Funder Factory Works 3, St Veit, Austria, 1988–9: sculpturally bursts out of its box

b Herzog and de Meuron, Ricola Factory, Laufen, Switzerland, 1986–7: the unconventional treatment of the exterior skin diverts attention from the functional form

c Ricola Factory: loading bay

d Funder Factory: entrance canopy

e Funder Factory: axonometric

f Ahrends Burton Koralek, Cummins Engine Company Ltd, Shotts, Lanarkshire, Scotland, 1975–83

g Kevin Roche John Dinkeloo & Associates, Cummins Engine Company Components Plant, Darlington, England, 1963–7

and sliced it through with the cowled forms of three high access spines, dividing the complex into four production areas and serving to buttress the building. Those four areas – classic deep-plan factory spaces – described the four stages of the production process: receiving and parts inspection; machining; assembly and stores; and testing.

The needs of the factory were extensively researched, 20 per cent of the workforce was interviewed, and a thirty-year low-energy strategy with heat reclaim implemented. Opened in 1983, the Cummins complex at Shotts was hailed as Scotland's finest post-war industrial scheme. However research and life-cycle costing are no talismans against changes in economic circumstances. The plant's working life was to be comparatively short: it closed in 1997.

Private companies without institutional shareholders to please are often capable of producing one-off industrial buildings of note. Examples in Britain are the circular stone-built David Mellor cutlery factory at Hathersage in Derbyshire, by Michael Hopkins & Partners, 1988–9; a startling change from the rectangular glass pavilion of a factory Hopkins had just produced for Solid State Logic outside Oxford, 1986–8. The two factories are on the cusp of Hopkins' move away from 'high-tech', apparently lightweight buildings (see also his partly mast-supported, fabric-roofed Schlumberger Research building outside Cambridge, England, 1982–92), towards a concern with weight and mass. The small rural factory takes its place in the Utopian tradition – Mellor both lived and worked at Hathersage, and his

workforce helped to make and build the Hopkins factory – and is seen as a means to employment. Thus a descendant of Hathersage is the Dr Martens shoe factory at Wollaston in Northamptonshire by Haworth Tompkins, 1994–6: small town, small factory, local industry, vernacular materials used in a contemporary manner.

If ABK's Cummins plant shows how vulnerable factories are to changing economic conditions; Hopkins' Schlumberger demonstrates the mutability of the concepts that originally inform the brief. The reason for the great caterpillar-like translucent-fabric central hall, built in the first phase of 1982–5, was to provide a daylit clear-span space for Schlumberger's test drilling equipment (the company being concerned with oil exploration). Drilling pits are sunk

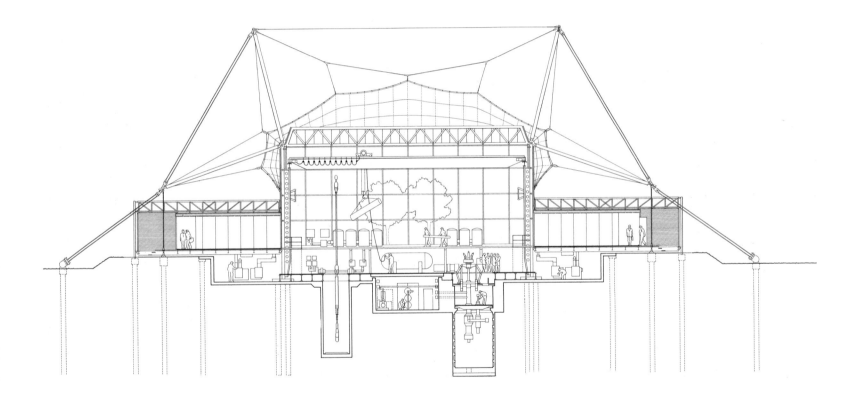

a   d

b c

Ways to get industry into the countryside, where employment is often badly needed:

a Michael Hopkins & Partners, Schlumberger Cambridge Research Centre, Cambridge, England, 1982–92: section

b Haworth Tompkins, Dr Martens Factory, Wollaston, Northhamptonshire, England, 1994–6

c Michael Hopkins & Partners, David Mellor Cutlery Factory, Hathersage, Derbyshire, England, 1988–9

d Schlumberger Cambridge: view towards the caterpillar-like central hall with its mast-supported fabric roof

b	d
a	c

a   Richard Rogers Partnership,
    Inmos Factory, Newport, South
    Wales, 1982: exterior

b   Inmos Factory: entrance

c   Inmos Factory: view of the
    central suspended structure
    and rooftop ductwork

d   Renzo Piano Building
    Workshop, Schlumberger
    Facilities Restructuring,
    Montrouge, Paris, 1981–4

into the ground beneath the building for this purpose, and a high level gantry crane moves heavy items of equipment about. Hopkins' decision to place the big test-rig hall in the centre of the complex, and allow everyone in the laboratories and offices around to see what was going on, was an inspired move and put into architectural form what the company was all about. The roof was a relatively early use of Teflon-coated glass fibre, transmitting about 13 per cent of daylight and – as importantly – glowing at night from within. Yet within a few years, Schlumberger found it could simulate most of its testing procedures on computer. The prime determinant of the building's form had shrivelled in importance. But the company continued to expand its Cambridge site and when Hopkins came to design the second phase in 1990–2, no such bravura gesture was needed to house the laboratories and offices required. So he played a subtler game, casting the exposed first-floor slab of the building in geometric stress-patterns recalling the work of Pier Luigi Nervi. As if to show that his technology, too, had moved on, Hopkins decided against continuing the aesthetic of the circus-tent roof for the atrium and meeting areas of the new block. Instead, the light-transmitting roofs here are inflated pillows of fluorocarbon film.

The tent roof became a trademark for Schlumberger in the early 1980s, since the Renzo

Piano Building Workshop adopted the form for the renovation of the company's large historic industrial site in Montrouge, southern Paris, 1981–4, thus slightly antedating Hopkins. In Paris, Schlumberger was already fully engaged in changing technological horses, from the making of heavy equipment to the making of electronic components. Piano accordingly demolished the old single-storey factories on the site, renovated the higher blocks around the perimeter for the new working methods, and placed a communal 'street' across the middle, its buildings earth-sheltered and with an undulating canopy of Teflon-coated fabric marking the spine route. In the old buildings, Piano exposed the frame and placed within (and sometimes behind) it a kit of brightly coloured parts out of which the new areas are made: a similar approach was to be taken with the Fiat factory at Lingotto in Turin. This was the first big project for the Building Workshop, and the first industrial building for Piano since, within the Piano and Rogers practice, he had helped designed the Patscentre research laboratories in Melbourn, England, 1976–83 – where the original idea was also for an earth-sheltered building, but where finally the bermed landscape was allowed to approach but not engulf it.

The Patscentre (for the PA Technology Group) is often overlooked in the development of Piano and Rogers, but the philosophy behind it is crucial in the

way it took both men in different directions. It led Piano to the earth-sheltered forms of Schlumberger in Paris, but it took Rogers towards the expressed-services solution of the Inmos microchip plant at Newport, South Wales. At first glance there is little in common between the two buildings – one with its understated, smooth carapace of interchangeable panels, the other with its frenetic disposition of suspension structure and rooftop ductwork. But Inmos, 1982, is, in a sense, the Patscentre turned upside-down. At the latter, the services are exposed beneath the elevated floor slab, under which cars park, and form an intrinsic part of the architecture; at the former, the slab sits on the ground, and all the services spill out of the roof – without them, the architecture would be almost nothing. Effectively nine suspension bridges in parallel carry the big roof, while their paired masts define a central circulation spine beneath, and a zone of exposed services on top. This was in the cause of ultimate flexibility of space and use, as was the by now familiar pattern of (this time square) interchangeable cladding panels – opaque for the sealed 'clean room' production areas on one side of the spine, dotted with windows for the office and recreation areas on the other. The logic seems impeccable, even if the effect is somewhat startling. But microchip production requires not only ultra-clean production areas – hence the high level of servicing for rapid air changes and filtration – but also freedom from vibration. Design measures thus needed to be taken to guard against the structure quivering in high winds – a precaution that would not have been necessary in a conventional building envelope. All the same, the experiment was successful enough for Rogers to repeat in greatly simplified form at the PA Technology Center, Princeton, New Jersey, 1982–5, where engineer Peter Rice's paring down of the structure, and the alignment of the services more precisely with the central spine, makes the piggy-back arrangement of served and servant elements very much clearer.

A decade or more on from those early 1980s projects, some of the imagery of those heroic times cropped up again in the work of others. In 1992

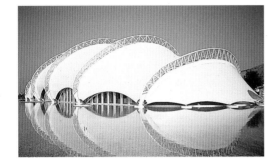

Samyn and Partners completed laboratories for M&G Richerche in Venafro, Italy, that looked again at the Piano and Hopkins idea of the tensile fabric roof. In their case, they used the technique to provide not just an element of a building complex, but the entire envelope. Six steel horseshoe arches increasing in size towards the middle serve to tension the PVC-coated polyester fabric of the roof from end to end, like a hooped skirt. Beneath the enclosure, freestanding buildings of one and two storeys do not touch the envelope. A broad moat surrounds the building, over which cooling air is drawn in summer and which serves to protect the membrane against casual vandalism (since it comes down to ground level, save for scalloped glazed openings) Later, Philippe Samyn's practice turned to timber technology for the

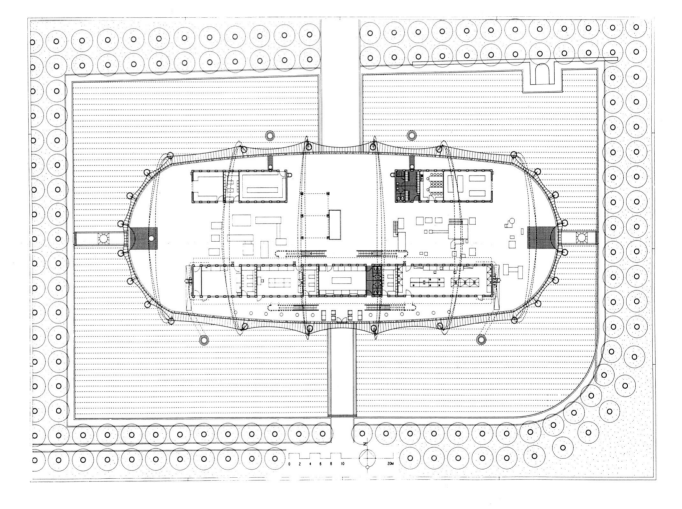

a   c

b   d
    e f

Convincing use of the hooped tensile structure:
a   Samyn & Partners, M&G Richerche Venafro, Venafro, Italy, 1989–92: six horseshoe arches tension the PVC fabric roof
b   M&G Richerche Venafro: plan
c   Samyn & Partners, Walloon Forestry Centre, Marche-en-Famenne, Belgium, 1992–5: sections
d   Walloon Forestry Centre: plan
e   Walloon Forestry Centre: exterior view
f   Walloon Forestry Centre: interior

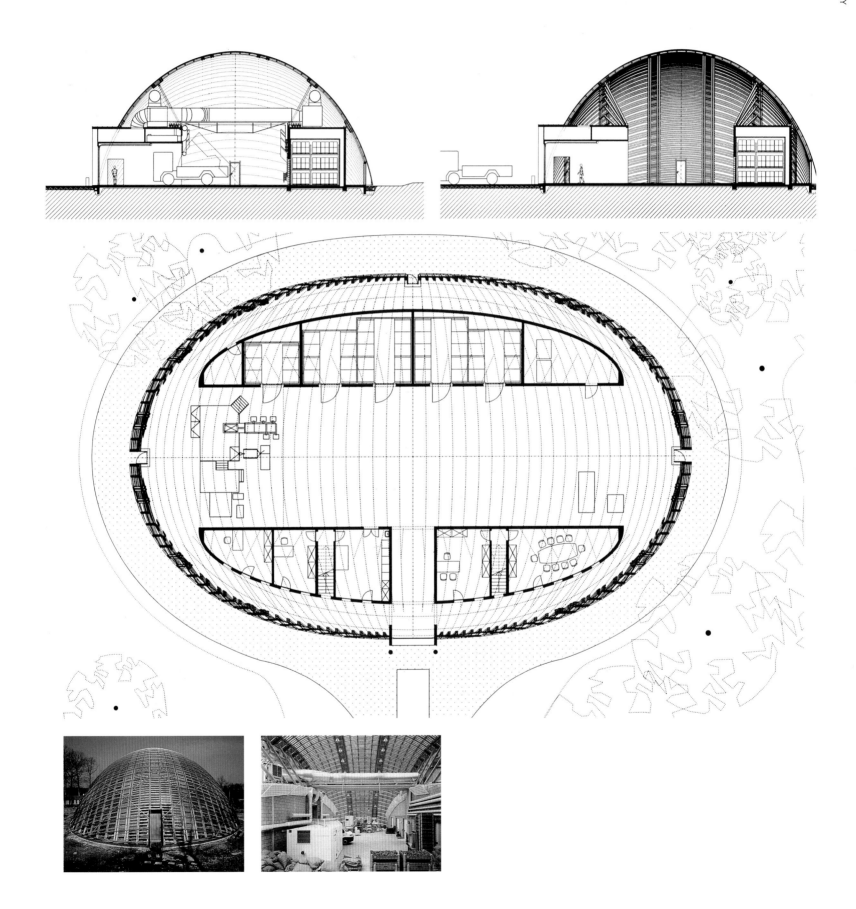

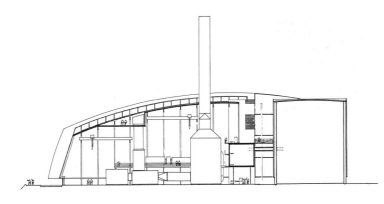

egg-shaped Walloon Forestry Centre in Belgium.

Industrial buildings occur in the public sector in the form of power and pumping stations, dams and refuse disposal plant. The potential of hydro-electric schemes has been convincingly demonstrated since Victorian times, not least in the titanic structures of the Tennessee Valley Authority from 1933 onwards. When power stations were small and coal-fired they convincingly employed the skills of architects as well as engineers – though the larger they become, the more the contribution of the former seems puny in comparison with the latter. The smooth intersecting metallic forms of Rotterdam's smoke cleaning plant, 1991–3, by Maarten Struijs – a new variation on the old trick of articulating sheer blank industrial walls – is a notable exception. Into this category also fits the 1993 electricity substation at Amersfoort in The Netherlands by Van Berkel and Bos, which achieves its effect by splitting the usual transformer box, slightly displacing the two interlocking halves and expressing them with different surface treatments, one being black basalt, the other silvery aluminium (representing respectively insulating and conducting properties). By subtly altering the external envelope in this way, the architect achieves a feeling of real power in what is usually a shallow building type. A similar approach works equally well at the Viborg

Architects become seduced by 'Big Industry' and express it rather than conceal it:

a Peter Kjelgaard and Thomas Pedersen, Viborg District Heating Plan, Denmark, 1993–6: longitudinal section

b Maarten Struijs (Public Works, Rotterdam), Smoke Cleaner, Brielselaan Refuse Combustion Plant, Rotterdam, The Netherlands, 1991–3: aerial view

c Smoke Cleaner: exterior

d Viborg District Heating Plant: exterior

e Van Berkel + Bos, Electric Substation, Amersfoort, The Netherlands, 1993

f John Outram Associates, Storm Water Pumping Station, Isle of Dogs, London, 1986–8

g Oswald Mathias Ungers, Tiergarten Pumping Station, Berlin, 1987: interior

h Tiergarten Pumping Station: exterior

District Heating Plant in Denmark, 1993–6, by Peter Kjelgaard and Thomas Pedersen. This acknowledges the fact that such large freestanding chunks of plant cannot easily or cheaply be hidden and that therefore the appropriate answer is to celebrate them. The plant with its central chimney and large cylindrical heat storage tank is therefore clasped by two clamshell walls, tilting inwards and clad with reflective ceramic tiles. Both walls dramatize and partly reveal the process of power generation, since slots of glazing are formed in the gaps between the shells, allowing passing motorists a glimpse of the machinery within. The composition is made all the more powerful by the fact that the big storage tank is separately expressed, just caught between the shells at the front as if emerging from within.

In the 1980s and 1990s pumping stations – which can be and often are invisible underground chambers – began to reclaim some of the glory that their Victorian forbears had enjoyed. Government regeneration agencies, usually dependent on private developers to invest in their former industrial and dockside areas, find that of the infrastructure they must put in, pumping stations and bridges offer the most opportunity. Bridges are in the civic realm, and will be dealt with in that section. Pumping stations, however, must be considered industrial, since the public seldom gains access to them. In this context

Oswald Mathias Ungers' Tiergarten Pumping Station in Berlin, 1987, sets the scene. This is a sewage pumping works, treating effluent from 680 hectares of the city. Most of the works are below ground but – in common with all building of the type - the works had to be ventilated to avoid a potentially explosive build-up of methane. The buildings that sit above such Stygian chambers need do little more than provide access for engineers and some kind of mechanical ventilation. Ungers, however, expresses his building on a heroic scale, with pure, unadorned forms: four tall chimneys inset slightly from the corners, a solid plinth, a dark pitched roof. It is enough; it abstracts the elements of its predecessors. In London's Docklands, John Outram in contrast applied his iconographic theories to a building of similar function, a storm-water pumping station, 1986–8: but turns it into a temple, complete with the complex language that is personal to the architect but which results in some original decorative details immediately appreciated by the public and which conceal the fact that this is a large, bomb-proof, windowless shed. A small, fast extractor fan would have vented the interior sufficiently, but Outram prefers a very large, slow-turning, multi-bladed number set into a cowling reminiscent of a turbofan jet engine, which is set right at the centre of the pediment.

The London Docklands Development Corporation also commissioned pumping stations from Nicholas Grimshaw and Richard Rogers. Grimshaw's is a steel-plate design, reminiscent of a surfacing submarine, while Rogers', 1977, is a jolly pair of concentric drums with an overlay of breezy maritime imagery. Of the London examples, Outram's most perfectly captures the mysterious romance of such places, but in Berlin, Gustav Peichl achieved a similar urban success by other means. His Phosphate Elimination Plant, 1980–5, is in fact a sewage treatment works, cleansing effluent before it flows into Lake Tegel. As befits a project from that city's International Building Exhibition of 1984, it is treated as an important object in the landscape, Peichl's joke being to make it into a great submerged ship, of which only the bridge and top-hamper is visible above the surrounding greensward, overlooking the purification tanks.

In the United States, aqueous industrial architecture has had a lot to live up to since 1932 when Gordon B Kaufman styled the Hoover Dam, on the Colorado River between Arizona and Nevada. Between 1978 and 1985 the practice Gatje Papachristou Smith (principally Hamilton Smith) did their damnedest with the Richard B Russell Powerhouse on the Savannah River between Georgia and South Carolina. The Powerhouse is a hydroelectric

power-generating dam built by the US Corps of Engineers. Hamilton Smith, who had previously worked for Eero Saarinen and Marcel Breuer, made the dam and power station into a highly sculptural and massive *in situ* concrete building in which the workings are on display – for instance the eight arched window openings on the downstream side, which give the dam the feel of a Roman aqueduct, related to eight giant turbines inside, clearly visible. Perhaps uniquely for an industrial project, it includes an open-air theatre, overlooking the water. Compare a project on this scale with Ingimundur Sveinsson's geothermal storage plant in Reykjavik, 1987–91 – a cluster of six cylindrical insulated tanks containing water piped from a nearby extractor plant, held here before being distributed as a heating medium throughout the city. Sveinsson arranged the six found tanks in a ring, put a glass dome over the central void, and there created a lush winter garden of hot-climate plants – making a civic space with upper levels devoted to a bar and observation deck. Again, the industrial process has been made public.

Farm buildings have been industrial buildings from the beginning, and as with all other forms of industry, centralized distribution and mechanization have made great differences to the appearance of agricultural architecture. Grain silos came to define America's Midwest just as much as its tall furnace

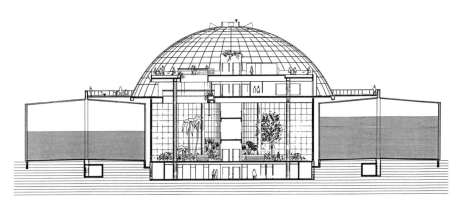

sheds spoke of the wealth of its Steel Belt. Today the low wide sheds of chicken and pig 'farms' are production plant in all but name, requiring large amounts of energy to run. Although occasionally an industrial loop can be closed – the small power station at Eye in Suffolk, England, 1990–4, by architects Lifschutz Davidson, for instance, is powered entirely by chicken litter, produces fertiliser as the product of combustion, and is architecturally ambitious. More usually agricultural buildings are of little architectural merit, integrated with no process other than their own.

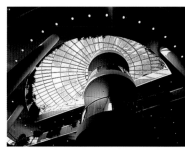

Exceptions include ecological farm complexes such as the Laredo Demonstration Farm, begun in 1987 on the Texan–Mexican border by the organization known as the Center for Maximum Potential Building Systems. Although a model for a sustainable eco-farm, Laredo is arranged not in the *ad hoc* fashion beloved of many environmentalists, but on a stern grid, using an equally stern system of component parts, and recycled and local materials. Its principal designers, Pliny Fisk and Gail Vittori, have a Kahn-influenced feel for buildings and their systems that works even at this relatively humble level. An important part of Laredo's function is to offer teaching, which is one reason why it has to appear serious and convincing. Perhaps this is why more conventional agricultural study centres are also more concerned than most farms with self-presentation. The Japanese

a Gustav Peichl, Phosphate Elimination Plant, Berlin, 1980–5: overlooking the purification tanks
b Phosphate Elimination Plant: aerial view
c Lifschutz Davidson, Eye Power Station, Eye, Suffolk, England, 1990–4: powered by a renewable resource and process waste is recycled
d Eye Power Station: exterior detail
e Eye Power Station: for such a small industrial building its aims are architecturally ambitious
f Ingimundur Sveinsson, Geothermal Plant, Reykjavik, Iceland, 1987–91: section
g Geothermal Plant: winter garden roof
h Geothermal Plant: six insulated tanks surround the central public space

a
b

c d e

f
g
h

born, French-based architect Masasaku Bokura adopted an aesthetic more usually associated with electronics companies for his Saint-Lo Agricultural Study Centre, Brittany, France. Here, low, single-storey aluminium-clad buildings with glazed apsidal ends stand alongside more conventional wide-span box buildings, their roofs hung from simple suspension masts. Surrounded by its own arable land on the edge of the city, most of the rest of that land has been swallowed up by a typical industrial park – a fact that Bokura's buildings both acknowledge and subvert.

Similarly, the Kumamoto Grasslands agricultural institute in Japan by the Anglo-Icelandic partnership of Tom Heneghan and Inga Dagfinnsdottir was conceived on a more elevated plane than usual as part of a programme of new public buildings, dubbed 'Art Polis', across this southern region. Moreover, it is in a glorious mountain setting (very unlike the flat suburban site of Bokura's Saint-Lo centre) which is a national park. The buildings, 1991–2, are barnlike in many senses, some with apsidal ends recalling great airship hangars. They are clustered into two distinct groups for dairy and beef farming, with a separate collection of research buildings. Each of the main buildings appears naturally to fall into the tripartite division of central nave flanked with aisles, familiar to large agricultural buildings across the world. Here, however, the aisles extend

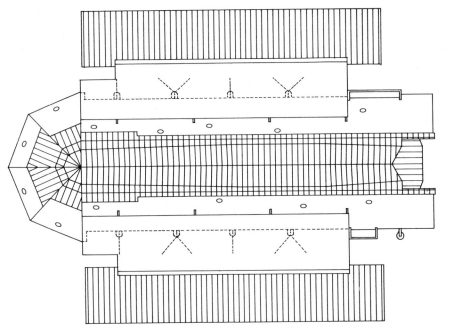
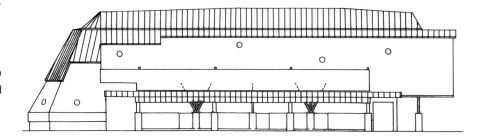

Enlightened new architecture in agriculture is even scarcer than in other industries:

a   Centre for Maximum Potential Building Systems (principal designers Pliny Fisk and Gail Vittori), Laredo Demonstration Farm, Texas, on US–Mexican Border, 1987: interior of farm buildings

b   Laredo Demonstration Farm: exterior

c   The Architecture Factory (Tom Heneghan and Inga Dagfinnsdottir) in association with Ojukai Furukawa Architects, Kumamoto Grasslands Agricultural Institute, Kumamoto, Japan, 1991–2: dairy building

d   Kumamoto Grasslands Institute: plan and elevation

e   Kumamoto Grasslands Institute: interior of dairy

	b c e
a	d

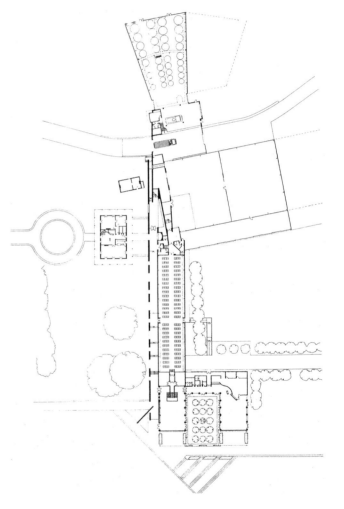

a d f		g i j
b e		k
c		
		h

A breed of new model industrialists began to emerge from the entrepreneurs of the 1980s and 1990s:

a   Allen Jack & Cottier, Penfold's Magill Estate, Adelaide, Australia, 1993–6: exterior

b   Allen Jack & Cottier, Domaine Chandon Winery, Coldstream, Australia, 1987–90: exterior

c   Domaine Chandon Winery: loading bay

d   Magill Estate: restaurant

e   Domaine Chandon Winery: site plan

f   Magill Estate: wine storage

g   Van Berkel + Bos, Karbouw Office and Workshop, Amersfoort, The Netherlands, 1990–2: the deconstructed shed

h   John McAslan & Partners, Max Mara Headquarters, Reggio Emilia, Milan, Italy, 1995–9

i   Karbouw Office and Workshop: the upper level shifts off the grid

j   Karbouw Office and Workshop: window and cladding detail

k   Afra + Tobia Scarpa, Benetton Factory, Treviso, Italy, 1993–5

into freestanding shelters for open cattle pens beneath aerofoil-section roofs.

Higher architectural budgets are possible in agriculture, as with other industries, when the product has an added value. Hence the agricultural equivalent of the 'luxury factory' such as Cartier or L'Oreal is the winery. In certain areas such as California, Bordeaux and Southern Australia, the wine industry produces added-value industrial buildings. A perfect diagram of the genre is provided by Allen Jack & Cottier's Domaine Chandon Winery at Coldstream in Australia's Yarra Valley, 1987–90, where a linear plan beginning with the shed-like forms of the production and storage areas (press, tanks, sieving vats) gives way to a long colonnade in costly looking brick and stone, leading to a spacious tasting room and restaurant overlooking the vines. Thus the winery is an exact architectural description of the path from raw materials, through production, to consumption and back, visually, to the raw materials again. The practice later added a glass-pavilion restaurant, with rich coloured and timber-veneer interiors, to Penfold's historic Magill Estate in Adelaide. This estate had become more of a tourist destination as its viticultural and wine-making activities had declined, a not uncommon example of an industrial complex becoming 'heritage' like many a Scotch whisky distillery.

The pursuit of the ideal factory continues,

especially in Europe. Italy, with its craft tradition, frequently produces places that are studios and showrooms as well as places of production or distribution. Into this category falls the MaxMara Group headquarters at Reggio Emilia, just south of Milan, by John McAslan & Partners, 1995–9, where the differing needs of offices, studios, showrooms and warehousing are expressed as discrete elements within a small company township set among a grid-pattern of landscaped olive groves and water courses. Emphatically not in this category, however, is the Benetton factory in Treviso by Afra and Tobia Scarpa – long-term architects to the Benetton empire. This is purely and simply a factory building. In plan, the Treviso factory, completed 1995, is remarkably similar to Rogers' Inmos plant – central circulation spine flanked by long bays, their roofs held by a succession of masts and cables. These bays gradually assume pitched roofs towards their ends as their flank walls taper down: but the impression of the building being just a collection of linked, long sheds is belied by the vast spaces of the interior. For all the single-minded nature of the building, this is still a factory shed considered in architectural terms. As such, it shows that even the most basic industrial buildings can be raised a few notches above the norm. It compares with others in the field such as the moderately deconstructed industrial shed outside Amersfoort in The Netherlands by

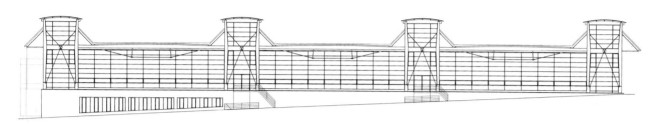

Ben van Berkel, where the upper level is wrenched slightly away from the orthogonal grid, and the tension between the levels then fruitfully exploited.

Very much more ambitious, however, are two industrial complexes in Germany – homeland of the advanced factory since Behrens. These are Thomas Herzog's Wilkhahn factory in Munder, 1989–92, and James Stirling and Michael Wilford's Braun complex in Melsungen, 1986–92. The Wilkhahn factory makes chairs and tables for the contract market, so perhaps the influence of Vitra in the south was starting to make an impression: in 1987 the company had built a sequence of pyramid-roofed industrial pavilions by Frei Otto. Because the Wilkhahn manufacturing philosophy is group-working, with a co-operative, profit-sharing structure, there are no production lines. As a result the factory adopts what is an ancient form – the virtually square, deep-plan production floor, familiar since Carmen's tobacco factory in Seville, built between 1728 and 1770. At Wilkhahn, Herzog provides three such floors in a row, with four high transverse nave elements containing stairs, offices and workshops serving to divide and bookend the spaces. The two-storey building is timber-framed and, on the administrative western side, partially timber-clad as well: although Herzog had previously worked mostly in steel, he had by this time, developed a system of timber high-tech. Accordingly the longer

span beams are here braced with steel chords. The fact remains, however, that the building looks a natural for total steel-framing – unlike Ernst Giselbrecht's carpenter's school in Murau, Austria, for instance, where the short spans and central pitched glass-clad spine lend themselves to timber used *au naturel*. One must assume, then, that for Wilkhahn, it was the image of the material, rather than any structural or economic benefits it might bring, that accorded best with the company philosophy. Its approach may be compared with that of the Phillips Plastics Factory, 1991, near New Richmond, Wisconsin. This, another organization with a humane, team-oriented approach to its manufacture, commissioned Julie Snow of the practice James–Snow to design its building – clad in masonry, but with large arched trusses to achieve the required clear span, the structure being exposed by cutbacks at the corners. Phillips wanted its offices on the factory floor in a non-hierarchical fashion: Snow designed fully glazed acoustic partitions to make this possible – so white and blue collar workers are in view of each other.

This might seem no great advance, but the 'democratic' factory is rare in the West: usually management offices are either placed separately from the factory, or designed to overlook the workers from a dominant position. Snow went on to design the QMR plastics factory at River Falls, Wisconsin, 1995 – with

its tilting roof and gable windows an interesting variant of the small rural factory type – and a third, not so overtly industrial, complex, the Origen Center, Menominee, Wisconsin, 1995, intended to be a training centre and factory space for start-up businesses. This is a very restrained reworking of the Miesian ideal, its rectilinear grid expressed in a series of pavilions on a shallow granite plinth, incorporating such non-industrial materials as cedar, cherrywood, and fabric ceilings: a manifesto production building.

Such non-hierarchical factories are more common in Japan, along with a philosophy that management and workers should enter by the same door and, as far as possible given the different nature of their activities, wear the same clothes. This is part of the concept of employer as cradle-to-grave carer, which often results in an employee living in company-built housing as well. This tradition came under strain in the 1990s as Japan's economy came off the rails and full employment ceased to be possible, but the concept persisted. When Japanese companies built factories overseas, they invariably exported this practice. Hence when the Sakata company set up a rice-cracker factory in Melbourne, Australia – effectively a bakery and packaging-distribution plant – Joseph Toscano architects studied the working practices and produced a building, 1993–5, that some have seen as Japanese in its simplicity, but which in

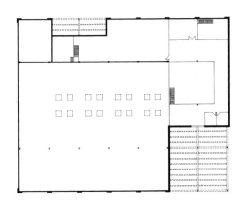

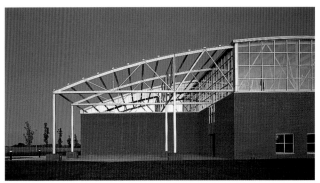

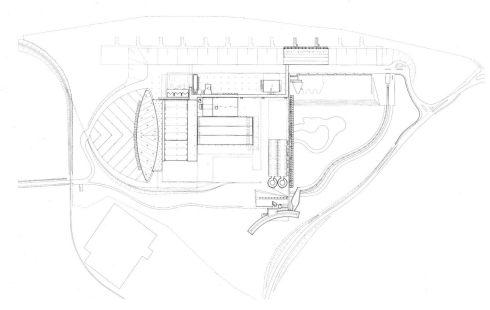

any event is an assured modelling of what in other hands would turn out to be a standard portal-shed form. The plan is ultra-simple: a linear progression from raw materials to finished products, with a small general office and company restaurant extruded beneath a sheltering roof at one side.

At Melsungen, James Stirling produced the last large-scale work he saw completed, one which, unlike Phillips in the United States or many Japanese equivalents, is unashamedly hierarchical in the paternalistic sense. The Braun complex was perhaps ideal for Stirling Wilford – here working with Walter Nageli – since it comprised a number of elements – factory, distribution warehouse, offices, car park, amenity buildings – that could be expressed as clearly distinct objects in an Arcadian landscape. If Nouvel's Poulain factory was land art, then Braun, for these architects, was a sculpture park. The company was far from being a producer of added-value goods: it made plastic medical components. The brief was for a large industrial centre: it got a disposition of objects in the tradition of the picturesque. The largest building here – the factory proper – is treated in understated fashion, its bulk reduced by being cut into the valley side. In compensation, the very much smaller, curving administration block with its parti-coloured window openings and upturned-cone *pilotis* is designed on a giant scale.

The distribution building, usually a bland affair for trucks to plug into, is here treated heroically as a long tilted oval dish of copper. A long, ceremonial pedestrian bridge on a forest of marching legs crosses the shallow valley from the entrance and car park to the factory. There is no worker housing here, yet this feels very much in the Owenite tradition of the Utopian community, since all the built elements are given equal architectural value. It is sad but perhaps not wholly surprising that such places are rare.

The image of the industrial building, be it a factory or power station, is today more powerful than its actuality. Few new industrial buildings can match the might and grandeur of the old, for the simple reason that production, storage and distribution processes have changed, and with them the need for large numbers of manual labourers. As the old buildings are demolished, converted – as with the German Design Centre at Essen in Germany's Ruhr, created in the huge, late 1920s boilerhouse of the Zollverein XII coal mine building by Foster and Partners in 1995-7 – and turned into museums of themselves, the spirit of industrial architecture is perhaps more to be found in buildings of other types. The industrial aesthetic is alive and well – but is as likely to be encountered in a house, bar or office block as it is in the world of manufacturing, where the most basic short-life enclosure is now usually thought to suffice.

c   e
       f
a   d   g
b

a   Joseph Toscano, Sakata
    Factory, Melbourne, Australia,
    1993–5: exterior
b   Sakata Factory: entrance
c   James Stirling Michael Wilford
    & Associates, in association
    with Walter Nageli, Braun
    Research and Production
    Headquarters, Melsungen,
    Germany, 1986–92: site plan

d   Braun HQ: distribution
    building
e   Braun HQ: factory or
    sculpture park?
f   Braun HQ: pedestrian bridge
g   Braun HQ: each of the
    elements of the factory
    are treated differently
    but without hierarchy

LEISURE *Theme parks, hotels & visitor centres* Tourism is the world's single biggest industry. Providing the hotels, resorts, theme parks and visitor centres to cope with huge global tidal flows of people, with high expectations of how they want to spend their leisure time, now represents a significant proportion of new building. In the late twentieth century the leisure industry would seem to be dominated by the Disney organization. But the themed environment spreads its tentacles wider, even into the earnest bastions of recent World Expos and innovative high-tech educational centres.

'I'm not "Walt Disney" anymore. Disney is a thing, an attitude, an image in the eyes of the public. I've spent my whole career creating that image, and I'm a great believer in what Disney is. But it's not me, the person.'

Walter Elias Disney quoted by his 'Imagineer', Marty Sklar, in 1996.

There is a picture of Salvador Dalí, nattily dressed and seated cross-legged like a Buddha, riding a miniature steam railway train in the back yard of Walt Disney's Burbank home. It was the early 1950s, and Walt's replica Canadian Pacific railway ride was his first stab at reproducing American history as a leisure event. Socially awkward himself, Disney found that the train gave him something to do at his own parties – and the planning of the little railroad, and the making of the models that went with it, provided a release from the increasingly irksome and union-plagued business of making animated feature films.

To protect his new hobby from prying eyes – though he said it was to protect his neighbours from the clatter and whistles of the train – he built an earth bank around his garden. Walt never let go of a good idea: all the later public Disney theme parks, whatever their content, featured some kind of railway in a park sheltered from the outside world by land-scaped earthworks. Dalí, one of a number of promi-nent artists patronized by Disney at the time, was

merely quick to exploit the surrealist potential offered by this fledgling genre.

Disney's personal back yard theme ride was developed at the same time as he was considering how best to cope with public demand for a 'studio tour', of the kind routinely provided by the live-action Hollywood movie companies. The business of animation being a dull, repetitive one with little visual interest, he conceived instead a pleasure park featuring characters from his films, set in a version of America that would be both cosily nostalgic and, in places, resolutely forward-looking. He set up a separate company, WED Enterprises, in 1952, to bring it into reality. Disneyland opened in Anaheim, California, on 17 July 1955. The company later became known as the 'Imagineers'. At the time of writing, the eighth and ninth Disney theme parks, in California next to the original, and in Tokyo, were in the intensive design stage. Each now costs around $1 billion, and takes up to seven years from concept to opening. They are massive pieces of urban planning and detail design. Leisure architec-ture – the architecture of tourism and affluence – cannot be ignored as a perhaps regrettable architec-tural sideline, not to be compared with serious stuff like art galleries and office blocks. Just as Walt Disney recognized early on that 'Disney' was not a person but an attitude, so our own response to that

attitude is changing, even if we still nurture a residual feeling that 'theming' is somehow not a pure form of architecture or design. Perhaps we are becoming aware of the historical evidence (Gothic or Italianate detailing of nineteenth-century Western public buildings, for instance, or the Moorish revival in the Middle East, or the temple references in many secular Japanese buildings) that theming has long been with us. Perhaps we are a little uncomfortable at the revisiting of the 'heroic modern' phase of architecture by some of today's architects, realizing that this is no less pastiche than vernacular, neo-classical or any other of architecture's 'isms'. The 1980s vogue for 'narra-tive architecture', which emerged in the projects, interiors and buildings of Nigel Coates and others, is more closely related to the normally despised theme parks than many realized at the time. Finally, while it is obvious that many shopping malls have now become themed environments, it is also now clearer than it used to be that Disney himself borrowed a great deal from the emerging mall architecture of the 1950s as pioneered by Victor Gruen and others. Shopping malls and theme parks have therefore been intertwined all the way through: a grudging critical respect for the urbanis-tic imperatives of both, while overdue, is nonethe-less beginning to emerge.

a

Inventing a history
from scratch:
a   Wimberly, Allison, Tong & Goo,
    'Palace of the Lost City',
    Bophuthatswana, South Africa,
    1990–2

Walt Disney World in Florida, for instance – comprising the differing but linked attractions of The Magic Kingdom, Epcot, the Disney-MGM Studio tours, Pleasure Island, three water parks, two shopping centres, Disney's offices, the emerging Celebration new town of 20,000 permanent inhabitants, and lashings of hotels of all types – covers over 35,000 acres and attracts 30 million visitors a year, many of whom stay for as long as a week. The Disney way to urbanism is now the subject of serious academic and anthropological study. The quasi-religious, ritual quality of Walt Disney World has been compared with Mecca, the aims of the organization regarded as alternately Utopian and fascist – but always capitalist. One of what the Disney people call 'Mickey's Ten Commandments' for making such places can sound chilling, but applies to all such environments: 'Organize the flow of people and ideas'.

Disney rules the roost when it comes to theming, but there are plenty of other operators working in this area: indeed, theming was one of fastest-growing influences on the urban realm during the thirty-year timespan of this book, going as ever hand-in-hand with the retailing boom. Even though it is so familiar, the excesses of theming can still be startling. Consider the 'Palace of the Lost City' in the Republic of Bophuthatswana, South Africa, by architects Wimberly, Allison, Tong & Goo. Built in 1990–2,

this is a hotel-based leisure complex themed upon a fictional narrative spun by the design architect – the buildings serving to 'rediscover' the style of a civilization that nobody, least of all the architects, pretended had ever existed there. The hotel, according to this model, is a recreation of an imagined 1,000-year-old royal palace. Its architecture is richly eccentric to beyond the point of decadence – it is as fanciful as anything dreamed up by Disney's architects and 'imagineers'. It effortlessly outperforms the same architects' comparatively restrained hotel at Disneyland Paris, and the 68-acre African site also includes an Olympic-sized swimming pool and two professional-standard golf courses – so relating it distantly to the history of sports-leisure venues such as the Roman baths of Caracalla and Diocletian.

European architects and critics tend to sneer at such projects, which are seen as exported examples of Las Vegas frippery. Yet this fictionalizing tendency is by no means confined to the New World. In 1989 the British architect John Outram was shortlisted in an international competition to design a rural opera house at Compton Verney near Stratford-upon-Avon, England. After all the usual suspects had been thrown out by the judges, Outram was finally in a head-to-head with the Danish architect Henning Larsen. Outram chose to theme his entire composition upon a notion of a lost Mughal empire, and

a Wimberly, Allison, Tong & Goo,
'Palace of the Lost City',
Bophuthatswana, South Africa,
1990–2: hotel interior
b 'Palace of the Lost City':
courtyard of hotel
Tourism by stealth:
c François Spoerry, Port
Grimaud, France, 1967–75: a
holiday village for the jet-set
d François Spoerry, Port Liberté,
Jersey City, New York, 1984
e Port Grimaud: aerial view

spent much time inventing the archaeological traces of this vanished kingdom as a landscape strategy, with the opera house itself as the rediscovered palace. I telephoned Outram at the time to discuss how the design was evolving. 'You'll like it,' Outram replied, equably. 'It's got elephants on it.' Yet Outram, though sometimes regarded as an eccentric maverick, is a deeply serious architect who needs the force of his symbolic narratives to drive his designs forward – be they a storm-water pumping station in London's Isle of Dogs, or a computer studies faculty building at Rice University, Texas. Outram's proposal was too gamey for the competition assessors. The declared winner was Larsen, with a rather sexless modern-classical design that remained unbuilt. Compton Verney was an example of what became rather too common in Britain in the 1990s – a competition involving the world's architects that brought prestige to the organizers and their advisors, but for a building that never stood a realistic chance of being financed.

One person's theming is another's historical revival. It could be argued that the concept of the Olympic Games since their revival in 1896 – 1,500 years after the original Ancient Greek Olympics were discontinued – is also based upon a largely fictionalized historical premise, and that the Olympics, which are undeniably touristic, are therefore as deeply

implicated in the business of theming as a Wild West shopping mall. You cannot chase this particular animal to ground: theming crops up everywhere, consciously or unconsciously, even in the hushed control rooms of nuclear power stations, where white-coated officials act out their version of a thousand science fiction and horror films as they stride on glistening floors between the dials, switches and blinking lights. Unconsciously or not, such places are designed theatrically.

Not all tourist-related architecture, of course, is themed. A concrete hotel on the Costa del Sol is the same as its equivalents anywhere else in the world: a glance at the holiday brochures soon reveals that these bastardized offspring of the International Style continue to sprout like fungal fruiting bodies wherever conditions allow. One can argue, perhaps, that such places have become a theme in themselves, that they represent a global package-holiday vernacular that carries with it the reassurance of familiarity; but as long ago as 1967, when François Spoerry began to design Port Grimaud on France's southern littoral near St Tropez, an alternative was on offer. Completed in 1975, this was a relatively early response to a growing recognition that the damaging impact of tourism is the flipside of the economic benefits it brings, and that therefore the design and siting of such places must be considered

with care. Port Grimaud can, depending on your point of view, be described as pastiche, as vernacular, as contextualist, as themed. True, it is an artificial Mediterranean fishing village for those with Sunseeker motor yachts moored outside their houses, but it marked a point at which it began to be felt that tourist developments should start to dig themselves into their locale. Spoerry later went to the United States to design Port Liberté in New York Harbour, 1984, an exercise in New England vernacular.

Today's inheritors of this tradition include the town of Seaside in Florida by Andres Duany and Elizabeth Plater Zyberk – which is governed by its own internal logic, guarded by building codes, and which thus evolves in a very controlled manner, very unlike the settlements of the past that it tips its hat to. Also in this vein is the Greek holiday resort of Pitiousa on the island of Spetses, by Demetri Porphyrios. This, like Seaside and a great deal of Disney's new town Celebration in Florida, is built in what the philosopher Roger Scruton describes as 'the classical vernacular', which he defines as an aesthetic building system that works adequately even in the hands of workaday, less than inspired, architects. There is no overcoming the fact, however, that such developments are highly self-conscious, and that this over-awareness of their own mission militates against the simultaneous desire for a kind

of invisibility and anonymity. Perhaps, in time, they will cease to be noticed, and so fulfil one of their stated aims. There are now plenty of post-Spoerry developments in the Mediterranean Olive Belt and elsewhere, built as close to the relevant local vernacular as rendered and painted concrete block will allow. They are generally given away by their marinas, golf courses, and high levels of perimeter security, but otherwise they blend into the landscape well enough. The headline developments, however, are less likely to find such welcome obscurity. They will probably continue to be regarded as model settlements, along the lines of the Utopian worker-village projects built by Western paternalistic land-owners and industrialists from the late eigteenth century through to the early twentieth century. Their greatest difficulty is to avoid seeming merely quaint: but until the modernist tradition can come up with a workable alternative, it seems that quaintness is the price we must pay for a reduced urban impact.

Geoffrey Bawa in Sri Lanka and Jean Nouvel in France (odd bedfellows) have emerged as architects prepared to respond creatively to context with touristic buildings. Bawa is usually regarded as 'regionalist' in his approach, with such buildings as the Triton Hotel in Ahungalla, 1982, with its big roofs and courtyards, influenced to an extent by the local vernacular. However, Bawa's architecture had

a c

b

d

e

a Demetri Porphyrios, Pitiousa
   Resort Village, Spetses, Greece,
   1993–5

b Tony Atkin, Beach pavilion,
   Seaside New Town, Florida,
   1987

c Leon Krier, 'Belvedere' House,
   Seaside New Town, Florida,
   1988

d Geoffrey Bawa, Triton Hotel,
   Ahungalla, Sri Lanka, 1982:
   local vernacular

e Triton Hotel: interior view

moved on by the time it came to the 150-bed Kandalama Hotel at Dambulla, 1991–5. Built deep in the dry-zone jungle of the interior, it is positively Miesian in the rigour of its timber-framed detailing, the horizontals extending into timber-slatted balconies and green planted roofs and terraces. However, it is not a rectilinear plan but a ribbon. Its narrow wings are cranked along a contour against a rock face, overlooking an extensive reservoir. It manages to be at one with its setting, probably precisely because of its ultra-simple post-and-beam construction, raised on *pilotis* above the otherwise undisturbed landscape. The Kandalama is an example of an 'eco-hotel', designed for minimum environmental impact, drawing water from its own wells and with its own sewage-treatment plant: a model for other regions.

Nouvel, the sophisticated Westerner, is not such a curious name to yoke with that of Bawa. Nouvel's Hôtel Les Thermes, 1990–2, in the spa town of Dax, southwest France, has an external facade of full-height timber shutters, a related solar canopy at eaves level, and big awnings all round the double-height common areas at the base – details drawn from, but not directly copying, the hot-climate indigenous architecture. Similarly his earlier Hôtel St James in Bordeaux, 1987–9, broken down into a cluster of smaller forms rather than being a single imposing structure as in Dax, sports an external grillage of oxidized steel. Instead of the folding external shutters of Dax, the grilles rise on gas struts where they cover the windows. The appearance of the complex makes clear reference to the tobacco-drying

sheds of the region. Inside, the rooms were finished in plain waxed plaster and concrete – an early example of the luxury monk's cell look that was to become one of the architectural clichés of the 1990s as 'minimalism' came back into fashion and architects led by John Pawson indulged in interiors of 'exquisite restraint' for exquisitely wealthy clients.

By 1997, even London's boutique hotelier Anouska Hempel had abandoned her other oriental cluttered chic look in order to create her eponymous minimalist-with-a-twist hotel, The Hempel. A noted stickler for detail, Hempel was quoted as saying, when her hotel was finished but not yet open: 'Terrible things go wrong when you're working in the minimalism [sic] because there's nothing for the eye to look at except light and shade, so it sees all the

```
a   c   d   f
            g
b       e
```

The 'boutique hotel' is now an established type:

a   Jean Nouvel, Hôtel Les Thermes, Dax, France, 1990–2: exterior view

b   Jean Nouvel, Hôtel St James, Bouiliac Bordeaux, France, 1987–9

c   Hôtel Les Thermes: swimming pool

d   Anouska Hempel Designs, The Hempel, London, 1997

e   Kisho Kurokawa, Hotel Kyocera, Kagoshima, Japan, 1991–5: the legacy of John Portman's atrium hotels

f   Philippe Starck, Penninsula Hotel, Hong Kong, 1987

g   Aldo Rossi, Hotel Il Palazzo, Fukuoka, Japan, 1987–9

mistakes.' There is the authentic voice of the interior decorator. The architects involved included Hugh Tuffley and Russell Jones of Hempel's design company. Such ostensibly 'modern' hotels, and their designerly equivalents such as the many hotels with interiors by Philippe Starck, must be regarded as fashion statements, to be considered with the rash of designerly restaurants that bloomed during the 1980s and 1990s. There are clear differences within the restaurant genre, however – a relatively restrained modern interior by an architect such as Rick Mather (the international Zen chain of Chinese restaurants in the 1970s and 1980s, and London's Avenue Restaurant of 1996) or Julyan Wickham (Bank Restaurant, London, 1996) is a rather different animal from the designer-led restaurant interior produced by, for instance, Mark Newson (Mash and Air, Manchester, 1997; Atlantic Bar and Grill, Coast, etc, London, 1995-6, see 'Consumerism').

On the hotels side, the fashion interiors could not be more different than, say, the almost overwhelmingly corporate-modern Hotel Kyocera in Kagoshima, 1991–5, by Kisho Kurokawa, which takes the glass-clad atrium office block as its model, but moulds it into an ovoid shape, thirteen storeys high. As with the pioneering hotels of John Portman in the 1960s, the rooms are arranged around this colossal atrium rather than focused on the external landscape, although such is the height and relative narrowness of the space that this is perhaps less of an event than it might be. Contrast this with the 1980s fashion in Japan for 'trophy architects' where developers acquired a taste for collecting famous Western names. Into this category comes Aldo Rossi's Il Palazzo Hotel in Fukuoka (with Morris Adjimi) 1987–9, in which Rossi's blind rationalist facade with its regular bays might as well be another of his famous ossuaries. Inside the funereal feel is continued, with rich sombre colours, mausoleum-like forms, and a bar with all the liveliness of a chapel of rest (but for the witty touch of the hotel's grid-like facade being reproduced, scaled down, as the reredos to the bar counter).

Nouvel, however, did not confine his touristic designs to hotels. His 'Pierre et Vacances' complex of 174 holiday apartments at Cap d'Ail, 1987–91, was a way of dealing with the old problem of the need for single-aspect housing – all anyone is

interested in is the sea view – by virtually hanging the strings of apartments off a cliff, like seagulls' nests, in three descending rows: the materials being chosen for their mineral qualities in order to relate them to the rocky background. This is tough, stratified architecture: Nouvel has said, in a comment that might have been made by Wright or Lautner: *'The density and rawness of the material combine with the volume and depth of space to make this building, inscribed in the cliff, a reminiscence, and inscription on our consciousness of what architecture has always been: a shelter, a strategic place in the face of the elements.'*

The hotel is a building form with a long history – as long as the history of travel. Some vast hotels were being built by the late nineteenth and early twentieth centuries, spurred by the development of the railways, but as early as 1855 the first tourist tie-in hotel appeared. This was the Hôtel du Grand Louvre on the Rue Rivoli in Paris – built for the largely forgotten Second International Exhibition of that year (the first, in London in 1851, having engendered the Crystal Palace exhibition hall). The Hôtel du Grand Louvre was described by commentators of the time as 'a little town', with its own shops, a large internal courtyard, vast public rooms, and 700 bedrooms (though only twenty lavatories). It was ahead of its time in everything but plumbing, but it was a

commercial failure as a hotel. Its shops took over, to the extent that it finally became a department store. The mix of facilities originally provided, and the reason for its construction, are familiar enough today, and are still prone to the same problems. When the Disney organization came to plan EuroDisney (now Disneyland Paris) in the 1980s, they made the same mistake of assuming that a big popular European attraction would yield dividends in the form of stop-over visitors – as they were accustomed to in the United States. They were, at least at first, wrong: EuroDisney, in the new town of Marne-la-Vallée, was built close to Paris with all its hotels and shops, and the vast majority of visitors to the new theme park in the troubled early years were day visitors only who preferred to return to the big city at night. So the resort hotels by Michael Graves (New York theme), Robert Stern (New England theme), Antoine Grumbach (mountain wilderness theme), Antoine Predock (New Mexico desert theme), and the Imagineers with Wimberly, Allison, Tong & Goo (fantasy-chateau theme), did bad business to begin with. Just how bad is reflected by the fact that the park was forced to make its name more site-specific in order to locate itself more firmly in peoples' minds.

Disneyland Paris, however, is remembered not primarily for its hotels – unlike its older equivalent in Florida, for instance, where Graves produced

his 'Swan' and 'Dolphin' hotels. Those in search of architects of repute who have taken the Disney shilling most usually head for Frank Gehry's Festival Disney restaurant and shopping mall, in which Gehry mostly dispenses with the iconography of the host organization and uses his trademark abstract forms and metallic cladding in a hot, Las Vegas, way (though Mickey is to be found zooming out of the complex aboard a space rocket). As Gehry was to remark, his contribution to the park was not meant to be themed – but later he saw that it was: the Frank Gehry theme. He himself had become a recognizable American trade mark and he had not realized it.

In an interview in 1996 with Karal Ann Marling and Phyllis Lambert at the Canadian Centre for Architecture in Montreal, Gehry made some telling comments about the process of Disneyfication, recounting how Robert Venturi had shocked the Disney organization by going literally too far down the Mickey Mouse path to be comfortable. The event took place at a joint presentation given by all the architects involved at Robert Stern's office, and Gehry's account is worth considering at some length because it lays open the whole curious and touchy business of how you treat Mickey as an icon:
'Venturi came in with his best Princeton professorial demeanour. He had the cardigan sweater. Of course

a Jean Nouvel, Pierre et Vacances holiday apartments, Cap d'Ail, France, 1987–91: stratified layers of apartments
b Pierre et Vacances holiday apartments: the mineral qualities of the building's materials are chosen to relate to the surroundings
c Frank O Gehry & Associates, Festival Disney, Disneyland Paris, 1988–92: Gehry's theme is Gehry himself; his architecture wields its own signature
d Festival Disney: Las Vegas forms in the French landscape
e Festival Disney: Mickey presides over the walkways in his space rocket

he doesn't smoke a pipe. He stood up and presented the fall line. An "allée" of 150-foot-high flat cutouts of Mickey Mouse and Minnie Mouse, every fifty feet on center, from the entry to the Castle ... he had pictures of it in relation to the distance between Place de la Concorde and the Arc de Triomphe. It was the same distance. You would be confronted with Mickey and Minnie frontally, holding hands across this "allée" every 50 feet, 150 feet high. It was breathtaking and spectacular.

'I guess in Disney's context it would have been the wrong thing to do, but it was so strong, so beautiful, and so to the point of what the whole thing is about. They would have, in one fell swoop, replanted the Champs-Elysées and taken control of it for Disney. It was just hilarious. Disney president Frank Wells got up and said, "You can't do this, Robert."'

Venturi had suffered an earlier setback with Disney in the mid-1980s when, asked to collaborate with Michael Graves on a pair of hotels at Walt Disney World in Florida, he had insisted instead on a competition between them – and lost. Graves was then at the height of his imagistic powers, and came up with the double-whammy of his 'Swan' and 'Dolphin' hotels (both 1987–90). Note that these, although themed buildings, were not themed on any particular Disney characters such as the Little Mermaid. Graves, who said he wanted imagery 'that

a child could identify with, but wasn't sappy', had turned to Bernini for baroque inspiration after his competition-winning designs were at first judged over-austere. Given that the pair of gilded swans atop one hotel were each 47 feet high, and the dolphins on the other scarcely less gargantuan, it is fair to say that Bernini may have helped design St Peter's in Rome, but never had an opportunity like this.

Graves quickly got over his Ivy League distaste of Disney characters with the Team Disney building in Burbank, California, 1985–91, where he employed the Seven Dwarfs as telamones. Six of them – Sleepy, Happy, Grumpy, Doc, Sneezy and Bashful – support the entablature while little Dopey takes pride of place in the apex of the pediment, seemingly holding up the roof. This is something of a classical irony, since it is not a place where visible support is needed and one would not normally find a caryatid or telamon there. Graves' earlier designs for the building were dwarf-free, and he more correctly proposed a free-standing statue (of Mickey Mouse) in the tympanum before being urged to 'lighten up' by Disney chairman Michael Eisner. Given the context of cartoon imagery, and the fact that Graves is not a classical architect in the accepted sense, the solecism should not matter. Classical rules, we are often told, are anyway made to be broken – otherwise, how did the likes of Hawksmoor and Vanbrugh ever get on?

Here, however, it does matter because Dopey looks all wrong up there on the pediment, his positioning and needlessly outstretched arms unfortunately suggesting a Crucifixion. If only there had been Six Dwarfs instead of Seven, Graves' problems would have been solved and a new Dwarf Order created to go into the classical casebooks.

Venturi, however, had played a different game in Paris by scaling Mickey and Minnie up to become Collossi, and repeatedly so. This was not 'lightening up', since at that level an air of menace was inescapable. One thinks of the giant-scaled scimitar-wielding forearms of the Iraqi leader Saddam Hussein, forming an arch across the main road into Baghdad, or the huge images erected of many another despotic leader around the world. As Gehry concluded:
'It pointed out to me something very important ... that Venturi plays close to their edge, but he does it in a way that is art, that is meaningful, that is relevant to where we are in the world and what we are doing. He tells the truth. There is an essence and a truth in Venturi's portrayal of this whole thing. That's why he could not work for them.'

Thus Venturi – who with his grasp of popular culture might be supposed a natural for Disney – found he had transgressed an unwritten code and was excluded, while Gehry – who with his high-art credentials might be thought an odd choice, and

a Michael Graves, Walt Disney World Swan Hotel, Lake Buena Vista, Florida, 1987–90: view across the lake
b Swan Hotel: interior of lobby
c Michael Graves, Walt Disney World Dolphin Hotel, Lake Buena Vista, Florida, 1987–90
d Michael Graves, Team Disney Corporate Headquarters, Burbank, California, 1985–91

a c
b
   d

who refused to design to any theme but his own – paradoxically found himself both involved and reasonably happy with the process. Significantly, Gehry's long-term artist collaborator, Claes Oldenburg, refused to work with him for Disney. Gehry's conclusion was that both Oldenburg and Venturi had the same problem: 'Those two get very close to the Mouse,' he said, 'but Oldenburg and Venturi are also commentators.' It was that implied commentary that the Disney organization could not take, and it was the lack of it in Gehry's case that they appreciated.

Venturi and Scott Brown agreed with Gehry's analysis of the situation when I put the transcript to them. 'Denise Scott Brown and I think Frank Gehry's reporting and interpretations are sound,' Venturi wrote, adding in parentheses: 'I remember also at a later meeting with the Disney Imagineers in California, Steven Izenour [another partner] and I were called vulgar …'

One pauses to consider the delicious irony of the Disney organization convincing itself that one of America's most academically inclined architects was a vulgarian. It is a mark of just how seriously Walt's empire takes itself that it could not recognize a parallel seriousness in the work of Venturi. He is clear on the credentials of his practice, concluding: *'There is the irony that Denise Scott Brown was the first "respectable" architect – along with Charles*

Moore – to acknowledge Disneyland, taking her UCLA students there in the mid-60s. And we both are fundamentally in our work as a whole (rather than just for Disney) employers of iconography, symbolism as valid (and historically substantiated) elements of architecture.'

Interestingly it is Gehry's view that the forbidden ironic view of Mickey, as proposed by Venturi, would have worked in France in a way that it could not in the United States, presumably on the grounds that the French, with their European self-awareness and un-American cynicism, would have noticed and appreciated the wry gesture.

Such national stereotyping works both ways. As Jean Baudrillard once acidly observed, Disneyland exists in order for Americans to believe that what lies outside it is real. What this stinging generalization overlooks is that the likes of Venturi and Gehry, with their Europhile scholarliness, are also 'Americans', no less than the perhaps more naive Robert Stern, of whom more in a moment, and Graves. However, the fact that Grumbach was the only European architect to get to build at EuroDisney – out of an initial trawl that also included Bernard Tschumi, Hans Hollein, Rem Koolhaas, Jean Nouvel, Jean-Paul Vigier and Aldo Rossi – tells its own story. Rossi got a certain way down the line but then resigned under pressure. He wrote to Eisner, astutely (especially given Graves'

built references to the same sculptor-architect in Florida) comparing his problems with those of Gian Lorenzo Bernini. Bernini had fallen foul of an over-demanding and petulant Sun King, Louis XIV, when asked to produce designs for the Louvre. Rossi told Eisner: 'I realize I am not Bernini, but you are not the king of France. I quit.'

Venturi makes no reference to his Parisian disappointment in his published writings, although there is a tantalizing essay, written in bursts from 1993 to 1995, comparing the Americanization of Paris with what he saw as the 'Parisification' of Philadelphia, his home city. In it he remarks, 'What if I were to say there's nothing wrong with the Champs-Elysées that a few billboards won't cure? Is that so different from saying how about *'grands projets'* for South Broad Street?' Despite the EuroDisney setback, the Mouse did not entirely forget Robert Venturi and Denise Scott Brown; the projects they got to do – 'in the interstices' as Venturi puts it – include a minor office building on the Burbank campus and a fire station, the ponderously named Reedy Creek Emergency Services Center at Lake Buena Vista, part of Walt Disney World in Florida.

At Lake Buena Vista, Venturi Scott Brown and Associates produced a building that looks as if it is a child's building-brick composition – a true

a   b c

      d
      e

a   Venturi Scott Brown and
    Associates, Reedy Creek
    Emergency Services Center,
    Orlando, Florida, 1992–4
b   Aldo Rossi, Celebration Place,
    Orlando, Florida, 1991–6:
    Rossi's office buildings at the
    heart of Celebration

c   Celebration Place: serious
    urban planning for Disney
d   Robert A M Stern, Masterplan,
    Celebration, Florida, 1991
e   Philip Johnson, Town Hall,
    Celebration, Florida, 1994–6

'decorated shed' in the Venturian tradition that acknowledges Disney history in the form of a wall covered with Dalmatian spots. This is in its way as much a reference to Venturi's earlier appliqué designs – the Best supermarket covered with flowers, for instance – as it is to the iconography of the commissioning client. Venturi, like Gehry or Rossi, is perfectly capable of theming a design upon himself. This, no doubt, is why Rossi was also given another chance: in 1995 he completed the commercial heart of Disney's new town of Celebration in Florida – next door to Walt Disney World – in his characteristic rationalist-classical-stage-set manner. The strangeness of a Rossi set-piece urban composition – the space between the buildings feels somehow warped, and one expects a raggle-taggle procession out of Fellini to appear at any moment – is appropriate to Disney, and besides, Celebration is one of Disney's serious pieces of straight urban planning rather than one of its equally serious but differently presented theme parks.

Disney always saw his fun-park developments, from the original Disneyland to EPCOT in Florida, as being the core of expanding new-town developments. However, the fun-park element always got in the way. EPCOT was conceived by Walt in 1966 as the 'Experimental Prototype Community of Tomorrow' – that 'Tomorrow' unconsciously or otherwise echoing Ebenezer Howard's famous garden

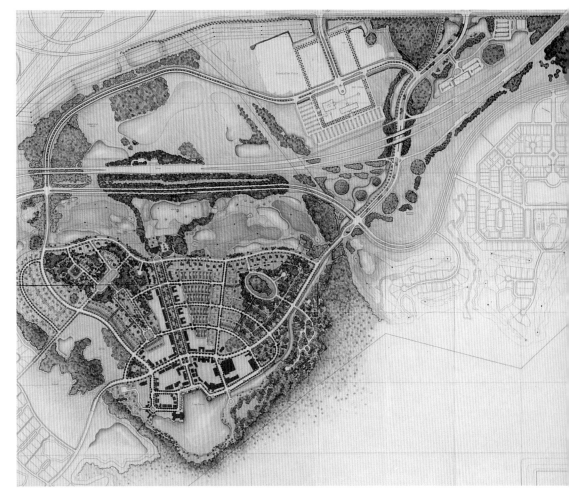

city manifesto of 1898, so closing a particular historical loop. Howard had spent five years in America
between 1872 and 1877 and had immersed himself
in the Utopian writings of Walt Whitman, Ralph
Waldo Emerson and Edward Bellamy. Thus America
was the inspiration for a phenomenon – the garden
city – that took root in the Old Country, and Disney
was merely returning to the subject to reclaim it for
the New. But he died too soon to see it reach the
kind of reality he had envisaged. EPCOT with its
monorail, Buckminster Fuller geodesic dome and
John Portman-inspired atrium hotel became merely a
futuristically themed fun park rather than a historically-
themed one. In contrast, Celebration is a serious
attempt to engineer an ideal community, even
though what brought it into existence was the
prosaic need to claim land as a buffer zone to
prevent undesirable non-Disney developments
getting too close to the Mouse's kingdom.

The Disney organization's courting of 'name'
architects – a policy initiated by Eisner when he took
over as chairman in 1984 – has had mixed results,
just as his predecessors found that all was not plain
sailing when it came to roping in serious artists and
musicians. At their best, these signature buildings
have a symbolic strength that communicates very
well through pictures: such as Arata Isozaki's Team
Disney headquarters in Florida, 1987–91, a design

that has all the traditional architectonic force of the
drum, cone and dome set against the rectilinear
block. In pictures it is as forceful an image in its way
as other twentieth-century buildings that play the
same trick: Lutyens' Viceroy's House in New Delhi, Le
Corbusier's Chandigarh, Asplund's Stockholm Public
Library, Jones and Kirkland's Mississauga City Hall,
Stirling and Wilford's Music Academy in Stuttgart,
and so on. What Isozaki brought to this ancient
game, apart from an accomplished post-modern jumbling of colourful cubic forms breaking through the
rectilinear grid in front of the rotunda, was an almost
too perfect glossiness. The building has a quality of
finish to rival Dalí that – as with Dalí's paintings –
works better in reproduction than in actuality. Like
Dalí's *The Metamorphosis of Narcissus*, the weird
transformation of traditional forms is reflected eerily
in the lake that was created in front of it. This is a
building that loves the large-format colour reproduction more than life itself.

Again, the question of theming came up.
The theme turned out to be time, and the rotunda
functions within as the biggest sundial in the world,
the gnomon of which projects horizontally across
the oculus at its apex. Unlike Graves, Isozaki was
happy to think of arranging statues of Disney characters around the floor of the rotunda – Pluto, Bambi,
Snow White and so on – but was dissuaded, and an

unadorned Japanese pebble garden now occupies
the space. What remained from his first designs for
this open-air interior, however, is the abstracted but
wholly recognizable 'Mouse ears' fanlight above the
main entrance to the building.

One can read much into the fact that Isozaki
never went to see his completed building. His stated
reason is that 'I saw it when I designed it – I saw it in
my mind'. This is fair enough, but this is also true of
all architects and all buildings. One remembers the
writer William Somerset Maugham (1874–1965) staying in India close to the Taj Mahal, but refusing to go
and see it on the grounds that it was bound to be a
disappointment after all the familiar chocolate-box
versions of it. Perhaps Isozaki felt the same. For sure
the images of his Team Disney building at Walt
Disney World, with their intense colours and magical
sheen, are so perfect that reality, with its weathering
and human wear and tear, could only be a let-down.
For Eisner and Disney, the building brought architectural respectability. Critics may have been a little –
or even very – unsure of the brash PoMo elements
of the Graves and Stern buildings, but here was an
authentic global architectural star, from another culture entirely, producing something that looked as if it
might have claims to being a masterpiece.

Robert Stern does not stand up so well in
such comparisons, despite the start he was given as

a   c

d

e

b

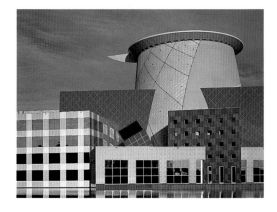

one of Eisner's favoured architects (he had designed Eisner's parents' apartment) and the fact that he is apparently described by Eisner as a 'Super-Imagineer', which means he is, in Gehry's phrase, 'close to the Mouse' in a different – that is, non-judgemental – way to Venturi and Oldenburg. Neither so flamboyant as Graves, so analytical as Venturi, nor so internationally acclaimed for cultural buildings as Isozaki, Stern produced a rather unsatisfactory building for the Walt Disney World Casting Center in Florida – a weak piece of what might be called 'Florida Venetian' with a harlequin chequerboard facade, abstracted-gothic fenestration, and a pair of openwork spires like formal garden ornaments that expose the lack of focus at the centre, where a dome, tower or taller spire is called for to strengthen the composition. Deliberately crude on the exterior – it was designed to be read in the rear-view mirror of cars passing at 55 mph on the Orlando Freeway – it does however work better on the interior, where Stern has had fun playing with scale and perspective in a memory of Disney's *Alice in Wonderland* (the 'talking face' door furniture, for instance, is taken directly from the film). The idea is to process wannabe actors through the distorting mirrors of Disney's world, complete with Disney characters and various unsettling *trompe-l'œil* effects, before they arrive, after a lengthy approach, at the reception with – centrally placed like a Holy

Grail – a model of Cinderella's Castle. By which time they will either be thoroughly in tune with the ethos and history of the organization, or presumably screaming to get out.

Again, the potentially sinister aspects of the organization are brought out, but so far as one can tell, Stern did all this seemingly with no hidden cultural commentary in mind. Thus he found himself embraced to the bosom of Disney and was rewarded by eventually being made joint masterplanner of Celebration with Jaquelin Robertson – while others like Venturi and Rossi, though eventually used, were kept at arms' length. Philip Johnson, right at the end of his lengthy and chameleon career, got to design Celebration's town hall, opened in 1996, in an abstracted-colonial style – so fulfilling an early ambition of Eisner's who had wanted Johnson on his team almost from the moment of taking hold of the Disney reins in 1984.

Externally at least, Stern did better on his next project, the Feature Animation Building in Burbank, 1993–5. This is the engine room of Disney, where the animators work. Previously they had been in a converted warehouse, and – rather than move them to a high-rise somewhere – Eisner briefed Stern to produce a creatively cluttered interior with space for people to lark around at ping-pong and frisbee rather than be chained to their desks. Stern did just

Architecture as PR, seen by millions from the freeways. Even non-public Disney buildings are made to work hard for their keep – image is all:

a   Robert A M Stern, Disney Feature Animation Building, Burbank, California, 1994–5

b   Arata Isozaki & Associates, Team Disney Building, Florida, 1987–91

c   Robert A M Stern, Disney Casting Center, Lake Buena Vista, Florida, 1987–9: view from the freeway

d   Disney Casting Center: exterior detail

e   Disney Casting Center: entrance canopy

this, but mixed his metaphors as well. The exterior is an amalgam of 1930s Moderne – a reference to Walt Disney's favoured architect of the 1930s, Kem Weber – and PoMo fantasy. Its great crown of parti-coloured profiled metal, seen by some as being a strip of film complete with sprocket-holes, is a reference to both the Mad Hatter's topper and, for that matter, Uncle Sam's, the whole composition leaning vertiginously. The entrance is marked with a spire based on Mickey's star-spangled conical hat as the Sorcerer's Apprentice in *Fantasia*. Although most of the complex consists of barrel-vaulted buildings that are very like warehouses, it is these images that persist – these and the more than somewhat over-the-top office of Roy E Disney, nephew of Walt and head of animation. This is a retina-searing, 1930s-referential confection that is how you imagine a Toontown executive's office might look – in a cartoon. It is also built inside the Sorcerer's Apprentice's hat.

The very public statement that the Animation building made – right on the Ventura Freeway in Burbank – served to re-establish the credentials of a group of people who had, during the 1970s and early 1980s, become disenchanted and demoralized: the animators themselves. After a string of feature film successes from then onwards under the Eisner regime – from *The Little Mermaid* to *Hercules* – they regained their status. This had its

a	c		e
b			f
		d	

a Michael Graves, Hotel New York, Disneyland Paris, 1988–92: complex seen across the lake

b Hotel New York: Downtown Athletic Club

c Robert Stern, Newport Bay Club, Disneyland Paris, 1988–92

d Antoine Predock, Hotel Santa Fe, Disneyland Paris, 1988–92: echoes of Wim Wenders' *Paris, Texas*

e Hotel Santa Fe: illuminated sign of Clint Eastwood above the hotel

f Hotel Santa Fe: site plan

g (pages 340–1) Las Vegas by night, with the illuminated Statue of Liberty of Gaskin and Besanski, New York, New York Casino, Las Vegas, 1997

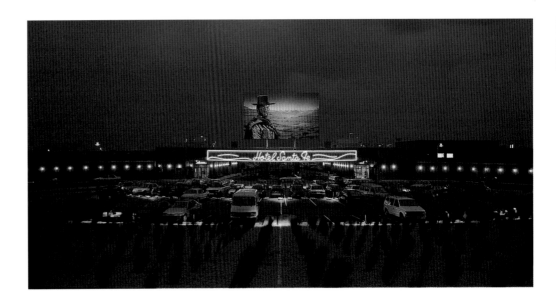

downside, in that the new building immediately
proved to be too small to house more than half of
the colossal team of animators, producing a feature
film a year, that Disney was by then employing. But
Stern had expressed a particular moment of
confidence partly by referring back to the glorious
pioneering pre-war years.

After that, it was theme business as
usual. Stern's New England style hotel at Disneyland
Paris – the Newport Bay Club – was pretty accomplished in a Williamsburg kind of way (he also did
a cowboy movie stage-set hotel, the Cheyenne),
while Graves got to do Hotel New York, comprising
facade elements in differing vertical strips to evoke
Manhattan skyscrapers. Grumbach – the only
European architect to make the cut there, but also
sporting the credentials of a Harvard and Princeton
architecture teacher – produced 'Sequoia Lodge',
an eco-hotel, recalling the lodges to be found in
American national parks. Built in the natural materials of timber, stone and copper, it is also a homage
to the American Arts and Crafts Movement as represented by Greene and Greene and the early Frank
Lloyd Wright. The most interesting of the hotels at
Disneyland Paris, however, because of the principled
and unshowy nature of the architect in question, is
Antoine Predock's Hotel Santa Fe. Yes, Predock was
chosen to 'theme' New Mexico with its adobe and

adobe-influenced buildings, but since he is the prime exponent of this particular regionalist architecture, it might be said that, as with Gehry, he was theming his building upon himself.

Acutely aware of the intellectual minefield of theming, Predock chose a pragmatic way out: rather than theme his building on the received, touristy images of Santa Fe, he chose to summon up the bleaker high-desert imagery explored in Wim Wenders' 1984 film *Paris, Texas*. This meant building in a certain sense of abandonment and decay. The result is a hymn to Route 66 – a road of legend that, as Predock was quick to observe, is now largely bypassed by tourists. Abandoned cars and trucks are half-buried in the hotel's precincts. Desert vegetation is planted in rigorous grids, but there are also chance weeds to be encountered. Much of the hotel is in small-scale pueblo blocks, and so on. Junked cars aside, it is on the whole a successful and largely abstract evocation of its area, even if the wet and cloudy climate of Paris means that it can never be seen in its true light. All Predock's intellectualizing is probably missed by 90 per cent of visitors, who will see only the entrance facade with its huge billboard of Clint Eastwood as 'the man with no name' in the desert, poncho flung over his shoulder. Clearly Eastwood directed by Leone was thought to press more buttons with the

a
b

c

public than Harry Dean Stanton directed by Wenders.

After all, Santa Fe is – in American travel terms – very close to Las Vegas, and one has to return to Las Vegas, as Venturi and Scott Brown did (see 'Consumerism') in order to appreciate how an entire city can be made out of nowhere, built on the artless use of symbolism and iconography, and still develop as a real organism. To describe Vegas as themed is the same as describing Paris or Rome as urban – it is not a surface finish, it is the thing itself. From Caesars Palace onwards, so many of its principal buildings have been the entertainment business' take on world monuments – perhaps most famously in recent years, the Great Pyramid of Veldon Simpson's hotel, the Luxor, which comes complete with a mighty Sphinx (opened 1993). It is a perfect, gleaming pyramid and a perfect, gleaming Sphinx as never seen by modern man: that is the power of Vegas. The fact that such buildings are but one step on from film sets is entirely appropriate. Film sets themselves took on a durability as soon as 'studio tours' were invented to satisfy the public's appetite to see behind the scenes of film-making: an interestingly Platonic case of wanting to see the physical unreality behind the apparent reality of the projected image. When film-set design invades 'real' architecture, and thus raises questions of durability and 'reality', it only serves to demonstrate what happens

everywhere anyway: that buildings are built, complete with their particular system of architectural symbolism – and in time are either demolished and replaced, or given a new set of clothes, or symbols. This process of 'churn' used to happen faster in the United States than anywhere, and faster in Vegas than elsewhere in the States – but as with skyscrapers, that distinction has now passed to the Far East.

So it was noteworthy, in the late 1990s, that Vegas should have taken the Manhattan skyline as one of its symbols, just as Disneyland Paris had done. The previously unquestioned American pre-eminence in this field had been transmuted into something discernible as a historic period, ripe for theming. While a slightly earlier development such as the Treasure Island casino and hotel complex by Joel D Bergman (with the Jerde Partnership and AA Marnell II) was safely in the fictionalized past, the 'New York, New York' development (also hotels and casinos) consists of a cluster of Manhattan towers and the Statue of Liberty grouped at much-reduced scale, just as Disney used to create Main Street, USA, at slightly reduced scale. A scary roller-coaster ride goes looping through this composite cityscape, making the experience of the place even more hallucinogenic. By Gaskin and Bezanski with Yates and Silverman – with various other designers also involved – this miniaturized but still vast rendering of Manhattan covers 20 acres and

cost $400 million. It opened in 1997. It is a curious case: in its way like the miniaturized cityscapes to be found in many theme parks including Legoland, but habitable, to the extent that its towers shoot above 500 feet – though all of them, like Stern's far smaller version of Manhattan at Disneyland Paris, are in fact just part of one vast building. It has been suggested that people 'suspend disbelief' when they go to such places, but this is nonsense. Nobody going there really thinks they are in the real New York, any more than someone in a themed Italian restaurant believes he is truly in Sorrento. It is the same exercise, writ large, merely the creation of a mood. Is a facade composed of nine shrunken faux-Manhattan towers more or less architecture than an eighteenth-century English country house cobbled together out of Palladio? One remembers Lord Hervey's biting comment on Burlington and Kent's Chiswick House, London, 1723–9, a villa which is a scaled-down reworking of Palladio's Villa Rotonda. It was, said Hervey, 'too small to live in, too big to wear on one's watch chain'. Belief or disbelief do not enter into the equation – one merely notes the architectural references and carries on. Sir John Summerson's description of Chiswick House – 'an architectural laboratory, a collection of expositions and experiments' – might very well describe Las Vegas.

Suspension of reality –
not disbelief:

a Joel D Bergman with the Jerde
   Partnership and AA Marnell II,
   Treasure Island Casino
   Hotel, Las Vegas, 1993:
   entrance gate

b Treasure Island Casino Hotel:
   the fictionalized past of pirates
   and lost treasure

c Veldon Simpson, The Luxor,
   Las Vegas, 1993

The architect Jon Jerde, with his MCA Universal City Walk in Los Angeles and his Fremont Street Experience in Las Vegas, is a key example of the cross-fertilization that goes on between the relatively 'straight' architecture of the shopping mall and the 'unreal' architecture of the themed world. Working fluently in both areas, Jerde Associates brings theming to shopping malls and mall design techniques to themed attractions. The Fremont Street Experience, 1995, for instance, is a very large but relatively conventional mall overlaid with a richer theme than usual. Far richer, for the theme in question is Las Vegas itself. The mall is supposed to recreate the naive early days of the Vegas strip, as it was back when Scott Brown and Venturi discovered and appropriated it. As it was before it became self-conscious. But commercially speaking, the Experience does what all good in-town shopping malls do: it acts as a magnet to correct the sprawl of the out-of-town world, in this case the new Vegas Strip to the south. As ever, big developer-led retailing is being used to shape a city, quite consciously – and so quite unlike the early days of Vegas itself, where anarchy prevailed. At the 1993-4 MCA Universal City Walk, in contrast, there was the pre-existing attraction of the Universal Studios, and the streets Jerde created were a way of spinning retail sales off the back of the enormous numbers of visitors. Just as Universal's film

sets of American towns were used for film after film, so Jerde uses the architecture of the whole of America in his mall design – not forgetting to give the whole a film-set quality. Thus does architecture eat itself.

If you seek reality in this peculiar but fascinating area, the place to find it is in an old-fashioned – indeed simply old – permanent mega-fairground, the Blackpool Pleasure Beach in north-west England. The Pleasure Beach has evolved over a century very like a real town, in that its 'rides' are frequently demolished and replaced by newer, better ones – but some of the very oldest rides, being very good, have simply been kept going and therefore perform the function of historic buildings in a 'real' town. There are surviving buildings there, including a casino, by the inter-war modernist Joseph Emberton, but several of the working rides – including the 1904 'Flying Machines' built by Sir Hiram Maxim, inventor of the Maxim machine gun – are older still. Because of an obscure British planning law which places fun parks in the same category as chemical refineries – that is, that they do not need planning permission to modify or replace even very large built objects, since these are deemed to be items of equipment rather than architecture – the Pleasure Beach has developed largely unhindered by the normal town planning and conservationist constraints. It is a complete 42-acre

township that effortlessly solves the problems of heritage versus fakery, tradition versus modernity, mechanized transport versus pedestrians. A town run by benevolent dictators (the same family firm for the past century) who install the latest ride technology while being – perhaps precisely because of their sense of their own personal history – fully aware of their built patrimony. Although relatively little-known outside the hermetic world of international roller-coaster fanatics, the Pleasure Beach is one of the largest such attractions in the world and makes a convincing case for unplanned development. When the giant roller-coaster known as 'The Big One' was built there in 1992-4 (at the time the world's tallest), its beguiling snaking, twisting form was dictated as much by the site boundaries and the need to place its giant feet carefully among the existing attractions, as by computer-designed gravity engineering. Design credits, as always for such non-building projects, are interestingly different from the usual. Arrow Dynamics of Utah designed the ride, Allot and Lomax engineers of Manchester bedded it into the existing urban fabric of the Pleasure Beach, and the multi-level 'station' for the cars was designed by architect Fiona Gilje. At a cost of £13 million, rising to a height of 235 feet, with a capacity of 1,700 passengers each hour, and creating a form on the flat coastline strangely reminiscent of the ranges of hills

a   Jerde Partnership
    International, Fremont Street
    Experience, Las Vegas, 1995:
    Las Vegas themes itself
b   Arrow Dynamics Inc (Utah,
    ride designers), Allott and
    Lomax (Manchester, engi-
    neers), Fiona Gilje (architect)
    in association with Philip
    England, 'The Pepsi Max Big
    One' ride, Blackpool Pleasure
    Beach, Blackpool, England,
    1992-4

                                                        a   b

rising behind, the Big One is architecture in everything but name. Its sense of theming is rooted in the world of the fairground barker: every ride has its own exotic identity, some with no discernible theme beyond the celebration of technology.

Even existing for a century, as the Pleasure Beach has, does not bring such places to the notice of most architectural historians. However, the six-month lives of World Expos with their similarly jostling scrum of structures are quite long enough to generate acres of commentary. This may seem unbalanced, but the Expos – from the first Great Exhibition of 1851 onwards – have always served as snapshots of architectural tastes. Moreover they are deemed to be 'educational' and to have a wider political role in generating international understanding, so their importance – though always overestimated – is nonetheless real.

It is now coming to be appreciated that Walt Disney synthesized the twin experiences of the shabby pleasure parks of his youth – the small-time American equivalents of Blackpool's resplendent Pleasure Beach – with the snootier but safer experiences of trade fairs and World's Fairs. The fault line between high and low culture has always been a difficult one to bridge, and those pleasure parks that start off with high ideals – from London's Vauxhall Gardens, opened in the 1660s, onwards – tend

relatively quickly to descend into raffishness. The undisputed success of Disney's theme parks has been never to go below a given quality threshold, and to mix screaming beer-and-skittles entertainment with a particular sense of vision and celebration. Now that Disney has become an important patron of new architecture by some of the world's finest architects, it is becoming increasingly difficult to distinguish between the aims of the theme park and the aims of the World Expo. But that has long been the case. Expo '67 in Montreal boasted a Buckminster Fuller geodesic dome – the American pavilion – with an exciting, futuristic-looking monorail running through it. Disney's EPCOT in Florida, planned during that Expo and opened in 1971, copied these features quite openly: the idea of EPCOT, once it had ceased to be thought of as a Utopian city for Disney employees, was to give exactly the same taste of the wold's cultures that a World's Fair did – only permanently. The Disney organization at first even tried to get the nations of the world to sponsor their themed attractions in the World Showcase section of EPCOT, opened in 1982. They would not, so this area became a kind of themed shopping-and-eating mall instead, tilting it towards the Las Vegas world view. A key architect in the design of the 1971 EPCOT was Welton Becket, the hotel architect, who devised an innovative programme of modularized hotel rooms to

be stacked and slung on A-frame structures. This, of course, was at the time of maximum world architectural interest in modular construction, something that – along with inflatable structures – informed many of the pavilions at Expo '70 in Osaka.

For both Expos and theme parks, huge numbers of visitors are required – more so by the Expos than by the theme parks, since their lives are so short. In both cases, the only way to achieve this is by offering a spectacle sufficiently dramatic to bring people flocking from far afield. In both cases they are themed – in Disney's case, usually on aspects of American culture, but in the case of Expos, on a given theme (it might be exploration, or nature) which always comes down to individual national themes based on individual national pavilions. The World Expo is to do with the countries of the world showing off their prowess to each other. Sometimes that prowess is to do with tradition, but more usually it is to do with the concept of technological progress. Largely discredited elsewhere, the idea that all technology is good, benign and getting constantly better and more exciting, is arguably now confined only to Expos.

The desire to seem go-ahead is most keenly felt by those nations with some catching up to do, and least keenly by those with nothing to prove. So at Expo '92 in Seville, Spain, the most arresting

a b   e f

c d   g

pavilion technologically was that of the United Kingdom, with its shimmering water wall rippling down its glass facade. Architect Nicholas Grimshaw had been specifically chosen for his 'high-tech' credentials by the Thatcher government, which badly needed world export orders. However the most impressive, and largest, pavilion, was Japan's, which had the reverse problem when it came to its balance of payments, and eschewed an overtly technological image in favour of Tadao Ando's great timber 'temple' with its awe-inspiring approach via a convex flight of steps. The Expo yielded a crop of smaller projects that in their way were more interesting, such as Santiago Calatrava's Kuwaiti Pavilion – a kinetic sculpture, a mechanical Venus Flytrap – or Imre Makovecz's Hungarian offering, a pavilion very reminiscent of one of his 'organic' churches. Much of the incidental design of the Expo was to do with dealing with the extreme summer heat of this part of Spain – for example the Avenue of Europe by Jean Marie Henning and Nicolas Normier, which used fabric cooling towers activated by mist sprays, within the confines of which was a 400-metre-long water wall by SITE architects. Both psychologically and actually, these devices made visitors feel cooler – a couple of degrees difference from the searing heat of the unprotected terrain was enough. Thus Expo '92 became, if nothing else, a demonstration project in

how to keep cool without air-conditioning, using many techniques present in Moorish architecture. There was a downside, however. Andalusia was suffering a crippling drought and the huge quantities of water required by the Expo, not least for its natural-cooling purposes, had the effect of depriving farmers of the region of much-needed irrigation water. As for what was inside many of the pavilions – nobody ever remembers that. The buildings are the thing, since they constitute the experience of going. For instance the 'Pavilion of the Future' by Oriol Bohigas of MBM, Barcelona, is remembered principally for the structural audacity of its slender loadbearing, freestanding screen of granite arches, held apparently impossibly in place with tensioned steel cables. These arches acted as suspension towers for a building behind, but that was unimportant: the image was what counted. Similarly the mast-suspended British pavilion at Expo '70 in Osaka by Powell and Moya, which floated free of the ground, is remembered mainly for the shelter it offered from the rainstorms which lashed the event. Recent world Expos, up until the last of the century, Expo 98 in Lisbon, Portugal, lacked a feature that was frequently present right up to the 1960s: the big landmark feature, be it the Crystal Palace in London in 1951, the Eiffel Tower and Palace of Machines of the Paris Expo of 1889, the Atomium of Brussels in 1958, or the 'Bucky Ball' of the American Pavilion of

Montreal '67. Montreal was the high point of post-war Expos, since it also featured the pioneering use of cable net structures by Frei Otto in the German Pavilion (a system nostalgically revived by others in the German Pavilion at Seville in '92). The lack of the big landmark in later expositions would certainly not have been understood by Walt Disney, who always insisted on what he called the 'wienie' – his term for the eye-catching central tall feature, usually but not always a fairytale castle – to draw people through the park.

Lisbon in 1998 learned some of the lessons both of the theme park and of earlier Expositions and World Fairs. It sported a landmark feature of sorts – the 120-metre Vasco da Gama tower, which was rather upstaged by the new Tagus bridge behind it. It placed national displays inside two large temporary building complexes rather than letting them compete as pavilions out in the open. However Alvaro Siza's Portuguese Pavilion, acting as the foyer for the whole event, naturally took centre stage and was notable for its audacious thin-shell catenary-curved concrete canopy over the ceremonial square. Close to it was a 15,000-seat auditorium for a multi-media 'experience' in the form of SOM's 'Utopia Pavilion': a grey metal-clad shark's head of a building with a highly successful all-timber interior. And it had the Oceanarium by Peter Chermayeff of Cambridge

Expos are theme parks, for all their high-mindedness:
a Nicholas Grimshaw, British Pavilion, Expo '92, Seville, Spain, 1990–2
b SITE, Water Wall, Avenue of Europe, Expo '92, Seville, Spain, 1992
c Powell and Moya, British pavilion, Expo '70, Osaka, Japan, 1970
d Antonio Cano, Pedro Silva and Manuel Alvarez, Bioclimatic Sphere, Expo '92, Seville, Spain, 1992
e Imre Makovecz, Hungarian Pavilion, Expo '92, Seville, Spain, 1992
f Nicolas Normier and Jean-Marie Henning, Avenue of Europe, Expo '92, Seville, Spain, 1992
g Cambirdge Seven Associates, The Oceanarium, Expo '98, Lisbon, 1997–8

Seven Associates – the largest aquarium in Europe, containing habitats from four of the world's climate zones, expressed in a robust late high-tech manner. Lisbon, then, was tightly organized as a place of mass entertainment and, crucially, all these key buildings were designed to be permanent features of the cityscape after the Expo closed.

Permanent attractions have to offer more than the rather two-dimensional fare provided by the pavilions of World Fairs and Expos, where the day visitor is often content merely to browse along the avenues. In some themed attractions, an element of 'authenticity' is sometimes present in a way that is very rare in the Disney venues. The Shakespeare Country Park at Maruyama in Japan, 1995–7, by Julian Bicknell is a re-creation of a village of Shakespeare's time, based loosely on Stratford-upon-Avon. Bicknell was almost archaeologically thorough in his re-creations (some of the buildings copied still exist in Stratford, others are stabs at long-demolished examples), and the buildings erected at Maruyama were built the medieval way, full-size, from English oak – invisibly strengthened with steel clasps, however, to guard against earthquakes. They do not pretend to be the actual houses they depict: for Bicknell, they are metaphors, 'an educational and cultural resource'. But the fact that their frames were made the old way in England before being shipped out to Japan like flat-pack furniture suggests that, for Bicknell's client, something more than Disney-style stage-set architecture was required, even if something rather less than absolute authenticity would do.

The problem is much the same with other visitor attractions that try to be educational, such as the plethora of cultural projects in the United Kingdom, part-funded by that country's National Lottery, built around the year 2000. These of course have their themes: sustainability in the case of 'The Earth Centre' outside Doncaster, with buildings by Future Systems, Alsop and Störmer, and Feilden Clegg; industrial renewal in the case of 'Magna', a project created out of a former steelworks in Sheffield, by Peter Clash; and botanical diversity in the case of 'Project Eden' in Cornwall – a mighty series of linked glasshouses curled around the precipitous interiors of a worked-out quarry, by Nicholas Grimshaw. All these and many more could not have

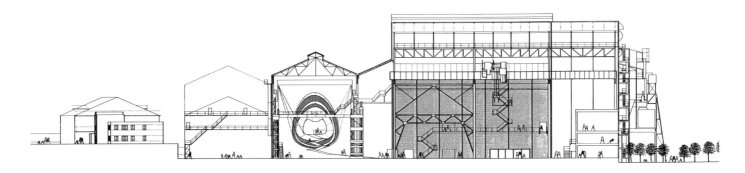

been built without the advent of Britain's Lottery – but despite some sophisticated market research, nobody really knew how popular with the public they would turn out to be. Would a 'Centre for Life' in Newcastle by Terry Farrell, predicated on the idea of genetics, really turn out to be a significant popular draw? The research said that it would.

It is a different problem with another very characteristic late twentieth-century building type, the visitor centre. Such buildings – apart from being relatively small – exist to contain and process people who are coming to see some pre-existing historic or cultural magnet. Like Edward Cullinan's visitor centre at Fountains Abbey in Yorkshire, 1987–92, like Henri Ciriani's 'Historiale de la Grand Guerre' at Peronne in the Somme battlefields, or like the range of

sophisticated visitor and interpretative centres built around Ireland, often in remote areas of archaeological interest, by that country's Office of Public Works, these are in a sense ancillary buildings – even if they also act as museums in their own right. They do not have to generate a new audience from scratch.

What all such buildings and developments recognize, wherever in the world they occur, is that tourism is the biggest single global industry, and moreover, involves the mass movement of people rather than information, money or manufactured goods. Building new theme parks and semi-educational centres, Expos, hotels and visitor centres is much the same as building factories: as in any processing plant, the trick is to ensure that there is not too much in the way of toxic residue.

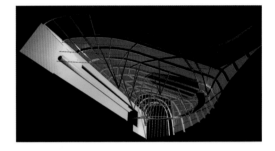

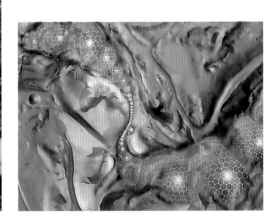

None of these schemes can be considered less 'genuine' than another:

a Julian Bicknell, Shakespeare Country Park, Maruyama, Japan, 1995–7

b Clash Associates, Magna, Sheffield, England, 1997–2000

c Nicholas Grimshaw, Eden Project, Cornwall, England, 1998–2000: the original scheme proposed one large enclosure

d Terry Farrell, Centre for Life, Newcastle-upon-Tyne, England, 1997: computer-generated model

e Centre for Life: computer-generated perspective

f Eden Project: the revised proposals are for a number of 'pods' enclosing different functions

		d
a	c	e
b		f

a Edward Cullinan, Fountains Abbey Visitors' Centre, Yorkshire, England, 1987–92: exterior

b Fountains Abbey Visitors' Centre: interior

c Henri Ciriani, Historiale de la Grande Guerre, Peronne, France, 1987–92: exterior

d Historiale de la Grande Guerre: gallery interior

e Mary MacKenna, Office of Public Works, Ireland, Ceidé Fields Cultural Centre, County Mayo, Ireland, 1990–3

f Ciarán O'Connor and Gerald O'Sullivan, Office of Public Works, Ireland, Blasket Island Cultural Centre, Dun Chaoin, County Kerry, Ireland, 1990–3

g Juhani Katainen Architects (Juhani Katainen and Olavi Koponen), Kolinportti Visitor Centre, Ahmovaara, Juuka, Koli, Finland, 1990–2

TRANSPORT *Airports, stations & shipping terminals* The story of modernity is the story of movement. The nodal points of the global movement network generate dynamic structures that very often go beyond their function to celebrate the fact of arrival, departure and transition. Providing some of the most successful partnerships of architect and engineer, airports, railway stations and shipping terminals of the late twentieth century are some of the purest examples of fine architecture. As in the nineteenth century, new transport infrastructure stimulates new buildings of a high order.

'Just as the ancients took their artistic inspiration from the elements of nature, so too must we – who are materially and spiritually artificial – find our inspiration in the elements of the new mechanical world that we have created.'
Antonio Sant'Elia, 1914.

The story of modernity is the story of

movement. The nodal points of the global movement network generate structures that very often go beyond their function to celebrate arrival, departure and transit. Rail and shipping terminals, bridges and airports provide some of the most successful partnerships of architect and engineer. Yet these buildings have to adapt to constant change: in the nature of the vehicles they serve, in patterns of travel, and in economic circumstances.

At the close of the twentieth century, the most important transport buildings are inevitably airports, and moreover a global consensus has emerged on the most profitable way to park planes and transfer passengers. After decades of experimentation, the preferred plan turns out to be a progression of long narrow wings – the first in the sequence having a passenger hall and retail mall at its centre and, where needed, with subsequent waves of departure malls being arranged in parallel echelons, reached via underground walkways or trams. Murphy Jahn

adopted this plan for their Terminal One complex at Chicago's O'Hare Airport, 1983-7, and the plan differs only in scale from Renzo Piano's Kansai Airport, 1988-94; Richard Rogers' proposed Terminal Five at Heathrow, 1989-2010; Gensler Associates' John Wayne International Airport in California, 1991, and Detroit Metropolitan Airport, 1989-95; or HOK's Fukuoka International Passenger Terminal in Japan, 1993-7 – all arranged in this way. As with Victorian railway stations, there also seems to be broad agreement as to how the main terminal halls should feel – big, light, busy, structurally audacious. But history suggests that this consensus will only hold for so long before travel patterns change, causing alternative architectural solutions.

For instance, airport terminals designed in the 1950s on the basis of expensive scheduled services by nationalized airlines found themselves, only a decade later, having to adapt to an entirely different air travel market – package holidays with charter aircraft. Shipping terminals, too, had to undergo a more radical and upmarket change with the complete cessation of long-haul scheduled services as transcontinental air travel took over. This was to some extent compensated for by a steady rise in the cruise-ship market, but was affected deeply by the closure of many traditional docklands departure points. In the meantime short-hop journeys – by air

b c	d e
a	f
	g

a Murphy Jahn, Terminal One, O'Hare United Airlines Airport, Chicago, 1983-7: aerial view
b Terminal One, O'Hare Airport: arrivals and departures
c Terminal One, O'Hare Airport: concourse
d Gensler Associates, John Wayne International Airport, Santa Ana, California, 1990: aerial view
e John Wayne International Airport: baggage reclaim
f Hellmuth Obata Kassabaum (HOK), Fukuoka International Passenger Terminal, Fukuoka, Japan, 1993-7: computer-generated perspective
g Fukuoka International Passenger Terminal: model

or by sea – boomed. From the 1980s onwards, car ferries became either much larger and more like cruise ships, or smaller and faster as waterjet catamaran designs attempted to compete with air and, where applicable, rail tunnel. The railways themselves – neglected in many parts of the world as internal air routes and new motorways stole their custom – underwent something of a revival in more densely populated parts of the world as new train and track designs enabled them to match the airlines for speed on the shorter inter-city routes. Everywhere, increasingly sophisticated interchanges between the various modes of transport became necessary. One of the principal arguments at the very lengthy public inquiry into Heathrow Airport's enormous proposed fifth terminal by Richard Rogers was the level of public transport necessary to service what had long been one of the world's busiest airports. The terminal would generate considerable extra demand and the designer had to consider whether sufficient capacity would be provided on rail express and metro links in order to avoid gridlock on the already overloaded road system in the area.

Airports are the buildings that most closely define the course of twentieth-century architecture, and the fifth terminal argument was really concerned with the problem of adapting to the constancy of change. Heathrow had seemed a long way out of

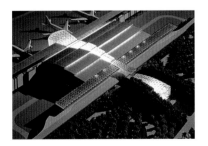

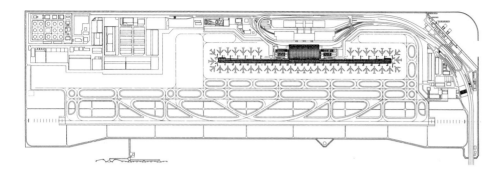

a
b
c

d
e
f

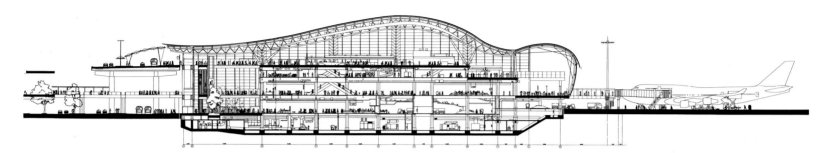

London when it was first seriously developed in the 1950s. Thirty years later, it was almost too close for comfort. Its history has some parallels with that of Berlin's most famous airport, Tempelhof, which was to fall victim to its location – it was originally a military parade ground, only two miles from the centre – despite the best efforts of its architects. The first Tempelhof Airport Terminal was a competition-winning design by Paul and Klaus Engler, built 1926–9. A sophisticated symmetrical modernist building, it was designed for expansion at either end – one of the few early airport buildings to be designed in anticipation of change. However, this was not to be, as Tempelhof just grew too fast. Its passenger numbers sextupled in a decade, making it the world's busiest airport, and the Engler building obstructed runway expansion. Finally, a complete rebuild was called for at the height of the Third Reich. Ernst Sagebiel, once a modernist working for Erich Mendelsohn, designed the new terminal in stripped-classical style in 1936–9, facing a triumphal piazza that was to form an element of Albert Speer's unbuilt north–south axis. It was huge, from the immense arrivals hall to the vast cantilevered canopy on the airside designed for planes to taxi underneath. Sagebiel's buildings – although immensely more spacious than necessary, thus allowing for internal expansion rather than the external extrusion that

his predecessors had pinned their hopes on – were not enough to save the airport from decline after its moment of history during the 1948–9 Berlin Airlift. It was intended to last until the year 2000 and it will, but not as the city's main airport. Too close to the centre, its landlocked egg-shaped landing field was incapable of taking longer runways, and it soon yielded to outlying Tegel. Thus its convenient location proved to be its downfall, although the story did not quite end there since the arrival of small, quiet 'city hopper' aircraft in the 1980s found it once again useful as part of a European-wide trend towards compact central business airports. Tempelhof is still an impressive airport to visit, and is one of the very few in the world to remain largely unchanged since it was built. To see the little inter-city planes pull up under the shelter of Sagebiel's huge canopy is instructive: the system still works exactly as it did in the run-up to the Second World War. Tempelhof, in the late 1990s, however, is finally slated to lose its airport function, its landing field now scheduled for redevelopment.

The comparison between Tempelhof and Heathrow, and from there to all modern airports, is informative. Airport buffs tend to categorize airport layouts in the twentieth century into six generations. The first were the earliest landing strips with passenger facilities in huts, the sixth are the big 'hangar'

The aerofoil form taken to extremity: by the late 1980s airports demanded their own territories:

a Renzo Piano Building Workshop, Kansai International Airport, Osaka, Japan, 1988–94: site plan

b Kansai International Airport: aerial view of island

c Kansai International Airport: roofscape

d Kansai International Airport: cross section

e Kansai International Airport: international departures hall

f Kansai International Airport: boarding wing showing curved rib structure

terminal buildings such as Renzo Piano's Kansai or
Norman Foster's Hong Kong International Airport,
1992–8, second terminal 2040, leading into their
long rows of departure gates. On this chronology,
Tempelhof, with its buildings on the perimeter, is
second or third generation; Heathrow, with its terminal cluster originally built right in the centre of the
runway configuration, is fourth; and the circular
Terminal One at Charles de Gaulle Airport, Roissy,
Paris, with its satellite mini-terminals (Paul Andreu of
Aéroports de Paris, 1967–74) is fifth. The Tempelhof
generation having been mostly pensioned off, it is
now the turn of the Heathrow generation to adapt or
die. Originally laid out in the 1940s, with its first passenger buildings by Frederick Gibberd dating from
the 1950s (some of which survive), Heathrow has
lasted longer, but in time has, like Tempelhof,
become landlocked, despite continuing attempts to
keep up with changing fashions in airport design.
Rogers' Terminal Five with its undulating roofline,
originally designed in 1989 and due to be built in
phases up to the year 2010, is to be its last development (at the time of writing it had not officially been
approved). Significantly, in the late 1990s British government economists were already factoring into their
calculations the economic effect on the capital of the
eventual closure of Heathrow, while simultaneously
new rapid rail links are being built to it. Airports, it

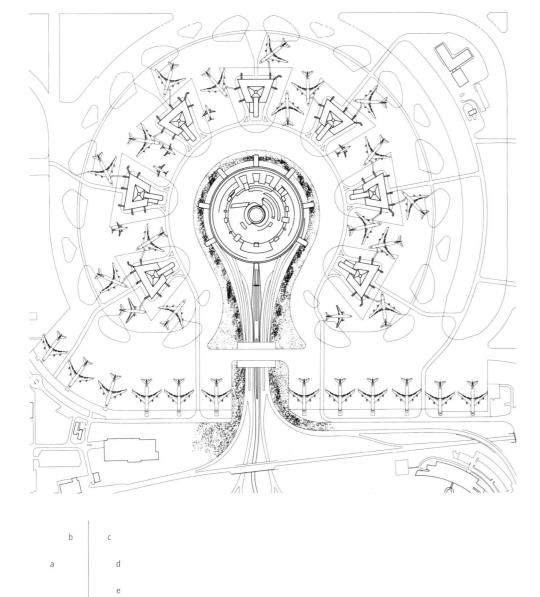

The apotheosis of the still current circular terminal:
a Aéroports de Paris
(Paul Andreu), Terminal One,
Roissy, Charles De Gaulle
Airport, Paris, 1967–74:
site plan
b Roissy Terminal One: the
approach by road
c Roissy Terminal One:
cross section
d Roissy Terminal One:
escalators cross the
central space
e Roissy Terminal One:
internal space

seems, are transitory features of the world's topography: like lakes, they are destined eventually to vanish as the silt they attract finally chokes them. Consequently, the world's newest and largest international airports have less and less to do with one particular city or another. Instead, they come to serve whole regions or countries. Such hubs are then supplied by feeder airlines from smaller airports which are closer to target destinations.

Getting an architectural fix on this forever mutating industry is tricky precisely because the actuality of air travel tends to run ahead of architectural ideas – or run on a different track entirely. In 1914 the Italian Futurist architect Antonio Sant'Elia set out what was to become a century-long vision of a romanticized integrated transport system. Railway lines at the base of Sant'Elia's airport provide the circulation feed. People then rise on funiculars and elevators past street level, eventually emerging onto the roof, between twin pairs of towers, whence they are whisked away in planes. As a layered diagram, this was astonishingly prescient: the rail–road–air sandwich is precisely how most major airports developed. However, like many architects of the early to mid-twentieth century, Sant'Elia made the mistake of thinking that things of the air should alight and take off from a roof. Endless architect-designed airports, including that in Le Corbusier's 1922 Ville

Contemporaine, also placed on the roof of a railway station, made the same understandable but erroneous assumption. This showed a complete ignorance of the ground-hugging, land-hungry nature of real airports, which even then was becoming apparent: because airports have always been about more than a terminal building and a launch pad. Huge amounts of hangars and ancillary maintenance and administration buildings are necessary. Taxi-ways have to be included. Wind direction may indicate use of one runway rather than another. Safety alone would suggest not landing civilian planes on an elevated deck in the middle of a city – even military aircraft carriers have the sea to ditch into. And the inflexibility of such rooftop designs meant that any changes in aircraft type – requiring longer runways, for instance – could not be allowed for, any more than Corbusier's Villa Savoye could accommodate a car of more than an absolutely specified size and turning radius. The notion of the runway in the sky, however, persisted among architects for a surprisingly long time after it was conclusively proved to be a silly idea. It survives today in all the buildings designed with a helicopter pad on the roof – which at any rate is practicable, if sometimes noisy and expensive.

Norman Foster's Hongkong and Shanghai Bank building of 1979–86 has more than a touch of

Sant'Elia about it, with the helicopter pad expressed as an intrinsic part of an ovoid architectural element that included private dining rooms and a viewing gallery: the final landing platform was not installed, however, as it was not permitted by the authorities. Even more overtly, Chemetov and Huidobro's Ministry of Finance at Bercy in Paris, 1982–90, returned to the brooding horizontalist masses of Sant'Elia. Roads – in one case a six-lane highway – sweep beneath this megastructure on both sides, a railway station slots in alongside, one end stands right in the Seine, providing an implied water gate, and the whole titanic mass rises to the helicopter pad on the roof, expressed as an oversailing disc. This is a building to be read at speed, when it is exhilarating: at close quarters, however, its details are crude. Although its function is to be an office complex for civil servants, its appearance is that of a multi-level transport interchange, and a heroic one at that. The Italian Futurists' influence does not end there. As late as 1995, a rooftop airport placed above a raised railway station was being proposed by the Bell Helicopter company to be used by a putative new generation of vertical take-off inter-city aircraft.

Once they engaged with airport reality, architects relatively quickly evolved a form of terminal or control building that became universally recognizable. The clean-lined block with control tower

became a leitmotif of modernism, so useful was the tower as a vertical foil to the horizontal mass. Of the endless variations on this theme, a mature and successful example – although by a very young architect – was Desmond Fitzgerald's terminal at Dublin Airport, 1937–41. Ireland came late to air travel, unlike pioneering Germany, and this was the first building for the new national airline Aer Lingus. As such it was a manifestation of national pride, with every detail right down to the cutlery in the restaurant being scrutinized by Fitzgerald's team at the Office of Public Works. A bilaterally symmetrical curving plan was given aileron-like cantilevered rectangular viewing platforms at either end at first floor level: the ends of the wings were rounded, and left unglazed on their top level, so exposing the columns as a form of wing strut. The horizontal bands of windows were relieved by vertical glazing placed centrally beneath the octagonal control room on top, so implying an embedded tower; and the whole thrust of the building was aimed towards the apron where the planes await. The radius of its curvature was similar to the wingspan of the Douglas DC3s that pulled up in front of it, and the approach road from the rear (also strictly symmetrical) provided the building with a 'fuselage' on plan, even kicking out at the ends to suggest a tailplane. The plan form of Fitzgerald's building was anything but whimsical – an almost

a

Great aeronautical metaphor,
or hamfisted orientalism?
a Eero Saarinen, Dulles airport,
   Washington, DC, 1958–63

identically planned and massed terminal at United Airport, Burbank, California by the Austin Company, 1930, proves that Fitzgerald cannot be accused of needlessly forcing a building into an aeroplane shape. But of all the many examples of airport buildings that express the symbolism of flight – inevitably Saarinen's terminals at Kennedy, 1956–62, and Dulles, 1958–63, airports loom large as abstract examples, and Nicholas Grimshaw's additions to London Heathrow and Manchester as literal ones – Fitzgerald's was one of the most successfully overt.

However, the problem remained: one still had to walk across the apron to board the plane – a problem that terminal buildings like the second Tempelhof with its high sheltering canopy could only partially solve. Experiments with moveable access corridors to aircraft had begun at Berkeley in California in the 1920s; however, the first building fully to exploit this technology came in 1936 at Britain's rural Gatwick Airport, known then as London South. Gatwick compensated for its great distance (twenty-five miles) from the city by being the first European airport with an express rail link. Architects Hoar, Marlow and Lovett devised a circular terminal – the hub – accessed via a subway from the rail station. Six 'gates' led to spokes radiating from this hub to waiting planes, via telescoping electric-powered passageways running on rails sunk

a

b

c

into the apron. Ironically, considering that the Gatwick Terminal was the forerunner of a series of airports of this radial pattern leading up to Paris' Charles de Gaulle airport in 1974, it was initially criticized for being impossible to expand. The idea of simply replicating it with more, linked hubs had not yet occurred. Even without such replication, the Gatwick terminal had a working life of twenty years, a long time in airport terms. Gatwick's new terminal built in the late 1950s placed its gates along a long narrow steel-framed spine building by architects Yorke, Rosenberg and Mardall: however the same practice returned to the hub form in the 1980s with its circular South Terminal, 1983–8, umbilically linked to its original via automatic tramcars.

Always, the architects and engineers of airport terminal buildings have to reconcile two opposing factors: to accommodate more and more planes, and therefore departure gates, while at the same time trying to reduce as much as possible the distance that passengers have to travel on foot within the terminal buildings. Piecemeal development over time always erodes this ideal, leading to confusing airports with a welter of moving walkways and remote waiting areas, combined with that old standby, buses across the tarmac to the waiting plane. Consequently, at regular intervals existing terminal complexes are abandoned and a new start made on

another side of the landing field. Or, where that is not possible, complete new airports are created on new sites. And since land is inevitably scarce, costly, and fought over by local residents and environmental interests, the idea of building on reclaimed land regularly crops up – from Amsterdam's Schipol, one of the first to be built on reclaimed land in 1919, to the end-of-century Far Eastern giants of Kansai and Hong Kong.

***Dirigiste* governmental regimes,**
however, have less difficulty getting new transport infrastructure built, and such was the case with Paul Andreu's Charles de Gaulle Terminal One at Roissy. Gatwick had been designed around a rapid rail link – not so much because of low car ownership in the 1930s, not a problem for the wealthy clientele of the fledgling airlines, but because a railway existed and roads were poor in the area. Heathrow, in the postwar years, relied on roads and did not connect itself to London's metro system until the late 1970s, or to mainline express railways until the late 1990s. Roissy, even more than Heathrow, was designed first and foremost for the motor car. Conceived well before the first oil crisis of the 1970s, its whole architecture is a homage to the car as much as the plane. As at the Villa Savoye, you could drive up to the great rotunda at Roissy, whip round it, and return whence you came like a slingshot. As with Frank

Lloyd Wright's unbuilt 'automobile objective' of 1925, this is a building you can drive into, spiralling upwards and arriving finally on the roof of the drum, which is given over to car parking. A related exercise was being carried out at Berlin's Tegel airport, 1965–75, by Meinhard von Gerkan, Volkwin Marg and Klaus Nickels: there the centre of a hexagonal terminal building was given over to layers of parking, leaving only a relatively thin rim to penetrate the plane stands. At Roissy, Andreu went a step further, by surrounding the central rotunda with seven freestanding 'satellites', each a mini-terminal, accessed by moving walkways in double-decker tunnels beneath the taxiways. The spiritual descendent of the 1936 Gatwick rotunda, the image of Roissy 1 was of process rather than product. The building had a sense of movement, highlighted by the criss-crossing walkway tubes at the central void of the torus, much favoured by sci-fi film makers. It is emphatically not a place to linger. Contemporaries of Roissy 1 include the great multi-hub airports of the United States such as Kansas City (Kivett and Myers, 1968–72) and Dallas–Fort Worth (Tippetts Abbett McCarthy and HOK, 1965–73), which again are experiments in movement as much as architecture.

The circular terminal layout recurs at intervals, for instance in Gensler's Palm Springs Regional Airport expansion, 1999, where linked octagonal

a Von Gerkan, Marg und Partner
with Nickel, Tegel Airport,
Berlin, 1965–75: runway
across roadway approach
b Tegel Airport: aerial view
c Gensler Associates, Palm
Springs Regional Airport
extension, California, 1999:
model

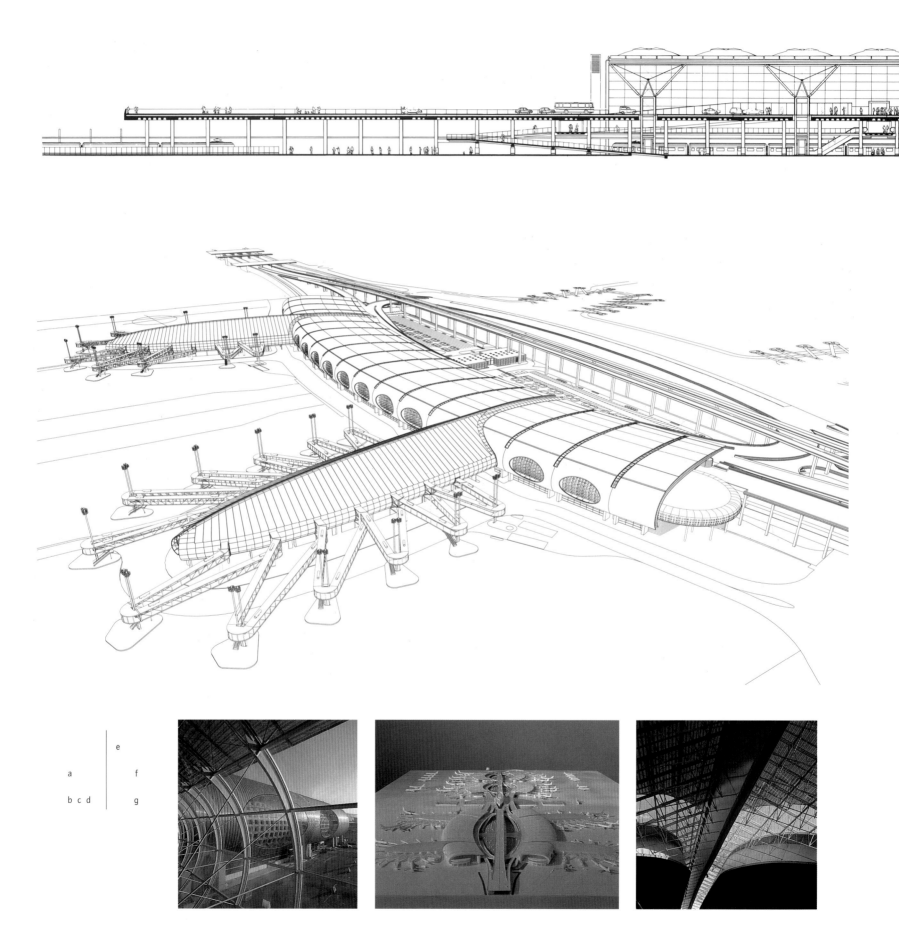

a

b c d

e

f

g

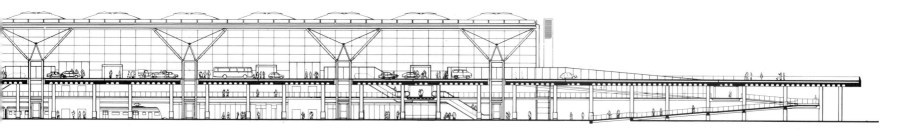

pavilions returned to the radial pattern of plane stands pioneered in the 1930s. However, for Roissy's second phase through to the mid-1990s, Andreu turned to a sequence of linked ellipses, with a multi-lane elevated highway forming the spine and the voids between the curved ranges of buildings given over to car parking. Despite its greater complexity, the basic movement diagram was still very simple: arrival – short perambulation across a building – departure; and vice-versa. However, for the latest phase of Roissy (Terminal 2F, 1989–98) Andreu was obliged to adopt a more conventional longer-walk approach, with a glazed 200-metre spine of gates projecting from the concrete shell of the terminal building: although the curvilinear feel of the earlier phases is (just) maintained, this looks like the end of Roissy's radicalism.

Four things served to upset the apple cart from the mid-1970s onwards. Public transport became more necessary as roads and car parks reached saturation point: international terrorism made stringent security checks necessary; airlines were deregulated in many countries, meaning they could no longer be told where to go and were free to set up their own terminals and points of transit; and, by the 1980s, airports were turning into shopping centres. The first of these factors had relatively little impact on airport architecture, since the expensive fix was to run a railway in under the new or existing buildings (at Norman

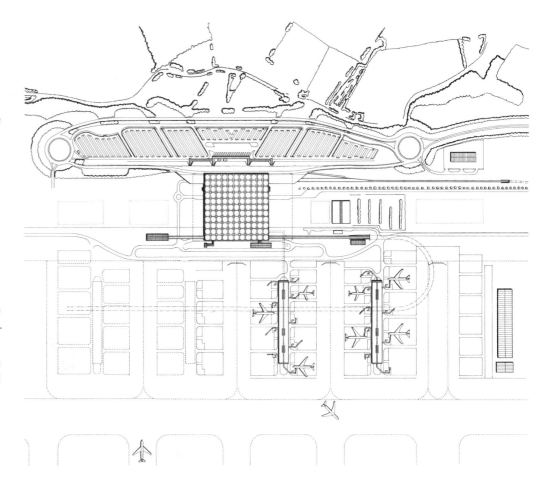

The spinal approach:
a Aéroports de Paris (Paul Andreu), Terminal 2F, Roissy, Charles de Gaulle Airport, Paris, 1989–98: perspective
b Terminal 2F, Roissy: view from across ramp back to main building
c Terminal 2F, Roissy: model
d Terminal 2F, Roissy: roof detail

The search for compactness and legibility:
e Foster and Partners, Stansted Airport, Essex, 1981–91: section
f Stansted Airport: site plan
g Stansted Airport: baggage reclaim

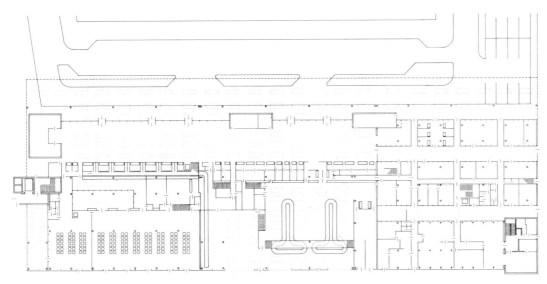

Foster's Stansted Airport, 1986–91 – London's third – the railway link was decided on at a late stage, while the building was advanced in design but still adaptable). But the other three factors in conjunction had a profound effect. Security checks mean bottlenecks and passengers milling around, so obstructing the movement from arrival to departure; airline deregulation makes it difficult to forecast traffic flow and integrate movement through a complete airport; and, worst of all for those who saw airport terminals purely as movement processors, the airport operators discovered that they could make much more money out of retail than they could out of landing and handling charges – which, after deregulation, were subject to such cut-throat competition that the mere handling of millions of passengers and cargo pallets could even show up as a loss on the balance sheet.

With the collapse of the previous municipal-national status of airports – where the facility was provided by the state and profitability was not an issue – the planning of airport buildings changed utterly, except in certain provincial towns and cities where traveller numbers are low enough to keep the retail tide at bay. This was the case at Riegler Riewe's minimalist airport terminal at Graz, Austria, 1989–97, which relies for its effect on precisely detailed good manners rather than any dramatics. The airport as retail mall was at first a British

phenomenon, consequent upon the privatization of the state airport operator, but quickly spread elsewhere.

Foster found himself on the cusp of two eras at Stansted. His idea of an upper medium-sized airport that retains the small-airfield visual link from arrival to departure, together with a dignified and elegant internal rhythm of structural 'trees' to support the unencumbered roof, was sorely tested by the need to put lots of shops in the concourse, with the inevitable visual clutter that a retail mall provides. His solution was to produce a system of structural 'cabins' for the retail, of a uniform height, to sit in the centre of the concourse. But the tide of clutter began to creep up even before the building opened, causing Foster to grumble publicly. Shortly afterwards Richard Rogers was to find himself faced with a similar challenge when charged with the task of designing a market-tested Terminal Five at Heathrow: when cheapness of build and maximum profitability in use are the main criteria, where does architecture go? The answer would appear to be to enclose a single large volume in such a way that the roof and its supports become the key visual architectural element: at Terminal Five, this is seen as an undulating, Aalto-esque roof that rises and falls over the central spine of the building, with related mini-waves over the parallel 'satellite' spines. This big roof was a relation of Rogers' similarly undulating glass roof over

London's pre-existing arts complex known as the South Bank Centre, designed in the mid-1990s. Such issues aside, the perceived need to retain people for longer within the airport concourse, rather than moving them through as rapidly as possible, makes a dramatic difference to the way such spaces are designed and the amount of space required. With airports increasingly resembling self-contained towns – complete with industry, office buildings, residential areas and of course transport links – the retail mall, with its captive clientele in the passenger concourses, was bound to follow sooner or later. Different cultures have different priorities, however: at the King Khaled Airport in Saudi Arabia, for instance, by Hellmuth, Obata and Kassabaum, 1975–83, the central building in the concourse – rising high above the areas of linked triangulated domes that cover the main concourse areas – is a mosque capable of holding 5,000 people. Anything further than the apologetic chapels always to be found tucked away somewhere in Western airports could scarcely be imagined. Moreover, by happy coincidence, the tall dome of the King Khaled mosque and its associated minaret anchored the low, sprawling mass of the airport complex rather as the control towers of the 1920s and 1930s did.

After the rotunda-terminals of America and Europe in the 1960s and 1970s, and acting as an

The symbolic gateway:
a Hellmuth, Obata + Kassabaum (HOK), King Khaled Airport, Saudi Arabia, 1975–83: aerial view
b King Khaled Airport: interior of airport mosque

The no-fuss people processor:
c Riegler Riewe (Florian Riegler and Roger Riewe), Graz Airport, passenger terminal and offices, Graz, Austria, 1989–97: site plan
d Graz Airport: minimalist and mannered exterior
e Graz Airport: entrance to concourse

alternative to the rigid big-shed terminal buildings emerging in the next two decades, two airports explored the different aesthetic of the tensile roof. SOM's Haj Terminal at Jeddah, Saudi Arabia, 1977–87, and Fentress and Bradburn's Denver Airport, 1992, however use the technology to different ends. The Haj terminal, part of the King Abdul Aziz Airport at Jeddah, was designed purely to handle the mass of pilgrims *en route* for Mecca every year. It is an open-sided transit area, handling pilgrims moving from planes to buses. Therefore its chosen aesthetic – of mast-suspended tented roofs in Teflon-coated glass fibre fabric – was appropriate in its suggestion of a temporary encampment, even if the use of the material dates it firmly as part of a 1970s architectural fashion. At Denver, however, Fentress & Bradburn

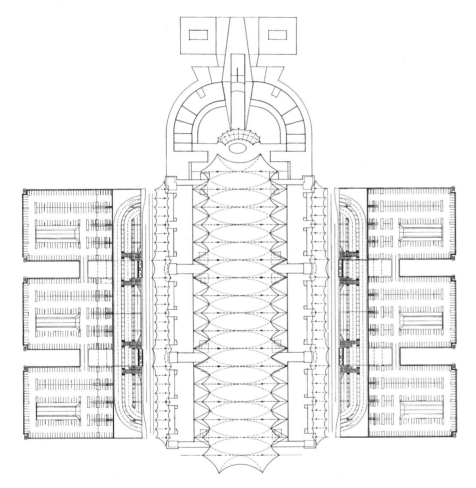

a c
   e   g
b   h i
   f
d   j

returned to the tensile roof technique – this time using a more sophisticated double-skin arrangement for thermal and acoustic purposes – in order to cover the concourse of what was at the time the largest international airport in the United States. Designed with engineers Severud Associates, the peaks of the roof – then the largest tensile roof in the world at 275 metres long – were intended to echo the snowy peaks of the Rocky Mountains rising in the distance from the Denver Plateau. Where the Haj Terminal suspended its roof via cables strung from external masts and is loose-fit, Denver is tensioned on internal masts and is sealed, with sophisticated pneumatic joints taking up the movement between flexing roof and rigid glazing. Although at first glance the roof seems to be a series of fabric domes, in fact there are two

ranges of these peaks, with wide fabric 'valleys' tensioned between them, spanning 50 metres between the parallel lines of masts. Denver Airport acknowledges that in any building of this kind, the roof is everything (the solid architectural elements are dull indeed). It also recognizes the high economic importance of such places. Its trading power, when all its ancillary high-tech building developments were built, was predicted to be more than the gross domestic product of some European nations. Such calculations depend very much on where you define the boundaries of an airport proper, and how widely you assume its gravitational field operates. What is not in question is that the economic pull of a transport interchange is huge. This much was true of the towns that sprang up on canal and railway junctions in the

eighteenth and nineteenth centuries, the 'intersection cities' to be found on motorways (see 'Consumerism'), and the huge retail developments associated with any new ground-based transport project. An example is the Channel Tunnel and its associated fast rail links, which include what is virtually a new town with a new name: Euralille in northern France.

At the end of the century all of the world's biggest airports have gone the same way, with variations: the big roof is the dominant image. Foster's system of structural 'trees' at Stansted, supporting an uncluttered roof beneath which activities can change freely, is one motif frequently repeated, not least by Rogers at his Heathrow Terminal Five, which despite its rippling roof owes more to Stansted than to Piano's Kansai. Kisho Kurokawa's

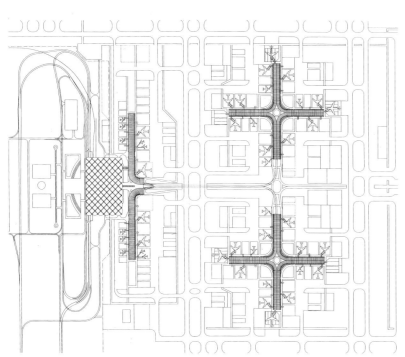

Tensile structures provide shelter and light for deep-plan terminals:

a C W Fentress J H Bradburn and Associates, Denver International Airport, Denver, Colorado, 1991–4: exterior view

b Denver International Airport: plan

c Denver International Airport: flexible pneumatic joints allow for movement between the fabric roof and the fixed glazing

d Denver International Airport: concourse

e Skidmore, Owings and Merrill (SOM), Haj Terminal, Jeddah, Saudi Arabia, 1977–87, 1992: exterior view

f Haj Terminal: passenger waiting areas

g Kisho Kurokawa, Kuala Lumpur International Airport, Kuala Lumpur, Malaysia, 1993–8: section

h Kuala Lumpur International Airport: site plan

i Kuala Lumpur International Airport: model

j Kuala Lumpur International Airport: model of glazing structure and 'trees'

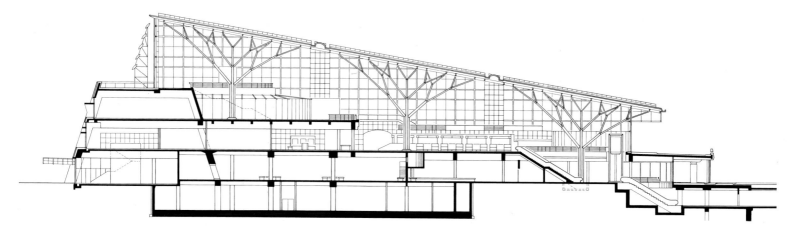

Kuala Lumpur International terminal, 1993-8, uses the 'trees' as a visual echo of the brand-new tropical rainforest planted as a thick green belt around the airport - his terminal plan, unusually, is cruciform, being two long spines crossing at right angles. The 1980-90 Stuttgart Airport by Von Gerkan, Marg and Partner deployed 'trees' at their most literal, supporting a sloping roof on an organically derived branching structural system. The later Oslo International Airport, 1993-8, by Aviaplan - a consortium including Niels Torp - is remarkably similar despite claiming a Nordic, specifically Norwegian, sensibility. Such big spaces frequently deploy - usually in conjunction with structural 'trees' - the long-span roof truss, which gives a deeper and busier roof structure but fewer columns. Bangkok's second airport, by Murphy Jahn, 1993-2000, envisages a colossal flat louvered roof formed in this way, while San Francisco's international arrivals hall (SOM and others, 1994-2000) deploys bowed trusses based on the Forth Bridge principle to give a shallow 'wingspread' roof profile. Trees and trusses can be combined, as by Von Gerkan, Marg and Partner at Hamburg International Airport, 1986-93, and most notably at Renzo Piano's Kansai, 1988-94. At Kansai, the trusses curve and swoop across the width of the main concourse like a spinal column, supported by two lines of 'trees' comprising raking struts

(this was the last project engineered by Peter Rice, who had first worked with Piano on Paris' Pompidou Centre). This sinusoidal curve visually ripples the building - and thus the passengers - towards the business end of the airport where the planes stand (and roots the building clearly in the 1990s, the decade of the wavy roof). The terminal building is, however, two structures rather than one since the boarding 'wing' at the front is a separate arrangement of toroidal latticed steel arches which, at 1.7 kilometres from end to end, was, at its opening, the longest enclosed space in the world. Where Kurokawa's Kuala Lumpur airport wraps itself in an environmental mantle of forest, Kansai isolates itself by virtue of being built on a complete artificial island in Osaka Bay - large enough to be visible from space.

Foster himself moved to the long-truss technique when it came to Hong Kong's new airport - like Piano's, built on a man-made island, called Chek Lap Kok - islands proving increasingly attractive for new airports as a way both of creating the enormous areas of land needed, and of removing the noise and pollution of planes from the inhabited city. It is an idea frequently mooted for Chicago and London, and adopted by Fentress and Bradburn for the new Seoul Metropolitan Airport in South Korea, 1994-2000. Superlatives are always called upon for these mega-airports: although Foster's did

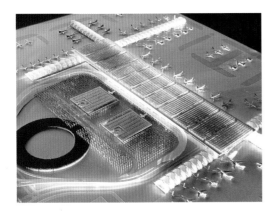

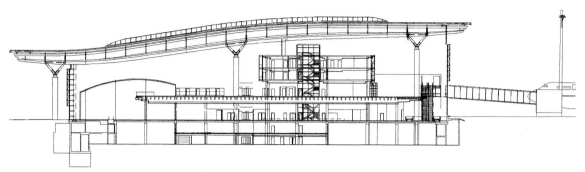

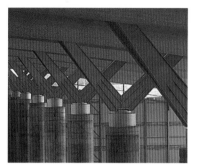

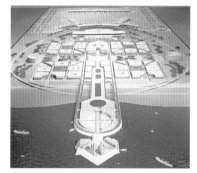

The tree, the truss, and their combinations:

a Von Gerkan, Marg und Partner with Karsten Brauer, Stuttgart Airport, Stuttgart, Germany, 1980–90: section

b Stuttgart Airport: interior

c Murphy Jahn, New Bangkok International Airport, Bangkok, 1993–2000: model

d Bangkok Airport: computer-generated interior perspective

e Aviaplan, Oslo International Airport, Oslo, Norway, 1993-8: section

f Von Gerkan, Marg und Partner with Karsten Brauer, Hamburg International Airport, Hamburg, Germany, 1986–93: trees and trusses combined

g Hamburg International Airport: entrance canopy

h Oslo International Airport: exterior view shows the depth of the roof structure

i Oslo International Airport: detail of truss–column connection

j C W Fentress J H Bradburn and Associates, New Inchon International Air Passenger Terminal Complex, Seoul, Republic of South Korea, 1994-2000

			h
a		e	i
b			j
		f g	
c d			

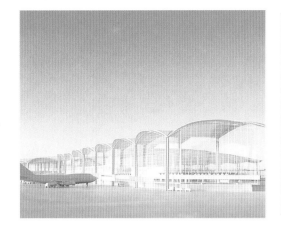

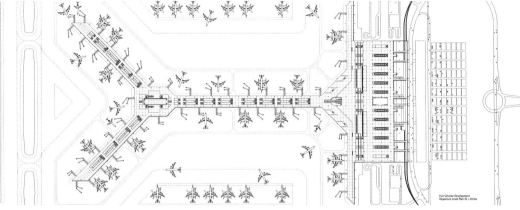

not attain the length of Kansai's boarding wing – his terminal was 200 metres shorter – it could claim to be the largest airport in the world when it came to passenger movements, as well as the world's largest single construction site. Completed in its first phase in 1998, the Hong Kong airport is planned to be expanded until, by the year 2040, it will be handling 87 million passengers, more than Heathrow and JFK combined. Where Piano created a single long boarding arm, Foster chose a Y-shaped configuration, which on plan is like a pair of aircraft wings.

The whole of Hong Kong airport's roof structure is based upon a repeated module of linked barrel vaults, each 36 metres across, and of steel shell construction on concrete support structure. For the main landside terminal building, these vaults rise up and over the main concourse before descending to the lower main spine out to the planes. On plan, this looks spindly but this is only because of the huge size of the entire building: the spine is a broad three-storey construction, raised to allow surface service vehicles beneath, and with twin tramways and service roads buried beneath the ground. Even so, and despite the colossal scale of the interior of the main concourse which can hardly fail to be stunningly impressive, Hong Kong suffers like all mega-airports from the sheer area it has to cover. Airport buildings cannot be tall. They have

very little by way of facades. Viewed from above, the Hong Kong airport looks as if a giant has taken a machete to a fieldful of Dutch glasshouses, and carved himself out an interesting pattern – vaguely reminiscent of a giant parked aircraft when viewed horizontally, very like a child's stick-figure of a human when seen vertically. Either way, it is another man-made symbol doubtless visible from space.

Such structural gymnastics might almost make one believe that there are, at most, only three ways to enclose an airport terminal. This may be true of the very largest, but on the smaller scale interesting alternatives are possible. Aldo Rossi's Linate airport project at Milan, Italy, 1991–3, was a visually heavyweight composition of columns, Vierendeel girders and masonry infill owing more to inter-war factory construction methods than high-tech computer wizardry. Deliberately austere in the way Rossi's buildings tend to be, it was nonetheless seen by the architect as holding symbolic importance. 'Antique writers spoke of the sky's limits but the sky is becoming an increasingly inhabited space,' he observed in 1994. 'Airports have therefore become the new gates of the cities and they should express their spirit and character and at the same time be ready for change.' A sentiment with which no architect, of whatever stylistic persuasion, would disagree.

a	c	d	f
			g
b		e h	

Lightweight, insubstantial, but huge:
a Foster and Partners, Hong Kong International Airport, Hong Kong, 1992–8: model
b Aldo Rossi, Linate Airport, Milan, 1991–3: Rossi attempts to impose solidity and permanence
c Hong Kong International Airport: plan

d Rafael Moneo, San Pablo Airport, Seville, Spain, 1987–92: site plan
e Forbes and Fitzhardinge, Stirling Station, Perth, Australia, 1992: site plan
f San Pablo Airport: exterior
g San Pablo Airport: interior of concourse
h Stirling Station: exterior view

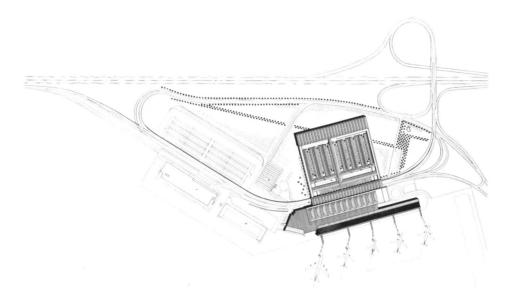

Similarly Rafael Moneo's San Pablo airport at Seville, Spain, 1987–92, was a deliberate exercise in the architecture of weight. Moneo determinedly rejected any avian or aeronautical metaphor. 'The perfection and lightness of flying machines have very little in common with the complex, functional mechanisms behind airports,' observed the 1997 Pritzker Prize winner. 'Airports belong to the world of things built on land, and not to the sky, and are by definition places of transit ... the idea is for the space defined by the vaults to act as a threshold to the sky.' To reinforce the point, the vaults of his departure concourse were painted deep blue. Outside, the terminal sports traditional pyramidal roof forms. Moneo's big arches do not span anything like the distance of Piano's or Jahn's roof trusses, but they hardly need to in this relatively modest regional airport. While Moneo's airport was at any rate 'modern' in the broad sense, other new airports, particularly in the United States, turned out to be rampantly historicist. Nantucket Memorial Airport, 1992, architects HNTB Corporation, for instance, is a shingled, mock-colonial theming exercise.

Airports are the city gateways of today but railways performed that function in the past and, to some extent, still do. In 1875, Britain's *Building News* observed:

'*Railway termini and hotels are to the nineteenth*

century what monasteries and cathedrals were to the thirteenth century. They are truly the only real representative buildings we possess ... Our metropolitan termini have been leaders of the art spirit of our time.' One could take this sentiment, replace 'railway' with 'airport' and the words would be as valid today, but for one thing: the late twentieth-century revival of the landmark railway station. This has, unsurprisingly, taken place in crowded regions where fast trains can compete on time and comfort with airlines. Hence their resurgence in Europe and the Far East, but their relative scarcity in North America and Australia. Fast railways came to assume high importance as physical links between the countries of the European Union, for instance, and central European funds were available to help finance them. There are exceptions to this European–Far Eastern rule, such as the Northern Suburbs Transit System in Perth, Australia, which has generated seven new stations. The best result of this programme was Stirling Station by Forbes and Fitzhardinge, completed in 1992. This is a successful composition of overlapping mast-supported butterfly roofs on a station placed unpromisingly in the gap between the two carriageways of a new freeway, served at high level by a curving bus and pedestrian bridge. Complete in itself for rail users, it also functions as a kind of speed-sculpture for passing drivers. This symbiotic

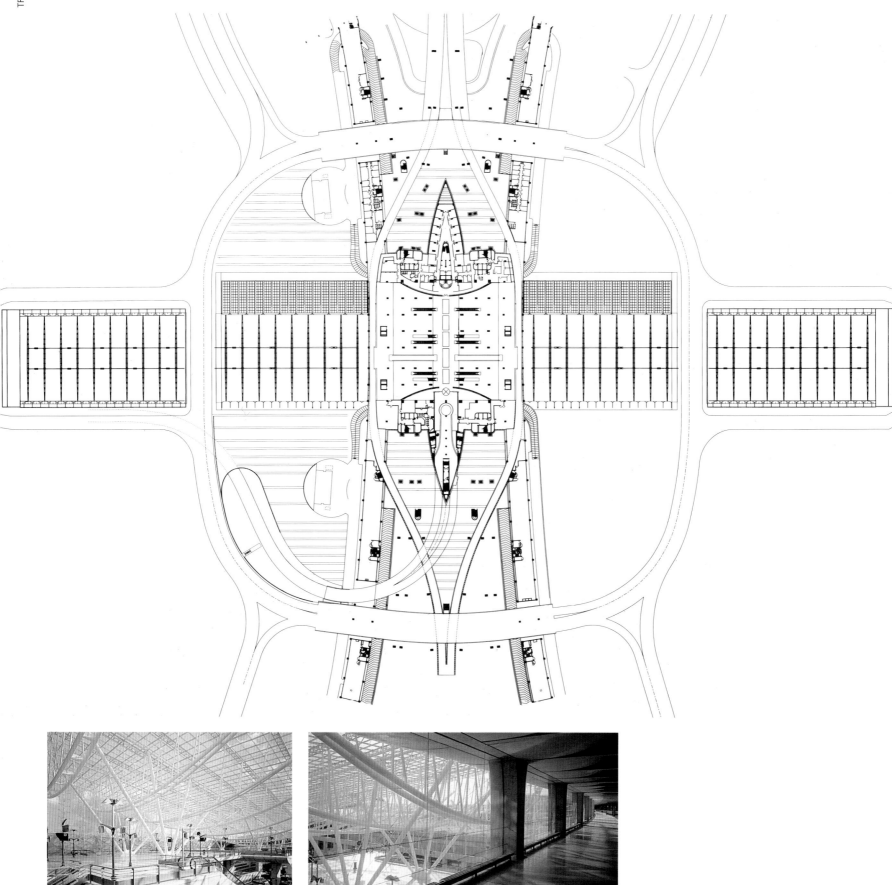

relationship between transport systems is one of the main factors ensuring the continued health of railway architecture.

The most successful examples can hold their own even in the context of flight, particularly if the same architect is involved. Paul Andreu's rail terminal at Roissy, Paris, whizzing through the terminal at right angles to its main road spine, acknowledges the crossing by building itself up in steel and glass wedges either side of the elongated oval of the station and airport hotel set on the axis. This simple gesture generates some powerful interlocking spaces. Again, the roof structure was a late work of Peter Rice (completed two years after his death in 1993), in this case a series of inverted bowstring trusses rather wilfully hung from the familiar 'trees' instead of being supported directly from below. The bows could equally well have been reversed and placed above the roof, but the effect of the tubes swooping low over the tracks and rising clear at the edges was what mattered, coupled with the stately rise of the trusses up towards the Roissy spine. The diagram of the inter-European express line slicing across the airport is very important. In global terms, London, Paris and Frankfurt are in fairly close proximity. With trains this fast serving Roissy, and a rail tunnel in operation under the English Channel, passengers can be enticed from both city's airports if the connections

are right. Where passengers go, trade inevitably follows, and the whole Roissy area was accordingly expectantly laid out for commerce.

At Euralille, a relatively short distance to the north, the French–German high-speed train network generated a famous knot of architecture. The new express rail line, thundering towards the Channel Tunnel, was not originally scheduled to pause at Lille until local interests campaigned to change the government's mind. As a result, a complete new commercial district, Euralille, was created, which like the original Berlin Tempelhof Airport was previously an area given over to the military. It was masterplanned by Rem Koolhaas of OMA with buildings by him, Jean Nouvel, Christian de Portzamparc, and others. The station is yet another to involve Peter Rice as an engineer (Rice was intensely productive in the years before his early death, here working with fellow engineers Jean-François Blassel of the RFR consultancy and Sophie Lebourva of Ove Arup), while the architects were Jean-Marie Duthilleul, Etienne Tricaud and Pierre Saboya. The station, Lille-Europe, started with a brief from Duthilleul, the chief architect of the French Railways, that it should recapture the sense of excitement apparent at those stations dating from the railways' nineteenth-century heyday. But for all the talent thrown at it and the importance attached to it, Lille-Europe does not succeed in its relationship

with the development it traverses nearly as successfully as Andreu and Rice's effort at Roissy. Ironically, this is partly because the engineered structure is so pure and insubstantial, the slender tubular steel arches supporting the obligatory 1990s wavy roof like bent canes. The almost wilful over-engineering of Roissy is absent, although at Lille-Europe the weight of the roof is communicated to the tops of the hoops via a little game of struts and cables that is meant to make the roof 'float' and is surely inspired by the unconscious engineering of the railways' overhead power lines. The overall effect, however, with its semi-translucent roof, is more that of a market hall than a glasshouse. This is a crucial difference, since the technology of the nineteenth-century terminals evolved directly from the great botanical glasshouses of a few years earlier. Moreover, by running along the spine of the Euralille development, with two big buildings and a road spanning it at high level, there is none of the tectonic force generated by Roissy's powerful cross-axis. While clearly ingenious, Lille-Europe is also strangely indeterminate.

The glasshouse railway aesthetic is much better handled at Chur in Switzerland, where the station is by Richard Brosi and Robert Obrist, 1985–92 for the first phase, though the engineering is by the familiar pedigree partnership of Peter Rice with Ove Arup and (for the glazing) RFR. A curved

Acknowledging the intersection:
a Aéroports de Paris (Paul Andreu), TGV Station, Roissy, Charles de Gaulle Airport, Paris, 1992–4: site plan
b TGV Station, Roissy: interior
c TGV Station, Roissy: croissant-shaped roof trusses are supported on 'tree' columns
d Jean-Marie Duthilleul with RFR and Ove Arup, Lille-Europe, Lille, 1988–94: concourse
e Lille-Europe: aerial view

d e

a

b c

glass roof, and nothing else, certainly not walls, it spans the railway and bus stations, and the idea is not to obstruct any view of the surrounding mountains, since this is a transhipment point for skiers on their way up to St Moritz – Brosi was from Chur, Obrist from St Moritz. This desire for transparency even extends to leaving the sides clear: the big curved roof is supported by rows of simple paired masts like rowers carrying an upturned boat. In order not to compromise the integrity of the roof with too much clutter, overhead lighting is provided from uplighters bouncing off angled flights of convex mirrors.

Until the ultima Thule of an all-glass structural canopy of this size is attained, Chur will continue to represent a very pure example of this particular design obsession. It is to be found again, for instance, at Chris Wilkinson's Stratford Market depot for London Underground trains, 1991–7, where Wilkinson, an emerging talent in the 1990s particularly noted for his bridge designs, flung a shallow barrel vault over a rhomboidal site containing the echelons of rail tracks needed for metro train storage, cleaning and maintenance. The depot is significant since it represents an example of the high architectural standards applied to London's Jubilee Line extension, due for completion in 1998, which swings south of the Thames and then east through the Canary Wharf commercial district built in the London Docklands, thence through the

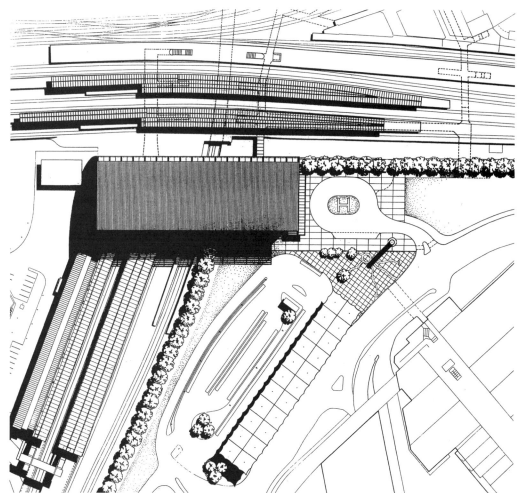

The glorification of arrival:
a Richard Brosi + Robert Obrist,
   Chur Station, Chur,
   Switzerland, 1985–92
b Chris Wilkinson Architects,
   Stratford Market Depot,
   London, 1991–7: interior
c Chris Wilkinson Architects,
   Stratford Station, London,
   1994–8: model
d Stratford Market Depot:
   site plan

	b	c
a		
	d	

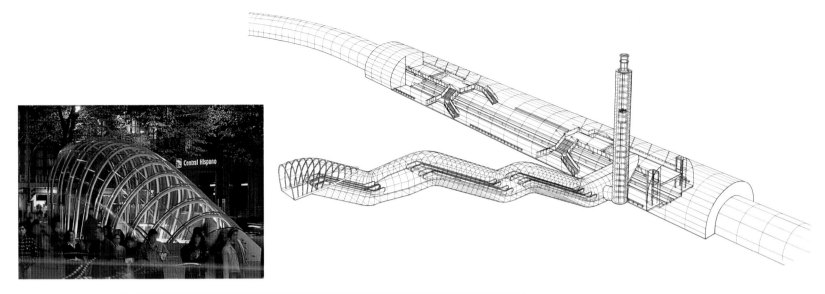

Millennium Exhibition site, Greenwich, before turning north to conclude at Stratford, East London. The London Underground's commissioning architect, Roland Paoletti, was largely responsible for a policy that – unlike previous London metro lines from the 1900s onwards – employed different architects for the various stations and associated buildings. Previously a 'house style' had always been adopted, either per line or (pre-nationalization) per metro company. This approach reached its flowering with the integrated city-wide London Transport design policy in the 1930s, masterminded by LT's Frank Pick with much of the work being designed by the practice of Charles Holden. Similar thinking informed the new metro system of Bilbao in Spain, where all the stations were designed by Sir Norman Foster and Partners, 1988–95. For the Jubilee Line extension, however, stations and other buildings were awarded to a roster of well-regarded architects, some of whom had never worked in the transport field before. They included Alsop and Störmer, Foster, Herron Associates, Michael Hopkins and Partners, MacCormac Jamieson Prichard, Ian Ritchie Architects, John McAslan, Van Heyningen and Haward, and Weston Williamson, as well as Chris Wilkinson. This was a startling departure, and in a sense acknowledged the plurality of architectural approaches existing at the time as well as acting as a metaphor for what seemed likely to be

a c   e
b   f

d

the break-up and privatization of the Underground network in the absence of a city-wide London authority (the Greater London Council and its strategic powers had been abolished in 1987). It was plurality, however, in a strictly confined sense since – although Richard MacCormac's architecture, for instance, was very different from Norman Foster's, likewise John McAslan's from Will Alsop's, and so on – all fell within the parameters of modernism. Therefore the Jubilee Line project, conceived at the end of the 1980s, can be seen as an indicator of the official reassertion of the modernist establishment in Britain after a decade of uncertainty. Had the post-modernists or classicists, or even the eclectic individualists, got a foothold here, then that would have indicated that the course of public architecture in Britain was going in a different direction. Alsop was perhaps the most extreme of the bunch, but only in British terms. His designs for North Greenwich station were regarded as daring indeed at first but, by the time of completion, had come to be seen in European terms as relatively mainstream, not least because public commissioning clients had by then emerged from their mid-1980s aesthetic bunkers and were doing things like commissioning Daniel Libeskind and Günter Behnisch to design museum extensions and concert halls. Alsop, furthermore, found his previously isolated station – built in the middle of cleared industrial wasteland in

anticipation of new development – suddenly in the thick of things as the British government declared its support for an Expo-style 'Millennium Experience' for the year 2000 on the Greenwich site. Thus Alsop's underground architecture was topped with a wing-shaped transport interchange designed by Foster to sit alongside Richard Rogers' Millennium Dome: an architectural triple-whammy.

Railway buildings will always represent engineering at its most architectural, and always have done. London's St Pancras Station of 1865–77 is conventionally attributed to George Gilbert Scott, and indeed the fantastical Gothic hotel at the front is his: but the station's still awe-inspiring column-free train shed behind, 100 feet high with a span of 243 feet, was by the Midland Railway Company's engineer William Henry Barlow with R M Ordish. Since the architectural competition for the hotel was held after the shed was designed – Scott remarking on Barlow's happy structural choice of a pointed arch for the shed, which suited his own Gothic sensibilities – and the hotel only built after the station was in use, there must have been a moment when Barlow's shed on its great brick plinth stood revealed as proudly as that of Chur does today. Curiously enough St Pancras – latterly a somewhat under-used London terminus, and at times threatened with demolition – was suddenly woken from its slumbers at the end of

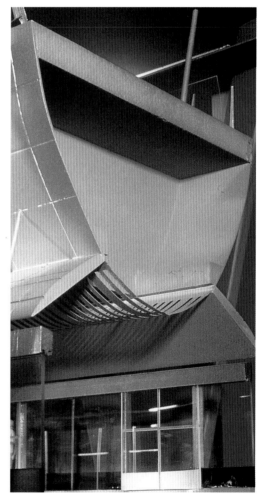

Making visual links to the surface:

a Foster and Partners, Metro System, Bilbao, Spain, 1988–95: entrance canopy

b Bilbao Metro System: escalators down to trains

c Bilbao Metro System: axonometric

d Bilbao Metro System: platform level

e MacCormac Jamieson Prichard, Southwark Jubilee Line station, London, 1993–8

f Alsop and Störmer, North Greenwich Jubilee Line station, London, 1991: model

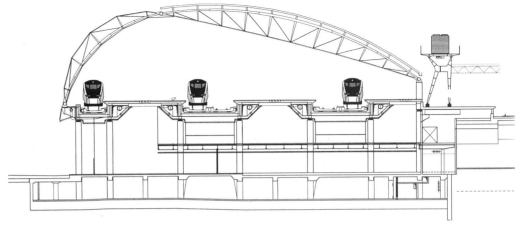

the twentieth century as the London conclusion of the new express rail link to the Channel Tunnel. This provided Sir Norman Foster with the ticklish challenge of adding an extension to Barlow's shed capable of sheltering the immensely long Eurostar trains.

Before the building of that rail link, however, London brought the Eurostars along old lines into a new terminal at Waterloo Station, 1988–93, designed by Nicholas Grimshaw, with the roof engineered by Anthony Hunt. Grimshaw immediately saw the terminal as the equivalent of a twenty-first-century airport. He had just completed a speculative airport terminal for the 1991 Venice Architecture Biennale – the underlying principle of which was to do away with the conventional 'gate' system, by taking passengers from a central terminal building out to their planes by train only when their plane was ready to take off. Similarly (though this was an operational coincidence) at Waterloo International, passengers move from waiting areas directly onto the trains, with no hanging around on the platforms. This was made possible by the fact that the terminal is in effect a two-storey curved building with trains arriving on its roof – above which is the asymmetrical canopy that is the building's principal aesthetic image. The fact that passengers are marshalled down below contradicts the received image of the bustling Victorian terminus. Although St Pancras was

also built up high, its undercroft was designed for transhipment of goods – the module of its columned bays calculated from the dimensions of the barrels of Burton beer stored there. Similarly Foster's Stansted Airport put its railway station, baggage handling and other services into the undercroft, so releasing passengers to wander freely beneath the terminal canopy.

In another railway station 'sandwich' – Hellmuth Obata and Kassabaum's New Penn Station in New York (scheduled for completion in 1999) – the passenger concourse is beneath the great arched tubular steel-framed roof, and passengers descend to trains beneath, just as they did at the original Pennsylvania Station, 1904–10, by McKim, Mead and White, which was demolished for air rights development in the 1960s. The irony is that HOK's new station was designed to slot into another, surviving, McKim, Mead and White creation – the adjacent James A Farley building, home of the United States postal service, completed in 1918. Grimshaw's Waterloo International works the other way round: the platforms are eerily deserted until the passengers are released in bursts from below to embark or disembark. The usual promenade down the platforms from the mouth of the shed is absent: that mouth, though left open and proudly visible from the main Waterloo station concourse, is guarded by a moat

c
d
a
b
e f

Layering a station's functions gives priority to people or trains, but seldom both:
a   Hellmuth Obata + Kassabaum, New Penn Station, New York, 1999: model
b   New Penn Station: perspective of interior
c   Nicholas Grimshaw and Partners, Waterloo International Terminal, London, 1988–93: section
d   Waterloo International Terminal: train shed
e   Waterloo International Terminal: Eurostar trains leaving Waterloo
f   Waterloo International Terminal: aerial view

and placed behind a glass wall. On such a tight site that the insertion of a complete new station was in itself something of a miracle (its snaking form defining the very edge of the available land) the high level of the tracks above ground was the only way to make space for the extra paraphernalia of customs and security contingent upon an international terminal. In another historical twist, St Pancras' shallower undercroft was, at the time of writing, due to be pressed similarly into international service, over a hundred and thirty years after it was built.

None of this mattered. The Grimshaw–Hunt train shed with its ingenious knucklebone engineering and asymmetrical, tapering form was almost universally acclaimed and immediately became a

beloved London landmark, with none of the usual frenzy of press-stimulated architect-bashing. Indeed, when at one point it appeared that the design, prior to even being built, was going to be stamped on by new office blocks *à la* Euralille, a petition was organized to 'save' it. This serves to demonstrate that the big train shed was always a symbolic rather than a practical architectural type. Platforms do not have to be sheltered in this expansive way – little separate canopies running along each one, as Santiago Calatrava modestly provided at Zurich's Stadelhofen station, 1984–90 – provide all the shelter necessary. Indeed, the enclosing roof was always an environmental problem in the era of smoky steam or diesel locomotives, something readily apparent even today at Isambard Kingdom Brunel and Matthew Digby

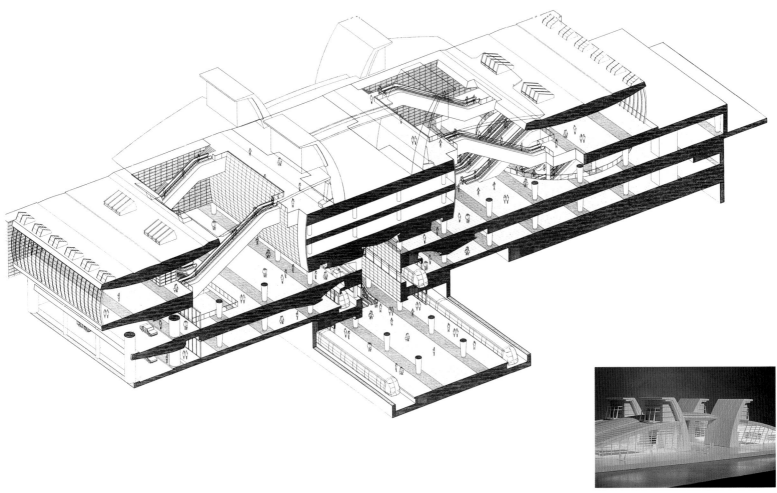

a

b   f   g

   d

c e   h

Wyatt's Paddington Station, 1852–4, terminus of the Great Western Railway. It is chokingly apparent here that the Great Western is still not electrified at the start of the twenty-first century. But railway companies wanted to advertise their presence in cities, and the spectacle of the big roof was, and is, the way to do it. Waterloo International represented the swansong of the nationalized British Railways as an architectural patron, and of Jane Priestman as effectively its last design director, since the network was sold off in pieces to private companies soon after. Priestman, who had previously held a similar post at the British Airports Authority – also privatized after her departure – went on to advise on the building of the Hong Kong metro system, which was handed over to China along with the rest of the colony in 1997. She would

be forgiven for thinking that the British government held a grudge against her: fortunately the buildings remain as a legacy. Terry Farrell's titanic transport interchange and commercial development at Kowloon in Hong Kong, 1992–8 – on the line out to Foster's airport – is an example. Farrell typically sets solid against void by interrupting what in other hands would be a continuous arched roof, inserting four curved masonry towers which define the axis of the station building (much of which is below podium level) and the whole development. As frequently happens, former partners find themselves designing buildings with similar functions in similar parts of the world: as Farrell was finishing his Kowloon interchange, Nicholas Grimshaw was commencing work on his also immense Pusan Bay interchange in

Korea, in which the roof is expressed as a giant compound 'eye' overlooking the sea.

So the big roof was revived for railway stations and transport interchanges at the same time that it was adopted for airports, taking sometimes highly sculptural forms – Farrell's in Kowloon; Calatrava's great winged head-dress at Lyon–Satolas airport, France, 1988–94, with its refined, bony concrete structure below; and Michael Wilford's Abando station and interchange in Bilbao, Spain, 1990–2000. At Abando the curved vault, 166 metres wide, is constructed as a diagonal latticework, with a strongly facetted skin, interspersed with other building forms both inside and outside including a funnel-shaped office building acting as conning-tower. Elsewhere, architects decided to consider older forms

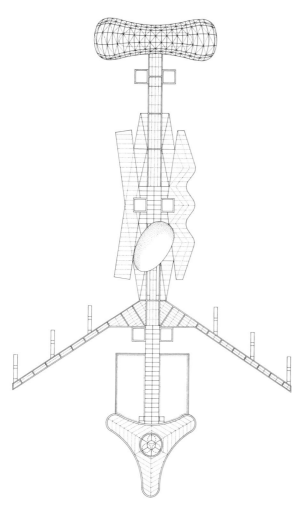

Transport interchanges continue to be spurs for city regeneration:

a Santiago Calatrava, Stadelhofen Station, Zurich, Switzerland, 1983–90
b Terry Farrell, Kowloon Station Interchange, Hong Kong, 1992–8: axonometric
c Santiago Calatrava, Lyon–Satolas TGV Station, Lyons, France, 1988–94
d Kowloon Station: model
e Lyon–Satolas: platform

f Michael Wilford & Partners, Abando Station Interchange, Bilbao, Spain, 1990–2000: concept plan
g Abando Station: model
h Nicholas Grimshaw, Pusan Bay interchange, Korea, 1993–

of the station vault – Santa Justa station in Seville, Spain, for instance (Cruz and Ortiz, 1988–92), has six parallel tall, narrow vaults stretching back from its austerely palatial brick-built concourse: a somewhat unexpected conclusion, given the enormously wide and shallow roof that spans the entire frontage of the station. The direct successor to Seville – built for the 1992 Expo – is the Calatrava-designed station for the 1998 Expo in Lisbon, Portugal. There, Calatrava roofed the concourse with a forest of structural 'trees', so serving to merge railway and airport building typologies still further, but also giving a Gothic feel to the elevated station that must please all those who see the Gothic mode first and foremost as a naturally derived structural system. Whereas at Abando Wilford embraced both trains and buses in his inclusive architecture, at Lisbon Calatrava chose to express the bus concourse in a different architecture of cantilevered canopies, set behind and at a lower level than the station. His characteristic response of concrete ground structure rising to lightweight steel superstructure – both treated in equally plastic fashion – is particularly appropriate here, given the 12-metre height difference between road and railway.

Others also tried to redefine the traditional form. Also in Lyon, Jourda and Perraudin had produced the influential Parilly metro station,

1985–92. As with Calatrava, concrete undercrofts rise to a lightweight roof. But the undercrofts are deliberately heavy and crude, with massive fluted stripped-classical columns – some impressively angled, and supporting a form of fan vaulting. The roof above, of coloured glass supported on delicate steel branches, was a gently curving square, semi-enclosed with a wall of glass that rose from the ground but stopped well short of the roof. This was a temporary covering, since the area above the station was zoned for commercial development. But its generative principle was permanent: the square lightwell provided by the canopy was placed at an angle to the rectangle of the station concourse just beneath the surface, so forcefully skewing the geometry.

In The Netherlands, Harry Reijnders bent over backwards in his efforts to find a new kind of station roof. The Rotterdam Blaak station, 1986–93, is crowned with a tilted glazed disc 35 metres in diameter – precisely a shallow dome like an upturned saucer – hung at its upturned front edge from a soaring curved arched truss, 62.5 metres long, that whizzes overhead to plant itself on the street edge. This assemblage defines the crossing point of railway and metro lines at different levels below ground. The disc follows the shape of the circular shaft down with its stairs and escalators. It is brightly and garishly lit with changing coloured lighting. This is in a part of

a d e
b
f h
c
g i

Placing the urban marker; stations rediscovering their civic role:

a Antonio Cruz + Antonio Ortiz, Santa Justa Station, Seville, Spain, 1988–92: entrance
b Santa Justa Station: escalators from platform to concourse
c Santa Justa Station: platforms and tracks
d Santa Justa Station: at the rear six vaults span the tracks

e Santiago Calatrava, Expo '98 Station, Lisbon, 1993–8: section
f Jourda & Perraudin, Station at Parilly Metro, Lyons, 1985–92: platform
g Enric Miralles, Entrance to Takaoka Train Station, Takaoka, Toyama, Japan, 1991–3
h Parilly Metro: canopy over entrance hall
i Harry Reijnders, Rotterdam Blaak, Rotterdam, The Netherlands, 1986–93

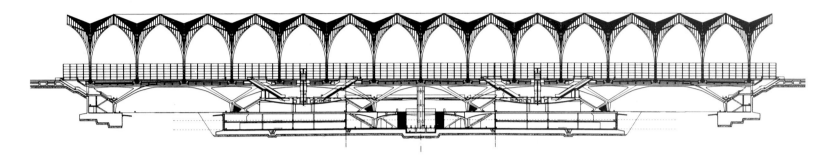

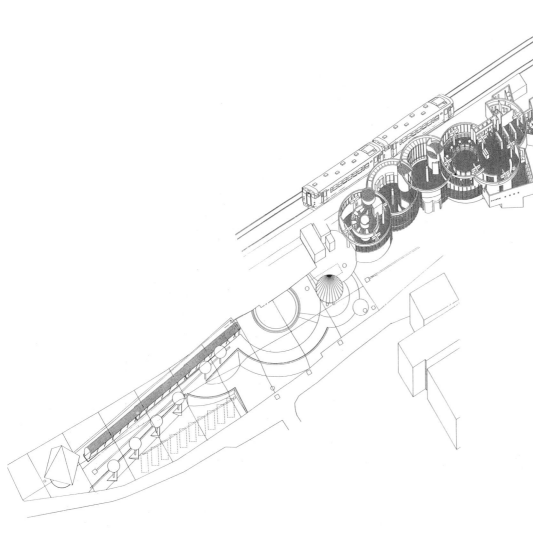

The Netherlands where startling geometrical gestures have mysteriously become the norm: not far away are Piet Blom's famous balancing-cube 'tree houses' (see 'Living'). The station can, then, be regarded as contextual, in a city where – like Tokyo – the only context would appear to be chaotic. Two stations in Japan respond to their differing contexts in this way: Enric Miralles' Takaoka Train Station, 1991–3, where Miralles makes a purely symbolic freestanding facade of twisting metal beams, recalling both tangled rail tracks and the city's looping overhead power lines; and Kuniaki Ito's Hanawa Station, Japan, 1996. Here a small rural halt takes the form of a group of linked conical and pyramidal huts with expressed heavy internal timber structure – the geometry responding to, but not copying, local building forms. Miralles' contribution in particular reminds us that individual architects can make telling contributions to the genre on a small scale, as Herzog and de Meuron did with their copper-banded signal box in Basel, 1989–94 – a veritable Faraday's cage for its occupants and a mystic totem for passing travellers – and Kate Diamond's (of Siegel Diamond) control tower at Los Angeles International Airport, 1993, with its heavily expressive sunshading cowls on angled struts making it a giant semi-organic treehouse. It spins off from the space-age fantasy of the nearby 1958 'Theme Building' – a circular

a c

b d

a Kuniaki Ito, Hunawa Station, Japan, 1996: plan
b Hunawa Station: the group of conical huts respond to local building forms
c Herzog and de Meuron, Signal Box, Basel, Switzerland, 1989–94
d Kate Diamond (Siegel Diamond), Control Tower, Los Angeles International Airport, Los Angeles, 1993

restaurant suspended from slender intersecting arches – by Pereira, Williams and Becket, which was an earlier attempt to glamorize the surroundings of a big airport which became an achingly fashionable rendezvous for the Hollywood set by the late 1990s.

The vernacular-inspired Hanawa station reflected other developments in railway design in Japan. The nation that invented the new generation of fast trains and at first traded on that idea of modernity both in the appearance of the trains and their stations, was the first to investigate a less technology-obsessed image. The Kyushu Railway company's trains of the late 1990s, though technically advanced with their tilt mechanisms, allowing high speeds on corners, were given a colourful snap-on body kit and interior treatment by Eiji Mitooka of Don Design Associates that ameliorated the usual airliner aesthetic. In response, the airlines started doing the same thing. Although the large Dallas-based Braniff International Airways had deployed informal 'non-liveries' designed by the architect Alexander Girard in the 1960s and 1970s, giving its planes bright individual colour schemes and liquorice-allsort interiors, corporatism generally held sway until the moment in 1997 when British Airways, one of the largest in the world, abandoned its stern and rigorously applied blue, white and red corporate livery for a looser, less nationalistic appearance. In

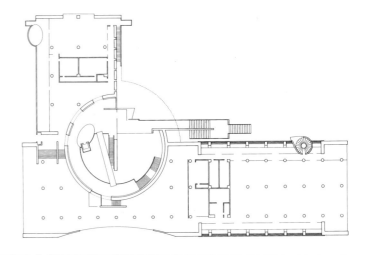

particular the tailplanes – usually given over to some kind of flag, monogram – or both in the case of BA, were turned over to spray-painted reproductions of contemporary artworks from around the world. Some saw this as a fatal move away from the one thing that distinguished the airline – its stiff-upper-lip Britishness. But for both the Sonic trains of the Kyushu Railway and the 747s of BA, the change was a fresh attempt to make a visual impact in the marketplace.

Other, long neglected, means of transport had begun to revive. New technology in shipping seemed for a long time to be confined to freight carriers: the return of profitability to passenger shipping began to change that. Alsop and Störmer's Hamburg Ferry Terminal derived from a competition win in

1987-8 for a crustacean-like building the practice called the 'shipfish'. As built, it transmogrified into an office building with the passenger-processing element much reduced: however, the new form this took was to extend what was already a long building to 500 metres, in anticipation of a cruise ship terminal being added. The final form was not so much the clichéd one of the ocean liner as the perhaps more valid image of the dockside industrial structure. Thus the building – with a striking nipped-in waist – jetties out at one end on angled struts as if it wished to be a loading gantry.

In Japan, Shin Takamatsu rejected maritime imagery completely with the interlocking geometrical forms of the Nagasaki Ferry Terminal, 1994-5, scoring a notable success with the cham-

fered concrete drum that anchors the composition and brings a superb quality of light washing down into the circular entrance hall. Upstairs in the waiting area – placed in the oval tube forming the sea frontage – a panoramic window is scooped out of the form as one might take a thin slice off a cucumber. This window provides a direct visual link with the shipping movements outside. The complex is rather calmer than the same architect's ferry terminal and museum at Mihonoseki, its waving roof forms pierced by a sharp cone and topped with a shiny egg. This wizard's concoction does however have a semi-mystical origin, since the only reason for its existence is the public interest in the town stirred up by the destructive arrival, in 1992, of a weighty meteorite in what had been a declining fishing village. The fame

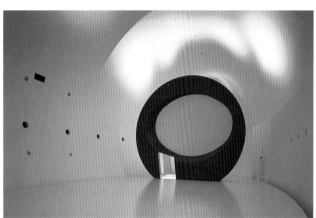
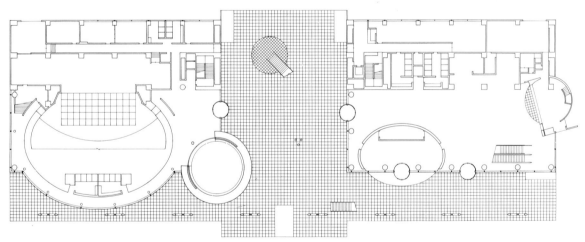

After years of decline, passenger shipping recovered its confidence and invested in new architecture:
a Shin Takamatsu, Nagasaki Port Terminal Building, Nagasaki, Japan, 1994-5: exterior
b Nagasaki Port Terminal Building: interior of entrance hall
c Nagasaki Port Terminal Building: plan
d Shin Takamatsu, Meteor Plaza and Shichiruiko Ferry Terminal, Mihonoseki, Shimane, Japan, 1994-5: the form marks the landing of a meteorite
e Meteor Plaza and Shichiruiko Ferry Terminal: plan
f Meteor Plaza and Shichiruiko Ferry Terminal: interior
g Alsop and Störmer, Hamburg Ferry Terminal, Hamburg, Germany, 1988-92: circulation
h Hamburg Ferry Terminal: exterior

a c
d f
b e h
g

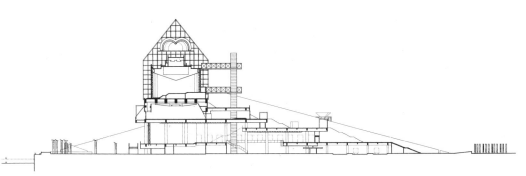

a c
b d | e g
f h

this astral visitation brought ensured the place not only a new ferry building, but also an integral museum (the egg-shaped element) to commemorate the event. Though whimsical, this complex has just a little in common with the strongly geometrical layout of Minoru Takeyama's Tokyo International Port terminal, 1991, with its stumpy cage-like tower of a terminal building acting almost as a navigation beacon.

More straightforwardly pragmatic than any of the foregoing marine buildings was the Sydney Overseas Passenger Terminal, 1983–7, by Lawrence Nield and Partners. This was an attempt to rectify the fact that the city's Sydney Cove Terminal – opened in 1960 to handle both cruise-ship passengers and large numbers of immigrants – had become under-used and under-maintained due to the rise of air

travel. As part of a re-appraisal of Sydney's quay area – Jørn Utzon's Opera House was nearby – the huge building had a third of its bulk removed to make a new public open space, and its remaining portal frame with secondary cantilevers was re-used in the new building, its previously opaque cladding replaced with glazing. From the harbour, this exercise in revealing and transforming an engineered structure of merit resulted in a terraced appearance, anchored at each end by circular tower forms. As so often with such buildings, much of the interest is created at the point where they connect up to ships: the extendible covered walkways sloping down from the building's flanks imply another, portable architectural element that will shortly arrive.

This is always the paradox of the transport

building: that the place where we really want to be is not there at all. Unless we are train, plane or ship-spotting, these buildings are not true destinations, merely points of transit. When the spur to development is the arrival of a new kind of vehicle – as in Manser Associates' series of low-budget ferry terminals linking Great Britain with Ireland, 1990–6, for the world's biggest waterjet ferry – then the vehicle rather than the place is what matters. The one constant and familiar piece of architecture, for instance, to be found at all the world's big airports was designed in 1969 by a team headed by one Joseph F Sutter. Sutter's architecture outlasted many conventional airport buildings, was modified into a number of different forms, and came to enjoy global recognition. It was called the Boeing 747.

a   Minoru Takeyama, Tokyo
    International Passenger
    Terminal, Tokyo, 1988–91:
    exterior view
b   Tokyo International Passenger
    Terminal: interior
c   Tokyo International Passenger
    Terminal: section
d   Tokyo International Passenger
    Terminal: the cage-like tower
    lights up like a beacon

e   Lawrence Nield + Partners,
    Overseas Passenger Terminal,
    Sydney, 1983–7: exterior view
f   Overseas Passenger Terminal:
    entrance canopy
g   Manser Associates,
    Southampton Airport,
    Southampton, England,
    1993–4
h   Manser Associates,
    Ferry Terminal, Holyhead,
    Wales, 1995–6

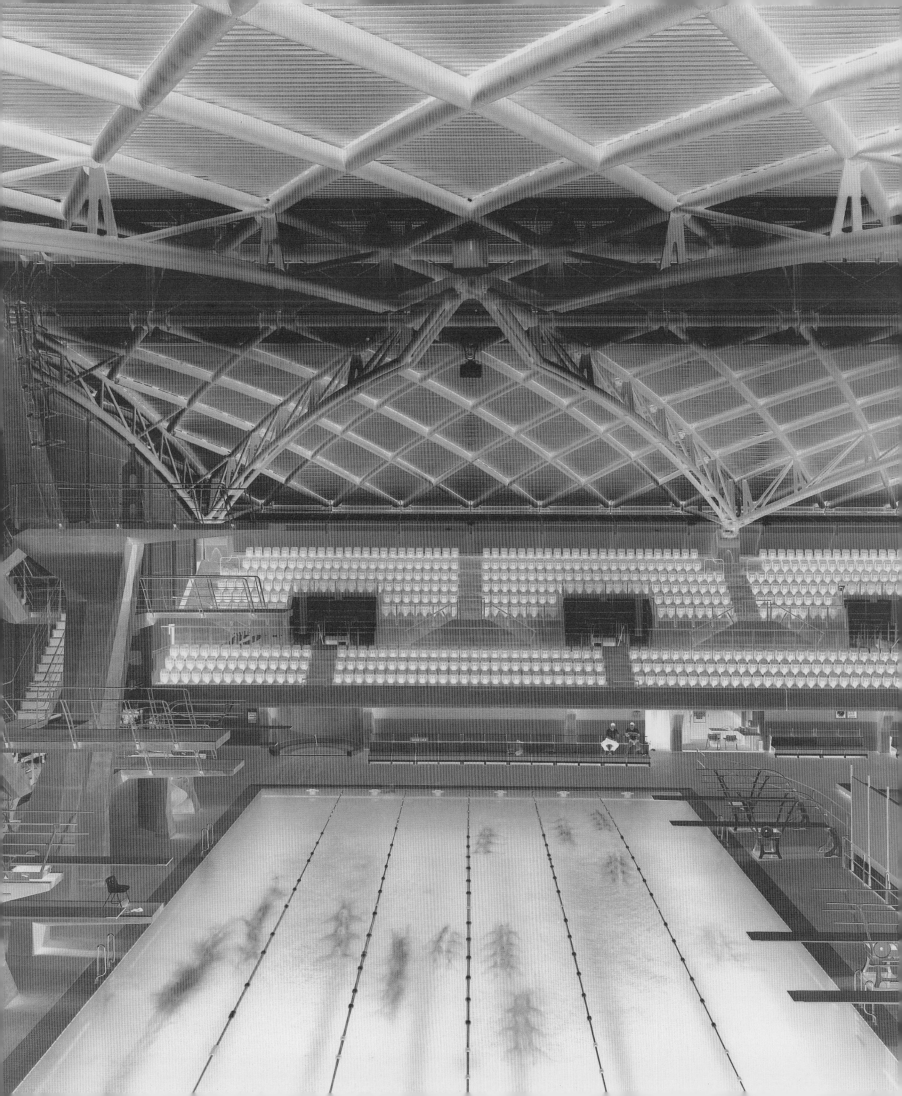

SPORT *Stadia, gymnasia & pools* Art and technology combine in the buildings that house sport, just as they do in the activity itself. From stadia to swimming pools, sports buildings have an aspirational as much as a practical function. In their handling of spectators and participants, they share certain attributes both with the performance buildings of 'high' culture and with those of 'low' culture where sport becomes leisure. But even a humble sports hall can become a building of international status and civic stature when nations chase the honour of hosting the next Olympic Games.

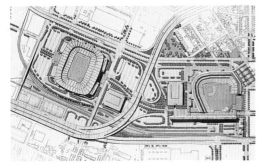

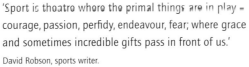

'Sport is theatre where the primal things are in play – courage, passion, perfidy, endeavour, fear; where grace and sometimes incredible gifts pass in front of us.'
David Robson, sports writer.

There is no immense difference between the aims of the Flavian Amphitheatre (better known as the Colosseum) in Rome, built in AD 72–80, and the Sydney rugby football stadium of 1988 by Philip Cox – or its larger contemporary, the San Nicola football and athletics stadium in Bari, Italy, 1987–90, by Renzo Piano. Convincing demonstrations were carried out in 1995 by engineer Chris Wise of Ove Arup that showed the method by which the Romans were capable of achieving retractable mast-supported fabric awnings on their stadia, nearly two millennia before this became commonplace for modern sports arenas. Similarly a Roman plunging into the Baths of Caracalla, AD 212–217, or the later and even larger Baths of Diocletian, would have had no trouble in recognizing the genre of building today known as the 'leisure pool'. Since hotels and inns can also trace their ancestry back to the xenodochium of classical times, then it quickly becomes apparent that the buildings associated with the art of recreation – meaning sport and leisure in their broadest senses – enjoy a more distinguished architectural pedigree than many other building types.

Art and technology combine as much in the buildings that house sport, as in the activity itself. From stadiums to athletics halls, sports buildings have an aspirational as much as a practical function. In their handling of spectators and participants, they share certain attributes both with the buildings of 'high' culture and with those of 'low' culture where sport becomes leisure. But whereas a theme park and a sports complex have common characteristics, only 'pure' sport provides buildings of civic and international stature. Thus, at one end of this spectrum, you have the supposedly lofty ideals of the Olympic movement expressed in buildings ranging from Pier Luigi Nervi's Palazzetto della Sport and Flaminio Stadium in Rome, 1959–60, through Kenzo Tange's Tokyo Olympics buildings of four years later, to the equivalent architecture of Arata Isozaki and others at Barcelona in 1992. At the other end of the spectrum, you find the themed hotels, leisure complexes and fun parks (discussed further in 'Leisure').

While both sports and leisure complexes are greedy for space, the large stadia required by sports buildings present particular difficulties in engaging with the urban grain. To take a typical late twentieth-century example: the Camden Yard Sports Complex in Baltimore, Maryland, USA, by RTKL Associates, completed in 1992, occupies eighty-five acres

International rivalry leads to prestige commissions by the host nation of major sporting events:
a RTKL Associates, Camden Yard Sports Complex, Baltimore, 1992: aerial view
b Camden Yard: site plan
c Kenzo Tange, Tokyo Olympic Gymnasium, Tokyo, 1964
d Renzo Piano Building Workshop, San Nicola Stadium, Bari, Italy, 1987–90: exterior view
e San Nicola Stadium: underside of concrete seating tier and staircase
f San Nicola Stadium: site plan
g San Nicola Stadium: inside the stadium

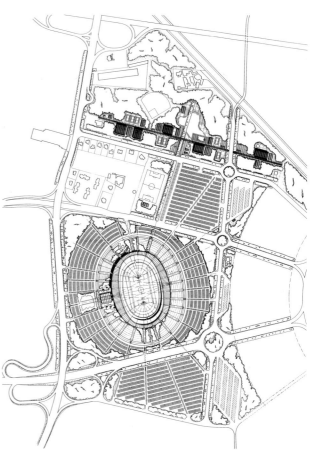

a c e f
b
d

of land downtown, near the Inner Harbour; the site bisected by an urban freeway. The usual two types of American stadium were required: a fan-shaped baseball park and a rectangular football ground (attempts to combine these two utterly different sporting activities at one venue, as at New York's 1964 Shea Stadium, are today usually regarded as unduly compromised projects). The baseball park was closer to the built centre of town and its site included a redundant 1,100-foot-long brick warehouse building. Accordingly the park was given a 'street edge' which consisted of the long warehouse on one side and a new contextual brick frontage on the other (though baseball parks, being an odd shape, never fit easily into any grid plan and usually leave an unresolved corner or two: here, it is where the sharply curving back of the grandstand collides at an angle with the centre of the warehouse facade). The football ground aspect of the masterplan, in contrast, was treated in a much more open manner, sitting amid acres of car parking – though not as much as many such stadia, given the routing of a light rail service past the site.

These two utterly different sports building types, yoked together, have come to define the downtown areas of numerous North American cities. The 'Cleveland Gateway', for instance, 1990–4, gives us the same pairing – covered football stadium by

Ellerbe Becket, open baseball ground by Hellmuth Obata and Kassabaum. This is a tighter composition in that an L-shaped multi-storey parking building mediates between the two, which are thus brought closer together than in Baltimore with its open parking. Here, though the football ground is the usual clamshell, no attempt has been made, as in Baltimore, to screen off the 'dead' end of the baseball stadium. Instead it is left open, facing the main road and a small urban park on the corner. Suddenly the only advantage of this curious sporting building type becomes apparent: passers-by can directly view the massed ranks of ball game fans staring straight back out at them. Very rarely do such large sports buildings give anything to their urban surroundings in this way since all but a few are wholly enclosed.

There are ways round this problem. Renzo Piano's San Nicola soccer stadium at Bari makes an architectural virtue out of the fact that it does not have a built edge of any kind – neither one that engages with an existing urban condition nor one that stands alone like a vast pavilion. The outside edge of the Bari stadium is merely an expression of its structure: the undersides of the concrete shell forms of the upper tiers of seating, free-flying staircases that descend from them, and the fabric roof which is tensioned across lightweight steel framing. Because the floor of the stadium and the lower tier

of seating is excavated, the building seems shallower than it really is, which contributes to its insubstantial appearance. It is, inevitably, in the tradition of the engineer Pier Luigi Nervi's Communal Stadium in Florence, 1930–2, an early expression of pure concrete structure in stadium design, though its quest for drama and beauty make it a very different proposition from, say, the 1989–94 Athletics Stadium in Madrid, Spain, by Cruz and Ortiz, which is an exercise in bare-minimum concrete structure. The tilted plane of the grandstand, its curved rim oversailing the accommodation tucked in below, is unmistakably a Platonic form. The grandstand can hold 12,500 spectators plus a further 8,000 on a lower tier arranged on the earth bank of the sunken stadium. When it was first opened, it had no roof to shelter it from the fierce sun of inland Spain: unlike bullrings, this was a place that is all *sol* and no *sombra*. All the built forms are of *in-situ* concrete, unpainted and unrelieved apart from the bright red splashes of the signage. It comes almost as a disappointment to learn that the structure was engineered to take a canopy at a later date – so uncompromising and effective was its original appearance as a paring-down of the essential forms of the genre. The Madrid Athletics stadium was conceived as the first part of a larger sporting complex intended to bring international events to Spain's

The stadium stripped bare:
a Antonio Cruz + Antonio Ortiz, Madrid Athletics Stadium, Madrid, 1989–94: exit ramp
b Madrid Athletics Stadium: circulation under the grandstand
c Madrid Athletics Stadium: grandstand
d Madrid Athletics Stadium: exterior of grandstand

e Hellmuth Obata + Kassabaum, Cleveland Gateway Baseball Stadium, Cleveland, Ohio, 1990–4: view of stand
f Cleveland Gateway Baseball Stadium: aerial view

capital for the first time – despite its extreme continental climate and smog problem – yet its solitary appearance as the first part of the plan was especially effective. In its simplicity it can be compared with another Spanish building, the Sports Centre in Girona by Esteve Bonell and Josep Gil, which again is an expression of the appropriate form – in this case, the large enclosed clear-span volume – but steering clear of tin-shed functionalism. Bonell (who with his then partner Francesc Ruis designed the well thought-of basketball stadium for the Barcelona Olympics of 1992) takes the stadium trick of sinking the arena into the ground, here cutting the volume of the hall into the sloping site to reduce its apparent volume. Placing a terrace of sloping seating against the south-east elevation also reduces the apparent bulk and gives an otherwise internalized building an eye on the outside world (compare David Morley's Indoor Cricket School at Lord's, London, later in this section). Its flanks are relieved by well-judged openings and canopies for escape stairs. The resulting relatively low building, finished in plain concrete set off with heavily veined local golden stone, is a calm presence in the landscape.

There is always a geometric problem involved with wrapping a building full of spectators around a given shape of games area. At the Colosseum in Rome, the Roman builders overcame

a   c

b   d

      e

Design engineering in the service of large-span enclosure:
a   RAN International Architects and Engineers (Rod Robbie with Michael Allen), Skydome, Toronto, 1989: Toronto skyline
b   Skydome: the roof retracts in sections
c   Lobb Partnership, McAlpine Stadium, Huddersfield, Yorkshire, England, 1993–5

d   Hellmuth, Obata + Kassabaum, Hong Kong Stadium, Hong Kong, 1991–5: underneath the arched lattice truss of the roof canopy
e   Hong Kong Stadium: aerial view

the problem simply by making the arena a perfect oval, which then dictated the whole plan of the building. But the Colosseum was built for spectacle, not competitive games, and thus has more in common with theatre or the modern-day boxing or wrestling ring. Most sports, however, have a given size and shape of playing area that makes such a beautifully simple solution as the Colosseum impossible. The difficulty with the fan shape of a baseball pitch, for instance, is that there is little point in fully surrounding it with seating as the action is concentrated at the apex of the fan. Thus a rough V-formation of seating is the normal response, though there are exceptions, such as Toronto's 1989 Skydome with its retractable roof of sliding and rotating sections, by architect Rod Robbie and engineer Michael Allen. But for most sports, the playing area is rectangular. Every architect thus faces the same choice: either to generate the shape of the stands and their roofs from the rectangle – which creates curious seating configurations and unsatisfactory sightlines in the corners, not to mention the sometimes desperate aesthetic measures needed to crank a deep cantilevered roof through 90 degrees – or to overlay an oval or circular geometry of seating, which can create 'dead' areas on either side of the rectangle.

The usual continental European solution to the problem – to incorporate an oval athletics track around the rectangular football pitch – has the drawback of distancing spectators from the action on the pitch, particularly at the ends. At England's 1924 Wembley Stadium, for instance – the national stadium that resulted from the Empire Exhibition of that year – some seats were placed so far back that the ball could simply not be seen. For all these reasons, many older football grounds tend to leave the corners open, and merely place four rectilinear stands on each face of the pitch. The resulting voids are then filled – if at all – in *ad hoc* fashion by electronic scoreboards and the like. In European football, the Arsenal Football Club in North London is a classic of this genre, its two flanking stands dating from the 1930s being squeezed onto such a tight site that spectators on the lower tiers sit virtually on the touchline and the style of play is constricted by the lack of run-off. A modern example is the Sir Alfred McAlpine Stadium in Huddersfield, Yorkshire, 1993-5, by the Lobb Partnership, where drama is introduced to an otherwise potentially unexciting layout by means of curving clear-span roofs running longitudinally and supported by grandly gestural arched trusses, one per stand. In such places the contribution of the structural engineer – in this case Stephen Morley, working under Anthony Hunt – becomes aesthetically crucial. A similar and even showier exercise in this vein is the Hong Kong

Stadium by Hellmuth, Obata and Kassabaum, where the arched lattice trusses – one per stand, again, but in this case there are only two covered stands, running each side of the rectangular pitch – describe a higher and wider arc than the Huddersfield example. As a consequence the roofs are much taller, even given the fact that they cover three tiers of seating apiece and the trusses continue their stride well beyond the circumference of the arena before finally making contact with the ground. As at Piano's Bari Stadium, much emphasis is given to expressing the bony concrete structure of the underside of the seating tiers. The siting of the stadium – in a former quarry on a wooded hillside looking across to the city's skyline – does no harm to the image, either. But one curious consequence of the design, with its pleated fabric roofs, is that it looks like – though is not – a potentially complete enclosure for the ground. One half expects the two shells to close together, clam-like, but this feat was not attempted.

Such virtuoso design input is sadly lacking in the biggest of British four-stand grounds, Ibrox Park in Glasgow (architects The Miller Partnership and Gareth Hutchinson). The home of Glasgow Rangers was rebuilt after a crowd-control disaster in the ground in 1971 that killed sixty-six people. It still boasts the frontage of its redbrick 10,000-seat south stand by the football architect Archibald Leitch.

Designed in 1927–9, the ground was then the largest and most lavish in the world but sadly the cumbersome trio of stands that joined it in the 1970s and 1980s do not compare. As built, the gaps between the corners of the four stands were left unresolved, whereas at the Sir Alfred McAlpine ground in Huddersfield this problem was neatly resolved by springing the single curved roof truss of each stand from shared pylons in the corners. The perhaps surprisingly high quality of design devoted to a relatively minor sports venue is explained by the fact that Huddersfield was the first built example of a previously hypothetical generic British stadium design system: one evolved by Lobb, Morley and Hunt with the British Government's Sports Council. This was in response to another football tragedy, the disaster in 1989 at Hillsborough Stadium in Sheffield, in which nearly a hundred spectators died, and which prompted a nationwide rebuilding programme to provide all-seater stadia, removing the danger areas of open terraces. Huddersfield was the first all-new product of that intense period of thinking: crucially, its design was influenced not only by safety criteria but also by the expressed views of spectators as to where they liked to sit, and what they liked to be able to see.

More usually, however, the demand for seats and the need to maximize income at top-ranking clubs meant that the pragmatic four-stands approach

to sports ground design became obsolete at this level: fully enclosed stadia being the best way to get enough customers in (Glasgow Rangers began to fill in the open corners at Ibrox with seating in the 1990s in response to this need). Again, the Colosseum is the high-density precedent. In an amphitheatre measuring only 188 metres long by 156 metres wide, rising to 48.5 metres high at the top ambulatory terrace, crowds estimated at between 50,000 and 70,000 could pack in, mostly seated on benches. A wholly permeable ground-level perimeter of eighty entrance arches, coupled with an advanced complex internal structure providing a separate 'service route' for performers, animals and equipment, meant that these numbers could be handled with remarkable ease and speed. Present-day rules governing the speed of evacuation of stadia in an emergency tend to lead to broadly similar design solutions. However, examination of the Greek Olympic stadium at Athens – the reconstructed survivor of the type used in the original Games – shows that high density is not the sole preserve of the enclosed arena. The Greek model, designed principally for running, is for a U-shaped arena, open at one end, rather than an endless loop, and can seat 50,000.

Tennis is one of only two major sports in the world where spectators are happy to sit all around

a   b   d

c   e

Fitting the shelter to the preferred spectator areas invites contortions. Tennis is in-the-round, other sports are not:
a   The Miller Partnership with Gareth Hutchinson, Ibrox Park, Glasgow, 1990s
b   Building Design Partnership, Number One Court, All England Lawn Tennis Club, Wimbledon, 1992–7: the dished torus roof allows a slot of light in around the perimeter
c   Philip Cox, Sydney Football Stadium, Sydney, 1988: exterior structure
d   Number One Court: grandstand building
e   Sydney Football Stadium: the saddle-shaped roof undulates on either side of the pitch
f   (pages 402–3) Sydney Football Stadium: the interior of the arena

the action rather than generally preferring the two longer sides; another such sport is Australian Rules Football, which plays on an oval pitch. Consequently the All England Lawn Tennis and Croquet Club – better known as Wimbledon after the south-west London suburb where the famous eponymous Grand Slam tennis championship takes place each year – makes an ideal case study of sports stadium design. Each of its two major arenas – Centre Court and Number One Court – takes an opposite approach to the other. Centre Court, seating 13,100, has evolved since 1922 in a number of hands as a rectangular stadium, its geometry originally generated by the shape of the tennis court. Its companion, the 11,000-seat Number One Court, 1992–7, by the Building Design Partnership, is in contrast a circular stadium, partly sunk into the ground to disguise its four-storey height. The seating does not quite follow the same circular geometry as the dished torus roof, instead being divided into wedges such that every seat is precisely angled towards the centre of the net dividing the court. Seating is also brought forward to fill the spaces left between the rectangle and the circle. There is consequently a sense of focus that is often absent in rectangular-format stadia. Moreover the roof, being expressed as a free-sailing element, allows a slot of light in through the perimeter. The result is far less claustrophobic than Centre Court

where seats are packed virtually up into the dark roof rafters at the back of the stands. However it was discovered, at the very first championship to be played there in 1997, that the new Number One Court did not generate quite the same fervent atmosphere as its older sibling. This was partly due to a lower density of people per square metre, but also because of the more open nature of the design. Number One Court is more of an arena, while Centre Court is more of a cockpit. This difference was apparent also to those watching on television, because in the new court it was more difficult to capture the crowd's reaction. This was to some extent intentional – the previous Number One Court had also had a more open character and was itself subservient to the Centre Court where it was always intended that the gladiatorial combat of the finals would continue to be played. But it confirms the instinctive belief that nothing creates atmosphere in the theatre of sport – as in the theatre of performance – more than packing the audience into the space as close as possible to the action.

Shaping a stadium to respond to the need for the shortest possible sight-lines between spectator and action – especially with a rectangular playing area, which means those seated at the back at each end are furthest removed – leads to further problems. Given that in most sports, spectators

would prefer to be seated on the sides rather than the ends, the obvious response is to reduce the tiers of seating at the ends and increase them at the sides. This, however, results in an uneven profile to the stands, particularly if the steepness of the rake is increased at the sides so as to give those right at the back a reasonable view. This matters little when the stands at each side are discrete buildings in the old-fashioned way. But where the stands wrap round the ground uninterrupted, the architectural response is usually to try to warp the usual flat doughnut, curving the sides up and in, and bringing the roof swooping up to meet it. Renzo Piano did this very subtly at his San Nicola football stadium in Bari, Italy, raising the sides gradually towards a modest peak at either side and bringing the metal frames of his (relatively vestigial) fabric canopy up in a smooth curve to mark the transition. In Sydney, Philip Cox chose a more radical solution, swooping his mast-suspended detached roof dizzyingly up and down to create a roofline with a pronounced saddle shape. The Sydney stadium goes to extremes because very little seating is placed at the ends, behind the goals, and by far the greater proportion of it is pushed up at either side. The roof not only undulates but – because of the lesser need for shelter at the ends – also narrows from its maximum width of 30 metres down to 10 metres. Its height at the peak is exaggerated by the

suspension masts, which are absent at the ends. As a diagram of the conflicting geometrical forces inherent in stadium design, it could not be bettered. And as at Bari, the roof is as much an architectural engineering gesture as it is a practical shield from the weather, yet there were complaints that it did not provide sufficient guard against the rain.

A more enclosed version of this 'saddleback' concept was designed by James Burland of Arup Associates – who had worked briefly with Cox – for the new stadium in Manchester, England, originally designed as part of an Olympic bid but intended as a subsidiary national stadium, (project, 1993–8). Burland combined the saddleback principle with an idea encountered in Italy and the United States: rapid and safe exit from the arena via spiral ramps.

This device is employed on Leo Finzi's San Siro Stadium in Milan, and the Joe Robbie stadium in Miami by Hellmuth Obata and Kassabaum, and by Burland himself for Arups' Johannesburg Athletics Stadium. It was also deployed as part of Lobb, Morley and Hunt's British 'stadium for the 1990s' scheme. For the Manchester project, Burland made a repetitive architectural feature of such spiral ramps by placing them all around his oval stadium, curling them around the masts that support the roof.

Another architectural response – to lift the roof so high above the stands that its integrity is entirely unaffected by the unequal disposition of seating below – risks taking the gesturalism inherent in canopy design to impractical extremes. The Stade de France at St Denis, Paris, the French national

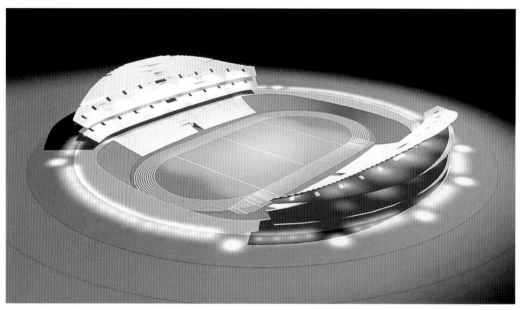

a Hellmuth Obata + Kassabaum, Joe Robbie Stadium, Miami, Florida, 1985–7: interior of the stadium

b Joe Robbie Stadium: spiral exit ramps

c Arup Associates (James Burland), Manchester Stadium, Manchester, 1993–8: computer-generated model

d Manchester Stadium: form continues the 'saddleback' concept of Sydney, with spiral ramps that curl around the roof masts

e Arup Associates, Johannesburg Athletics Stadium, Johannesburg, 1993–5: plan

f Johannesburg Athletics Stadium: canopy detail

g Johannesburg Athletics Stadium: aerial view

h Henri & Bruno Gaudin, Charlety Stadium, Paris, 1991–4: site plan

i Charlety Stadium: exterior

stadium for soccer and rugby, completed for the 1998 soccer World Cup, raises its elliptical disc of a glass roof on eighteen masts, 43 metres up. The architects Macary, Zublena, Regembal and Costantini took the view that sufficient weather protection could be afforded by making the disc very broad, so that it projects as far outside the stadium perimeter as it projects inwards. Thus the need to spring the roof from or near the back of the stands was theoretically obviated. At the time of writing, the Stade de France with its giant Frisbee of a hat has not yet been tested by the public in severe weather conditions: in Sydney, extra weather protection in the form of tensioned fabric vertical spats ¦had to be designed after the stadium had been in use for a while, in order to cope with wind-driven

rain through the slot between roof and stands. There is no doubt, however, that this solution is urbanistically better than the fully enclosed alternative, as demonstrated by a number of North American 'domes' and by Amsterdam's Ajax soccer club stadium outside Amsterdam with its retractable roof, 1990–6 (by architects Rob Schuurman and Sjoerd Soeters with engineers Grabowsky and Poort). Far from trying to sink its bulk into the ground, the Ajax stadium is perched on top of a car park – the 'ground' starting 10 metres up – so making it highly visible for many miles around in the flat landscape. Despite its flaring elevation following the shape of the internal stands, this structure does not read as a sports venue at all: ill-proportioned and sinister, it looks more like an assembly building for giant planes

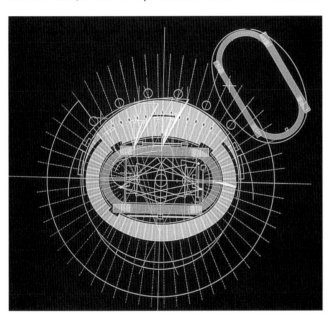

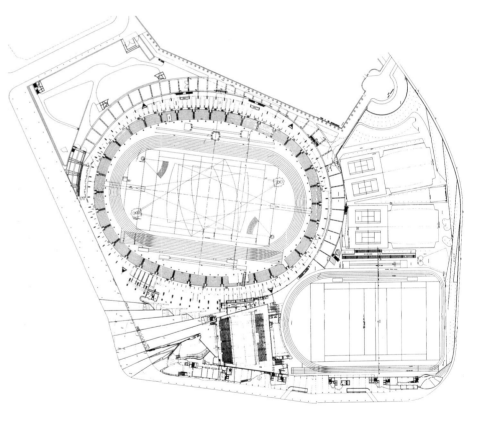

or spaceships. Four external stairways each bear twin pylons from which spring the two main roof trusses. Although the Stade de France can hold twice as many spectators – up to 100,000 – and covers a much greater land area, it is saved by its evident gracefulness. In contrast the lumpen Amsterdam stadium is to become the centrepiece of an American-style 'gateway' development, complete not only with a 600-metre boulevard of offices and shops, but also a theatre, cinema and concert hall. These later buildings may help to redeem this part of south-east Amsterdam and are intended to mitigate the initial raw bulk of the stadium by clustering around it as foothills. However, the relationship is one-sided; unlike the 'Cleveland Gateway' in Ohio, let alone the Bari and Paris stadia, the Ajax stadium itself gives little to its surroundings.

All of these more or less successful theatrical attempts to heighten the drama of the sporting event must be considered in relation to the Munich Olympic Park, completed in 1972, by the architect Günter Behnisch and the engineers Frei Otto and Fritz Leonardt. Otto's cable-net structures defined the 1972 games and resolved the problem of the wall-roof connection by, effectively, doing away with the walls. The draped forms provided a type of facade as well as a roofscape, and proved to be adaptable to many of the key buildings of the

Games. For the stadium, Behnisch and Otto decided to shift the centre of gravity. Instead of an oval with largely equal tiers of seating all round, the seating was shifted up so that most of it was on the southern side. The cable-net roof then wrapped around this taller half of the stadium, leaving the far side in the open. In those days before Teflon-coated fabric or architectural PVC, Otto's solution using plexiglass panels, fixed to the cable net like fish scales, was daring. By the end of the century the great Munich roofs, covering 8.5 hectares in all, were badly in need of repair – even so, they had lasted longer than the designed life of their more commonplace and simpler-to-use fabric successors, and were unexpectedly and nostalgically revived on the German pavilion at Expo '92 in Seville. Meanwhile the notion of the asymmetrical stadium was revisited at the Johannesburg Athletics centre by James Burland of Arup Associates: as well as the undulating ribbon of a Cox-like roof, an additional broad mast-suspended roofing element in scimitar shape was added over the highest and deepest part of the stand. The shape is a pure one, in contrast to the peaks and troughs of Munich, but the intention is broadly the same. Something of the same layered-canopy approach was tried out a few years earlier at the Charlety stadium in Paris by Henri and Bruno Gaudin, and completed in 1994.

The Munich Games were architecturally important as much for what the buildings were not, as for what they were. These were the first Olympic Games to be held in Germany since the notorious 1936 event, where the monumental architecture of Werner March's Berlin stadium as communicated through the lens of Leni Riefenstahl became more associated with Nazi propaganda than sporting prowess. March deserves better publicity, since his design was a relatively advanced steel-frame structure, and in the modern manner, the sports field was sunk into the ground to lessen the stadium's bulk. Moreover, he wanted to give the stadium a modernist carapace of lightweight cladding. However, Hitler disapproved and his architect Albert Speer ordered a stone colonnaded exterior instead, to give it the monumental approach. The Italians feared no ghosts in returning to this classical model for their stadium for the 1960 Olympics (by Annibale Vitellozzi) but Germany had more to be haunted by. Consequently, the Behnisch–Otto design was a clean break with tradition – although they did not invent the idea of 'weighting' the ellipse towards one side: that was a feature of both Tokyo in 1964 and Mexico City in 1968, each of which, like Berlin in 1936, were rebuilds of existing stadia. Nor for that matter was this the first use of such a mast-suspended roof, since Otto had deployed a similar, if smaller, roof on the

a

b

c

a Günter Behnisch, Frei Otto and
   Fritz Leonardt, Munich Olympic
   Park, Munich, Germany,
   1968–72: view of the park
b Macary, Zublena, Regembal
   and Costantini, Stade de
   France, Paris, 1995–7
c Munich Olympic Park:
   the cable-net roof wraps
   around the higher southern
   side of the stadium

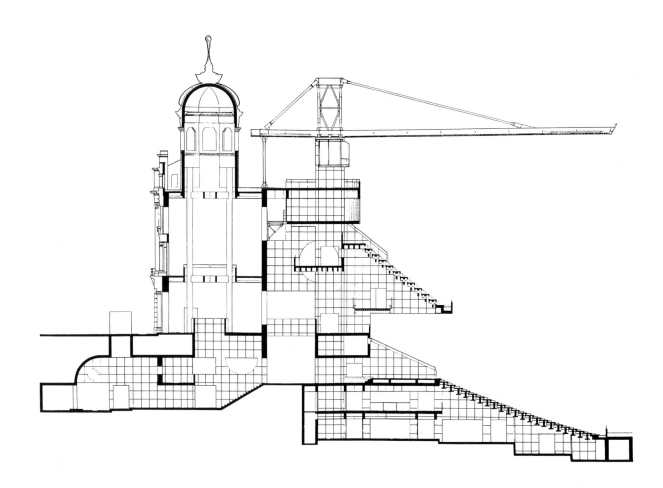

a d | f
       g i
b   h k
c e   j l

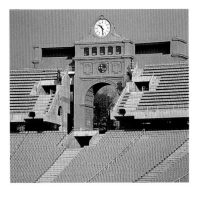

a Gregotti Associati International
   and Partners, Olympic
   Stadium, Barcelona, Spain,
   1983–9: side view of stand
b Olympic Stadium, Barcelona:
   cross section
c Olympic Stadium, Barcelona:
   circulation space
d Olympic Stadium, Barcelona:
   aerial view

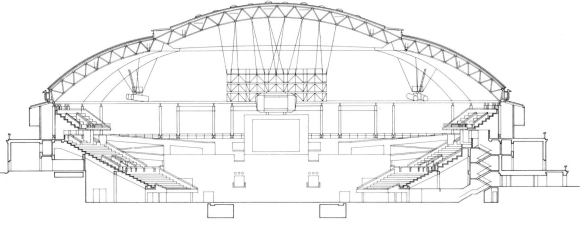

e Olympic Stadium, Barcelona:
   exit from the stands
f Ricardo Bofill, Physical
   Education Centre, Barcelona,
   Spain, 1989–91: gymnasia
g Physical Education Centre:
   the classical facade
h Arata Isozaki & Associates,
   Palau D'Esports San Jorda,
   Barcelona, Spain, 1983–90:
   interior of sports hall

i Palau D'Esports San Jorda:
   section
j Palau D'Esports San Jorda:
   entrance
k Palau D'Esports San Jorda:
   circulation space
l Santiago Calatrava, Olympic
   Flame,Barcelons, Spain, 1992

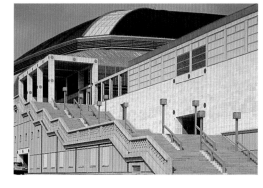

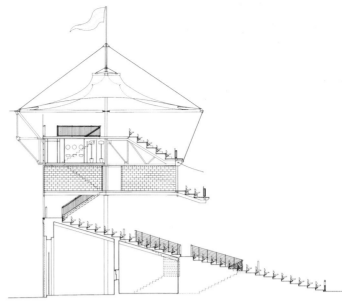

German Pavilion in Expo '67 in Montreal, and this in turn built upon his own experiments from 1955 onwards, and related American projects of the time by Eero Saarinen, Bruce Goff and others. Kenzo Tange's National Gymnasium for the 1964 Tokyo Olympics can also stake a claim, since Tange hung concrete roof panels from cables spiralling from a single offset mast – a larger-scale version of Goff's 1950 Bavinger House. But by bringing all these ideas together into an amoebic cable-net city, such that the undulating landscape of the reclaimed Munich Olympiapark was echoed in the undulations of the roofline, a complete 'organic' entity was formed. Ironically in view of the ghastly Arab–Israeli terrorist incidents that blighted the 1972 games, the Behnisch–Otto Olympic buildings successfully suggested a peaceful competitive environment rather than an arena for nationalist preening. Behnisch was to become a master at such humane architecture in other forms, to the extent that he was the natural choice to design the then West German parliament building in Bonn (see 'Civic Realm').

Perhaps the least expected, and least successful, Olympian successor to Munich, however, was the extraordinary Montreal Olympic stadium of 1976, though completed only in 1988, where a vast leaning tower suspended an oval fabric roof over the entire stadium from a fan of cables. The idea

that the roof could simply be pulled up and away when needed was a very direct homage to another of Otto's projects, the similarly engineered, but considerably smaller, roof covering to the Open Air Theatre at Bad Hersfeld in Germany, 1967–8, where the square roof, hung from a single mast, could be pulled down to cover the roofless ruined abbey that constituted the theatre. However, not only was the Montreal stadium roof not completed until more than a decade after the relevant Games, but it has hardly ever been opened since – unlike Otto's theatre roof. Montreal, in fact, marked the point when the decadent political pastime of striving for international kudos by building ever more spectacular Olympics buildings was shown to be fraught with danger. After Goff, Tange, Otto and Behnisch, it would perhaps have been wise not to try to go one better with the same system.

Stadia are frequently adapted for changing circumstances, as we have seen, and nations can try to cut costs by making use of an existing arena for the Olympics. This is what they did in London in 1948 (with the adaptation of the 1924 Wembley Stadium by its original engineer, Sir Owen Williams) and also in Barcelona in 1992 (the same year Spain also held an international Expo, in Seville). Both events were seen as means to urban regeneration, which was not the way Olympiads had been

regarded, at least up until the public spending fiasco of Montreal '76. For Barcelona, the Montjuic stadium left over from the Barcelona World's Fair of 1929 was pressed into use – though in reality the architect Vittorio Gregotti left only the original facades relatively untouched: everything inside the shell was redesigned. He adopted a simple cantilevered roof for the main grandstand, its proportions reflecting the massing of the 1929 entrance frontage behind. 'Modification has gradually assumed a special importance as the conceptual instrument that presides over the project of architecture,' Gregotti was to write later. 'It might be considered the most continuous and structural element of the changes that have occurred within the theory of architectural design during the past thirty years.' For Gregotti, modification of an existing building helped to preserve a sense of belonging and avoid feelings of displacement – but he also saw it as a chance to take breath during what he described as 'the unbearable supertechnical and superstylistic chatter of recent architectural production'. In addition it happened to suit Barcelona's frugal budget, and was, for all its heaviness, considerably more of an aesthetic success than Ricardo Bofill's nearby Physical Education Centre, a weak classical composition complete with underscaled pedimented portico atop overscaled flights of stairs.

a b   c
              d
              e

              f

The pavilion rather than the stadium:

a Michael Hopkins & Partners, Mound Stand, Lord's Cricket Ground, London, 1984–91: Hopkins' stand curves around with the plinth of the original building

b Mound Stand: cross section

c GAPP Architects & Urban Designers with ACG Architects, Hartleyvale Hockey Stadium, Cape Town, South Africa, 1994–6: elevation

d Hartleyvale Hockey Stadium: view of pitch

e Hartleyvale Hockey Stadium: detail of end of stand

f Hartleyvale Hockey Stadium: section

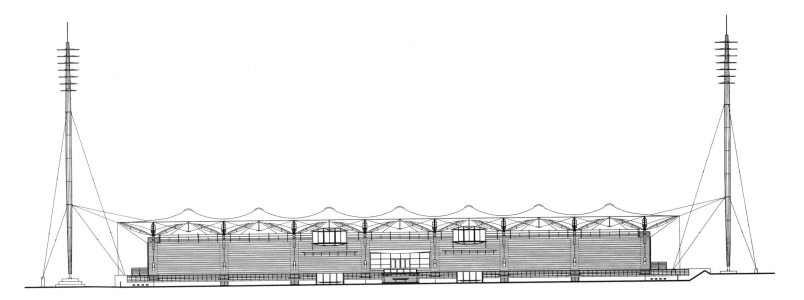

Similarly, in 1986, Vienna's Prater Stadium of 1928–31 – constructed as an open ellipse – was given a compression-tension ring roof, rather like a spoked bicycle wheel, by architects Erich Frantl and Peter Hoffstätter. This project is interesting because the sometimes over-busy roofscape generated by a forest of stubby suspension masts is counterbalanced by the simple expedient of linking the tops of all the masts with a continuous slender ring beam, thereby creating an abstracted cornice. In 1990, Vitellozzi's 1960 Rome stadium was tweaked in almost exactly the same manner by the engineer Massimo Majowiecki, in this case using fabric tensioned over horizontal struts in a manner the ancient Romans would have recognized from the Colosseum.

Gregotti ought, one feels, to approve of one of the iconic British sporting buildings of the 1980s: the Mound Stand at Lord's cricket ground in London by Michael Hopkins, 1984–91. This grandstand serves to fuse Hopkins' apparently paradoxical twin interests in lightweight structures and loadbearing masonry. The starting point was an existing c1890 curved brick wall with seven infilled arches at ground level, retained from the otherwise demolished stand undercroft by Frank Verity, a prolific architect of theatres and cinemas. Hopkins decided to complete an arcade as Verity might have originally intended, using it as a plinth from which to build a stand that became progressively lighter as it rose, culminating in a mast-supported tensioned fabric roof, still following the same curve round one radiused corner of the roughly square 150-year-old playing field. The whole edifice is balanced on a row of only six steel columns which terminate as the masts. The natural tendency of the building to tip forward under the weight of its projecting concrete seating tiers is counterbalanced with tension rods running down the back, pinning the rear of the slabs to the ground. This remarkable leanness of structure, by engineers Ove Arup, is not readily apparent to the casual user, perhaps because of the reassuring presence of that massive ground-level arcade. As a result of this layering, the Mound Stand is one of the few examples of an essentially introverted type to be more visually interesting from the outside than from within. It created something of a 'school' of grandstand design, aesthetically if not necessarily structurally. The Hartleyvale hockey stadium in Cape Town, South Africa (GAPP and ACG Architects, 1994–6) is a clear descendant, with its sequence of tented roofs. Although not set on the curve as Hopkins' stand is, and lacking the earlier building's crown of suspension masts, being instead tensioned from beneath, the stadium is undoubtedly the more dramatic for its context of river and mountains, and was accordingly used as a symbol for South Africa's bid for the 2004 Olympics.

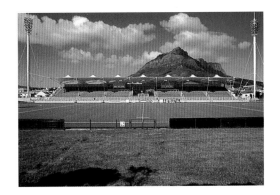

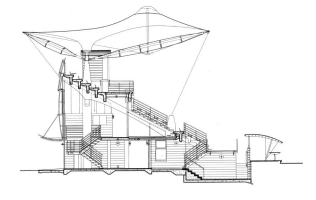

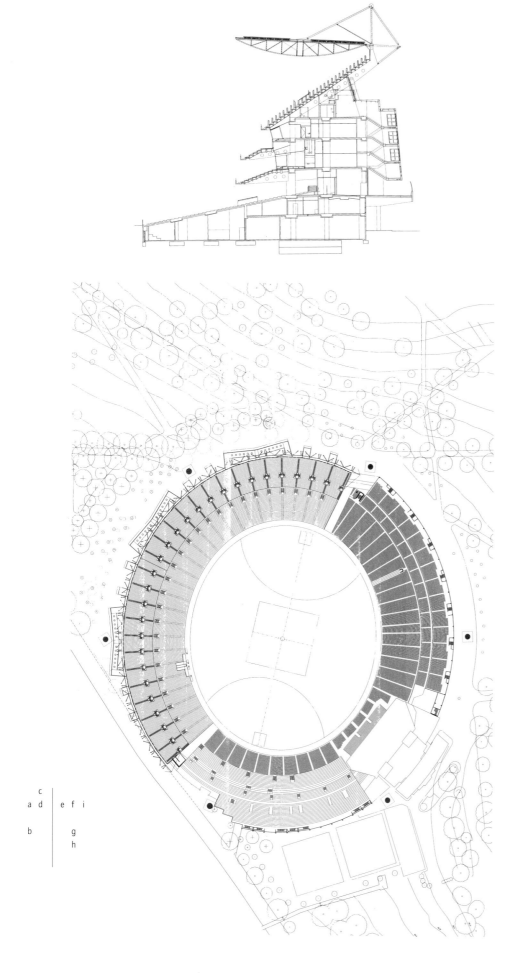

c
a d | e f i

b | g
h

Lord's is famed as the home of MCC
(Marylebone Cricket Club), the ruling body for the
game, one of the most conservative sporting organizations on earth. Despite its occasionally fearsome
reputation, MCC has pursued a policy of enlightened
architectural patronage at Lord's, starting with
Hopkins. The decision was made early on that the
ground should not become a stadium, and that it
should remain a mix of separate stands and pavilions, relatively loosely arranged around the ground
as they had evolved over the years. This was the
assemblage that Sir Nikolaus Pevsner, the architectural historian, primly described in 1950 as 'a jumble
without aspirations, quite unthinkable in a country
like Sweden or Holland'. Being German born and
bred, Pevsner was understandably not attuned to
the village-green basis of cricket, the *ad hoc* tents
and pavilions of which form a folk memory which
pervades the game to the highest level. This is the
case at least in England, India and the Caribbean,
for this is a game that went with much of the old
British Empire. (Australia, another cricketing nation
resulting from that era, has, however, gone over to
stadia for the game, witness Daryl Jackson's great
floodlit bowl of the Melbourne Cricket Ground,
1988–91.) When Lord's began to rebuild, it accordingly invited different architects for different buildings. After Hopkins (who masterplanned the first

phases of the changes) came David Morley with his Indoor Cricket School and English TCCB Cricket Board Offices, 1994–5, and Future Systems (Jan Kaplicky and Amanda Levete) with their aluminium-hulled Media Centre, 1996–8, raised high on columns as the television and press gallery. Then, as if determined to provide a building that would be structurally even more audacious than Hopkins' (visually at least), Nicholas Grimshaw arrived. His contribution (phase 1, 1995–8) replaces the previous 1926 stand by Herbert Baker, and faces the Mound Stand across the greensward. Hopkins' roof was tethered by a series of booms running the width of the building from the six masts. However, Grimshaw's, designed a decade later, has a single, central mast supporting the entire roof via a longitudinal lattice beam. Where the Hopkins imagery was tents and yachts, Grimshaw's is aeronautical: the roof is a wing. One would be interested to hear Pevsner's views today: Lord's is now consciously rather than unconsciously a jumble, and aspiration has not so much crept as marched in.

The individual stand, as opposed to the complete stadium, has life in it yet outside the rarefied atmosphere of cricket. Two of the best examples in recent years are built on the proceeds of horse racing. The stand at the Selangor Turf Club, Sungei

a Daryl Jackson, Melbourne
   Cricket Ground, Melbourne,
   Australia, 1988–91: cross
   section
b Melbourne Cricket Ground:
   site plan
c Melbourne Cricket Ground:
   interior of stadium
d Melbourne Cricket Ground:
   exterior
e David Morley, Indoor Cricket
   School, Lord's Cricket Ground,
   London, 1994–5: exterior

f Indoor Cricket School:
   practice areas
g T R Hamzah & Yeang, Selangor
   Turf Club, Sungei Besi,
   Malaysia, 1989–92
h Nicholas Grimshaw and
   Partners, New Stand, Lord's
   Cricket Ground, London,
   1995–8
i Future Systems, NatWest
   Media Centre, Lord's Cricket
   Ground, London, 1996–8

RE·ADMISSION TO ENCLOSURE
BY WRIST STRAP ONLY
ENCLOSURE   ENCLOSURE
TURNSTILES   TURNSTILES

Besi, Malaysia, by T R Hamzah & Yeang, 1989-92, is topped with a parasol rather than an umbrella: there, the need was to shade spectators from the sun as much as to protect them from the rain. Consequently the roof – notable for its delicate tapering latticed cantilevers – projects rather further forward than the grandstand roofs of more temperate climates. Equally, a greater proportion of its spectator area is climate-controlled behind glass. Ken Yeang's environmental concerns would suggest that the shading roof is a device to reduce the need for the high energy consumption of artificial cooling in the sealed areas.

Racecourse stands owe more to the tradition of the galleried building than to the arena or stadium, since they tend to have to contain rather more ancillary areas for entertainment, betting and so forth, with less of an emphasis merely on providing banks of seating. The numbers of spectators involved are also far smaller. The Queen's Stand at Epsom racecourse, England, completed in 1992 by architect Richard Horden, has a capacity of only 5,000 – far fewer than its equivalents in the world of soccer. Its function, in theatrical terms, is to provide the private boxes for the top end of the market, while the mass seating of football stands represent the cheaper seats in the stalls and circle. The Queen's Stand is thus a vertically stacked building, each level expressed in projecting balconies on three sides,

with a relatively small amount of raked seating at the front. Consequently it does not have the characteristic grandstand feature of a large roof – indeed its only roofs are modest little articulated affairs to shelter spectators on the top two decks. Its exaggeratedly tall twin masts, which fold backwards when necessary, also serve to heighten the atmosphere. The ensemble effect of the wall of faces, the pavilion-like roofscape, and the closeness to the action, is much more akin to a galleried Shakespearian theatre: a sea of groundlings spread out in front of rising vertical tiers of wealthier punters.

Although some stadia are enclosed, or have retractable roofs, particularly in Canada (for climatic reasons) and the United States, the full enclosure of a grassed playing area is fraught with problems; especially with the transmission of natural light to the growing surface. The retractable roof avoids this particular problem by standing open most of the time, as it is only closed during periods of bad weather: its disadvantage is the high cost of a building component that is only used occasionally. Anyhow, it is best suited to a relatively compact playing area such as baseball: over entire multi-use sports stadia it is usually an unaffordable luxury. Air-supported roofs are one cost-effective way of covering stadia – the 1973 Silverdome in Pontiac, USA, has

just such a Teflon-coated glass fibre fabric roof, strengthened by a net of cables (architects and engineers: Howard Needles Tammen and Bergendoff). Higher air pressure within the stadium than outside keeps the roof aloft while the cable net would hold it just clear of spectators in the event of pressure loss. A quarter of a century on, the technology has improved and research is being conducted into stadium roofs made of inflatable cushions of clear ETFE foil with high transmission of natural light. In the meantime, however, the pragmatic state of the art was represented by the Georgia Dome in Atlanta, 1990-2, built for the 1996 Olympics, which contrived a translucent fabric roof supported by a 'tensegrity' rigid cable-supported structure. Three architects were involved – Heery International, Rosser Fabrap International, and Thompson, Ventulett, Stainback Architects and Engineers – and eight other firms of consultants, making it the kind of collaborative effort inherent to such huge sports buildings, particularly when the deadline of an Olympic Games presses. The Georgia dome has a number of rare design details, such as angled five-storey atria at each corner to draw light into the plan, but the roof, as always, is what holds the interest. Where Buckminster Fuller conceived his tensegrity structures as pure domes or spheres, in Atlanta the concept is expanded and an elliptical form is used. The components were

a Richard Horden, Queen's
   Stand, Epsom, 1992:
   the wall of faces is like an
   Elizabethan theatre
b Heery International, Rosser
   Fabrap International and
   Thompson, Ventulett,
   Stainback Architects and
   Engineers, Georgia Dome,
   Atlanta, Georgia, 1990–92:
   the elliptical translucent fabric
   roof is a 'tensegrity' rigid
   cable-supported structure
c Georgia Dome: exterior

b c

a

assembled at ground level, then lifted and finally jacked into place in a manner related to Arata Isozaki's athletics arena for the 1992 Olympics.

Smaller arenas have always been enclosed, for example, gymnastics halls and swimming pool buildings. Here the challenge is to span a relatively large space without columns, using conventional means. Examples are the two circular buildings engineered by Pier Luigi Nervi at the 1960s Rome Olympics: the large Palazzo della Sport (architect Marcello Piacentini) and its baby brother, the Palazzetto della Sport (Annibale Vitelozzi). The big building conceals its ingenuity within, while the Palazzetto is the more successful externally, with its domed concrete-shell roof meeting the ground via thirty-six modernist flying buttresses. The Nervian tradition of the sports building as pure structure was continued by such architects as Norman Foster in his unbuilt Frankfurt Sports Hall project of 1981–6. For Foster, the idiom was appropriate for athletics because of its attempt to combine maximum strength with minimum weight – an almost spiritual goal. The curving form, partially sunk into the ground to reduce its bulk, was later to recur in his American Air Museum at Duxford near Cambridge, England, 1995–7: a demonstration that large clear spans, if using an arched or domed structure, do not necessarily demand a paraphernalia of masts and cables.

However, the goal of structural purity came to be challenged by those who sought a less understated architectural input into such buildings. Of these, the sports buildings of Enric Miralles in Spain are notable. Miralles' contribution to the Barcelona Olympics was confined to the poetics of his sun-shading 'Icaria pergolas' on the central avenue of the Olympic Village and the Olympic Archery Range buildings. Outside of the Olympics, he did rather better. His Huesca Basketball Stadium, 1988–94, and Alicante Eurythmics Centre, 1989–93, are buildings that, though fully expressive of their structure, are conceived, like the pergolas, as metaphorical responses to their settings. At Huesca the arched trusses from which the roof is hung, and the concrete pylons on which they bear, have a redundancy of structure that turns them into sculpture, since the materials make shapes that have little to do with their absolute function. Miralles noted that the area covered by the hall and its ancillary open spaces was roughly equivalent to the area of the wooded hill it abutted. Thus in his mind the roof structure with its masts became influenced by the trees, and the banked earth used as a basis for the seating was a response to the hill. As Sir Denys Lasdun once observed, every architect needs his own personal myth. Beneath all the slightly frenzied external activity is an entirely conventional basketball court with rational tiers of seating. Pulling

A frantic search for new forms to enclose old uses, these Spanish sport buildings nonetheless helped to re-invigorate the genre:
a Enric Miralles and Carme Pinós, National Training Centre for Rhythmic Gymnastics, Spain, Valencia, 1989–93
b Enric Miralles and Carme Pinós, Icaria Pergolas, Olympic Village, Vall d'Hebron, Barcelona, 1989–92
c National Training Centre for Rhythmic Gymnastics: section
d Enric Miralles and Carme Pinós, Olympic Archery Range, Olympic Village, Vall d'Hebron, Barcelona, 1989–92: plan and elevation
e Enric Miralles, Augustin Obriol, Carme Pinós and Robert Brufau, Huesca Basketball Sports Hall, Huesca, Spain, 1988–94: site plan
f Olympic Archery Range: competition building
g Olympic Archery Range: sunshading
h Huesca Basketball Sports Hall: exterior

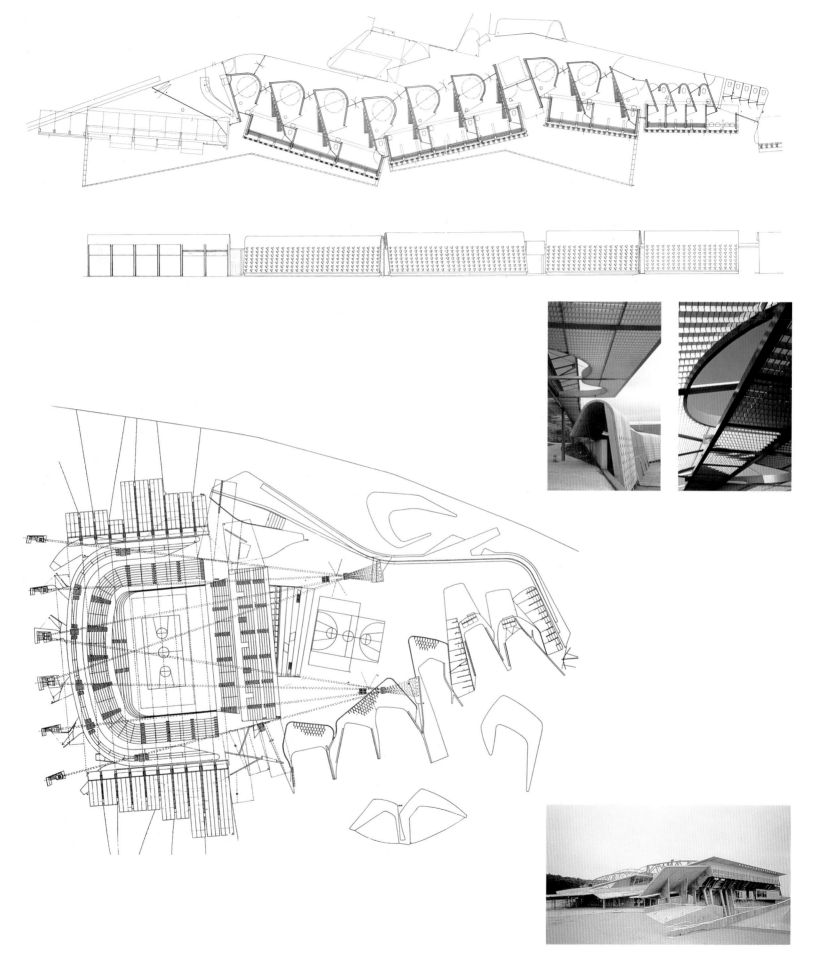

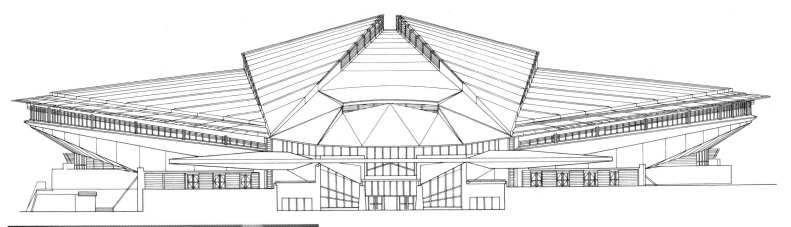

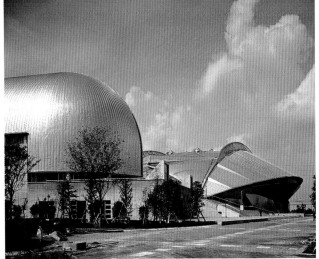

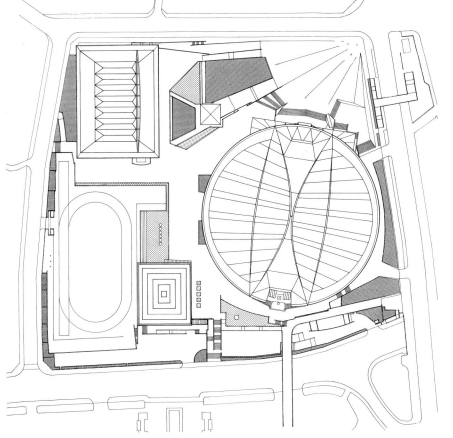

a
b
c   d
      e   f g

out the varying volumes of the changing rooms as 'fingers' protruding unevenly beyond the main building envelope is a curiously endearing gesture. Miralles' spidery drawings can at times appear to be produced by a stream of consciousness, and indeed, for him buildings exist as much through process as through final product.

Following hard on the heels of Huesca came the Eurythmics Centre at Alicante. Again, a mass of activity around and above the building leaves a calm, clear space at its heart. The broken entrance facade with its approach ramps are to Miralles like a sprawled human body, heavy with religious imagery. Yet inside are found wholly witty touches such as his unequally tilted tripartite columns with their little feet, perfectly evocative of rhythmic gymnasts struggling to maintain a pose. The extraordinary railway-bridge aesthetic of the roof structure – as at Huesca, both mast-suspension and arched trusses are employed – coupled with devices such as raking columns to support the exposed underside of a tier of seating, suggests that Miralles sees engineering structures in what an engineer would see as an impure way – as decorative devices, here echoing in their undulations the form of the mountain ranges in the middle distance.

A contemporary modernist architect such as Stephen Hodder used just one unifying engineering motif at his swimming pool building at Colne, England, 1990–1: a deliberately unbalanced structure of overlapping shells is tethered to a single external anchor like a line of mountaineers leaning backwards on a rope, engineered by Stephen Morley of Anthony Hunt. On a larger scale, but with a similar aim in mind, Graeme Law's Netball Centre in Victoria, Australia, 1995, tethers each of its overlapping roof shells separately and sets them at 45 degrees to the grid of the four courts beneath. In both cases the gaps between the overlaps, made by the depth of the steel roof trusses, are used as clerestories to bring natural light into what would otherwise be large unrelieved spaces beneath – and a bit of syncopation is provided by means of one of the masts and tapering trusses being placed in reverse to the others. Hodder later developed the engineering principle of structural 'beaks', with engineers Whitby and Bird, for the unifying roof element of his larger and more sophisticated Clissold swimming and leisure centre in London's Stoke Newington, 1996–9 – the 'beaks' once more being employed as a daylighting device as well as a solution to the eternal big-roof problem. In contrast to such relatively restrained one-principle structural measures, at Alicante Miralles was happy with a riotous confusion of engineering methods, each working individually. Meanwhile in the Canberra suburbs,

Daryl Jackson and Alastair Swayn stole a trick from superstore design by treating the Tuggeranong pool building, 1989–94, more as a neutral box, instead opting to concentrate attention on the facade. This 'head' of the usual pool ancillary functions is indicated by a skewed and pointed freestanding canopy somewhat reminiscent of Zaha Hadid's famous private fire station at the Vitra headquarters in Germany. Here the grid is displaced in characteristic 1990s style: a hallmark as associated with the era as Art Deco was to the 1930s.

The 'both-and' rather than 'either-or' ideology evident in Miralles' work is nonetheless one demonstration of the plurality of approaches in the broad church known as modernism at the end of the century. Standing midway between these two extremes is the work of an architect such as Fumihiko Maki, whose Fujisawa Gymnasium, 1984–6, is more in the sculptural tradition of Kenzo Tange's 1964 Olympic buildings. At Fujisawa, Maki produced a complex of buildings sheathed in forms that recall samurai armour or astronautical equipment, depending on your point of view. Using a relatively pure structural system to create the clear-span spaces within, Maki nonetheless created very strong external forms, using his then favoured cladding material of ultra-thin stainless steel sheeting. Anything but recessive in the Fosterian sense, certainly not wildly exuberant in the

Where the spaces are given, the roof form becomes all-important:

a Fumihiko Maki, Tokyo Metropolitan Gymnasium, Tokyo, Japan, 1990: elevation

b Fumihiko Maki, Fujisawa Municipal Gymnasium, Fujisawa, 1984–6: the sheathed forms recall samurai armour

c Fujisawa Municipal Gymnasium: interior

d Tokyo Metropolitan Gymnasium: site plan

e Tokyo Metropolitan Gymnasium: exterior

f Hodder Associates, Swimming Pool, Colne, England, 1990–1

g Hodder Associates, Clissold Leisure Centre, London, 1996–9

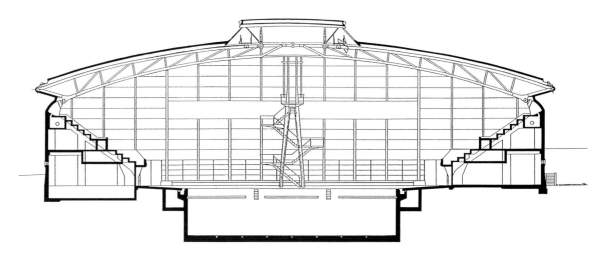

Miralles sense, the Fujisawa Gymnasium is what Maki calls 'a more subtle relationship between structure and expression, a search for the power that details within abstract figures seem to suggest.' He repeated the trick with the Tokyo Metropolitan Gymnasium of 1990, where the same imagery recurs in the arena building with its characteristic folded metal roof. Elsewhere on the site, the swimming pool was expressed as a rectangular box and a smaller arena in the form of a ziggurat. But the main building is interesting because of its clearly anthropomorphic and biological nature. Even more than at Fujisawa, it has a 'face' with clearly defined eyes, nose and mouth. The purpose of such a building demands an axial organization, but on these large legible spaces Maki overlaid the Japanese principles of 'mujokan', defined as a pattern of discontinuous and deflected movement inspired by notions of mutability. Maki's imagery is multivalent, but one is still tempted to conclude that no other architect but a Japanese one could produce such a place. However, one would be wrong, for a very similar, if slightly less complex, response is apparent in Niels Torp's Hamar Olympic Hall in Lillehammer, Norway, built in 1992 for the 1995 Winter Olympics. Torp's hooped helmet-like structure is given an overlapping jointed carapace like a trilobite or armadillo, its backbone descending to

a point at ground level. In the case of both Maki and Torp, then, it is the expression of the roof as shaped by the dynamics of the underlying long-span structure that has led to such an unexpected similarity between two sports buildings at opposite sides of the world.

The swimming pool building has generally not received as much design attention as other sports or leisure types, for two reasons. Firstly, the capital cost of providing pools with their water filtration, sterilizing, heating and ventilation systems is very high and tends to eat into the budget for the building envelope, particularly since so many of them are public-sector financed. Secondly, the evolution of the 'fun pool' means that interiors – and often exteriors – are frequently dominated by the specialist manufacturers of water slides, wave effects, flume rides and such like. So, to return to the analogy made at the start of this section, if 'conventional' rectangular pools for exercise fall into the Olympian camp, then the fun pools partake of the theme park ethos. It is quite difficult to indulge in any serious swimming at a fun pool: contrariwise, larking about at the sports-and-fitness-oriented variety is frowned upon. Architects of pools tend to be specialist firms, some good; Britain's Faulkner Browns consultancy has produced pool buildings of merit ranging from the 'serious' and

structurally impressive Pond's Forge International Sports Centre in Sheffield, 1991 – designed for the Commonwealth Games - to the 'fun' pool-and-ice-rink complex of the Dome leisure centre in nearby Doncaster, unexpectedly powered by coal from the local pits but also using heat-transfer technology between cold ice and warm water. Pond's Forge was an example of a former industrial site reclaimed by the leisure industry, and can be directly compared with Richard Dattner's Asphalt Green Aqua Center, 1990–3, on New York's Upper East Side - part of a sports complex made out of a former riverside asphalt plant that still includes a parabolic arched industrial structure by Ely Jacques Kahn and Robert Jacobs, 1942. Internally, Dattner's 50-metre pool, the first of its size in New York, is conventional enough, and structurally could be regarded as a lean-to version of the pin-jointed arch of the Pond's Forge building. Outside, however, it is of interest since the pool volume is treated as the long side - parallel with the East River - of a triangular mass that rises to a five-storey brick administrative and fitness centre at its apex. One corner of the pool breaks through the plan, and so the wall curves to accommodate it - a device repeated for its own sake elsewhere in the building, combined with ribbon windows, to give it something of a Moderne feel. More importantly, pushing up

a

d

b   c

a   Faulkner Browns, Pond's Forge International Sports Centre, Sheffield, England, 1991: section

b   Niels Torp, Hamar Olympic Hall, Lillehammer, Norway, 1992

c   Richard Dattner, Asphalt Green Aqua Centre, New York, 1990–3

d   Pond's Forge International Sports Centre: diving boards

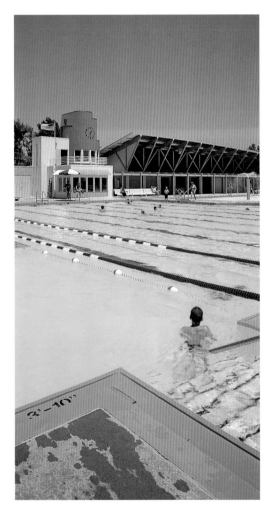

the bulk to one corner overcomes one of the perennial problems of this building type: that they are usually low-lying warehouse-like structures which do not necessarily achieve the necessary urban presence. Another method is successfully tried by architects Shaughnessy Fickel and Scott for their Maryville Aquatic Center in Missouri, 1993–5, where the pool is outside but a big roof, as if lifted at one corner, defines the changing rooms and restaurant alongside. The roof rises to a freestanding clock tower like a ship's bridge which houses the complex's offices.

Occasionally non-specialized 'name' architects such as Britain's Stephen Hodder win competitions and break into this aqueous market, but as with all such specialisms (shopping centres and hospitals are typical examples) technical experience is generally prized above architectonic ability – except when an international sporting event is looming. The exceptions usually have to find ingenious means, as Daryl Jackson does, to escape from the cheap-shed image of the standard portal-frame pool building. Alsop and Lyall's 'Splash' pool, completed 1988, at the seaside resort of Sheringham in Norfolk, England, is an example of an architect – then with little built and lacking the international reputation Alsop was later to acquire – thinking of ways to reconcile architecture with a rock-bottom budget for a local client

(Alsop lived in the town). They devised a throwback timber structural system, using the material in both latticed and laminated forms. This, coupled with a patented colour-stained plywood external cladding system and some unusual details such as massively oversized rainwater spouts and hoppers, resulted in a building that was jolly without being kitsch and is the nearest Alsop got to the 'PoMo' style.

The high-tech style is more usual when it comes to throwing a roof over a number of disparate elements. As a unifying device, it works pretty well at the pool complex at Kolding in Denmark by Nøhr and Sigsgaard, 1994–8, where the big wavy roof serves to pull together old and new buildings alike (this is much the same thinking as Richard Rogers' proposed enclosure for London's South Bank Centre arts ghetto – see 'Civic Realm'). As usual, the architecture at Kolding is compromised by the worm-like form of the flume ride, an imported piece of equipment that architects of sensibility always dread. More effective in its way, however, is the underground swimming baths in Helsinki by Hyvämäki-Karhunen-Parkkinen, 1993, where a curving entrance canopy leads you into a cavern hollowed out of a granite mountainside, occupied by a slightly festive swimming pool. This is Finnish pragmatism: such caverns were made as nuclear shelters at the height of the Cold War, and were so costly to excavate that

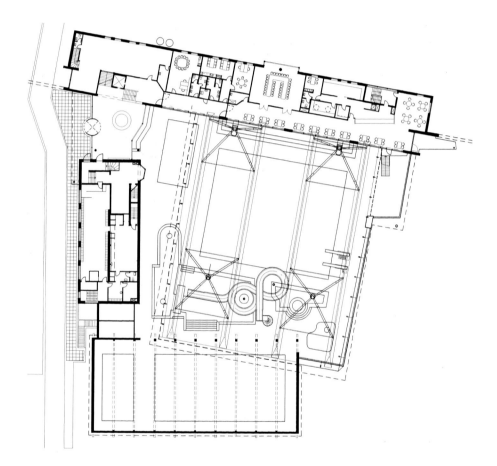

alternative continuous uses such as this were found for them. The Finns, living in a cold watery country, developed an almost Roman delight in warm communal bathing, and thus produced above-ground pool buildings of equal quality, such as Helin and Siitonen's baths at Forssa in the south-west of the country, 1988–93, or – in mildly deconstructivist mode – the equivalent in Siilinjärvi by Esa Laaksonen of the same period. Whereas in many nations such pools are placed on the edges of town, in Finland they are more usually treated as town-centre object buildings because of their important social function.

The pool complex is a building form undergoing mutation into something altogether more sybaritic. For instance the traditional Japanese bath house – by no means merely a place for washing even at its most historic – lends itself to becoming, like the Scandinavian sauna, a place associated with indulgence, even of the most innocent kind. The twin late twentieth-century obsessions of the moneyed classes are fitness and spending – hence a project such as the 'Video Sento', 1996 onwards, by Klein Dytham Architects of Tokyo – a 'sento' being the traditional name for a bath house. The proposal, at the time of writing, is for the complex – in fashionable pod-on-stilts style – to house a health club and café as well as the baths. A twist is added by the proposal to build mirror-image buildings, on either side of a road:

one for women, one for men. The sliced off end walls of each building would then form video walls (another late twentieth-century architectural fad). It is a relief to turn from such metropolitan 'lifestyle' buildings to something as severely well-made as Peter Zumthor's Thermal Baths at Vals in Switzerland, 1989–97. This is a complex arranged around the hot springs found high in the Alps, and is as much an act of landscaping as of architecture – or perhaps, in the light of some of Zumthor's other projects, a piece of ready-made archaeology. The key is that sort of austerity, favoured by some of the wealthier members of society, where there are no superflous details, no glitz, no obvious comfort signals in the riven-gneiss and concrete public spaces, but warmer and costly materials where they count: the changing rooms are lined in polished red mahogany and have curtains of soft black leather, doors and other fittings are of bronze. The indoor sequence of watery rooms achieves its effects through the masterly handling of light and space. Cave-like but lit with shafts of light from above, they are very like the rediscovered Roman baths of earlier times, set as they are well below modern-day ground level. Zumthor manages to replicate that sense of mystery and sensuality, even of history, in a modern building that could be described as austere.

a   d   f

b

c

     e   g

From the sublime to the ubiquitous.

It is odd that the commonest sporting meeting-place of the affluent Western world – the golf clubhouse – should not have received better treatment from its custodians. One wonders if there is something in the game itself that is innately philistine. It is a curious omission, considering that boating and yachting clubhouses have a distinguished history of fine design from the early modernist era to late twentieth-century exercises such as Ian Ritchie's London Docklands Sailing Centre, 1996–9; Marks and Barfield's Liverpool Watersports Centre, 1992–5; Mario Botta's Water Sports Centre on the shores of Lake Maggiore in Switzerland, 1990–3; and Lindsay Clare of Clare Design's Ski 'n' Skurf Centre, Bli-Bli, Queensland, Australia, 1994. Going against the trend, a rare piece of good *fin-de-siècle* golf architecture is Sheila O'Donnell and John Tuomey's Blackwood Golf Club, 1992–4, at Clandeboye near Bangor in Northern Ireland, which is a highly sophisticated 'constructed landscape'. Each element in the composition of the buildings receives a different architectural treatment in timber, rendered masonry and metal, with the complex as a whole treated as a village. As a sensitive response to building in a contemporary vein in the rural landscape, it compares with such Scandinavian

examples as Lund Hagem's deceptively simple ski-slope cabin at Kvitfjell in Norway, 1990–3: both were initially contentious in planning terms.

Any building, in any discipline, stands an equal chance of achieving greatness, in theory at least. The odds, however, are conventionally more in favour of cultural buildings with their large budgets and prestige associations, than they are with a humble sports hall. This, however, is a situation that shows signs of changing. In the late twentieth century it is notable that stadia in particular – like bridges – have become the focus of attention by the best architects instead of the journeyman trade specialists. Sport has become glamorous enough to be considered cultural, and it is part of the health and fashion industries. Sport can transcend class and, often, wealth differences. Sport is primarily a television medium, thus must be well dressed. It has also become, like world Expos, a spur to urban regeneration – hence the keen competition to host the Olympics for economic, as well as image, reasons. Those economists who note the beneficial spin-off of a new concert hall also note the financial leverage of a significant sporting venue (and as a sideline the desirability of a healthy population and fully-occupied youth). Therefore some cities go all out for art, and some for sport: excellence and crowd-pulling capability being the aim in both cases.

Governments are more popular when their national teams are winning: so encouraging sport is politically expedient. Sport, now, is no longer cold and faintly disreputable. This is why an architect such as Rafael Viñoly – Uruguayan-born, American-based, called upon to build internationally – was given a free hand to design something as modest as a student gym for Lehman College in New York's Bronx, 1989–94. Modest? This gym cost $40 million. It is 608 feet long and occupies a prime site on the campus, marking the edge between town and college and so also forming a portal gate to the college. Viñoly noted that a fine gym was now as much of a reason to choose one college over another as a fine library, and he himself persuaded the academic authorities not to tuck the building away in the usual corner. The college realized that the building could be used by the public as well as by students, which was good both for income and public relations. The resulting long, low building with its tough concrete masonry wall facing the Bronx and its mill-finished stainless-steel roof curving down to the college campus behind like a great aerofoil section, is a built expression of the new-found acceptability of sport architecture. As with the wonderful library or gallery, you don't even have to go in. But you feel good, knowing that it exists. It has an equal cultural value.

a Marks and Barfield Architects Ltd, Liverpool Watersports Activities Centre, Liverpool, England, 1992–5
b O'Donnell + Tuomey, Blackwood Golf Centre, Bangor, Northern Ireland, 1992–4: interior
c Blackwood Golf Centre: entrance approach
d Clare Design, Ski 'n' Skurf Centre, Bli Bli, Queensland, Australia, 1994
e Helin & Siitonen, Forssa Swimming Hall, Forssa, Finland, 1988–93
f Rafael Viñoly, Lehman College Physical Education Facility, New York, 1991–4: sport as gateway to the campus – no longer concealed but glorified
g Lehman College PE Facility: basketball hall

THE CIVIC REALM *Public space & structures* The State has always expressed its power, influence and benevolence through its public buildings – government offices, city halls, law courts, embassies and hospitals. The civic realm, however, is as much to do with public space and the way it is perceived and manipulated, by privately funded agencies as well as public organizations. From large-scale masterplans for new towns and inner-city regeneration to sculptural landmark bridges or small pedestrian ones, this is a most important factor in the revitalization of many declining urban centres.

'The building should not assume power,
but deserve it.'
Ada Karmi-Melamed, architect of the
Supreme Court Building, Jerusalem

The State has always expressed its power and
influence through its buildings – palaces, government
offices, city halls, law courts, embassies, cultural
pavilions, prisons, even hospitals. The civic realm is,
however, to do with more than buildings, and more
than the State: it is also concerned with the connections between buildings and places – the streets,
squares, parks, roads and bridges that make up
public open space, and their equivalents in privately-
financed developments, from shopping malls and
business parks to certain city-centre atria. These, the
places in between, became the focus of attention
from the 1970s onwards and became associated with
two key words: 'urbanism' and 'masterplanning'.

The difference between these terms is mostly,
though not entirely, semantic. 'Masterplanning' is
an American term while 'urbanism' emanates from
Europe, most notably from France. Consequently,
given the power of the private sector in America, and
the power of the centralized state in France, the
former is more often applied to large-scale commercial developments, the latter more to public-sector
projects. However, there is another difference.

'Masterplanning' usually concerns real-life, fee-paying
projects (some famous architectural offices make
most of their money this way, and start to lose that
money when they are obliged to design and super-
vise the construction of actual buildings), while
'urbanism' is quite likely an academic, theoretical
exercise. There is however considerable overlap
between the genres.

The architect David Chipperfield wrote a
straightforward enough description of masterplanning, apropos his Aalemann Kanal housing block in
Berlin, 1994–97:
'The project began with a series of master-planning
workshops organized by the developer. Eight architects participated and developed a strategy for
twenty-four individual commissions. The master-plan
provided clear volumetric limitations for each block,
and tight space and cost requirements that made
efficient planning necessary. Each block faces an
access street on one side and a landscaped garden
on the other. Car parking is separated from the main
residential area in a similar way to the urban designs
conceived for New Towns, with circulation intended to
be primarily pedestrian.'

Such a description is admirably clear and
pragmatic, and indeed makes a useful distinction
between the masterplan and ordinary old 'efficient
planning'. The first establishes the parameters

common to all the architects taking part, the second
is what each individual architect must engage with
in detail. Urbanism, on the other hand, would appear
to be a far more intellectual and aesthetic exercise,
moreover one in which the cost element – identified
by Chipperfield as being an important aspect of
masterplanning – need not necessarily be present. A
final clue: while large urban developments, from the
1980s onwards, increasingly named an architect as
'masterplanner' – who determined the overall disposition of the development, probably contributed one
building, but invited in a roster of other architects to
do all the rest – this person was never given the title
of 'urbanist'. Urbanism can thus be seen as more of
a state of mind – a way of thinking about the city –
while masterplanning is a transitive, dirty-hands
exercise that comes into the architect's scheme of
work. Urbanism can be seen in the work of the
Luxembourg-born Krier brothers, Rob and Leon, who
seem happy to design their pre-industrial utopias
as independent exercises in idealism; masterplanning
in Cooper, Eckstut Associates' Battery Park City,
1983–90, a commercial quarter in New York.

The Kriers differ: Leon has a stronger classicist bias than his sibling, who is more concerned with
the bones of city making, the relation of public to
private space. But occasionally they are invited into
the real world by real clients, and when that happens

a Cesar Pelli, World Financial
   Center, New York, 1980–1:
   the towers combine with a
   sophisticated ground-level
   public realm
b World Financial Center:
   there is a considered approach
   to external and public space at
   street level
c World Financial Center:
   the Winter Garden forms
   the public space between
   the towers

a

b

c f

d e

Masterplanning burgeoned in importance alongside one-off public commissions:
a Studio Granda, Reykjavik Town Hall, Reykjavik, Iceland, 1987–92: interior of council chamber
b Reykjavik Town Hall: the civic approach
c Moore Ruble Yudell, Playa Vista Master Plan, Los Angeles, California, 1987–: masterplan of area

d Leon Krier, Poundbury Master Plan, Dorset, England, 1989–: the town itself has developed relatively quickly
e Poundbury Master Plan: rendered aerial perspective
f Playa Vista Master Plan: perspective of proposed buildings

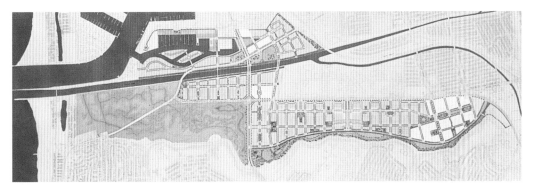

the boundaries between urbanism, architecture and masterplanning blur almost totally. Leon Krier's Atlantis project for a new town in Tenerife, 1987–8, was designed down to the very last detail of each individual building and its intended use, lacking only technical drawings in order to get started on site. There was a real client, too, committed to building a settlement that would provide a 'model for the art of living'. Inevitably financial difficulties meant that it was never built. Indeed Leon Krier never got to build very much at all, unlike Rob with his Berlin housing masterplans (Ritterstrasse, 1982–, Rauchstrasse, 1982–4) and individual homes. Leon Krier's remarks on this are ambivalent. In 1992 he wrote:
'I have in twenty-five years made over 10,000 architectural drawings and with all that achieved the building of a small house for myself, three podiums for Rob's sculptures and have received planning permission for a small town ... The weight of paper used in my publications and drawings probably exceeds that of my building materials. The kerosene consumed travel-feeding this paper tiger is probably enough to set on fire all the buildings I will ever be able to dislike. In short, a life of waste and failure, a modern life.'

The small town was Poundbury, outside Dorchester in Dorset, England, 1989–, parts of which have been built by others. Yet in his plans for Poundbury Krier established a pattern for a mixed-use development, a town of linked individual neighbourhoods, that showed a clear understanding of how to reduce car-dependence and reduce the pressure on existing overloaded town centres. Moreover this was a genuine masterplan, in that the architecture of individual buildings was always intended to be carried out by many hands. Like many urbanists, Krier follows Leone Battista Alberti (1404–72) in regarding the house as a city in microcosm (from *De re aedificatoria*, 1452, published in 1485) and seems to have no trouble at all in gearing up from the small-scale single house to the complete integrated community. Yet the difficulties of such exercises were emphasized by the one building that Krier reserved for himself at Poundbury: the civic marker that was to replace the church tower in settlements of a new age. Krier was adamant that the village needed such a symbol, which he saw as a 'market tower', and designed according to the Golden Section. The building had an open gothic porch at its base, a meeting room in its shaft lit by triangular dovecote-like apertures, and a composite crown comprising an attic storey of Egyptian columns surmounted by four obelisks. Yet settlements that are wholly in the commercial realm – as Poundbury is, despite the close involvement of a multi-millionaire royal patron, Prince Charles – cannot justify building desirable but ultimately useless civic monuments. Krier's market

tower remained on paper as a reminder that the past really is another country. Leon Krier built a small house for himself at Seaside in Florida, a settlement masterplanned by the like-minded architects Andres Duany and Elizabeth Plater Zyberk. Like the Disney town of Celebration, also in Florida (see 'Housing' and 'Leisure') this is a slightly unnerving exercise in rigorously policed and rather brittle idealized living in which it is assumed that tight controls are needed to prevent a slide into regrettable sprawl and low aesthetic standards. This is true, but it consequently means that such places, unlike their historic forbears, can only be wholly artificial.

More interesting, perhaps, are the continuing attempts to grapple with an existing, notoriously uncontrolled city: Los Angeles. As Peter Reyner Banham pointed out in 1971 (*Los Angeles: the Architecture of Four Ecologies*), LA has long been a planned city – it is just that the plans have a habit of not sticking, which is normal in most places. In a pre-echo of Leon Krier, Banham observed:
'The failure rate of town planning is so high throughout the world that one can only marvel that the profession has not long since given up trying: the history of the art of planning is a giant wastebin of sumptuously forgotten paper projects.'

However, a section of LA began to be planned in 1987, and construction began, in

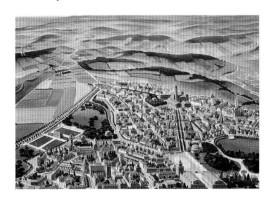

consultation with local residents, from then on: this was Playa Vista, the largest New Town in the USA (in fact a sizeable residential and commercial district covering 957 acres). The masterplanners were Moore Ruble Yudell, Charles Moore's firm, which saw Playa Vista rather as Krier saw Poundbury: as self-sufficient and mixed-use, a place not depending on the car (ironic, regarding its LA location). To this is added another element of 'greenness': the preservation of existing wetlands at one end of the site, and the use of renewable materials in some of the (generally low-rise) building work. The circle was closed by the involvement of a Krier connection, Elizabeth Plater Zyberk, on the wider multi-disciplinary team, but in fact Moore Ruble Yudell, who also completed the 6-acre Plaza las Fuentes in Pasadena in 1992, take more of a Rob Krier line in identifying the key urban typologies – the spaces – and working up from there. This line of thought goes back through the elder Krier to Camillo Sitte (1843–1903) and his theories of handling empty spaces (*Der Städtebau*, 1889). Today, it is enough of a victory just to have a mixed-use development accepted, since the post-war tendency has leaned towards rigorous zoning and separation of activities, and the coincident assumption of road-building to link them. Playa Vista, as an urban typology, is not too far removed from the original nineteenth-century grid-plan of urban blocks:

a sequence of spaces, some public, some private, with a relatively modest central focus in a largely decentralized layout.

A pervading factor in many such developments (as with airports) is to design according to maximum walking time. There is a consensus on this. From Leon Krier's Poundbury in England to RTKL's 388-acre residential new town outside Jakarta, Indonesia, 1994 onwards, it was decided to be ten minutes. According to this theory large developments therefore must be divided up into neighbourhoods, each with its local centre. Similarly, Balkrishna Doshi's Aranya low-cost housing project at Indore, India, 1983–6, was divided into six neighbourhoods, plugged into a spine containing schools, surgeries, shops and so on. More ambitiously, Doshi's 1995 masterplan for Bombay's International Finance and Business Centre envisaged 25 per cent of the building to be residential and the rest commercial, not only in order to reduce commuting, but also to ensure that the centre did not become deserted after office hours. There, the plan was for homes to be no further than five minutes' walk from a bus stop, running on a loop system. Allow another five minutes on the bus, and the magic ten-minute figure from home to work resurfaces. However, Doshi's plan – like most such plans in the commercial realm – was not ideally balanced. For 190,000 jobs, there was

provision for a resident population of just 20,000.

Nonetheless, the idea of combining work with homes is not wholly alien to the large-scale developers and their masterplanners. Battery Park City in New York, one of the biggest planned developments in Manhattan's history, covers 92 acres of spoil created when they dug the foundations of Minoru Yamasaki's adjacent World Trade Center, 1966–73. Battery Park City is known for its World Financial Center, 1980–88, a complex of office towers by Cesar Pelli, but less well known for its apartment blocks and town houses by a number of architects working to Stanton Eckstut's guidelines, among them James Stewart Polshek, Charles Moore, Mitchell Giurgola, Conklin and Rossant, Ulrich Franzen, Gruzen Stanton Steinglass, and Davis, Brody and Associates. The significance of Battery Park City is that it was stitched into the pattern of the existing city rather than being viewed as a defensible enclave. Its residential buildings verge on the nostalgic and its public areas are lavish. These include Eckstut's Esplanade, over a mile long, and the South Cove Park by Eckstut, artist Mary Miss, and landscape architect Susan Child – from which is available an awe-inspiring view of Manhattan of the kind previously only available from Central Park. They also include Pelli's huge Winter Garden within the Financial Center, which stages public concerts and

a b   c d

          e

exhibitions. Like the 1930s Rockefeller Center, the
base of Pelli's buildings are given over to the public
along with the office workers.

London's attempt to mimic Battery Park
City at Canary Wharf, 1987–99, in its former docklands area was masterplanned by Skidmore, Owings
and Merrill. Its central tower by Pelli was a taller version of his New York exercise, and its landscaping
was by the same firm used at the World Financial
Center, Hanna Olin. But despite being much larger
than its New York cousin, its very formal public open
spaces and relatively small-scale public interior
spaces do not compare. This indicates contrast
between the urban cultures on either side of the
Atlantic, even though many of the same developers
and designers are involved.

In many parts of the world, architecture and
town planning have become two separate profes-
sions with different career paths. The supposed creativity of architects thus came to be held in check by
the supposedly constraining influence of the planners
– whose job it became to police what others had
designed. The fact that it is usually possible for one
person to be qualified in both disciplines – just as it
is possible for an architect to be an engineer and
vice-versa – does not alter the fact that, in most
cases, one tends to fall into either category. This professional split is all the more marked in countries

a RTKL Associates, Wanakerta
   Residential Masterplan,
   Jakarta, Indonesia, 1994–:
   aerial perspective of
   masterplan
b Wanakerta Residential
   Masterplan: perspective view
   of typical street

London's Docklands
redevelopment achieved
very different results to
Battery Park City:
c Skidmore, Owings and Merrill,
   Canary Wharf, London
   Docklands, London, 1987–99:
   public squares
d Canary Wharf: Canada Square,
   at the foot of Pelli's Canary
   Wharf Tower
e Canary Wharf: aerial view

a c   d e
b

        f

that do not have a strong public sector design set up – depending on private practices – but which do have powerful restrictions on what may or may not be built. Different countries have systems that vary to such an extent that this theme can be taken no further than to note that 'masterplanners' are nearly always, first and foremost, architects.

Moreover, the 'master' prefix is important. The word, though perhaps originally intended merely to convey the broad-outline nature of the job, has by virtue of its association with master-class, master-race and so on, come to mean superiority. The masterplanner is more important than any of the other architects involved in the project, even if he or she does not personally contribute the majority of the buildings. Thus Rem Koolhaas is forever associated with the Euralille transport interchange and commercial district in northern France. Those other architects involved – Nouvel, Portzamparc, Andreu – are merely bit-players, as are the distinguished architects who worked under Rob Krier in Berlin. Similarly, when Norman Foster masterplanned a large (and ultimately abortive) commercial and residential development north of London's King's Cross in the late 1980s, the involvement of such other architects as Nouvel (again) and Jourda and Perraudin scarcely had a chance to register before the plug was pulled on the scheme. The title is therefore a coveted one:

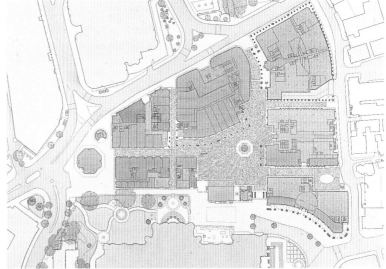

so much so that, for the second of three successive masterplans, 1987–97, to rebuild the commercial office district just north of London's St Paul's Cathedral, no fewer than three of the participating architects were called masterplanners: Terry Farrell and John Simpson from the UK, and Thomas Beeby from the United States. Perhaps to resolve potential conflict, Farrell was named 'superintending master-planner'. That scheme, like the one before it by Arup Associates, was abandoned. The third scheme for the site, presented in 1997, was masterplanned by the veteran historic-modernist William Whitfield, and included buildings by Michael Hopkins and Richard MacCormac (both of whom had been involved in the Arup scheme), Allies and Morrison, and John Simpson, a classicist brought forward from the Farrell scheme. Whitfield, a reticent and diplomatic individual who dated from a pre-superstar era in architecture and who had previously been Surveyor to the Fabric of St Paul's, hardly fitted the modern notion of the masterplanner as hero. Nonetheless the scheme was 'his' in the accepted sense.

The Paternoster Square saga was salutary because so much of it was to do with matters of both style and politics, and how the two meshed. An early public consultation exercise by Arup (winners of the original competition), setting out the loosest possible ground rules for the site in order to get maximum input from interested parties, counted for nothing because a rival architect, Simpson, designed a complete classical scheme without the benefit of any such consultation, and put it on public display. Arup's scheme, consisting at that stage merely of planning diagrams, did not capture the public's attention as Simpson's beguiling sunny perspectives did, and from that moment – although they clung on grimly through a change in site ownership – their scheme was doomed. Neither project was ultimately realized. In 1990, Simpson went on to design, and subsequently quit, a commercial office project called London Bridge City, facing the Tower of London across the Thames. Based on St Mark's Square, Venice, complete with Doge's Palace and campanile, this marked the high-water mark of classical pastiche in Britain, oddly enough on a site previously earmarked for a piece of Tudorbethan kitsch by Philip Johnson. In 1998 a remarkably similar scheme by others – with the addition of a towering hotel, the 'Venetian' – was proposed for Las Vegas at a cost of $2.5 billion, where it looked quite at home.

An equally explosive economic climate surrounded the development of Paris' Les Halles district in the late 1970s. The closure, and controversial demolition, of Baltard's nineteenth-century iron-and-glass market pavilions left an ugly wound in the city centre that took a very long time to heal.

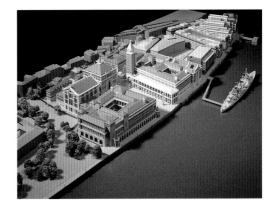

a   Rem Koolhaas, OMA,
    Le Grand Palais, Lille, France,
    1990–4: detail of exterior
b   Le Grand Palais: the congress
    hall was part of Koolhaas'
    masterplan for the Euralille
    district

c   Christian de Portzamparc,
    Crédit Lyonnais, Lille,
    France, 1991–5
d   William Whitfield, Paternoster
    Square, London, 1997:
    perspective view
e   Paternoster Square: site plan
f   John Simpson, London Bridge
    City Scheme, London, 1990

The architectural competition to re-plan Les Halles was, like Paternoster Square in London, a defining moment for the nation's architecture, when a new guard (Paul Chemetov, Henri Ciriani, Henri Gaudin, Yves Lion, Christian de Portzamparc and Jean Nouvel among them) made their presence felt. Not a moment too soon: in 1971, Richard Rogers had been advised, by the French chairman of the competition jury for the Pompidou Centre, not to employ any French architects because of their low standards. The period from the early 1970s onwards was, for this the most centrally-planned of cities, a time of architectural *scandales*, from the Montparnasse Tower of 1973 through the growth of the La Défense business district, the Les Halles affair, the Pompidou Centre, the museum and park of La Villette, and finally the *grands projets* under President François Mitterrand culminating in the new National Library by Dominique Perrault. But Les Halles caused the biggest row of them all.

Les Halles was at first intended to be a new central high-rise business district (the Paris Bourse is at one end). A conservation battle was fought, very similar to the battle in London to save the Covent Garden Market: but Baltard's pavilions were felled in 1971 despite enormous protest, and a colossal hole excavated to build an underground express railway station. This hole became a symbol of the

Parisian planning struggle and when Giscard succeeded Pompidou as president in 1974, he initiated a competition for the site, which he declared should be mostly a park. Ricardo Bofill won, albeit with modifications, but there was a backlash by the breakaway architects' body named the Syndicat de l'Architecture, in which Nouvel was a leading member. The Syndicat launched its own ideas competition in 1979, receiving 600 international entries. But the end result was a botched compromise typical of such overheated corners of the public realm. A sunken shopping centre by Vasconi and Pencreac'h, dating from before the Syndicat's contest, was built on top of the buried station, and surrounded by a slightly whimsical urban park, itself ringed with dull mansard-roofed office and apartment buildings. The controversy had saved central Paris from overscaled redevelopment, but had provided little of particular merit in its place.

It was noted that Piano and Rogers' Pompidou Centre, named in memory of the modernistically inclined president who had approved it, had become the most popular visitor attraction in Paris after its opening in 1977. The building stole most of the thunder of the later, rather indeterminate, Les Halles quarter by creating a discrete object on a public piazza in what had previously been a notorious slum district. Giscard had briefly considered

cancelling the project in 1974, but let his predecessor's decision stand. Instead he started to consider his own monument – which in true Parisian fashion was to be much more than just a building. This was the project known as La Villette and involved three competitions, consisting of the science museum, built in the hulk of a colossal under-used abattoir complex, the surrounding 35-acre park, and a concert hall. Adrien Fainsilber won the museum commission, Christian de Portzamparc the concert hall, known as the Cité de la Musique (to counterbalance the Cité des Sciences of Fainsilber) and Bernard Tschumi the park. It was all built between 1980 and 1995, and again a new president – this time Mitterrand – let his predecessor's decision stand while continuing with his own projects.

La Villette deserves study, in particular as an exercise in creating a civic sense of place. In this it succeeds in a way that Les Halles does not. It was a cruel outcome for the former markets area, which as a permeable private kingdom was by all accounts one of the magical places of Paris, its tall iron and glass pavilions as evocative as the earlier glazed galleries – still to be found – that were the prototypes for the fin-de-siècle department stores. La Villette, in contrast, was not an existing piece of city centre that the authorities decided had to be remade. It was an industrial complex conceived – or rather,

misconceived – in what some might see as a typically centrist French way. The vast abattoirs for this meat-eating city, planned during the earlier De Gaulle presidency, were designed on the assumption that live animals had to be brought in from the countryside and killed locally for distribution to the shops. The invention and universal adoption of the refrigerated truck, however, made a nonsense of this premise. The stockyards and unfinished buildings, placed beside a canal junction, became redundant. This area became the Parc de la Villette with its scattering of buildings large and small: a late twentieth-century version of John Nash's Regent's Park in London. And the key determinant of the feel of the place – like the villas that Nash envisaged in his park – is Tschumi's matrix of red-painted buildings described as 'folies'. Each differs in appearance; each derives its form from a basic 10-metre cube; and none is quite as useless as the word 'folie' might suggest, since each houses a function such as an information centre, café, cinema, sports pavilion, play area, and so on. Some, it is true, are little more than a kind of habitable sculpture, but on Tschumi's grid, placing the pavilions 120 metres apart, there was room for everything. About twenty-five have been built at the time of writing, and this was enough to give the necessary sense of definition to what had previously been a very bleak open space

Re-making the city:
a Christian de Portzamparc, Cité de la Musique, La Villette, Paris, 1984–95: this aerial view of the west wing of the Cité also shows Bernard Tschumi's 'folies' and Adrien Fainsilber's Cité des Sciences et de l'Industrie (top right)
b Bernard Tschumi Architect, Parc de la Villette, Paris, 1982–91: the 'folies' are more useful than their name might suggest

c Parc de la Villette: some of the 'folies' house functions such as cinema, café or play area
d Parc de la Villette: the 'folies' also mark points of arrival and departure

b c d

a

between the science and music complexes at opposite ends of the site.

Mitterrand's monument-building was more famous, because it involved more that was central to Paris, not least I M Pei's work at the Louvre which proved to be both a popular and critical success. (Though it was not always so. In the early days when Pei's pyramid was first announced, one French magazine asked of Mitterrand: 'Who does he think he is, Rameses II?' a dig that led the president, with his acknowledged preference for pure form of the Boullée–Ledoux variety, to be dubbed 'Mitterramses' ever after). If the Grand Louvre project (not finally completed in all its ramifications until 1998) was a success, then the Opéra Bastille by Carlos Ott was widely regarded as a failure and the Grande Arche at La Défense by Johan Otto von Spreckelsen as an intriguing enigma. This last project was perhaps the most obvious attempt by the French government to finally get a grip on the business district that had first been declared in the mid-1950s and which had become such a hot potato in the early 1970s when the big towers started to impinge on the view down the grand axis from the centre. The notion of creating a visual barrier to the axis by placing a building right across it (the commercial towers were kept to either side) led to a competition in 1982, won by Spreckelsen with his open-cube design, 1984–9, com-

pleted posthumously. His simple device two chamfered office towers joined with an identical horizontal lid – became surprisingly popular even though it proved hard to find tenants (the Government moved a department in). Equally the building deliberately missed the point: it does not terminate the great axis, merely frames it, thereby implying that the colossal boulevard continues out to the west. Moreover its enormous bulk, when seen from an angle rather than face-on, is only too apparent from the gardens of the nearby Bois de Boulogne. However its simplicity and scale, along with the Rice-Francis-Ritchie 'nuages' cable-net canopy suspended within the arch, and the glass-tube lift shooting up to an observation gallery in the roof, made this a popular symbol with the public. Paris and Mitterrand now had three platonic forms: the shiny sphere of the 'Géode' Omnimax cinema by Fainsilber at La Villette, the Pei pyramid of the Louvre, and the cube of Spreckelsen's Grande Arche at La Défense (to which Nouvel, with Emmanuel Cattani, appended his design of a pure cylinder, the unbuilt 1989 'Tour Sans Fins' or Endless Tower, 420 metres high, which is discussed further in 'Towers').

For all the magnitude of such projects, however – and no city in the world had a similarly state-sponsored building programme to compare with France's at this time, or anything like its paradoxical

idea of 'new monuments' – the successive French presidents were merely adding to an existing coherent urban fabric, and not nearly so radically as architects in the era of Napoleon III and Haussmann. A rather different prospect faced the newly reunified state of Germany in 1990, following the crumbling of the former Communist East German regime upon the collapse of the Berlin Wall in 1989.

With Berlin divided into four sectors following the Second World War (American, British, French and Russian), it effectively became a two-part city when the Wall was constructed in 1966, namely East and West. From that point onwards, Berlin developed two centres. In the smaller eastern sector, the government of the German Democratic Republic was, broadly speaking, based around the original city centre and possessed most of the cultural buildings remaining after the War. Here in 1973-6, the architects Heinz Graffunder and Karl-Ernst Swora built the sprawling white marble and reflective glass Palast der Republik on the banks of the Spree. The building now stands empty because of its association with the old Communist regime but is by no means the worst example of gubernatorial architecture of the period, East or West. In West Berlin, therefore – with no national government function, following the removal of the West German government to Bonn, and no arts district to speak of either – it was necessary to

a

b

a Johan Otto von Sprecklesen,
Grande Arche de la Défense,
Paris, 1984–9: a macro-scale
urban event
b Grande Arche de la Défense:
the suspended RFR-designed
cable-net canopy

start to create a separate city. This happened commercially out west around Zoo station, which became the shop and restaurant district, and also towards the east, close up to the Wall as near to the old centre as was possible, where the new cultural area was laid out.

It was there that Hans Scharoun, placed in charge of the city's reconstruction, conceived the idea of a 'cultural forum' that might one day serve to reunite the city. He built the Philharmonie concert hall, 1956–63, and State Library, 1964–79 (completed posthumously), and designed a large and prominent Chamber Music Hall as an adjunct to the Philharmonie that was finally built in 1968–87. Here Mies van der Rohe contributed his New National Gallery, 1965–8, and later James Stirling

and Michael Wilford built the more introverted Wissenschaftszentrum or Science Centre, 1984–8, replete with monumental Berlin quotations including sly references to the Third Reich architecture of Ernst Sagebiel in the window surrounds. However, as a cultural forum, these different buildings do not cohere; each stands as a discrete object despite their propinquity and the guiding hand (in the early days) of Scharoun. Odd weed-covered plots of land between them remain unbuilt on at the time of writing. But in a sense Scharoun was right: with the collapse of the Wall, his Cultural Forum was very close indeed to the biggest re-creation of the civic realm seen since the war: the reconstruction of the adjacent Potsdamer–Leipziger Platz area.

It is difficult to over-estimate the importance – symbolically, aesthetically and commercially – of this giant project, which at its height in the late 1990s represents one of the largest single building projects in the world, and which is the nearest Europe has come at this time to the huge city-building projects of the Pacific Rim, or to the earlier city-making exercises of Brasilia and Canberra. When the buildings, by such architects as Renzo Piano, Helmut Jahn, Arata Isosaki, Richard Rogers, Giorgio Grassi, Rafael Moneo and Hans Kollhoff, began to appear, it was equally difficult not to feel disappointed. To a certain extent this was because they were partly laid out according to a deeply conservative competition-winning urban design plan by the Munich architects Hilmer and Sattler, 1992–4, but

c
    e
a   b   d

then nobody could really complain about those architects' desire to recreate the original radial street plan of the area, once so fundamental to movement throughout the city. Their espousal of the traditional low-rise Berlin multi-use block – typically around 50 metres square with a layer of uses from retail at ground level to offices and housing above, usually set around a courtyard – was less appealing to the commercial interests that owned the three large parcels of land making up the site. These developers – Sony, ABB, and (the largest) Daimler Benz – at first acted jointly by commissioning a rival masterplan from Richard Rogers. It was rejected by the city fathers, though some elements found their way into a modified Hilmer and Sattler plan. The developers then signed up different planners and architects for

their respective portions, though the scale of the operation, combined with the creation of a new rail link underneath it, was such that the work had to be carefully co-ordinated. Building of the city's new central railway station on the banks of the Spree a little to the north (a veritable glass cathedral, complete with transepts, by Von Gerkan, Marg and Partner, 1993–2002) began soon after, along with the new government quarter. The estimate of thirty million passengers annually passing through the new Berlin Central indicates the astonishing level of development activity here.

In a sense the whole Potsdamer Platz exercise was doomed to be unsatisfactory because, like Les Halles in Paris, it was just too large, too much in the public eye, and people were too nervous about it.

Moreover, with the exception of its transport infrastructure, it was and is an entirely commercially led piece of city making. Will Alsop, an entrant in the 1991 urban design competition, believes that cities evolve riskily and chaotically, and that therefore it is fruitless to attempt to get things exactly right. In 1992, considering the situation in Berlin, Alsop wrote in his notebook:

'What is happening in Berlin? There is great confusion which has resulted in a return to conservative views and expectations mixed with nationalism. What should happen in Berlin? The city should take the unique opportunity it has to develop a test bed for a continuing experiment into urban and suburban life, forms and structures. With uncertainty: there is no guarantee that any proposal would work. Once this

Berlin became the world's biggest building site: but it attracted architects long before the fall of the Wall:
a James Stirling Michael Wilford & Associates, Wissenschaftszentrum, Berlin, 1984–8: makes overt reference to past times
b Wissenschaftszentrum: courtyard view

c Hilmer & Sattler (with Johannes Modersohn), Potsdamer–Leipziger Platz masterplan, Berlin, 1992–4
d Von Gerkan, Marg und Partner, Lehrter Bahnhof, Berlin, 1993–2002
e Richard Rogers Partnership, Daimler Benz Building, Berlin, 1992–9

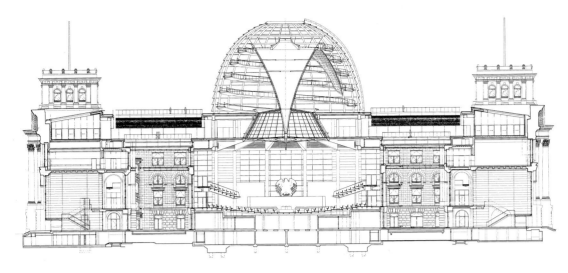

qood principle is accepted there is no reliance on history. Dare you imagine it, let alone realise it?' Later he added the rider:

'We live with the disastrous failures of proposals guaranteed to work. In Berlin above all it should be acknowledged that there are no certainties. They have crumbled all around: how many times, how many ways, in the memory of the century?'

The building of Potsdamer–Leipziger Platz continued as a curious mixture. On the one hand it was the kind of public–private mega-development familiar from such places as La Défense in Paris, Battery Park in New York, Canary Wharf in London, and Euralille in Northern France. On the other hand it was deeply traditionalist, in keeping with the buildings around the octagon of Leipziger Platz itself, slightly away from the main development. Here a plan was approved to rebuild the Wertheim department store as an exact replica of its pre-war, nineteenth-century state, right down to the construction techniques. At Pariser Platz behind the Brandenburg Gate, a few yards to the north of Potsdamer Platz, similarly historicist buildings were constructed (with modern techniques) to the designs of Paul Kleihues, in memory of those that had been lost in the war: an approach that disappointed other German architects such as Günter Behnisch who wanted a more contemporary approach. Given that Berlin's pre-war building codes and height restrictions continued to be respected far more in the old eastern quarter than the west (with some notable exceptions such as the East German TV Tower and high-rise apartment blocks) this sudden lowering of scale had a historic piquancy to it as a means to mark the old division between East and West.

Tucked away behind Kleihues at the Brandenburg Gate, Frank Gehry was commissioned to design a new headquarters for Deutscher Bank, also keeping low, if not exactly traditional. Christian de Portzamparc was later commissioned to add his French Embassy, 1997–2001, to the mix and this reserved its architectural exuberance for a circular internal courtyard. As it turned out, only one true tower was built in this whole sea of development: set well back at the south end of the Daimler-Benz development, this was by Renzo Piano in his sober brick-and-glass mode. Piano let himself go a little more in his low-rise theatre scheme nearby, but more typical were the urban blocks by Isozaki, Rogers *et al*, including a hotel by Moneo. Forced together, and obliged by the city planners not to misbehave, their relationship was slightly uneasy, leading one to the heretical thought that things might not have turned out so very differently if the usual cheap and cheerful commercial architects, unencumbered by celebrity or aesthetic ambition, had been left to get on with things. Berlin

a Christian de Portzamparc,
   French Embassy, Berlin,
   1997–2001: perspective
b French Embassy, Berlin: model
c Foster and Partners, New
   German Government Reichstag
   Project, Berlin, 1992–9: section
d Reichstag Project:
   photomontage

e Axel Schultes + Charlotte
   Frank, Federal buildings,
   Spreebogen, Berlin, 1989–:
   masterplan
f Spreebogen: model of the
   Bundeskanzleramt or
   Chancellory Building of the
   unified German Government

c   d
a
b   e
     f

had been this way before, with many world architects invited in over the years to design new housing and related developments for the IBA project. Some were good, some indifferent: looking at them now, it is apparent that the most successful IBA exercises in terms of urban mending were carried out by architects not trying to make too much of a point.

All this was only part of what was going on in the area. Because the unified Germany moved its Government back to Berlin – but not, for largely ideological reasons, into the 1970s Palast der Republik built for the former East German president Erich Honecker – a large-scale parliamentary building programme began in parallel with the commercial developments. Some existing buildings were to be re-used: first among them Paul Wallot's Reichstag (1884–94, rebuilt 1958–72 with insertions by Paul Baumgarten). This was once again rebuilt, this time to the designs of Sir Norman Foster who gave it a new glass dome and viewing gallery to replace Wallot's dome burnt down by the Nazis in 1933 and not replaced since then. Foster's dome, with its internal spiral ramp, also contains an inverted cone supplying light and natural ventilation to the plenary chamber below. This scheme was rather lower-key than Foster's original competition entry, which envisaged an enormous open canopy over the entire building and surrounding area as a symbolic public

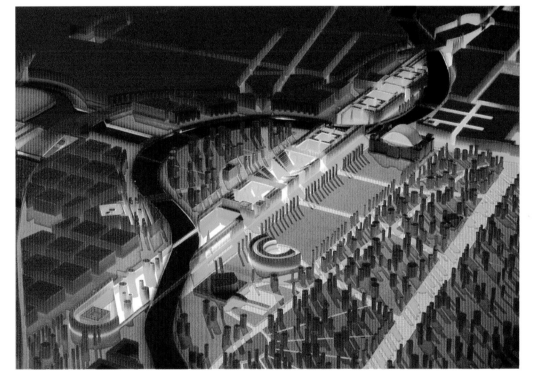

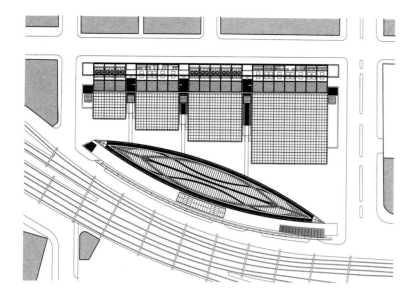

gathering place. However, an equivalently grandiose scheme was taking shape alongside the Reichstag. There architects Axel Schultes and Charlotte Frank won a competition in 1989 to build a 'Federal Ribbon' of buildings, in effect a new 1.5-kilometre grand axis running straight across the northern Tiergarten just north of the Reichstag, leaping twice over bends in the River Spree. This ribbon – part buildings, part bridge, part hard landscape – includes offices for the Bundestag members and the Federal Chancellor. A separate oval presidential building, designed by Martin Gruber and Helmut Kleine-Kraneburg, was built further west in the Tiergarten in 1994–8. Elsewhere in Berlin – mostly in older buildings in the former eastern sector – other government departments moved in. The Federal Ministry of Finance, for instance, moved into Ernst Sagebiel's 1936 Air Ministry.

All this, combined with new underground roads and the intersecting railways with an imposing main station, amounted to a re-ordering of a capital city of a kind not seen since the reconstruction projects of the immediate post-war years. The feeling in the city was that the great rebuilding would serve to remove, rather than re-create, the one-time atmosphere of Berlin. There was a feeling, too, that it was a city still waiting for its moment. As Daniel Libeskind, himself responsible for Berlin's new Jewish

Museum, expressed in 1997:
'Berlin is like a mystery town – it is similar to that strange silence that always comes up in the airplane shortly before landing when the "Fasten Seat Belt" sign lights up and everybody forgets to chat.'

In Tokyo, a city notoriously lacking public space, the opportunities for calm public space as provided by Takefumi Aida's Furusato Village Hall of 1994 are rare. For this outlying community, the architect provided five buildings offering different town hall services, from welfare and health centre to library – and shuffled these into an intriguing composition of varying wall planes, arranged so that views appear and disappear as one moves around the site. Recalling Alberti, this is the small building as city in microcosm, since the freestanding structures jointly give an impression of a crowded townscape of intersecting streets. In scale and expression, if not in ambition, it is the exact opposite of the Tokyo International Forum. The 1990 competition for the building provided the opportunity to create a village hall on a super-scale, since seven acres of city-centre land were liberated by the demolition of the old city hall by Kenzo Tange (who also designed the new one, see 'Workplace'). The winner of the competition was Rafael Viñoly, Uruguayan born and American-based.

Viñoly made a very simple diagram: the descending size of the auditoria required could be

a   Rafael Viñoly, Tokyo
     International Forum,
     Tokyo, 1990–6: site plan
b   Tokyo International Forum:
     bridges criss-cross the interior
     of the atrium
c   Tokyo International Forum:
     a 'village hall' for one of
     the world's great cities, its
     success lies in its simplicity
d   Tokyo International Forum: the
     atrium at the heart of the
     building is urban theatre

a

b   c   d

balanced against the slanting edge of the site, allowing a perfect elongated oval of enclosed public space, and a sequence of open landscaped courts, to be created between the two. The great event of the building is therefore the architecture of this enclosed oval space, crossed by walkways which then lead over the open courts to the auditoria. It is an extraordinary piece of urban theatre, comparable with the great railway stations and botanic glasshouses of the past, but with the massive steel trusses of the roof curving down rather than up: the effect is like looking up at the hull of a ship, or airship. The result is that Tokyo – which is like Los Angeles only in its lack of apparent centre – has a 'there'. The Forum, opened in 1997, lives up to its name.

The construction of a new Parliament
Building is usually a protracted process, one almost certain to provoke public controversy, and one which, due to the international competition system, increasingly involves architects foreign to the countries in question. Hence Foster designing the Berlin Reichstag. Hence the East Coast American firm of Mitchell Giurgola winning the competition for Australia's Parliament House in Canberra – itself a new city designed by Americans in 1911, namely Walter and Marion Griffin who had worked with Frank Lloyd Wright. Mitchell Giurgola entered with the Australian architect Richard Thorp, and built

what became the nation's largest building in the 1980s, in time for its bicentennial celebrations.

The scale of the building is massive. This, coupled with its hilltop setting in a mature 'garden city' arrangement of radial avenues, is enough to provoke comparisons with the roughly contemporary New Delhi, laid out by Lutyens and Baker: the difference is that Lutyens' Viceroy's House, 1913–24, was built as soon as possible, while Canberra's politicians spent fifty years in a temporary building waiting for the right conditions to build their eventual workplace. Its ordering of spaces owes something to Louis Kahn's 1963 Dacca Parliament Building in Bangladesh, while the identification of this site by the Griffins in 1911 as the location for a 'capitol' gives a Washingtonian flavour. Certain classical devices – the strict symmetricality of the layout, the grand approach, the mighty portico with the flag fluttering high above an implied dome – are universal symbols of government. Inside, certain visual cues establish links with the nineteenth-century British Houses of Parliament, on which the Australian parliamentary democracy was modelled: the Senate or Upper Chamber is in deep red like the original House of Lords, while the House of Representatives (lower chamber) is in green like the British House of Commons. The building thus ends up encoded with various American,

British and Australian messages, but succeeds by over-stressing none of them.

The cleverness of the composition, with its butterfly plan of two long walls placed back to back, is compelling. The effect of this simple plan is to divide the building into quadrants – relating to the upper chamber, the lower chamber, administration, and the public areas. The sweep of the long stepped walls serves to embrace the outside world and draw the eye, while at the same time screening one element from another. Only from a plane can the full extent of the complex be seen, not least because it is shaped to follow the contours of the site and thus can appear smaller than it is: the tilted walls to either side of the public entrance portico fade away into the ground, for instance, rather than kicking up into Lutyensesque end pavilions. This understatement is compensated for by the extreme prominence of the central flagpole, borne aloft by four angled stainless-steel legs like the armature of a dome. However the Beaux-Arts use of geometrical forms – circle, square, triangle – both as planning devices and decoratively, is much in evidence. One of the chief successes of the design is that it is to an extent divorced from its period – this, after all, was the time of flashy post-modernism, a style that even found its way into the public sector in the form of Michael Graves' Public Service building in Portland, Oregon,

a Mitchell Giurgola & Thorp
   Architects, Parliament House,
   Canberra, Australia, 1980–8:
   site plan
b Parliament House, Canberra:
   landscape is an integral
   element
c Parliament House, Canberra:
   interior

b c

a

1980-3. Where Graves took abstracted notions of classical grandeur and applied them in a thin veneer to the cladding of an otherwise standard foursquare steel-framed block, Mitchell Giurgola and Thorp paid some heed to the competition brief calling for a building to last two hundred years. No building is timeless, however: the stepped curving walls of the Canberra building with their rectangular cut-outs, and the freestanding screen-colonnade of the formal entrance, provide the clues to its era.

In India, Charles Correa took a more directly historicist model for his State Assembly for Madhya Pradesh in Bhopal, India, first phase, 1980-96. This takes a circular form, incorporating several other shapes relating to the uses within, especially the large dome over the Vidhan Sabha or Lower

Chamber, which consciously reflects the great domed Buddhist stupa at nearby Sanchi. Moreover, Correa took the Hindu mandala (temple) pattern of nine square within a square, but juxtaposed the nine elements within a circle. Correa and other architects in the Indian subcontinent can achieve a synthesis of tradition and modernity – and use rich decoration and overt symbolism – in an assured manner that seems beyond the grasp of most Western architects, who it seems must needs fall into 'traditional' or 'modern' camps. Thus Geoffrey Bawa's Parliament Building in Colombo, Sri Lanka, 1980-3, while consciously and obviously in the tradition of the hipped-roof temples and village halls of the region, was on a larger scale, arranged more formally and – once more – followed an internal layout like

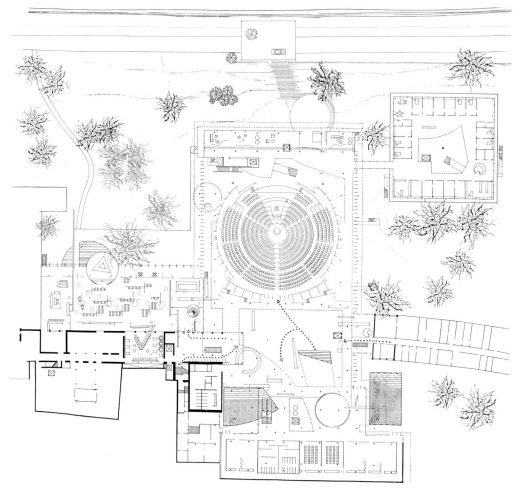

a Charles Correa, State Assembly, Madhya Pradesh, Bhopal, India, 1980-96 (first phase): exterior
b State Assembly: interior
c Günther Behnisch & Partner, West German Parliament Building, Bonn, 1992: interior
d West German Parliament Building: site plan
e Henning Larsen, Ministry of Foreign Affairs, Riyadh, Saudi Arabia, 1982-4: plan
f Ministry of Foreign Affairs, Riyadh: entrance
g Geoffrey Bawa, Parliament Building, Colombo, Sri Lanka, 1980-3: loggia
h Parliament Building, Colombo: the building reflects its roots in the surrounding landscape
i Ministry of Foreign Affairs, Riyadh: interior circulation

that of the British House of Commons. This is a physical layout which has done much to foster confrontational politics around the world, particularly suiting two-party states. It is, however, a design rejected by those countries with governments comprised of a multitude of small parties and, often, no overall majority. Thus the German Government – both in Bonn, in Günter Behnisch's building, and in its new incarnation in the Berlin Reichstag as remodelled by Norman Foster – disposes its representatives in-the-round.

The question of national characteristics for government buildings is a notoriously tricky one for overseas architects to address and only a few – Lutyens, Le Corbusier and Kahn among them – could ever manage the task with sufficient aplomb. One

wonders just how different Henning Larsen's Ministry of Foreign Affairs in Riyadh, Saudi Arabia, 1982–4, would have turned out if its attempt to absorb Arabic vernacular architecture had been made instead by an architect of the region such as the Jordanian Rasem Badran. Generally regarded as successful, Larsen's building is certainly better than most of the commercial buildings produced by foreign architects in the Middle East during the period – most of which were standard floorplate buildings with patronizing cut-out 'Islamic' motifs in their cladding. In many ways it is even better than many buildings produced by indigenous architects, which can tend to copy Western techniques. But Larsen's intellectual reworking of the idea of the thick-walled massive sheltering form and internal courtyard – a kind of Moorish fortress – cannot

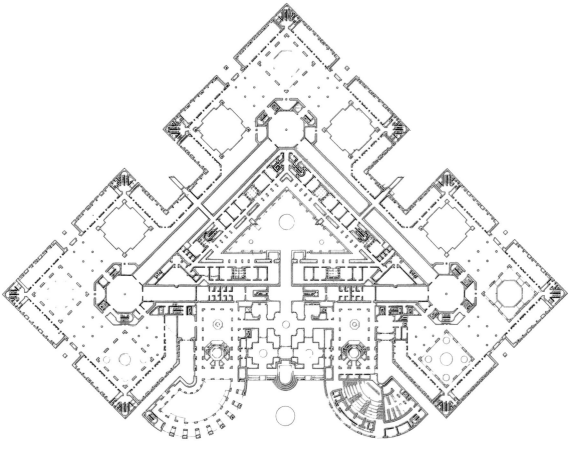

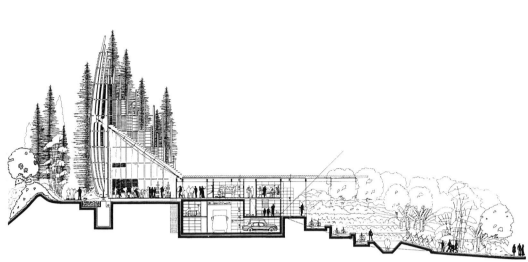

escape the charge of condescension either, however unfair that may be. In this sense Larsen's compatriot Jørn Utzon's 1972 National Assembly Building in Kuwait was more successful. This, with its many small departments placed in top-lit cubes either side of a central covered street, was a valid adoption of the idea of the bazaar, which is why its low bulk is not unlike that of a modern shopping centre. Some have seen the curving shapes of its twin roofs as reminiscent of desert tents or the sails of the traditional Arab trading boat, the dhow: but as with his Sydney Opera House, Utzon's forms in Kuwait were personalized, abstract responses and thus perhaps rather more appropriate as an outsider's take on a locality with its distinctive traditions and motifs. More successful, perhaps because more low-key, is Kohn Pedersen Fox's new Government House in Cypress, 1995-8, which does not condescend to the local vernacular and is the better for it. Both of these examples, however, fade into insignificance compared with the astonishing *tour de force* of Renzo Piano's Tjibaou Cultural Centre in Nouméa, New Caledonia, 1991-7.

New Caledonia was a French colony in the Pacific, heading for independence: the centre is devoted to the culture of the Kanak people who are concentrated there; the brief was to connect the culture's past with its future. It is significant that this

little project took shape at the same time as Piano's vast Potsdamerplatz redevelopment in Berlin, and clear that he regarded it as being of equal importance. Piano jettisoned his own cultural preconceptions and started from scratch: like a Method actor, he thought himself into the skin of a Kanak. The outcome is an assemblage of buildings and landscape on a peninsula, blending modern materials with those found on the island – in particular the local timber, iroko. The largest 'hut' with its curving, shell-like form stands as high as a nine-storey building. Naturally ventilated, the buildings are tuned to respond to the wind: they hum like the surrounding forests. Piano said of his scheme:

'The dread of falling into the trap of a folkloric imitation, of straying into the realms of kitsch and the picturesque, was a constant worry ... it was not feasible to offer a standard product of Western architecture, with a layer of camouflage over the top: it would have looked like an armored car covered with palm leaves.'

Instead he aimed for universality as informed by the spirit of place, and by doing so he succeeded.

Local architects are in certain circumstances able to reverse this process, moving from the particular to the general. Consider the Supreme Court Building in Jerusalem, 1986-95, by Ada Karmi-Melamed and Ram Karmi, a case of historical

synthesis by a brother and sister partnership. This was the result of a competition between mostly – though not exclusively – Jewish architects, from both overseas and Israel. Given the history of the area, there was no clear historical model for a court building. Indeed, there was such an overlay of styles and periods of architecture to draw upon that almost any response could in some way be regarded as contextual, even the Bauhaus aesthetic popular in the Palestine of the 1930s. Moreover the building was to be sited on Government Hill, close to the Knesset parliament building at a point where several important urban axes intersected. Thus it could be seen as a place of mediation between the city and its rulers. Several contestants turned to the Bible in search of inspiration but that scarcely narrowed down the possibilities: a myriad abstract and metaphorical references could be gleaned from it concerning the notion of the law, but nothing that gave any clue as to the architectural components of the scheme. The winning architects took the scale of Jerusalem's buildings as their starting point, stating: *'Throughout the world, monumentality is congruous with power. But not in Jerusalem. Here there is a sense of the unknown rather than of power. You look at buildings, part of which are hidden from view by the city wall. You see their skyline, but not where they touch ground. You always retain the sensation of*

a b

c

Responding to the spirit of place:
a Renzo Piano, Tjibaou Cultural Centre, Nouméa, New Caledonia, 1991–7: site section
b Tjibaou Cultural Centre: exterior view
c Ram Karmi + Ada Karmi-Melamed, Supreme Court Building, Jerusalem, 1986–95

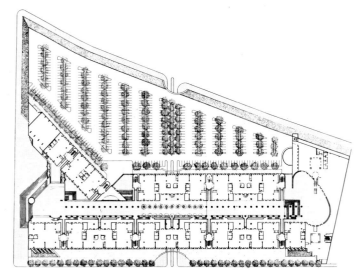

hidden layers and indefinite heights. This imparts a certain mystique to the buildings. Anywhere else in the world it would be called monumentality.'

A sense of the unknown, a sense of mystique, a sense of topography and hierarchy – these are qualities that the Jerusalem Supreme Court Building shares with the Parliament House in Canberra, along with the use of the dominant wall both as an ordering device within the building, and to root it in its landscape. In most other respects – particularly its asymmetry – the court building is completely different, and it certainly nods more towards the past, but both succeed in being austere with a stern beauty. The most successful civic buildings achieve this. As with Le Corbusier's government complex in Chandigarh, India, so with Teodoro González de Leôn's Supreme Court in Mexico City, 1987–92, which likewise treats concrete as a poetic medium suitable for a poor country, employing it in a sequence of portals and pergolas.

None of the above remarks on locality apply to the Hôtel du Département in Marseilles, 1990-5, also known as 'Le Grand Bleu', and (to local taxi drivers at least) as 'Le maison des Stroumphs' after the blue comic dwarf-characters, also known as Smurfs, that are unaccountably popular in Europe. This, the regional government headquarters of the Bouches-du-Rhône department, was a competition win by

Alsop, Lyall and Störmer (now Alsop and Störmer) Will Alsop's painterly approach to architecture is well documented, and is often characterized as an absolute reversal of the 'form follows function' dictum. This is perhaps overstated: Alsop draws or paints according to a very clear view of what the function of the building, and its hierarchy of uses, is to be: 'form swallows function' as the architectural critic Paul Finch noted at the time. But at first the building certainly appears to be wilfully different from standard city-hall models, and moreover flaunts its otherness by the use of its ultramarine cladding – International Klein Blue or IKB as the artist Yves Klein (1928-62) called it, while claiming to have patented the shade. The colour is important to the Alsop building because of what it says about the architect's attitude both to context and to conventional 'good taste'. Until quite late in the design process the building was white, as it remained internally, and in a hot sunny Mediterranean climate the adoption of a heat-absorbing dark colour was quixotic, to say the least. But it is important because it also tells us that, if the building can be ultramarine, it can be any other colour as well. It could be red, like Tschumi's 'folies' at La Villette. It could be bright yellow, like some mid-period Anthony Caro sculptures. It could be all-over orange, like the jacket of the book Alsop produced on the building. But what it

certainly could not be, finally, was a sensible heat-reflecting white, or the brown and russet tones of the surrounding buildings and landscape. Nor could it be anything as rational as the colour of its materials. Like Klein, Alsop applies his blue over virtually everything – structural steelwork, concrete, aluminium and glass cladding. One is surprised to encounter the occasional external element that is left unblued. Given its highly articulated nature, this is a building that looks as if it could march over to a giant sheet of paper and roll on it to produce a Klein body print. In fact, it has done just that: against the dry landscape the effect is uncannily like one of Klein's 'anthropometries' on burnt paper. So, it is not contextual. The sea and the sky are very seldom that colour, though we might like to think so, and landscape and cityscape are never that colour (Corb's nearby Unité is the contextual building here); moreover, nothing in the town is at all like that shape. The very confined site, landlocked by busy roads, militates against both the sprawling built form and the generous axial approaches seen in Canberra and Jerusalem.

The association with Caro and Tschumi is informative. Sculpture can be contextual, most strongly perhaps in the work of Andy Goldsworthy, but is more usually a three-dimensional statement set against its surroundings – which is precisely why the siting of open-air sculpture is so important. The

a b   c d

e

An act of bravura that put the city back on the architectural map:

a Teodoro González de Leôn, Supreme Court, Mexico City, 1987–92: exterior view

b Supreme Court, Mexico City: plan

c Alsop and Störmer, Hôtel du Département, Marseilles, 1990–4: interior

d Hôtel du Département: section

e Hôtel du Département: exterior

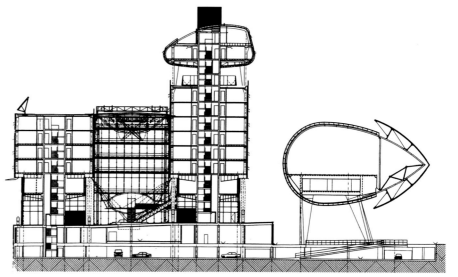

references, if any, to the surroundings can be implied or concealed. Le Grand Bleu is therefore not a 'foil' to its neighbours in the manner beloved of post-war modernists, but a sculpture representing authority, which also just happens to be an exploded diagram of its own working elements. Alsop pulls the functions apart and expresses each differently: therefore the building is readable and visually permeable from a distance. In use, a second set of values comes into play as one is drawn up the gentle slope into the equally sloping floor of the main concourse, where all is cool and rational. In a way, this outside to inside switch, and the clustering of disparate built elements, gives Alsop something in common with Frank Gehry. What it gives the Département des Bouches-du-Rhône is a symbol of the kind that French municipal and regional leaders – in this case Lucien Weygand, president of the council – love. Such architectural hard talking, regardless of the language, works the world over: for many, the Canadian town of Missisauga was unknown until the architects Ed Jones and Michael Kirkland won a competition to build its new city hall, and achieved one of the few convincing examples of post-modern classicism, a structure broken down into separate building elements of cube, drum, triangle and tower.

Such expressions of power can, of course, send out the wrong message, hence the wise

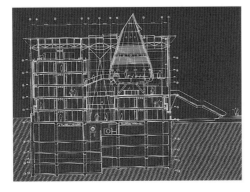

Symbols of nationhood and the power of the state:

a   Richard Rogers Partnership, European Court of Human Rights, Strasbourg, France, 1989–95

b   Richard Rogers Partnership, Bordeaux Law Courts, Bordeaux, France, 1993–8: section

c   Bordeaux Law Courts: building in progress

d   Harry Seidler (with Marcel Breuer), Australian Embassy, Paris, 1975: plan

e   Denton Corker Marshall, Australian Embassy, Tokyo, 1987–90

f   Allies & Morrison, British Embassy, Dublin, Ireland, 1995

g   Australian Embassy, Paris: looking towards Eiffel Tower

h   Arquitectonica, US Embassy, Lima, Peru, 1988–5

comment of Ada Karmi-Melamed that state buildings should deserve power rather than assume it. For an example of a building that both assumes and exudes power of a perhaps unintentionally menacing nature, one can take a late building by Kenzo Tange – the bastions of the Tokyo Metropolitan Government Headquarters, completed 1991. It is the largest single set of buildings to be constructed in Japan in the twentieth century, a titanic fortress complex – an example of how not to construct an interface between government and people. The City of Tokyo wanted a clear image of power to distinguish it from the national government buildings in the same city – rather as the Greater London Council built its massive headquarters in Edwardian times directly across the Thames from the Houses of Parliament – but

appeared not to rate very highly the notion of the accessible public face. Better – again because, as with Alsop in Marseilles and Jones and Kirkland in Missisauga, the differing functions of the building are readable – are Richard Rogers' European Court of Human Rights in Strasbourg, and subsequent (very different) Law Courts in Bordeaux, where in both cases the forms of the courts are expressed as separate elements within the overall composition.

The world is scattered with embassies where countries try to express, however ponderously and unconvincingly, something of their perceived international importance. Very often, these commissions are far from being their architects' finest work – due to government interference, perhaps. There are exceptions, such as Harry Seidler's Australian embassy in

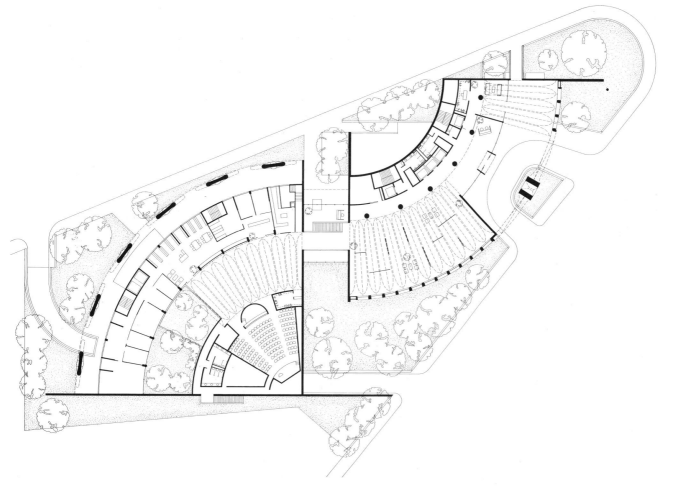

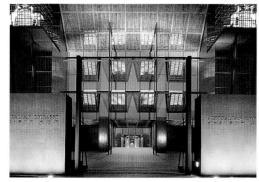

Paris, a Breueresque composition somewhat over looked at the time of its completion in 1975 because of the modishness of the contemporary Pompidou Centre; or Denton Corker Marshall's later Australian Embassy in Tokyo, or Arquitectonica's United States Embassy in Lima, Peru, 1988–95. The British architects Allies and Morrison combined a convincingly domestic-scaled, big-roofed building with the demands of high security for the British Embassy in Dublin in 1995, but perhaps none of these gestures – because their hallmark must be a seeming permanence – generally succeed so well as the (usually) short-life pavilions the same countries put up for Expos. The British government chose the solid virtues of Michael Wilford for its Berlin Embassy, 1995–, following the unification and enhanced importance of that city. For its Moscow Embassy, following the collapse of the Soviet regime, it selected the veteran modernist practice of Ahrends Burton Koralek, noted for its university work; but for Expo '92 in Seville it chose the glass, steel and cascading water on offer from Nicholas Grimshaw: a typically British allocation of horses for courses, the exportable high-tech style being fine for a forward-looking Expo but apparently wrong for the overseas expression of the historic state. Expo thinking understandably won out when it came to choosing a design for Britain's Millennium celebrations. The Millennium Dome, 1996–9, by the

Richard Rogers Partnership – principally Mike Davies – is technically not a dome, but a mast-supported cable-net structure of vast proportions, the ultimate circus Big Top. It is also a memory of Buckminster Fuller's city-enclosing bubbles, though its engineering is entirely different. As with so many such events, the presence of the landmark structure promised to be more memorable than the contents of the exhibition inside it, and the same problem remained of exactly what to do with it after the event.

The civic realm is in the end concerned with much more than government buildings, expressions of national pride, and large-scale planning. A Hungarian dancing barn by Dezsî Ecker, from that country's organic school of architects, is part of it. Piers Gough's public lavatory-cum-flower shop in West London, 1993, combines function and frivolity seamlessly. A fire station such as Toyo Ito's in Yatsushiro, 1992–5, or his old people's home of 1992–4 in the same town, is equally relevant. Peter Zumthor's obsessively understated timber-slat pavilions built to shelter the Roman ruins at Chur in Switzerland, 1985–6, are also public spaces. Visitor and information centres are vital to interpret towns or other buildings – and in Berlin, Schneider and Schumacher's elevated big red 1995 'Info Box' has served for five years as a centre for interpreting the construction site that the reunited Berlin has become.

a c | d f

b | e g

a Richard Rogers Partnership, Millennium Dome, Greenwich, London, 1996–9: photomontage
b Toyo Ito, Yatsushiro Fire Station, Yatsushiro, Kumamoto, Japan, 1992–5
c Tadao Ando, Fukuhara Clinic, Setagaya, Tokyo, 1982–87
d Morphosis, Cedars-Sinai Comprehensive Cancer Center, Los Angeles, California, 1985–6
e CZWG (Piers Gough), Public Lavatory, Westbourne Grove, London, 1993: plan
f Toyo Ito, Old people's home, Yatsushiro, Kumamoto, Japan, 1992–4
g Public Lavatory: florist's shop and public facilities

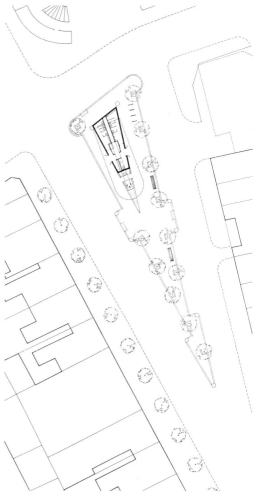

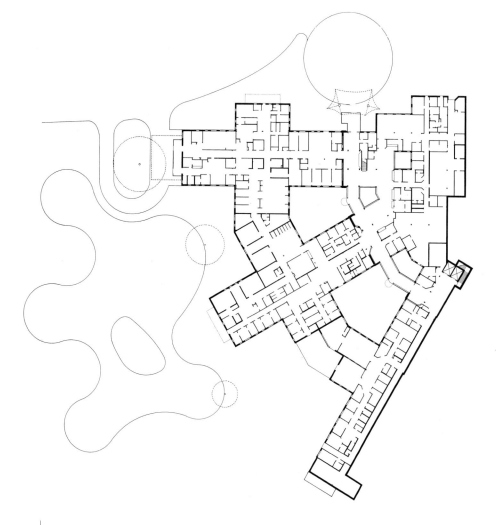

Much more problematic are city hospitals and clinics. These are usually no-go areas for good architecture, despite such precedents as Johannes Duiker's and Bernard Bijvoet's Zonnestraal Sanatorium in Hilversum, The Netherlands, 1926–8, or Alvar Aalto's Paimio Sanatorium of 1929–33. Of note in this area are such vastly differing buildings as Miguel Angel Roca's series of sometimes vivid Bolivian health centres, 1988–90; Morphosis' Cedars-Sinai Cancer Center in Los Angeles, 1985–6; Tadao Ando's Fukuhara Arthritis Clinic in Tokyo, 1982–7; Ahrends Burton Koralek's attempt to marry human-scale wards and public art and landscape with a glittering stainless-steel skin at their low-energy St Mary's Hospital, Isle of Wight, England, 1982–91; or, from the architectural mainstream, RTKL's John Hopkins Bayview Medical Center, 1994, in Baltimore. The impersonality of post-war city hospitals in the West is only now beginning to be addressed: health buildings at a small scale that are less set apart from their contexts are therefore either community experiments (such as Edward Cullinan's Lambeth Community Care Centre, London, 1980–5, or Hodder Associates' City Road surgery in Hulme, Manchester, 1995–6) or in less industrialized nations where such buildings are smaller-scale and unafraid of the regional vernacular, such as André Ravereau's mud-walled Mopti Medical Centre, 1970, in Mali. The

a c   e

b   f h

     d g

a Ahrends Burton Koralek, St Mary's Hospital, Newport, Isle of Wight, 1982–91: exterior

b St Mary's Hospital: plan

c RTKL Associates, John Hopkins Bayview Medical Center, Baltimore, 1994

d André Ravereau, Medical Centre, Mopti, Mali, 1970

e O'Donnell + Tuomey, Group 91, Irish Film Centre, Temple Bar, Dublin, 1987–92: plan

f Irish Film Centre: projection wall

g Hodder Associates, City Road Surgery, Hulme, Manchester, 1995–6

h Irish Film Centre: ticket office

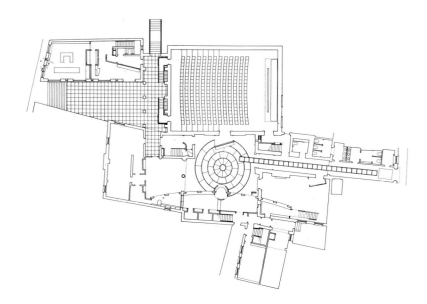

influence of Duiker–Bijvoet and Aalto is surprisingly small, considering the health claims made for the first wave of modern architecture: however, the undulating, ribbon-windowed white hospital of Bruck in Austria by architects Domenig Eisenköck, 1987–94, is happy to wear its homage on its sleeve.

The painstaking patchwork-mending of a decayed existing urban area, though such work lacks the media impact of comprehensive redevelopment, has the virtues of continuity and evolution. Into this category comes the Temple Bar project in Dublin, first phase 1987–92, by various Irish architects under the 'Group 91' banner and including O'Donnell and Tuomey's Irish Film Centre; Joachim Eble's Nuremberg mixed development with its glazed public courtyards; and the Barrio del Canyeret project in Lerida, Spain, 1982–91, by Amado-Domenech Architects, (reminiscent in one way of some of the late Brazilian work of Lina Bo Bardi, in another of the Urbino projects of Giancarlo de Carlo since 1962). Even the signature buildings of Eric Owen Moss in Culver City, Los Angeles (see 'Workplace') are part of this mending process, standing outside comprehensive redevelopment or regeneration schemes. Such projects were and are both necessary and rewarding exercises in acknowledging and reviving the civic realm. In the case of Dublin's Temple Bar, a once neglected but characterful area which – like London's Covent

Garden market – was saved from demolition in the 1970s became almost too popular for its own good once the revival was established: its once deserted alleys became overrun with tourists. Success in the urban realms thus tends to breed its own problems.

From the late 1980s onwards, governments and cities had discovered a highly visible and nearly always immensely popular way to build big in the public eye. Bridges appear not to be 'architecture' and moreover embody a highly appropriate, convenient and universally recognized symbolism. Ben van Berkel's Erasmus Bridge in Rotterdam, 1990–6, linking formerly derelict areas of docklands, was as much a symbol of regeneration as the giant harp form of Santiago Calatrava's Alamillo Bridge in Seville, 1987–92, built as a lasting residue of Expo '92, or

Christopher Wilkinson's deceptively ingenious Hulme Arch in Manchester, 1995–7. The Hulme bridge, a road over another road, was designed to link what had become a no-go area of social housing with the city centre. The structure has a diagonally placed arch and opposing sets of cables resulting in an almost kinetic, sculptural object. Wilkinson and his partner Jim Eyre became almost unbeatable in British bridge competitions, being responsible for one of the most notable of a clutch built in the mid to late 1990s in London's Docklands (other designers involved here being Lifschutz Davidson, Eva Jiricna, Nicholas Lacey, Future Systems, and the engineer Tony Hunt). It was belatedly acknowledged that, in the commercially driven exercise of docklands regeneration, a high standard of design in the public realm

was necessary to create the right matrix for investment. That lesson was applied in a small handful of other British regeneration projects in the 1990s, from Will Alsop's involvement in the Cardiff Bay Barrage and its associated structures, to the Millennium Bridges in London and Gateshead. Of these two the former was a taut ribbon, won by Sir Norman Foster with the sculptor Sir Anthony Caro, the latter a rotating 'eyeball' design by Wilkinson that neatly resolved the problem of making an openable bridge work aesthetically open as well as it did shut.

It is arguable but probable that the explosion of interest in architect-designed bridges in the 1990s would not have happened to anything like the same extent, were it not for the lyrical possibilities opened up by the architect-engineer Santiago Calatrava in

his work in this area. This remains the most successful of his output, since Calatrava's organic approach appears to work most happily on essentially horizontal structures. Despite the earlier twentieth-century example of bridges by Robert Maillart (1872–1940), Eugène Freyssinet (1879–1962), Eduardo Torroja (1899–1961) and others, the fact remains that, by the 1980s, too much bridge design work had descended to the level of unimaginative value engineering. Calatrava reminded everyone of the civic and sculptural value of the bridge form. At the same time, growing resistance to new roads in Europe meant that bridges took on a fresh environmental importance: hence the commissioning of Foster for perhaps the most dominant new bridge in France for decades, the Grand Viaduc du Millau marching

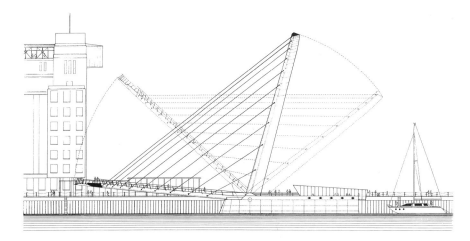

Architects reclaimed bridges from engineers as the civic importance of these structures was rediscovered. Would this have happened without Calatrava?

a Santiago Calatrava, Alamillo Bridge, Seville, Spain, 1987–92

b Van Berkel + Bos, Erasmus Bridge, Rotterdam, The Netherlands, 1990–6

c Chris Wilkinson Architects, South Quay bridge, London Docklands, 1994–7

d Future Systems, Docklands Bridge, London, 1996

e Chris Wilkinson Architects, Tyne Millennium Bridge, Gateshead, England, 1996–2000: computer-generated perspective

f Tyne Millennium Bridge: section

g Chris Wilkinson Architects, Hulme Arch, Manchester, 1995–7

h Foster and Partners, Grand Viaduc du Millau, Tarn, France, 1996–

a

b c d

f

e g

h

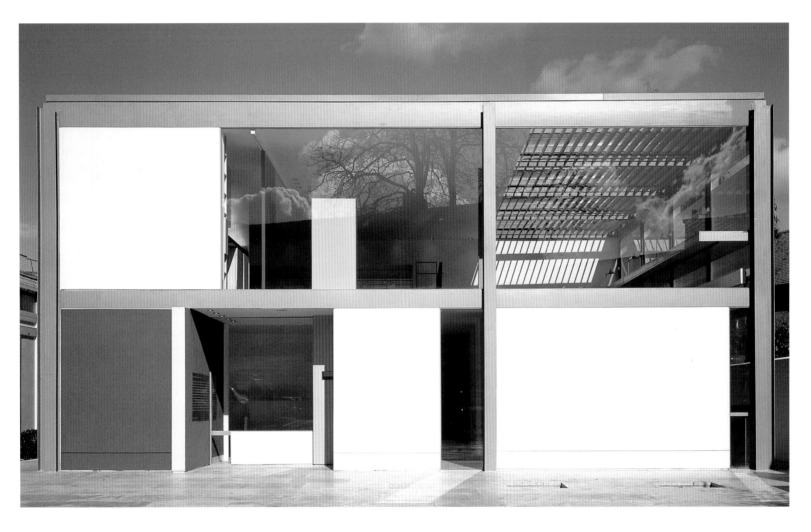

b   e

a

c d f g

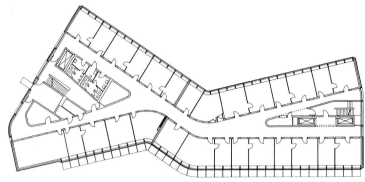

across the Tarn gorge. As Foster pointed out, with its road deck reaching a maximum height of 275 metres (and the A-frame cable-stay masts going 90 metres above that), the Grand Viaduc with its coupled columns was taller than his Commerzbank in Frankfurt – then Europe's tallest tower. But its height seemed incidental to its length of 2.5 kilometres, a distance covered in seven strides of 350 metres each.

Foster had come to the Millau Bridge with a reputation as an ennobler of civic forms – his Collserola communications tower, 1988–92, on the ridge overlooking Barcelona, designed with engineers Ove Arup, gathered the usual clutter of aerials and dishes into one structure – but in the years prior to the burgeoning of Calatrava, bridges were most usually seen as the province of highway engineers rather than architects and their favoured structural engineers. So far did the art of bridge design then advance in a short time that now it is hard to credit the international impact of Calatrava's modest little La Devesa pedestrian bridge in Ripoli, Spain, 1989–91, designed later but completed earlier than his Alamillo Bridge in Seville, and contemporary with his more conventional Lusitania Bridge in Mérida. By the simple act of tilting the bow of the La Devesa arch sideways – with all the structural implications that this gesture implied – Calatrava freed the bridge once more from its functionalist shackles. Although

stimulating a legion of imitators, he upped the stakes once more in 1997 with the opening of his gravity-defying Nervion pedestrian bridge in Bilbao, where the double-curved glass deck and its tilting arch both spring insouciantly from the graceful cantilevers of the approach ramps. This slender apparition in the midst of Bilbao's riverside dereliction is – as so often with bridges – a symbolic precursor of the area's regeneration rather than a response to any pressing pedestrian need.

There might, in the end, appear to be little to link such creatures of the civic realm as Arthur Erickson's craggy Vancouver Civic Centre, Bolles-Wilson and Partner's wriggling local government offices in Münster, Germany, Gabriel Bramante's Miesian Citizens' Advice Bureau in Chessington, England, Juan Navarro Baldeweg's rubble-and-render law courts in Mahon, Menorca, a covered timber bridge in Murau, Austria, by Marcel Meili and Markus Peter, or the remarkable range of rural and urban visitor centres designed by Ireland's Office of Public Works. A vast range of styles from the high-tech to the wholemeal. But nevertheless there is a link, which is that all these places are for the use of the people, with a greater or lesser degree of freedom. They are not private fiefdoms of industry, desk-working, or domesticity. Sometimes directly, sometimes in oblique ways, they all partake of the notion of *civitas*.

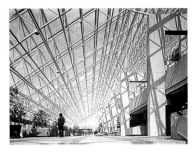
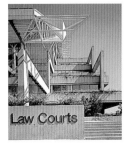

TOWERS *Vertical cities* Supertowers dissolve the boundaries of building types. They are entire city districts, vertically extruded. Once mono-cultural, they have steadily become mixed-use, containing offices, apartments, shops, hotels, recreation and public space. Inevitably they have a symbolic meaning as markers for the global economy, with the race to build the world's tallest tower being a strong expression of financial machismo. Their importance transcends that distinction, however: if the world is not to be wholly urbanized, the supertower could be our eventual salvation if ecological needs are to be met.

'Of all mankind's achievements in the field of architecture in the twentieth century, probably the skyscraper has emerged as the most dramatic, exciting, and profound.'

Jan Kaplicky, Future Systems, 1985.

Will all building types, in the end, boil down
to separate departments within megalopolises of great towers? Many predict that the economic and population growth of the world is such that the only salvation for humanity is to concentrate in great cities, building higher and higher in order to spare vital food-producing land and gambling on the long-predicted arrival of the sustainable eco-scraper. There are plenty of indications to support this contention. The growth of Tokyo – the paradigm of a great city uncomfortably shoehorned into limited space – has thrown up a succession of ideas for supertowers, many of them even built out in the sea. Tokyo Bay has been the subject of fantastical building projects since the early 1960s but the latest crop of proposals – from Shin Takamatsu's Future Port City of 1990, an island with airport, to Nikken Sekkei's 1994 'Soft Landing Island', an atoll of super-buildings, via Norman Foster's Tokyo Millennium Tower of 1989 with a harbour at its base – are all based around the need to create entire cities in high-rise form, away from existing land.

Such concepts were once science fiction, but are now structurally perfectly possible: which is not to say that financing them is any easier than the political will needed to realize them. Mixed use or monocultural, what is certain is that the progress of the ultra-tall building, which halted for nearly twenty years after Chicago's Sears Tower was finished in 1974, resumed in earnest as the new century loomed: and made its greatest leaps forward on the far side of the Pacific Rim from its American birthplace.

In any discussion of building types, the skyscraper tends to be considered only in its function as an office building, residential tower, or communications armature. Many of the world's best and tallest (the one by no means implies the other) are purely corporate buildings and are considered here. It is unusual for entirely domestic towers to achieve global recognition, usually because these tend to be smaller, low-cost, low-quality buildings: an exception might be made for Richard Rogers' Korean prefabricated housing tower project of 1992, or his Montevetro apartment building in London, 1994-9. But increasingly, the skyscraper can be regarded in its own right, both as a particularly demanding built form, and as an example of the ultimate urbanism: vertical city-making. At first this is a concept that may seem to be a particular concern of the 1990s, but in truth the skywards city arrived, if not quite

with the Empire State Building in 1930-1 (that being exclusively offices) then certainly in 1970 with the mixed-use John Hancock Center in Chicago, of which the artist Jeff Koons later observed: 'Mozart would have had a condo on 93rd.'

The Hancock tower had (and has) offices, apartments, shops, a hotel, even its famous swimming pool on the fortieth floor. The tenants who live there may well choose to leave the building often but have no compelling reason, in the normal run of their lives, ever to need to do so. Thus the emerging technology of super-tall buildings met the Corbusian dream of inclusive living and working: the Unité. Architect Bruce Graham and engineer Fazlur Khan of SOM, caused the Hancock to have as much to do with the emerging high-tech movement as it did with the nineteenth-century origins of the American skyscraper. Although the building underwent a period of eclipse, it can now be seen to have been extraordinarily influential.

No other kind of building is so
circumscribed – and so liberated – by available technology. Slender towers are possible even in mud construction – those of the Yemen are notably daring – and medieval cathedral towers and Renaissance campaniles tested the structural properties of masonry, frequently to destruction. The skyscraper as it is commonly understood, however, was made possible by

a   b

c   d

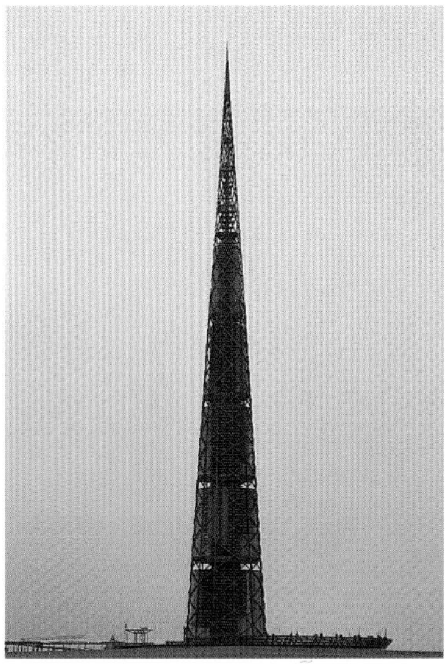

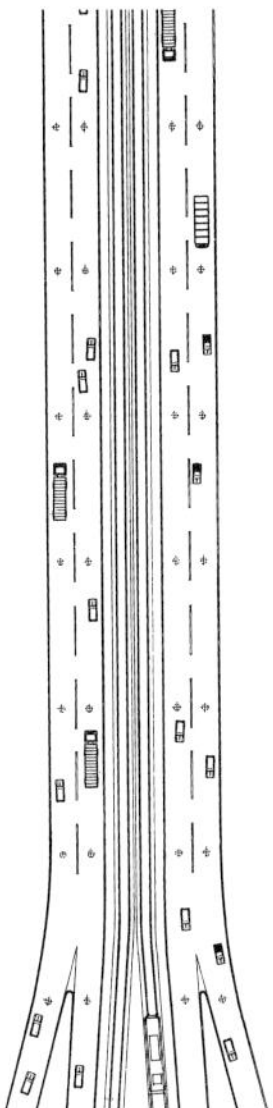

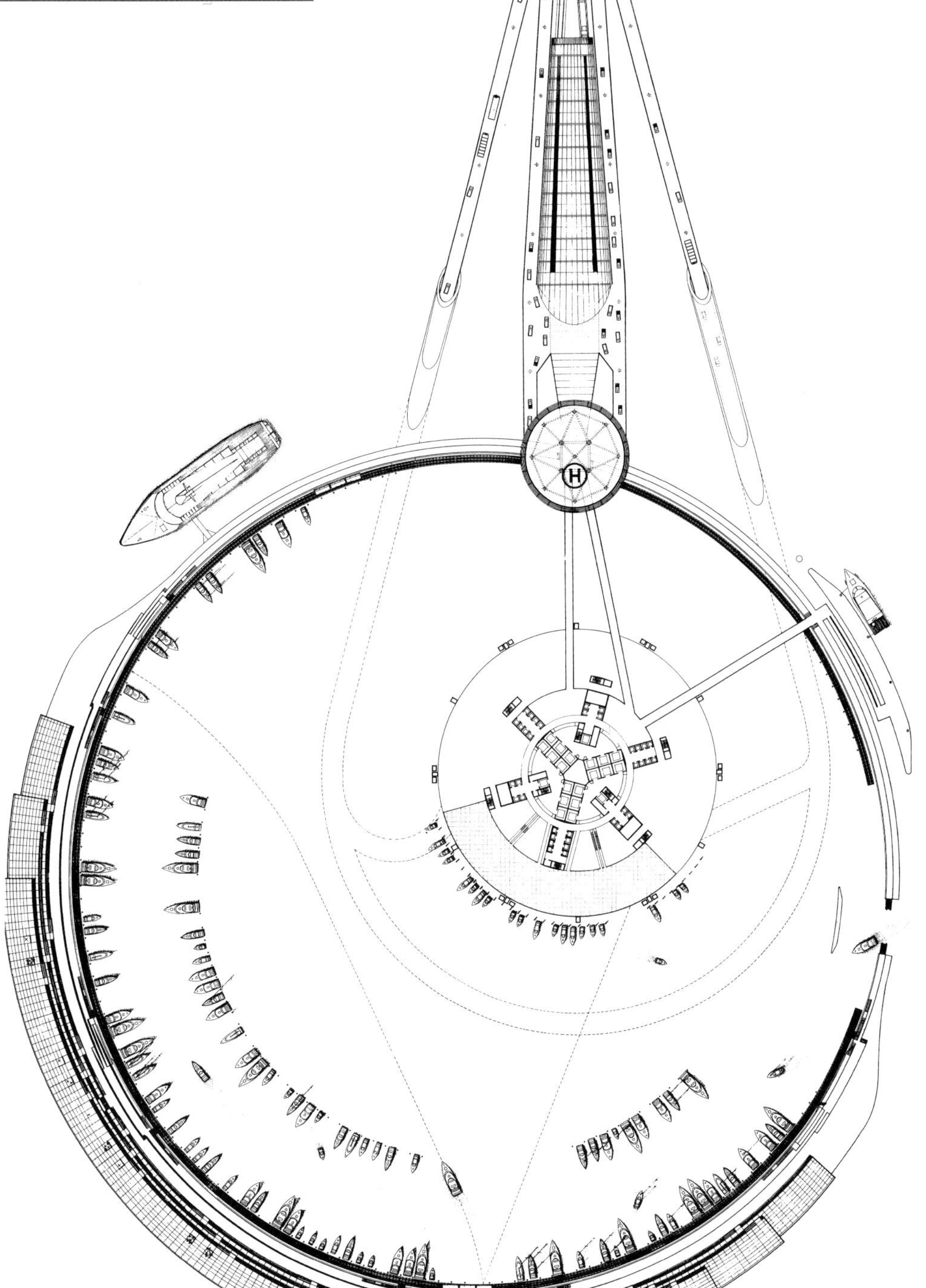
H

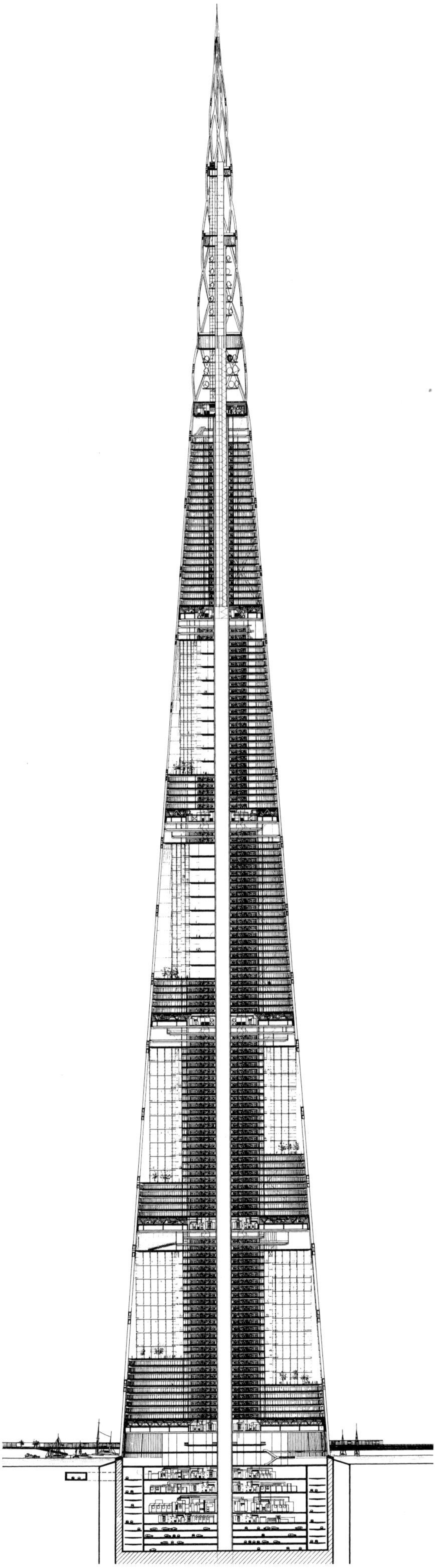

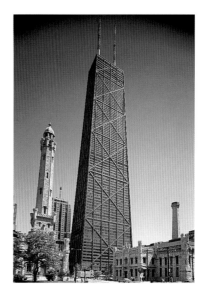

the invention of the high-speed elevator, coupled with the progressive refinement of the steel-frame structure. Today, the latter is no less vital than the former, since going steadily higher not only requires an equally steady improvement in the speed and efficiency of vertical transport, but also demands an increasingly stiff structure which simultaneously must not consume too much of the floor area of the lower regions. The higher you build, the less efficient the net-to-gross floorspace ratio of the entire building tends to become, as the structure thickens towards the point of maximum load (for services as well as structure) at the base. Similarly, the higher you go, the more it costs per gross square foot to build, and the more it costs to run the finished building. Therefore from the economic standpoint, skyscrapers are a very strange way of achieving large amounts of covered space – unless land is very scarce and expensive indeed, and ground conditions are favourable.

Both conditions apply in rocky, sea-girt Manhattan and to a lesser extent in lakeside Chicago, but a financial or corporate district does not have to be physically restricted and geologically helpful in order for its buildings to go high. Proximity of the main institutions is more often what counts, and as these expand on their historic sites, up is the only way to go. As a we shall see, saving land is becoming increasingly crucial for other reasons, most of them

residential as much as commercial. Finally and inevitably, the symbolic value of the tall building – to an institution, to a city, or to a nation – can be sufficient to outweigh any purely financial or space consideration. Macho it most certainly is. The feminist critic Camille Paglia claimed in 1993 that it was impossible to imagine a skyscraper designed by a woman. Nobody contradicted her.

Primitive powered elevators were relatively common in British factories and warehouses by 1835, transferred soon after to hotels. They were transformed in the United States when, in 1851, Elisha Graves Otis devised a safety brake to halt the car if the hoisting rope broke. Confidence in the modern elevator arrived at the New York Crystal Palace exhibition in 1853-4, when Otis personally cut the rope of his steam-powered elevator in the observation tower, and visibly did not plummet to his death. Around this time, the technology of high-pressure water and gas pipes, and steam-heating systems, had also evolved to a point where they were safe for use in high-rise buildings. Hydraulic power for elevators arrived in 1870 (and was used on the Eiffel Tower in 1889) and finally, by the turn of the century, reliable electric power. In the late 1990s cable-free electro-magnetic lifts, able to move laterally as well as vertically, are being developed, liberating towers such that they can do almost anything.

Even before this technology was adopted, the 1990s had already seen an extraordinary outbreak of tower-building, much of it in the Far East. The trend is inevitably ever upwards. Moreover, it is becoming normal for such buildings to have a layered mix of uses – retail, offices, housing, hotels being the usual ingredients, sometimes combined with a telecommunications function – each normally requiring its own entrance lobby at the relevant height. While mixed-use developments can function at almost any size, skyscrapers seems to work better on a large scale: the different functions are stacked rather than shuffled.

Frank Lloyd Wright claimed to have been there first, of course. He toyed intermittently with towers all his life – the unbuilt National Life Insurance scheme of 1924 was a stratified twenty-five-storey tower clad in permeable copper and glass screens – and in 1933 he conceived the idea of a half-mile high building to house the entire Chicago World's Fair. He conceived it as:
'a great skyscraper in which the Empire State Building might stand free in a central interior court space ... Instead of the old stage-props of the previous fairs, the same old miles of picture buildings faked in cheap materials, wrapped around a lagoon, fountain or theatrical waterfall in the middle ... let there be, for once, a genuine modern construction.'
After the Fair, he suggested, the tower could

a   b | c

d

Only now are architects beginning to come near Wright's prophecy of 1956:
a Jean Nouvel, Tour Sans Fins, Paris, 1989–93: model
b Skidmore, Owings and Merrill (SOM), John Hancock Center, Chicago, 1965–70
c Pei, Cobb, Freed & Partners, Bank of China, Hong Kong, 1985–90
d Frank Lloyd Wright, Mile High Tower, Illinois, 1956

house all the administrative departments of the City of Chicago.

There is no doubt about the graphic reality of Wright's 26-foot high rendering of the 'Mile-High Illinois' in 1956, a tower that proved to be strikingly prophetic. Building almost literally on the earlier idea, Wright proposed to put all the state departments of Illinois into it, and much more besides. It would be over 500 storeys high, contain a 100,000 people, 15,000 automobiles, and 100 helicopters. It would be nuclear-powered. He remarked: 'No one can afford to build it now, but in the future no one can afford not to build it'. Later he added: 'The Mile High would absorb, justify and legitimize the gregarious instinct of humanity.'

Wright appeared to think that by losing a lot of people and activities within the Mile High, land could be freed up for his earlier big idea – Broadacre City, his rurbanian 1930s riposte to Le Corbusier's Ville Contemporaine, 1922, in which Wright proposed that everyone would have an acre of land to farm. The vertical, in other words, would provide room for the horizontal, and this too was by no means an ill-judged theory. By the 1990s it had become apparent that, in order to maintain enough agricultural land to feed the rapidly expanding populations of the Third World and Far East, those populations would have to be concentrated in cities – and, in order to

accommodate the masses, those cities were going to have to be built very high. Others would farm the acre of land, but the idea was the same: the tower would spare the field.

Various construction methods are employed to achieve the necessary strength with height, but the commonest is the skeleton frame, developed from its nineteenth-century origins into the sophisticated stressed-skin structures of today. Of the alternatives, the relatively rigid central core or 'mast' with canti-levered floors survives despite its tendency to con-sume usable floorspace (a twin-core arrangement was proposed in 1989 for Jean Nouvel and Emmanuel Cattani's externally cylindrical Tour Sans Fins project at La Défense in Paris) while the solution of massive loadbearing walls ended with the nineteenth century. The turning point came with Bradford Lee Gilbert's Tower Building in New York, 1888-9 – in reality a very narrow eleven-storey slab, with an expressed tower frontage. Gilbert found that if he followed the New York building codes for wall thicknesses, so much floorspace would be lost at the lower levels that the building would be uneconomic. Instead he proposed a wind-braced iron frame. The structural diagram of this simple structure with its asymmetrical diagonal bracing, the beams diminishing in gauge the further up the building they appeared, is an aes-thetic prediction of such structurally expressive later

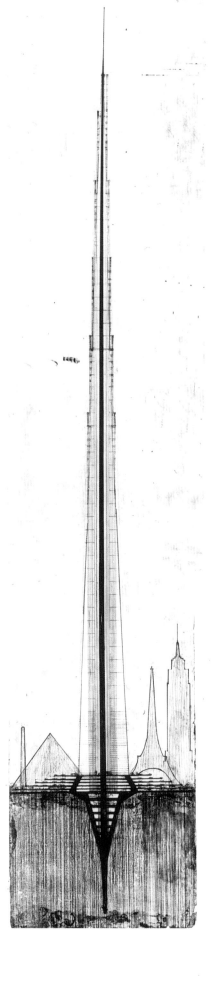

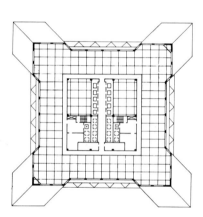

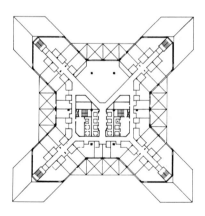

buildings as the Hancock Tower, or I M Pei's Bank of China, 1985–90, in Hong Kong. Gilbert, however, hid his structure behind a conventional masonry facade; much the same can be said of the granite-clad 1993 Landmark Tower in Yokohama, Japan's tallest at 296 metres, by Stubbins Associates. This acknowledges the main servicing problem of a skyscraper – the need for large vertical cores in the lower sections – by starting wide and tapering as it rises.

Gilbert's Tower Building was already much more advanced structurally than the three 1895 Chicago examples more commonly associated with the birth of the modern skyscraper – William Le Baron Jenney's ten-storey Home Insurance Building, Daniel Burnham's Reliance Building with fifteen storeys of relatively conventional semi-rigid riveted

steel frame but which had a highly glazed modern-looking external skin, and Adler and Sullivan's Guaranty Building – the square block aspiring to the condition of the tower. None of these attempted to tackle wind loading in the way that Gilbert did on the east coast.

New York being New York, Gilbert's pioneering construction was demolished as early as 1914. Building inspectors and engineers gathered to examine the building as it was dissected, and they concluded that Gilbert's famed cross-bracing was unstable and insecurely fastened, and that what had really held the building upright for 25 years was the weight of the masonry flank walls. This was of no consequence: by adopting the space-saving braced frame, Gilbert won his client an extra $10,000 a

year in rent in the 1890s. Such economics are frequent determinants of skyscraper design. Fazlur Khan's externally braced solution to the Hancock Tower, which allowed cheaper steel to be used more sparingly, is claimed to have saved $15 million over a conventionally engineered tower of the same height, while the bundled 'tube' engineering principle of his and Bruce Graham's 1974 Sears Tower, also determined by economics, led to its distinctive external setbacks. The Sears held the record as the world's tallest for more than twenty years. Savings of a different kind prevailed at Norman Foster's Hongkong and Shanghai Bank tower, 1979–86, long famed as the most costly building per square foot in the world (see also 'Workplace'). There, the decision to cool the building with seawater piped through a tunnel from

Hong Kong's harbour – rather than using conventional chillers – saved 25,000 square feet of space and recouped its extra capital cost within ten years, with considerable long-term ecological benefits.

After a century when tall building technology was a predictable battle between New York and Chicago, with New York taking the honours for most of the century, the situation became more complicated. For four decades, the 381-metre Empire State Building in New York by Shreve, Lamb and Harmon had held the title. It lost it to the 344-metre John Hancock Center in Chicago in 1969, and snatched it back in 1972 with Minoru Yamasaki's 417-metre twin-towered World Trade Center, 1966–73, the apparent blandness of which concealed an advanced stressed steel-mesh skin. In 1974, Chicago and SOM regained

a   Skidmore, Owings and
    Merrill, Sears Tower, Chicago,
    1974
b   The Stubbins Associates,
    Landmark Tower, Yokohama,
    Japan, 1993: plans
c   Landmark Tower:
    contextual view

d   Skyline of Hong Kong
    showing Pei Cobb Freed &
    Partners, Bank of China,
    Hong Kong, 1985–90;
    Foster and Partners, Hongkong
    and Shanghai Bank,
    Hong Kong, 1979–86

a

b   c   d

a c d
b

the trophy with the 443-metre Sears Tower, and there it rested until 1997, when Cesar Pelli – an architect who came to skyscrapers relatively late in his career – completed the twin pagodas of the 450-metre Petronas Towers in Kuala Lumpur, Malaysia. Named after the state petroleum company, the Petronas Towers were the first in a new series of the 'world's tallest building' contest, a game played now between China, Taiwan, Japan, Korea and Australia. A game that is, as it was before, all to do with prestige: for architects, their clients, the host city, the host nation.

The post-modern era brought back the notion of the 'classical' skyscraper. That is, a building that is not just a kind of extruded tube or faceted crystal, but one which has a clearly defined bottom, middle and top. The aptness of the tower as an inhabited classical column was explored by Adolf Loos with his giant Doric pillar in the *Chicago Tribune* competition of 1922: curious that the winning design in that famous competition – by Raymond Hood and John Mead Howells – should have been superficially gothic, so relating it to architecture's other great structural system (but this was truly 'Gothick' in the Walpole manner: an architectural principle reduced to decorative cladding). Hood and Howells played the game rather more successfully in one key aspect: the base of the building was

regarded as being of the street, and treated as if it were a four-storey city block turning the corner. Then came the vertical shaft – not unreminiscent of Barry and Pugin's Victoria Tower at the Palace of Westminster, 1835–52 – and finally the octagonal lantern top, poached from Ely Cathedral, with added flying buttresses. Such a search for historic precedents for the skyscraper building differed only in its lack of irony from Philip Johnson's famous 'Chippendale Skyscraper', the AT&T building of 1978–83 with its broken pediment and *mélange* of classical, gothic and Deco motifs, which became a touchstone in architectural debate (also discussed in 'Workplace'). Raymond Hood, as it happened, abandoned historicism soon after. Regardless of the elevational treatment, skyscrapers continued to separate into the two types: the extruded and the horizontally layered. The World Trade Center in New York, the 1974 Fiat tower at La Défense in Paris by Roger Saubot and François Jullien with SOM, and Nouvel's unbuilt Tour Sans Fins, also intended for La Défense, are extrusions *par excellence*: in contrast Johnson's AT&T building and Foster's Hongkong and Shanghai Bank have their tripartite division in common, if nothing else.

The social dimension of a skyscraper need not be, but often is, associated with its permeability or otherwise to the city around. The multi-use

Hancock Tower was designed to have its own internal life-patterns, and largely excluded the city, while the monocultural Fiat Tower in Paris, rising shiny and black from the La Défense podium like a missile emerging from its silo, is as purely corporate and exclusive as it is possible to get: so uncompromising, so sleek, and so intensely powerful as a result. It is unlike most American skyscrapers, which have a tradition of bringing in public space at lobby level. The Miesian plaza, as explored in the Seagram building of 1954–8, is not the typical New York response, which has rather more to do with the inclusive ground-life of the Rockefeller Center (Raymond Hood going modern with a consortium of others, 1931–40). Now here was a model: a complete assemblage of city uses at low level, including entertainment in the form of a music hall and the Radio City movie house, plus a two-level public square – part of which later became a winter ice rink – with shops, plus an underground shopping plaza and a variety of terraces. From this rose the tall and slender seventy-storey RCA tower, limestone-clad but stripped of historic accretions, acknowledging the spirit of the age by gently stepping back to form an understated pinnacle. But to those at street level, the tower might as well not be there, so little does it impinge: that is the usual New York trick, and it is one that the later slab-and-podium solution, pioneered by Gordon Bunshaft of

The move towards greater
articulation of towers
carries the danger of cultural
condescension:
a Cesar Pelli, Petronas Towers,
   Kuala Lumpur, Malaysia,
   1992–7: aerial perspective
b Petronas Towers:
   contextual view
c Petronas Towers: plans
d Minoru Yamasaki, World Trade
   Center, New York, 1966–73

b

e

a

c d

SOM's widely copied Lever House of 1950–2, could not manage nearly so successfully.

Mies would have none of it, rejecting even the mediating device of the podium block: his towers were designed to be seen full-on, though they were usually made permeable at ground level by the device of raising the block on *pilotis*. Norman Foster to some extent goes the Miesian route in the setting of his Hongkong and Shanghai Bank, but there the public space of Statue Square is made to sweep right underneath the building, the belly of which is transparent. Bunshaft, revisiting the genre for his National Commercial Bank of Jeddah in 1979–83, slyly placed the podium – a low-rise circular building – alongside the tower, which thus acted as a detached campanile. This historical moment – the tower hops down off its podium, like the sculpture of David Smith in the late 1950s – was overlooked because of the brilliance of Bunshaft's other new tricks. By now over seventy years old, at Jeddah he invented the cut-out skyscraper by slicing three huge square holes in its solid flanks – two one side, one on the other, all three together combining to provide daylight on every floor. This marked the birth of the 'sky lobby'. Aesthetically speaking, the building could be disassembled and rearranged as three blocks, side by side. It took Foster some years to catch up with Bunshaft's late-flowering creativity, but he managed it in his

Commerzbank tower in Frankfurt, 1991–7, Europe's tallest, where the 'bites' are taken out of the tower in spiral fashion and faired-in behind glazing like sports car headlights (see 'Workplace').

If the Chippendale skyscraper represented one return to the street-aware towers of the inter-war period, then Hugh Stubbins' Citicorp Center of 1977 was an attempt to create another Rockefeller. By starting the tower high in the air on four vast columns – placed not at the corners but at the centres of each side – Stubbins made room both for a new church (this was all previously church land) and a successful, if small, open plaza; but also a very good seven-storey public atrium, complete with shops and restaurants. European atrium buildings very seldom open to the public: here, the Citicorp atrium succeeds in achieving some of the public vitality of the Rockefeller Center. True, you cannot ignore the huge tower rising above you in all its fifty-seven storeys of dazzling white aluminium cladding: its powerful cantilevered bottom corners hover rather menacingly high above the plaza. The chamfered top to the Citicorp tower succeeds in imparting character with none of the theatricality of a Johnson building (his 'Lipstick' tower, clad in shiny red granite, is nearby) and moreover it has a purpose, containing a 400-ton concrete damper block that slides on a film of oil, controlled by hydraulic rams, to counteract its

tendency to sway in high winds. The engineers Ove Arup later devised a 'pendulum' for a similar purpose in Nouvel's Tour Sans Fins in Paris, intended to be on public display in the top-floor restaurant. This potentially alarming device has yet to see the light of day.

The smaller skyscrapers, which are less dependent on large-scale structure than those in the 'supertall' league, tend to offer more architecturally: from Gio Ponti and Pier Luigi Nervi's beautiful slender Pirelli Tower of 1958 in Milan – a stretched hexagon in plan – to Kohn Pedersen Fox's 333 Wacker Drive in Chicago, a curvilinear building of 1979–83 that attempts some of the same tricks in unrelieved reflective curtain walling, and with some success. It is certainly more memorable than the same practice's massively taller octagonal 311 South Wacker Drive tower, 1990. Perhaps nobody worked harder at re-inventing the skyscraper, however, than Norman Foster, and no building of this type in the world was so heavily, intensely designed as the Hongkong and Shanghai Bank, 1979–86. There is a touch of Raymond Hood's RCA tower in the way the building is conceived as a bundle of vertical slices, although one would be hard pressed to find any other resemblance. The Hong Kong bank is in the Eiffel tradition of a tower derived from bridge technology. In this case the whole building is supported from eight steel masts via suspension trusses and vertical hangers,

a Philip Johnson, 'Lipstick' building, New York, 1981–6
b Kohn Pederson Fox, 333 Wacker Drive, Chicago, Illinois, 1979–83
c The Stubbins Associates, Citicorp Center, New York, 1977: contextual view
d Citicorp Center: street level
e Foster and Partners, Century Tower, Tokyo, 1987–91

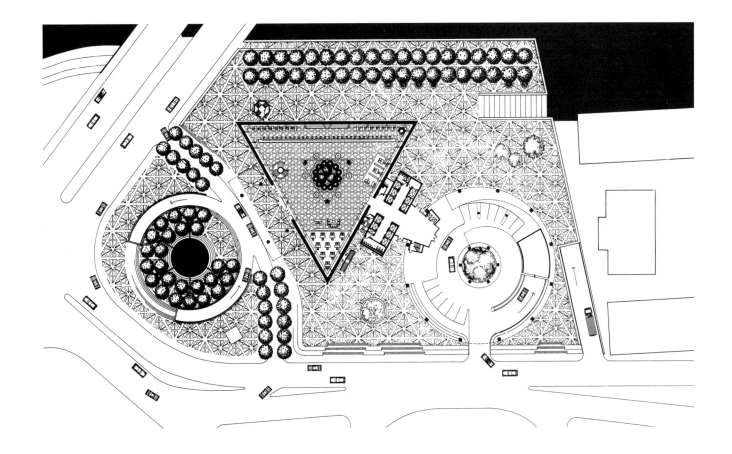

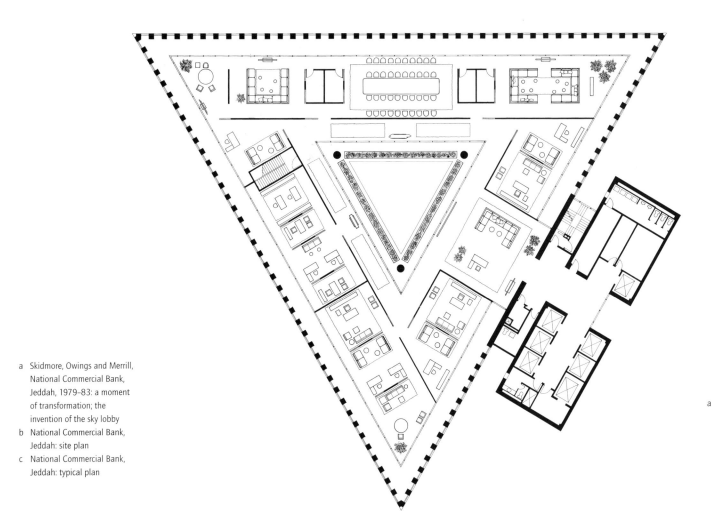

a   Skidmore, Owings and Merrill,
    National Commercial Bank,
    Jeddah, 1979–83: a moment
    of transformation; the
    invention of the sky lobby
b   National Commercial Bank,
    Jeddah: site plan
c   National Commercial Bank,
    Jeddah: typical plan

b

a | c

and this structure – as with the cross-bracing of the Hancock Tower – is fully expressed externally. Internally, a series of double-height spaces coincides with the intervals of the deep trusses with their associated cross-bracing running through the depth of the building. An internal atrium rising a third of the way up is partially daylit via a periscope arrangement involving a 30-ton rectangular 'sunscoop' slung off the south side of the building tracking the sun. With the vast majority of its components prefabricated all over the world and shipped in, this was an example of the globally sourced, high-technology building, an image rendered all the stronger by the fact that, during construction, it was shrouded in bamboo scaffolding tied together with string – the traditional Asian method, and one capable of withstanding hurricanes.

The aesthetic of the Hongkong bank is wholly a result of its method of construction, an aesthetic that is not confined to the exterior, but permeates the whole internal life of the building. At every point you are reminded how you are being suspended in the sky: every visable structural conponent evidently has an important role within the load bearing capacity. It is both earnest and restless, and quite unlike a conventional tower, where big efforts are made to make the internal spaces as neutral as those found in any low-rise building. As usual, a process of

unarguable logic led Foster through many permutations to the final built design. It raises the question: did the skyscraper need to be reinvented in this beefy engineering-led aesthetic? After all, subsequent Foster buildings used their own unarguable logic to arrive at rather different solutions. This reinvented skyscraper turned out not to be an easily reproduced kit of parts, as at first it might appear, but – as usual with the Great Leaps Forward of the high-tech set – a very highly crafted one-off item. Of course some of the lessons learned here were applied elsewhere – not least in Foster's own earthquake-proof Century Tower in Tokyo, 1987–91 – but this was not to be a repeatable, steadily refined design approach of the type that Mies accomplished.

The corporate skyscraper, for so long a symbol of competing companies in New York and Chicago – and of the rivalry of those two cities – had finally come to Europe relatively late in the twentieth century to play the same game. Paris, London and Frankfurt indulged in fitful bursts of tower building from the 1960s onwards. The cluster of towers, as an urban form, came to imply prosperity and available floorspace. The height of the buildings did not necessarily have to match the economic importance of the city: indeed London, routinely acknowledged as one of the three main centres of world finance (the others being New York and Tokyo), is strangely ambivalent

about the form, with the result that many London examples are half-hearted. Nonetheless, when Frankfurt built Helmut Jahn's Messeturm, 1985–91, to be Europe's tallest at 251 metres, the City of London saw it as a challenge to its power. While it had never bothered much about Paris in the 1970s when its La Défense office district began to sprout heavenwards along with the separate 229-metre Montparnasse tower, Frankfurt was seen as a real challenger to the might of London's financial district in a way that Paris – with its relatively unimportant Bourse – had not been. Much was made of the fact that the Messeturm was even taller than London's Canary Wharf tower by Cesar Pelli, and opened slightly earlier than that gleaming obelisk. For his part, Jahn insisted that the height of the building was not the prime consideration: he had to house a given number of workers, German building codes insisted that office workers must be seated near a window – so a deep plan was out – and so the tower, much influenced by the jazz-age skyscrapers of Manhattan, rose high and slender.

By 1996, the Messeturm was about to be eclipsed in Frankfurt by Norman Foster's slightly taller Commerzbank tower, and the Norwegian-owned Kværner group duly gave Foster the opportunity to design London a related Millennium Tower, complete with a bifurcated headpiece of apartments

a

b

a   Murphy Jahn, Messeturm,
    Frankfurt, Germany, 1985–91
b   Foster and Partners,
    Millennium Tower, London,
    1996: photomontage

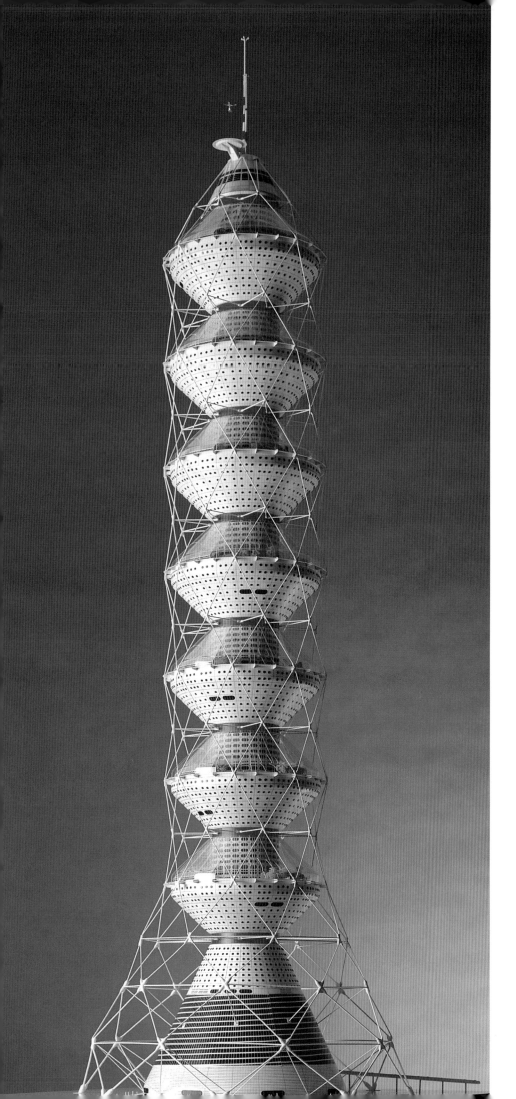

on top that would bring the crown to the United Kingdom. London refused the offer: the tower was seen as being simply too bulky, and Foster had to design a smaller building for the site instead. Given that the number of people employed in the financial services industry alone in London was by that time higher than the entire population of Frankfurt, this kind of 'mine's bigger than yours' exercise, popular in the 1980s, had come to be seen by many in the conservation-minded British Establishment as rather vulgar and unnecessary.

Yet other factors were at play. London undoubtedly had a shortage of a particular kind of large-floorplate office space at the time, when an economic boom was under way and financial institutions were jostling for position in the Square Mile. The proximity factor started to make itself felt. Foster's tower design could be seen as no more than an elegant block graph demonstrating supply and demand: if desire for good office space and a prestigious address increases to a certain level in a confined and wealthy financial centre, and if there are no artificial constraints, then up shoots the graph, and the tower gets higher accordingly. In the centre of London, however, artificial constraints do apply, more strongly than in most world cities. To make a parallel with economics, the London planning system is Keynesian rather than monetarist. The physical result of this

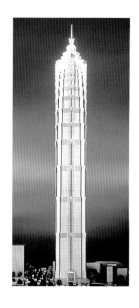

compression was to force the new office space out sideways – either in the form of deep-basement 'groundscrapers' in the traditional City, or into another location altogether. Canary Wharf, in London's previously derelict Docklands a few miles east, fitted the bill. It took a healthy amount of the City overspill, and recreated the old London tradition of having newspapers cheek by jowl with finance houses, as the City had rubbed along with Fleet Street. Squeezed out of their ancient home to make way for groundscrapers, several British national newspapers found a home in Pelli's Canary Wharf tower instead.

The posturings of European cities were minor-league in comparison. European towers were usually monocultural – either offices or homes, very seldom mixed, although there are quirky exceptions such as the 1976–9 David Murray John Tower in Swindon, England, which is an aluminium-clad double-decker sandwich of flats over offices, in turn sprouting from a retail mall, designed by Douglas Stephen and the Building Design Partnership. Not until Foster's swiftly abandoned London Millennium Tower project was this typically American high-rise arrangement of retail-corporate-residential seriously proposed again in the UK. Frightened by the prospect, London's planners then introduced anti-tower guidelines to make sure nothing similar happened again. Sporadic projects for European great towers continued to pop up,

particularly in former Eastern bloc cities such as Warsaw and Moscow, but the big shift that has happened in skyscraper pre-eminence towards the end of the twentieth century leapfrogged Europe *en route* from America to the Pacific Rim.

Some of the early research on the emerging breed of mixed-use supertower was, however, Anglo-American. In 1985 the theory-based Future Systems – then comprising Jan Kaplicky in London and David Nixon in Los Angeles, and working for NASA on the design of a space station, moon base, and extendible orbiting structures – devised a modular, repeatable, and potentially very tall mixed-use tower named 'Coexistence'. Kaplicky and Nixon deliberately photo-montaged their design into the skylines of both New York and London, in order to emphasize its universality. Unlike previous tower visionaries such as Wright, who cared little for dull things like construction feasibility, they took very great care with the nuts and bolts of the scheme, right down to the building methods and sequence. As their starting point they took a United Nations report predicting (correctly) that by the year 2000 half of the world's population would be city-based, and that many of those cities would start to coalesce into eighteen or twenty megacities. Kaplicky and Nixon designed Coexistence to combine high-density housing with both offices and public open space. The pair knew

that the office and homes mix was nothing new, at least not in the United States, and they acknowledged the precedent of the John Hancock Tower: but the way the two elements were differently expressed within the building, and the creation of open space in the sky, was highly original.

Future Systems' optimistic view of technology was clear in its description of the project: *'The concept proposed ... combines a wide range of human activities in a single giant "mother-structure" of the future – a structure conceived in the belief that people can live and coexist in self-contained communities in the sky, nurtured and protected by twenty-first-century construction technology.'* They placed their accommodation in a series of doughnut-shaped units dropped onto a central service and structural mast. The lower half of each doughnut ring, forming an inverted cone, would be offices, the upper half residential. While the offices filled their conic volume, the apartments were taken back into a cylindrical form, surrounded with gardens, the resulting open space protected by an openable transparent enclosure. Therefore neither offices nor homes would overlook each other. A larger cone of entertainment, hotel and parking space would form the base, while educational institutions and civic offices would be right at the top. The resulting stack of city pods was to be tensioned by an external

a   Future Systems, 'Coexistence' research project, New York and London, 1985: an influential project that completely reinvented the idea of the mixed-use tower
b   Cesar Pelli, Canary Wharf, London, 1988–91
c   Skidmore, Owings and Merrill, Jin Mao Tower, Shanghai, 1993–8

b   c

a

cylindrical truss structure, tied down to the ground like a television mast.

It was not such a great step from here to the Far East, with Norman Foster's more famous Millennium Tower project of 1989. This was the one designed not for London but for a site near Tokyo, intended not to be the tallest in Europe, but in the world – and, at twice the height of the Sears Tower, by a considerable margin. Intended to accommodate 50,000 people, living and working, the Millennium Tower, designed for the Obayashi Corporation, was intended to work in a way quite like the earlier Coexistence. Much of the thinking was along the same lines: the central mast, the clumps of accommodation separated by 'skyparks', the basket-weave external structure to stiffen it. It looked entirely different, however – a proportionally slender cone, its external structure arranged helically – reflecting perhaps the greater structural engineering input. Where Coexistence could in theory extend on upwards indefinitely – but would in reality be halted by the far higher wind loadings at great height – the Millennium Tower diminished to a point beyond which it could not go, its height determined by the width of its base. The taper was an elegant response to the problem of wind loading, offering less resistance the higher it rose. The designed project was scaled to rise to 840 metres – still lower than Wright's 'Mile High', but beginning to approach it in ambition. To emphasize its land-saving aspects, the tower was depicted rising from a man-made lagoon in the middle of Tokyo Bay.

Few of the very tall towers now being designed and built approach this for purity of line. SOM, once so restrained, had by the 1990s loosened up considerably, with dubious aesthetic consequences. Their octagonal 88-storey Jin Mao Tower in Shanghai, 1993–8, ostensibly designed in accordance with the principles of geomancy or *feng shui* – and sometimes compared to a bamboo shoot – came out looking even more pagoda-like than Cesar Pelli's Petronas Towers in Kuala Lumpur. The design unease was reminiscent of Western architects' efforts to come to grips with Islamic motifs in the Middle East in the 1970s. Elsewhere, symmetry was abandoned in the 457-metre Chongqing Tower by Haines, Lundberg, Waehler of New York, completed in 1997, which snitched the 'world's tallest' crown from Pelli's

Petronas Towers by just 7 metres. There, a polygonal shaft breaks away into a tall atrium and rectilinear hotel at the summit. Other towers that had confidently started out as 'world's tallest' lost the crown before they even gained it, such as Kohn Pedersen Fox's gracefully chamfered Shanghai World Financial Tower, 1997–2001, close to SOM's offering. But though KPF could not win in pure height terms, this practice's record in re-thinking the external appearance of the skyscraper stood it in good stead. Where its early buildings unashamedly derived from the Manhattan of the 1930s, its more recent buildings – such as their 1993 DG Bank building in Frankfurt, sharing the skyline with the throwback Messeturm – have been more of their own time. The DG Bank engages a square tower with a taller cylinder, both

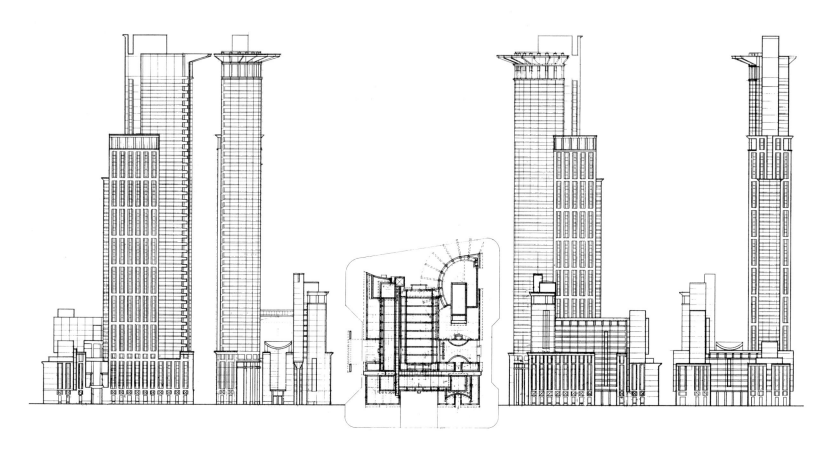

a Kohn Pedersen Fox, Shanghai World Financial Centre, Shanghai, 1997–2001: the huge aperture reduces wind resistance

b Kohn Pedersen Fox, DG Bank Headquarters, Frankfurt, Germany, 1993: elevations and plan

c DG Bank HQ: exterior view

c

a   b

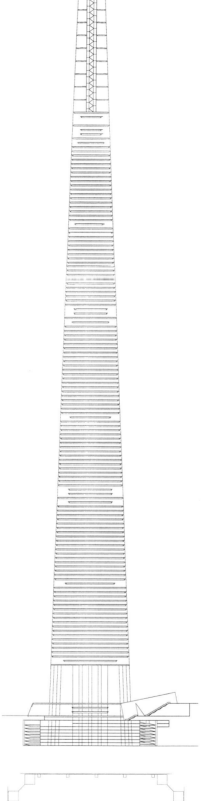

rising, as is the Frankfurt way, from a wider floorplate block on the building line of the street, and the whole building is topped with a huge Statue-of-Liberty headpiece that is overscaled to say the least. The Shanghai Tower is far better because it makes a virtue out of one particular structural necessity. The need to reduce wind resistance at very high level, solved by others with a tapering form, is here achieved by means of a large circular aperture marking the observation deck above the hotel element.

This return to relative design simplicity, if not modesty, was also signalled by the veteran Australian architect Harry Seidler with the first 1996 version of the super-tall Melbourne Tower – rigorously geometric within a strongly expressed tapering frame – and then by Denton Corker Marshall with the preferred second, more ethereal, version. Unusually, the two were put out to public vote by the tower's promoter, Bruno Grollo, who had funded DCM's earlier Governor Phillip and Macquarie Towers in Sydney. Denton Corker Marshall's Melbourne Tower, 1996 onwards, is intended to be 680 metres tall, comfortably the world's tallest so far. A four-sided obelisk, its cladding cantilevers out beyond the edge of each face to form a re-entrant angle in which scenic lifts will run. As with Nouvel's Tour Sans Fins project in Paris, the tower continues on above the final inhabited level as a dematerializing glass screen, lit from within

as the *ne plus ultra* of lighthouses. But more importantly for the development of the tower form, it is conceived as a mixed-use building – apartments, shops, offices, auditoria, restaurants, hotel and, of course, observation decks. Like a greatly enlarged version of Stubbins' Citicorp Center in New York, the building will stand on four legs and start high up in the air – 35 metres from the ground, allowing it to straddle a public garden within a park, rather as the Eiffel Tower does. The section of the building is simple: like Bunshaft's National Commercial Bank in Jeddah, it is three buildings on top of each other, but in this case three towers instead of three blocks, each with its own lobby. All are served by a complex vertical transport network including triple-decker lifts.

Such projects depend on a boom economy and are inevitably delayed or abandoned as soon as the world's financial winds turn chill. These, of course, blow on the bad projects as well as the good. It is inescapable that most of the very tall towers in the world – for instance Central Plaza in Hong Kong (Ng Chun Man and Associates, 1992), the Nina Tower (1994 on, Kwok and Associates) or their Taiwanese equivalents – have little going for them except their height. They do not necessarily come to define the cities or countries they bloom in. Few people know what Frankfurt's Messeturm looks like – its existence is curiously as much statistical as

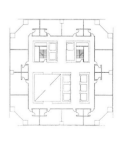

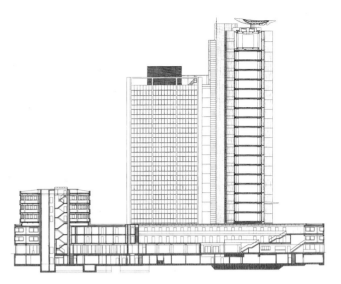

physical, a characteristic it shares with Pei Cobb Freed's First Interstate Bank tower in Los Angeles, 1984-6, which may be the tallest building in the western United States, may sport a curious crown on top, but which is so banal, it manages to slide out of everyone's consciousness. The Rialto Centre in Melbourne by Gérard de Peu and Partners, 1985, is at the time of writing Australia's tallest sharing with Kenzo Tange's 1986 Oub Building in Singapore (that country's tallest) a well-justified anonymity. What this tells us is that skyscrapers are now so common as not necessarily to be considered as individually special as they used to be: most of them are merely the building-blocks of the city, working as an ensemble.

In contrast, everyone knows the unique shape of San Francisco's Transamerica Pyramid by William Pereira, 1972, which although relatively short, makes an aesthetic virtue out of its movement-absorbing earthquake-protecting structure. All tall towers, in fact, perform reasonably creditably in quakes, owing to the vertical flexibility of their high steel frames; conventional low masonry structures are far more dangerous. Pereira however made much of his above-ground triangulated shock absorbers, which although scarcely subtle, fit in neatly with the triangular geometry of the building. It has come to define San Francisco as much as the Golden Gate Bridge: perhaps because the ostensible reason for its

appearance is directly related to the fault-line mentality of that city. Such one-offs happen as seldom as they ever did: the best one can usually hope for are the sleeker constructions of the better traditional sky-scraper practices, such as the tapering oval of Ellerbe Becket's Graha Kuninghan tower in Jakarta, Indonesia, 1995-9, or KPF's spiral-glazed constructions planned for Beirut and Malaysia.

Malaysia was the birthplace of the 'bioclimatic skyscraper' as pioneered by Ken Yeang of T R Hamzah and Yeang. His relatively tiny 1989-92 cylindrical office tower in Kuala Lumpur, Menara Mesiniaga, festooned with vegetation, equipped with an ascending spiral of open 'sky-courts', and designed to capture cooling breezes, became a symbol of high-rise eco-architecture in a way that his larger mixed-use Y-shaped MBF Tower in Penang, 1990-3, did not. Partly this was because the Kuala Lumpur building chimed in more with the aesthetic preoccupations of Western architects, who themselves were working in this direction. Yeang's 1994 Hitechniaga tower project took this thinking further, but the true test of its success lies in the fact that SOM's 66-storey Post and Telecom Tower project in Xiamen, China, 1996-2000, adopted the Yeang look with its spiralling sky lobbies on a far larger scale, although it was supposedly inspired by the wave-forms of radio frequencies. Instantly, it seemed,

this eco-style had hit the mainstream. Wind-tunnel-tested, naturally ventilated skyscraper schemes then became as commonplace in the Far East as double-skinned chimney-effect blocks by Piano, Foster et al became in Europe (see 'Workplace'). Piano designed a wind-cooled mixed-use tower, 1996 onwards, on Macquarie Street, Sydney, with sail-like flanks: another nautical metaphor for Sydney Harbour.

In Berlin, the young practice of Sauerbruch and Hutton instead plumped for cross-ventilation combined with a solar chimney effect in their very narrow-plan GSW Tower, 1991-9, for the city's public housing agency. This is notable for the painterly effect of its internal mesh solar screens behind the west-facing facade, and also for the fact that it dares to revive the idea of the slab and podium. However, the very slender tall curving slab form was chosen for historical as much as passive solar reasons: it is sited on the vanished line of the old Berlin Wall where a dialogue takes place between the showpiece residential towers of the former East and the ostentatiously affluent office towers of the old West. It is consequently both a mediating device and a commentary on a moment in history: building after the Wall.

Architects and engineers began to tinker with the idea of rooftop wind turbines to help reduce the enormous power consumption of such large buildings: coincidentally the technology of

Mixed-use, a template for the twenty-first-century city:

a Denton Corker Marshall, Melbourne Tower, Melbourne, Australia, 1996: section

b Melbourne Tower: plans

c Melbourne Tower: photomontage

d Sauerbruch Hutton, GSW Headquarters Office Tower, Berlin, 1991-9: section. Attempts at an eco-scraper; can a truly sustainable tower be achieved?

e Denton Corker Marshall, Governor Phillip Tower, Melbourne, Australia, 1996: exterior

f Governor Phillip Tower: lobby

g Skidmore, Owings and Merrill et al, Post and Telecom Tower project, Xiamen, China, 1996-2000: model

	c	d g
a		
b		e f

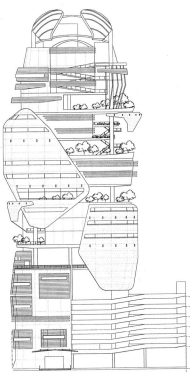

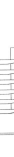

photo-voltaic panels reached a point at which they could be made translucent, even near-transparent. This brought tantalizingly nearer to reality the dream of the sustainable skyscraper, using its great height to generate its own cooling and power needs from wind and sun combined. Yeang was quick to research the possibilities of photovoltaic 'fritting' in glass – the frits, or applied dots, serving both to generate power and to act as solar shading – and in 1995 he estimated that 60 per cent of a building's power needs could be met in this way. This technological development had a further implication: given the highly polluted air of many cities – which makes natural ventilation a poisonous business – self-generated air-conditioning would deal with the problem inside while not adding to it outside. At the time that this book went to press, such an ideal balance had yet to be struck in any significantly tall building, not least on grounds of cost: yet it appears a realistic medium-term proposition.

When it comes to the new generation of giants, architects either struggle to put an appropriate jacket on the chosen structural solution, or go with the flow and let the structure dictate the aesthetics. Either way the outcome, successful or unsuccessful, can work only at the macro scale. The normal architectural concerns of detail at the human scale, of fine detailing, become irrelevant. Therefore – if we

are to regard supertowers as a form of city planning rather than architecture, and increasingly we must – it follows that their designers must be regarded principally as masterplanners. It follows equally that other architects should be called in to design specific elements within the overall tower: elements that – were it a horizontal city – would conventionally be regarded as 'buildings'.

The single biggest shift in architectural patronage this century has undoubtedly been the separation of external architecture and internal fit-out. This dubious distinction between inside and outside, spurred by the corporate sector's speculative building frenzy, has resulted in some bizarrely schizophrenic buildings – cool modern interiors with encrusted post-modern skins, and high-tech blocks with faux-Regency boardrooms. There are architects who design only the outer three inches of a building, and others who only create environments within them. Well, so be it: the practice stands a chance of redemption in the logical conclusion of the twenty-first-century supertower. The skyscraper skin, under this new dispensation, ceases to be 'architecture' at all, and becomes instead an enveloping device, the equivalent of the old city wall. The burgeoning of ever-greater towers at the world's node points is a cause for optimism rather than despair. Within them, a very great deal of new thinking is possible.

a c

b d

a　T R Hamzah & Yeang, Hitechniaga Tower project, 1994: model
b　Hitechniaga Tower: elevation
c　T R Hamzah & Yeang, MBF Tower, Penang, Malaysia, 1990–3
d　William Pereira, Transamerica Pyramid, San Francisco, 1972: a form that was to prove prescient

SELECT BIBLIOGRAPHY

TYPOLOGY

General

Forsyth, Alastair, *Buildings for the Age –
New Building Types, 1900–1939*,
London, 1982

Kronenbourg, Robert, *Portable
Architecture*, Oxford, 1996

Pevsner, Nikolaus, *A History of Building
Types*, London, 1976

Saxon, Richard, *Atrium Buildings*,
London, 1986

Visual Arts

Brawne, Michael, *Kimbell Art Museum
by Louis I Kahn*, London, 1992

Davis, Douglas, *The Museum
Transformed*, New York, 1990

Martin, Wagenaar, and Welkamp, (eds),
*Mendini, Starck, de Lucchi, Coop
Himmelblau in Groningen*,
Groningen, 1995

Montaner, Josep, *New Museums*,
London, 1990

Steele, James, (ed), *Museum Builders*,
London, 1994

Performance

Mulryne, Ronnie, and Margaret
Shewring, *Making Space for Theatre*,
Stratford-upon-Avon, 1995

Neumann, Dietrich, (ed), *Film
Architecture*, Munich, 1996

Steele, James, (ed), *Theatre Builders*,
London, 1995

Sydney Opera House, London, 1995

Learning

Koolhaas, Rem, *2 Bibliotheques: Jussieu*,
(private printing)

Library Builders (introduction by
Michael Brawne), London, 1995

Jacques, Michael, (ed), *La Bibliothèque
Nationale de France*, Basel, 1995

Weston, Richard, *Schools of Thought –
Hampshire Architecture 1974–1991*,
Winchester, 1991

Religion

Bruegmann, Robert, (ed), *Modernism at
Mid-Century: the Architecture of the
United States Air Force Academy*,
Chicago and London, 1994

Drew, Philip, *Church on the Water and
Church of the Light by Tadao Ando*,
London, 1996

Frishman, Martin, and Hasan-Uddin
Khan, (eds), *The Mosque*,
London, 1994

Norman, Edward, *The House of God:
Church Architecture, Style and History*,
London, 1990

Serageldin, Dr Ismail, and James Steele,
*The Architecture of the Contemporary
Mosque*, London, 1996

Spence, Basil, *Phoenix at Coventry – The
Building of a Cathedral*, London, 1962

Zabalbeascoa, Anatxu, *Igualada
Cemetery*, London, 1996

Consumerism

Gruen, Victor, *Urban Environment –
Survival of the Cities*, Chicago, 1973

Maitland, Barry, *The New Architecture of
the Retail Mall*, London, 1990

Manser, Jose, *Joseph Shops, Eva Jiricna*,
London, 1991

Wenz-Gahler, Ingrid, *Café Bar Bistro –
Design und Gastlichkeit*,
Stuttgart, 1993

Living

Betsky, Aaron, *Drager House*,
London, 1996

Frampton, Kenneth (photographs by
M Freeman and P Rocheleau), *The
Twentieth-Century American House:
Masterworks of Residential
Architecture*, London, 1995

Goldberger, Paul and Richard Rogers,
Richard Meier Houses, London, 1996

Kronenburg, Robert, *Houses in Motion*,
London, 1995

Lloyd, Peter, and Keith Collie, *San
Francisco Houses after the Fire*,
Cologne, 1997

Mead, Christopher, *Houses by Bart
Prince*, Albuquerque, 1991

Muthesius, Hermann, *The English
House*, Berlin, 1911

Muthesius, Stefan, *The English Terraced
House*, New Haven and London, 1982

Norberg-Schulz, Christian, *The Concept
of Dwelling: On the Way to Figurative
Architecture*, New York, 1985

Oliver, Davis, Bentley, *Dunroamin: the
Suburban Semi and its Enemies*,
London, 1981

Overy, Paul, *et al*, *The Rietveld Schröder
House*, London and Naarden, 1988

Pearson, Clifford A, (ed), *Modern
American Houses*, New York, 1996

Steele, James, *Eames House: Charles
and Ray Eames*, London, 1994

Welsh, John, *Modern House*,
London, 1995

Zabalbeascoa, Anatxu, *The House of the
Architect*, Barcelona, 1995

Workplace

Duffy, Francis, *The New Office*,
London, 1997

Duffy, Francis, *The Changing Workplace*,
London, 1992

Lambot, Ian, *The New Headquarters for
the Hongkong and Shanghai Banking
Corporation*, Hong Kong, 1986

Pelegrin-Genel, Elisabeth, *The Office*,
Paris, 1996

Powell, Kenneth, *Lloyd's Building
by Richard Rogers Partnership*,
London, 1994

Powell, Kenneth, *Vauxhall Cross*,
London, 1992

Industry

Abel, Chris, *Renault Centre*,
London, 1991

Jenkins, David, *Financial Times Print
Works*, London, 1991

Jenkins, David, *Schlumberger Cambridge
Research Centre*, London, 1993

Perry, Victoria, *Built for a Better Future:
the Brynmawr Rubber Factory*,
Oxford, 1994

Leisure

Dunlop, Beth, *Building a Dream –
The Art of Disney Architecture*,
New York, 1996

Friebe, Wolfgang, *Buildings of the World
Exhibitions*, Leipzig, 1985

Marling, Karal Ann, (ed), *Designing
Disney's Theme Parks*,
Paris and New York, 1997

Transport

Binney, Marcus, *Architecture of Rail:
the Way Ahead*, London, 1995

Bode, Steven, and Jeremy Millar, (eds),
Airport, London, 1997

Lawrence, David, *Underground
Architecture*, London, 1994

Parissien, Steven, *Station to Station*,
London, 1997

Richards, Brian, *Transport in Cities*,
London, 1990

Zukowsky, John, *Building for Air Travel*,
Zurich, 1996

Sport

Bale, John, *Sport, Space and the City*,
London, 1993

Gaudin, Henri and Bruno Gaudin,
Le Stade Charlety, Paris, 1994

Inglis, Simon, *The Football Grounds of
Europe*, London, 1990

The Civic Realm

Fitzgerald, Alan, *Canberra and the New
Parliament House*, Sydney, 1983

Beck, Haig, (ed), *Parliament House,
Canberra: A Building for the Nation*,
Sydney, 1988

Myerson, Jeremy, (ed), *New Public
Architecture*, London, 1996

Rogers, Richard and Philip Gumuchdjian
(eds), *Cities for a Small Planet*,
London, 1998.

Sharon, Yosef, *The Supreme Court
Building, Jerusalem*, Jerusalem, 1993

Spens, Michael, *William Alsop – Le
Grand Bleu, Marseilles*, London, 1994

Towers

Bennett, David, *Skyscrapers: The World's
Tallest Buildings and How They Work*,
London, 1995

Glendinning and Muthesius, (eds),
Tower Block, New Haven and
London, 1994

Goldberger, Paul, *The Skyscraper*,
New York, 1981

Golding, William, *The Spire*,
London, 1964

Huxtable, Ada Louise, *The Tall Building
Artistically Reconsidered: The Search
for a Skyscraper Style*, New York, 1984

Landau, Sarah Bradford, and Carl W
Condit, *Rise of the New York
Skyscraper 1865–1913*, New Haven
and London, 1996

Sabbagh, Karl, *Skyscraper, the Making
of a Building*, London, 1989

Yeang, Kenneth, *The Skyscraper,
Bioclimatically Considered*,
London, 1995

GEOGRAPHICAL LOCATION

Asia

Gavin, Angus, and Ramez Maluf, *Beirut Reborn*, London and Beirut, 1996

Hillenbrand, Robert, *Islamic Architecture*, Edinburgh, 1994

Khan, Hasan-Uddin, *Contemporary Asian Architects,* Cologne, 1995

Kroyanker, David, *Jerusalem Architecture*, London, 1994

Mitchell, George, (ed), *Architecture of the Islamic World: Its History and Social Meaning*, London, 1995

Steele, James, *Architecture for Islamic Societies Today*, London, 1994

Tillotson, Giles, *The Tradition of Indian Architecture*, New Haven and London, 1989

Australia

Jahn, Graham, *Contemporary Australian Architecture*, Sydney, 1994

Europe

Alsop, McLean, Störmer, *City of Objects – Designs on Berlin*, London, 1992

Balfour, Alan, (ed), *World Cities: Berlin*, London, 1995

Barker, Felix, and Ralph Hyde, *London As It Might Have Been*, London, 1982

Becker, Olley, Wang, (eds), *20th century Architecture – Ireland*, Munich and New York, 1997

Beret, Chantal, (ed), *Architectures en France – Modernité, Post-Modernité*, Paris, 1981

British Architects Today: Six Protagonists, Milan, 1991

Contemporary European Architects I, Cologne, 1994

Fraser, Derek, *Berlin*, Manchester, 1996

Gleiniger, Matzig, Redecke, (eds), *Paris Contemporary Architecture*, Munich and New York, 1997

Ibelings, Hans, *20th Century Architecture in the Netherlands*, Rotterdam, 1995

Jodidio, Philip, *Contemporary European Architects III, IV,* Cologne, 1995, 1996

Hans Kollhoff and Helga Timmermann: Projects for Berlin, Antwerp, 1994

Meyhöfer, Dirk, *Contemporary European Architects II*, Cologne, 1995

Nairn, Ian, *Nairn's London*, Harmondsworth, 1988

Powell, Kenneth, (ed), *World Cities: London*, London, 1993

Tafuri, Manfredo, *History of Italian Architecture, 1944–1985*, Cambridge, MA, 1989

Thorne, Martha, and Pauline Saliga, (eds), *Building in a New Spain, Contemporary Spanish Architecture*, Madrid and Chicago, 1992

Tzonis, Alexander, and Liane Lefaivre, *Architecture in Europe Since 1968*, London, 1992

Japan

Bognar, Botond, (ed), *World Cities: Tokyo*, London, 1997

Bognar, Botond, (ed), *The New Japanese Architecture*, New York, 1990

Coaldrake, William H, *Architecture and Authority in Japan*, London, 1996

Contemporary Japanese Architects I, Cologne, 1995

'Japanese Architecture I, II, III', *Architectural Design*, Nos 73, 99, 107, London, 1988, 1992, 1994

Kurokawa, Kisho, *New Wave Japanese Architecture*, London, 1993

Nitschke, Günter, *From Shinto to Ando: Studies in Architectural Anthropology in Japan*, London, 1993

Stewart, David B, *The Making of a Modern Japanese Architecture, 1868 to the Present*, Tokyo, 1987

Tange, Kenzo, and Noboru Kawazoe, *Ise: Prototype of Japanese Architecture*, Cambridge, MA, 1965

North America

Anderton, Frances, and John Chase, *Las Vegas: The Success of Excess*, London, 1997

Anyone Corporation, 'Seaside and the Real World: A Debate on American Urbanism,' *Architecture New York*, No 1 (July/August 1993)

Bluestone, Daniel, *Constructing Chicago*, New Haven and London, 1991

Cohen, S, *Chicago Architects*, Chicago, 1976

Experimental Architecture in LA (introduction by Frank Gehry), New York, 1991

Hays, Michael, and Carol Burns, (eds),

Thinking the Present. Recent American Architecture, New York, 1990

Hess, Alan, *Viva Las Vegas: After Hours Architecture* (foreword by R Venturi, D Scott Brown and S Izenour), San Francisco, 1993

Huxtable, Ada Louise, *The Unreal America: Architecture and Illusion*, New York, 1997

Jacobs, Jane, *The Death and Life of Great American Cities*, New York, 1961

Jodidio, Philip, *Contemporary Californian Architects*, Cologne, 1995

Jodidio, Philip, *Contemporary American Architects I, II,* Cologne, 1993, 1996

Jordy, William H, *American Buildings and their Architects, Vol 4: The Impact of European Modernism in the Mid-Twentieth Century*, New York, 1972

Mohney, David, and Keller Easterling, (eds), *Seaside: Making A Town in America,* New York, 1991

Steele, James, *Los Angeles Architecture: The Contemporary Condition*, London, 1993

Toy, Maggie, (ed), *World Cities: Los Angeles*, London, 1994

Tzonis, Alexander, Liane Lefaivre and Richard Diamond, *Architecture in North America Since 1960*, London, 1995

South America

Holston, James, *The Modernist City, an Anthropological Critique of Brasilia*, Chicago, 1989

Pendleton-Jullian, Ann M, *The Road That Is Not a Road and the Open City, Ritoque, Chile*, Cambridge, MA, 1996

General

Cohen, Jean-Louis, *Scenes of the World to Come – European Architecture and the American Challenge 1893–1960*, Montreal and Paris, 1995

Davidson, Cynthia D, and Ismail Serageldin, *Architecture Beyond Architecture, The Aga Khan Award for Architecture*, London, 1996

Economakis, Richard, (ed), *Building Classical: A Vision of Europe and America*, London, 1993

Kulterman, Udo, *Architects of the Third World*, Cologne, 1980

ARCHITECTS MONOGRAPHS

Alvar Aalto
Weston, Richard, *Alvar Aalto*,
London, 1995;
Alvar Aalto, London, 1978

Ahrends Burton and Koralek
Ahrends Burton Koralek (introduction
by Peter Blundell Jones), London,
1991;
Vance, Mary, *Ahrends Burton Koralek*,
Monticello, Illinois, 1985

Allies & Morrison
Allies & Morrison, Ann Arbor,
Michigan, 1996

Alsop & Störmer
Gooding, Mel, *William Alsop:
Buildings and Projects*, London, 1992;
Spens, Michael, *Le Grand Bleu*,
London, 1994

Tadao Ando
Dal Co, Francesco, *Complete Works:
Tadao Ando*, London, 1995 (includes
articles by and on Ando);
Pare, Richard, *Tadao Ando: The
Colours of Light*, London, 1996

Architecture Studio
*Architecture Studio, Selected and
Current Works*, Victoria, 1995

Alfredo Arribas
*Alfredo Arribas Arquitectos Asociados:
works 1991–95*, Wasmuth, 1995;
Alfredo Arribas, Barcelona, 1991

Arquitectonica
Dunlop, Beth, *Arquitectonica*,
New York, 1991

Arup Associates
Dunster, David (ed), *Arups on
Engineering*, Berlin, 1997;
Brawne, Michael, *Arup Associates*,
London, 1983

Gunnar Asplund
Cruickshank, Dan (ed), *Masters
of Building: Erik Gunnar Asplund*,
London, 1988

Shigeru Ban
Shigeru Ban, Barcelona, 1997

Lina Bo Bardi
Carvalho Ferraz, Marcelo, *Lina Bo
Bardi*, Milan and Sao Paulo, 1994

Luis Barragán
Rispa, Paul (ed), *Barragán: The
Complete Works*, London, 1996;
Riggen Martinez, Antonio, *Luis
Barragán: Mexico's Modern Master
1902–1988*, New York, 1996;
Ambasz, Emilio, *The Architecture of
Luis Barragán*, New York, 1976

Geoffrey Bawa
Brace Taylor, Brian, *Geoffrey Bawa*,
London, 1992

Günter Behnisch
Gauzin-Müller, Dominique, *Behnisch &
Partner 50 Years of Architecture*, Berlin
and London, 1997;
Kandzia, Christian (ed), *Behnisch
and Partner: Designs 1952–87*,
Stuttgart, 1987

Ben van Berkel
Ben van Berkel: Mobile Forces,
Berlin, 1994

Gunnar Birkerts
Kaiser, Kay, *The Architecture of
Gunnar Birkerts*, Washington and
Florence, 1989

Ricardo Bofill
James, Warren A (ed), *Ricardo Bofill,
Taller de Arquitectura: Buildings and
Projects 1960–1985*, New York, 1988

Gottfried Böhm
Darius, Veronika, *Der Architekt
Gottfried Böhm: Bauten der sechziger
Jahre*, Düsseldorf, 1988;
Gottfried Böhm, Stuttgart, 1988;
Raev, S (ed), *Gottfried Böhm: Bauten
und Projekte 1950–1980*,
Cologne, 1982

Bolles-Wilson & Partner
Bolles-Wilson, Barcelona, 1994;
*Architekturburo Bolles-Wilson Projekte
1988–92*, Münster, 1993;
Architekturburo Bolles-Wilson,
Barcelona, 1991

Mario Botta
Nicolin, Perluigi, *Mario Botta:
Buildings and Projects 1961–1982*,
New York, 1984;
Pizzi, Emilio, *Mario Botta, The Complete
Works*, vol. I, *1960–1985*, Basel, Boston
and Berlin, 1993; vol. 2, *1985–1990*,
1994

Branson Coates
Poynor, Rick, *Nigel Coates, The City
in Motion*, London, 1989

Richard Buckminster Fuller
Pawley, Martin, *Buckminster Fuller*,
London, 1990

Santiago Calatrava
Sharp, Dennis, *Santiago Calatrava*,
London, 1996

Alberto Campo Baeza
Alberto Campo Baeza (introduction
by Kenneth Frampton), Boston, 1996

Giancarlo de Carlo
Mioni, Angela, and Etra Connie
Ocihialini, *Giancarlo de Carlo: imagini
e frammenti*, Milan, 1995;
Maki, Fumihiko, *Giancarlo de Carlo:
architect of harmony between the old
and the new*, Tokyo, 1987

David Chipperfield
Chipperfield, David, *Theoretical
Practice* (introduction by Joseph
Rykwert), London, 1994;
David Chipperfield, Barcelona, 1992

Henri Ciriani
Henri Ciriani (foreword by Richard
Meier, introduction by François
Chaslin), Rockport, 1997;
Chaslin, François, *et al*, *Henri Ciriani*,
Paris, 1984

Coop Himmelblau
*Coop Himmelb(l)au: From Cloud to
Cloud*, Klagenfurt, 1996;
*Blaubox, Coop Himmelblau:
Wolf D Prix, H Swiczinsky*,
London, 1988;
*Coop Himmelblau: die Faszination der
Stodt* (foreword by Frank Werner),
Darmstadt, 1988

Charles Correa
Correa, Charles, and Kenneth
Frampton, *Charles Correa*,
London, 1996;
Cantacuzino, Sherban, *Charles Correa*,
London and Singapore, 1984 (2nd
edn, 1987)

Antonio Cruz + Antonio Ortiz
Cruz/Ortiz (introduction by Rafael
Moneo), New York, 1996;
Antonio Cruz y Antonio Ortiz,
Barcelona, 1991

Edward Cullinan
Powell, Kenneth, *Edward Cullinan
Architects*, London, 1995

CZWG
Sudjic, Deyan, *et al*, *English Extremists*:
*The Architecture of Campbell
Zogolovitch Wilkinson & Gough*,
London, 1988

Decq + Cornette
Melhuish, Clare, *Odile Decq Benoît
Cornette*, London, 1997

Denton Corker Marshall
Beck, Haig, and Jackie Cooper,
*Australian Architects: Denton Corker
Marshall*, Canberra, 1987

Günther Domenig
Raja, Raffaele, *Günther Domenig:
Werkbuch*, Salzburg, 1991

Balkrishna Doshi
Curtis, William, *Balkrishna Doshi:
An Architecture for India*,
Ahmedabad, 1988

Mary and Peter Doyle
The Architecture of Mary & Peter Doyle 1970–1990, Dublin, 1990

Andres Duany and Elizabeth Plater Zyberk
Mohney, D, and K Easterling (eds), *Seaside: Making a New Town in America*, London, 1991

Charles and Ray Eames
Kirkham, Pat, *Charles and Ray Eames: Designers of the Twentieth Century*, Cambridge, MA, 1995

Edmond + Corrigan
Hamann, Conrad, *Cities of Hope: Australian Architecture and Design by Edmond and Corrigan, 1962–92*, Melbourne, 1993

Peter Eisenman
Eisenman Architects: Selected and Current Works, Mulgrave, 1995;
Bedard, Jean-François (ed), *Cities of Artificial Excavation: The Work of Peter Eisenman 1978–1988*, Montreal and New York, 1994;
Moneo, Rafael, *et al*, *Wexner Center for the Visual Arts: The Ohio State University*, New York, 1989

Abdel Wahed El-Wakil
'The Mosque: Architecture of El-Wakil', *Albenaa*, vol. 6, no. 34, 1987

Craig Ellwood
McCoy, Esther, *Craig Ellwood*, Venice, 1968

Richard England
Abel, Chris, *Transformations – Richard England, 25 Years of Architecture*, Malta, 1987

Ralph Erskine
Egelius, Mats, *Ralph Erskine, Architect*, Stockholm, 1990;
Collymore, Peter, *The Architecture of Ralph Erskine*, London, 1982

Terry Farrell
Terry Farrell: Selected and Current Works, Mulgrave, 1994;
Terry Farrell, London, 1993

Hassan Fathy
Steele, James, *Hassan Fathy*, Architectural Monograph, London, 1988;
Richards, J M, I Serageldin and D Rastorfer, *Hassan Fathy*, London, 1985

Sverre Fehn
Norberg-Schultz, Christian, *Sverre Fehn: opera completa*, Milan, 1997;
Fjeld, Per Olaf, *Sverre Fehn: The Thought of Construction*, New York, 1983

Norman Foster
Treiber, Daniel, *Norman Foster*, London, 1995;
Lambot, Ian (ed), *Norman Foster ... Buildings and Projects, vol. 1, 1964–1973*, Godalming, 1991, *vol. 2, 1971–1978*, Hong Kong, 1990, *vol. 3, 1978–1985*, Hong Kong, 1990

Massimiliano Fuksas
Massimiliano Fuksas: neue Bauten und Projekte, Zurich and London, 1994

Future Systems
Pawley, Martin, *Future Systems – Story of Tomorrow*, London, 1993

Frank Gehry
Futagawa, Yukio (ed), *Frank O Gehry*, Tokyo, 1993;
Arnell, Peter, *et al*, *Frank Gehry: Buildings and Projects*, New York, 1985

Bruce Goff
Saliga and Woolever, (eds), *The Architecture of Bruce Goff*, Munich and New York, 1995

Teodoro González de Leôn
Heyer, Paul, *Mexican Architecture: The Work of Abraham Zabludovsky and Teodoro González de Leôn*, New York, 1978

Michael Graves
Michael Graves; Buildings and Projects 1990–1994, New York, 1995;
Vogel Nichols, Karen, Patrick J Burke and Caroline Hancock, *Michael Graves: Buildings and Projects 1982–1989*, New Haven and London, 1990

Allan Greenberg
Allan Greenberg, Selected Work, London, 1995

Vittorio Gregotti
Tafuri, Manfredo, *Vittorio Gregotti: progetti e architetture*, Milan and New York, 1982

Nicholas Grimshaw
Architecture, Industry and Innovation: The Early Work of Nicholas Grimshaw and Partners (introduction by Colin Amery), London, 1995;
Moore, Rowan (ed), *Structure, Space and Skin, The Work of Nicholas Grimshaw & Partners*, London, 1993

Walter Gropius
Giedion, Sigfried, *Walter Gropius*, New York, 1992

Gwathmey Siegel
Gwathmey Siegel, Buildings and Projects 1982–1992, New York, 1993

Zaha Hadid
Futagawa, Yukio (ed), *Zaha Hadid*, Tokyo, 1986;
Zaha Hadid 1983–1991, El Croquis monograph, Madrid, 1991

Hiroshi Hara
Stewart, David B and Yukio Futagawa (eds), *Hiroshi Hara*, Tokyo, 1993

Itsuko Hasegawa
Itsuko Hasegawa, 1993;
Itsuko Hasegawa: Recent Buildings and Projects, Basel, 1997

Zvi Hecker
Feireiss, Kristin (ed), *Zvi Hecker: die Heinz-Galinski Schule in Berlin*, Tübingen, 1996

John Hedjuk
Five Architects: Eisenman, Graves, Gwathmey, Hejduk, Meier, New York, 1972

Ron Herron
Banham, Reyner, *The Visions of Ron Herron*, London, 1994

Herman Hertzberger
Herman Hertzberger: Accommodating the Unexpected: Projects 1990–1995, Rotterdam, 1995

Herzog & de Meuron
Herzog & de Meuron, Tokyo, 1995;
Herzog & de Meuron, Madrid, 1993;
Wang, Wilfried, *Herzog & de Meuron*, Zürich, 1992;
Wang, Wilfried, *Herzog & de Meuron, Projects and Buildings 1982–1990*, New York, 1990

Hodgetts + Fung
Hodgetts + Fung: Scenarios and Spaces (introduction by Kurt Foster), New York, 1997

Steven Holl
Steven Holl, Tokyo, 1996

Hans Hollein
Pettena, Giani, *Hans Hollein: Works 1960–1988*, Milan, 1988;
Architekten Hans Hollein, Stuttgart, 1987;
Mackler, Christoph, *Hans Hollein*, Aachen, 1978;

Michael Hopkins
Davies, Colin, *Hopkins: The Work of Michael Hopkins and Partners*, London, 1993

Ingenhoven, Overdeik, Kahlen & Partner
Hochhaus RWE AG Essen, Düsseldorf, 1997

Kazuhiro Ishii
Kazuhiro Ishii, Tokyo, 1990

Arata Isozaki
Doi, Yoshitake and Arata Isozaki, *Arata Isozaki: opere e progetti* (preface by Francesco Dal Co), Milan, 1994; Futagawa, Yukio (ed) (criticism by Kenneth Frampton), *Arata Isozaki, Vol. 1: 1959-1978*, Tokyo, 1991; Stewart, David B and Hajime Yatsuka, *Arata Isozaki: Architecture 1960-1990* (preface by Richard Koshalek), New York, 1991

Franklin D Israel
Hines, Thomas S and Franklin D Israel, *Franklin D Israel, Buildings and Projects* (introduction by Frank O Gehry), New York, 1992

Toyo Ito
Toyo Ito (introduction by Charles Jencks), London, 1995

Helmut Jahn (Murphy Jahn)
Miller, Nory, *Helmut Jahn*, New York, 1986; *Helmut Jahn 1982-1992*, Tokyo, 1992; *Murphy Jahn, Master Series*, Mulgrave, 1995

Eva Jiricna
Eva Jiricna Designs, London, 1987; Pawley, Martin, *Eva Jiricna: Design in Exile*, London, 1990

Philip Johnson
Jacobus, John M, *Philip Johnson: Architecture*, New York, 1979; Knight, Carleton, *Philip Johnson John Burgee Architecture 1979-85*, New York, 1985; Kipnis, Jeffrey (ed), *Philip Johnson: Recent Works*, London, 1996

Jourda et Perraudin
Mardaga, Pierre (ed), *Jourda et Perraudin*, Liege, 1993

Louis I Kahn
Scully, Vincent, *Louis I Kahn*, New York, 1962; Ronner, Heinz, Sharad Jhaveri and Alessandro Vesella, *Louis I Kahn: The Complete Works 1935-1974*, Boulder, 1977; Brownlee, David and David G De Long, *Louis I Kahn: In the Realm of Architecture*, New York, 1991; Buttiker, Urs, *Louis I Kahn: Light and Space*, Basel, 1993

Josef Paul Kleihues
O'Regan, John, *Josef Paul Kleihues*, Dublin, 1983; Shkapich, Kim (ed), *Josef P Kleihues, The Museum Projects*, New York, 1989; Mesecke, Andrea and Thorsten Scheer (eds), *Josef Paul Kleihues: Themes and Projects*, Basel, 1996

Kohn Pedersen Fox (KPF)
James, Warren A (ed), *KPF: Kohn Pedersen Fox: Architecture and Urbanism 1986-1992*, New York, 1993; Chao, Sonia R and Trevor D Abramson (eds), *Kohn Pedersen Fox: Buildings and Projects 1976-1986*, New York, 1987

Hans Kollhoff
Hans Kollhoff, Barcelona, 1991

Rem Koolhaas OMA
OMA/Rem Koolhaas, 1987-1992, Madrid, 1992; Goulet, Patrice, *OMA, Rem Koolhaas: Six Projects*: Paris, 1990; Lucan, Jacques, *OMA, Rem Koolhaas*, Milan and Paris, 1990

Tom Kovac
Tom Kovac, London, 1998

Leon Krier
Economakis, Richard (ed), *Leon Krier: Architecture and Urban Design 1967-1992*, London, 1992

Rob Krier
Frampton, Kenneth (ed), *Rob Krier*, New York, 1982

Shiro Kuramata
Shiro Kuramata 1967-1987, Tokyo, 1988

Kisho Kurokawa
Kisho Kurokawa: Abstract Symbolism (preface by Aldo Castellano, introduction by Kisho Kurokawa), Milan, 1996; *Kisho Kurokawa: Selected and Current Works*, Mulgrave, 1995

Denys Lasdun
Curtis, William JR, *Denys Lasdun, Architecture, City, Landscape*, London, 1994

John Lautner
Escher, Frank (ed), *John Lautner, Architect*, London, 1994

Le Corbusier
Le Corbusier, Architect of the Century, London, 1987; Curtis, William JR, *Le Corbusier: Ideas and Forms*, London, 1986

Juha Leiviskä
Webb, Michael (ed), *Juha Leiviskä*, Tokyo, 1995

Ricardo Legorreta
Attoe, Wayne, *The Architecture of Ricardo Legorreta*, Austin, 1990; Mutlow, John V (ed), *The Architecture of Ricardo Legorreta*, London, 1997

Daniel Libeskind
Libeskind, Daniel, *Radix: Matrix: Works and Writings of Daniel Libeskind*, New York, 1996; Libeskind, Daniel, *Daniel Libeskind: Countersign*, London, 1992

Berthold Lubetkin
Allan, John, *Berthold Lubetkin*, London, 1992

Fumihiko Maki
Maki, Fumihiko, *Maki and Associates: Recent Major Work*, Tokyo, 1990; Salat, Serge, *Fumihiko Maki, an Aesthetic of Fragmentation*, New York, 1988

Imre Makovecz
Edwin Heathcote, *Imre Makovecz*, London, 1997; János, Frank, *Imre Makovecz*, Budapest, 1979

Werner March
Schmidt, Thomas, *Werner March: Architekt des Olympia Stadions 1894-1976*, Berlin, 1992

Martorell, Bohigas, Mackay
Drew, Philip, *Real Space: The Architecture of Martorell, Bohigas, Mackay, Puig*, Berlin, 1993

Rick Mather
Pearman, Hugh, *Rick Mather: Urban Approaches*, London, 1992; Welsh, John, *Zen Restaurants: Rick Mather*, London, 1992

Mecanoo
Somer, Kees, *Mecanoo architecten*, Rotterdam, 1995; *Mecanoo architekten*, Madrid, 1994

Richard Meier
Flaggel, Ingeborg (ed), *Richard Meier in Europe*, Berlin, 1997; Blaser, Werner, *Richard Meier Details*, Basel, 1996; Jodidio, Philip, *Richard Meier*, Cologne, 1995; Rykwert, Joseph, *Richard Meier, Architect*, New York, 1986 (vol 1), 1991 (vol 2)

Ludwig Mies van der Rohe
Blaser, Werner, *Mies van der Rohe*, Basel, 1997; Schultz, Franz, *Mies van der Rohe: A Critical Biography*, Chicago and London, 1985

Enric Miralles
Tagliabue, Benedetta, *Enric Miralles: Opere e progetti*, Milan, 1996; Tagliabue, Benedetta (ed), *Enric Miralles*, London, 1995

Mitchell Giurgola Architects
Mitchell Giurgola Architects, New York, 1983

Rafael Moneo
Rafael Moneo: Contra la indiferencia como norma, Santiago, 1995; *Rafael Moneo*, Tokyo, 1989; *Rafael Moneo 1990-1994*, Madrid, 1994

Charles Moore
Charles W Moore: Buildings and Projects, 1949-1986, New York, 1986

Moore Ruble Yudell
Steele, James (ed), *Moore Ruble Yudell*, London and Berlin, 1993

Morphosis
Weinstein, Richard, *Morphosis: Buildings and Projects II*, New York, 1994; Cook, Peter and George Rand, *Morphosis: Buildings and Projects*, New York, 1989

Eric Owen Moss
Eric Owen Moss, Buildings and Projects 2, introduction by Anthony Vidler, New York, 1996; *Eric Owen Moss*, London, 1993; *Eric Owen Moss, Buildings and Projects 1* (foreword by Philip Johnson, introduction by Wolf Prix), New York, 1991

Glenn Murcutt
Fromonot, Françoise, *Glenn Murcutt: Works and Projects*, London, 1995; Farrelly, E M, *Three Houses*, London, 1993; Drew, Philip, *Leaves of Iron: Glenn Murcutt, Pioneer of an Australian Architectural Form*, Sydney, 1985

Juan Navarro Baldeweg
Lahverta, Juan José, Angel González García and Juan Navarro Baldeweg, *Juan Navarro Baldeweg: opere progetti*, Milan, 1990; 2nd edn, 1996 (Spanish edn, Madrid, 1993); *Juan Navarro Baldeweg*, Madrid, 1995

Pier Luigi Nervi
Louis de Irizarry, Florita Z, *Work and Life of Pier Luigi Nervi*, Monticello, Illinois, 1984

Jean Nouvel
Boissière, Olivier, *Jean Nouvel*, Basel, 1996'
Goulet, Patrice, *Jean Nouvel*, Paris, 1994;
Jean Nouvel: Ra obra reciente 1987-1990, Barcelona, 1990

Frei Otto
Schanz, Sabine (ed), *Frei Otto, Bodo Rasch, finding form*, Stuttgart, 1995

John Pawson
John Pawson (introduced by Bruce Chatwin and Deyan Sudjic), Barcelona, 1992

I M Pei (Pei Cobb Freed & Partners)
Cannell, Michael, *IM Pei: Mandarin of Modernism*, New York, 1995; Wiseman, Carter, *The Architecture of I M Pei*, London, 1990

Gustav Peichl
Gustav Peichl: neue Projekte, Basel, 1996; *Gustav Peichl: Buildings and Projects*, Stuttgart, 1992

Cesar Pelli
Pelli, Cesar: *Selected and Current Works* (introduction by Michael J Crosbie, Mulgrave), 1993; Gray, Lee Edward and David Walters, *Pattern and Context, Essays on Cesar Pelli*, Charlotte, NC, 1992; Goldberger, Paul, *et al*, *Cesar Pelli: Buildings and Projects 1965-1990*, New York, 1990

Dominique Perrault
Michael Jacques (ed) *La Bibliothèque Nationale de France*, Basel, 1995; *Dominique Perrault*, London, 1994

Renzo Piano
Piano, Renzo, *The Renzo Piano Logbook*, London, 1997; Buchanan, Peter, *Renzo Piano Building Workshop: Complete Works*, 1994 (vol 1), 1996 (vol 2), 1997 (vol 3); Goldberger, Paul, *Renzo Piano and Building Workshop: Buildings and Projects 1971-89*, New York, 1989

Demetri Porphyrios
Demetri Porphyrios: Selected Buildings and Writings, London, 1993

John Portman
Goldberger, Paul, *GA57: John Portman and Associates*, Tokyo, 1981

Christian de Portzamparc
Généalogie des formes, les designs de Christian de Portzamparc, Paris, 1996; *Christian de Portzamparc, Institut Français d'Architecture*, Paris, 1984

Antoine Predock
Antoine Predock, London, 1997; *Architectural Journeys - Antoine Predock*, New York, 1995 Collins, Brad and Juliette Robbins, *Antoine Predock Architect*, New York, 1994

Bart Prince
Mead, Christopher, *Houses by Bart Prince*, Albuquerque, 1991

Raj Rewal
Brace Taylor, Brian, *Raj Rewal*, London, 1992; *Raj Rewal*, Paris, 1986

Peter Rice
Rice, Peter, *Exploring Materials - the Work of Peter Rice*, London, 1992

Ian Ritchie
Ritchie, Ian, *(Well)Connected Buildings*, London, 1990

Miguel Angel Roca
Broadbent, Geoffrey (ed), *Miguel Angel Roca*, London, 1994

Richard Rogers
Burdett, Richard, *Richard Rogers Partnership*, Milan, 1995; Sudjic, Dejan, *The Architecture of Richard Rogers*, London, 1994 Appleyard, Bryan, *Richard Rogers, A Biography*, London, 1986

Aldo Rossi
Ferlenga, Alberto (ed), *Aldo Rossi: opera completa 1993-1996*, Milan, 1996; Morris Adjmi (ed) *et al*, *Aldo Rossi: Drawings and Projects*, New York, 1993; Rossi, Aldo, *Aldo Rossi Architect*, Berlin, 1993; *Aldo Rossi: The Complete Buildings and Projects 1981-1991*, London, 1992; Ferlenga, Alberto (ed), *Aldo Rossi: architetture 1959-1987*, Milan, 1987

RoTo
RoTo, Michigan Architecture Papers I, Ann Arbor, 1996

Eero Saarinen
Nakamina, Toshio, *Eero Saarinen*, Tokyo, 1984

Stanley Saitowitz
Bell, Michael (ed), *Stanley Saitowitz*, postscript by Lars Larup, Houston, 1996

Philippe Samyn
Samyn & Partners: Architecture to be Lived, Milan, 1997

Antonio Sant'Elia
Da Costa Meyer, Esther, *The Work of Antonio Sant'Elia*, New Haven and London, 1995

Carlo Scarpa
Los, Sergio, *Carlo Scarpa*,
Cologne, 1993;
Dal Co, Francesco and Mazzariol,
(eds), *Carlo Scarpa: The Complete
Works*, New York, 1986

Hans Scharoun
Blundell Jones, Peter, *Hans Scharoun*,
London, 1995

Rudolph Schindler
March, Lionel and Judith Sheine,
*R M Schindler, Composition and
Construction*, London, 1993

Karl Friedrich Schinkel
Bindman, David and Gottfried
Riemann, (eds), *Karl Friedrich Schinkel
'the English Journey'*, New Haven and
London, 1993

Scogin, Elam and Bray
Linder, Mark (ed), *Scogin, Elam and
Bray: Critical Architecture/Architectural
Criticism*, New York, 1992

Harry Seidler
Frampton, Kenneth, *Harry Seidler: Four
Decades of Architecture*, London, 1992

Kazuo Shinohara
Kazuo Shinohara (introduction by
Irmtraud Schaarschmidt-Richtor),
Berlin, 1994;
Kazuo Shinohara, New York, 1981

SITE
Restany, Pierre and Bruno Zevi, *SITE:
Architecture as Art*, London and
New York, 1980

Alvaro Siza
Castanheira (eds), *Alvaro Siza: opere e
progetti*, Milan, 1996;
Fleck, Brigitte, *Alvaro Siza*,
London, 1995;
Trigueiros, Luiz (ed), *Alvaro Siza
1986-1995*, Lisbon, 1995;
de Llano, Pedro and Carlos
Dos Santos, José Paulo (ed), *Alvaro Siza:
Works and Projects 1954-1992*,
Barcelona, 1993

Skidmore Owings & Merrill
*Skidmore, Owings & Merrill: Selected
and Current Works*, Mulgrave, 1995;
Herselle Krinsky, Carol, *Gordon
Bunshaft of Skidmore, Owings
& Merrill*, Cambridge, MA, and
London, 1988;
*Skidmore Owings & Merrill:
Architecture and Urbanism
1973-1983* (introduction by Albert
Bush-Brown), London, 1984

Alison and Peter Smithson
Webster, Helena (ed), *Modernism
without Rhetoric: the work of Alison
and Peter Smithson*, London, 1997

Snøhetta
Bibliotheca Alexandrina, Oslo, 1995

Sir Basil Spence
Spence, Basil *Phoenix at Coventry –
The Building of a Cathedral*,
London, 1962

Philippe Starck
Bertoni, Franco, *The Architecture
of Philippe Starck*, London, 1994;
Philippe Starck, Cologne, 1991

Robert A M Stern
Robert A M Stern: Buildings,
New York, 1996;
Robert A M Stern: Selected Works,
London, 1991

James Stirling
James Stirling and Michael Wilford,
London, 1994
Arnell, Peter and Ted Bickford (ed),
*James Stirling: Buildings and Projects
1950-1980*, New York, 1984

Hugh Stubbins
Ludman, Diane M, *Hugh Stubbins and
his Associates: the First Fifty Years*,
Cambridge, MA, 1986

Studio Asymptote
Asymptote: Architecture at the Interval,
New York, 1995

Studio Granda
Studio Granda, London, 1992

Shin Takamatsu
*Shin Takamatsu: Architecture
and Nothingness*, Milan, 1996;
Guillot, Xavier, *Shin Takamatsu*,
Paris, 1989

Takasaki Masaharu
*Takasaki Masaharu: An Architecture of
Cosmology*, Princeton, 1997

Minoru Takeyama
Bognar, Botond (ed) *Minoru
Takeyama*, London, 1995

Kenzo Tange
Kultermann, Udo, *Kenzo Tange*,
Barcelona, 1989;
Boyd, R, *Kenzo Tange*, New York
and London, 1962;
Kultermann, Udo (ed), *Kenzo Tange
1946-1969: Architecture and Urban
Design*, Zurich and London, 1970

Yoshio Taniguchi
Taniguchi, Yohio, *The Architecture of
Yoshio Taniguchi*, Kyoto, 1996

Quinlan Terry
Aslet, Clive, *Quinlan Terry: The Revival
of Architecture*, London, 1986

Bernard Tschumi
Bernard Tschumi, Tokyo, 1994

Oswald Matthias Ungers
Klotz, Heinrich, *OM Ungers,
1951-1984, Bauten und Projekte*,
Brauschweig and Weisbaden, 1985

Ushida Findlay
van Schaik, Leon and Paul Carter
(eds), *Ushida Findlay – 2G
Monograph*, Barcelona, 1998;
Parallel Landscapes, Tokyo, 1996

Jørn Utzon
Sydney Opera House, London, 1995;
Jørn Utzon, Houses in Fredensborg,
Berlin, 1991

**Venturi Rauch and Scott Brown &
Associates**
*Venturi Rauch Scott Brown Associates:
On Houses and Housing*,
London, 1992;
von Moos, Stanislaus, *Venturi Rauch
and Scott Brown: Buildings and
Projects*, New York, 1987

Von Gerkan, Marg und Partner
Marg, Volkwin, *Neue Messe
Leipzig/New Trade Fair Leipzig*,
Basel, 1997;
Von Gerkan, Marg & Partner,
London, 1993

Michael Wilford
James Stirling and Michael Wilford,
London, 1994

Owen Williams
Cottam, David, *Sir Owen Williams
1890-1969*, London, 1986

Frank Lloyd Wright
McCarter, Robert, *Frank Lloyd Wright,
Architect*, London, 1997;
Gill, Brendan, *Many Masks, a Life of
Frank Lloyd Wright*, London, 1988

Minoru Yamasaki
Doumato, Lamia, *Minoru Yamasaki*,
Monticello, 1986

Ken Yeang
Balfour, Alan and Ivor Richards,
Bioclimatic Skyscrapers/Ken Yeang,
London, 1994;
Powell, Robert, *Ken Yeang:
Rethinking the Environmental Filter*,
Singapore, 1989

FURTHER READING

Historical

Benevolo, Leonardo, *History of Modern Architecture*, 2 Vols, Cambridge, MA, 1971

Benton, Charlotte, *A Different World – Emigré Architects in Britain, 1928–58*, London, 1995

Cruickshank, Dan, (ed), *Sir Banister Fletcher's A History of Architecture*, London, 1996

Curtis, William J R, *Modern Architecture Since 1900* (third edition), London, 1996

De Jong, Cees, and Erik Mattie, *Architectural Competitions, 1792–1949, and 1950–Today*, Cologne and Naarden, 1994

De Witt, Dennis, and Elizabeth De Witt, *Modern Architecture in Europe*, London, 1987

Ford, Edward R, *The Details Of Modern Architecture Volume 2: 1928–1988*, Cambridge, MA, 1996

Frampton, Kenneth, *Modern Architecture: A Critical History*, New York and London, 1980 (revised and enlarged, 1985; third edition, 1992)

Gossel, Peter, and Gabriele Leuthauser, *Architecture in the 20th Century*, Cologne, 1991

Jacobus, J, *Twentieth-Century Architecture: The Middle Years 1945–1965*, New York, 1966

Koulermos, Panos (and James Steele, (ed)), *Twentieth-Century European Rationalism*, London, 1995

Lampugnani, Vittorio Magnano, (ed), *Encyclopaedia of 20th Century Architecture*, Stuttgart, 1983

Peter, John, *The Oral History of Modern Architecture*, New York, 1994

Pevsner, Nikolaus, *Pioneers of the Modern Movement*, London, 1936, republished as *Pioneers of Modern Design from William Morris to Walter Gropius*, New York, 1949, reprint 1975

Samuel, Raphael, *Theatres of Memory*, London, 1994

Sharp, Dennis, *Modern Architecture and Expressionism*, London, 1966

Steele, James, *Architecture Today*, London, 1997

Tafuri, Manfredo, and Francesco Dal Co, *Modern Architecture*, New York, 1979

Theoretical

'Aspects of Minimal Architecture', *Architectural Design*, No 110, London, 1994

Banham, Reyner, *A Critic Writes*, San Francisco, 1996

Banham, Reyner, *Los Angeles: The Architecture of Four Ecologies*, London, 1971

Banham, Reyner, *The Architecture of the Well-Tempered Environment*, London, 1969

Betsky, Aaron, *Violated Perfection, Architecture and the Fragmentation of the Modern*, New York, 1990

Brand, Stewart, *How Buildings Learn – What Happens After They're Built*, New York, 1994

Corn, Joseph J, (ed), *Imagining Tomorrow – History, Technology and the American Future*, Cambridge, MA, 1986

'Deconstruction in Architecture, II, III', *Architectural Design,* No 72, 77, 87, London, 1988, 1989, 1990

Duffy, Francis, and Alex Henney, *The Changing City*, London, 1989

Farmer, John, *Green Shift – Towards a Green Sensibility in Architecture*, Oxford, 1996

Frampton, Kenneth (and John Cava, (ed)), *Studies in Tectonic Culture*, Cambridge, MA, 1995

Ghirardo, Diane, *Architecture After Modernism*, London, 1996

Giedion, Sigfried, *Space, Time and Architecture*, Cambridge, MA, 1941

Hitchcock, Henry-Russell, and Philip Johnson, *The International Style*, New York, 1932 and 1966

Howard, Ebenezer, *Garden Cities of Tomorrow*, London, 1898 and 1902

Jencks, Charles, *Architecture of the Jumping Universe*, London, 1996

Jencks, Charles, *The Language of Postmodern Architecture*, London, 1977

Jencks, Charles, *Modern Movements in Architecture*, New York, 1973

Jenks, Burton, Williams, (eds), *The Compact City – a Sustainable Urban Form?*, London, 1996

Johnson, Philip, and Mark Wigley, *Deconstructivist Architecture*, New York, 1988

Koolhaas, Rem, *Delirious New York: A Retroactive Manifesto for Manhattan*, New York, 1978 and 1994

Koolhaas, Rem, and Bruce Mau, *S, M, L, XL*, New York, 1995, Rotterdam, 1996

Krier, Rob, *Urban Space*, London, 1979

Larson, Magali Sarfatti, *Behind the Postmodern Facade: Architectural Change in Late Twentieth-Century America*, Los Angeles, 1993

Macrae-Gibson, Gavin, *The Secret Life of Buildings: An American Mythology for Modern Architecture*, Cambridge, MA, 1988

Norberg-Schulz, Christian, *Architecture: Meaning and Place*, New York, 1988

Papadakis, Andreas, (ed), *Theory and Experimentation*, London, 1992

Papanek, Victor, *The Green Imperative: Ecology and Ethics in Design and Architecture*, London, 1995

Pawley, Martin, *Theory and Design in the Second Machine Age*, London, 1990

Rassmussen, Steen Eiler, *Experiencing Architecture*, Boston, 1957

Rogers, Richard, *Cities for a Small Planet*, London, 1997

Rogers, Richard, *Architecture, a Modern View*, London, 1990

Riewoldt, Otto, *Intelligent Spaces – Architecture for the Information Age*, London, 1997

Rossi, Aldo, *The Architecture of the City*, (translated by Diane Ghirardo and Joan Ockman), Cambridge, MA, 1982

Rowe, Colin, *The Architecture of Good Intentions: Towards a Possible Retrospect*, London, 1994

Rowe, Colin, *The Mathematics of the Ideal Villa*, Cambridge, MA, 1976

Rudofsky, Bernard, *Architecture without Architects*, London, 1981

Stern, Robert A M, *Modern Classicism*, London, 1988

Sudjic, Deyan, *The 100 Mile City*, London, 1992

Tafuri, Manfredo, *Architecture and Utopia: Design and Capitalist Development*, Cambridge, MA, 1976

Tschumi, Bernard, *Architecture and Disjunction*, Cambridge, MA, 1994

Tschumi, Bernard, *The Manhattan Transcripts*, London, 1985, 1995

Turner, J F, *Housing by People: Towards Autonomy in Building Environments*, London, 1976

Tzonis, Alexander, and Liane Lefaivre, *Classical Architecture: The Poetics of Order*, Cambridge, MA, 1986

Unwin, Simon, *Analysing Architecture*, London, 1997

Venturi, Robert, *Iconography and Electronics upon a Generic Architecture*, Cambridge, MA, 1996

Venturi, Robert, *Complexity and Contradiction in Architecture*, New York, 1966

Venturi, Robert, Denise Scott Brown and Steven Izenour, *Learning From Las Vegas*, Cambridge, MA, 1972, 1977

Wilson, Colin St John, *The Other Tradition of Modern Architecture*, London, 1995

Wilson, Colin St John, *Architectural Reflections*, London, 1992

General

Chesterton, G K, *The Napoleon of Notting Hill*, London, 1904

Herzog, Thomas, (ed), *Solar Energy in Architecture and Urban Planning*, Munich and New York, 1996

Holden, Robert, *International Landscape Design*, London, 1996

Jellicoe, Geoffrey, and Susan Jellicoe, *The Landscape of Man*, London, 1987

Lubbock, Jules, *The Tyranny of Taste*, New Haven and London, 1995

Mackintosh, Iain, *Architecture, Actor and Audience*, London and New York, 1993

Moore, Suzi, and Terrence Moore, *Under the Sun – Desert Style and Architecture*, New York and Toronto, 1995

Nanji, Asim, (ed), *Building for Tomorrow: The Aga Kahn Award For Architecture*, London, 1995

Rand, Ayn, *The Fountainhead*, New York, 1943

Rice, Peter, *An Engineer Imagines*, London, 1993

Robbin, Tony, *Engineering a New Architecture*, Cambridge, MA, 1996

Rosenthal, Ruth, and Maggie Toy (eds), *Building Sights*, London, 1995

Scheuermann, Rudi, and Keith Boxer, *Tensile Architecture in the Urban Context*, Oxford, 1996

Wigginton, Michael, *Glass in Architecture*, London, 1996

Wolfe, Tom, *From Bauhaus to Our House*, New York, 1981

INDEX

Page numbers in **bold** refer to the illustrations
All buildings listed by architect, followed by practice name in parentheses where applicable.

510

ACKNOWLEDGEMENTS

AUTHORS ACKNOWLEDGEMENTS

This book, being a critical anthology, owes thanks to more people than can be individually mentioned: to other authors, not just of the books listed in the bibliography, but of numerous magazine articles from many countries. I am grateful to *The Sunday Times* newspaper in London for giving its architecture critic the scope to tackle this enterprise; to my editors David Jenkins, Iona Baird and Vivian Constantinopoulos at Phaidon Press for their patient guidance; to my picture researchers Sophia Gibb, Jemima Rellie and Laura Cleobury for tracking down some recalcitrant images; to Thomas Manss and David Law of Thomas Manss & Company for their excellent design and clear understanding of the text; to Hilary Bird for her formidably impressive index – a pleasure in itself; to Kate Hobson for cataloguing my own previously chaotic library such that it became a valuable resource; also to her and the rest of my family for all the lost evenings and weekends.

ILLUSTRATION CAPTIONS

Jacket Illustration: Rafael Viñoly, Hall A, Tokyo International Forum, Tokyo, 1990-6
p4: Günter Behnisch & Partner, Hysolar Research Building, University of Stuttgart, Stuttgart, Germany, 1987
The solarized images which open each chapter are as follows:
Visual Arts p20: Frank O Gehry & Associates, Guggenheim Museum, Bilbao, Spain, 1991-7
Performance p66: Rafael Viñoly, Hall A, Tokyo International Forum, Tokyo, 1990-6
Learning p102: James Stirling Michael Wilford & Associates, University of California Science Library, Irvine, California, 1988-94
Religion p136: Mario Botta, Church at Sartirana, 1987-95
Consumerism p170: Jean Nouvel, Galeries Lafayettes, Berlin, 1991-6
Living p202: TR Hamzah & Yeang, Roof-roof' House, Selangor, Malaysia, 1983-4
Workplace p246: Foster and Partners, Hongkong and Shanghai Bank, Hong Kong, 1979-86
Industry p282: Nicholas Grimshaw and Partners, Rank Xerox Headquarters, Welwyn Garden City, Hertfordshire, England, 1988
Leisure p320: Frank O Gehry & Associates, Festival Disney, Disneyland Paris, 1988-1992
Transport p352: Nicholas Grimshaw and Partners, Waterloo International Terminal, London, 1988-93
Sport p392: Faulkner Browns, Pond's Forge International Sports Centre, Sheffield, 1991
The Civic Realm p426: Henning Larsen, Ministry of Foreign Affairs, Riyadh, Saudi Arabia, 1982-4
Towers p464: Kohn Pederson Fox, 333 Wacker Drive, Chicago, Illinois, 1979-83

ILLUSTRATION ACKNOWLEDGEMENTS

All illustrations supplied by architects unless otherwise specified. Photographic sources are listed where possible, but the publisher will endeavour to rectify any inadvertent omissions.
Aerocamera/Michel Hofmeester BV: 308cl; Aga Khan Trust for Culture: 50tl; 155tl,bl; Aga Khan Trust for Culture/©AKAA Reproduction: 154cl; Aga Khan Trust for Culture/J Betant: 154bc; Aga Khan Trust for Culture/©Jahangir Mazlum-Yazdi:154tl; Architecten-bureau Alberts & Van Huut: 261cl,cr; Dirk Alten: 208c,bl; Tadao Ando: 139tc,tr,c; 164; 165cr,br; 238cl; 239t,c,br; 456tr; J Apicella/CP+A: 472bc; Arcaid/Alex Bartel: 32; Arcaid/Belle/Simon Kenny: 329tr; Arcaid/Ian Bruce: 70; Arcaid/©Richard Bryant: 11bl; 30tl,ct; 44cr; 56; 73bl; 74; 75; 85tl; 102; 119tr; 124c,b; 140bc, br; 148cl; 197cr; 213l,r,c; 222, 240c; 245cl,cr; 249b; 258bl; 263tc; 267; 268tr; 269cr; 274cl; 277bl,br; 309tr; 319tr,cl,cr,br; 327l,r; 346tl,br; 352; 381br; 398t; 409br; 416cl; 437tc; 439; 440cl,cr; 449tr,cr,br,bc; 451; 478; Arcaid/©Stefan Buzas: 168tl,cl,bl Arcaid/Jeremy Cockayne 101cr,l; 211; 251tr; 350ctl,cbl; Arcaid/Stephane Couturier: 54c; Arcaid/Colin Dixon: 214tc; Arcaid/©Richard Einzig: 33cr; 77cr; 148br; 208ct; Arcaid/Mark Fiennes: 410tl; Arcaid/Chris Gascoigne: 251tl,bl; Arcaid/©Dennis Gilbert; 127cr,br; 133tr; 414; 430c; Arcaid/Richard Glover: 438tl; Arcaid/©Martine Hamilton-Knight: 184tr; Arcaid/Annet Held: 230tl,tc; Arcaid/©Ben Johnson: 347tr; Arcaid/Nicholas Kane: 37; 198tc; 347tl; 462; Arcaid/Ian Lambot: 199tr; Arcaid/John Edward Linden: 50r; 375tc; 382br; 460c; Arcaid/Trevor Mein: 122tr; 201tl; Arcaid/Viv Porter: 52ct; Arcaid/Prisma: 198cl; Arcaid/Paul Raftery: 12-13; 20; 163tl,c,b; 382bl; Arcaid/Natalie Tepper: 381bl; Arcaid/©Richard Waite: 256b; 302br; Arcaid/Alan Weintraub: 215r; 216; 217; Archipress/Stephane Couturier: 60cl; Archipress/Franck Eustace: 274bc; Arch Photo Inc/Eduard Hueber: 209bl; ARFO: 52br; 132br; Arquitectonica: 219br; ©Arup Associates: 404c,b; 405tl, cl,bl; Assassi Productions: 172tr; Bastin & Evrard: 307bl; Herbert Beckhard: 9tl; Tom Bernard: 326cl; D Biggi: 295; ©Helene Binet: 315tr; Olivier Boissiére: 228br; Tom Bonner: 18t; 249c; 272cl,tr; Bookart: 144; N Borel: 89br; Dave Bower: 114b; Bitter Bredt Fotografie: 42tr,tc; Steven Brooke Studios: 332t,b; 333t; Judith Bromley: 125; Tim Brotherton: 241cr; J Brough-Schamp: 394tl; ©Frederico Brunetti: 192bl; Richard Bryant/©HLT: 426; Canary Wharf Ltd: 433tl,tc,cr; Robert Canfield: 31c,tcr, bcr; Mario Carrieri: 36tl; Rob Casey: 400; Martin Charles: 60tcl; 87bc,br; 458tl; Andy Chopping: 302bc;

Finn Christoffersen (DK): 423tr,tl; Clare Design: 228tc, tr; 424tr; Nigel Coates: 53t; H J Commerell: 460bl; Felipe Condado: 347br; John Connell: 196cl; Terence Conran: 198tl, Graham Cook/JLEP: 379t; Peter Cook: 276cl; 381t; 455bc; 459c,cr; C M Correa: 448tl,cl; Stephane Couturier: 266tc; 405br; ©Roderick Coyne: 379cr; 422tl,tr; William Curtis: 151t; Marco D'Anna: 136; 160cr Mark Darley: 286cl; 287t; Richard Davies: 241ct; 293c,cr; 372tr; 378tl,c; 443t; 460br; 467tl; 480l; Daylight & Liege sprl: 307bc; ©M Denance: 39br; 232cl,bl; 281t; 194br; 395c; Jan Derwig: 315tl,tc; ©Design Archive: 189tl,r; ©Willem Diepraam: 264br; John Donat: 209tl; 301tr; James Dow: 114tl; Max Dupain: 8b; 455tr; Peter Durant: 133l,br; Michael Dyer: 349r; Edge Media, New York: 482b; Chris Edgecombe: 83; 383cr; Richard England: 166br; H G Esch: 279tl; ESTO: 463bcr,br; ESTO/©Peter Aaron: 92b; 152t,br; 258tr; 320; 331tl, bc; 337t,cr,br; 338tl,cl,tr; 339tr,bl; 455br; 338tr; ESTO/Peter Aaron/©The Walt Disney Company: 335tl,tr; 336t; ESTO/©Wayne Andrews: 179; ESTO/Scott Frances: 44bl; 205tl,bl,r; 244c,bl; 401bc,br; 402-403; ESTO/©John Paul Getty Trust/Scott Frances: 24; 26; 27; ESTO/©Jeff Goldberg: 28tl,tr, c,br; 33bl; 289t,bl,br; 333b; 420br; 425t,br; ESTO/Wolfgang Hoyt: 476; ESTO/©Peter Mauss: 45c,b; 248cl; 382l; ESTO/©Jack Pottle: 159tl,tr; ESTO/©Ezra Stoller: 9tr; 361; ESTO/©Ezra Stoller Associates: 16; 44cl; 60b; 361; 470tl; Marcelo Carvalho Ferraz: 150tl, tc,bc; 200tr; Luis Ferreira Alves:127tl,tr; Georges Fessy: 120cl,bl; 131tl; 266tl; 468tl; Mark Fiennes: 431bl; Frederick Fisher and Partners: 54br; ©Mark Fisher: 201bc,br; Alberto Flammer: 273tl; ©Foto-Service SBB, GS Berlin: 376; K Frahm: 371c; Scott Frances: 221tc; Bob Freund: 126tr,cl; Katsuaki Furudate: 42cb; 78tc,tr; 280t; 390tl,cl,c; ©Gianni Berengo Gardin: 81tr; 194bc; 395tl; Chris Gascoigne: 457br; Claude Gaspari: 325tl; ©Gaston: 193cr; W-D Gericke: 370cr; ©Luigi Ghirri: 108tl; 166tl; ©Dennis Gilbert: 15bc; 19t; 109cr; 120cr; 365br; 378b; 483tr; Richard Glover: 197t,tr; John Gollings: 158; 201tr; 391tl,bl; 412utr,ltr; 447tr; 455bl; 484tc; 485bl, br; David Grandorge: 212cl; Graphix Images/©A Da Silva: 406bc; Tim Griffith: 123; 318cl,bl; Paul Groh: 69t,b; Philippe Guignard: 436; Lars Hallen: 276tc,tr; Lawrence Halprin: 183cr; T R Hamzah & Yeang:18b; Jiri Havran: 420bc; Hayes Davidson: 377tc; 441br; Hayes Davidson/Chorley Handford: 456tl; Hedrich Blessing: 23t,cr,b; 145tl; 290cl,bl,br; Hedrich-Blessing/Scott McDonald: 355tc; Anouska Hempel Design: 329cl; Paul Hester: 38br,c; ©Hickey-Robertson: 39cr; Christopher Hill: 424cl,bl; Pedro Hiriart: 452tl;

Kanji Hiwatashi: 356c; ©HLT/Richard Bryant: 426; Studio Hollein/Sina Baniahmad: 48b; 182cr,b; Ariel Huber/Studio Libeskind: 42cl; ©Greg Hursley: 312, 313tl; ©Timothy Hursley: jacket; 19b; 45tr; 48ct,tr; 49c,b; 61c,b; 66; 72bl; 73tl,tr; 77br; 80t,b; 94cl,cr; 104tl,tr; 126br; 127cl,bl; 128bl,bc; 145bl; 146; 147; 153tc,tr; 219tr,cr; 224b; 227t,bl,cr; 255; 262; 263tl; 291tr,c; 340-1; 343; 344; 354cl,tr; 368tl,tc,bc; 387b; 415tl,tc; 428tc,tr; 429; 444cl; 445l,r; 487; INDEX/ Cantarelli: 192c; T Isaksen: 371tr,cr; ©S Ishida: 395br; Yasuhiro Ishimoto: 63tl,tc,cr; 142tl,bl; 336b; 409cl,cr,bl; JLEP: 377tl; Mimmo Jodice: 408tl,tr,bl,br; Ron Johnson: 371cr; ©Douglas Kahn: 422cl; Christian Kandzia: 4; 93cr; 116tr,br; 406tl, 407; 448bl; Barbara Karant: 464; 474tc; Hiroyuki Kawano: 174cr; Katsuhisa Kida 233tl, bc,br; 454bc; Ken Kirkwood: 264tl,tc; 292tl; 304cl,cr,t; Toshiharu Kitajima: 97t; 177; 357cr; ©Toshiharu Kitajima/Arch Photo: 418cb; K L Ng Photography: 202; 210tc; 278tr,cr,br; 413cr; 486tl,tr; Toshiyuki Kobayashi: 117c,br; 280bc,br; 389tl,tr, Balthazar Korab: 128tr; 183tr; 185tr; 473; Erich Koyama: 284tc,c; 285; ©Ian Lambot: 8ct; 246; 252tl,bl; 253; 270; 271tl; 475; Ian Lawson: 399tl; Natasha Le Comber: 461c; Lourdes Legorreta: 152cl; 226tl,tr,b; 273cr,b; 294t,b; ©Heiner Leiska: 441bl; ©Dieter Leistner: 316tr; Lenscape Inc: 398cl; Ronnie Levitan: 411ctr,cbr; William Lim: 174tl,tr; Fotograf Ake E:son Lindman Ab: 373tr; Christopher Little: 459bl; Mark Lohman: 363tr; Charalambos Louizides: 124tr; Max MacKenzie: 458tr; ©Duccio Malagamba: 106tr; 107; 373cr; 384tl,tr,cl,bl; 396tl,tr,c,b; 417c,cr; 463bl; ©Antonio Martinelli: 76bl; 120br; Mitsuo Matsuoka: 64tl; 76br; 176; ©Paul Maurer: 183br; 358tr; 364bl,br; 374bl,bc; Mayska, Mönchengladbach: 48tl; ©Norman McGrath: 72cr; 180-181; 219l, 474br; 481tl; Andrew McKinney: 218cl,bl,r; Rahul Mehrotra: 52bl; ©Norbert Miguletz Fotografie: 220t; Tom Miller: 479; ©Jean-Marie Monthiers: 51c,bl,br; 350tc,bc; Jonathan Moore: 419tl; James H Morris: 34-5; 118; P&G Morisson: 71tl; ©Grant Mudford: 266br; 457tl; ©Osamu Murai: 101br; 248tc; 259cr; 394tr; Pino Musi: 59cr,b; 160bl,br; 161cl, cr,br; 163cr; 196t; Nacasa & Partners Inc: 198bl; 275cl, cr,tr; 388t,b; NAI: 375tr; Voitto Niemelä: 84; Courtesy of Nikko Hotels: 470br; Robert Oerlemans: 261tr; Shigeo Ogawa: 64tc; Tomio Ohashi: 58c; 62tl,c, bl,bc; 64c; 79c; 230bl,bc; 329bc; 369cr,br; Eamonn O'Mahony: 263b; Paul Ott: 367tr,cr; Paschall/Taylor: 258tc; ©Richard Payne: 100c,b; 122cl; 258cl; 474cl; Prof Gustave Peichl: 310tl,cl; ©Matteo Piazza: 306cl; Paolo Portoghesi: 157tr; Armando Salas Portugal: 7b; Atelier Christian de

Portzamparc: 88; 89t,cr,c; 442tl,bl; Positive Image: 461cr; Proto Acme Photo: 260cr; ©Andrew Putler: 29cr; 315bl; 419tc; Uwe Rau: 362cl; Yacov Rechter: 90t,b; 91cl,cr; Robert Reck: 94b; Jo Reid & John Peck: 241cl; 282; 286tr; 287bc,br; 288tl,bl,br; 297tl; Mandy Reynolds: 115tr; ©Christian Richters Fotograf: 14; 15tl; 41cl,c,cr,br; 105c,bc,br; 110tl,cl,bl,tr; 112; 113; 131cr; 194tr; 195; 434cl; 463tl; Simo Rista: 166tr; ©Juan Rodriguez: 57tr; P A C Rook: 308bl; ©Steve Rosenthal: 98tl; 99c,b; Paolo Rosselli: 160cl; Aldo Rossi Studio di Architettura: 55t; 76tr; ©Philippe Ruault: 22; 86c,bl,bc; 121tr; 193cl, bc; 228c,bl; 266bl,bc; 299tl,br; 328tl,bl,br; 330tl,tc; ©Graham Sands: 373br; ©Durston Saylor: 72tl; Shinkenchiku-sha: 10cb; 58tl,tr, 59tl; 122br; 134tl, bl; 140tl; 143; 233c; 234cl,cr,bl,br; 235tr; 236tl,c; 259cl; 356br; 357br; 418; Shinkenchiku-sha/Taisuke Ogawa: 418tl; Roger Simmons: 349tr,tc; ©Jerome Schlomoff: 298l,t; ©Shotenkenchikusha Co, Ltd/ Shinichi Sato: 348c; Julius Shulman: 121br; ©Axel Shultes Architekten: 57b; 443br; Axel Schultes Architeckten + Charlotte Frank: 443cr; Roger Simmons: 349tr,tc; Stephen Simpson: 174cl; Skidmore, Owings, & Merrill LLP/Steinkamp/Ballogg: 481tr; Heide Smith: 447tl; Timothy Soar: 209tr; Margherita Spiluttini: 40tl; 41t; 55c; 300cl,bc; 387t; 463bcl; ©Steinkamp/Ballogg Photograhy: 370bl; 485tr; Tim Street-Porter: 9b; 206c,b; 210tl; 243; The Stubbins Associates/Edward Jacoby: 474bl; David Suchere: 184tc; ©Hisao Suzuki: 169cl; 385b; Ryoji Suzuki: 175tc; Ingimundur Sveinsson: 311c,b; ©Tate Gallery, London 1998: 17tc; 54tr; William Taylor: 335b; Wes Thompson: 184tl; Jussi Tiainen: 167cr; 351; 423bl, bc,br; Bill Timmerman: 130t,b; 141; ©Stefano Topuntoli: 372bl; Rauno Träskelin: 424br; Hiroshi Ueda: 64b; Prof O M Ungers Architekt: 309cr,br; Eddie Valentine-Hames: 172tl,b; 175tl; Valode & Pistre Architects: 296tl,tr; Frank Van Dam: 385br; ©Ger van der Vlugt: 265tr; Herman H Van Doorn: 96; Venturi Scott Brown & Associates: 11t; VIEW/©Peter Cook: 10t; 37br; 52cl; 77tl; 122bl; 132tl, tr; 135; 256tl,tc; 421; 469tl; 471c; VIEW/©Dennis Gilbert: 46b; 47; 95c,cr; 188tl,tc; 303; 359c,b; 413tl;tc, tr; 430tl; D von Schaewen: 305tr; Morley von Sternberg: 186l,r; 391cr; 454t; 460bc; ©Paul Warchol: 156; 157tl; 198br; 199tl; 263tr; 274cr; Matt Wargo: 36cb; 37cb; 334t; Rob Weiner: 355tl; Alan Weintraub: 224tc; ©Hans Werleman: 57tl; 92t; 207; Joshua White: 78br; Don F Wong Photography: 317tr,cl,cr,bl,br; Charlotte Wood: 401tl,tr; ©1998 The Frank Lloyd Wright Foundation: 469r; Mr. Syuji Yamada: 97bc; Nigel Young: 382cr; ©Gerald Zugmann: 300tl,tr; ©Kim Zwarts: 309tl

Phaidon Press Limited

Regent's Wharf

All Saints Street

London N1 9PA

© Phaidon Press Limited 1998

ISBN 0 7148 3743 1

A CIP Catalogue for this book is available from the British Library

All rights reserved. No part of this publication may be reproduced,
stored in a retrieval system or transmitted, in any form or by any
means, electronic, mechanical, photocopying, recording or otherwise,
without the prior permission of Phaidon Press Limited

Printed in Singapore